FULHAM
A COMPLETE
RECORD
1879-1987

A COMPLETE RECORD
1879-1987

DENNIS TURNER & ALEX WHITE

Breedon Books Sport

Hope springs eternal in the human breast;
Man never is, but always to be blessed.
The soul, uneasy, and confined from home,
Rests and expatiates in a life to come.
Alexander Pope

First published in Great Britain by
The Breedon Books Publishing Company Limited
45 Friar Gate, Derby DE1 1DA
1987

ISBN 0 907969 28 3

Printed by Butler and Tanner Limited, Frome
Jacket designed by Graham Hales
and printed by Echo Press (1983) Limited, Loughborough.

Contents

Acknowledgements

The idea for a book such as this has had a gestation period of many years, since in fact we both reluctantly accepted that we would not fulfil our true ambition of playing for Fulham. There has, therefore, been an element of self-indulgence in documenting the club's complete history. Our association with Fulham, however, through the production of the official programme, has convinced us that such a publication would be of interest to more people than just ourselves and some of our equally eccentric colleagues. The articles on Fulham's history in the programme generate more correspondence than any other feature, raising questions which can rarely be answered from the fragmented records kept by the club. We therefore saw it as our mission in life to fill the many gaps which existed in the understanding of Fulham's affairs.

Whilst we have nurtured for a long time the desire to make available to the world the fruits of our research, the stimulus to do so only came towards the end of 1986. In the nine months that it took to put this book together, we have ruthlessly exploited the good nature and generosity of friends and other Fulham supporters and football historians. Of these, Dennis Bone, a Fulham supporter for over 60 years, was especially helpful, letting us borrow his marvellous collection of inter-war programmes (with the team changes marked) and treasured schoolboy scrapbooks of press cuttings and memorabilia. These solved many of our problems. Similarly, Ken 'Super Snaps' Coton, club photographer for over 20 years, kindly allowed us to pillage his unique collection of photographs, whilst Bill Vose spent untold hours patiently copying photographs which we had borrowed. We are also grateful to the Fulham secretary, Yvonne Haines, for the support she has given and the access we have been allowed to the club.

There are, in addition, many others who contributed willingly and to whom a barely adequate acknowledgement must suffice. In particular, we would like to thank Douglas Lamming, Jim Creasy, Bob Lillman, Dave Sullivan, Alex Ferguson, Wendy Gannon, Jack Rollin, Jack Mills, Graham Blackman, Graham Haynes, Roy Shoesmith, Michael Whelan, Michael Featherstone, Mike Davage and Richard Wells.

Dennis Turner
Alex White

July 1987

Notes on the text

In common with other football club historians, we have had to cope with the lack of official records, conflicting evidence from various sources and the need to adopt a standardised approach to problems such as the numbering/position of players and the treatment of substitute appearances. There are two obvious examples of how reconciling contradictory information from several sources has led us to revise two of Fulham's long-established club records. For many years, it has been assumed that the goalscoring record for a season was Frank Newton's 41-goal tally in 1931-2: we have, however, established to our satisfaction that he scored 43 goals that season. Similarly, Johnny Haynes' career total was 157 goals not 156, as has generally been thought.

These conclusions, and the resolution of numerous other statistical problems, were reached after sifting a wide range of sources. Newspapers, national and local, were a vital starting point, and these have been supplemented by reference to many secondary sources, such as players' biographies/autobiographies, statistical annuals and the various helpful publications of the Association of Football Statisticians. We have also had access to virtually every Fulham programme since 1907, together with the annual handbooks, but their lack of attention to statistical accuracy, particularly in the years before 1970, have often confused rather than enlightened. These have frequently been the source of the myths that have continued up until now. Where it has not been possible to find the definitive answer to any problem, we have taken the majority view or, where we could, consulted those with longer memories than our own.

We have adopted the conventional approach to the numbering of players (which was not compulsory before 1939), i.e. the 2-3-5 formation for outfield players. For substitute appearances, only those who came on during a match have been shown: non-appearances by the number 12 have been excluded. Appearances and goal tallies include the competitive games in the Southern League First Division, Football League, FA Cup and League/Milk/Littlewoods Cup, whilst competitions such as the Full Members Cup and Freight/Rover Trophy are shown separately but not in the players' career totals. The three Second Division games of the aborted 1939-40 season are classed as wartime, and included in that section and omitted from the players' career aggregates.

Foreword
by Johnny Haynes

In common with everybody who is interested in football, I was absolutely horrified when I learned of the proposal to merge Fulham with Queen's Park Rangers. The news was especially poignant for me because I spent my entire playing career at the Cottage, 20 very happy years. I was therefore delighted and relieved when my old team-mate, Jimmy Hill, put together a group which bought the club and ensured its survival. The reunion of old players, which Jimmy organised to mark his taking over as chairman, was a marvellous occasion for all of us and the reception we got from the supporters was genuinely moving.

In my opinion, the whole episode illustrates the mistake of trying to apply strict commercial principles to football whilst ignoring the importance of tradition. Over the years, Fulham has earned a special place in the affections of football supporters. This is perhaps attributable to the unique environment of the Cottage, which seems to allow players to express themselves in their own individual way. This has made it a happy club, and the sense of enjoyment we had as players spread to the crowd, which in turn encouraged our idiosyncracies. The reaction to the merger proposal showed how deep were the public's feelings for Fulham's traditions.

When I left school, I had offers from several clubs, but chose Fulham. Once I was established in the team, I was aware of approaches from bigger English clubs and from European sides, but I wanted to stay at Craven Cottage. In the end, this may have cost me League and Cup medals, but I do not regret it. I was as happy at Fulham as I could have been anywhere else, probably more so. Although we won no trophies in my 20 years, I played with some of the finest players in the country, and with some of the most amusing characters. Now, nearly 20 years on, these memories are as valuable as any medal I could have won elsewhere.

The publication of this book is a timely and fascinating reminder of the history of one of English football's best-loved clubs. Anyone who has been associated with Fulham in any capacity will delight in being able to recall their own favourite matches and players. It has certainly stirred many memories for me and I am proud to have contributed to what were probably the 20 most exciting years of the club's existence.

Johnny Haynes celebrates a goal against Plymouth Argyle at Craven Cottage in September 1969. It was his 156th for Fulham and extended the record he had set a week earlier.

THE FULHAM STORY

Hope Springs Eternal....

Introduction

WHEN the proposed merger between Fulham and Queen's Park Rangers was announced in February 1987, it sparked off a wave of protests which clearly surprised those behind the deal. Virtually all the ensuing publicity focussed, perhaps unfairly, on the consequences for Fulham rather than the change in identity implied for Rangers. This reflected the peculiar affection felt for Fulham throughout football, even amongst supporters of other clubs. Over the years, the Cottagers have enjoyed a reputation for fairness, good humour and for placing a higher priority on entertaining than winning. These attitudes reaped their reward when help came from all quarters to fight the merger.

A second long-running theme throughout the club's history has been a fight for financial survival. From the early years of the century, when mergers with Chelsea and Arsenal were proposed, to the present day, Fulham have had to struggle to compete with wealthier neighbours to maintain a separate identity. These pressures intensified in the late 1970s and culminated in the attempt to move Fulham from Craven Cottage to Loftus Road, where it would become the junior partner in a new club. The fact that Fulham's playing fortunes were probably at their lowest ever ebb in the winter of 1987 did not deter some very committed supporters from backing a consortium to try to save the club as an independent entity.

This, therefore, is an appropriate time to consider how Fulham reached crisis point, both on and off the field, after 108 years in existence. What were the influences that created the unique atmosphere at Craven Cottage; where did it all go wrong; who are the heroes and villains; and what, if anything, does the future hold? These, and other questions, are discussed in this introductory narrative.

Morning, 1879-1914

LIKE many clubs which began life in the last quarter of the 19th century, Fulham's origins lay in the church, the link apparent from the club's first name, Fulham St Andrews, which was shortened to the present title in 1888. The precise date of formation cannot be traced, but one of the founders, H.D.Shrimpton, stated categorically in his 'Foundation History' of the Cottagers, that "The Fulham Club was founded in 1879 — not 1880 as sometimes published."

Until 1896, Fulham were indistinguishable from many amateur sides of the period and had more in common with a park team than the Blackburns and Prestons which achieved success in League and Cup. Fixtures were arranged on a haphazard basis and the games were rough-and-tumble affairs of no fixed duration, played on pitches of varying sizes and dubious quality. The colours were, moreover, unspecified, the laws liberally interpreted and most matches were friendlies. The competitions that existed were local rather than national, and of these, Fulham won the West London Cup in 1886-7, the West London Observer Cup in 1891 and the West London League (of

Above and below: Fulham manager Harry Bradshaw and some of the experienced players he signed for the club. Also pictured is club secretary Mr H.E.Jackson, who later committed suicide.

which Fulham were one of the ten founder members) in 1892-3.

It was between 1896 and 1903 that Fulham took the series of steps which paved the way for entry to the Football League in 1907. The acquisition of a permanent home, Craven Cottage, came in 1896, as did participation in the London League and FA Cup. The Cup debut was at Swanscombe in October 1896 and resulted in a 5-0 defeat. Although the club did not win the London League, it enjoyed two relatively successful seasons, which led to entry to the Southern League in 1898, the year in which professionalism was adopted. Whilst this was not accepted unanimously, and some club members resigned, it was a turning point. Then, in 1903, the club was floated as the Fulham Football and Athletic Company Limited, with a share capital of £7,500. Prominent on the first board were chairman John Dean, whose family have maintained a connection with the club up to the present day, (Sir) Henry Norris and local MP, William Hayes Fisher.

These off-the-field activities were matched by changes on the playing front. New players were signed, many with League experience. The most important were goalkeeper Jack Fryer, a veteran of three Cup Finals with Derby, and Liverpool's tough-tackling Scottish wing-half, Billy Goldie, winner of a League Championship medal in 1900-01. In 1904, Fulham appointed their first full-time manager, Harry Bradshaw, who joined the club having achieved considerable success with Arsenal.

Bradshaw virtually rebuilt the Fulham side and guided the club to the quarter-finals of the FA Cup in his first season and then to two consecutive Southern League championships. He was active in the transfer market, taking to the Cottage many former League players, a high proportion of whom were Scottish. Amongst these was Jimmy Sharp, a Scottish international full-back, the outstanding Fulham player of this era, and rated by contemporaries as the finest back in the country. In the Southern League championship sides of 1905-07, Arthur (Pat) Collins and Billy Morrison made their marks and, with Goldie, completed a superb half-back line.

Action at Elm Park, Reading, during the goalless FA Cup match in February 1905. Fulham players, left to right, are Albert Soar, Willie Wardrope, Billy Goldie, Harry Thorpe, Bob Haworth, Billy Morrison, Bobby Graham, Harry Ross and Jack Fryer.

11

Manchester United under pressure during an FA Cup match at Craven Cottage in 1905.

Fulham playing staff for the club's first season in the Football League. Back row (left to right): J.Bradshaw, H.Crossthwaite, P.Waterson, H.Ross, W.Morrison, J.Hogan, J.Hindmarsh, A.Wilkes. Standing: J.Norris (asst. secretary), T.Pyne (steward), R.Armstrong, J.Hird, Mr W.G.Allen, J.Fryer, Mr J.Dean, F.Threlfall, Mr J.Watts, A.Collins, L.Skene, G.Mullett, Mr H.Bradshaw, J.Hamilton (trainer). Seated: T.Walker, W.Goldie, A.Fraser, E.Charlton, F.Bevan, A.Lindsay, T.Walker, J.Hullock. On ground: E.Ward, A.Hubbard, T.Leigh, R.Dalrymple, W.Freeman, W.Thompson.

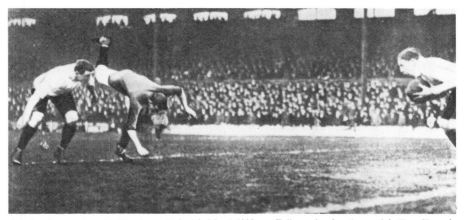

Another Cup meeting with Manchester United, in March 1908, saw Fulham win a fourth-round tie. Here, Skene, in the Fulham goal, collects the ball.

Football League status was achieved in 1907, following the success in the Southern League. The first match was at the Cottage on a Tuesday afternoon in September against Hull: Fulham lost 1-0. Bradshaw continued to strengthen the squad and amongst the 13 new signings were Scottish international goalkeeper Leslie Skene and Bob Dalrymple, a much-travelled Scottish striker. These were two of the stars of an impressive debut season in which Fulham finished fourth in the Second Division and reached the FA Cup semi-finals. There were two memorable Cup victories, over the two First Division Manchester clubs, both of which attracted huge crowds to the Cottage. A mid-season signing, Fred Harrison from Southampton, was the principal marksman in the Cup run, which ended in disaster at Liverpool. Against the mighty Newcastle, Fulham conceded three goals in the first five minutes and any hopes of getting back in the match were lost when goalkeeper Skene was injured. The final score was 6-0, still the highest recorded at this stage of the competition.

It had, nevertheless, been a highly encouraging first season for Fulham. It was exactly 50 years before the Cottagers were again to do as well in both League and Cup in the same season and then they missed out on both. After his considerable success, Bradshaw stayed just one more season, preferring the secretary's job at the Southern League to the offer of a second five-year contract at Fulham. He had done a remarkable job and passed on to his successor, Phil Kelso (who had followed Bradshaw at Arsenal as well), a club that was in good health.

The new manager was careful with his inheritance. Kelso stayed for 15 years, the longest period any individual has had sole control of the club. His time at the helm splits into three phases: the six years up to World War One, the four years of war football and, finally, the five peacetime years up to 1923-4. Under Kelso, Fulham consolidated their position in the Second Division up to World War One, finishing regularly in mid-table. In the Cup, the achievements were just as modest, with only one run creating any excitement. In 1912, Fulham got to the quarter-finals before losing at West Brom, but on the way had the satisfaction of beating First Division Liverpool.

In spite of the lack of trophies, Kelso's sides were attractive, skilful and committed to attack. He encouraged the close-passing game associated with his native Scotland and, in Jimmy Torrance, Wattie White and the returning Jimmy Sharp, found players with

13

Fulham 1909-1910. Back row (left to right): Mr S.D.Evans (director), L.Skene, F.Mavin, T.Leigh, J.McCourt, S.Archer, T.Pyne (resident steward). Standing: J.Hamilton (trainer), Mr J.E.Norris (assistant secretary), J.Price (assistant trainer), H.Lee, J.McEwen, Mr P.Kelso, J.Smith, J.Fryer, W.Freeman, J.Flanagan, J.Wayment, Mr H.G.Norris (director), unknown, unknown. Mr W.Hall (chairman), A.Berry, R.Suart, R.Prout, E.Charlton, A.Collins, H.Lipsham, R.Dalrymple, W.Barton, J.Sharp, A.Lindsay. On ground: J.Goldie, B.Millington, J.Peacock, F.Mouncher, H.Brown, F.Harrison, T.Walker (groundsman).

the necessary skills. Up front, two Englishmen, Tim Coleman and Bert Pearce, formed a marvellous striking partnership, while in goal, Arthur Reynolds took up residence between the posts and outlasted even Kelso. Although the initial burst of enthusiasm which followed entry to the League had moderated, Kelso's Fulham teams, which typically comprised a blend of home-produced talent and some famous personalities near the end of their careers, comfortably held their own in the Second Division. When the war came, it ended the mid-table complacency that appeared to have enveloped the Cottage and, when competitive football was resumed four years later, it was a very different world.

Afternoon, 1919-1939

ALL but four of the 20 inter-war seasons were spent in the Second Division. The exceptions were from 1928-32, when Fulham had their first taste of Third Division football. The period opened with the final years of Kelso's long tenure and ended during Jack Peart's almost equally lengthy term as manager. The period in the middle, however, was marked by an unusually high rate of turnover amongst managers and players, from which Fulham emerged considerably strengthened.

Kelso had another five years in charge when League football was resumed in 1919. Just ten of the pre-war squad returned, of whom only Torrance, Reynolds and White made a contribution beyond the first season. There was, therefore, an influx of new faces and amongst Kelso's best signings were winger Frank Penn, who was to serve the club as player and trainer for almost 50 years, full-back Alec Chaplin, wing-half Harry Bagge and centre-forward Donald Cock.

This new-look team flourished briefly in the early 1920s, finishing sixth in 1919-20 and seventh in 1921-2. The addition of experienced internationals such as Andy Ducat, the legendary Danny Shea and the discovery of youngsters like Frank Osborne made Fulham serious promotion contenders in 1921-2. Kelso had paid a club record of £3,500 for Sunderland's centre-forward Barney Travers. He was an immediate success, scoring 17 goals in 30 games in a dashing style which made him a great favourite with the supporters. Fulham's challenge and Travers' career came to grief, however, in

14

March 1922, when he was implicated in an attempt to bribe an opponent before a crucial game at South Shields. Travers was banned for life and, without his fire power, the Cottagers' promotion push fell away.

This scandal overshadowed Kelso's two remaining seasons. His last season at the helm, 1923-4, was his poorest and precipitated his retirement. Relegation appeared a real possibility for the first time and only a fine run in the last month of the season, when only one of the last seven games was lost, lifted them into the safety of 20th position. A 20,000 crowd saw Fulham make certain of retaining Second Division status by beating Stockport 1-0 on the last day of the season.

Andy Ducat was the popular choice to succeed Kelso, the first ex-Fulham player to manage the club. He was also a county cricketer (for Surrey), one of a number who played for the Cottagers in the 1920s and 1930s: Bob Gregory (Surrey), Percy Fender (Surrey), Bert White (Warwickshire), Fred Avey (Essex), Jim Hammond (Sussex) and John Arnold (Hampshire) were the others. In spite of his playing abilities and popularity, Ducat's time as manager was not a happy one and ended after two seasons. The only highlight was a run in the FA Cup in which three First Division sides (Everton, Liverpool and Notts County) were beaten, before Fulham fell, at home, to Manchester United in the sixth round. These matches established the young third-team goalkeeper, Ernie Beecham, as a Fulham folk hero, whose career (and much of his subsequent life) was effectively ruined by a broken neck sustained in a match against Exeter in 1928.

The dismissal of Ducat in 1926 inaugurated a period of managerial instability that saw Joe Bradshaw, Ned Liddell, James McIntyre and Jimmy Hogan come and go before Jack Peart's appointment in 1935. In 1928, during Bradshaw's second season, Fulham were relegated for the first time, largely as a result of an appalling away record

Fulham goalkeeper Arthur Reynolds gathers the ball from a West Ham forward during a Second Division match at the Cottage in 1922.

Fulham in 1925-6. Back row (left to right): White, Borland, Fleming, McKenna, Beecham, Doyle, Riddell, Dyer, Brooks. Standing: Edelston, Barrett, Oliver, E.Craig, Probert, Wolfe, Pike, McNab, Chaplin. Seated: Kennedy, Lancashire, F.Craig, Bagge, Torrance, Prouse, Penn, Wood. On ground: Packham, Ferguson, Edmonds, Ruffell, Ranson.

Fulham in 1929. Back row (left to right, players only): Unknown, Barrett, Mason, Meeson, Ward, Allen, Unknown. Standing: Steele, Dyer, McNab, Bird, Craig, Frewin, Unknown, Ferguson. Seated: Oliver, Haley, Lawson, Penn, Rosier, Unknown, Blake, Hammond. On ground: Temple, Price, Avey, Proud, Charles.

in which 20 of the 21 games were lost. Paradoxically, centre-forward Sid Elliott set a new club goalscoring record that season, with 26 goals. Bradshaw's departure in 1929 and Liddell's brief tenure did little to promise a speedy return to Division Two. Although the club finished in the top half of the table, promotion was never a serious prospect.

There were a few consolations, particularly the emergence of some players who were to form the nucleus of the team in the 1930s. Len Oliver and Albert Barrett played a combined total of around 900 games between 1924 and 1936, and both were capped for England whilst Third Division players. With Syd 'Carnera' Gibbons, they formed an imposing half-back line which was the backbone of the side for many seasons. At inside-forward, Johnny Price and Jim Hammond made their mark in the Third Division, but enjoyed greater success at a higher level. Jack Finch, a utility forward, was another who first appeared in Division Three, but who made a greater contribution in Division Two.

The arrival of manager James McIntyre in April 1931 heralded the much-needed change in performances. He made two crucial signings, centre-forward Frank 'Bonzo' Newton and winger Billy Richards, and within 12 months had steered Fulham to the Third Division title. Newton's contribution to the record 111-goal haul was 43, also a Fulham record. In 1932-3, it seemed as if Fulham would go straight into Division One. The signings of Mike Keeping and John Arnold from Southampton added depth and quality to the squad. The promotion drive petered out in the final month, but it was as close as Fulham had ever been to the First Division.

After this near miss, McIntyre inexplicably sold Newton to Reading, a move which was to cost him his job. To succeed him, the board made the highly innovative appointment of Jimmy Hogan, a coach rather than manager, who, although a former Fulham player, had made his name on the Continent. The players, however, did not respond to his novel methods and in the spring of 1935 he was sacked after less than a season in the job.

The club turned next to Jack Peart, whose style was more conventional and whose skills were largely administrative. He was more durable than his five immediate predecessors and remained in office for over 13 years. Much of this was lost to the war,

'Bonzo' Newton is carried off with a broken leg in the friendly match against FK Austria at Craven Cottage in December 1934. The injury ended his career.

17

Alf Tootill gathers the ball during a Second Division match at West Ham in October 1937. The other Fulham
defenders to the right of Tootill are Joe Birch, Mike Keeping and Syd Gibbons.

Still in Division Two, Ronnie Rooke drives the ball past Chesterfield goalkeeper Ray Middleton at Craven Cottage
in September 1938. Rooke's effort was disallowed, however, for offside, but he scored once in Fulham's 2-0 win.

but he steered the club through that difficult phase and just months after his death, his team won the Second Division title. Peart's major achievement came in his first season, 1935-6. After beating Brighton and Blackpool in the third and fourth rounds of the Cup, Fulham eliminated First Division Chelsea and Derby in thrilling ties to reach the semi-finals for only the second time. They were drawn against Sheffield United, also from the Second Division, but on the day played below their best, losing 2-1 at Molineux. Ironically, five days later the clubs met in a League game at Bramall Lane and Fulham won 1-0.

The club in the 1930s, as in the 1950s and 1960s, was noted more for its personalities than its achievements. To the likes of Hammond, Arnold, Finch, Keeping and Gibbons were added goalkeeper Alf Tootill (the 'bird-catcher'), wing-half Jimmy Tompkins and forwards Eddie Perry and Trevor Smith, all of whom have a special place in Fulham's history. Perhaps Peart's best signing was Crystal Palace's reserve centre-forward, Ronnie Rooke. After scoring a hat-trick on his debut against West Ham in November 1936, he became a one-man goal machine, topping Fulham's scoring lists for each of the 11 seasons (including the war years) that he was a Fulham player. In December 1946, he was transferred to Arsenal, and in that season he was top scorer for both Fulham and the Gunners.

The club began the final inter-war season with a flourish, heading the Division Two table through the autumn. Attendances soared and in October 1938 a record of 49,335 witnessed the top-of-the-table clash with Millwall. Fulham could not sustain their League form once winter set in, but in a remarkable third round Cup tie against Bury at the Cottage in January 1939, Rooke brought this era in the club's history to a fitting close, scoring all the goals in a 6-0 win.

Fulham 1938-9. Back row (left to right): Clarke, Evans, Bacuzzi, Turner, Keeping, Tompkins, Voisey (trainer). Front row: Higgins, Woodward, Rooke, Finch, Arnold, Hiles.

Fulham 1946-7. Back row (left to right): Woodward, Rooke, Freeman, Hinton, Taylor, Lewin, Beasley, Penn (trainer), Peart (manager). Front row: Stevens, McCormick, Watson, Wallbanks, Shepherd.

Newcastle goalkeeper Swinburne punches clear from Ronnie Rooke at Craven Cottage in November 1946.

Evening, 1945-1968

FULHAM shared in the general prosperity enjoyed by English football in the immediate aftermath of World War Two. In fact, the period up to 1968 was something of a halcyon era for the club, when its playing fortunes were at their zenith, personalities abounded and attendances soared. First Division status was won and lost twice in this time, on two occasions Wembley was missed by a whisker and, of the 230 international caps won by Fulham players, more than half came during these 24 years.

Jack Peart was still at the helm when the war ended in 1945. As there was insufficient time to organise a resumption of the Football League, the 1945-6 season continued on a regional basis, although the guest system was ended. Not surprisingly, the first couple of post-war seasons were unsettled. Fulham finished mid-table in both years with a team which comprised a few players from the pre-war era (Bacuzzi, Freeman, Pitts, Hiles, Woodward and Rooke were the only players who had pre-war League experience with Fulham), some wartime discoveries (particularly Arthur Stevens, Len Quested and Jim Taylor) and a few new signings, including Irish goalkeeper Ted Hinton, Bury defender Jack Watson and Northumberland miner, Harold Wallbanks. For just £750, Peart secured the services of the experienced Pat Beasley, a former Arsenal, Huddersfield and England inside-forward, who became captain and a very influential figure in these years.

Goalscoring was a problem in these early post-war years, particularly after the controversial sale of Ronnie Rooke in December 1946, to Arsenal, who paid £1,000 plus Dave Nelson and Cyril Grant. Whilst Rooke went on to greater things, Fulham struggled. Doug McGibbon, signed as a replacement from Southampton, scored a

Bob Thomas scores one of his two goals in Fulham's 5-0 home victory over Queen's Park Rangers in October 1948, the first win under new manager Frank Osborne.

21

Everton's Harry Catterick finds himself in some discomfort as Fulham goalkeeper Hinton clears during the fifth round FA Cup tie at Craven Cottage in February 1948.

hat-trick on his Fulham debut (as had Rooke), but he could not match his predecessor's scoring rate. The arrival of inside-forward Bob Thomas, from Plymouth in the summer of 1947 for £4,000, improved Fulham's scoring record, but he lacked an effective striking partner.

Whilst League form was generally frustrating, the Cup was more interesting. In 1945-6 (the FA Cup was re-started a season earlier than the League), Fulham were involved in a unique result. For the only time in its history, the Cup was played on a two-legged basis, and in January 1946, the Cottagers met Charlton in the third round. In the first leg at The Valley, the Haddicks won 3-1, but Fulham had the edge in the return, 2-1. Charlton, nevertheless, went through 4-3 on aggregate, and eventually got to Wembley, only to lose 4-1 to Derby, after extra-time. Charlton thus became the only club to reach the Final of the FA Cup after losing a match in an earlier round.

In 1947-8, Fulham reached the quarter-finals, defeating Doncaster, Bristol Rovers and (most memorably) Everton on the way. Before the Bristol Rovers tie, director Tommy Trinder offered an overcoat to the scorer of a hat-trick. When Arthur Stevens scored his third goal, Trinder was seen hanging over the balcony of the Cottage, displaying the coat. The matter was later investigated by the authorities, who suspected that an illegal payment may have been made. In the sixth round, however, Fulham, reduced to ten men after 20 minutes when Freeman was injured, lost 2-0 at home to Blackpool.

After a tragic opening, 1948-9 was to prove the most memorable in Fulham's history. With just four games played, manager Jack Peart died after a short illness. A month later, director and former player Frank Osborne succeeded him. He appointed

Fulham, Divison Two champions 1948-9. Back row (left to right): E.Perry, H.Freeman, L.Quested, D.Flack, J.Taylor, J.Bacuzzi, A.Beasley, F.Penn (trainer). Front row: R.Lewin, A.Stevens, R.Thomas, G.A.Rowley, S.Thomas, J.McDonald, D.Bewley.

Fulham's Bob Thomas and Liverpool's Laurie Hughes battle for the ball in the first Division One meeting between the clubs, at Craven Cottage in October 1949. Liverpool won 1-0.

another former player, Eddie Perry, as team manager. When Osborne took over, the team was in mid-table, and he made immediate changes, bringing in goalkeeper Doug Flack and inside-forward Bedford Jezzard. He also moved on the transfer market, swapping Ernie Shepherd for West Brom's centre-forward Arthur Rowley. This was the missing piece of the jigsaw, for Rowley was to prove the genuine successor to Rooke, and a most effective partner for Thomas, with 19 goals in 22 games. In a thrilling climax to the season, Fulham took 21 points out of a possible 26 to pip West Brom and Southampton for the Second Division title. An unsung hero was third-choice goalkeeper Larry Gage, a former Canadian paratrooper, who played in the last three games when Flack was injured. These matches, all against London clubs, attracted a total of 130,000 people: Gage played superbly as Fulham won five out of six points, and the championship. They proved to be his only League appearances for Fulham.

The club failed to make the necessary adjustment to the demands of the First Division, and the three years from 1949-52 were a struggle. The manager of Southampton, who had just missed out on promotion, Bill Dodgin, went to the Cottage in the summer of 1949 as team manager, and for 12 months he and Osborne relied on the squad which won promotion. The only newcomers were a trio signed from the troubled Belfast Celtic: defender Robin Lawler, goalkeeper Hugh Kelly and winger Johnny Campbell were all to win Irish caps whilst with Fulham.

In the summer of 1950, Dodgin entered the transfer market, signing the Lowe brothers from Aston Villa, Scottish wing-half Archie Macaulay as a replacement for skipper Pat Beasley, goalkeeper Ian Black from Southampton and Irish international inside-forward Bobby Brennan from Birmingham. An estimated £40,000 was spent on these transfers, including a club record of £20,000 on Brennan, but the results were no more successful: Fulham finished 18th, one place lower than in the previous season.

The following season was to prove the last in this first spell in the top flight. Only 27 points were taken from 42 games, 23 games were lost, and Fulham spent most of the campaign propping up the table. The statistics do not tell the whole story, however. Injuries were a problem throughout, and Dodgin could rarely field a full team, whilst 16 of the defeats were by the odd goal. New blood was introduced, particularly Bobby Robson at inside-forward and new signings Charlie Mitten and Jimmy Hill, who all made a significant impact, but too late to preserve First Division status. The highlight of this spell amongst the elite was a Cup run in 1951, which again ended in the sixth round, again at the hands of Blackpool, but this time at Bloomfield Road, to a fourth-minute Allan Brown penalty.

In spite of the relative lack of success, the crowds flocked to the Cottage. Attendances averaged over 32,000 in all three seasons, and the crowds saw plenty of goals. This trend continued over the next seven years, from 1952-9, when the club returned to the Second Division. In 294 League games, Fulham scored 621 goals, and conceded 510, an average of almost four goals in every game. For the first five of these seasons, the club was in mid-table, but in 1957-8, there was a distinct improvement in its form.

There were major changes in these years. Bill Dodgin left in the autumn of 1953, and was not replaced until January 1956 when Dug Livingstone came as team manager from Newcastle: Frank Osborne combined the roles of general and team manager in-between times. A brilliant young inside-forward, Johnny Haynes, emerged in 1952-3, and was to dominate the club for almost 20 years. He developed a superb understanding with Robson and Jezzard, and with wingers Stevens and Mitten, to form Fulham's most exciting and prolific forward line. It lasted less than four seasons, however, and was broken up in 1956, by Robson's transfer to West Brom for £25,000 and an injury to Jezzard which ended his career.

These came just months after a magnificent Cup tie at the Cottage, when holders

In October 1954, Fulham beat Birmingham 2-1 at home. A timely interception by full-back Robin Lawler saved the situation, with goalkeeper Ian Black stranded.

Fulham's 1959 promotion squad, minus a goalkeeper. Back row (left to right): Stevens, Cohen, Stapleton, Lowe, Johnson, Bentley, Lawler, Langley, Mullery, Penn (trainer), Jezzard (manager). Front row: Key, Barton, Hill, Cook, Haynes, Chamberlain.

Newcastle won a thrilling game 5-4. Just weeks after this match, Newcastle's team manager, Livingstone, took over at Fulham and in two years restructured the team into one which challenged for promotion. He signed Chelsea's England centre-forward Roy Bentley and converted him to a half-back; introduced youngsters like goalkeeper Tony Macedo and full-back George Cohen; and signed full-back Jim Langley from Brighton and centre-forward Maurice Cook from Watford.

For much of 1957-8 it seemed as if Fulham would win promotion. In the end, the club missed out as a result of a fixture pile-up caused by an extended FA Cup run, when the semi-finals were reached for the third time. Manchester United, recently devastated by the Munich disaster, provided the opposition and in a memorable game at Villa Park, the honours were shared. In the replay, however, some inexplicable lapses by Macedo, and a controversial refereeing decision which denied Fulham a goal when the score stood at 3-4, cost the Cottagers a Wembley place.

Livingstone left in the summer of 1958 and was replaced by Bedford Jezzard. He signed Scottish international winger Graham Leggat for £15,000 from Aberdeen, and from the first game of the season when Stoke were thrashed 6-1, promotion was on the cards. Haynes took over as chief goalscorer, as well as creator, and his total of 26 included four hat-tricks. Other than Leggat, the only significant addition to the side was the introduction of teenager Alan Mullery at wing-half in February 1959. He played a major part in the run-in which secured the runners-up position behind Sheffield Wednesday.

In spite of some gloomy predictions, Fulham managed to retain First Division status for nine seasons. It was, however, a close call on more than one occasion and

Trevor Chamberlain hammers home a penalty past Birmingham City goalkeeper Colin Withers at Craven Cottage in August 1963. Chamberlain scored both goals in Fulham's 2-1 victory.

Penalty action at the other end. This time Fulham goalkeeper Tony Macedo fails to stop Third Division Walsall's Tony Richards scoring in an FA Cup match at the Cottage in January 1962. Walsall went 2-0 up, but First Division Fulham eventually levelled the scores and won the replay.

Fulham pictured in August 1963. Back row: Robson, Keetch, Mullery, Macedo, Cohen, Langley. Front row: Key, Leggat, Brown, Cook, Haynes, O'Connell.

breathtaking relegation battles became commonplace at the Cottage in the 1960s. Only once, in 1959-60, did the club finish in the top half of the table and three times the drop was avoided by just one League place. These were, nevertheless, exciting years. The team was a better one than the statistics implied, but was usually two or three players short of a quality First Division line-up. The old habit of selling off the best players was resisted in the cases of Haynes and Cohen but not Mullery, whose £72,500 move to Spurs in March 1964 was negotiated without the manager's knowledge.

Osborne and Jezzard both retired in the autumn of 1964, but not before they had steered Fulham to another Cup semi-final. In 1962, Burnley were the opponents and the London club should have won the first game at Villa Park: a blatant penalty, when goalkeeper Blacklaw brought down Cook with the goal gaping, was denied by the referee. In the replay, Burnley deservedly won 2-1. This Cup run sparked off a revival in League form, however, and in a tense climax to the season, relegation was narrowly avoided. A poor refereeing decision also cost Fulham the leadership of Division One for the only time, in December 1959. In a home match with Spurs, a win would have put the Cottagers on top, but they could only draw. It might have been different, however, had the referee given a penalty rather than a corner when Spurs' Peter Baker punched a goalbound shot over the bar. This was the high water mark of Fulham's First Division career.

Arthur Stevens held the fort during the period between Jezzard's departure and the appointment of his successor in January 1965, Vic Buckingham. The new manager had impeccable credentials, but his tenure was short and unhappy. He cleared out many of the established players, such as Cook, Leggat, Keetch, Langley, Marsh and O'Connell, most of whom showed with their new clubs that they had a few seasons still left in them. With one exception (Allan Clarke), his signings comprised older players whose best years were behind them. Mark Pearson and Terry Dyson were the obvious examples.

Whilst the team did, on occasions, produce football of the highest quality, it was too inconsistent to aspire to more than survival in the First Division. In 1965-6, the Cottagers produced their most dramatic relegation escape, winning 20 points from a possible 26 in a gripping finalé to the season. The climax came in April 1966, with a 4-2 win at Northampton, which virtually relegated the Cobblers and kept Fulham up. This result turned on one crucial incident when Northampton were leading 2-1 and Fulham were attacking in numbers. The home side broke away and, with most of the Fulham players and the referee stranded at the other end of the pitch, had a shot which beat McClelland in the Fulham goal but hit the underside of the bar. Fulham scrambled the ball clear, but Northampton claimed a goal. Unfortunately for them, the linesman had slipped over and had missed the incident and the referee, still in the Northampton half, was in no position to give a goal.

Much of the success for Fulham's revival in the winter of 1966 was credited to the new coach, Dave Sexton, who had been sacked as manager by Orient. He had brought in youngsters like Steve Earle and Les Barrett, who were still there the following season when Sexton left for Arsenal. Buckingham's final 18 months saw a further deterioration in results, until, in the winter of 1967-8, it was obvious that relegation could no longer be staved off. The manager departed when his three year contract expired and, to replace him, the board turned to a former player who had retired six months earlier and gone to work in Canada.

It was Bobby Robson's first managerial job — and it proved to be a traumatic one. He inherited a demoralised side, firmly rooted at the bottom of the table and which had lost its captain, George Cohen, with the injury which ended his career. Not surprisingly, Robson could not turn the tide and in the remaining three months of 1967-8, he tried to build the basis of a team which might challenge for promotion at the first attempt.

Allan Clarke finds the net at Maine Road in March 1968. Unfortunately, Manchester City scored five as they pushed on for the League title and Fulham were finally relegated.

In over 20 years as club photographer, Ken Coton took thousands of pictures. This is his favourite, Les Barrett scoring Fulham's only goal against Cardiff in December 1968 at the Cottage.

Night, 1968-1987

In the years since 1969, Fulham have experienced sharp fluctuations in their fortunes, but have failed to recapture a place in the top flight. It has been a period of instability, with five changes in League status, eight managers and, reflecting the growing financial problems, five chairmen, each of whom has established a new board of directors. There have been occasional breaks in the cloud, the promotions of 1971 and 1982 and a Cup Final appearance in 1975, but generally the trend has been downwards.

Relegation from Division One in 1968 did not end the uncertainty at the Cottage. In the following season, the problems multiplied, and ten years and one day after winning promotion to the First, Fulham were relegated to the Third Division. An appalling start, in which a reserve full-back converted to centre-forward, Malcolm Macdonald, made a brief impression, left the club floundering at the foot of the table and, after just ten months in the job, manager Robson was sacked. He was succeeded briefly by Haynes, who took on the role of player-manager on a temporary basis until a permanent appointment was made.

Bill Dodgin (junior), a former player, and son of a previous manager, took over in December 1968. He began the enormous task of rebuilding the club, but could not avoid the slide into Division Three, for only the second time in the club's history. An indication of the uncertainty that prevailed in the years between 1967 and 1969 is apparent from the fact that in two seasons 39 players were tried, of whom ten played their first and last games for the club. There was a sense of panic about some of the new signings and promising youngsters, like Macdonald and John Ryan, were allowed to drift away, having failed to make an immediate impact in a bad team.

The first season back in the Third Division, 1969-70, began inauspiciously, but ended in a run which took Fulham into fourth place. The highlight of the year was undoubtedly an 8-0 win at Halifax, in which Steve Earle equalled Jimmy Hill's record of scoring five goals in an away League match. Earle, with Jim Conway, Les Barrett and new skipper Barry Lloyd, provided the thrust in Dodgin's attack-minded side. At the back, Reg Matthewson, Fred Callaghan and Stan Brown brought some stability, whilst Haynes was the most notable casualty. He ended his illustrious career in January 1970, in a 1-1 draw against Stockport in front of 7,500 people.

This sojourn in Division Three was brief, ending after just two seasons. For much of 1970-71, Fulham, Preston and Aston Villa fought for the two promotion spots and Fulham clinched a place with a 3-2 win in the penultimate game at Bradford City. Dodgin had added Irish wing-half Jimmy Dunne and Scottish winger George Johnston to the side, and in the final match, the Cottagers needed only a draw against Preston to clinch the title. They lost 1-0 before a 25,700 crowd.

Dodgin's belief in attacking football was tested to the limit on the club's return to Division Two. Only a desperate last-minute rally prevented an immediate return to the Third and this owed more to the team's defensive qualities than attacking skills. There were two important signings made in the second half of the season, goalkeeper Peter Mellor from Burnley and, more controversially, Alan Mullery on loan from Spurs. Mullery's signing led to protests from other relegation strugglers and it proved a turning point. Fulham wanted to sign him permanently, but Spurs were reluctant to let him go and in his brief spell at the Cottage, he helped the club win six priceless points.

Days after relegation had been avoided, Dodgin was sacked. This led to calls from the Supporters' Club for chairman Tommy Trinder's resignation. His response was to abolish the Supporters' Club and to appoint Alec Stock as manager. In his four years at the helm, the wily Stock consolidated Fulham's position as a mid-table Second Division club; guided them to their first Wembley Final; dealt successfully and imaginatively on the transfer market; and brought a little glamour back to the Cottage. With the shrewd assistance of coach Bill Taylor, Stock's Fulham averaged exactly a

Steve Earle (left) watches as skipper Barry Lloyd (hidden by goalkeeper) scores Fulham's second goal against Chesterfield in September 1970. Earle scored the first goal in the 2-0 win at Craven Cottage.

West Ham's Tommy Taylor (left) is on hand as Alan Slough (centre) battles with Billy Bonds during the 1975 FA Cup Final at Wembley.

point-a-game between 1972 and 1976, and whilst promotion was never a realistic possibility, nor was relegation a serious threat.

The manager's two most important signings were Alan Mullery during the 1972 close season and Bobby Moore in March 1974. He allowed Earle to move to Leicester for a six-figure fee and bought and sold, at a profit, defender Paul Went. Promising youngsters like Les Strong, John Lacy and John Mitchell were brought into the side to replace the likes of Matthewson, Brown and Callaghan. The pinnacle of Stock's achievement at Fulham, and probably of his entire career, came in 1975, when he steered his nondescript group of Second Division journeymen to a Wembley Final. It was a fitting climax for a man who had made his reputation managing clubs in the lower divisions and who had specialised in giant-killing feats.

Fulham's road to Wembley was the longest of any previous Finalist, 11 games in all, and all the victories came in away matches. It took seven games to dispose of fellow Second Division clubs Hull and Nottingham Forest before the Cottagers were pitched against First Division leaders Everton at Goodison. For the third time, Fulham achieved an unexpected but thoroughly deserved Cup win over the Toffeemen, thanks to two Viv Busby goals. Goalkeeper Mellor was the star of the sixth round victory at First Division Carlisle, which gave Fulham a semi-final tie at Hillsborough against Birmingham.

The London club had, at that time, the unenviable record of reaching more semi-finals than any other club without making it to the Final. When Birmingham defender Joe Gallagher equalised John Mitchell's spectacular goal, Fulham supporters had visions of a repeat of 1958 and 1962. In the replay, dour defending in which Mullery and Moore were outstanding, kept the scoresheet blank. Extra-time was going the same way until, with less than a minute remaining, a rebound from goalkeeper Latchford struck Mitchell and rolled tantalisingly over the line. At this stage it was quantity, not quality, that mattered and it set up a romantic all-London Final, in which Moore faced his old West Ham colleagues.

The Final itself was an anti-climax. Fulham, although not overawed by the occasion, played below their best and conceded two goals from elementary defensive

Fulham's 1975 FA Cup Final squad. Back row (left to right): Woolnough (physiotherapist), Lloyd, Strong, Howe, Lacy, Mellor, Dowie, Busby, Mitchell, Fraser, Taylor (coach). Front row: Conway, Slough, Mullery, Stock (manager), Moore, Barrett, Cutbush.

33

Roger Brown's magnificent header which won Fulham promotion in the dramatic match against Lincoln in May 1982.

Fulham in 1982-3. Back row (left to right): Lock, Reeves, Hopkins, Gale, Peyton, Brown, Stannard, O'Driscoll, Tempest, Houghton, Coney. Front row: Harford (coach), Davies, Scott, Wilson, Macdonald (manager), Lewington, Parker, Carr, Wright (physiotherapist).

errors. It was, nevertheless, a great achievement marred only by an injury to Les Strong two weeks before the Final. He had played in all the previous 53 games that season, but was forced to watch the big match from the sidelines.

The following season proved to be Stock's last in charge: a boardroom reshuffle prompted his departure and the succession of coach Bobby Campbell. Following Mullery's retirement in 1976, Fulham signed George Best and Rodney Marsh in an attempt to stimulate interest. The two veterans displayed their considerable talents intermittently and whilst the home gates were boosted by an average of 5,000 per game, the impact on away attendances was even greater.

Campbell took over in December 1976 and his appointment coincided with a nose-dive towards the Second Division basement. Relegation was avoided in the final fortnight, but it proved to be only a stay of execution. In both 1977-8 and 1978-9, respectable mid-table positions were achieved, but the trapdoor to Division Three opened again in 1979-80. The manager was a paradox. His style and personality did not endear him to the supporters — although he was widely respected by the players as a coach, and youngsters like Tony Gale, John Margerrison and Robert Wilson came through his period of office. He also dealt extensively and generally shrewdly on the transfer market, selling John Lacy, Terry Bullivant, Richard Money and Teddy Maybank for huge fees and buying Gordon Davies, Kevin Lock, Maybank, Money and John Beck for next to nothing. He seemed unable, however, to weld the individuals into a cohesive whole, and his idiosyncratic style led to the premature departure of many players. His own insecurities seemed to be transferred to the team, and a loss of confidence was apparent.

He was sacked in October 1980, after a dreadful opening spell in Division Three, and was succeeded by former player Malcolm Macdonald. In spite of his cavalier image as a player, 'Supermac' proved to be a thoughtful, articulate manager, whose open style and commitment to cultured and attacking football revived the club's fortunes and won many admirers. He made only a few changes to the side (he never spent a penny on transfers in three-and-a-half years as manager), but introduced youngsters like Dean Coney, Jeff Hopkins and Paul Parker. In defence, Gale and Roger Brown dominated, in midfield Sean O'Driscoll, Wilson, Ray Lewington and Peter O'Sullivan were the engine room of the side, whilst Coney and Davies up front formed a lethal partnership.

After just two seasons in the Third, Fulham again won promotion, but only after a nail-biting climax. In a piece of pure theatre, Fulham needed at least one point from the final match to go up, whilst opponents Lincoln needed all three to overhaul the Cottagers. Over 20,000 were at the Cottage for this midweek finalé and saw skipper Roger Brown, his shirt covered in blood from a gashed forehead, score the goal which earned a point and won promotion.

For much of the following season, it seemed as if Fulham would jump back into Division One at the first attempt. Only Ray Houghton, a free transfer from West Ham, was added to the squad, and Macdonald's young side was never out of the top three until the final month of the season. A 1-0 home defeat by challengers Leicester in March was a crucial turning point, but it was at the Baseball Ground in the final minutes of the final match that the real drama occurred.

Fulham needed to win to go up, and Derby were fighting to avoid relegation. With two minutes to go, the home side were leading 1-0. The huge crowd had spilled over on to the touchlines and, thinking mistakenly that the referee had blown the final whistle, invaded the pitch. The referee was forced to take the teams off, and when it proved impossible to re-start, he admitted that he had in effect abandoned the game. Fulham appealed to the League to have the match replayed and Macdonald could cite a precedent of a Cup semi-final in which he had been involved at Newcastle against Nottingham Forest. The weight of evidence and balance of the argument were clearly in Fulham's favour, but the League authorities took the line of least resistance and allowed the result to stand. The reasons seemed fatuous (Fulham would not have scored two goals in the remaining time and that it was not possible to re-create the conditions of the last Saturday of the season when promotion and relegation issues were settled) and to many impartial observers the decision was a triumph of expediency over principle and a victory for 'hooliganism'.

Since that controversy, Fulham's playing fortunes have declined at an alarming rate, the result primarily of off-the-field financial problems. Malcolm Macdonald lasted less than a year after the Derby debacle and, whilst the team's League form was inconsistent in 1983-4, they took Liverpool to three games in the Milk Cup, losing to an extra-time Souness goal. For reasons largely unconnected with football, Macdonald left the Cottage in March 1984 and was replaced by coach Ray Harford. His baptism as a manager was every bit as traumatic as Bobby Robson's almost 20 years earlier and it had the same outcome, relegation to Division Three and the departure of the manager.

Harford was desperately unlucky. He had been responsible for the development of many of the players since they were juniors and he clearly had a marvellous relationship with them. The club's dire financial straits, however, meant that anyone who was warm and breathing was available for transfer and few players were prepared to re-sign once their contracts expired. Consequently, there was a mass exodus and between 1984 and 1986, an entire team was sold or allowed to leave (Peyton, Lock, Lewington, Brown, Wilson, Gale, Davies, Houghton, O'Driscoll, Tempest, Rosenior and Sealy). It is a measure of the quality of the players Fulham lost that five went to First Division clubs and three to other Second Division sides.

With the ground effectively cut from under his feet, Harford, for all his proven coaching skills, could not make a silk purse out of a sow's ear. Relegation was inevitable months before it became a statistical reality in April 1986, and during the close season Harford left to take over as coach at First Division Luton. Within weeks, the Clay family sold Fulham to the SB Property Company, a subsidiary of Marler

Kevin Lock scored twice against Bruce Grobbelaar from the penalty spot in the 1983-4 Milk Cup. This one, at Anfield in the third round replay, levelled the scores at 1-1 and put the game into extra-time.

Estates, and the critical action in 1986-7 had little to do with football.

In spite of promises about the club's future, the new owners' ambitions to develop the Craven Cottage site became apparent after only a few months. (These events are chronicled elsewhere in this book). They quickly persuaded themselves that Fulham's decline was terminal and euthanasia was the most merciful solution. The huge public outcry following the announcement of a merger between Fulham and Queen's Park Rangers showed they had clearly misjudged public opinion; and they were forced into discussions with yet another group of would-be owners and a deal was concluded in April 1987.

A New Dawn? 1987-

DERRY Quigley is a genial Irishman who has been responsible for Fulham's very successful youth development programme. Over the last 25 years, he has worked as hard and cared as much about the club as anyone, but has seen it pushed to the brink of disaster on several occasions. Derry, however, is a supreme optimist and puts a uniquely Fulham interpretation on the saying that the darkest hour is just before dawn. He believes that in times of crisis, the spirits of the club's founders congregate at midnight in 'J' block in the old Stevenage Road stand to decide what should be done. Then, as if by divine intervention, events take an unexpected course and Fulham is pulled back from the abyss.

If SB Property Company's plans were Fulham's darkest hour, the emergence of Jimmy Hill and his consortium was as unexpected, as it was welcome, and represents a new dawn for the club. The spirits have, apparently, been working overtime.

The off-the field activities overshadowed most of the playing events during 1986-7. The season started with some optimism, with a popular new manager, Ray Lewington, and a squad which had gained experience in the Second Division. Any promotion aspirations were quickly dispelled, however, and once the uncertainties behind the scenes emerged and a crop of injuries occurred, the club nosedived towards the Third Division basement. Not even the return of Gordon Davies or the emergence of promising youngsters like Kevin Hoddy and Roddy Brathwaite could halt the apparent slide towards the oblivion of Division Four. Record defeats at the hands of Liverpool (10-0) in the Littlewoods Cup and Port Vale (6-0 at home in the League) underlined the parlous condition of the club.

The change of ownership and the new spirit of optimism engendered by Jimmy Hill and his group brought about an end-of-season revival. Some spirited performances, which relied heavily on enthusiasm and endeavour, garnered critical points which lifted Fulham to safety by the close of the campaign. Great as the relief was, there was no denying that the final position was the lowest in the Cottagers' 80-year history, and any euphoria was more about the fact the club had survived to fight another day than a sense of pride in the actual playing achievement.

There are, nevertheless, grounds for believing that the spirits had done their work and could now go into recess. The new board is more involved in and committed to the club, and the proposed second tier of control, a board of management, will be able to draw on a broader base of expertise than has ever been at the club's disposal before. As Liverpool and the various clubs managed by Brian Clough have shown, getting things right off the field is the first and most critical step to building a winning team. The squad, currently too large (almost twice as big as Queen's Park Rangers', for example), needs pruning, but contains enough potential to suggest that given a stable environment and the right leadership, it can challenge for honours in 1987-8. It will be a long road back, but there are precedents, and if the recipe for success includes professional management, enthusiasm for the club, ambition and a nucleus of talented, young players, Fulham has most of the key ingredients already at hand.

*The original Craven Cottage, destroyed by fire in 1888.
It stood on what is now the centre-circle area of the
football ground.*

The Ground, The Board and Money

M OST Fulham supporters have been angered, confused or saddened by the events of the last two or three years. The press has carried many depressing articles about the problems off the field, whilst the fans have seen for themselves the effect on the team's performance following the mass exodus of players. This culminated in the attempt to merge Fulham with Queen's Park Rangers in February 1987.

Whilst the suddenness of the announcement surprised many people, as did the extent of Fulham's financial problems, it was a situation that had been building up for years. It could in fact be traced to the turn of the century, when proposals were made first to move Fulham to Stamford Bridge and then to merge with Arsenal. The struggle the Cottagers have had to maintain an independent existence at Craven Cottage has been a feature of their history virtually since the club took over the site. Although not strictly about football, this is such an integral part of the Fulham story, it warrants telling in detail. It is a tragedy in three parts: the ground, the men who controlled the purse strings and the financial background against which these games were played. The three strands all came together towards the end of 1984 to produce the denouement of 1987.

The Ground

THE link between football club and ground is arguably stronger in the case of Fulham and Craven Cottage than for many other League teams. The friendly atmosphere and modest surroundings have created a unique environment for football, quite distinct from the usual crowded urban industrial developments which characterise most League grounds. That the Cottage is often described as having a 'homely' feeling is appropriate, since it was for many years used as a home for members of the staff.

Yet Craven Cottage was Fulham's ninth home and was not acquired until the mid-1890s. The earlier grounds served only to emphasise the club's amateur status, and none could be flattered with the title of a stadium. The club's wanderings did not take them very far: all the eight temporary grounds were within a couple of miles of Craven Cottage. Star Road near Earl's Court was the first from 1879-83, to be quickly followed by Eelbrook Common (1883), Lillie Road (1884), Putney Lower Common (1885), Ranlagh House, near Putney Bridge (1885-88), Barn Elms (1888-90), Pursur's Cross (1890), back to Eelbrook Common (1891) and then the Half Moon, Putney.

This nomadic existence was clearly inappropriate for a successful club with ambitions of becoming a footballing force in West London. A derelict site on the banks of the Thames was available, belonging partly to the Church Commissioners and partly to the Dean family (who were to feature prominently in Fulham's subsequent history). The original Craven Cottage, which had been built by the sixth Baron Craven in 1780, had been burnt down in 1888. The residents of that Cottage included Charles King, a money-lender, Sir Ralph Howard, and Edward Bulwer-Lytton, who wrote *The Last Days of Pompeii* whilst the occupant. By the time Fulham took over this land for a home ground in 1894, it had become a wilderness, the result of six years of neglect.

It took two years to turn the site into an area suitable for football. Full use was made of the excavations from the Shepherd's Bush underground to provide banking at the Hammersmith and Putney ends, and on the riverside. In addition, a stand was built on the Stevenage Road side, popularly known as The Rabbit Hutch. A firm owned by the Mears family was prominent in the construction of this building, and they subsequently tried to get Fulham to move to a new ground they had built, Stamford Bridge. When they were rebuffed, they started their own club. The first match played at the Cottage was on 10 October 1896, a Middlesex Senior Cup tie against Minerva, which Fulham won comfortably, 4-0.

These new surroundings lasted less than nine years. Once the club turned professional and joined the Southern League, it outgrew these facilities, and in 1905 the board appointed Archibald Leitch to remodel the ground. A man who spent much of his professional career designing football grounds, he has received posthumous recognition (Simon Inglis — *The Football Grounds of England and Wales*), and his work for Fulham is now of sufficient interest to have justified a preservation order on his structures in 1987.

Crowd's view of the Fulham-Brentford match at the Cottage in April 1905, showing the old stand.

England met Wales at the Cottage in 1907.

Leitch designed the current Stevenage Road stand and improved the banks of terracing on the other three sides of the ground. Most importantly, he built the present-day Cottage which has served at various times as a home, offices, dressing-rooms and players' bar. The new ground, which cost £15,000, was unveiled in September 1905 when Fulham and Portsmouth played out a 0-0 draw in a Southern League game. The football authorities were impressed enough with the new Cottage to use it for England's international against Wales in 1907.

This was basically how the ground remained until the early 1960s. There were only slight changes, such as the Cottage being connected for electricity in 1933 and concrete replacing the asphalt terracing in 1949. More ambitious plans, particularly the building of a second stand along the riverside, were rejected, once in 1935 (when Leitch's firm was once more involved) and again in 1950, on the grounds of cost. In 1935, the estimate was £11,000, and in 1950, £40,000.

The return to Division One in 1959 led to some modest improvements. The terracing at the Hammersmith end was first extended and then partially covered in 1965, whilst in 1962, Fulham installed floodlights, the last First Division club to do so. The money was raised by the Supporters' Club, and the club spent its funds on a player (Bobby Robson). Sheffield Wednesday were the Cottagers' first visitors under lights, in September 1962, and a Maurice Cook hat-trick helped Fulham to a 4-1 win.

In February 1972, the club opened the long-awaited Riverside Stand, the only significant alteration to Leitch's 1905 development. It was in many ways an admirable stand, but it was hopelessly mistimed. Attendances were well past their peak when it was built, the team was hovering perilously close to the Third Division, and the cost added a burden which the club's finances could not support.

Since then, the changes to the ground have been cosmetic (an electronic scoreboard which had a fatal seizure when Fulham scored five goals against Manchester City in 1984); enforced, by the Safety of Sports Ground Act; or practical, particularly the cell-system pitch, installed in 1983 and paid for by the Greater London Council. The real issue about the ground in recent years, however, is that ownership of the freehold passed from the Church Commissioners to the club in 1985. This fact, and the crippling financial problems arising out of the building of the riverside stand, have changed the nature of the debate about ground development. The issues have lately been how much commercial building there will be on the 6.3 acres site and whether football can continue to be played there.

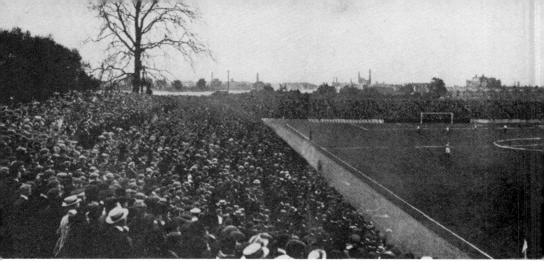

▲ *Craven Cottage pictured in 1906, just after rebuilding.*

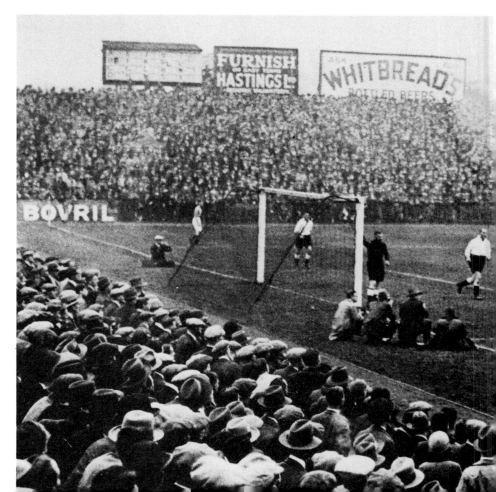

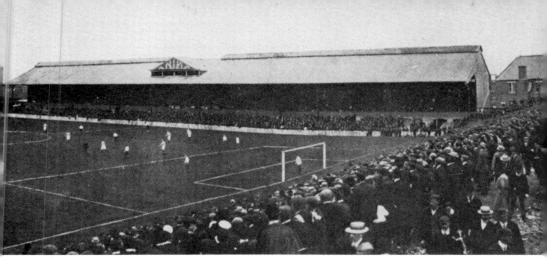

View of Craven Cottage taken during a League game in 1932.

Fulham v. Doncaster Rovers

Ruskin Spear is well known for his uncommon pictures of the commonplace. But, oddly, this most companionable Academician had never recorded a Soccer scene until we invited him to look at the Fulham ground—Craven Cottage—yesterday.

Ruskin Spear 1957

In 1957, The Observer *newspaper invited Ruskin Spear RA to look at Craven Cottage. The Academican had never before recorded a soccer scene. The above is his interpretation of a match-day at the Cottage.*

Fulham chairman John Dean acknowledges the crowd massed below the directors' box after the game against Exeter City in May 1932. They were celebrating promotion, which had been won the previous week against Bristol Rovers. The directors' box was then in the Stevenage Road Stand, where the press box is today.

44

The Board

MANY professional football clubs owe their original development, subsequent growth and (often) current survival to a rich patron. There has been considerable speculation as to the motives of these individuals, particularly recently as the financial stakes have increased. What is undeniable, however, is that the growth of the 'People's Game' has had more to do with the behaviour and attitudes of a wealthy oligarchy than with democratic principles. Fulham's history reflects this general trend. For much of its existence, the club has been under the control of one individual or clique, whose dictatorial style has varied only in the benevolence shown to the manager, players and supporters.

For a club which has spent most of its professional life outside the First Division, Fulham has had several chairmen and directors who have attracted a great deal of public attention, often more than the team. In some ways, this has helped to create the unique character of the club. Viewed from the outside, the Cottagers have usually appeared eccentric, inconsistent, humorous or frustrating, but rarely boring. It has, on the other hand, cost Fulham dear. Just as the team has often seemed naïve on the pitch, so has the club displayed a child-like innocence off it, placing its trust misguidedly in those who sought to take advantage for their own ends. The events of 1987 led to a reaction to this treatment and the establishment of a radically new structure.

For most of the period up to World War One, William Hall was the chairman, but the real power was Henry Norris (who was later knighted). Although he held only 50 shares in the new company, he exercised enormous influence. Norris was briefly chairman (from immediately prior to joining the League until 1908), but outside commitments led him to hand over to Hall. For seven years, Norris was Mayor of Fulham, and from 1918-22, MP for Fulham East. He made his money from property, and a company he owned with another Fulham director, George Allen, built some 2,000 houses in West London, including those artisan dwellings close to Craven Cottage which now change hands for six-figure sums in what has become 'yuppieland'.

Norris was labelled a soccer 'Czar'. He was wealthy, charismatic, outspoken and ruthless, a man who considered no opinion other than his own. He possessed a vaulting ambition, and, as might be expected of a politician, delighted in behind-the-scenes intrigue and manoeuvres. His lobbying was instrumental in gaining Fulham entry to the League in 1907. He also resisted the Mears' attempts to get Fulham to move to Stamford Bridge. This was not, however, because he was opposed to the principle of a

Henry Norris

William Hall

45

merger, for in 1909-10, he proposed either merging Fulham with the financially-troubled Arsenal or getting the clubs to share Craven Cottage or the White City. These proposals were blocked by the football authorities following protests from other London clubs and, thereafter, Norris' ambitions switched from Fulham to the Gunners.

He and Hall, whilst remaining Fulham directors, took over Arsenal and were behind the move from Plumstead to Highbury. More controversially, his wheeling and dealing got Arsenal back into the First Division in 1919, despite the fact that they finished in sixth place in Division Two in 1915. Norris' behaviour caught up with him, however, for in 1927-8 he (and Hall) were banned for life from football following financial irregularities in his dealings at Highbury. He died, an outcast from football, in 1934.

The next power to emerge on the Fulham board was a local businessman, John Dean. He had been a founder member of the company in 1903 (with 100 shares) and was the first chairman. He resigned from the board in 1908 following a disagreement with Norris and only returned when chairman James Watt resigned in 1925. Dean and his son, Charles Bradlaugh Dean, remained in the chair until 1958, and after that, his two grandsons were on the board until the upheaval in 1977.

Dean was as much a dictator as Norris, but his style was different. His fortune came from the family business of manufacturing blinds for shops, offices and homes, the London operation of which was based in Putney. He was committed to Fulham throughout his life, and was generous with his time and money. He rarely missed a match, home or away, ran regular and efficient board meetings and financed the debts the club accumulated season after season. In 1928, he even purchased the assets of the Craven Cottage Syndicate (which had financed the ground development) for £21,000. The money was originally meant as a loan for a 12-month period, but it extended well beyond the original date. Then, in February 1933, he paid from his own pocket the £5,100 transfer fee which brought Arnold and Keeping to the Cottage.

With his waxed moustache and wing collars, Dean's image was cast in the Victorian-Edwardian mould. This was reflected in his character and management style, which,

John Dean

Tommy Trinder

whilst authoritarian, was also paternalistic. He could be ruthless in his dealings with managers, but, at the same time, was considerate to many players who served the club well by giving them jobs when their careers came to an end. He viewed the club very much as his own possession, to the extent that he was known to involve himself in the preparation of the pitch, and even to have his lunch from a table specially placed in the centre-circle.

He died in 1944, without seeing the fulfilment of his ambition, taking Fulham into the First Division. He was succeeded by his son, Charles, who held the office until his death in 1958. During this period, the chairman continued the pattern established by his father. Although the Cottagers reached Division One in 1949, they did not indulge in big transfer fees. The £40,000 spent in the 1950 close season on five players was certainly substantial by Fulham standards, but it was modest for the time (the record fee for one player was £26,000) and pales into insignificance when averaged out over the number of years when the club refrained from any purchases. There was also relatively little expenditure on the ground and this raises an issue which is hard to resolve. In a period when attendances averaged 30-35,000, and players' wages were restricted (although playing staffs tended to be much larger), why were Fulham apparently so hard-pressed for funds?

Charles Dean's period of office was for the most part enjoyable and uncontroversial. Supporters were upset when Bobby Robson was sold to West Brom in 1956 for £25,000: the reason given was the club's financial condition. Although an isolated incident in the 1950s, it foreshadowed trends in later decades.

As fellow board members, Dean inherited bandleader Noel 'Chappie' D'Amato and appointed comedian Tommy Trinder amongst other directors. These two were Fulham supporters long before they were show-business personalities and it recognised a long-standing link between Fulham and the entertainment world. In recent years, disc jockey David Hamilton and rhythm and blues singer Alan Price have been directors whilst other actors, writers and singers such as Ray Brooks, Willis Hall, bandleader Ted Heath, Annie Ross, Honor Blackman, Ralph McTell, Terence Alexander and Dominic Guard have all been regulars at the Cottage. Fulham, moreover, are probably the only League club which has been supported by the title characters in three popular television series (all comedies), *Budgie, Citizen Smith* and *Minder.*

When Charles Dean died in December 1958, the season promotion was won back to Division One, he was succeeded by Tommy Trinder. An established stage, screen and television personality, Trinder's love of Fulham became part of his act. He was chairman at a critical time in the club's history: his term of office began with promotion to Division One and ended just after the 1975 Cup Final appearance. Trinder's high public profile brought Fulham to audiences other chairman could not reach, and his references to the Cottagers were invariably witty and affectionate. He helped to create the modern image of the club, and he was a chairman who was liked by the players.

Whilst Trinder was clearly at home in a public relations capacity, he was less comfortable with business matters and towards the end of his term, he lost the comedian's most priceless asset, a sense of timing. Little money was spent on either the ground or players, and Fulham were usually three or four players short of a quality First Division side. The practice of selling promising players to ease the financial problems became more common in the 1960s and 1970s, and when the club did purchase to try to avert the slide, there was an air of panic about it.

Trinder brought some new directors on to the board, people he believed could add a sharper business perspective to the club's affairs. The most notable of these was Eric Miller (later Sir Eric), a man who headed the property company, Peachey Corporation, and who was an Arsenal season-ticket and shareholder and well connected in Harold Wilson's Labour Party (echoes of Henry Norris). He used his influence with the Church Commissioners and the construction company, McAlpine, to build the riverside stand, from which most of Fulham's modern financial troubles stem. The financial consultant to McAlpine, Derek Budden, joined the board, as did City stockbroker, Guy Libby, a Fulham supporter and friend of Miller.

In spite of reaching the Cup Final in 1975, Fulham's debts mounted (see next section) and tensions on the board began to surface. Miller substantially increased his shareholding and was the major shareholder. Libby had alternative plans for financing the debt (to raise the share capital to £1 million through the issue of loan stock and converting the McAlpine debt into this longer-term form) but he failed to get the necessary 75 per cent of the votes to have his proposal adopted. When Trinder gave up the chair at the end of 1976, to become life president, Libby succeeded him, but it brought to a head the divisions on the board.

The summer of 1977 saw a public and highly acrimonious split. Libby, Budden, Trinder and the two Dean brothers, Tony and Charles, resigned, leaving Miller effectively in charge. When he put a bullet through his brain in September (on Yom Kippur, the Jewish Day of Atonement), a crisis loomed. Fulham claimed later that Miller had an agreement with McAlpine that he would place building contracts their way in lieu of payment for the stand, something the builders denied when they pressed for payment. It was left to another of Miller's associates to pick up the pieces after his death.

It was in July 1976 that Ernest Clay first appeared on the Fulham scene and in a little over 12 months he had taken over as chairman. In spite of having few friends at court, he emerged the victor from the bloody boardroom battle when most of the old guard were swept away in the summer of 1977. Clay remained in office for nine controversial and divisive years, during which time he continually provoked the football authorities and tried new ideas for making Fulham pay. In the end, his plans were thwarted by the

Ernie Clay *David Bulstrode*

48

local authority, but he gained substantial financial recompense by selling his interests in the club to the SB Property Company Limited for £4 million in May 1986.

This most visible of Fulham chairmen was a blunt Yorkshireman whose family business interests included an insulating materials manufacturing company in Reigate and Huddersfield and an hotel in Portugal. His first direct connection with football, albeit a tenuous one, came in 1963, during George Eastham's dispute with Newcastle United. Ernie, a friend of George Eastham senior, gave George junior a job with his company, which helped sustain him during the protracted legal battle. His involvement with Fulham, however, can be traced indirectly back to the late 1930s, when he was associated with a man who later became the father-in-law of (Sir) Eric Miller. When Miller committed suicide in 1977, Clay took over his shareholdings.

Viewed either from a distance or at close quarters, Clay is an enigma. Some people doubted his motives, whilst others questioned his methods. Nobody felt neutral about him. A case can be made, however, for claiming he was far-sighted, and in his efforts to inject some financial realism into football, he succeeded in shaking the soccer establishment from its complacency. Ernie admitted his lack of education, his small-business view of the world and his lack of southern sophistication, yet, at the end of the day, he sold his interest in a bankrupt Third Division football team to more subtle London operators for £4 million. Whilst he certainly took more risks with his own and his family's money than most football club directors did with theirs, in the end, his reward was commensurately greater.

Ernie's detractors would claim that from the first day he walked into the Cottage, his one goal was to turn the ground into a building site. He immediately appreciated the potential of the 6.3 acres of land on the banks of the Thames and all his actions, according to some of his critics, were designed to acquire the freehold of the Cottage and realise the development potential. Alec Stock, for example, in his autobiography, *A Little Thing Called Pride*, wrote that on his first day as chairman, Ernie Clay announced to the players at training: "We shall all be rich one day when we have a BUPA Hospital and a Hotel on the ground." Stock quickly concluded that the chairman had plans to sell up and move the club to another part of London. Similarly, several former players were quite outspoken in their criticisms of Clay and the way he ran the club after he sold it to SB Property. According to them, he was content to run the club down, to sell off the best players and let Fulham die from neglect.

Hindsight is a very precise science and it is easy now to construct a coherent scenario out of what in all probability were a series of *ad hoc* responses to specific situations. The conspiracy theory also overlooks the extent of Fulham's financial woes and the part played by other parties who contributed to the emergence of the SB Property Company. Some of the criticisms of Clay's policies, moreover, were based on a dislike of his forthright and earthy manner: his management style had a lot in common with a 19th-century mill-owner. He could also claim, with some justice, that the exodus of players between 1984 and 1986 owed as much to freedom of contract as to disaffection with his regime.

What is undeniable is that the life-support machine on which Fulham had depended for almost 15 years was turned off in 1986. When Clay's plans for perimeter development of the ground were rejected by the local authority, he could no longer afford to pump money into the club. Publicly, he talked of moving to a new ground, allowing the full development of Craven Cottage, but privately, as the depleted team slipped into the Third Division, he was negotiating with another buyer.

In May 1986, it was announced that Clay had sold out his controlling interest in Fulham to SB Property Company, the subsidiary of Marler Estates which also owned Stamford Bridge. The new chairman of Fulham was David Bulstrode, the chairman of both Marler and its subsidiary. His connections with Fulham were remote, but his initial promises impressed people at the start of 1986-7. His commitment continued for as long as another property company had a legal interest in partial development, but when the council rejected this application in February 1987, he revealed his plans to merge Fulham with Queen's Park Rangers and develop the Craven Cottage site.

From the ensuing outcry, one man emerged with a plan to save the club: former player Jimmy Hill. He moved quickly to mobilise support and within weeks had struck a deal with Bulstrode. In April 1987, he took over as chairman, Fulham's third in less than 12 months. In a short space of time, he brought an integrity and professionalism to the running of the club's affairs that had been missing for generations, and his infectious enthusiasm and progressive ideas offer the club its best hope of salvation. Never one to let the grass grow under his feet, Hill has harnessed the public reaction against property developers with his own skills as a football executive and communicator. His blueprint for Fulham's future is imaginative and innovative, giving all groups with an interest in the club a chance to participate in its management. His message to supporters when he took over was 'Happy Days Are Here Again', and the spirit running through the club from that time suggests that they just might be.

Jimmy Hill

50

Pages from the original Memorandum of Association in 1903.

Money

FROM their earliest days as a company, Fulham have struggled to be financially viable. They have been a modest club in every respect. The ground is noted more for its charm than its comfort, the team for entertaining more than winning, and crowds for their humour rather than their size. A modest club with much to be modest about is probably a realistic assessment, if a little harsh.

This is due as much to a lack of finance as a lack of ambition. As early as 1909-10, the board reported a loss to the shareholders, of £723, which raised the club's overdraft to £3,113. Financial losses continued until World War One, with the exception of a small (£88) profit in 1913-14. These sums seem trifling now, but in those days a season's gate receipts rarely exceeded £9,000 and the most expensive season ticket cost just £1.60 (£1.05 for ladies). In 1914-15 alone, expenditure of £9,046 was £2,770 above income, and the deficit represented well over half the season's total receipts.

The inter-war period saw a continuation of these trends. Expenditure regularly exceeded income and the recurring deficit imposed obvious limitations on plans for ground improvements and buying new players. In the five seasons between 1930 and 1935, for example, the total losses amounted to £12,132. This was at a time when the gate receipts for a home game rarely produced more than £1,000 and there was little scope for increasing income from outside sources.

The club therefore had to rely on the generosity of wealthy benefactors, usually the chairman or directors. From 1925 until 1959, this meant the Dean family, which used its private resources to keep Fulham going. In the immediate post-war era, the high attendances, and Fulham's promotions to Division One, eased the pressure, although the debt was never very far away. In the 1950s and 1960s, the usual response to a cash problem was to sell a player, of which Bobby Robson and Alan Mullery were the two best-known examples.

Attendances peaked in this period, and with the abolition of the maximum wage (in which Fulham's Jimmy Hill and former Fulham full-back Cliff Lloyd were the leading Players' Union personalities) and spiralling of transfer fees, the pressure on costs rose. The 1970s ushered in a period of accelerating inflation, which pushed up interest rates and increased the burden of the debt. These general economic conditions coincided with the Fulham board's decision to build a long-promised stand on the river side of the ground, which resulted in a quantum leap in the financial problems in the 1970s.

The ground has been at the centre of the events which led, almost inexorably, to the merger proposal of February 1987. It was the primary cause of the escalation of the financial problems in the 1970s and became the proposed solution of the 1980s. The building of the costly riverside stand in 1971-2 added significantly to Fulham's rising debts. Various schemes were put forward for developing parts of the ground to clear these debts, but none came to fruition. By the time SB Property Company paid the best part of £9 million for a bankrupt Third Division club in the 1986 close season, there was only one way they were likely to get a profitable return on their huge investment.

As Table 1 shows, Fulham's income rose steadily during the 1970s, but was at least 20 per cent short of the annual expenditure. These deficits could have been financed by transfers, but in fact in only two years were net transfers sufficient to make up the shortfall. Clearly, the club could not continue indefinitely spending £90,000 or so a year more than it was earning, but the sums were not so large as to threaten Fulham's continued existence.

Table 1:   Selected indicators of Fulham's financial performance, 1973-85, figures are in £000s.

Year ending June 30	Income	Expenditure	Net transfers	Profit (loss) for year	Current liabilities*
1973	164	246	−135	(217)	758
1975	349	434	+2	(83)	806
1977	393	488	−103	(146)	1,028
1979	445	560	−127	(193)	1,103
1981	388	798	+426	(177)	1,181
1983	926	1,058	+2	(404)	2,037
1985	658	890	+326	(88)	3,383

*Comprises bank overdraft, secured loans and accrued interest, creditors and accruals.

The riverside stand was the central issue. It added an enormous amount to the club's already large accumulated debt, which was growing bigger every year with the regular trading deficits. The club's annual accounts show that from 1973, the stand was the single largest item of debt and by 1979, this amounted to £434,000. In addition, there was a bank overdraft in excess of £200,000, and loans from directors had risen from £25,000 in 1973 to £170,000 by the end of the decade.

The club, therefore, had a huge debt, which was getting larger annually not only from the annual losses, but also from the non-payment of interest. By 1979, the annual interest on the debt amounted to £159,962, equivalent to 44 per cent of the gate receipts for the season. This meant that of every 20 people passing through the turnstiles, nine were used to stop the existing debt rising further. The problem was that the other 11 were insufficient to meet the necessary expenditure, and thus the debt rose anyway.

Fulham, therefore, went into the 1980s in bad shape. The team was relegated to Division Three and faced the prospect of falling attendances, whilst the club's liabilities (i.e. its overdraft, loans and creditors) rose to £1.1 million. The only significant asset in the balance sheet was the lease (which did not expire until 2094), valued at almost £725,000, but this could not be realised to pay off the debts.

One man who continued to increase his financial involvement in the club, and therefore his control over it, was the chairman. In August 1979, the assignees of the McAlpine (the builders of the riverside stand) debt, Financial and General Securities Limited, were paid in full by a loan provided by Ernest Clay Holdings, which was secured by a debenture, giving a floating charge over the assets of the company. Clay, moreover, increased his shareholding at every opportunity. In 1977, he had just 200 of the 15,000 shares, but by 1979 he held 7,898: by 1984, his own holding was up to 10,729. This was something no previous director had felt compelled to do and, for some time, it was difficult to see why he was doing it, or how he would get his money back.

The situation deteriorated rapidly in the early 1980s. A substantial sum (c.£600,000) was lost on a short-lived foray in Rugby League and, after missing out on promotion in 1982-3, gate receipts levelled off and then fell. Thus the pressure on costs continued to rise, whilst the income declined. The interest on the debt alone reached £178,000 in 1984, and the amount owing to creditors falling due within 12 months rose to £2.3 million. Over 70 per cent of this debt was to Ernest Clay Holdings Limited and it was clear that the chairman's family companies were suffering as a result of having to fund Fulham. The club, moreover, was up to its limit on its own overdraft and at the end of 1983-4 recorded a loss for the year of £326,000.

It seemed a dubious asset that chairman Clay had acquired, but in November 1984, the whole picture changed. Fulham had been tenants at Craven Cottage of the Church Commissioners: they had a long lease (110 years) at a peppercorn rent of £2,000 a year. While these were clearly generous terms, Fulham's options for reducing their debts were limited. The extent to which commercial development could be undertaken was restricted: a proposal to build flats at the Putney end in the early 1980s was given serious consideration, but eventually dropped. As long as Fulham continued to play football, their future at the Cottage was guaranteed by the lease with the Church Commissioners. The escalation in London property values offered the prospect of a profitable commercial development of two sides of the ground, but, as tenants of Craven Cottage, Fulham would not have benefitted to the full extent of any new buildings. The Church Commissioners' co-operation with Fulham did not extend to assisting the club financially by allowing it to exploit the development value, which, they claimed, belonged to them.

After years of trying, and with the help of respected public figures and Fulham supporters like Peter Pitt of the GLC, and Tom Wilson of St Quintin, Clay finally got the Church Commissioners to sell the freehold of the whole 6.3 acres of the Cottage site to Fulham FC. In November 1984, he agreed to pay £900,000, a £20,000 option in January 1985 and the balance six months later. Although advised by a number of independent people close to the club, and legally able to do so, the Church Commissioners chose not to insert restrictive covenants on any part of the ground. They could, for instance, have excluded the area of the pitch from any future development proposals, which would have virtually ensured the continuation of football on the site. As it was, the terms of the sale of the freehold gave the Fulham board two options, partial or perimeter development which would probably yield sufficient profit to clear the existing debts, or to move the club to an alternative ground and develop the whole Craven Cottage site, a vastly more profitable proposition.

The 18 months that followed the option to purchase the freehold in January 1985 were marked by hectic negotiations, political manoeuvering and financial wheeling and dealing. The chronology is relatively straightforward, but the simple events have been subject to several interpretations. The bare facts are as follows:

January-July 1985
Discussions were held with a number of developers, both to develop the whole site and for partial development. In addition, Clay approached the local council to suggest a joint development of the site, but was rejected. The Clays did not have sufficient funds to pay for the balance (£880,000) of the freehold as the deadline approached, a deal was struck with a Manchester-based firm, Kilroe Industrial Enterprises, of which Sir Matt Busby was a director. The total cost of the freehold acquisition was £972,000, which was met by a loan from Kilroe.

July-December 1985
Kilroe prepared their plans for a partial development of the ground, covering the Putney end and the riverside. This would have preserved football at the Cottage, yielded the developers their normal profit, and the club in the region of £3.5m-£4.0m, sufficient to clear all the debts.

Fulham, meanwhile, had reported more huge losses in 1985. Expenditure exceeded income by £232,000, to which had to be added £210,000 in interest charges. The overall deficit, however, was reduced to £88,000 by the sale of players, which contributed £326,000 to club funds. The overall debts were increased by the loan for the freehold (£972,000), and rose to £3.23 million. This was five times higher than the income for the year, clearly a position which could not be sustained for very long. The critical difference in the 1985 accounts, however, was that balance sheet showed fixed assets (the ground) valued at £4.02 million.

January-March 1986
Kilroe's plans became a political issue at the turn of the year with the death of local Conservative MP, Martin Stevens. The residents in the area around the ground were opposed to the development, and the Conservatives on the council (who had a majority on the planning committee), did not want to jeopardise their party's chances in the parliamentary by-election by supporting an unpopular proposal. When Kilroe's application was heard by the council's planning committee, it was rejected 7-0.

March-May 1986
Following the council's decision, the Clays felt there was no option but to move the club from Craven Cottage. The family interpreted the planning rejection as evidence that the community did not want a football club in its midst. The only way they could get their money back was to move the club and develop the whole site. The Labour candidate's victory in the parliamentary election and the return of a Labour council two months later, committed to maintaining three football clubs in the borough on three sites, offered Fulham a glimmer of hope.

May 1986 — February 1987
Within weeks of the end of the season, Clay surprised everybody connected with the club by selling his shares to SB Property Company, a subsidiary of Marler Estates plc. The new owners paid approximately £9 million (£5.5 million for the shares and £3.5 million, including the loan from Kilroe, to Fulham's creditors) for the club. This worked out at about £367 per share, which made Ernie Clay's holding worth close on £4 million. To finance the deal, SB Property Company had a rights issue, the prospectus for which showed that Craven Cottage was valued independently at £4 million on the basis of its continued use as a football ground, but at £11 million as a

vacant site. Since they had paid £9 million for it, it was obvious how SB Property Company intended to make a return on their outlay.

Since this same company also owned the Stamford Bridge site, it was generally assumed that Fulham had been purchased in order to offer alternative accommodation to Chelsea. The new chairman, David Bulstrode, made soothing noises about his intentions when the 1986-7 season opened. This may have been an expedient, however, since he did not have a free hand. Kilroe were contractually entitled to submit a revised development, which they did to the new council's planning committee in February 1987. Before a decision was taken, however, the proposal was withdrawn, and effectively died.

Just a week or so later, Bulstrode dropped his bombshell. He negotiated the purchase of Queen's Park Rangers from Jim Gregory, and with this deal his companies owned two West London clubs and three grounds. To meet the League's objections about having interests in more than one club, he proposed to merge Fulham with Queen's Park Rangers, and then develop the whole Craven Cottage site. The announcement led to a furore: the press, Football League, PFA, politicians and football personalities were all vociferous in condemning the involvement of property developers in football generally and the demise of Fulham in particular.

It is not unlikely that SB Property never intended to close Fulham down. The proposal contained two separate objectives, the first to clear the Craven Cottage site and the second to merge the football club with Queen's Park Rangers. The first was the most important to Bulstrode and his shareholders and was not conditional on achieving the second. They could therefore consider negotiating on Fulham's survival without jeopardising their principal goal. If they could get some assurances on ground development, they could concede the continuation of the club, something about which they were probably indifferent, so long as it played somewhere else and some other group was prepared to finance it. These tactics could also have a beneficial public relations effect, since SB Property could be seen to bowing to public pressure. So, within a fortnight of the announcement of the merger, Bulstrode indicated that he was prepared to sell the football club whilst retaining the freehold rights to the Craven Cottage site.

The Football League Management Committee made this change of heart easier by blocking the merger. For several weeks, there was much speculation about consortia interested in purchasing Fulham. In reality, there was just one serious contender, led by Jimmy Hill, who worked closely with local MP, Nick Raynsford, council leader Gordon Prentice and former Fulham full-back and the head of the City surveying firm, St Quintin, Tom Wilson. In April, the basis of a deal was agreed and Jimmy Hill took over as chairman of Fulham FC. He got financial backing from a small group of supporters, who, although wealthy, had no experience of running a Football League club. Hill agreed to act as chairman for a temporary period to help with the transition, particularly the restructuring of the club.

It is too early to assess the likelihood of success for the new board, and some of the details of the agreement with SB Property must stay confidential. There remain, however, several outstanding questions about these events and only those most directly involved know the answers. In particular:

a. Why did the Church Commissioners sell the freehold of the ground without any restrictive convenants?

b. Why did the council reject Clay's offer to develop the ground jointly?

c. Why did the council reject Kilroe's planning applications?

d. When did Bulstrode and Clay begin negotiating?

e. Why did SB Property Company pay so much for Fulham? Clay had said openly he would go if his debts were paid, but in fact he got much more. The fact that millions of pounds were effectively taken out of the club in this deal severely constrains the new board's options.

f. When did Bulstrode and Jim Gregory begin negotiating for the sale of Queen's Park Rangers, the announcement of which came only days after Kilroe's second planning application was withdrawn?

These questions are largely academic as far as the future of Fulham is concerned. The club must now put this unhappy episode behind it and look to the future. All supporters must hope that under Jimmy Hill's dynamic leadership, the new board will, in its financial dealings, put the interests of the club first; hope that the manager can build a promotion-winning team; hope that the youth policy will continue to produce high-quality youngsters; and hope that the players will once again wear the Fulham shirt with pride. For hope, as all Fulham supporters know, springs eternal.

Work underway on the 'cell-system' pitch, laid at Craven Cottage in the close season of 1983. The cost of £140,000 was paid for by Ken Livingstone's GLC; the company which installed it included Denis Thatcher on its board.

The Fulham Managers

JUST as the history of a country is often seen in terms of kings, presidents or prime ministers, so the history of a football club can be viewed from the perspective of its managers, the men who are popularly thought to determine its fortunes. Before looking at the careers of the individuals who have been at the helm at the Cottage, it is interesting to make some overall assessment of their records. The table below shows the League record of each Fulham manager, excluding caretakers such as Joe Edelston and Johnny Haynes and incumbent Ray Lewington, on the basis of two points for a win. There is also an element of double counting, since Frank Osborne was assisted at times by three team managers, and the playing record of the period is shown against both.

The table shows that there is a wide variation in the individuals' periods of office. The 19 managers span 71 playing seasons, an average of 3.7 seasons per manager, or 4.3 years if the war years are included. Frank Osborne (16 years), Phil Kelso (15 years) and Jack Peart (13 years) are the longest serving, whilst Jimmy Hogan and Bobby Robson, two of the most famous names on the list, lasted less than 12 months. Although James McIntyre heads the table, he would have been overhauled by Harry Bradshaw if the results of Bradshaw's first three seasons are included. Between 1904 and 1907, Fulham twice won the Southern League championship before joining the Football League.

There are some interesting common denominators between many of the managers. The first is the high proportion who were former Fulham players: Ray Lewington is the ninth, following Ducat, Joe Bradshaw, Osborne, Hogan, Jezzard, Robson, Dodgin (junior) and Macdonald. In addition, Vic Buckingham guested during the war and the caretaker managers were all players or former players. Another common factor is a connection with Arsenal. Bradshaw (senior), Kelso, Ducat, Liddell, Dodgin (junior), Stock, Campbell and Macdonald all gained playing, coaching or management experience at Highbury before going to the Cottage. There are five internationals on the list (Ducat, Osborne, Jezzard, Robson and Macdonald), whilst only Bradshaw (senior) and Kelso had never been League players. Finally, two father and son teams, the Bradshaws and the Dodgins, have managed Fulham.

MANAGERS' SUCCESS-RATE

	Manager	Period	Div	Pld	W	D	L	Goals For	Ag	Total pts*	Goals /game	Points /game
1	James McIntyre	1931-34	2 & 3	119	59	25	35	238	181	143	2.00	1.20
2	Harry Bradshaw	1904-09	2	76	35	16	25	140	97	86	1.84	1.13
2	Dug Livingstone	1956-58	2	96	45	19	32	207	115	109	2.16	1.13
4	Malcolm Macdonald	1980-84	2 & 3	151	61	44	46	228	185	166	1.51	1.10
5	Ned Liddell	1929-31	3	77	33	17	27	151	147	83	1.96	1.08
6	Bill Dodgin (junior)	1968-72	2 & 3	154	60	40	54	211	205	160	1.37	1.04
7	Jimmy Hogan	1934-35	2	31	17	10	10	49	42	32	1.58	1.03
8	Phil Kelso	1909-24	2	438	172	99	167	582	517	443	1.33	1.01
8	Jack Peart	1935-48	2	256	95	69	92	383	349	259	1.50	1.01
10	Frank Osborne	1948-64	1 & 2	682	262	155	265	1182	1152	679	1.73	0.99
10	Alec Stock	1972-76	2	186	63	59	64	213	202	185	1.15	0.99
12	Bedford Jezzard	1958-64	1 & 2	274	103	62	109	448	486	268	1.64	0.98
13	Joe Bradshaw	1926-29	2 & 3	126	47	25	54	227	252	119	1.80	0.94
14	Ray Harford	1984-86	2	90	34	14	42	125	138	82	1.39	0.91
15	Andy Ducat	1924-26	2	84	26	22	36	87	133	74	1.04	0.88
16	Bill Dodgin (senior)	1949-53	1 & 2	181	51	50	80	258	299	152	1.43	0.84
16	Bobby Campbell	1976-80	2	163	47	43	73	180	226	137	1.10	0.84
18	Vic Buckingham	1965-68	1	123	35	27	61	189	247	97	1.52	0.79
19	Bobby Robson	1968	1 & 2	36	6	10	20	39	75	22	1.08	0.61

*Two points for a win throughout

57

Harry Bradshaw
1904-1909

FULHAM'S first full-time manager, and one of the most successful, was Harry Bradshaw. He was in charge for five seasons, and took the club from the Southern League into the Football League, and to a semi-final place in the FA Cup. In addition, the Craven Cottage site was redeveloped, with the building of the Stevenage Road stand and the Cottage itself.

One of football's earliest pioneers, Bradshaw first made his name with Burnley from 1891 to 1899 before coming south to manage the ailing Woolwich Arsenal. In a relatively short space of time, he brought about a remarkable transformation in that club's fortunes, building a team which won promotion to the First Division as well as halting the slide into bankruptcy. It was something of a surprise therefore, when Bradshaw was lured to Fulham from Plumstead in 1904. The club had only just become a limited liability company and acquired professional status.

The Bradshaw style at Arsenal and Fulham owed much to the old Scottish formation of short accurate passing and dribbling. In his first few months, he signed seven new players, six of them Scots, and he got results. In his second season, 1905-06, Fulham won the Southern League championship, a feat they repeated the following year, even more convincingly. These successes paved the way for admission to the Football League in 1907, where the club proved immediately that it was not out of its depth. Not only did Bradshaw's side reach the FA Cup semi-final, but it was also just three points short of promotion.

It was by any standards a remarkable debut amongst soccer's elite, and it was exactly 50 years before Fulham had an equally successful season in both competitions. The remainder of Bradshaw's tenure was anti-climatic: mid-table League positions and early eliminations from the Cup. When his contract expired in 1909, he chose not to renew it, preferring instead to become secretary of the Southern League. His son Joe, a player at Fulham, also left, but was to return in the 1920s as manager. Bradshaw senior, a good administrator, shrewd businessman and (as far as the term could be applied in Edwardian times) clever tactician, put Fulham on the football map, just as he had Arsenal. He died in 1921, still running the Southern League.

Phil Kelso
1909-1924

WHEN Bradshaw left Arsenal, the Woolwich club turned to Phil Kelso to replace him, and when Bradshaw left the Cottage in 1909, it was Kelso the Fulham board appointed as his successor. (This Fulham - Arsenal link has been maintained up to the present day). Although he was only 40 when he took over at Fulham, Kelso already had an established reputation in football management. A stern, abrasive Scot, he was with Hibernian before coming to London with Arsenal in 1904, helping them to two FA Cup semi-finals. After four years, he returned to Scotland, to take over a hotel in Largs, in the Firth of Clyde, but 12 months later the Fulham board enticed him back to football, and London.

He was to stay for 15 years, a period which spanned World War One. This was the longest term any one manager has had sole control of Fulham's affairs. Although few trophies were won, he helped the club consolidate its position in the Second Division, and successfully steered it through the difficult years of the World War. The financial pressures which have dogged Fulham's history were evident in Kelso's time, and he helped the Cottagers to survive a proposed merger with Arsenal. Some of his dealings in the transfer market were highly imaginative. He brought a number of famous internationals, who, although past their best, added a lot of glamour to West London and who blended in with some locally developed talent.

Kelso was a man of firm views and had a reputation as a disciplinarian. He had a paternalistic attitude towards players' drinking and smoking, and he also wanted them to live in London but spend the night before a match away from the bright lights. More than one player left after clashes with the manager, but most regarded him as fair but strict, and a bit remote.

In his long period of office, Kelso built two fine teams, one either side of World War One. His last couple of seasons were the least successful and relegation was a threat. He also lost a lot of credibility in the Barney Travers bribery scandal: many people felt the player carried the can for carrying out the instructions of others. In 1924, Kelso retired for the second and last time. He stayed in the area and took over a pub, where he stayed until his death, at the age of 64 in 1935.

Andy Ducat
1924-1926

THE popular choice to succeed Kelso as manager in 1924 was club captain Andy Ducat. He was the first Fulham player to take over the helm and, like his two predecessors, had been with Arsenal. Ducat was one of the most distinguished figures on the English sporting scene for a quarter of a century, and is one of only 17 men this century to win caps for England at both football and cricket.

Born in Brixton in February 1886, Ducat was raised in Southend, and his first club as a player was Westcliff Athletic. He then joined Southend Athletic before Phil Kelso signed him for Arsenal in February 1905. He was then a centre forward and marked his Football League debut with a hat-trick against Newcastle. It was at wing-half, however, that Ducat established himself and, in 1910, won the first of his international caps.

A serious financial crisis forced the Gunners to sell him to Aston Villa in June 1912 for £1500. Although at his peak, his career was interrupted by a broken leg, which kept him out of Villa's Cup-winning side of 1913, and by World War One. He came back in 1919 to lead Villa to an FA Cup triumph over Huddersfield and to win back his England place. Then, 12 months later, a dispute with the Villa board about living closer to the club led to his transfer to Fulham, signed once again by Kelso.

Ducat immediately took over as club captain on his arrival in June 1921, and went on to make 68 appearances in three seasons. He was a classical wing-half, a master of positional play, especially good in the air and, in spite of a bulky frame, very graceful. He had an unrivalled reputation for fair play and was in the tradition of the old Victorian gentlemen sportsmen. These same qualities were a disadvantage when he took over as manager. He survived only two seasons and in 1925-6 relegation was avoided only on the last day of the season. A spirited Cup run that season, when Fulham beat First Division Notts County, Liverpool and Everton before going out in the quarter-finals to Manchester United, was the only bright spot in his tenure of office.

In 1926, Ducat paid the price for failure and was the first Fulham manager to be sacked. He continued playing cricket for Surrey, scoring over 23,000 runs, including 52 centuries, between 1906 and 1931. He also coached cricket at Eton, turned to journalism and became a licensee. In 1942, at the age of 56, he collapsed and died whilst batting at Lords.

Joe Bradshaw
1926-1929

IT was to a familiar figure that the Fulham board turned for a successor to Andy Ducat. In the first couple of League seasons, 1907-09, Joe Bradshaw had played a handful of matches for the club when his father was manager. In 1909, when Bradshaw senior moved on, Joe made the short journey to Stamford Bridge, where he made half-a-dozen League appearances in 1909-10. From there, he went to Southend, as player-manager, but after overseas service in World War One, he was back in the Football League, managing Swansea until 1926.

He came to the Cottage at a difficult time. Ducat's teams had come perilously close to relegation and a number of the established players were clearly past their best. There was also a new chairman to contend with, the dynamic John Dean replacing James Watts. The Deans were to be an influential family in Fulham's affairs right up to the 1970s. There was also a major change in the offside law, which increased substantially the number of goals scored in football generally.

The combination of these events proved too much for Fulham and Bradshaw. He made changes, clearing out many older players, but unfortunately their replacements did not perform any better. Whilst most clubs set scoring records with the change in the offside law, Fulham managed just five more goals in 1926-7. In 1927-8, Fulham were relegated for the first time, largely because of an appalling away record. The introduction of Third Division football to the Cottage led to more sweeping changes and, in Bradshaw's third season, a century of goals was scored for the first time. It was not enough to win promotion, however, or save the manager's job. When his contract expired in 1929, he left Fulham for Bristol City, where he stayed until 1932. He then left football to work in insurance.

Edward (Ned) Liddell
1929-1931

FULHAM'S third manager in five years was Ned Liddell, and he was destined to stay less time than either of his immediate predecessors. He is the only one of Fulham's previous managers whose whole period of office was spent in the Third Division, and in each of the two seasons under his control the club finished in a lower position than it had 12 months earlier.

Born in the North-East in 1878, Liddell worked in the shipyards and played amateur football in his youth. The first of his many clubs was Southern League Southampton in 1905-06, and subsequently he played for Gainsborough Trinity, Clapton Orient, Southend and Arsenal. After World War One, Liddell went back to Southend as manager and had a spell as Queen's Park Rangers' manager (their first in the Football League), before joining Fulham as a scout in 1922.

He was, therefore, part of the Cottage set-up when he was invited to replace Bradshaw. In spite of playing open, attractive football, Liddell's Fulham teams made no serious promotion challenge. He made one or two useful signings, like Jake Iceton and Syd Gibbons, but generally he kept the same side. The relationship between Liddell and Chairman John Dean was a very uneasy one and it is clear from the minutes of the board meetings who had the upper hand.

When it became apparent that 1930-31 was going to be another unsuccessful season, the directors invited James McIntyre to take over as manager, but asked Liddell to stay on in his previous scouting capacity. It was clearly an untenable position for him and shortly after McIntyre's arrival, in April 1931, he left to continue his wanderings. His post-Fulham career saw Liddell serve West Ham, Luton (manager), Chelsea, Portsmouth, Brentford and Spurs, usually as a scout. He was active in football up to the time of his death, at the age of 90, in 1968.

James McIntyre
1931-1934

STATISTICALLY Fulham's most successful manager, James McIntyre had a long and varied career in football, but only a relatively short stay at the Cottage. Walsall born, he began as a player with his local club and then had spells with Notts County, Reading, Coventry and Northampton, where he was a playing colleague of the legendary Herbert Chapman. Like the famous Arsenal manager, McIntyre had a reputation for being outspoken and effective.

In 1907, he became trainer at Coventry, a post he held for seven years. He then moved on to Southampton in a similar capacity, but, when League football was suspended during World War One, he went back to Coventry to work in a factory. On the resumption of football in 1919, he returned to The Dell, but as manager, and guided the Saints to promotion from the Third Division. In 1924 he retired and went to run an hotel in Scotland. Within four years, however, he was back in England, and in football, as Coventry's manager, where he stayed for three years until his appointment as Fulham manager in April 1931.

In his first full season in charge, 1931-2, he guided the club to the Third Division (South) title, the first manager to achieve this feat twice with different clubs. It was a record-breaking season for the Cottagers and was followed by an equally thrilling season when promotion to the First Division was missed by a whisker. Much of the credit was due to McIntyre. His new signings made all the difference to a side which had failed to make an impact on the Third Division in the previous three seasons.

One of these was free-scoring centre-forward Frank 'Bonzo' Newton from Stockport, who set a club record of 43 goals in the championship season. Within 18 months, McIntyre surprisingly sold Newton to Reading, and to replace him paid £2,500 for Arsenal's Jack Lambert, who was clearly past his best. A run of poor performances followed, and in February 1934, the manager was dismissed. The reason, according to the board minutes, was because 'of his unprecedented action in transferring, entirely on his own initiative, F.Newton to Reading for the impossible price of £650'. The Fulham board allowed McIntyre's successors much less discretion, whilst he left football for good, to work in Southampton for a company called Follands.

Jimmy Hogan
1934-1935

THE man who has the dubious distinction of being Fulham's shortest-serving manager is also one of the most distinguished figures in football history. Jimmy Hogan took over as manager-coach in the summer of 1934, and although it was his first post in England, he was already recognised internationally as an outstanding coach. His reputation counted for nothing at the Cottage, however, when his techniques proved too unorthodox for the board and players. After only 31 League matches, he was relieved of his duties.

Born in Nelson, Lancashire in 1883, Hogan began his playing career with his local club, and then had spells with Rochdale, Burnley, Bolton and Swindon. Southern League Fulham signed him in 1905, where he won two championship medals and made a handful of Football League appearances in 1907-08. Although not an outstanding inside-forward, Hogan's interest in tactics stemmed from his playing experiences at the Cottage, where he was influenced greatly by the club's ball-playing Scots. After leaving Fulham, he served several other clubs before moving to Europe, and in 1912 he took up a coaching assignment in Holland. Two years later, he went to Austria to take charge of the national side and began a famous partnership with Hugo Meisl.

Interned in Budapest during World War One, he remained on the Continent in the 1920s, coaching in Hungary, Germany and Austria. In his 20 years in Europe, he was given much of the credit for developing the game to the point where, technically, it outstripped the British. Hopes were high when he returned to the Cottage as manager in the 1934 close season. He deplored the stifling effect of Herbert Chapman's third-back game control, close intricate passing and dribbling were at the heart of Hogan's philosophy.

The response he got was the typical British reaction to anything new. The players did not like his unconventional training methods and tactics and the board did not believe mature players needed coaching. In spite of an improvement in results, and the goal tally, Hogan did not last the season. Very little credit attaches to the Fulham board for the way they handled his dismissal. He learned of his fate while recuperating in hospital from an operation. What started as a bold and imaginative experiment failed, almost certainly for a want of trying.

Hogan returned to the Continent and guided Austria to the Olympic Final of 1936. He subsequently led Aston Villa to promotion in 1938 and the FA Cup semi-final. After the war he was involved with Celtic, Brentford and Villa. His reputation increased as he grew older, particularly after the Hungarian side which defeated England 6-3 at Wembley in 1953 acknowledged the contribution he had made to their game. When he died in January 1974 at the age of 90, he was widely regarded as one of the outstanding coaches in the history of football.

Joe Edelston
1934 & 1935

ONE of the most popular and best-known figures at the Cottage during the inter-war period was Joe Edelston. In a long football career, he served six clubs in a variety of roles, but he was generally associated with Fulham. He was never given complete control of club affairs, nor did he reach the heights as a player. He took over on a temporary basis on several occasions, but for the most part he remained assistant or reserve-team manager.

He was born in 1891 and played for Hull and Manchester City before signing for Fulham in 1920. Edelston was a wing-half, and in the early 1920s formed an impressive half-back line with Andy Ducat and Jimmy Torrance. All three were over the age of 30, but they were the backbone of a promotion-chasing team. In all, Edelston made 67 appearances in four years, but impressed people with his organisational abilities and knowledge of the game. He was made captain and coach of the reserves in 1925, and continued in that role for 12 years, earning a reputation as a survivor, serving under six managers in this period.

As important as his work with the reserves, was Edelston's willingness to step into the breach when a manager left suddenly. The first such occasion followed McIntyre's departure in February 1934, and the second came 12 months later when Hogan was dismissed. Many people at the Cottage hoped he would get the job permanently, but the board opted for Jack Peart. This was the beginning of the end of Edelston's career at Fulham.

With the prompting of Hogan, he had become a qualified FA coach, one of the very first. This was at a time when the manager's role was essentially administrative and directors were unconvinced about the value of coaching. Matters came to a head in November 1937, when the first team languished at the foot of the Second Division, whilst the reserves were riding high in the Combination table. Edelston was accused of countermanding Peart's tactical instructions and was advised to look for another appointment.

It was an unhappy end to his stay. When he left, he took his son Maurice, an inside-forward but later a BBC commentator, with him. Edelston senior subsequently worked for Brentford, Reading and Leyton Orient, but finished his working life in a clerical job in Deptford. He died, aged 78, in 1970.

John George (Jack) Peart
1935-1948

THE 11 years of managerial instability that began in 1924 ended with the appointment of Jack Peart. After the imaginative choice of Hogan, the board opted for a safe and conventional successor. Peart was to remain at the Cottage until his death 13 years later and he ranks as the third longest-serving Fulham manager, although seven seasons were lost to World War Two.

He was born at South Shields in October 1889. A centre-forward, he began his playing career with the local side South Shields Adelaide in 1905 and ended it at Rochdale as player-manager in 1924. Peart was one of football's nomads, spending brief periods at Sheffield United (May 1907), Stoke (1911), Newcastle (March 1912), Notts County (February 1913), Birmingham (November 1919), Derby (January 1920), Port Vale (January 1922) and Norwich (cs 1922). He also had a short spell as player-manager of Ebbw Vale (1920-22). He joined Rochdale as player-manager in March 1923, but gave up playing in the 1924 close season, and he remained at the Spotland ground until the summer of 1930. He then took over at Bradford City, where he stayed until his appointment as Fulham manager in May 1935.

Peart was a quiet, knowledgeable man, an administrator rather than a tactician. He had learned his craft in the lower divisions of the Football League and, whilst he may have lacked vision, even ambition, he brought stability to the club and guided them through the difficult war years. His role was spelt out by the board on his appointment: to act as the principal adviser to the board, to control all matters relating to players and matches, to secure new players and 'to dispose of any surplus or unwanted players'. For this, he was offered a salary of £600 and the same bonuses as the players.

Fulham's major achievement in Peart's time came in his first season, when the club reached the FA Cup semi-final for only the second time: Sheffield United won 2-1. In September 1948, after a brief illness, Peart died. Ironically, Fulham went on to win the Second Division championship that season, virtually with the team that he had built. Peart's legacy was, therefore, a sound one, for in spite of the lack of honours, the club was undoubtedly stronger at the time of his death then it had been when he arrived.

Frank Osborne
1948-1964

WHEN Frank Osborne reluctantly accepted the invitation to step into Peart's shoes in October

1948, it completed an unusual series of appointments. He first signed for Fulham in 1921 and became the first Fulham player to win an England cap, when he played against Ireland in 1922. He moved to Spurs 15 months later, spending seven and a half years at White Hart Lane, before ending his playing career at Southampton in 1933.

He had not severed his connections with Fulham, however, for he was working as a sales representative for chairman Dean's blinds company and, when he finished playing, he became a Fulham director in 1935. He was still on the board when Peart died, and thus 'stepped down' to become manager. So unusual was the appointment that it needed special permission from the FA. Osborne was to remain at the helm until his retirement in October 1964, and his 16 years in charge made him Fulham's longest-serving manager. He was, however, assisted by several team-managers, and his title varied from manager to secretary-manager to general manager.

A South African from Wynberg, Osborne was born in October 1896, and came to England in 1911. Until his retirement 53 years later, he was continuously involved in football and, in many ways, his period as manager was the most successful. In his first season, 1948-9, Fulham won the Second Division title and, after being relegated in 1952, were promoted again in 1959. In his time, the club also reached two FA Cup semi-finals. Osborne's era, however, is remembered for more than these successes: his teams were the highest scoring of any in Fulham's history and the football played, particularly in the 1950s, amongst the most attractive. The family atmosphere associated with Craven Cottage owed much to his attitude, where players were given the freedom to express themselves and entertain the crowds.

Osborne was reputedly a nervous character, often unable to watch the closing minutes of tense matches. He was also subject to the players' superstitions. In the exciting promotion push of 1949, Osborne was in Scotland, scouting. As a result of getting his hair cut, he missed the train connection and the game he was going to watch. Fulham won that day, and from then until the end of the season, he had to repeat the routine for away games.

He retired on his 68th birthday in October 1964, since when he has had little contact with Fulham. Today, at the age of 91, he lives in Epsom, Surrey, and is the oldest surviving Fulham player. (See *Fulham Stars A-Z*).

Bill Dodgin (senior)
1949-1953

FOR much of his long tenure, Frank Osborne was assisted in his managerial duties by a team manager. The second of these, but the first to have control over playing affairs, was Bill Dodgin. He went to the Cottage in 1949, just after promotion to Division One had been achieved, although an attempt had been made to secure his services several months earlier.

As a player, Dodgin was a workmanlike rather than outstanding wing-half. Born in Gateshead in 1905, he began his career with Huddersfield in the 1920s, at a time when the Yorkshire club was one of the most powerful in the country. He then moved on to Lincoln, where he captained the Imps, before joining Charlton in the 1930s for the most successful part of his playing career. Under Jimmy Seed's shrewd guidance, the 'Haddicks' won promotion from the Third to the First Division in consecutive seasons and almost took the League title the following year.

In 1939, Dodgin was transferred to Southampton, where he ended his playing days and began his managerial career. Success came quickly in the post-war era. In 1947-8 and 1948-9, the Saints finished third in Division Two, just missing out on promotion. In the second of these seasons, they led the table for much of the year, but were finally edged out by Fulham and West Brom. Nevertheless, Dodgin was in charge of a First Division club when the 1949-50 season opened following his move to the Cottage.

Fulham stayed in the top flight for just three seasons and had one good Cup run, to the sixth round in 1950-51. The club never adjusted to the demands of the higher grade and struggled constantly. Given the limited resources at his disposal, it is unlikely that many managers would have done better than Dodgin. Some of his signings, like Ian Black and Eddie Lowe, were to prove valuable acquisitions, but only after the manager's departure. Similarly, a number of the promising youngsters he signed, most notably Johnny Haynes and Bobby Robson, matured after he had gone. Many fans were incensed, moreover, when he let the popular wing-half Len Quested move to Huddersfield in the autumn of 1951.

After relegation in 1951-2, Dodgin was given one season to get the club back up. When he failed, the axe fell in October 1953. He went on to manage Brentford and Bristol Rovers and returned to the Cottage as Rovers' manager in 1970 when his son Bill was the Fulham boss. Today, in his eighties, Bill senior is still a frequent and welcome visitor to the Cottage, where he talks without bitterness or regret of his spell at the helm.

Dugald Livingstone
1956-1958

IT was two and a half years before Dodgin was replaced as team manager, Frank Osborne assuming responsibility for both the administration and the team. In February 1956, the board decided to split the job in two and appointed Dug Livingstone to look after the playing side of the club. He stayed for just over two years, but in that time he made some critical changes which laid the foundations for the success of the late 1950s and early 1960s. He is arguably Fulham's most underrated manager.

A Scot, from Alexandria, near Dumbarton, Livingstone was born in February 1898. An undistinguished player, he served Tranmere, Everton (100 games from 1921-26), Plymouth, Aberdeen and Celtic, before going to Exeter as trainer in 1935. The following year, he moved on to Sheffield United in a similar capacity, and stayed until 1949. He then had his first spell abroad, as coach to Sparta of Rotterdam, before being appointed manager of the Irish national side in 1951. It was back to the Continent in 1953, to manage the Belgium national team. He was in charge during the 1954 World Cup Finals, when Belgium drew 4-4 with England. Towards the end of 1954, Livingstone returned to England, as manager of Newcastle and six months later led them to an FA Cup final victory over Manchester City.

His reward for this success was to be relieved of any say in team selection and his departure was predictable. He came to the Cottage early in 1956 when the club was in its fourth season back in Division Two and had not mounted a serious promotion challenge. When his first full season began in August 1956, Livingstone had lost two of his star players, Bobby Robson to West Brom and Bedford Jezzard to injury. Two seasons later, Fulham had narrowly lost in the FA Cup semi-final and missed promotion by a whisker. It came right 12 months later, however, by which time he had moved on.

Livingstone was an unflappable, happy-go-lucky character, a marked contrast to the nervous, worrying Dodgin, and his attitude was reflected in the team's play. The Fulham board had no hesitation in offering him a new contract in the summer of 1958, but his wife had been unable to settle in the south. He moved on to manage Chesterfield, where he remained until his retirement. He maintained an interest in football right up to his death. A week before he died, at Marlow in January 1981, he attended a Reading v Carlisle match, clubs managed by Roy Bentley and Bob Stokoe, two of his former players.

Bedford Jezzard
1958-1964

OF Fulham's 21 managers, past and present, more than half have been former Fulham players, and none has contributed more to the club in the two roles than Bedford Jezzard. In spite of having his playing career cut short by injury, he set up a club goalscoring record and then, as manager, took Fulham into the First Division, kept them there and got within a whisker of Wembley.

When a broken ankle, sustained on an FA tour of South Africa in the 1956 close season, ended his playing career, Jezzard was offered the role of coach to Fulham's juniors. Within 12 months he took over as team manager, the popular choice to succeed Livingstone in the summer of 1958. Osborne remained the general manager and acted as a father figure to Jezzard, who was responsible for managing his former colleagues.

The previous season, Fulham had reached the FA Cup semi-final, and only missed promotion as a result of the consequent fixture pile-up. In 1958-9, with virtually the same team (the signing of Leggat and departure of Dwight were the major changes), Fulham were amongst the pace-setters all year, and promotion was won comfortably. The next five seasons under Jezzard's control were all in the top flight and he somehow contrived to maintain Fulham's senior status. Although not a subtle player, he was able, as a manager, to harness the skills of some disparate talents and personalities into an effective team. His easy-going style won the respect of the players, who still speak reverentially of 'Jezzard the manager.'

He managed on slim resources. Fulham were always three or four players short of being a good First Division side, but rather than spend money to strengthen the squad, the board were more inclined to sell to balance the books. The transfer of Alan Mullery to Spurs in March 1964 was negotiated without Jezzard's knowledge and led to his eventual departure. When Osborne retired in October 1964, Jezzard took on both roles, but only for a month. He preferred instead to leave football and concentrate on running his family's successful pub, a couple of miles away from the ground. He continued doing this until his recent retirement. Jezzard was an infrequent, but welcome visitor to the Cottage in subsequent years, impressing all who met him with his knowledge of football and his quiet, modest and unassuming manner. (See *Fulham Stars A-Z*).

Vic Buckingham
1965-1968

AFTER a brief interregnum, and a lengthy interview process, the board appointed Vic

Buckingham to succeed Bedford Jezzard in January 1965. He was an experienced manager, and someone widely respected as one of the game's deep thinkers. He was given a three-year contract and he completely overhauled many aspects of the club's affairs. Unfortunately, the results were even less impressive than in previous years and he lasted only the duration of his first contract.

Greenwich-born Buckingham started his professional career as a wing-half with Spurs in 1934-5 and remained at White Hart Lane until 1950. A stylish wing-half, he made 204 League appearances for Spurs, but, in the war years, had frequently guested for Fulham. He began coaching with the Middlesex County FA and then guided the combined Oxford and Cambridge University side, Pegasus, to victory in the 1951 Amateur Cup Final.

This led to his introduction to Football League management, a 20-month stint at Bradford. In February 1953, he stepped into the First Division and in his first full season. the Throstles won the FA Cup and finished runners-up in the League. The subsequent seasons were less successful and in 1959 he went to Holland to manage Ajax. He was appointed Plymouth Argyle manager in March 1961, but could not take up the post because of contractual problems. His return was only delayed until May of that year, when he took over at Sheffield Wednesday.

He came to Fulham in January 1965 with impressive credentials. Of his predecessors, perhaps only Hogan had a better tactical brain and Livingstone and Dodgin as much experience. Yet Buckingham's tenure was not a happy one and relegation from Division One was a constant threat, which finally materialised just months after his departure. He tried to make too many changes too soon and succeeded only in upsetting almost everyone. Even the credit for the memorable escape from relegation in 1965-6 is usually given to a change in coach, the introduction of Dave Sexton. By the time his contract expired in January 1968, Fulham were firmly rooted at the foot of Division One. It was no surprise when he left and went back to Europe to manage, first in Greece, later in Spain.

Bobby Robson
1968

ON the surface, it appears strange that the man who ranks as the least successful Fulham manager should go on to become one of the leading club managers in the country and then to take over the national side. The superficial view, however, overlooks the traumatic state of affairs Robson inherited and the fact it was his first managerial position.

Born in Sacriston, County Durham, in February 1933, Bobby Robson first joined Fulham in May 1950. He formed an exciting inside-forward partnership with Jezzard and Haynes, before he was sold to Vic Buckingham's West Brom in March 1956. In six years at the Hawthorns, he was converted to wing-half, made almost 300 appearances and won 20 England caps. He returned to the Cottage in the summer of 1962 and played for another five seasons before retiring. He crossed the Atlantic to manage Vancouver Royals in the 1967 close season, but within six months joined Fulham for the third time, as manager and successor to his previous boss, Vic Buckingham.

It is an understatement to say that a challenge awaited Robson at the Cottage in January 1968. With relegation a near certainty he had little option but to take short-term measures to stem the tide of defeats. He had little success in the transfer market, buying players who were past their best or lacked First Division quality. His principal asset, Allan Clarke, he sold to Leicester, but came off second-best in the deal when he accepted Frank Large, valued at £50,000, as part of the package. Finally, it was not easy for him to handle former colleagues, some of whom were not responsive to the new manager's approach.

There was little respite when Second Division football returned to the Cottage in August 1968. A series of poor performances raised the spectre of relegation for the second consecutive season. Robson tried many new players, re-organised the backroom staff and even dropped Johnny Haynes, but all to no avail. The seeds of disintegration had been sown years earlier, and he reaped the harvest. After ten months in the job he was sacked, rumours being rife about the role and motivation of certain directors. It was a while before Robson got another managerial position, but when he did, at Ipswich, he proved his ability. Now, as England manager, he has reached the pinnacle of his profession. Not for the first, or last, time had Fulham discarded a person who subsequently went on to greater things. (See *Fulham Stars A-Z*).

Bill Dodgin (junior)
1968-1972

FOLLOWING the traumas of the first 11 months of 1968, during which Fulham had three managers, a period of relative stability began with Bill Dodgin's appointment just before Christmas. A former Fulham and Arsenal player, like so many of his predecessors he was also the son of a previous Fulham manager, the second father-son succession in the club's history.

Born at Wardley in November 1931, young Bill began his career with Southampton. Whilst an apprentice draughtsman at an aircraft factory, he turned out for Saints' junior team at the time his father was manager at The Dell. In April 1949, Dodgin (senior) took over at the Cottage and six months later followed him to London. After a spell in the juniors and National Service, he made his League debut, at full-back in November 1951.

In the 12 months that followed he bore the brunt of the fans' dissatisfaction with his father's handling of a struggling team. He moved on to Arsenal, where he made 210 appearances, and won an Under-23 cap against Italy in 1954. When he lost his place at Highbury, he returned to the Cottage, in March 1961. He was centre-half in the side which reached the FA Cup semi-final in 1962. A broken leg shortly afterwards virtually ended his career and his last game, ironically, was a 4-1 defeat by Arsenal.

He then jumped on the coaching and management roundabout. After a spell with Millwall, he joined Queen's Park Rangers, and helped them from the Third to the First Division, and to a League Cup Final victory in 1967. Towards the end of 1968 he was back at the Cottage for the third time, as manager on the recommendation of caretaker player-manager Johnny Haynes. The club's fortunes were at a low ebb, and he joined too late to stop relegation to the Third Division, just 12 months after relegation from the First. Within two seasons, however, he built a team which won promotion, and only missed the championship on the last day of the season.

Dodgin was a firm believer in attacking football, and the goal tallies, both for and against, of his clubs were always amongst the highest in their divisions. Attractive as this philosophy was, it proved his undoing 12 months later. Fulham's return to the Second Division was marked by a relegation battle, which was only won with a 0-0 draw in the final match. Within days he had lost his job, despite protests from the Supporters' Club. His successor was a playing colleague of his father's in the 1930s and his own mentor at Loftus Road in the 1960s, Alec Stock. Dodgin himself later managed Northampton and Brentford with the same uncompromising commitment to attack, with similar consequences for himself. Today, he runs a golf club in Surrey. (See *Fulham Stars A-Z*).

Alec Stock
1972-1976

ONE of the most respected men in football, Alec Stock took over as Fulham's manager in a highly-charged situation. Relegation had been narrowly avoided and the Supporters' Club had been disbanded by the board following protests at Dodgin's dismissal. In addition, financial problems associated with the building of the riverside stand were coming to the fore. Stock brought consistency to the club's League results and inspired them to unconquered peaks in the Cup, but, when he left, the situation off the field became even more turbulent.

Born in Surrey in 1917, Stock played Rugby Union at school and was a trainee bank-clerk when he began playing football for Wilmington Village and then Redhill. He had three games for Spurs as an amateur before turning professional with Charlton in 1936. He had two seasons at The Valley before joining Queen's Park Rangers for the first time. In the war, he rose to the rank of major with the Royal Armoured Corps and in 1946 began his managerial career, as player-manager of Southern League Yeovil. Then, in 1949, it was back to London, with Leyton Orient, where he stayed for ten years, except for brief interludes as assistant manager at Arsenal (Feb-April 1956) and team manager of AS Roma (Aug-Dec 1957). He seemed happiest with small clubs, and in 1959 returned to Loftus Road, where he guided Queen's Park Rangers from the Third to the First Division, and to a League Cup Final victory at Wembley. Luton was the next stop, from 1968-72, where he again won promotion from Division Three.

Stock had a superb track record managing clubs in the lower divisions and had gained success in both League and Cup competitions. He was a master of dealing on the transfer market and was able to handle talented players, like Rodney Marsh and Malcolm Macdonald, far better than most managers. In his four years at Fulham, he re-established the club in the Second Division, and brought some glamour back to the Cottage, with imaginative signings such as Alan Mullery, Bobby Moore and George Best. His greatest triumph, however, was taking Fulham through 11 FA Cup games in 1975, to the Final against West Ham. Of the many giant-killing feats he had inspired since his days at Yeovil, this was the most remarkable.

Off the field, however, Fulham's financial problems worsened, and a major boardroom shake-up in 1976 marked the beginning of the end for Stock. His old-world charm and good manners were in marked contrast to the more aggressive, financially-motivated approach of the new regime and in December 1976 he departed. He was the last of a long line of Fulham managers noted for their character and gentlemanly style as much as their understanding of the game. From 1977 until his retirement in 1986, he had spells as caretaker-manager and director of Queen's Park Rangers and as manager and director of Bournemouth, and is today a welcome visitor to the Cottage.

Bobby Campbell
1976-1980

THE financial pressures that affected Alec Stock intensified under his successor, Bobby Campbell. Results on the field were less consistent however, and as the problems mounted, the atmosphere at the Cottage became increasingly tense. To a certain extent, this was aggravated by the manager's personality. He was a tough, no-nonsense character, but prone to losing his temper, revealing a sense of insecurity.

As a player, Campbell learnt his trade at Anfield. He won England Youth honours and had a handful of games for Liverpool between 1958 and 1960. The bulk of his career was spent at Portsmouth (1961-66), and was ended at Aldershot (1966-69) by injury. He turned to coaching, first with Portsmouth and then at Queen's Park Rangers. It was at Loftus Road between 1972 and 1974 that he made his reputation. Working with Gordon Jago, he helped Rangers back into the First Division and then in 1974 moved on to Highbury to work with Bertie Mee. He was initially fancied to take over as manager when Mee left two years later, but the post eluded him and he went to the Cottage in the summer of 1976.

Initially, he was coach to manager Alec Stock, as successor to Bill Taylor. From the start, he had to overcome some resistance, since the job was originally meant for Alan Mullery. Within months, Campbell was promoted to manager when Stock departed, the victim of a boardroom upheaval. Fulham's results deteriorated under the new manager and the second half of the 1976-7 season was marked by a fight against relegation, which was ultimately successful. For the next two seasons, there were occasions on which the team promised much, but it lacked consistency and finished in mid-table. Then, in 1979-80, the growing tension at the club was reflected in the results and Fulham were relegated to the Third Division. Within months of the opening of 1980-81, after a disastrous start to the season, Campbell was on his way.

Few people doubted his abilities as a coach, and many promising youngsters developed under his guidance. He also wheeled and dealed on the transfer market, showing a significant profit over his five years. This, however, seemed to have an unsettling effect on the squad, and the turnover of players was remarkably high. Campbell's major weakness was man-management. He was abrasive and inflexible, and in the end lost the confidence of the players. Since leaving the Cottage, he has had further spells as coach and manager at Portsmouth and as a coach at Queen's Park Rangers.

71

Malcolm Macdonald
1980-1984

THE successor to Campbell came from within the club, and it was one of the most colourful characters of the previous decade. Malcolm Macdonald had been born just a goal-kick away from Craven Cottage, in January 1950. In the summer of 1968, he joined Fulham as a player, a right-back from Tonbridge. Manager Bobby Robson converted him to centre-forward, and in the early months of the traumatic 1968-9 season he showed his potential as a goalscorer.

When Robson left, Macdonald fell out of favour, and he was allowed to move on. Alec Stock signed him for Luton, where his 49 goals in 88 League games attracted the attention of First Division clubs. In May 1971, he went to Newcastle for £180,000, and his 95 goals in 187 League games made him a hero in the Gallagher or Milburn mould. He was back in London in July 1976, with Arsenal, for £333,333, and continued scoring, on average once in every two of his 84 games. He also played 14 times for England (and once scored five in a match), as well as in two FA Cup Finals and one League Cup Final. Injury ended his career in 1979, and he returned to the Cottage as Fulham's marketing executive.

There were many sceptics when he became manager, but all were proved wrong. The brash, arrogant centre-forward quickly became a thoughtful, articulate manager. He looked the part, with the sideburns shaved off and dressed in smart suits and spectacles. He was comfortable with the press, honest with supporters and, if results are any indication, respected by the players. In his first few months, Macdonald steered the club clear of relegation to Division Four. He then put a promotion-winning side together in 1981-2, which so nearly got into the First Division the following season. The team played with a style and flair that won many admirers, and he had not spent a penny on transfers.

The 1983-4 season was a reaction to the success of the previous years and the team struggled. For Macdonald, events reached a climax in March 1984, with publicity about his private life. He left within a month, to run a pub in Worthing, and Fulham were the poorer for it. He had restored the club's pride and had brought a measure of success without compromising the club's traditions. The press paid attention to Fulham when Macdonald was in charge in a way that was only equalled in Alec Stock's time. It seemed Macdonald was destined for managerial success at the highest level, but it is now three years since he left the game and, with each passing year, a return becomes harder.

Ray Harford
1984-1986

FEW people at Fulham paid much attention to the appointment of a new youth-team coach at the start of the 1981-2 season. Ray Harford came from Colchester, highly recommended to Malcolm Macdonald and, following George Armstrong's departure 12 months later, he stepped up to first-team coach. The Fulham team which played with such style and enjoyed success between 1981 and 1983 owed much to the influence of Harford, acknowledged as one of the best coaches in the country.

He enjoyed a lengthy, but only modestly successful playing career, as a defender, mostly in the lower divisions. In 11 years, he made almost 400 first-class appearances, for Charlton (1964-66), Exeter (1966-67), Lincoln (1967-71), Mansfield (1971), Port Vale (1971-73) and Colchester (1973-75). He had two cartilage operations in quick succession at Colchester and decided to hang up his boots. He got his full FA coaching badge the same year and his first opportunity to use it at Layer Road.

As a coach, Harford had an immediate impact at Fulham, with promotion to Division Two in his first season, and so nearly promotion again the following year. When Macdonald left before the end of 1983-4, Harford was given the job for the rest of the season: five wins in six matches secured the appointment on a more permanent basis. It was, however, to prove a baptism of fire as Fulham's financial problems continued to mount.

Few people are as knowledgeable about football, or as dedicated to it, as Harford. He never misses any opportunity to see a game, or to discuss ideas with anyone who will listen. He is most at home with players, or other football people, and he was never as comfortable with the Press or supporters as Macdonald. Pressure from the board, moreover, forced him to sell most of his best players, with predictable results. Harford kept an average Fulham team up in 1984-5, but, with the ground cut from under him, relegation was inevitable in 1985-6. He left that summer, to step up into the First Division, as coach to Luton Town. Although managing a struggling side, Harford's skills as a coach were generally admired, and Luton have clearly benefitted from his influence.

Ray Lewington
1986-

FEW managers could have had as difficult a debut season in charge as Fulham's Ray Lewington in 1986-7. The popular choice to succeed Ray Harford, Lewington saw the club change hands, be closed down and then drop perilously close to Division Four before a winning run in the closing weeks pulled the Cottagers clear at the same time as a rescue deal was underway to save the club's very existence.

It was in the summer of 1986 that he became Fulham's first player-manager (excluding Johnny Haynes' temporary assignment) and it is hardly fair to judge Lewington's performance on the strength of one, remarkable, campaign.

As the 1987-8 season began, he could at least be sure of one thing, however: that Fulham supporters were willing him to succeed. (See also *Fulham Stars A-Z*).

Just as many Fulham managers have had previous experience with Arsenal, so have several Southend managers been former Fulham players. Joe Bradshaw, Eddie Perry, Ernie Shepherd, Arthur Rowley and Bobby Moore were all managers at Roots Hall having spent parts of their playing careers at the Cottage.

Fulham Stars A-Z

Arnold's main claim to fame was to have represented England at both football and cricket. After performing well in an England soccer trial, he was picked to play against Scotland at Hampden Park in April 1933. England lost 2-1 and it proved to be his only cap. Arnold had earlier played in a Test match, in 1931 against New Zealand at Lord's. Born at Cowley near Oxford on 30 November 1907, he joined non-League Oxford City and played cricket for Oxfordshire. In 1928, Arnold moved to Southampton and also joined Hampshire CCC. He spent five years at The Dell, playing 120 games and scoring 47 goals. He joined Fulham in 1933, with Mike Keeping, for a joint fee of £5,100, a club record. A natural left-footer, he was fast and direct, with an eye for goal. Arnold helped Fulham to the FA Cup semi-final in 1936, when they lost to Sheffield United, and made his last appearance for Fulham in 1945. He also played 396 matches for Hampshire between 1929 and 1950, scoring 21,831 runs, including 37 centuries, and was appointed a first-class umpire in 1961. He died on 3 April 1984, within weeks of Mike Keeping's death.

JOHNNY ARNOLD

	LEAGUE		FA CUP		TOTAL	
	App	Gls	App	Gls	App	Gls
1932-33	13	6	0	0	13	6
1933-34	31	6	2	1	33	7
1934-35	34	8	1	1	35	9
1935-36	24	9	4	3	28	12
1936-37	36	12	1	0	37	12
1937-38	30	8	1	0	31	8
1938-39	34	9	2	0	36	9
	202	58	22	5	213	63

Bacuzzi was born in King's Cross on 25 September 1916. He won representative honours with Islington Schools, Middlesex and London Boys and joined Isthmian League side, Tufnell Park, from school, where he spent two seasons. He also played a few 'A' team games for Arsenal, but never signed for the club. He joined Fulham as an amateur in 1935 and signed professional in April 1936. This was the beginning of a 30-year association with the Cottagers. He developed into a stylish full-back, strong in the tackle and with outstanding positional play but always ready for a foray upfield. He made 70 appearances before war was declared in 1939. During the war, he gained 13 England caps but was unable to gain a full cap in peacetime. He played in 104 wartime games for Fulham and appeared in the Arsenal side which played the prestige match against Moscow Dynamo in November 1945. Bacuzzi formed a fine full-back partnership with Harry Freeman after the war. When a nagging knee injury ended his career in the summer of 1956, he was appointed trainer and remained at the Cottage until 1965. His son, David, played full-back for Arsenal, Manchester City and Reading.

JOE BACUZZI

	LEAGUE		FA CUP		TOTAL	
	App	Gls	App	Gls	App	Gls
1936-37	2	0	0	0	2	0
1937-38	26	1	0	0	26	1
1938-39	42	0	2	0	44	0
1945-46	0	0	2	0	2	0
1946-47	18	0	0	0	18	0
1947-48	39	0	5	0	44	0
1948-49	41	0	1	0	42	0
1949-50	38	1	1	0	39	1
1950-51	34	0	5	0	39	0
1951-52	26	0	0	0	26	0
1952-53	15	0	0	0	15	0
1953-54	0	0	0	0	0	0
1954-55	1	0	0	0	1	0
1955-56	1	0	0	0	1	0
	283	2	16	0	299	2

A hard-working, defensively-minded half-back who was an essential part of the Fulham side in the early 1920s, Bagge was born in Tottenham in 1896 and joined his local side, Spurs, as an amateur in World War One. Bagge was unable to gain a first-team place during his stay at White Hart Lane and decided to try his luck at Craven Cottage. He made his Fulham debut in a wartime London Combination game against Clapton Orient, and, on the resumption of League football in August 1919, found himself in the first team for the opening game against South Shields. However, he made only five more first-team appearances that season and it was not until the following campaign that he established himself. He remained a regular until 1925-6 and scored his one and only goal for Fulham in a 3-0 victory over Stoke in April 1924. Bagge went to Sheffield Wednesday in 1926 but played only for the reserves. The following year, he moved to Spain to take a coaching post.

	LEAGUE		FA CUP		TOTAL	
	App	Gls	App	Gls	App	Gls
1919-20	7	0	0	0	7	0
1920-21	35	0	5	0	40	0
1921-22	31	0	3	0	34	0
1922-23	30	0	1	0	31	0
1923-24	40	1	3	0	43	1
1924-25	26	0	0	0	26	0
1925-26	10	0	0	0	10	0
1926-27	0	0	0	0	0	0
	179	1	12	0	191	1

HENRY (HARRY) BAGGE

Born at West Ham on 11 November 1903, Barrett attended Park School, West Ham, and later played soccer for Fairbairn House Boys Club. He won representative honours with West Ham Boys, appearing in three English Schools Shield Finals, and was capped for England Schoolboys against Scotland in 1917. He later played soccer for the Fairbairn House Boys club which won the London Minor Cup before joining Leytonstone in 1921-2 where he gained four England Amateur caps. Barrett had brief spells with West Ham and Southampton before joining Fulham as a professional in August 1925. He became an automatic choice for the next ten seasons, playing over 400 games. Easily recognisable with his blond hair, Barrett was a cool, stylish wing-half with a flair for attack. He also played occasionally at left-back. He toured South Africa with an FA XI in the summer of 1929, and won his one and only full cap against Northern Ireland in 1930. He won a Third Division South Championship medal in 1932 and played in the losing FA Cup semi-final team against Sheffield United in 1936. After retiring from playing in 1937, Barrett rejoined Leytonstone as coach. He had trained as an accountant whilst at Fulham and worked for chairman John Dean in this capacity. He emigrated to South Africa in 1954.

ALBERT BARRETT

	LEAGUE		FA CUP		TOTAL	
	App	Gls	App	Gls	App	Gls
1925-26	36	2	4	0	40	2
1926-27	30	0	2	0	32	0
1927-28	39	0	1	0	40	0
1928-29	31	0	2	0	33	0
1929-30	34	1	5	4	39	5
1930-31	42	5	4	0	46	5
1931-32	30	5	3	0	33	5
1932-33	41	2	1	0	42	2
1933-34	40	1	2	0	42	1
1934-35	42	0	1	0	43	0
1935-36	19	0	5	1	24	1
1936-37	4	0	0	0	4	0
	388	16	30	5	418	21

Les Barrett was one of a dying breed, a fast and naturally skilful winger with good control and able to centre accurately or cut in and have a go himself. He was a very popular player with the crowd because of his cool attitude to the game and his 'electric' speed. Born in Chelsea on 22 October 1947, he was brought up on East Hill Estate, Wandsworth, and attended Eltringham and Wandsworth schools. His Fulham debut came in January 1966, in a side struggling against relegation from the First Division. He formed an exciting front line with Steve Earle and Allan Clarke and won an England Under-23 cap against Greece in 1967. Barrett seemed to have a great career ahead of him but Fulham dropped to the Third Division, and although there was talk of Manchester United trying to sign him, the move never materialised. Barrett was top scorer in Fulham's promotion season of 1970-71 and gained a FA Cup runners-up medal in 1975. He made almost 500 appearances before signing for Millwall in October 1977 for a £12,000 fee. After a brief spell in the USA he signed as player-coach to Woking and retired at the age of 39.

	LEAGUE		FA CUP		FL CUP		TOTAL	
	App	Gls	App	Gls	App	Gls	App	Gls
1965-66	12/2	4	0	0	0	0	12/2	4
1966-67	33	8	3	0	3	1	39	9
1967-68	40	8	3	0	6	2	49	10
1968-69	29	2	2	0	1	0	32	2
1969-70	44	7	1	0	2	0	47	7
1970-71	46	15	1	0	6	3	53	18
1971-72	42	8	3	0	2	0	47	8
1972-73	39	6	1	0	4	0	44	6
1973-74	42	7	3	1	4	3	49	11
1974-75	41	5	12	1	3	2	56	8
1975-76	32/1	1	1	0	1	0	34/1	1
1976-77	20	3	1/1	1	4	1	25/1	5
1977-78	0	0	0	0	0	0	0	0
	420/3	74	31/1	3	36	12	487/4	89

LESLIE BARRETT

Barton was born in Sutton on 8 April 1937. One of a family of nine (one brother guested for Bristol City in World War Two and another played for Carshalton in the Corinthian League), he represented London Boys and the Surrey County FA. Barton also won an England Schoolboy cap against Scotland and represented England Youth on five occasions. He joined Fulham as a 13-year-old, but played for Sutton United in 1953-4. Signing professional for Fulham in May 1954, Barton had already made his debut at Lincoln an hour earlier. Moving to Nottingham Forest in December 1959 he made 22 appearances before another move, to Portsmouth, in December 1961. Barton scored 37 goals in 144 appearances for Pompey. He joined their coaching staff in 1966 but made his first big impact in management with Aston Villa, a club he joined in 1980 as assistant-manager. Promoted to team manager in February 1982, he guided the Midlands club to a European Cup Final victory only four months later. After he was sacked in June 1984, Barton became Northampton's manager a month later. After a heart attack, he moved to Southampton as assistant to Chris Nicholl in September 1985.

	LEAGUE		FA CUP		TOTAL	
	App	Gls	App	Gls	App	Gls
1953-54	1	0	0	0	1	0
1954-55	12	2	0	0	12	2
1955-56	7	1	0	0	7	1
1956-57	1	0	0	0	1	0
1957-58	13	3	0	0	13	3
1958-59	15	2	0	0	15	2
	49	8	0	0	49	8

TONY BARTON

Born in Stourbridge on 27 July 1912, Beasley played for Brierley Hill Schools and Cookley before joining local club, Stourbridge, in the Birmingham League. Signed by the legendary Arsenal manager, Herbert Chapman for £550 in May 1931, Beasley won a League Championship medal with Arsenal in 1933-4 but missed out on two Cup Final appearances. He scored 24 goals in 89 appearances for the Gunners before moving to Huddersfield Town in October 1936 for £750. He played in Town's 1938 FA Cup Final side which lost to Preston, and won his only England cap against Scotland in April 1939 as a left-winger. He spent much of the war overseas but signed for Fulham in December 1945 and was appointed captain. Although small and slight, Beasley tackled enthusiastically and was a constant inspiration in his new position of wing-half. He led Fulham to the Second Division Championship in 1949 as his astute captaincy welded the team into a cohesive and winning unit. He moved to Bristol City as player-manager in August 1950, hanging up his boots just before his 40th birthday. Manager of Birmingham City for two and a half seasons from February 1958, he ended his career as Dover manager in the summer of 1964 and died in March 1986.

	LEAGUE		FA CUP		TOTAL	
	App	Gls	App	Gls	App	Gls
1945-46	0	0	2	0	2	0
1946-47	40	9	1	0	41	9
1947-48	37	3	5	0	42	3
1948-49	39	1	1	0	40	1
1949-50	37	0	2	0	39	0
	153	13	11	0	164	13

ALBERT 'PAT' BEASLEY

JOHN BECK

A midfield schemer, Beck was dangerous at free kicks and a good crosser of the ball. Born at Edmonton on 25 May 1954, he joined Queen's Park Rangers as a professional in May 1972 after two seasons as an apprentice. His debut came on Boxing Day 1972 in the home match against Orient, as substitute. Beck made his big breakthrough into first-team football in 1974-5 playing 29 games. He moved to Coventry City in June 1976 for £40,000 and immediately won a regular place, making 78 appearances and scoring six goals. He joined Fulham for £80,000 in October 1978 and quickly fitted in with manager Campbell's style. A regular until 1981 when he was dropped by manager Malcolm Macdonald, Beck moved on to Bournemouth, initially on loan, but permanently in February 1983. After 115 games and 13 goals for the Cherries (plus an Associate Members Cup-winners' medal in 1984), he moved to Cambridge United in the close season of 1986.

	LEAGUE		FA CUP		FL CUP		TOTAL	
	App	Gls	App	Gls	App	Gls	App	Gls
1978-79	32	1	3	0	0	0	35	1
1979-80	40	2	2	0	2	0	44	2
1980-81	37	8	1	0	2	0	40	8
1981-82	4/1	1	0	0	2	1	6/1	2
	113/1	12	6	0	6	1	125/1	13

Beecham was a brave and fearless goalkeeper who possessed huge hands and a massive kick. He was born in Cromwell Road, Hertford, on 23 July 1896 (hence his middle name as he was the first baby born in this road). He attended Cowper School and joined local club, Hertford Town, in the Spartan League just after the war, gaining Herts County honours. Initially he joined Fulham as a reserve in October 1923 but signed professional in April 1924. After playing brilliantly in Fulham's Cup run of 1926 and winning London Combination honours, Beecham toured Holland with an England XI in 1927 before receiving a serious spinal injury diving at the feet of an Exeter forward named Death in October 1928. He was troubled by this injury for the rest of his life, and needed several operations. Eventually he made a comeback but was never the same 'keeper. He moved to Queen's Park Rangers in May 1932, playing almost a 100 games before breaking his arm. He decided to retire but was soon persuaded back by Brighton in September 1935 and moved to Swindon in November. Another illness the following March finally ended his career. Beecham managed Ware of the Spartan League in 1947 and died of cancer in August 1985, still residing in the house where he was born.

ERNEST (CROMWELL) BEECHAM

	LEAGUE		FA CUP		TOTAL	
	App	Gls	App	Gls	App	Gls
1925-26	25	0	5	0	30	0
1926-27	42	0	2	0	44	0
1927-28	42	0	1	0	43	0
1928-29	13	0	0	0	13	0
1929-30	35	0	5	0	40	0
1930-31	6	0	0	0	6	0
1931-32	9	0	0	0	9	0
	172	0	13	0	185	0

ROY BENTLEY

Bentley was a wandering centre-forward who possessed great acceleration and was good in the air. Born at Shirehampton near Bristol on 17 May 1924, he captained Bristol Schools and played for both Bristol clubs, signing professional for City in 1941. For much of the war he was on active service and on his demob signed for Newcastle United in June 1946 for an £8,500 fee. Bentley moved to Chelsea in January 1948 and gained many honours whilst at the Bridge, including 11 England caps (amongst which were appearances in the 1950 World Cup Finals). He scored nine goals for England. He also gained a 'B' international cap, represented the Football League and played for Great Britain against the Rest of Europe in August 1955. Probably his greatest achievement was captaining Chelsea to the League Championship in 1955. After scoring 149 goals in 366 appearances for the Blues, Bentley moved to Fulham in September 1956 for an £8,600 fee, where he was converted into an outstanding half-back. He helped Fulham back to the First Division in 1959 and to the FA Cup semi-finals in 1958. He moved to Queen's Park Rangers in June 1961 and later took up management at Reading, from 1963 to 1969, and Swansea, from 1969 to 1973. Since then, he has worked as club secretary at Reading and Aldershot.

	LEAGUE		FA CUP		FL CUP		TOTAL	
	App	Gls	App	Gls	App	Gls	App	Gls
1956-57	32	14	2	1	0	0	34	15
1957-58	31	7	7	1	0	0	38	8
1958-59	35	0	4	0	0	0	39	0
1959-60	29	2	2	0	0	0	31	2
1960-61	16	0	1	0	1	0	18	0
	143	23	16	2	1	0	160	25

Best burst on to the football scene when only 17 with Manchester United. Born in Belfast on 22 May 1946, this dark-haired, blue-eyed, good looking but somewhat shy boy's career was to hit a peak then fizzle out early. His brave and thrilling darts for goal tormented many a defence. Best possessed a marvellous sense of balance, amazing ball control, a deceptive swerve and an accurate shot. He helped United to two League Championships in seasons 1964-5 and 1966-7 and the European Cup in 1968, in a memorable victory over Benfica at Wembley, as well as gaining 37 caps for Northern Ireland. Best was voted the British and European Footballer of the Year in 1968. Sadly, he was unable to cope with the pressures of stardom and he headed down the slippery slope. His career had hit rock bottom by 1975 and after brief comebacks at Stockport County and Cork Celtic, he headed for the USA. Fulham were to sign him from Los Angeles Aztecs in September 1976 and he gave some fine performances before arguments over money saw his return to the States. He later had spells with Hibernian in 1977, San José Earthquakes, Bournemouth in March 1983 and Tobermore in the Republic of Ireland in February 1984.

	LEAGUE		FA CUP		FL CUP		TOTAL	
	App	Gls	App	Gls	App	Gls	App	Gls
1976-77	32	6	2	0	3	2	37	8
1977-78	10	2	0	0	0	0	10	2
	42	8	2	0	3	2	47	10

GEORGE BEST

JOE BIRCH

Birch was born in Hednesford and started his career at Birmingham in 1927. A resolute defender who tackled enthusiastically and could kick a ball a great distance, he was weighty (12st 7lb) but exceptionally fast and able to recover quickly when caught out of position or beaten in the tackle. After only one appearance at St Andrews, Birch was transferred to Bournemouth in the close season of 1929. He made 26 appearances for the South Coast club before Fulham signed him in 1931 to fill a problem position. This he did with great efficiency for South Championship medal in his first season at the club. d a half seasons, winning a Third Division He adapted well to Second Division football and was a regular performer at right-back, except in season 1935-6. He moved to Colchester United in July 1938 and played in their Southern League Championship side of season 1938-9.

	LEAGUE		FA CUP		TOTAL	
	App	Gls	App	Gls	App	Gls
1931-32	32	0	5	0	37	0
1932-33	35	0	1	0	36	0
1933-34	33	0	2	0	35	0
1934-35	29	0	1	0	30	0
1935-36	10	0	0	0	10	0
1936-37	35	0	1	0	36	0
1937-38	13	0	0	0	13	0
	187	0	10	0	197	0

Black was born in Aberdeen on 27 March 1924. As a youngster, he played in the Scottish Juvenile Cup Final for St Clements against Thorneywood United. He joined his local club, Aberdeen, in 1944 but whilst serving in REME, he was able to compete in wartime soccer for Chelsea and Southampton. Black played in the 1945 League South Cup Final at Wembley when Chelsea beat Millwall. He moved to Southampton in December 1947 for a fee of £1,000 after losing his place in the Dons' League team. Just four months later, Black was capped by Scotland against England in a 2-0 defeat at Hampden Park. This proved to be his only cap. He was signed by Fulham manager Bill Dodgin (who had managed him at Southampton) in August 1950 in a player-exchange deal involving Hugh Kelly. Black was a tall, stylish 'keeper with safe, reliable hands, good anticipation and considerable courage, but was sometimes vulnerable on crosses. He became the only Fulham goalkeeper to score a goal, after injury forced him to play at centre-forward against Leicester in August 1952. After losing his place to Tony Macedo, he moved to Southern League Bath City in August 1959. He coached Brentford's junior side in the 1960s, but Black currently runs a bowling club at Tolworth.

	LEAGUE		FA CUP		TOTAL	
	App	Gls	App	Gls	App	Gls
1950-51	42	0	5	0	47	0
1951-52	39	0	1	0	40	0
1952-53	37	1	1	0	38	1
1953-54	32	0	3	0	35	0
1954-55	27	0	0	0	27	0
1955-56	34	0	2	0	36	0
1956-57	37	0	2	0	39	0
1957-58	15	0	0	0	15	0
	263	1	14	0	277	1

IAN BLACK

BOBBY BRENNAN

Born in Belfast on 14 March 1925, Brennan joined Distillery in the Irish League from school. He won an Irish Cup runners-up medal in 1946 and also represented the Irish League before coming to England to join Luton Town. Here he gained the first of his five Irish caps, against Wales in 1949. After scoring 22 goals in 67 League games for the Hatters, Brennan moved to Birmingham City for a £20,000 fee in July 1949. He stayed one season at St Andrews before joining Fulham for a similar fee in June 1950. He won three more caps whilst at the Cottage. A fast, clever and creative inside-forward, Brennan possessed a lot of deft touches and a deceptive body swerve and was a schemer rather than a goalscorer. He did not settle at the Cottage and once Johnny Haynes had established himself, Brennan moved on to Norwich City in July 1953. Here he teamed up with former Fulham teammate Archie Macaulay, then, the Canaries' manager. Brennan played 222 League games for City scoring 44 goals and helping them in their marvellous Cup run of 1959 before joining King's Lynn later that year as coach. He still lives in the Norwich area.

	LEAGUE		FA CUP		TOTAL	
	App	Gls	App	Gls	App	Gls
1950-51	22	3	5	3	27	6
1951-52	19	7	1	0	20	7
1952-53	32	3	1	0	33	3
	73	13	7	3	80	16

Born in Bedford on 4 May 1924, Gordon joined Luton Town from Bedford St Clements just three months before World War Two was declared. Unable to play much football in the war years, Brice rejoined Luton in 1946 and scored 13 goals in 46 appearances before signing for Wolves in May 1947. Brice is the first to admit that he did not have a happy time at Molyneux. "The trouble was that they had paid £10,000 for me and increased my wages from £5 to £11 per week and being the successor to the great Stan Cullis was a hell of a responsibility." He was relieved when Ted Drake signed him for Reading in March 1948. Brice played over 200 games for the Elm Park club before moving to Fulham in December 1952. He loved his time at the Cottage, and whilst Fulham were not famous for their defensive play in this period, Brice gave some great displays at centre-half. He joined Ayr United in the summer of 1956 where he also ran an hotel for a spell. Brice nicknamed 'Whiz', also played county cricket for Northants, and in 1987 is living in Bedfordshire.

	LEAGUE		FA CUP		TOTAL	
	App	Gls	App	Gls	App	Gls
1952-53	4	0	0	0	4	0
1953-54	42	0	3	0	45	0
1954-55	27	1	1	0	28	1
1955-56	14	0	2	0	16	0
	87	1	6	0	93	1

GORDON BRICE

ARTHUR BROWN

Born in Gainsborough on 6 April 1885, Brown joined his local Second Division club, Gainsborough Trinity, early in 1902. Sheffield United were quick to see his potential and signed him after only three games for Trinity for a large fee. He made his international debut at only 18, against Wales in 1904, and was the youngest-ever England international until Duncan Edwards in the 1950s. After six highly successful seasons with United, in which he scored 96 goals in 174 appearances, he moved to Sunderland for a world record fee of £1,600 in 1908. Brown had twice topped 20 goals in a season at Bramall Lane. He scored 17 goals in his first term at Roker Park but lost his place the following season. Fulham stepped in to sign him in October 1910, but his career was now in decline. He gave some good performances but could not find the net regularly. Brown played only four games for Middlesbrough after moving to Ayresome Park in the summer of 1912 and what had looked a highly-promising career at 18 had petered out at the early age of 29. He died in Gainsborough in June 1944.

	LEAGUE		FA CUP		TOTAL	
	App	Gls	App	Gls	App	Gls
1910-11	16	4	1	0	17	4
1911-12	25	5	4	3	29	8
	41	9	5	3	46	12

Born in Northampton in November 1883, Brown joined Northampton Town from a local church side St Sepulchres in 1902. He was a regular in their Southern League side until his departure to West Bromwich Albion in December 1903. Albion were relegated to the Second Division at the end of his initial season at the club. After losing his place, Brown moved to Southampton in April 1905. He was soon on the move again a year later, to Newcastle United, where he reached the pinnacle of his career when the Magpies won the League Championship in season 1906-07. Brown had cost £380 and he rewarded their investment with eight goals in 22 appearances that season. Brown was on the move again in October 1907 to Bradford for a £250 fee and arrived at the Cottage in March 1908. Although small, Brown packed a fierce shot and was soon scoring regularly for Fulham. His final move was back to Southampton in September 1910 but he retired in 1912 because of poor eyesight and ran a pub. He finally went blind and died in Nuneaton in February 1934.

	LEAGUE		FA CUP		TOTAL	
	App	Gls	App	Gls	App	Gls
1907-08	7	5	0	0	7	5
1908-09	19	6	0	0	19	6
1909-10	27	10	2	0	29	10
	53	21	2	0	55	21

HARRY BROWN

ROGER BROWN

Brown holds Fulham's goalscoring record for a defender, with 12 goals in 1981-2. Born in Tamworth in Staffordshire on 12 December 1952, Brown joined his local club, Walsall, in 1970 as an apprentice but failed to make the grade. He became a production manager in an engineering firm based in Leamington and joined the local club as a semi-professional. Bournemouth resurrected his Football League career at the age of 25 when they signed him from AP Leamington in February 1977. A powerful, dominant central defender, Brown was soon spotted by First Division club Norwich City and moved to Norfolk in July 1979 for a fee of £85,000. He stayed eight months before joining Fulham for a £100,000 fee but was injured on his debut against Chelsea. Brown became a great favourite at the Cottage and was an inspirational leader in Fulham's promotion season of 1981-2 when he scored the vital goal against Lincoln in the last match to ensure a return to the Second Division. He fell out of favour with manager Malcolm Macdonald and he moved to Bournemouth in December 1983 in a £35,000 deal. Brown won an Associate Members Cup-winners' medal in 1984.

	LEAGUE		FA CUP		FL CUP		TOTAL	
	App	Gls	App	Gls	App	Gls	App	Gls
1979-80	1	0	0	0	0	0	1	0
1980-81	39	2	3	0	2	0	44	2
1981-82	46	12	2	0	6	0	54	12
1982-83	42	4	3	0	4	1	49	5
1983-84	13	0	0	0	0	0	13	0
	141	18	8	0	12	1	161	19

Brown was known as the professional's professional, an adaptable, utility player who was probably appreciated more by his team mates than the Fulham crowd. Born at Lewes on 15 September 1941, Brown still lives in the area today. As a youngster, he captained East Sussex Boys and first came to Fulham in 1957. He signed professional in May 1959 and made his debut in a disastrous 1-6 home defeat against Sheffield Wednesday in January 1961, Alan Mullery managing to score an own-goal after 30 seconds without the opposition touching the ball. Although only 5ft 7in, Brown was a fine header of the ball and a consistent and dependable player who was always making himself available to his colleagues. Stan was equally effective in defence, midfield or attack. After almost 400 games for Fulham, he moved to Brighton on loan in October 1972 and joined Colchester permanently two months later. He signed for Wimbledon in the summer of 1973 and later spent many years in the Sussex League as a player and manager with Haywards Heath, Burgess Hill and Ringmer, before retiring from playing in 1981 at 40 years of age. His brothers Alan and Irvine played for Brighton and Bournemouth respectively.

STAN BROWN

	LEAGUE		FA CUP		FL CUP		TOTAL	
	App	Gls	App	Gls	App	Gls	App	Gls
1960-61	1	0	0	0	0	0	1	0
1961-62	0	0	0	0	0	0	0	0
1962-63	34	7	2	0	3	1	39	8
1963-64	15	0	0	0	0	0	15	0
1964-65	35	1	2	0	3	0	40	1
1965-66	36	3	1	0	2	0	39	3
1966-67	40	0	3	0	3	0	46	0
1967-68	42	1	3	0	6	0	51	1
1968-69	35/1	0	2	2	1	0	38/1	2
1969-70	44/2	3	1	0	3	0	48/2	3
1970-71	35/1	1	1	0	5	0	41/1	1
1971-72	28/1	0	0	0	1	0	29/1	0
1972-73	3	0	0	0	2	0	5	0
	348/5	16	15	2	29	1	392/5	19

Born in South East London on 23 September 1957, Bullivant joined Fulham as an apprentice in April 1972 and signed professional forms in May 1974. He made his debut as substitute at Bristol City a week before Fulham's FA Cup Final appearance in 1975. The breakthrough as a first-team regular came in season 1976-7 when his ball-winning role in midfield was essential to the make-up of any team in the mid-1970s. His tenacity, courage and enthusiasm often inspired his colleagues and there are many who felt that his departure to Aston Villa in November 1979 was the cause of Fulham's relegation to the Third Division that season. Villa paid £220,000 for his services, but he had an unhappy time at Villa Park, playing only 14 games in two and a half seasons. In the summer of 1982 he moved to Charlton Athletic where he teamed up with Alan Simonsen for a season. After joining Brentford in July 1983, Bullivant appeared at Wembley in their Associate Members Cup Final side of 1985. He also played briefly on loan for Reading in March 1984. Bullivant rejoined Fulham in August 1986 as part-time youth team coach and in the 1987 close season was appointed first-team coach.

TERRY BULLIVANT

	LEAGUE		FA CUP		FL CUP		TOTAL	
	App	Gls	App	Gls	App	Gls	App	Gls
1974-75	0/1	0	0	0	0	0	0/1	0
1975-76	1/2	0	0	0	0	0	1/2	0
1976-77	18/1	1	1	0	3	0	22/1	1
1977-78	32/3	1	1	0	2	0	35/3	1
1978-79	28	0	3	0	2	0	33	0
1979-80	15	0	0	0	2	0	17	0
	94/7	2	5	0	9	0	108/7	2

Busby was born in High Wycombe on 19 June 1949 and joined local club Wycombe Wanderers after an unsuccessful trial at Fulham in 1969. Luton Town saw his potential and signed him in January 1970. He went to Newcastle on loan in December 1971 but was not signed permanently after a disastrous FA Cup defeat at non-League Hereford United. Busby had scored 16 goals in 77 appearances when former Luton manager, Alec Stock, signed him for Fulham in August 1973 for £25,000, along with Alan Slough. Busby possessed fine ball skills and was fast when running with the ball but did not hit the net often enough. He did score some vital goals in helping Fulham to the Cup Final in 1975, however, none more so than the two at Goodison which beat Everton. With the return of Rodney Marsh, Busby moved to Norwich City for £50,000 in September 1976. He then became something of a nomad, signing for Stoke City in November 1977, Tulsa Roughnecks (USA) summer 1979, Sheffield United on loan in January 1980, Blackburn Rovers February 1981 and finally York City in August 1982. After retiring from playing, Busby became assistant-manager at York and in the 1987 close season went with Dennis Smith to Sunderland. He had scored 83 goals in 311 League and Cup games between 1973 and 1980.

VIV BUSBY

	LEAGUE		FA CUP		FL CUP		TOTAL	
	App	Gls	App	Gls	App	Gls	App	Gls
1973-74	34/4	12	2	0	2	0	38/4	12
1974-75	38	11	12	6	3	1	53	18
1975-76	37	6	1	1	3	0	41	7
1976-77	5	0	0	0	2	0	7	0
	114/4	29	15	7	10	1	139/4	37

A wholehearted player, Callaghan endeared himself to the supporters who gave him the nickname of 'Tank' because of his thunderous runs down the left wing which were a feature of Fulham's play in the late 1960s. Born in Fulham on 19 December 1944, Callaghan was raised in Avalon Road and attended St Marks Secondary School. After representing West London Schools, he joined Fulham's groundstaff, signing professional in August 1962. Progressing through the juniors and reserves, his great chance came with the departure of Alan Mullery to Spurs in March 1964. Initially a wing-half, it was at left-back that Callaghan found a regular first-team place in season 1966-7. Although Fulham went from the First to the Third Divisions in consecutive seasons, Fred was one of the few players to survive and be part of the recovery. His most important goal was the late equaliser at The Valley in April 1972 which sent Charlton down to the Third Division instead of Fulham. Callaghan was a regular choice until the summer of 1973 when a slipped disc virtually ended his playing career. He spent several seasons as manager of Enfield and Woking before taking up management of a League club, Brentford, from March 1980 to February 1984. Currently a taxi driver and scouting for various clubs.

	LEAGUE		FA CUP		FL CUP		TOTAL	
	App	Gls	App	Gls	App	Gls	App	Gls
1963-64	8	0	0	0	0	0	8	0
1964-65	12	0	0	0	2	0	14	0
1965-66	9	0	0	0	1	0	10	0
1966-67	34/1	3	3	1	3	1	40/1	5
1967-68	35	0	3	0	6	1	44	1
1968-69	40	2	2	0	1	0	43	2
1969-70	28/1	1	1	0	2	0	31/1	1
1970-71	45	0	1	0	6	0	52	0
1971-72	42	3	3	0	2	0	47	3
1972-73	38/1	0	1	0	4	0	43/1	0
1973-74	0/1	0	0	0	0	0	0/1	0
	291/4	9	14	1	27	2	332/4	12

FRED CALLAGHAN

Born in Belfast on 28 June 1923, Campbell went to a school in Londonderry which played only Gaelic football. He began to play soccer whilst working as a fitter's mate and he joined Foyne Harps. Campbell signed professional for Derry Celtic and moved to Belfast Celtic in 1945. He scored over 100 goals in his three seasons at the club. He once scored three goals in three minutes against Shelbourne and was Irish Footballer of the Year in 1946. He also gained an Irish Cup-winners' medal in season 1946-7 when Belfast Celtic beat Glentoran 1-0. One of his favourite memories was scoring both goals against Scotland in a 2-0 victory whilst touring the United States with the Belfast club. Campbell moved to Fulham in March 1949 with Robin Lawler and Hugh Kelly. He played in every forward position for Fulham and won two Northern Ireland caps in 1951 against England and Scotland. He had previously represented the Irish League. A serious and sudden illness in 1953 ended his playing days. Fulham made him their Irish representative after his recovery, where despite poor health, he kept his eyes on the local talent until his untimely death in January 1968.

	LEAGUE		FA CUP		TOTAL	
	App	Gls	App	Gls	App	Gls
1949-50	13	1	0	0	13	1
1950-51	23	2	5	2	28	4
1951-52	25	1	1	0	26	1
1952-53	1	0	0	0	1	0
	62	4	6	2	68	6

JOHNNY CAMPBELL

One of Fulham's most popular players, Chamberlain's reputation as a joker has tended to overshadow his ability as a left-winger. He was born in Camden Town in 1933, and won representative honours as a left-back for schools sides in Islington. As a left-winger, he played for Middlesex, London and England Boys (once scoring three goals in four minutes against the Republic of Ireland). In 1948, his club side, White Lion Play Centre, had a cup final at the Cottage, and Chamberlain caught the eye of Fulham manager Jack Peart. After a spell on the groundstaff, where he won England Youth honours, Chamberlain turned professional, and in 1954, after two years National Service, he made a sensational League debut. With his first kick in the first minute, he scored against Lincoln. In December 1955, he established himself as first choice, and held the position for five years. His partnership with his old schoolfriend, Johnny Haynes, was as amusing as it was effective. As well as a great sense of fun, Tosh had skill, and was the possessor of a ferocious shot. He scored a memorable hat-trick in a 1956 Cup-tie against Newcastle, probably the greatest match ever seen at the Cottage. A one-club player who cared deeply about Fulham, Chamberlain is a frequent and welcome visitor to the club today.

	LEAGUE		FA CUP		FL CUP		TOTAL	
	App	Gls	App	Gls	App	Gls	App	Gls
1954-55	6	1	0	0	0	0	6	1
1955-56	21	11	1	3	0	0	22	14
1956-57	39	15	2	0	0	0	41	15
1957-58	27	13	6	1	0	0	33	14
1958-59	24	7	0	0	0	0	24	7
1959-60	27	6	2	1	0	0	29	7
1960-61	11	1	1	0	1	0	13	1
1961-62	14	2	0	0	2	0	16	2
1962-63	3	0	0	0	1	0	4	0
1963-64	7	2	0	0	0	0	7	2
1964-65	8	1	1	0	0	0	9	1
	187	59	13	5	4	0	204	64

TREVOR 'TOSH' CHAMBERLAIN

Chaplin, who was born in Dundee in February 1892, came to Fulham in 1919 and stayed to become something of a local celebrity. He was from a footballing family: his two brothers were both professionals, one winning a Scottish cap with Dundee and the other playing for Huddersfield in the 1920s. After playing for Dundee Hibs, Chaplin came to London to work in a munitions factory during World War One. Whilst playing for Napier in the Munitions League, he was spotted by Fulham's manager Phil Kelso, who was watching his son. Chaplin signed for Fulham and made his debut at the age of 27 in the first post-war League match. He succeeded his brother-in-law Jimmy Sharp, in the left-back position. A stylish player, he was club captain and member of Fulham's successful defence of the early 1920s. He was quite at home at the Cottage — literally — for the upstairs of Craven Cottage was home to Alec, his wife and four children for several years. When Joe Bradshaw became manager in the 1926 close season, Alec moved on to become player-coach at Northfleet, Spurs' nursery team, and helped them to the Kent Senior Cup twice in three years. When he retired, he returned to his previous trade, plastering, and from 1944 to 1959 he served as a Labour member on the Fulham Borough Council and was a noted local horticulturist. Right up until his death in March 1986, at the age of 94, he was a regular at the Cottage, a proud and independent old man, who was always a delightful companion.

ALEC CHAPLIN

| | LEAGUE | | FA CUP | | TOTAL | |
	App	Gls	App	Gls	App	Gls
1919-20	39	0	1	0	40	0
1920-21	39	0	5	0	44	0
1921-22	41	0	3	0	44	0
1922-23	41	0	1	0	42	0
1923-24	36	1	3	0	39	1
1924-25	34	0	1	0	35	0
1925-26	29	0	3	0	32	0
	259	1	17	0	276	1

Better known as 'Taffa', Charlton was born at Southwick near Sunderland around 1885. He joined his local club as an amateur and moved to the Cottage in the summer of 1906. Charlton gained a Southern League Championship medal in his first season at the club but almost left for Glossop in 1907 following a dispute with the club's management. His transfer was blocked, but he lost his place in the first team in Fulham's first season in the Football League whilst his future was being decided. Charlton gained a regular place in season 1908-09 and played in an international trial match in January 1909 for the South versus the North at Craven Cottage. He won a London Challenge Cup-winners' medal in season 1909-10. An effective full-back who often started attacks with accurate passes out of defence, he was also a permanent fixture in the Fulham first-team until 1920 when injury forced his retirement. Charlton was the first Fulham player to make 200 Football League appearances for the club.

TED CHARLTON

| | F LEAGUE | | STHRN LGE | | FA CUP | | TOTAL | |
	App	Gls	App	Gls	App	Gls	App	Gls
1906-07	0	0	20	0	4	0	24	0
1907-08	9	0	0	0	0	0	9	0
1908-09	28	4	0	0	2	0	30	4
1909-10	37	2	0	0	3	0	40	2
1910-11	37	1	0	0	1	0	38	1
1911-12	29	0	0	0	4	0	33	0
1912-13	13	0	0	0	0	0	13	0
1913-14	24	0	0	0	1	0	25	0
1914-15	34	0	0	0	2	0	36	0
1919-20	18	0	0	0	1	0	19	0
	229	7	20	0	18	0	267	7

An arrogant, natural goalscorer, Clarke earned the nickname 'sniffer' because of his ability to sniff out half chances. Born at Willenhall on 31 July 1946, Clarke had four footballing brothers, Frank, Derek, Kelvin and Wayne. Joining Walsall from school, he made his debut when only 16. Fulham, then a First Division club, negotiated his transfer for £35,000 in March 1966. Clarke was the leading scorer for the next couple of seasons, and also won six England Under-23 caps and represented the Football League during his spell at the Cottage. When Fulham were relegated in May 1968, Clarke demanded a move and Leicester paid a record £150,000 for his services. Although they appeared in the FA Cup Final in 1969, they were also relegated, and so Allan moved to Leeds United in a £165,000 deal. At Elland Road, he won 19 England caps, a League Championship medal in 1974, an FA Cup-winners' medal in 1972 and runners-up medals in 1970 and 1973, a UEFA Cup-winners' medal in 1971 and a European Cup runners-up medal in 1975. Clarke joined Barnsley in June 1978 and became manager a year later. He also had managerial spells at Leeds United in 1981 and Scunthorpe United in 1983, but returned to Barnsley in 1985.

	LEAGUE		FA CUP		FL CUP		TOTAL	
	App	Gls	App	Gls	App	Gls	App	Gls
1965-66	7/1	1	0	0	0	0	7/1	1
1966-67	42	24	3	3	2	2	47	29
1967-68	36	20	3	2	6	5	45	27
	85/1	45	6	5	8	7	99/1	57

ALLAN CLARKE

BRUCE CLARKE

Clarke possessed a delicate touch on the ball for a player who was 6ft 2in tall. Born in Johannesburg in South Africa on 4 October 1910, Bruce spent most of his childhood in Scotland. He joined Hillside Junior Club as a youngster and spent two months with Montrose before joining Third Lanark in 1928. After gaining a regular first-team place he impressed a Fulham scout with his seven goals in 27 appearances in season 1933-4, and he came south to the Cottage that summer for a £550 fee. Clarke played at right-half, inside-right and on the right wing for Fulham and was a great artist on the ball. He eventually lost his place to James Evans in 1937. His best seasons were 1934-5 and 1936-7 when he played 40 and 39 games respectively. He scored his only goal for Fulham in the 4-1 win over Blackpool at the Cottage in September 1934. Clarke left Fulham in the summer of 1939 to carry on his trade as a joiner.

	LEAGUE		FA CUP		TOTAL	
	App	Gls	App	Gls	App	Gls
1934-35	40	1	1	0	41	1
1935-36	26	0	0	0	26	0
1936-37	39	0	1	0	40	0
1937-38	5	0	0	0	5	0
1938-39	2	0	0	0	2	0
	112	1	2	0	114	1

Born at Hayle, Cornwall on 10 July 1896, Donald, like his brother Jack, was to become a prolific goalscorer. Cock played for Brentford in World War One but joined Fulham in the summer of 1919. His brother Jack had guested for Fulham in the war years but made his name with Chelsea and Huddersfield in the 1920s, winning two England caps. Donald never quite reached international standard but played in an international trial at Craven Cottage in 1922 and scored over 100 goals during his career. He had a fine goalscoring record for Fulham, nearly a goal in every two games and scored 25 goals in his first season. After losing his place, he moved to Notts County in October 1922 and helped them to the Second Division Championship that season with 11 goals. He kept scoring at the highest level and Arsenal signed him near the end of season 1925-6. He was not a success at Highbury and moved to Clapton Orient in October 1925. Cock scored 30 goals in two seasons at Homerton but wanted First Division football again and joined Wolves in the close season of 1927, but played only three games. He died at Bradmore near Wolverhampton on 31 August 1974.

DONALD COCK

	LEAGUE		FA CUP		TOTAL	
	App	Gls	App	Gls	App	Gls
1919-20	33	25	1	0	34	25
1920-21	29	10	4	1	33	11
1921-22	23	8	2	0	25	8
1922-23	1	0	0	0	1	0
	86	43	7	1	93	44

GEORGE COHEN

The last Fulham player to win an England cap was George Cohen, who was a member of the World Cup-winning side in 1966. He was born in Kensington on 22 October 1939. He attended the Henry Compton School, Hammersmith and played for West London Boys, London Boys and Middlesex Youth at left-half. He joined Fulham as an amateur in 1955, and signed professional the day after his 17th birthday, in October 1956. His debut came in March 1957, a home match against Liverpool, but it was another nine months before he made the right-back spot his own. From November 1957 until December 1967, only injury kept him out, and for never more than seven games in a season. In these years, Fulham reached two FA Cup semi-finals and the First Division. Cohen's quiet, unobtrusive style, and his tremendous speed, made him a natural choice for Alf Ramsey's 'wingless' England team. He won his first cap in May 1964 against Uruguay and went on to play in 37 of the next 42 internationals. Then, in a game against Liverpool at the Cottage in December 1967, Cohen received the knee injury which virtually ended his career before he was 30. After retiring, he was briefly a coach with the juniors, but left to develop his business interests in building and property. Cohen has also battled against cancer with the same determination and as much success as he took on wingers in the 1960s, and he retains his interest in football, and Fulham.

	LEAGUE		FA CUP		FL CUP		TOTAL	
	App	Gls	App	Gls	App	Gls	App	Gls
1956-57	1	0	0	0	0	0	1	0
1957-58	26	0	7	0	0	0	33	0
1958-59	41	1	4	0	0	0	45	1
1959-60	42	0	2	0	0	0	44	0
1960-61	41	0	1	0	1	0	43	0
1961-62	41	1	8	0	2	0	51	1
1962-63	38	0	2	0	1	0	41	0
1963-64	41	1	2	0	1	0	44	1
1964-65	40	2	2	0	2	0	44	2
1965-66	39	0	1	0	3	0	43	0
1966-67	35	1	3	0	3	0	41	1
1967-68	17	0	0	0	5	0	22	0
1968-69	6	0	1	0	0	0	7	0
	408	6	33	0	18	0	459	6

Born in Kettering in 1880, he joined the local Southern League side as a youngster. 'Tim' was to become one of the most-travelled players of his time. His first move was to Northampton in 1901. A season later he went to Plumstead to play for Woolwich Arsenal. He stayed for almost six seasons scoring 85 goals in 190 games and played in three international trial games before winning a full cap against Ireland in February 1907: he also represented the Football League on two occasions. He was on the move again in March 1908 to Everton. Sunderland was his next port of call, where he stayed only one season. He arrived at the Cottage in July 1911 and immediately struck up a fine goalscoring partnership with Bert Pearce. He topped 20 goals in a season on five occasions, the last being in 1912-13 with Fulham, including hat-tricks in consecutive games. Moving to Nottingham Forest in 1914, the war soon halted his career. He joined the Football Battalion and was at one time reported missing-in-action. He returned to play for Tunbridge Wells Rangers in 1919 and died in an industrial accident on 20 November 1940.

	LEAGUE		FA CUP		TOTAL	
	App	Gls	App	Gls	App	Gls
1911-12	31	15	4	3	35	18
1912-13	36	20	1	0	37	20
1913-14	27	10	1	0	28	10
	94	45	6	3	100	48

JOHN, GEORGE 'TIM' COLEMAN

ARTHUR 'PAT' COLLINS

An Edwardian dandy, 'Prince Arthur' was always immaculately dressed and greatly admired by the ladies for his elegance and good looks. Born in Leicester in 1883, Collins joined Leicester Fosse at the turn of the century, playing 82 games before being signed by Fulham manager Harry Bradshaw in the summer of 1905. Helped to make up one of Fulham's best-ever half-back lines with Billy Morrison and Billy Goldie, which won two Southern League Championship titles between 1905 and 1907. He was a perfect foil for Goldie. His cultured, graceful style contrasted with the more gritty and dour Goldie. The Fulham defence conceded only 15 goals in the 1905-06 season thanks largely to the half-back trio. Collins played in three England trial matches but never made the full international side and many critics of his time felt that he was very unlucky not to be capped. Later in his career Collins also appeared at centre-half for Fulham. After almost 300 games in a white shirt, he moved to Norwich City in the summer of 1914 and he retired during World War One after 29 appearances for the Canaries.

	F LEAGUE		STHRN LGE		FA CUP		TOTAL	
	App	Gls	App	Gls	App	Gls	App	Gls
1905-06	0	0	31	0	2	1	33	1
1906-07	0	0	32	0	4	0	36	0
1907-08	32	0	0	0	6	0	38	0
1908-09	34	0	0	0	2	1	36	1
1909-10	36	1	0	0	3	0	39	1
1910-11	32	0	0	0	1	0	33	0
1911-12	30	3	0	0	0	0	30	3
1912-13	28	3	0	0	1	0	29	3
1913-14	5	1	0	0	0	0	5	1
	197	8	63	0	19	2	279	10

90

A talented centre-forward who supplies his colleagues with many chances, with deft touches and skilful play, Coney was born in Dagenham on 18 September 1963. He attended Erkenwald School and represented London and Essex Boys. After signing as an apprentice in April 1980, he became a professional in May the following year. After some impressive displays for the junior and reserve teams, Coney made his debut against Newport County in March 1981. He instantly found a rapport with Gordon Davies. In his first full season he helped Fulham to promotion with 19 goals in League and Cup games, but the following season the goals dried up and he went 15 months without scoring in the League. Coney won four England Under-21 caps, the first being against Turkey in November 1984. He was Fulham's top scorer in season 1985-6 with 12 League goals and renewed his fruitful partnership with Gordon Davies the following season. In the 1987 close season, he made the short journey to Loftus Road with Paul Parker.

DEAN CONEY

	LEAGUE		FA CUP		FL CUP		TOTAL	
	App	Gls	App	Gls	App	Gls	App	Gls
1980-81	7	3	0	0	0	0	7	3
1981-82	42	13	2	2	7	4	51	19
1982-83	37	4	3	2	4	1	44	7
1983-84	26/1	7	0	0	2	0	28/1	7
1984-85	24	7	1	0	3	2	28	9
1985-86	37	12	1	0	4	1	42	13
1986-87	36/1	10	4	2	4	2	44/1	14
	209/2	56	11	6	24	10	244/2	72

JIMMY CONWAY

One of the few Fulham players who survived the traumas of relegation from the First to the Third Divisions, Conway was a key member of the 1971 promotion side who was also in the team which got to Wembley in 1975. He was one of a family of 17, born in Dublin in August 1946. Conway won caps at Schoolboy, Youth and Amateur levels, and joined Irish League club Bohemians whilst still in his teens. Just before his 20th birthday, in May 1966, he joined Fulham, and five months later he was in the first team. This same month, October 1966, he won the first of his 19 international caps, 18 of which were won whilst he was with Fulham. Conway was a genuine midfield player, not a wing-half or inside-forward, and was more effective operating wide on the right. He could be a regular goalscorer, as in 1969-70 when he topped the list with 23 goals, but generally was more of a provider. Conway also had more than his share of injuries, particularly in 1971-2 and 1972-3, but he fought his way back to fitness, and to Wembley. He had one more season at the Cottage after the Cup Final, and followed coach Bill Taylor to Manchester City. After only four months at Maine Road (14 games and 1 goal), Conway left to try his luck in the USA.

	LEAGUE		FA CUP		FL CUP		TOTAL	
	App	Gls	App	Gls	App	Gls	App	Gls
1966-67	30	3	3	0	1	1	34	4
1967-68	42	4	3	0	6	0	51	4
1968-69	34/1	5	1	0	1	0	36/1	5
1969-70	46	21	1	0	3	2	50	23
1970-71	29	8	0	0	2	2	31	10
1971-72	22	8	3	1	0	0	25	9
1972-73	13/1	4	1	0	0	0	14/1	4
1973-74	25/2	3	2	0	0	0	27/2	3
1974-75	32	4	10	1	3	0	45	5
1975-76	39	7	1	1	3	1	43	9
	312/4	67	25	3	19	6	356/4	76

Although not as skilful as some of his colleagues (he once asked manager Osborne for a transfer because he felt he was not good enough to play in the same side as Johnny Haynes), Cook was nevertheless an integral part of the successful Fulham team of the late 1950s and early 1960s. Cook was born in Berkhamstead on 10 December 1931, he began is career with his home-town club after playing for Potten End School and Hertfordshire Boys. National Service came next, after which he signed for Watford in May 1953. In four and a half years at Vicarage Road, Cook missed only three matches, and scored 84 goals in 215 matches. He was noted for his versatility, playing in all five forward positions, full-back and in goal. Then, in February 1958, he signed for Fulham, to strengthen their promotion challenge. Although the Cottagers missed out in 1957-8, they got it right the next season, and Cook made a major contribution with 17 goals. Nobody could accuse him of being subtle or graceful. He was hard, direct and brave, an old-fashioned centre-forward. What he lacked in control or speed, he made up for in perseverance. Vic Buckingham's arrival meant the end of his Fulham career. He went to Reading for £5,000, but stayed at Elm Park for only one season, scoring three goals in 17 games. He returned to the Watford area to run a pub, but was unlucky in some of his business affairs. Cook remains popular, but is only an occasional visitor to Craven Cottage.

	LEAGUE		FA CUP		FL CUP		TOTAL	
	App	Gls	App	Gls	App	Gls	App	Gls
1957-58	15	9	0	0	0	0	15	9
1958-59	41	17	4	0	0	0	45	17
1959-60	17	8	2	1	0	0	19	9
1960-61	32	12	1	0	1	1	34	13
1961-62	35	15	8	4	2	0	45	19
1962-63	35	15	2	0	2	0	39	15
1963-64	29	5	2	1	1	0	32	6
1964-65	17	8	0	0	2	1	19	9
	221	89	19	6	8	2	248	97

MAURICE COOK

Born at Stewarton in Scotland on 9 February 1903, Craig played in Scottish junior football prior to coming to Craven Cottage in December 1924. He scored on his debut at Middlesbrough on New Year's Day 1925 in a fine 3-1 victory. Over the next three and a half seasons, Craig rarely missed a game for Fulham. A schemer rather than a goalscoring inside-forward, Craig's best season for goals was 1927-8 when he scored ten. Fulham were relegated that season and Craig lost his place in the Third Division side. Bristol City manager Joe Bradshaw, who had been Craig's manager at Fulham, signed him in September 1930 for a fee of £550, but when Bradshaw was sacked in March 1932, it also marked the end of Craig's career at Ashton Gate. He moved to Halifax Town that summer and was converted to wing-half. He missed just eight League games in the next seven seasons for the Yorkshire club, playing a total of 289 League games for the Shaymen before retiring shortly after the outbreak of war in 1939. Craig played 487 Football League games in all, scoring just 38 goals, between 1924 and 1939.

	LEAGUE		FA CUP		TOTAL	
	App	Gls	App	Gls	App	Gls
1924-25	20	2	2	0	22	2
1925-26	34	7	5	1	39	8
1926-27	37	5	2	1	39	6
1927-28	39	10	1	0	40	10
1928-29	13	3	0	0	13	3
1929-30	7	2	0	0	7	2
	150	29	10	2	160	31

TEDDY CRAIG

92

Easily picked out on the field by his bald head, Croal was a typical Scottish inside-forward who was renowned for his artistry and ball control. Born in Glasgow on 27 July 1895, Croal joined Falkirk at an early age. He won Scottish international honours, making his debut against Ireland in Dublin in a 2-1 victory in March 1913. He made two other appearances for Scotland, against Wales in February 1914 and England in two months later, helping the Scots to a 3-1 victory at Hampden Park. Croal also won a Scottish Cup-winners' medal in 1913 when Falkirk beat Raith Rovers 2-0 in the Final. He joined Chelsea in the summer of 1914 where his stay was interrupted by the war but he played 130 League and Cup games, including the 1915 FA Cup Final and scored 22 goals for the Pensioners. There were many critics who felt that Croal should have scored more goals. He moved to Fulham in March 1922 but was probably past his best by this time. Died by his own hand at South Petherton in Somerset on 16 September 1939 at the early age of 44.

	LEAGUE		FA CUP		TOTAL	
	App	Gls	App	Gls	App	Gls
1921-22	11	2	0	0	11	2
1922-23	19	4	0	0	19	4
1923-24	6	0	0	0	6	0
	36	6	0	0	36	6

JIMMY CROAL

JOHN CUTBUSH

Cutbush came from a footballing family, his father Dennis having been an England Amateur international left-half who played for Maidstone and the Royal Navy. His father was a chief petty officer in the RN and stationed in Malta when John was born there on 28 June 1949. After representing Kent Schoolboys, he signed as an apprentice for Spurs in July 1965 and became a professional in September 1966. John never made the Spurs first team and he moved to Fulham on a free transfer in August 1972. He soon found a regular spot at right-back having previously been a midfield player. Cutbush won admiration for his surges upfield to support the forwards and his indomitable and staunch defending. He played in Fulham's Wembley Cup run in 1975, winning a runners-up medal. The arrival of Peter Storey saw Cutbush's departure to Sheffield United for a £20,000 fee in March 1977. He played 129 League games for the Blades but relegation to the Fourth Division saw his release at the end of season 1980-81. Cutbush also played for Wichita Wings in the summer of 1979 in the USA.

	LEAGUE		FA CUP		FL CUP		TOTAL	
	App	Gls	App	Gls	App	Gls	App	Gls
1972-73	34/1	0	0	0	2	0	36/1	0
1973-74	34	2	0	0	4	0	38	2
1974-75	24/1	1	9	0	2	0	35/1	1
1975-76	22	0	1	0	2	0	25	0
1976-77	17/1	0	2	0	4	0	23/1	0
	131/3	3	12	0	14	0	157/3	3

93

He was described by a contemporary as untiring as a wolf and ravenous for work, his skill and shooting were exceptional. Born at Paisley in Glasgow in 1881, Dalrymple was an experienced campaigner on arrival at the Cottage in the summer of 1907. His first senior club was Hearts, with whom he won a Scottish Cup runners-up medal in 1903 when they lost to Rangers after two replays. He moved south to join Plymouth Argyle that summer, where he was a regular for two seasons before returning to Scotland again to join Glasgow Rangers in 1905. Portsmouth were the next club to use his undoubted talents. One of many fine Scottish inside-forwards to grace a Fulham shirt, Dalrymple scored 22 League and Cup goals in his first season at Fulham, including three hat-tricks. Although goals did not come quite so regularly in future seasons, he still maintained a healthy goal-tally until his transfer to Clapton Orient in January 1911. He stayed at Millfields Road until he was almost forty years old, retiring in 1920 after 139 League games and 37 goals for Orient.

	LEAGUE		FA CUP		TOTAL	
	App	Gls	App	Gls	App	Gls
1907-08	33	19	6	3	39	22
1908-09	31	13	2	0	33	13
1909-10	29	6	2	1	31	7
1910-11	5	2	0	0	5	2
	98	40	10	4	108	44

ROBERT DALRYMPLE

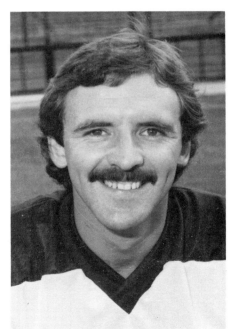

GORDON DAVIES

One of Fulham's most prolific goalscorers, Davies is affectionately known as 'Ivor' by the fans. He was born in Merthyr Tydfil on 8 August 1955 and joined Manchester City as an apprentice in 1972. After failing to make the grade, Davies studied for a teaching qualification in geography and settled down to a career in part-time soccer. Fortunately for Fulham and Davies, he was signed from Southern League Merthyr Tydfil for a bargain £4,000 in March 1978 and was soon scoring regularly in Second Division soccer. International recognition was just around the corner as he won his first cap in Turkey in 1980. At present 'Ivor' has 18 caps including playing against England at Wembley. After 126 goals in 289 League and Cup games for Fulham, Davies decided to try his luck in the First Division. He was unlucky at Chelsea not to be given more opportunities and was doing well at Manchester City until manager Billy McNeill decided to leave for Aston Villa. Just two years after leaving the Cottage, he returned to Fulham in October 1986, but was unlucky with injuries during the rest of 1986-7.

	LEAGUE		FA CUP		FL CUP		TOTAL	
	App	Gls	App	Gls	App	Gls	App	Gls
1977-78	4/1	1	0	0	0	0	4/1	1
1978-79	32	9	3	1	2	1	37	11
1979-80	39	15	2	0	2	1	43	16
1980-81	45	18	6	3	2	1	53	22
1981-82	41	24	2	0	7	1	50	25
1982-83	38	19	3	0	3	1	44	20
1983-84	35/1	23	2	0	5	3	42/1	26
1984-85	10/1	5	0	0	3	1	13/1	6
1986-87	18/3	6	3	3	0	0	21/3	9
	262/6	120	21	7	24	9	307/6	136

A tall and powerful defender, Dempsey played most of his soccer in West London. Born in Hampstead on 15 March 1946, he signed as an apprentice for Fulham in October 1962, signing professional forms in March 1964 and was an instant success. He had a spell at centre-forward for a period in season 1965-6, and once scored a hat-trick against Northampton in the League Cup. It looked as though he would remain Fulham's pivot for many years but was surprisingly transferred to Chelsea for £70,000 in January 1969. He achieved many successes at Stamford Bridge playing in probably Chelsea's best-ever side. He won an FA Cup-winners' medal in 1970, a European Cup-winners' medal in 1971, when he scored one of the goals which beat Real Madrid in the Final replay in Athens, and a League Cup runners-up medal in 1972. In all, Dempsey made 207 appearances for the Blues and won 13 international caps for the Republic of Ireland, the first seven as a Fulham player. Signed by Philadephia Furies in March 1978, Dempsey has recently been managing Maidenhead United and Egham Town.

JOHN DEMPSEY

	LEAGUE		FA CUP		FL CUP		TOTAL	
	App	Gls	App	Gls	App	Gls	App	Gls
1964-65	4	0	1	0	0	0	5	0
1965-66	38	2	1	1	4	3	43	6
1966-67	42	0	3	0	3	0	48	0
1967-68	38	1	3	0	6	0	47	1
1968-69	27	1	0	0	1	0	28	1
	149	4	8	1	14	3	171	8

BILL DODGIN

	LEAGUE		FA CUP		FL CUP		TOTAL	
	App	Gls	App	Gls	App	Gls	App	Gls
1951-52	21	0	1	0	0	0	22	0
1952-53	14	0	0	0	0	0	14	0
1960-61	9	0	0	0	0	0	9	0
1961-62	37	0	5	0	1	0	43	0
1962-63	16	0	0	0	2	0	18	0
1963-64	7	0	0	0	0	0	7	0
1964-65	0	0	0	0	0	0	0	0
	104	0	6	0	3	0	113	0

A member of a famous football family, Bill Dodgin was born at Wardley on 4 November 1931. He began playing for St Mary's College, Southampton, and, at the age of 14, played for the Catholic College of Britain against the Belgium Colleges. When he left school, Dodgin became an apprentice draughtsman at an aircraft factory, and played for Southampton's junior team, where his father was manager. When he left The Dell for the manager's job at Fulham in 1949, young Bill followed. After National Service, he made the breakthrough, his debut coming at Preston in November 1951. He was a full-back in a struggling side, and the fans' anger at his father's decision to let Len Quested move to Huddersfield was directed at Bill junior. After 36 games he moved on, to Arsenal, where he spent the next eight seasons. In all, he made 210 appearances for the Gunners, at full-back or centre-half, and played in the first-ever Under-23 international, against Italy in 1954. In March 1961, he returned to the Cottage and featured in Fulham's 1962, Cup semi-final side. In November 1962, he broke his leg at Villa Park, and played in only seven more games. Ironically, his final appearance was in a 4-1 home defeat by Arsenal. Bill was a solid if at times ungainly central defender, whose height gave him a considerable advantage in the air and compensated for a lack of speed. When he stopped playing, he turned to coaching and management, joining Fulham for a third time in 1968. (See *Fulham Managers*).

An underrated central defender, Dunne was an accurate
passer and a wholehearted player. A little unconventional
at times, he once got into trouble with the authorities
for lowering his shorts to the crowd at Sunderland after
they had given him some abuse. On another occasion,
he had a fight with Alan Mullery after the defence had
given away a simple goal at the Cottage. Born in Dublin
on 1 December 1947, Dunne joined Shelbourne Rovers
as a lad. It was Millwall scout, Bill Dodgin, who
discovered him and Dunne signed for Millwall for
£1,500. He was never given a first-team chance and
moved to Torquay United in July 1967. Fulham signed
him for £15,000 in July 1970. He won his only Republic
of Ireland cap in 1971 against Austria and was a regular
at the Cottage until 1974, when he decided to emigrate
to South Africa. Things did not work out and he
returned to Fulham reserves in October 1975, moving
back to Torquay in 1976 for £4,000. He retired in 1979
with 247 League games for United under his belt.

	LEAGUE		FA CUP		FL CUP		TOTAL	
	App	Gls	App	Gls	App	Gls	App	Gls
1970-71	45	2	1	0	6	0	52	2
1971-72	30	0	3	0	2	0	35	0
1972-73	32	0	1	0	4	0	37	0
1973-74	35/1	0	3	0	3	0	41/1	0
	142/1	2	8	0	15	0	165/1	2

JIMMY DUNNE

ROY DWIGHT

Born in Belvedere in Kent on 9 January 1933, Dwight
joined Fulahm in June 1950 after some experience at
Hastings United. It took him almost five years to make
his debut, scoring in a 3-2 defeat at Birmingham City in
March 1955. Dwight was unable to gain a regular first-
team place until Bedford Jezzard was forced to retire
through injury. He scored 26 and 24 goals respectively
in seasons 1956-7 and 1957-8 before moving to Nottingham Forest in July 1958 for a £6,000 fee. He scored in
the 1959 FA Cup Final against Luton Town but broke
his leg later in the game. He had appeared a year earlier
in a for Fulham, when they lost 5-3 to Manchester
United. Dwight had to leave League football for two
seasons because of his injury and appeared for Gravesend
and Northfleet in the Southern League. It was ex-
teammate and Coventry manager Jimmy Hill who
revived his career when he signed him for City in
January 1962. Dwight signed for Millwall two years
later but retired soon afterwards. He managed Tooting
& Mitcham United in their FA Cup runs in the early
1970s. Dwight has a famous nephew in Elton John, the
rock star and chairman of Watford. A triple heart
by-pass operation led to his early retirement at the age
of 51.

	LEAGUE		FA CUP		TOTAL	
	App	Gls	App	Gls	App	Gls
1954-55	4	2	0	0	4	2
1955-56	4	5	0	0	4	5
1956-57	34	25	2	1	36	26
1957-58	30	22	6	2	36	24
	72	54	8	3	80	57

96

Earle was one of Fulham's most consistent players in the troubled years of the late 1960s, and one of the key reasons for their prompt return to the Second Division. Born in Feltham, Middlesex, on 1 November 1945, Earle nearly joined Crystal Palace before going to the Cottage when he left school in July 1961. He made his debut at Forest in February 1964, and scored in his first senior game at the Cottage the following week, against Blackpool. It was not until the second half of the 1965-6 season, however, that he established himself in the first team. This coincided with the arrival of a new coach, Dave Sexton, who inspired the club to a breath-taking escape from relegation. Thereafter, Earle was a regular, sharing the striking duties with various partners, including Allan Clarke, Les Barrett and Jimmy Conway. His best season was 1969-70, when he scored 23 goals, including five in an 8-0 win at Halifax (see *Match to Remember no.17*). After over 300 games in 11 seasons in three divisions for six managers, Earle moved to Jimmy Bloomfield's Leicester for £100,000. An elegant, polished performer, who relied more on pace and control than power, he fitted in well at Filbert Street. He made 115 appearances and scored 26 goals before leaving in March 1978, to try his luck in the United States.

STEVE EARLE

	LEAGUE		FA CUP		FL CUP		TOTAL	
	App	Gls	App	Gls	App	Gls	App	Gls
1963-64	12	5	0	0	0	0	12	5
1964-65	4	2	0	0	0	0	4	2
1965-66	15	11	0	0	0	0	15	11
1966-67	36/2	12	3	0	2	1	41/2	13
1967-68	26/1	5	3	0	5	3	34/1	8
1968-69	13/2	0	2	0	0	0	15/2	0
1969-70	41	22	1	0	2	1	44	23
1970-71	42	13	1	0	6	1	49	14
1971-72	41	11	3	0	2	3	46	14
1972-73	40	15	1	0	3	0	44	15
1973-74	15/1	2	0	0	2	1	17/1	3
	285/6	98	14	0	22	10	321/6	108

A prolific goalscorer who used his heading abilities to great effect, Edmonds was born in Holborn in London on 4 April 1893. He spent much of his early life living in the St Albans area. He joined the local club in 1910 and moved on to Watford in 1912. Watford won the Southern League Championship in season 1914-15, Edmonds scoring 18 goals in 35 appearances. They were runners-up in the season after World War One, with Edmonds scoring 20 goals in that campaign. Wolves were impressed and paid a large fee for his services in the summer of 1920. He scored regularly in a struggling Second Division side. Edmonds appeared in the 1921 FA Cup Final against Spurs but was marked out of the game by future Fulham colleague Charlie Walters and Wolves lost 1-0. With Wolves relegated to Division Three in 1923, Edmonds moved to Fulham in October of that year. He was unlucky with injuries during his spell at the Cottage and was not the success that was expected. He returned to Watford in the close season of 1926 and retired at the end of that season. He scored 120 goals in 288 Southern and Football League appearances.

GEORGE EDMONDS

	LEAGUE		FA CUP		TOTAL	
	App	Gls	App	Gls	App	Gls
1923-24	23	13	3	2	26	15
1924-25	26	7	2	1	28	8
1925-26	17	3	2	0	19	3
	66	23	7	3	73	26

A strong, useful type of half-back who never knew when he was beaten, Evans was born in Merthyr and was a Welsh Schoolboy international trialist. He played in the Merthyr League as an amateur and worked as a coal-miner until he was 18 years old. He played two games for Merthyr Town in season 1929-30 before moving to Hereford United in the Midland League. Arsenal signed him in the mid-1930s and loaned him to their nursery club, Margate, which played in the Southern League. They had a fine FA Cup run in season 1935-6 beating Crystal Palace in the first round. Evans scored a hat-trick in this game with a penalty, a volley and from a free kick. He returned to Highbury in September 1936 but appeared for the reserves only. Given a free transfer in the summer of 1937, Evans signed for Fulham. He immediately gained a regular first-team place but his career was soon ruined by the war. However he played for Fulham throughout the war years, playing his last game in season 1945-6.

	LEAGUE		FA CUP		TOTAL	
	App	Gls	App	Gls	App	Gls
1937-38	31	1	1	0	32	1
1938-39	40	4	2	0	42	4
	71	5	3	0	74	5

JAMES EVANS

RAY EVANS

A fine attacking full-back who also knew how to defend, Evans was born in Edmonton on 20 September 1949 and was soon making a name for himself in local schools football. He joined Spurs as a professional in June 1967 and won England Youth international honours the following year. The highlight of his career at Tottenham was playing in the UEFA Cup Final side in 1974 which finished runners-up to Feyenoord. Evans played a total of 171 League and Cup games for Spurs before moving to Millwall in January 1975 for a £40,000 fee. After 91 appearances for the Lions, he moved to Fulham for a £35,000 fee in March 1977 in a successful bid to stave off relegation. Evans, a firm favourite with the supporters, once created all the goals in 6-1 victory over Orient in May 1977. He left to find First Division football with Stoke City in August 1979, Fulham receiving £120,000 for his transfer. Evans also played in North American soccer during the summer. He retired in 1982 with almost 450 games under his belt.

	LEAGUE		FA CUP		FL CUP		TOTAL	
	App	Gls	App	Gls	App	Gls	App	Gls
1976-77	12	0	0	0	0	0	12	0
1977-78	39	4	1	0	0	0	40	4
1978-79	35	2	2	0	0	0	37	2
	86	6	3	0	0	0	89	6

Evanson was born at Newcastle-under-Lyme on 10 May 1947, beginning his career with Towcester and joining Oxford United as an amateur in 1964. After signing professional in February 1965, he made his League debut against Bournemouth in 1966. He finally established himself in the second half of season 1970-71. In February 1974, after ten years and 160 League and Cup games, he left Oxford to join Blackpool for a £40,000 fee. He played on the left side of the midfield in 67 games for Blackpool before being given a free transfer in the summer of 1976. It was whilst he was playing summer soccer for Miami Toros that Evanson signed for Fulham. For the next three seasons, he was a regular feature of the midfield. He was also tried as a striker on a number of occasions. Evanson moved to Bournemouth in a £20,000 deal in July 1979 playing 53 games for the South Coast club before joining Poole Town in 1981.

	LEAGUE		FA CUP		FL CUP		TOTAL	
	App	Gls	App	Gls	App	Gls	App	Gls
1976-77	29/2	1	2	0	5	0	36/2	1
1977-78	39/2	3	1	0	2	0	42/2	3
1978-79	16/7	1	0	0	2	0	18/7	1
	84/11	5	3	0	9	0	96/11	5

A one-club man whose name was synonymous with Fulham in the 1930s, Jack Finch was a versatile forward who was most effective on the wing. A Londoner, from West Ham, he was born on 3 February 1909 and played for his Gainsborough Road School team and St Margarets in the West Ham JOC League. He then moved on to Isthmian League amateurs, Walthamstow Avenue for a season, when a job as a coach driver took him to Lowestoft, and the local club for two seasons. By the time he returned to the Avenue, he had developed a reputation, and Fulham beat several other clubs to obtain his signature in November 1930. Within a month he was in the first team, and established himself in September 1931 following a superb display in a 10-2 win over Torquay. He won a Third Division Championship medal that year, and played on the left-wing. When Johnny Arnold was signed the following season, Finch switched to the right flank, with equal effect. Over the next six years he played in every forward position, but his dribbling skills and ability to cross a ball accurately whilst running at top speed made him a natural winger. A staunch teetotaller and non-smoker, he had a reputation as a practical joker and driving was his principal hobby. When war broke out, he was Fulham's longest-serving player, yet he was only 30. Although he played in many wartime games, his career had ended when League football was resumed in 1946.

	LEAGUE		FA CUP		TOTAL	
	App	Gls	App	Gls	App	Gls
1930-31	18	1	0	0	18	1
1931-32	39	11	5	0	44	11
1932-33	42	6	1	0	43	6
1933-34	36	7	2	0	38	7
1934-35	39	8	1	1	40	9
1935-36	30	10	5	0	35	10
1936-37	21	1	0	0	21	1
1937-38	34	4	1	0	35	4
1938-39	21	2	0	0	21	2
	280	50	15	1	295	51

JOHN EVANSON

JACK FINCH

Flack was born in Staines, Middlesex on 24 October 1920 and won a scholarship to Spring Grove Grammar School, Isleworth. One of his teachers was Bernard Joy, who introduced him to Fulham. Flack initially joined the office staff in 1935 before learning his trade as a goalkeeper. He played as a guest 'keeper all over London between 1939 and 1942 when he joined the RAF, spending three years in the Far East. Demobbed in 1946, he returned to the Cottage where there was plenty of competition for the goalkeeper's jersey. Flack made his big breakthrough in the Championship season of 1948-9, playing on 29 occasions but missing the vital last three games through injury. He moved to Walsall in August 1953, where he finished his playing career at the age of 34. Flack became a qualified FA Coach in 1947 and took on a coaching post with Corinthian Casuals in 1954. In his first season, he took them to the Final of the FA Amateur Cup in which they lost to Bishop Auckland. He moved to Tooting & Mitcham United as manager in 1964, retiring in 1970 after 35 years of service to football, and currently works for an aircraft instrument company.

DOUG FLACK

	LEAGUE		FA CUP		TOTAL	
	App	Gls	App	Gls	App	Gls
1948-49	29	0	1	0	30	0
1949-50	17	0	0	0	17	0
1950-51	0	0	0	0	0	0
1951-52	3	0	0	0	3	0
1952-53	5	0	0	0	5	0
	54	0	1	0	55	0

TOM FLEMING

A plasterer by trade, Fleming also helped to fill the cracks in the Fulham defence between 1922 and 1925. Born in Glasgow, Tom was playing Scottish non-League soccer for Shettleston when Dundee signed him in the close season of 1920. They finished fourth in the Scottish League in the two seasons he played for them. He signed for Fulham in January 1922 and struck up an instant rapport with full-back partner Alec Chaplin who, not only was a plasterer, but had also played in Dundee football. Solid and dependable, Fleming rarely missed a game in the next three and a half seasons, except 1923-4 when injury kept him out for a while. He moved on to Wigan Borough in the Third Division North in October 1925, with Fulham colleague Jimmy Riddell. He made 16 appearances in season 1925-6, but only five the following season and was given a free transfer in the summer of 1927.

	LEAGUE		FA CUP		TOTAL	
	App	Gls	App	Gls	App	Gls
1921-22	17	0	0	0	17	0
1922-23	37	0	1	0	38	0
1923-24	23	0	0	0	23	0
1924-25	32	0	2	0	34	0
1925-26	2	0	0	0	2	0
	111	0	3	0	114	0

A clever footballer who used his dribbling skills to score as well as create goals, Fraser was born in Inverness in 1883, and started his football career at Inverness Thistle. He joined Newcastle United in the early years of the century but was unable to make the first team. It was at Fulham, a club he joined in October 1904, that Fraser made his first big impact in soccer. Playing mainly as an inside-left, but occasionally at centre-forward, Fraser found the net regularly over the next three seasons. He won two Southern League Championship medals in seasons 1905-06 and 1906-07 but lost his place when Fulham won entry to the Football League in 1907. Fraser moved to Bradford in March 1908, but made only 23 appearances for the Park Avenue club before moving to Darlington in 1909. Middlesbrough was his next club, signing in February 1912, but his career came to a premature end when he fell heavily after a tackle from Bolton defender Jennings; this injury finished his career. He then joined the North Eastern Railway Company as a boiler-maker.

	F LEAGUE		STHRN LGE		FA CUP		TOTAL	
	App	Gls	App	Gls	App	Gls	App	Gls
1904-05	0	0	21	8	9	3	30	1
1905-06	0	0	21	8	2	1	23	9
1906-07	0	0	27	3	0	0	27	3
1907-08	10	5	0	0	1	0	11	5
	10	5	69	19	12	4	91	28

ALEX FRASER

Freeman was born in the Oxfordshire village of Woodstock in November 1919. He was playing for his local club when he was recommended to Fulham by the brother of Leslie Skene, the Cottagers' goalkeeper of Edwardian days. A month before his 18th birthday, Freeman began his association with Fulham that was to last into the 1950s. He made just one appearance before the war, when he replaced the injuried Mike Keeping in a 1-1 draw with Newcastle in March 1939. During the war, he served in the Royal Fusiliers and played for Fulham as often as military duties permitted, and on his demob he went straight into the League side. He and Joe Bacuzzi formed an effective and consistent partnership at full-back for the best part of five seasons, and Freeman was denied full international honours only by the form of Alf Ramsey and Laurie Scott. He did, however, play for the FA, against the Navy in 1948 and on tours of Spain in 1949 and Canada in 1951. His strength as a full-back was his anticipation which compensated for a lack of speed. He was strong in the tackle and possessed a ferocious shot, scoring a few spectacular goals. One of these, against Charlton in the Cup in 1950, led to a rare display of emotion by the usually taciturn Freeman; he did a handstand in the middle of the pitch. In October 1952, he left Fulham for Walsall, but he stayed only one season at Fellows Park, making 21 appearances. For a brief period in the middle of the 1950s he returned to the Cottage groundstaff and subsequently worked in the baking trade before retirement in Oxford.

	LEAGUE		FA CUP		TOTAL	
	App	Gls	App	Gls	App	Gls
1938-39	1	0	0	0	1	0
1945-46	0	0	2	0	2	0
1946-47	42	3	1	0	43	3
1947-48	30	1	5	0	35	1
1948-49	37	1	1	0	38	1
1949-50	41	1	2	1	43	1
1950-51	18	0	0	0	18	1
1951-52	10	0	0	0	10	0
1952-53	0	0	0	0	0	0
	179	6	11	1	190	7

HARRY FREEMAN

101

A big, strong and fearless goalkeeper, Fryer used his height and weight (6ft 2½ins, 13st 8lb) to great effect. Born in Cromford in 1877, he played minor league soccer with Abbey Rovers and Cromford before being signed by Derby County in 1897. Fryer played in three losing FA Cup Finals for Derby, in 1898, 1899 and 1903; the last one proved to be his last game for the Rams. Bury hit a record six goals, three of them past an unfit Fryer, as Derby used a trio of 'keepers in an attempt to stem the flood. He had made 199 League and Cup appearances for Derby when he moved to Fulham a month later. Over the next four seasons, he let in only 96 goals in 125 Southern League games and gained two Southern League Championship medals. Fryer received a nasty injury at the end of season 1906-07 and was unable to play again for some time. After retiring in 1910, he ran a pub near Stamford Bridge. He had played in 52 FA Cup ties in his 370 appearances. Fryer maintained his links with Fulham until his death in December 1933.

	F LEAGUE		STHRN LGE		FA CUP		TOTAL	
	App	Gls	App	Gls	App	Gls	App	Gls
1903-04	0	0	28	0	7	0	35	0
1904-05	0	0	31	0	9	0	40	0
1905-06	0	0	30	0	1	0	31	0
1906-07	0	0	36	0	4	0	40	0
1907-08	0	0	0	0	0	0	0	0
1908-09	11	0	0	0	2	0	13	0
1909-10	8	0	0	0	3	0	11	0
	19	0	125	0	26	0	170	0

JOHN SPENCER 'JACK, STRING' FRYER

A cultured, well-balanced player who possesses great natural ability, Gale is always cool under pressure and is a fine passer of the ball. Born in Pimlico on 19 November 1959, he signed schoolboy forms for Fulham as a 13-year-old. He made his first-team debut when only 16 and was soon captaining the England Youth side, winning nine Youth caps in all. Gale took over from Bobby Moore at Fulham when he retired, and in many ways is a similar player. Although he gained just one England Under-21 cap, against Poland in 1982, he showed the ability to win further representative honours. He had already made 318 appearances for Fulham when he moved to West Ham for a £225,000 fee in August 1984 at the age of 24. Fulham's failure to gain First Division status in 1983 ultimately led to his departure. Ever-present for West Ham in season 1985-6, Gale may yet win full international recognition despite his critics claiming that he is too slow for international football.

	LEAGUE		FA CUP		FL CUP		TOTAL	
	App	Gls	App	Gls	App	Gls	App	Gls
1977-78	38	8	1	0	2	0	41	8
1978-79	36	2	2	0	2	0	40	2
1979-80	42	4	2	0	2	0	46	4
1980-81	40	1	5	0	2	1	47	2
1981-82	44	1	2	0	7	0	53	1
1982-83	42	2	3	0	4	1	49	3
1983-84	35	1	2	0	5	0	42	1
	277	19	17	0	24	2	318	21

TONY GALE

Gibbon was tragically killed in a motor-cycle accident near Deal in Kent on 8 April 1935. He had been at the Cottage since March 1929 and his death came as a great shock to everyone at Fulham. Born in Merthyr Tydfil in the winter of 1910, Gibbon's father was the chairman of Merthyr Football Club. The club was in financial difficulties and Sonny was made a professional so that a transfer fee could be obtained. After winning a Welsh Amateur international cap, against England as a centre-forward, Aberdare Athletic, a club which had just left the Football League, signed him. His next move was to Merthyr Town in 1928 where he played 25 League games before his transfer to the Cottage for a £700 fee. Gibbon was a well-built, fairly skilful full-back who possessed unabounded enthusiasm for the game and he established himself very quickly into the first team. Ever-present in season 1930-31, he gained a Third Division South Championship medal in 1931-2. He played mainly for the reserves thereafter until his death.

	LEAGUE		FA CUP		TOTAL	
	App	Gls	App	Gls	App	Gls
1928-29	6	1	0	0	6	1
1929-30	29	0	5	0	34	0
1930-31	42	0	4	0	46	0
1931-32	22	0	4	0	26	0
1932-33	1	0	0	0	1	0
1933-34	14	0	0	0	14	0
1934-35	0	0	0	0	0	0
	114	1	13	0	127	1

SAMUEL 'SONNY' GIBBON

One of the most dominating characters at the Cottage in the 1930s was centre-half Syd Gibbons, nicknamed 'Carnera' because of his imposing physique. Born in Darlaston in Staffs in 1903, he began his career with Cradley Heath in 1924 and in 1926 played for England Juniors against Scotland in 1926. Before turning professional with Manchester City that year, he worked in a foundry, which helped develop his strength. In four years at Maine Road, he made only ten appearances and in the summer of 1930 dropped down to the Third Division with Fulham. After overcoming initial home-sickness, he established himself in the side, and became a firm favourite of the supporters. With Len Oliver and Albert Barrett, he formed the superb half-back line which helped win the Third Division title in 1932, and he was in the 1936 semi-final side, one of the few Fulham players who did justice to his reputation that day. He was a human dynamo of a player, whose rugged all-action style was in sharp contrast with the 'stopper' centre-half so popular in the 1930s. Off the field, he was quiet and unassuming, enjoying cricket, bowls and gardening. He left the Cottage in the 1938 close season to become player-manager of Worcester City but returned to West London after the war to run a tobacconists in Putney and do some scouting for Fulham. This new career did not last, for he collapsed and died at the age of 50 in July 1953.

	LEAGUE		FA CUP		TOTAL	
	App	Gls	App	Gls	App	Gls
1930-31	32	0	3	2	35	2
1931-32	42	0	5	0	47	0
1932-33	42	3	1	0	43	3
1933-34	38	3	2	0	40	3
1934-35	42	5	1	0	43	5
1935-36	39	1	6	0	45	1
1936-37	42	1	1	0	43	1
1937-38	22	0	0	0	22	0
	299	13	19	2	318	15

SYD GIBBONS

"When danger threatened Goldie was always there. He did his work with grace of accomplishment which endeared him to the Fulham crowd." So said Merula in the Fulham programme of the time. A dour, defensive wing-half who rarely smiled, Goldie was born in Hurlford, Scotland in 1878. He joined the local club, Hurlford Thistle, in 1895 and moved to Clyde two years later. Liverpool signed Goldie in 1898, joining his brother Archie who had made the same trip three years earlier. Billy played 174 League and Cup games for the Reds, winning a League Championship medal in season 1900-01 when he was ever-present. Fulham signed him in January 1904 and he rarely missed a game until his departure to Leicester Fosse in the close season of 1908. Once, when suspended by the FA, he needed an interpreter at his enquiry as he had such a strong Scottish accent. Goldie won two Southern League Championship medals and another brother, John, also played for Fulham. He retired in 1911 to run a pub after almost 500 games.

	F LEAGUE		STHRN LGE		FA CUP		TOTAL	
	App	Gls	App	Gls	App	Gls	App	Gls
1903-04	0	0	18	0	1	0	19	0
1904-05	0	0	31	4	9	0	40	4
1905-06	0	0	34	0	2	0	36	0
1906-07	0	0	38	1	4	0	42	1
1907-08	36	0	0	0	6	0	42	0
	36	0	121	5	22	0	179	5

WILLIAM GOLDIE

WILLIAM HALEY

Haley proved a successful goalscorer for Fulham after three and a half barren years with Derby County. He has the distinction of having scored four hat-tricks in season 1929-30, against Bristol Rovers, Norwich City, Watford (four goals) and Merthyr Town. He was born in Bexleyheath in 1904, and joined Bostall Heath FC as a lad. He was soon spotted by Charlton Athletic, joining them in May 1924. Derby County signed Haley in February 1925 after he had scored nine goals in his first season. Alas, in three and a half years at the Baseball Ground, Haley made the first team only 11 times and scored only one goal against Middlesbrough in December 1925. Fulham snapped him up on a free transfer in June 1928 and he was soon scoring regularly. Haley scored 54 goals in three seasons at the Cottage, forming a fine goalscoring trio with Fred Avey and Johnny Price. Queen's Park Rangers signed him in May 1931 but after one season at the White City he moved to Dartford in the summer of 1932. His final club was Sheppey United whom he joined in August 1935. Haley died in Rochester on 2 January 1960.

	LEAGUE		FA CUP		TOTAL	
	App	Gls	App	Gls	App	Gls
1928-29	35	19	3	0	38	19
1929-30	30	21	3	2	33	23
1930-31	28	10	2	2	30	12
	93	50	8	4	101	54

This bustling striker was most appreciated at Sunderland where he played in their giant-killing Wembley win over Leeds in the 1973 FA Cup Final. Halom was born in Swadlincote near Derby on 3 October 1948, and started his football career in London, with Charlton Athletic in January 1966. He moved to Orient in August 1967 for a £3,000 fee. Halom gained a fine reputation at Brisbane Road and Fulham manager Bobby Robson just beat Brian Clough for his signature in November 1968, costing Fulham £35,000. His stay was plagued by injuries, but he played an important role he promotion side of 1970-71. In September 1971, he joined Luton Town and then moved to Sunderland in February 1973. At Sunderland, Halom won a Second Division Championship medal in 1975-6 as well as a Cup medal. His wanderings continued to Oldham in July 1976, Rotherham United in February 1980, and Fredrikstad (Norway) in 1982 before starting on a managerial career with Barrow in 1983. This was followed by two years at Rochdale. Halom made 451 League appearances scoring 130 goals in all.

	LEAGUE		FA CUP		FL CUP		TOTAL	
	App	Gls	App	Gls	App	Gls	App	Gls
1968-69	10	3	1	0	0	0	11	3
1969-70	23/1	11	0	0	1	0	24/1	11
1970-71	30/5	8	1	0	6	2	37/5	10
1971-72	3	0	0	0	1	1	4	1
	66/6	22	2	0	8	3	76/6	25

VIC HALOM

Of the six established county cricketers who played for Fulham in the inter-war period, Jim Hammond made the largest contribution to the Cottagers. Born at Hove in Sussex on 7 November 1907, he was an amateur with Lewes when he signed for Fulham in 1928. He had won England Schoolboy and Amateur caps, both against Wales. He made his League debut in 1929 against Merthyr and over the next ten years became the club's highest and most consistent goalscorer. In all, he scored 142 League and nine Cup goals, the first Fulham player to complete a century of goals, and a total only beaten by Jezzard and Haynes. He scored four goals in two matches and hat-tricks in eight others, and in seven of his eight full seasons was either the leading or second highest scorer. Hammond was a large man, 6ft 2in tall and weighing over 13st, forceful in the air, difficult to shake off the ball and the possessor of a strong shot in either foot. To the supporters he was known as the 'Galloping Hairpin', and it was his attitude as much as his skill which made him so popular. His conduct was always exemplary and he helped set standards for sportsmanship for which Fulham are noted. His cricketing career was spent with Sussex and between 1928 and 1939 scored over 4,000 runs (ave 28.72) and took 428 wickets (ave 28.71). His left-wing partner at Fulham was Johnny Arnold, another cricketer, and the two were both appointed first-class umpires in 1961. His football career ended through injury in 1938, by which time he had collected a Third Division Championship medal and was 12th man for England against Austria in 1932; he also played in the 1936 semi-final. Hammond died in July 1986, at the age of 78.

HERBERT EDWARD (JIM) HAMMOND

	LEAGUE		FA CUP		TOTAL	
	App	Gls	App	Gls	App	Gls
1928-29	8	5	0	0	8	5
1929-30	31	16	5	1	36	17
1930-31	36	14	4	2	40	16
1931-32	42	31	5	2	47	33
1932-33	38	10	1	0	39	10
1933-34	41	15	2	1	43	16
1934-35	40	22	1	0	41	22
1935-36	40	15	6	3	46	18
1936-37	21	7	1	0	22	7
1937-38	19	6	1	0	20	6
	316	141	26	9	342	150

Harrison shares the record of scoring five goals in a game for Fulham with Bedford Jezzard, Jimmy Hill and Steve Earle. He achieved this in September 1908 against Stockport County, scoring all the goals in a 5-1 victory. Harrison was born in Winchester around 1882 and joined Southampton as a youngster. He played in two international trial games, for the South v North in January 1904 and the Professionals v Amateurs two years later, but never gained a full cap. After scoring seven goals in a reserve match, he quickly gained a reputation as a prolific scorer for the Saints. When he moved to Fulham with Fred Mouncher in November 1907, Harrison had scored 89 goals in 165 games for Southampton. Unable to find the net so often for Fulham, he was heavily criticised by the press, but remained a popular figure with the crowd. Harrison moved to West Ham with full-back George Redwood in April 1911, and then to Bristol City in the summer of 1913. He eventually scored 155 goals in 341 League matches. Harrison won a Southern League Championship medal in season 1902-03 and a London Challenge Cup medal in 1909-10 with Fulham.

FRED HARRISON

	LEAGUE		FA CUP		TOTAL	
	App	Gls	App	Gls	App	Gls
1907-08	24	12	6	6	30	18
1908-09	32	13	2	0	34	13
1909-10	35	14	3	1	38	15
1910-11	30	8	1	0	31	8
	121	47	12	7	133	54

JOHNNY HAYNES

	LEAGUE		FA CUP		FL CUP		TOTAL	
	App	Gls	App	Gls	App	Gls	App	Gls
1952-53	18	1	1	0	0	0	19	1
1953-54	41	16	3	2	0	0	44	18
1954-55	37	8	1	1	0	0	38	9
1955-56	40	18	2	1	0	0	42	19
1956-57	33	4	2	0	0	0	35	4
1957-58	38	15	7	1	0	0	45	16
1958-59	34	26	4	0	0	0	38	26
1959-60	31	10	2	0	0	0	33	10
1960-61	39	9	1	0	1	0	41	9
1961-62	38	5	6	1	1	0	45	6
1962-63	8	0	0	0	0	0	8	0
1963-64	40	8	2	0	1	0	43	8
1964-65	39	5	2	0	2	0	43	5
1965-66	33	6	1	0	4	1	38	7
1966-67	36	6	3	1	2	0	41	7
1967-68	34	5	3	1	5	1	42	7
1968-69	28	1	2	1	1	0	31	2
1969-70	27	3	1	0	3	0	31	3
	594	146	43	9	20	2	657	157

Fulham's most famous son, and one of the outstanding post-war inside-forwards in British football, Johnny Haynes is the dominant figure in Fulham's history. In a career which stretched from Boxing Day 1952 to January 1970, he set most of Fulham's individual records: most appearances, highest goalscorer and most capped (56 — 22 as captain). Born at Edmonton on 17 October 1934, he had played for England at every level from Schoolboy through to full cap before his 20th birthday. Despite the interest of Arsenal and Spurs, he joined Fulham in 1950, following his schoolfriend 'Tosh' Chamberlain to the Cottage. Haynes played for Feltham, Wimbledon and Woodford Town in the Middlesex, Isthmian and Delphian Leagues to prepare him for professional football. Then, for almost 20 years, he was the central figure in Fulham teams, dictating the play from midfield with his magnificent distribution and control. The maestro was idolised by Fulham supporters, and he resisted offers from other First Division clubs and from abroad to remain a one-club man. His exaggerated gestures at the shortcomings of lesser colleagues were often misunderstood outside Craven Cottage, for, far from being arrogant or conceited, he was a perfectionist who was as hard on himself as he was on others. His England career ended in 1962, in the World Cup Finals. A car crash which kept him out for the best part of a season and the appointment of Alf Ramsey as manager cost him his place. His Fulham career continued for another eight years, however, until in 1970 he went to South Africa, to play for Durban City. In 1987, Haynes, now residing in the UK, enjoys a comfortable lifestyle in Edinburgh where he can maintain his interest in football and pursue his hobby of golf.

Described by journalist Brian Glanville as a quick, virile and imaginative winger who worked the ball very well, Henderson was born in Johnshaven in Scotland on 17 January 1932. He never played soccer as a schoolboy but joined a youth club side at Kirkintilloch as a teenager. Portsmouth were quick to spot his potential and signed him in January 1949 when they were one of the most successful sides in Britain. Henderson was soon a first-team regular, initially playing as a centre-forward. He won the first of seven Scottish caps in May 1953 against Sweden. After 226 appearances and 73 goals for Pompey, Henderson moved to Wolves in March 1958 but stayed only eight months before another move, to Arsenal. Henderson captured some of his old form at Highbury in a more suitable position on the right wing. He went to Fulham in January 1962 for £14,000 but proved to be one of many players signed at this time who were past their best. His final move was to Southern League Poole Town in the summer of 1964.

JOHN 'JACKIE' HENDERSON

	LEAGUE		FA CUP		FL CUP		TOTAL	
	App	Gls	App	Gls	App	Gls	App	Gls
1961-62	18	5	7	1	0	0	25	6
1962-63	23	2	2	0	2	1	27	3
1963-64	4	0	0	0	0	0	4	0
	45	7	9	1	2	1	56	9

Few people have had such a long and varied career in football as Jimmy Hill. At various times he has been a player, union leader, manager, director, television personality and business man. A Londoner born in Balham on 22 July 1928, Hill first tried his luck with Fulham as a 15-year-old school-leaver in 1943. He had played for Henry Cavendish's and then Henry Thornton's schools sides in Clapham as well as turning out for the Denmark Hill Police and Boys Brigade teams. He did not make the grade first time around and spent two years working as a clerk in the City with an insurance company and stockbrokers, but, whilst doing National Service was spotted by Reading manager Ted Drake and invited to Elm Park on his demob. It was, however, Brentford who signed him as a professional and between 1949 and 1952 be made 87 appearances for the Bees. He moved to the Cottage in March 1952 where he spent the rest of his playing career. Wholehearted and enthusiastic rather than skilful, Hill nevertheless was a key member of the 1957-9 side which won promotion to Division One and so nearly got to Wembley. In March 1958 he set a club record of scoring five goals in an away match at Doncaster. Some indication of his other skills came when, as chairman of the Players' Union, he negotiated the abolition of the maximum wage. Having represented the 'workers', he then turned his hand to management with equal success, guiding Coventry from the Third to the First Division. His subsequent career has included a spell as managing director at Highfield Road, a director of Charlton, a television executive and a wide range of other business activities. He also finds time to enjoy golf, tennis and riding. He made a dramatic return to Fulham in April 1987, as chairman of the driving force behind the group which saved the club from extinction.

JIMMY HILL

	LEAGUE		FA CUP		FL CUP		TOTAL	
	App	Gls	App	Gls	App	Gls	App	Gls
1951-52	6	1	0	0	0	0	6	1
1952-53	30	0	1	0	0	0	31	0
1953-54	33	2	3	1	0	0	36	3
1954-55	32	1	1	0	0	0	33	1
1955-56	31	4	2	1	0	0	33	5
1956-57	37	5	2	0	0	0	39	5
1957-58	37	16	7	6	0	0	44	22
1958-59	32	6	4	2	0	0	36	8
1959-60	25	5	1	1	0	0	26	6
1960-61	13	1	0	0	0	0	13	1
	276	41	21	11	0	0	297	52

107

Born in Sunderland in 1908, Hindson represented Sunderland Schools as a youngster. He joined Hylton Colliery as a miner and played for their football team in the Wearside League. Hindson joined Sunderland but, failing to make the grade, returned to non-League football with Spennymoor United. After a short period with Middlesbrough as an amateur, Hindson signed professional forms with Fulham in September 1930 and made his debut against Gillingham in January 1932. A serious injury at Blackpool, when he fractured his fibula early in season 1932-3, hindered his career for a while. Hindson was third choice behind Mike Keeping and Joe Birch and it was usually through injury that he made the first team. His best seasons were 1934-6; in the latter he made 38 League and Cup appearances. These included Fulham's FA Cup run to the semi-final where they lost to Sheffield United, thus denying him an appearance at Wembley. He retired from playing in 1938 and joined Fulham's training staff. Hindson was, however, dogged by ill health and died on 6 May 1950 after a long illness.

	LEAGUE		FA CUP		TOTAL	
	App	Gls	App	Gls	App	Gls
1931-32	6	0	1	0	7	0
1932-33	10	0	0	0	10	0
1933-34	20	0	1	0	21	0
1934-35	27	0	0	0	27	0
1935-36	33	0	6	0	39	0
1936-37	4	0	0	0	4	0
1937-38	4	0	1	0	5	0
	104	0	9	0	113	0

JAMES HINDSON

TED HINTON

Hinton was a strongly-built goalkeeper who always dominated the penalty area. He was born in Belfast on 20 May 1922, and joined Glentoran as an amateur in 1937, turning professional four years later. Hinton played in goal for Glentoran in their 1942 Irish Cup Final defeat by Linfield. He was transferred to Distillery in 1943 after which he crossed the Irish Sea to join Fulham in August 1946. He missed only one game in season 1947-8 but lost his place to Doug Flack the following season. He decided to move to Millwall in July 1949 for a small fee of £1,500. Hinton gained the first of his Irish caps against Scotland in a 0-0 draw in November 1946. He won seven caps in all including helping Northern Ireland to a memorable 2-0 victory over Scotland in October 1947 and holding England to a 2-2 draw at Everton the following month. After 91 appearances for the Lions, Hinton moved back to Ireland to join Ballymena in February 1953. Bangor signed him that summer and he played finally for Ballymena United from August 1956.

	LEAGUE		FA CUP		TOTAL	
	App	Gls	App	Gls	App	Gls
1946-47	31	0	0	0	31	0
1947-48	41	0	4	0	45	0
1948-49	10	0	0	0	10	0
	82	0	4	0	86	0

Hopkins was the driving force behind the 1987 side. A player with great enthusiasm and fight. The team always played with more determination when Hopkins was in the side. He was born in Swansea on 4 April 1964 but lost his Welsh accent as the family moved to Berkshire when he was very young. He joined Fulham as an apprentice in June 1980 after a period with Wokingham reserves to toughen him up for the rigours of professional football. Hopkins was still an apprentice when he made his debut at Huddersfield in May 1981. He established himself as a right-back but, after the departure of Roger Brown, was converted to centre-half. Initially, he struggled, especially in the air, but time and experience produced a fine central defender. Hopkins gained five Welsh Under-21 caps as well as Youth honours. He made his full international debut against Northern Ireland in May 1983 and in 1987 had appeared 14 times for Wales. His best performance for Wales was against Brazil the month following his debut when he marked the dangerous Eder out of the game in a 1-1 draw.

| | LEAGUE | | FA CUP | | FL CUP | | TOTAL | |
	App	Gls	App	Gls	App	Gls	App	Gls
1980-81	1	0	0	0	0	0	1	0
1981-82	31/4	0	2	0	7	1	40/4	1
1982-83	41	1	3	0	4	0	48	1
1983-84	31/2	0	2	0	5	0	38/2	0
1984-85	40	2	1	0	3	1	44	3
1985-86	23	0	1	0	4	0	28	0
1986-87	20	1	3	0	0	0	23	1
	187/6	4	12	0	23	2	222/6	6

JEFF HOPKINS

RAY HOUGHTON

Houghton is a fine midfield player who can dribble in the old Scottish style, pass a ball with great accuracy and score explosive goals with his thunderous shooting. He was born in Glasgow on 9 January 1962 but his family moved to London when he was ten-years-old. He joined West Ham as an apprentice in 1979 and had made only one appearance when John Lyall, the Hammers' manager, gave him a free transfer in May 1982. Fulham jumped at the chance to sign such a talented player and Houghton was soon making a big impact at the Cottage. He had made 145 appearances and scored 21 goals before his transfer to Oxford United for the ludicrously-small fee of £125,000. His value has since quadrupled as his displays earned him international recognition. Houghton was frustrated by Scotland's lack of interest in him and when Republic of Ireland manager, Jack Charlton, offered him a place, because his father is an Irishman, he jumped at the chance. Ironically, Houghton helped the Republic of Ireland beat Scotland at Hampden Park in the European Championship in February 1987. Houghton also scored a goal in Oxford's League Cup Final victory over Queen's Park Rangers in 1986.

| | LEAGUE | | FA CUP | | FL CUP | | TOTAL | |
	App	Gls	App	Gls	App	Gls	App	Gls
1982-83	42	5	3	1	4	1	49	7
1983-84	40	3	0	0	5	0	45	3
1984-85	42	8	1	2	3	1	46	11
1985-86	5	0	0	0	0	0	5	0
	129	16	4	3	12	2	145	21

Iceton was described by a contemporary as 'a courageous 'keeper with class and a big fellow who can take the knocks'. He was born in West Auckland on 22 October 1903 and went down the pits after leaving school. Iceton joined Hull City around 1928. He failed to make the first team and was released, and he joined Shildon FC. Iceton was rediscovered by Fulham in the close season of 1930 and he made his League debut at the age of 26 against Watford in August 1930. He was the first choice 'keeper for the next two and a half seasons until Alf Tootill's arrival in November 1932. Iceton won a Championship medal in season 1931-2 when Fulham won the Third Division South. He was given a free transfer in May 1935 and was signed by Aldershot. Mainly a reserve at the Recreation Ground, Iceton moved to Clapton Orient where he made 40 appearances before retiring at the outbreak of war. He died in 1981.

	LEAGUE		FA CUP		TOTAL	
	App	Gls	App	Gls	App	Gls
1930-31	36	0	4	0	40	0
1931-32	33	0	5	0	38	0
1932-33	19	0	0	0	19	0
1933-34	2	0	0	0	2	0
	90	0	9	0	99	0

One of Fulham's best-ever centre-forwards, who went on to become one of the club's most successful managers, Jezzard's name is indelibly printed on the 1948-64 period of the Cottagers' history, arguably their most successful period. Born in Clerkenwell in October 1927, he grew up in Croxley Green near Watford, and as a teenager played for Watford Boys and, on three occasions, for Watford's first team in the wartime League as an amateur. After 18 months military service in India towards the end of the war, he took up a post as assistant secretary to the Old Merchant Taylors Sports Club. In the summer of 1948, however, he was brought to the Cottage by full-back Joe Bacuzzi and signed as an amateur. After only three games in the reserves, he was selected for the League side and turned professional. In his first season, he won a Second Division Championship medal, and was a regular throughout the three First Division seasons. It was in the next four Second Division seasons, from 1952 to 1956, that he blossomed as a prolific goalscorer. Supported by inside-forwards Bobby Robson and Johnny Haynes, Beddy averaged 0.76 goals per game, and scored a total of 154 League goals, a record which still stands. His old fashioned skills of speed, strength, bravery and directness made him an ideal centre-forward to partner the subtler skills of the young inside-forwards. He won two England caps and also played for the Football League and England 'B'. It was whilst on a tour of South Africa with an FA XI that he received the ankle injury which prematurely ended his playing career in 1956 at the age of 28. (See *Fulham Managers*).

	LEAGUE		FA CUP		TOTAL	
	App	Gls	App	Gls	App	Gls
1948-49	30	6	1	0	31	6
1949-50	39	8	2	0	41	8
1950-51	35	9	3	0	38	9
1951-52	27	8	1	0	28	8
1952-53	42	35	1	0	43	35
1953-54	42	38	3	0	45	38
1954-55	39	23	1	0	40	23
1955-56	38	27	2	0	40	27
	292	154	14	0	306	154

JAKE ICETON

BEDFORD JEZZARD

110

Fulham have had a long line of distinguished left-backs, and amongst the best of these was Mike Keeping, captain for much of the 1930s. Born in Milford-on-Sea on 22 August 1902 he began his career with the local amateur side. In December 1920, he signed for Southampton, then in the Third Division, and spent 12 years at The Dell. Saints were managed at that time by James McIntyre, who was to sign him for Fulham in February 1933. Keeping got into Southampton's first team in 1925, and made almost 300 appearances for the South Coast side. He also picked up representative honours, playing on the FA Tours of Canada in 1926 and South Africa and Rhodesia in 1929. He also played for England against The Rest, for the Professionals against the Amateurs and, in 1931, for the Football League against the Irish League at Blackpool. His move to Fulham came just days after a drawn League game between the clubs at The Dell. A fee of £5,100 was paid for Keeping and Arnold, to strengthen the Cottagers promotion push. Although in the end promotion was missed, it proved a good investment because both players were regulars up until the outbreak of war. A big man in every sense of the word, Keeping was an old-fashioned full-back. He was not averse to using his weight, but was always scrupulously fair: it was said of him that he never committed a deliberate foul in his 19 years as a professional. After the war, Mike coached Real Madrid and later spent some time in South Africa. His family had a thriving motor business in Hampshire, where he lived whilst a Fulham player.

	LEAGUE		FA CUP		TOTAL	
	App	Gls	App	Gls	App	Gls
1932-33	14	0	0	0	14	0
1933-34	17	0	1	0	18	0
1934-35	26	0	1	0	27	0
1935-36	35	3	6	0	41	3
1936-37	40	2	1	0	41	2
1937-38	37	0	1	0	38	0
1938-39	36	2	2	0	38	2
	205	7	12	0	217	7

MIKE KEEPING

Keetch was a paradoxical character: outside football he was heavily involved in the art and antique world and the jet-set life-style which goes with it, whilst on the pitch he was an uncompromising and tough-tackling centre-half. It was said that the better the opposition the bigger the boots Keetch would wear. He was born in Tottenham on 25 October 1941 and joined West Ham as a youngster. He seemed to be getting nowhere at Upton Park and joined Fulham in April 1959. Keetch loved his years at the Cottage and was broken-hearted when Vic Buckingham gave him a free transfer in May 1965. Initially, he even retired, but Queen's Park Rangers persuaded him to join them and he played a part in their rise from the Third to the First Division. His life-style outside football was featured in a daily newspaper under the title of 'The Four Faces of Bobby Keetch' with four photographs depicting him as the Connoisseur, the Player, the Gourmet and the Man-about-Town complete with Lotus Elite sports car. Keetch retired from playing when he was only 27. Nowadays he travels all over the world as an importer.

BOBBY KEETCH

	LEAGUE		FA CUP		FL CUP		TOTAL	
	App	Gls	App	Gls	App	Gls	App	Gls
1961-62	0	0	0	0	1	0	1	0
1962-63	12	0	0	0	2	0	14	0
1963-64	38	2	2	0	1	0	41	2
1964-65	37	0	1	0	3	0	41	0
1965-66	19	0	1	0	3	0	23	0
	106	2	4	0	10	0	120	2

Kelly would probably wish to forget his international debut for Northern Ireland against England at Maine Road in November 1949. He let in nine goals as the Irish lost 9-2, Jack Rowley scoring four of England's goals. Kelly was born in Belfast on 17 August 1919 and joined Belfast Celtic during World War Two, where he won two Irish Cup-winners' medals. The first was in 1943 when Glentoran were beaten 1-0 and then second in the following year, when Linfield were defeated 3-1. Kelly also won Irish League representative honours. When Celtic folded in March 1949 after a riot at their ground, he, along with Lawler and Campbell, joined Fulham. He had to wait until the following September for his debut, against Chelsea in a 1-1 draw at the Cottage. Kelly gained four caps in total for Northern Ireland before Ted Hinton, his predecessor at Fulham, took his place in the side. Kelly stayed only one season at the Cottage before moving to Southampton in exchange for Ian Black in August 1950. He was never a regular at The Dell and moved on to Exeter City in June 1952. He made 99 League appearances for the Grecians before calling it a day in 1955.

	LEAGUE		FA CUP		TOTAL	
	App	Gls	App	Gls	App	Gls
1949-50	25	0	2	0	27	0
	25	0	2	0	27	0

HUGH KELLY

JOHNNY KEY

Key was a direct winger who loved to beat a full-back for speed and cross accurately for his forwards. He was born in Chelsea on 5 November 1937 and came to Fulham straight from school, signing professional in May 1956. Key was a good athlete and won the Southern AAA long-jump championship. He made his debut against Yeovil Town in the FA Cup in January 1958, Fulham winning 4-0. Key was to score 37 goals in 181 League and Cup games during the next eight seasons. His most memorable performance was against Spurs in January 1965 when Fulham won 4-1 and he scored a great goal from 25 yards. He was one of many Fulham stalwarts who were allowed to leave prematurely at this time by manager Vic Buckingham. He was given a free transfer and moved to Coventry City in May 1966 where Jimmy Hill was manager. In his first season Key won a Second Division Championship medal as City moved into the First Division for the first time. He moved to Orient in March 1968, retiring the following year to become a taxi-cab driver. He now lives a couple of doors away from Bedford Jezzard and tennis is his main sporting interest.

	LEAGUE		FA CUP		FL CUP		TOTAL	
	App	Gls	App	Gls	App	Gls	App	Gls
1957-58	0	0	1	1	0	0	1	1
1958-59	6	2	1	0	0	0	7	2
1959-60	25	4	0	0	0	0	25	4
1960-61	28	5	1	0	1	0	30	5
1961-62	9	0	1	1	1	0	11	1
1962-63	22	4	1	0	2	3	25	7
1963-64	27	5	1	0	1	1	29	6
1964-65	26	4	2	1	1	1	29	6
1965-66	20	5	0	0	4	0	24	5
	163	29	8	3	10	5	181	37

A late starter in football, Lacy gained a BSc in Economics before turning professional with Fulham. He was born in Liverpool on 14 August 1951, and football did not become important to him until he went to university at the London School of Economics. He played for the university or travelled home to Liverpool to play for Marine. For two seasons, Lacy played as an amateur for Fulham but signed professional forms in June 1971. At 6ft 3in tall, Lacy dominated in the air. He played an important role in Fulham's march to the Cup Final in 1975 and formed a good partnership with Bobby Moore. Lacy wanted First Division football and when Spurs offered £200,000 for his transfer in July 1978, he jumped at the chance. John found the transition a little difficult and his limitations on the ground were exploited, but he did play 125 games for Spurs in his five seasons at White Hart Lane. Lacy moved to Crystal Palace in June 1983 but his contract was cancelled with the club in November 1984. There were rumours that he would rejoin Fulham, but nothing came of them. After two years out of the game, Lacy rejoined John Mitchell at St Albans City.

	LEAGUE		FA CUP		FL CUP		TOTAL	
	App	Gls	App	Gls	App	Gls	App	Gls
1972-73	3/1	0	0	0	0	0	3/1	0
1973-74	32/1	0	3	0	3	1	38/1	1
1974-75	39	2	11	0	2	0	52	2
1975-76	26/1	1	1	0	0	0	27/1	1
1976-77	26/1	2	0	0	1	0	27/1	2
1977-78	38	2	1	0	2	0	41	2
	164/4	7	16	0	8	1	188/4	8

JOHN LACY

DEREK LAMPE

Lampe was a highly-promising central defender whose career was ruined by injury. He was born in Edmonton on 20 May 1937 and attended the local Montague School. When he was 15-years-old, he played for London Schools against Yorkshire Schools and later toured Germany with them. Lampe also played for Middlesex Schools. In July 1952, he asked Fulham trainer, Frank Penn, for a trial and was signed immediately afterwards. Lampe won further representative honours with Middlesex Youth and won six England Youth international caps. His greatest distinction was to captain England's Under-20 team against Hungary in a 2-1 victory at White Hart Lane. He made his Fulham debut against West Ham in August 1956. This proved to be his best season, for he played 42 League and Cup games. Sadly his career went downhill after this as increasingly he became dogged by one injury after another. Lampe finally called it a day in the summer of 1964.

	LEAGUE		FA CUP		FL CUP		TOTAL	
	App	Gls	App	Gls	App	Gls	App	Gls
1956-57	40	0	2	0	0	0	42	0
1957-58	13	0	2	0	0	0	15	0
1958-59	2	0	0	0	0	0	2	0
1959-60	14	0	0	0	0	0	14	0
1960-61	11	0	0	0	0	0	11	0
1961-62	5	0	3	0	0	0	8	0
1962-63	3	0	0	0	1	0	4	0
	88	0	7	0	1	0	96	0

Only the second full-back in the Football League to score 50 goals, Jim Langley was one of the more effervescent personalities in the Fulham sides of the 1950s and 1960s. Born in Kilburn, London, on 7 February 1929, Langley was evacuated to West Drayton during the war. His first club was Yiewsley, which was followed by spells with Hayes and Brentford as an amateur. During his National Service in 1947-8, he represented the Hampshire FA, and on his demob joined Southern League Guildford. Three years later, he got his chance with a League club, Leeds United, and played nine games on the left-wing, scoring three goals, for the Elland Road side in 1952-3. He then moved to Brighton and was converted to full-back and in four years made 174 appearances, scoring 15 times. Although in the Third Division, he won three England 'B' caps and played for the Football League. He was signed by Fulham in February 1957 and over the next eight years, this crew-cut, bow-legged player became a great favourite with the crowd. He had a wide range of tricks, such as a bicycle-kick, overhead-kick, an enormous throw-in and a superb slide-tackle. He was noted for his sportsmanship and sense of fun, as well as his ability. He won three full England caps, and in his time at the Cottage he helped Fulham to two FA Cup semi-finals and promotion to the First Division. Langley was sold prematurely by Vic Buckingham to Queen's Park Rangers in 1965 and at Loftus Road won a Third Division Championship medal and a League Cup-winners' medal. He left League football in 1967, after almost 650 appearances, to manage Hillingdon Borough, whom he took to Wembley in 1971. One of the great characters in Fulham's history, Langley is still a popular visitor to the Cottage.

JIM LANGLEY

	LEAGUE		FA CUP		FL CUP		TOTAL	
	App	Gls	App	Gls	App	Gls	App	Gls
1956-57	12	1	0	0	0	0	12	1
1957-58	38	4	7	0	0	0	45	4
1958-59	40	7	2	0	0	0	42	7
1959-60	42	3	2	0	0	0	44	3
1960-61	42	5	1	0	1	0	44	5
1961-62	35	2	5	2	2	0	42	4
1962-63	42	4	2	0	3	0	47	4
1963-64	31	1	2	0	1	0	34	1
1964-65	41	4	2	0	3	0	46	4
	323	31	23	2	10	0	356	33

In 1949, three Irishmen signed for £30,000 from the bankrupt Belfast Celtic. Of these, blond-haired wing-half/full-back, Robin Lawler, gave Fulham the best service. After a school career that encouraged the Gaelic code, Lawler joined a well-known junior club, Home Farm. After five seasons, when he was 18-years-old, he joined Irish League Distillery, but stayed only 18 months. He next had brief spells with Transport FC and Drumcondra before signing for Belfast Celtic in 1945. When he came to Fulham, he had to wait three seasons before establishing himself, but he began 1952-3 as first-choice left-half, later switching to left-back. He was one of the most consistent players of these years, noted for his uncanny anticipation, accurate distribution and long throw-in. His talents won international recognition. In March 1953, he got the first of eight caps for the Republic of Ireland, in a 4-0 win over Austria. Lawler was the first Fulham player to play for the Republic, although he had already won Junior and Irish League honours. Injuries cost him his place in 1960, and in the summer of 1962 he left for Southern League Yiewsley. He later worked for Fulham chairman Charles Dean's company but was forced by ill-health to retire early. Lawler still lives very close to Craven Cottage and continues to follow the fortunes of the club.

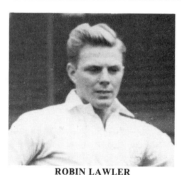

ROBIN LAWLER

	LEAGUE		FA CUP		FL CUP		TOTAL	
	App	Gls	App	Gls	App	Gls	App	Gls
1949-50	2	0	0	0	0	0	2	0
1950-51	4	0	0	0	0	0	4	0
1951-52	5	0	0	0	0	0	5	0
1952-53	33	0	0	0	0	0	33	0
1953-54	42	0	3	0	0	0	45	0
1954-55	39	0	1	0	0	0	40	0
1955-56	37	0	2	0	0	0	39	0
1956-57	41	0	2	0	0	0	43	0
1957-58	25	0	6	0	0	0	31	0
1958-59	29	0	4	0	0	0	33	0
1959-60	16	0	0	0	0	0	16	0
1960-61	7	0	0	0	0	0	7	0
1961-62	1	0	0	0	0	0	1	0
	281	0	18	0	0	0	299	0

The last Fulham player to win a Scottish cap was Graham Leggat, a fast, direct goalscoring winger/centre-forward. He was born in Aberdeen on 20 June 1934, and played for Aberdeen Schools, Scotland Youth and the Banks of Dee club before joining Aberdeen when he was 19. After only two games for Dons' reserves, he was in the first team, in September 1953. He won Scottish League, Cup and League Cup medals (he scored the winning goal against St Mirren in the 1955 League Cup Final) before signing for Fulham for £15,000 in the 1958 close season. He had scored 90 goals in 140 games at Aberdeen and played for Scotland and the Scottish League. At Fulham, he scored on his debut and went on to become the club's fourth highest-ever scorer. His eight hat-tricks is Fulham's post-war best, and one of these, against Ipswich on Boxing Day 1963, came in only three minutes, a First Division record. He was very fast, competitive, superbly fit (as might be expected of a PE teacher) and very brave. Although only 5ft 9in and weighing under 11 st, Leggat never shirked a tackle or flinched from a challenge. He was prepared to play in any forward position and this versatility undoubtedly cost him more Scottish caps. Over Christmas 1966, he came in for the injured Steve Earle and scored five goals in two games. Vic Buckingham promptly sold him to Birmingham: he later played for Rotherham, but made only 32 appearances after he left Fulham. Leggat is now in Canada, working as a journalist and in television.

GRAHAM LEGGAT

	LEAGUE		FA CUP		FL CUP		TOTAL	
	App	Gls	App	Gls	App	Gls	App	Gls
1958-59	36	21	4	1	0	0	40	22
1959-60	28	18	2	2	0	0	30	20
1960-61	36	23	0	0	0	0	36	23
1961-62	31	13	8	1	0	0	39	14
1962-63	33	10	1	0	1	0	35	10
1963-64	25	15	2	1	1	0	28	16
1964-65	17	4	0	0	2	0	19	4
1965-66	32/1	15	1	0	3	0	36/1	15
1966-67	13/2	8	0	0	1	2	14/2	10
	251/3	127	18	5	8	2	277/3	134

RAY LEWINGTON

Ray Lewington was born in Lambeth in September 1956, and although a West Ham supporter as a youngster, he joined Chelsea straight from school, signing professional forms at Stamford Bridge in February 1974. After captaining the junior and reserve sides, he made his League debut in February 1976 and went on to make 86 full appearances for Chelsea, playing in Eddie McCreadie's promotion-winning side of 1976-7. He left Stamford Bridge in 1979 and after a spell in the North American Soccer League, when he helped Vancouver Whitecaps win the North American Soccer Bowl, he returned to London in September 1979 to join Wimbledon. Lewington made just 30 appearances for the Plough Lane club before joining Fulham in March 1980. He came too late to save Bobby Campbell's side from relegation but was a key figure in Malcolm Macdonald's rebuilding programme. A forceful, ball-winning midfielder, he was generally at the centre of the action, breaking up an attack, or starting one for Fulham. A hard but scrupulously fair player who has had his share of injuries, Lewington took over the captaincy when Roger Brown left the Cottage and his leadership qualities were much in evidence. In the summer of 1986, he joined the exodus from Fulham and spent a season at Bramall Lane where he played 41 games for Sheffield United. Fulham missed his influence and in the summer of 1986 he returned as player-manager. (See *Fulham Managers*).

	LEAGUE		FA CUP		FL CUP		TOTAL	
	App	Gls	App	Gls	App	Gls	App	Gls
1979-80	10	1	0	0	0	0	10	1
1980-81	19/1	0	2/1	0	2	0	23/2	0
1981-82	31	4	2	0	7	1	40	5
1982-83	42	10	3	1	4	0	49	11
1983-84	32/1	0	2	0	4	1	38/1	1
1984-85	38	5	1	0	3	0	42	5
1986-87	25	0	0	0	4	0	30	0
	197/2	20	10/1	1	24	2	231/3	23

Lipsham was a speedy, orthodox winger who had a powerful shot and used his fast, accurate crosses to good purpose. He was born in Chester on 29 April 1878 and was discovered by his local club, Chester, playing in church football for St Oswalds. He moved to Crewe Alexandra in 1898 and on to Sheffield United in February 1900. Lipsham appeared in two FA Cup Finals for the Blades, against Spurs in 1901 (lost 3-1 after a replay) and against Southampton the following year (won 2-1). He gained an England cap against Wales in March 1902 and represented the Football League. Lipsham played 259 League and Cup games for United scoring 34 goals before joining Fulham in April 1908. He had plenty of competition for the left-wing position, and when he was offered the Millwall managerial post in 1910 he moved on. Lipsham continued to play until 1913 and left Millwall around 1915. After the war he coached West Norwood in 1921 and managed Northfleet from July 1922. He emigrated to Canada in 1923 but was dogged by misfortune. He lost his right hand in a timber-yard accident in Toronto, then died in a train crash in 1932.

	LEAGUE		FA CUP		TOTAL	
	App	Gls	App	Gls	App	Gls
1907-08	5	1	0	0	5	1
1908-09	35	3	1	0	36	3
1909-10	16	1	2	0	18	1
	56	5	3	0	59	5

HERBERT LIPSHAM

Captain of Fulham's 1971 promotion side, Lloyd was unlucky to miss out on several major honours. Born at Hillingdon in February 1949, he joined Chelsea in 1964 after a successful schools career, which included Middlesex Boys and a South of England XI: Lloyd signed professional at the Bridge in 1962 and made his debut in April 1967 against West Brom. He made only 14 appearances in three seasons for Chelsea, and so stepped down a division in February 1969 to join Fulham to get first-team football — Lloyd plus £35,000 were exchanged for John Dempsey. Several months later, he was made captain, but Fulham had then become a Third Division club. In midfield he beavered away, much more of a team player than an individualist, and promotion came in two seasons. Just as he was unlucky not to play for England Schoolboys, so a Third Division Championship medal eluded him on the last day of the 1970-71 season. Similarly, in 1975, he spent Cup Final day on the substitutes bench after playing in most of the games up to Wembley. Lloyd left the Cottage in October 1976 for Hereford but returned to London when his old mentor Bill Dodgin took over at Brentford in 1977, the Bees winning promotion that season. After almost 350 first-class appearances, Lloyd tried his hand at management, starting with Yeovil and Worthing. In 1986, he was appointed successor to his old Fulham colleague, Alan Mullery, as manager of Brighton.

	LEAGUE		FA CUP		FL CUP		TOTAL	
	App	Gls	App	Gls	App	Gls	App	Gls
1968-69	15	3	0	0	0	0	15	3
1969-70	30/4	7	0	0	0/2	0	30/6	7
1970-71	46	9	1	0	6	0	53	9
1971-72	42	3	3	0	2	0	47	3
1972-73	32/1	1	0	0	4	1	36/1	2
1973-74	34/2	2	2	0	4	0	40/2	2
1974-75	25/1	1	1/2	0	3	0	29	1
1975-76	25	3	0	0	2	0	27	3
	249/8	29	7/2	0	21/2	1	277/12	30

BARRY LLOYD

A stylish, unflurried player who was a shrewd passer of the ball, Lock was born in Plaistow on 27 December 1953. He joined West Ham as an apprentice in July 1969, signing professional in December 1971. Lock won nine England Youth caps, including a winners medal in the FIFA World Youth Tournament in 1971. He took over from Bobby Moore in 1974 and had an outstanding game for the Hammers against Fulham in the 1975 FA Cup Final. Lock won the first of his four Under-23 caps on a European tour in 1973 but missed out on West Ham's European Cup-winners' Cup Final appearance in 1976. Lock moved to Fulham in the 1978 close season for £60,000 after 157 games for the Hammers. He became the regular penalty-taker for Fulham and whereas he scored only two goals for West Ham, Lock scored 29 for the Cottagers. He featured in Fulham's promotion season of 1981-2 and by this time had been converted from a central defender into a left-back. After 237 appearances for Fulham he moved to Southend United in 1985 as a player and coach to the junior side.

	LEAGUE		FA CUP		FL CUP		TOTAL	
	App	Gls	App	Gls	App	Gls	App	Gls
1978-79	39	3	3	0	2	0	44	3
1979-80	38	5	0	0	2	0	40	5
1980-81	29	5	6	0	1	0	36	5
1981-82	25/1	5	0/1	0	1/1	0	26/3	5
1982-83	34	2	0	0	3	0	37	2
1983-84	15	2	0	0	3	2	18	4
1984-85	30	5	1	0	2	0	33	5
	210/1	27	10/1	0	14/1	2	234/3	29

KEVIN LOCK

The player who has the second highest appearances total for Fulham had already played 113 games (for Villa) and won three England caps before he signed for the Cottagers. Edmund Lowe was born in Halesowen, near Birmingham, in July 1925. He began with the Napier Aircraft Company, Finchley and Kynoch, before signing for Villa in May 1945. In his second season, he won his England honours, one of which was a 10-0 win over Portugal. In the 1950 close season, he and his brother Reg signed for Fulham for a combined £15,000 fee. He was virtually an automatic choice for 13 seasons, at full-back or wing-half, although towards the end of his career he was a most effective centre-half. Eddie, or 'Sticks' as he was nicknamed, was a very fit player; he thrived on hard work, and was usually first out and last in for training. He was also tenacious in the tackle and could mark the best inside-forwards out of a game. His leggy stride and balding head were seen for the last time on a sentimental occasion at the Cottage in May 1963. Birmingham, the visitors, scored five of the goals in a 3-3 draw. In his last season, he was placed fourth in the poll for Footballer of the Year. He left the Cottage to manage Notts County, where he stayed until April 1965. He left football to work as a purchasing manager for a company in Nottingham, where he still lives today.

	LEAGUE		FA CUP		FL CUP		TOTAL	
	App	Gls	App	Gls	App	Gls	App	Gls
1950-51	40	0	5	0	0	0	45	0
1951-52	39	4	1	0	0	0	40	4
1952-53	36	0	1	0	0	0	37	0
1953-54	39	1	3	0	0	0	42	1
1954-55	36	0	1	0	0	0	37	0
1955-56	39	0	2	0	0	0	41	0
1956-57	42	0	2	1	0	0	44	1
1957-58	35	1	1	0	0	0	36	1
1958-59	32	0	4	0	0	0	36	0
1959-60	33	0	2	0	0	0	35	0
1960-61	34	0	1	0	1	0	36	0
1961-62	40	2	8	1	2	0	50	3
1962-63	28	0	2	0	2	0	32	0
	473	8	33	2	5	0	511	10

EDDIE LOWE

117

McClelland was a solid and reliable goalkeeper who spent much of his time at the Cottage playing in the reserves. He was born in Lurgan on 19 May 1940 and joined Glenavon in the Irish League as a youngster. He crossed the Irish Sea to join Arsenal in October 1960 as reserve to Jack Kelsey. He appeared in the Gunners' first-team in 46 League games. He made his international debut for Northern Ireland in October 1960 against West Germany before he had made his League debut. McClelland won six caps in all, one of these as a Fulham player. He had joined Fulham in December 1964, but had to wait a year for his debut, at Stoke City, and he played a leading role in Fulham's 'Great Escape' from relegation in 1966. He moved to Lincoln on loan in December 1968 but returned to the Cottage four months later due to a goalkeeping crisis. He was given a free transfer in May 1969 and joined Barnet; McClelland played at Wembley in 1972 in Barnet's FA Trophy defeat by Stafford Rangers. He died in the late 1970s, after a brief illness, from cancer.

	LEAGUE		FA CUP		FL CUP		TOTAL	
	App	Gls	App	Gls	App	Gls	App	Gls
1965-66	21	0	1	0	1	0	23	0
1966-67	8	0	1	0	2	0	11	0
1967-68	8	0	0	0	1	0	9	0
1968-69	14	0	0	0	0	0	14	0
	51	0	2	0	4	0	57	0

JACK McCLELLAND

JACK McDONALD

McDonald was a tall, ambling Yorkshireman who scored regularly with his powerful left foot. He cost Fulham a club record £12,000 when he joined from Bournemouth in 1948. He was born at Maltby on 27 August 1921 and joined Wolves just before World War Two. He played regularly for Bournemouth from 1939 to 1941 before seeing service abroad with the armed forces. Returning in 1945, McDonald played for Chelsea in a wartime Cup Final at Wembley and the following season won a Third Division South Cup-winners' medal with Bournemouth, scoring the winning goal in the Final. He scored 57 goals from 1945 to 1948 for the Cherries and was ever-present in season 1947-8 before his transfer to Fulham in June 1948. McDonald missed only one game in Fulham's Second Division Championship side of 1948-9 but struggled in First Division football. He joined Southampton in August 1952 for a £5,000 fee, moved to Southend United in May 1953 and retired the following year.

	LEAGUE		FA CUP		TOTAL	
	App	Gls	App	Gls	App	Gls
1948-49	41	9	1	0	42	9
1949-50	24	5	2	1	26	6
1950-51	5	1	0	0	5	1
1951-52	5	4	0	0	5	4
	75	19	3	1	78	20

Probably Fulham's best-ever goalkeeper, Elio (Tony) Macedo was the son of a famous Barcelona player and Spanish international. Born in Gibraltar in February 1938, his family came to England and settled in North London when Tony was only two. As a lad, he played for his school team, Burghley Road in Tufnell Park, and represented St Pancras District Schoolboys. He also had two trials for the England Youth side and played for Middlesex. When he left school, Macedo became an apprentice cabinet-maker and joined Fulham's groundstaff in 1954. He played regularly for the juniors and occasionally for the reserves, but, although he signed professional in 1956, his League career was delayed by National Service. When, however, Ian Black was injured in November 1957, Fulham paid Macedo's £14 air fare from his RAF station in Germany for a match against Bristol City. He played superbly and held his place, and kept five clean sheets in his first seven games. In almost 400 games over the next ten years, Macedo's highly-individualistic play was a feature of Fulham's game. Brave, acrobatic, but prone to lapses in the continental tradition, Macedo used to prowl the penalty-area like a nervous cat. With Cohen and Langley, he made up an outstanding rearguard, but unlike them, he never got a full cap: he had to be satisfied with ten Under-23 caps. He was dogged by injuries later in his career, and in 1968 joined Colchester. After one season (39 games), he left and went to South Africa, where he still lives.

	LEAGUE		FA CUP		FL CUP		TOTAL	
	App	Gls	App	Gls	App	Gls	App	Gls
1957-58	23	0	7	0	0	0	30	0
1958-59	37	0	3	0	0	0	40	0
1959-60	39	0	2	0	0	0	41	0
1960-61	31	0	0	0	0	0	31	0
1961-62	38	0	8	0	2	0	48	0
1962-63	42	0	2	0	3	0	47	0
1963-64	24	0	2	0	0	0	26	0
1969-70	40	0	2	0	2	0	44	0
1965-66	21	0	0	0	3	0	24	0
1966-67	33	0	2	0	1	0	36	0
1967-68	18	0	3	0	3	0	24	0
	346	0	31	0	14	0	391	0

TONY MACEDO

McNabb was Fulham's captain and attacking centre-half for five seasons, in which he rarely missed a match. He was born in Cleland, Lanarkshire on 2 December 1897 and was playing for Newart Hill Thistle in the Lanarkshire Junior League when a Portsmouth scout saw his potential and signed him as a professional in March 1923. Fulham signed him in July 1925 after he had played only nine games for Pompey. His brother John, a Scottish international, played as a wing-half for Liverpool at this time. McNabb made his debut at Barnsley in October 1925 after which he became a first-team regular. He scored 20 goals for Fulham in his time at the Cottage and he loved supporting the forwards in their quest for goals. Much of his Fulham career was spent playing in struggling sides. He moved to Coventry City in the summer of 1930 for a £500 fee, £200 of this going to McNabb as a benefit. He played nine games for City before moving to Llanelli where he spent five seasons before retiring to take up engineering. McNabb was last heard of in 1956 living in Mitcham where he was the local bowls champion.

DAVID 'JOCK' McNABB

	LEAGUE		FA CUP		TOTAL	
	App	Gls	App	Gls	App	Gls
1925-26	30	3	5	0	35	3
1926-27	38	9	1	0	39	9
1927-28	38	3	1	0	41	3
1928-29	30	6	1	0	31	6
1929-30	22	0	3	0	25	0
	158	21	11	0	169	21

Marsh was the clown-prince of soccer, a flamboyant, precocious talent who should have won more than the nine England caps he gained. Unfortunately, his style did not fit in with Alf Ramsey's plans. He was born in Hatfield on 11 October 1944 and joined Fulham as a professional on his 18th birthday; he scored a magnificent volleyed goal on his League debut. His career was making rapid progress when he sustained a serious injury at Leicester in February 1965 which left him partially deaf. After losing form, he was allowed to join Queen's Park Rangers in March 1966 for a paltry £15,000. Marsh played a major part in Rangers' rise from the Third to the First Division, and he won a Third Division Championship medal and League Cup-winners' medal in 1967, scoring one of the goals in a sensational victory over West Brom. He also gained England Under-23 honours in 1968. Manchester City paid £200,000 for Marsh in March 1972. He won another League Cup medal when City lost to Wolves 2-1 in the 1974 Final. Marsh next moved to the United States, to join Tampa Bay Rowdies, and later managed them after retiring from playing. He returned to Fulham briefly in September 1976 to team up with George Best but injury dogged his stay.

RODNEY MARSH

	LEAGUE		FA CUP		FL CUP		TOTAL	
	App	Gls	App	Gls	App	Gls	App	Gls
1962-63	1	1	0	0	0	0	1	1
1963-64	4	1	0	0	0	0	4	1
1964-65	41	17	1	0	2	0	44	17
1965-66	17	3	1	0	1	0	19	3
1976-77	16	5	2	1	4	0	22	6
	79	27	4	1	7	0	90	28

ALFRED MARSHALL

Marshall was a formidable half-back whose career was reaching its peak when World War One ruined his progress. He was born in Darlington in the early months of 1888. He joined Darlington St Johns in 1906 and moved to Darlington St Augustine the following year. Marshall joined the Cottagers in September 1909 with Billy Walker and made his debut at Bradford in February 1910. He did not play regularly until season 1912-13. Occasionally called upon to play at centre-half, Marshall's favourite position was in a defensive wing-half role. He appeared very rarely for Fulham from 1914 to 1919, spending much of this time in the services. His best season was 1919-20 when he made 39 appearances. Marshall had gained the nickname of 'Rubberneck' for reasons that can now only be guessed at. He moved to First Division Oldham Athletic in the summer of 1920, where he made 66 appearances in the next three seasons. However, whilst at home for the summer in Darlington, Marshall died suddenly on 30 June 1923 at the age of 35.

	LEAGUE		FA CUP		TOTAL	
	App	Gls	App	Gls	App	Gls
1909-10	2	0	0	0	2	0
1910-11	9	0	0	0	9	0
1911-12	9	0	4	0	13	0
1912-13	21	0	1	0	22	0
1913-14	18	0	1	0	19	0
1914-15	3	0	0	0	3	0
1919-20	38	0	1	0	39	0
	100	0	7	0	107	0

Matthewson was a solid, methodical central defender, who, although short of height, was good at marshalling and organising the defence. He joined his home-town club, Sheffield United, in June 1958 after representing Sheffield Boys. Matthewson was born in the city on 6 August 1939. He made his debut at the Cottage in March 1962, and was giving the runaround by Maurice Cook who scored a hat-trick. Matthewson made 148 League appearances for the Blades before moving to Fulham in February 1968 in a £30,000 deal. He played during some of the most traumatic times in Fulham's history but helped in the comeback in season 1970-71 when promotion from the Third Division was achieved. He played 50 times that season and scored his only goal for Fulham, against Torquay. With the arrival of Paul Went, Matthewson became dissatisfied with reserve team football and moved to Chester in January 1973. He was later a player-coach at Bangor City from 1978 to 1980, assistant-manager at Shrewsbury 1980-81 and Wrexham's coach. He left football after this to take up an operative job in Ellesmere Port.

	LEAGUE		FA CUP		FL CUP		TOTAL	
	App	Gls	App	Gls	App	Gls	App	Gls
1967-68	10	0	0	0	0	0	10	0
1968-69	24	0	2	0	1	0	27	0
1969-70	39	0	1	0	1	0	41	0
1970-71	43/1	1	1	0	5	0	49/1	1
1971-72	39/1	0	3	0	2	0	44/1	0
1972-73	1	0	0	0	0	0	1	0
	156/2	1	7	0	9	0	172/2	1

REG MATTHEWSON

FRED MAVIN

Born at Newcastle-upon-Tyne in 1885, Mavin was destined to follow the natural trade of that town of engineers, but the allure of football was too strong and, after winning his spurs in the Newcastle Reserve team, he came south to New Brompton in 1905. For four years, at centre-half, he was one of the mainstays of the Kentish team, playing 115 games. Mavin joined Fulham in the summer of 1909 and like many centre-halves before him the offside rule was changed, played in an attacking role. He held the record for a defender of scoring the most goals in a season for Fulham for 70 years, twice getting ten in a season. He was also club captain. Fred joined Bradford in December 1913 and returned to the Cottage as a guest player during the 1915-19 period. After the war, he played for Reading for two seasons before retiring to take up management. Mavin managed Crystal Palace just after their entry into the League and he rejoined his old club Gillingham as secretary from January 1932 to May 1937, after which he managed Exeter City.

	LEAGUE		FA CUP		TOTAL	
	App	Gls	App	Gls	App	Gls
1909-10	32	2	3	0	35	2
1910-11	34	10	1	0	35	10
1911-12	37	10	4	0	41	10
1912-13	28	2	1	0	29	2
1913-14	9	3	0	0	9	3
	140	27	9	0	149	27

Mellor will mainly be remembered for his great displays on Fulham's road to Wembley in 1975. He was an eccentric goalkeeper with a lot of character, and was popular with the Fulham crowd, something he had not enjoyed at Burnley. Mellor was born in Prestbury on 20 November 1947, and joined Manchester City as an apprentice from school. He won an England Youth cap against Wales in 1966 but failed to make the grade at Maine Road. He joined Witton Albion in 1968 where he completed his apprenticeship as a motor mechanic. Burnley stepped in with £1,750 for his transfer in April 1969 and he was ever-present in season 1969-70. However, the crowd started to barrack him, so Mellor moved to Fulham in February 1972 for £20,000. Between 1972 and 1976 he missed only nine games for Fulham, but after sustaining a nasty injury against Notts County in November 1976, he fell out with manager Bobby Campbell and left Fulham under a cloud for Hereford United in September 1977. After a season at Edgar Street, Mellor enjoyed three happy seasons at Fratton Park before retiring with 424 League appearances under his belt. He is now living and working in Florida.

	LEAGUE		FA CUP		FL CUP		TOTAL	
	App	Gls	App	Gls	App	Gls	App	Gls
1971-72	13	0	0	0	0	0	13	0
1972-73	42	0	1	0	4	0	47	0
1973-74	38	0	3	0	2	0	43	0
1974-75	42	0	12	0	3	0	57	0
1975-76	42	0	1	0	3	0	46	0
1976-77	13	0	0	0	5	0	18	0
	190	0	17	0	17	0	224	0

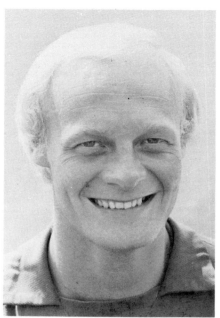

PETER MELLOR

JOHN MITCHELL

'Mitch' scored the important goal at Maine Road which took Fulham to Wembley for the first time in 1975. Born on 3 March 1952, Mitchell represented Hertfordshire Boys and joined Carlton, the youth team of his home-town club, St Albans City, when he left school. He progressed to City's first team and was spotted by a Fulham scout. He moved to the Cottage in February 1972 for a fee of £3,000. In his first season, Mitchell scored 11 goals but he was then struck by a loss of form followed by a series of injuries. He missed the early rounds of the FA Cup in 1975, but scored in both semi-final matches against Birmingham City. His brave and battling style earned him goals that did not seem possible. In June 1978, Mitchell was transferred to Millwall for £100,000 and he was greatly missed. At the Den, he was again beset by injuries and finally had to retire in 1982. Mitchell scored 18 goals in 81 League appearances for the Lions. In 1987, he was managing St Albans, where he began his career, and working as a representative for a sports equipment firm.

	LEAGUE		FA CUP		FL CUP		TOTAL	
	App	Gls	App	Gls	App	Gls	App	Gls
1972-73	36	11	1	0	0	0	37	11
1973-74	11/2	2	1	0	4	0	16/2	2
1974-75	8/8	5	5/1	2	0/1	0	13/10	7
1975-76	26/1	10	1	0	2/1	0	29/2	10
1976-77	38	20	2	0	3	2	43	22
1977-78	39	9	1	0	2	0	42	9
	158/11	57	11/1	2	11/2	2	180/14	61

A colourful and controversial figure, Mitten was a cultured left-winger who made his name with Manchester United and came to Fulham via Bogota. Although he was nearly selected for Scotland, Mitten was born in Rangoon in India on 17 January 1921, where his father was serving with the Royal Scots Guards. He later lived in Scotland, where he played junior football for Strath-allen Hawthorne and Dunblane Rovers, before going to Old Trafford in 1936. During World War Two, he guested for Tranmere, Southampton, Aston Villa and Chelsea, helping the Blues to two Cup Finals. On his demob, he was a key figure in Manchester United's resurgence and Mitten played in 161 matches, including the 1948 FA Cup Final. He also became the second player to score a hat-trick of penalties in a First Division match (v Aston Villa). For 18 months, in the early 1950s, he was out of football, following an excursion to South America and subsequent suspension. When it was over, he came to Fulham in January 1952, where his control and dribbling delighted crowds and teased opponents. Mitten, who was one of the game's most colourful characters, left the Cottage in 1956, to become player-manager of Mansfield, where he made 102 appearances. His next stop was St James' Park where he managed Newcastle from 1958 to 1961. When he left football, he returned to Manchester and managed the White City greyhound stadium. His son John was a professional with Newcastle.

| | LEAGUE | | FA CUP | | TOTAL | |
	App	Gls	App	Gls	App	Gls
1951-52	16	6	0	0	16	6
1952-53	40	7	1	1	41	8
1953-54	41	9	3	0	44	9
1954-55	36	6	1	0	37	6
1955-56	21	4	1	0	22	4
	154	32	6	1	160	33

CHARLIE MITTEN

RICHARD MONEY

The £333,333 Liverpool paid for Richard Money in April 1980 is the record transfer fee received by Fulham. He was a utility player at the Cottage, playing in midfield, right-back and centre-half, but performed at left-back at Anfield. Born in Lowestoft on 13 October 1955, he joined the local club as a youngster. Scunthorpe United signed him in July 1973 and Richard made 179 appearances for the South Humberside club before his transfer to Fulham in December 1977 for a fee of £50,000. With his quiet, determined and authoratative displays, Money was soon noticed by the bigger clubs. He followed in the footsteps of Kevin Keegan and Ray Clemence when he signed for Liverpool, all having started their careers at Scunthorpe. Sadly, he never established himself at Anfield and played only 17 games. After a loan period at Derby County in early 1982, he signed for Luton Town in April of that year for £100,000. A year later he moved to Portsmouth, but a broken leg inhibited his career and he eventually moved back to Scunthorpe in October 1985, once again finding regular first-team football. Early in 1987 he took over as caretaker player-manager.

| | LEAGUE | | FACUP | | FL CUP | | TOTAL | |
	App	Gls	App	Gls	App	Gls	App	Gls
1977-78	23	2	0	0	0	0	23	2
1978-79	42	1	3	0	2	0	47	1
1979-80	41	0	2	1	2	0	45	1
	106	3	5	1	4	0	115	4

A tall, well-built, fair-haired Londoner, Bobby Moore was a most talented footballer and truly great captain. During the 1966 World Cup, his captaincy was inspirational, with his cool temperament steadying his fellow players as he led by example. Moore was born in Barking on 12 April 1941 and in his younger days won 18 England Youth international caps. He then played eight times for the Under-23s. He has the unique distinction of leading three Cup-winning sides in successive years to Wembley, West Ham when they won the FA Cup in 1964 and the European Cup-winners' Cup a year later, and, of course, England when they won the World Cup in 1966. He was voted Footballer of the Year in 1964 and besides his 108 caps for England also represented the Football League on 12 occasions. Moore played a total of 642 League and Cup games scoring 27 goals before his move to Fulham in March 1974 for £20,000. He inspired Fulham's march to Wembley in 1975 and played some fine games before retirement. He managed Oxford City for a while, then worked in Hong Kong before returning to manage Southend from February 1984 to April 1986.

	LEAGUE		FA CUP		FL CUP		TOTAL	
	App	Gls	App	Gls	App	Gls	App	Gls
1973-74	10	1	0	0	0	0	10	1
1974-75	41	0	12	0	3	0	56	0
1975-76	33	0	1	0	3	0	37	0
1976-77	40	0	2	0	5	0	47	0
	124	1	15	0	11	0	150	1

BOBBY MOORE OBE

The Fulham side which won entry to the Football League in 1907 was built around a magnificent half-back line of Arthur Collins, Billy Morrison and Billy Goldie. Morrison was born in West Benhar in Lanarkshire in 1879. Joining West Calder FC as a youngster, he moved after three seasons to Edinburgh club St Bernard's in 1902, who were in the Scottish League at this time. Morrison was one of many Scots signed by manager Harry Bradshaw in August 1904. In his first season at the club, Fulham won their way through to the FA Cup quarter-finals before losing to eventual winners Aston Villa. Morrison won two Southern League Championship medals in the next two seasons, and then played regularly in Fulham's first season in the Football League. After losing his place following a disastrous 3-2 home defeat by Glossop in the opening game of season 1908-09, he moved to that club in September 1908. Morrison appeared 76 times scoring two goals for Glossop in the next two seasons before moving to Clyde. Raith Rovers signed him around 1913 and he won a Scottish Cup runners-up medal that year when they lost to Falkirk in the Final. Morrison's final move was to Falkirk the following year.

	F LEAGUE		STHRN LGE		FA CUP		TOTAL	
	App	Gls	App	Gls	App	Gls	App	Gls
1904-05	0	0	20	2	8	0	28	2
1905-06	0	0	33	3	2	0	35	3
1906-07	0	0	38	2	4	0	42	2
1907-08	30	1	0	0	6	1	36	2
1908-09	1	0	0	0	0	0	1	0
	31	1	91	7	20	1	142	9

WILLIAM MORRISON

The driving force behind Fulham's Wembley run in 1975, Alan Mullery enjoyed two successful spells at Craven Cottage either side of an eight year stint at White Hart Lane. Born in Notting Hill on 23 November 1941, Mullery first joined Fulham in June 1957 after winning schoolboy representative honours for West London, All London and Middlesex Schools. He signed professional in December 1958 and was in the League side two months later, helping Fulham clinch promotion to Division One. An aggressive, all-action right-half, it was apparent his ability matched his self confidence and he became a target for other clubs. In March 1964, he moved to Spurs for £72,500 to ease Fulham's financial problems. Whilst with the North London club, Mullery played 372 games, won an FA Cup-winners' medal (1967), League Cup-winners' medal, a EUFA Cup-winners' medal and 35 England caps. In October 1971, he received a mysterious stomach injury, which kept him out of the Spurs side, and in March 1972 he came back to Fulham, controversially on loan. He showed the same appetite for the game as he had as a 17-year-old, and he helped stave off the threat of relegation. When Alec Stock took over at Fulham that summer, he brought Mullery back permanently for £65,000 and made him skipper. In his last four seasons, he helped stabilise the club's Second Division status, get Fulham to Wembley and win for himself the Footballer of the Year award and the MBE. When he retired in 1976, he did not get the job at Fulham he had expected and Stock had promised. Instead, he went to manage Brighton, and subsequently Charlton, Crystal Palace and Queen's Park Rangers, before going back briefly to the Goldstone in 1986.

ALAN MULLERY MBE

	LEAGUE		FA CUP		FL CUP		TOTAL	
	App	Gls	App	Gls	App	Gls	App	Gls
1958-59	14	0	0	0	0	0	14	0
1959-60	36	2	2	0	0	0	38	2
1960-61	37	1	1	0	0	0	38	1
1961-62	40	6	7	0	2	0	49	6
1962-63	38	1	2	0	2	0	42	1
1963-64	34	3	2	1	1	0	37	4
1971-72	6	1	0	0	0	0	6	1
1972-73	40	8	1	0	2	0	43	8
1973-74	40	2	3	1	4	1	47	4
1974-75	42	9	12	0	3	1	57	10
1975-76	36/1	4	1	0	3	1	40/1	5
	363/1	37	31	2	17	3	411/1	42

FRANK 'BONZO' NEWTON

	LEAGUE		FA CUP		TOTAL	
	App	Gls	App	Gls	App	Gls
1931-32	39	43	5	4	44	47
1932-33	31	27	0	0	31	27
1933-34	4	2	0	0	4	2
1934-35	9	5	0	0	9	5
	83	77	5	4	88	81

For many years, the record books have showed that Frank Newton scored a record 41 goals in season 1931-2 for Fulham. However, more recent research has shown that he actually scored 43 League goals that season, in only 39 games. A weighty, bustling player, Newton got his forwards moving well and was an unselfish trier. He was born in Romiley on 12 November 1902, and ran away to sea as a boy. He later joined the Army, representing them at soccer, rugby, hockey and as a good light-heavyweight boxer. Newton joined Ashton National FC from the Army and moved to Stockport County in 1928. He scored 77 goals in only 94 League appearances for County before moving to Fulham in the summer of 1931 for a fee of £575. Newton was the vital ingredient missing in the Fulham side, and they won the Third Division South Championship in his first season at the club. In September 1933, he was inexplicably transferred to Reading for only £650 by manager James McIntyre. This ultimately led to his dismissal as manager. A year later Newton was back at the Cottage. Unfortunately, a broken leg received playing in a friendly with FK Austria in December 1934 was to end his career. Newton died in the Tameside area in the autumn of 1977.

O'Callaghan was a clever ball artisté who scored plenty of goals with both feet, and was full of boyish enthusiasm. He was born in Ebbw Vale on 6 October 1906 and became a protégé of Jack Peart. When Peart was player-coach of Ebbw Vale in the early 1920s, O'Callaghan used to run errands for his wife, and when he was old enough, joined the club. He arrived at Spurs in 1924 and was loaned out at first to Barnet and Northfleet. He became a favourite of the White Hart Lane crowd and scored 94 goals in 252 League appearances for Spurs. He also won 11 Welsh caps, with his best performance coming against Scotland in October 1932 when Wales won 5-2 and O'Callaghan scored two of the goals. After ten years at Spurs, he was transferred to Leicester City in March 1935. He won a Second Division Championship medal in season 1936-7 and when Jack Peart came to Craven Cottage as manager, he signed O'Callaghan in October 1937. He played his last game for Fulham in season 1945-6, then joining the training staff, working with the reserves until his death on 4 July 1956. He was always a jovial character and a great influence in the dressing room.

	LEAGUE		FA CUP		TOTAL	
	App	Gls	App	Gls	App	Gls
1937-38	26	4	1	1	27	5
1938-39	13	2	2	0	15	2
	39	6	3	1	42	7

EUGENE 'TAFFY' O'CALLAGHAN

BRIAN 'PAT' O'CONNELL

Brian O'Connell was a regular performer for Fulham in their First Division days. He was born in Earls Court on 13 September 1937 and joined Fulham as a professional in March 1956 after representing West London Schools and Middlesex Youth. O'Connell made his debut as an inside-right at Stoke in December 1958. A versatile player, O'Connell later played as a left winger and at left-back in his last season at the Cottage. Goals were always difficult to come by for O'Connell, and by his own admission, he was not a good finisher; however, he did score ten goals in season 1960-61. In July 1966, he was given a free transfer and joined Crystal Palace. After one season at Selhurst Park, he moved to Canada to play for Vancouver, who were managed by Ferenc Puskas. O'Connell returned to England to play for the now defunct Brentwood, who had a fine FA Cup run to the third round in 1969-70, beating Reading on the way. O'Connell also played for Dover, Wimbledon and Epsom & Ewell who he also managed until the early 1980s. He appeared at Wembley in an FA Vase Final for them in 1975. Today, he drives a taxi and coaches at Spencer Park School, Wandsworth.

	LEAGUE		FA CUP		FL CUP		TOTAL	
	App	Gls	App	Gls	App	Gls	App	Gls
1958-59	1	0	0	0	0	0	1	0
1959-60	6	2	0	0	0	0	6	2
1960-61	26	10	1	0	1	0	28	10
1961-62	31	8	7	0	1	0	39	8
1962-63	31	2	0	0	2	0	33	2
1963-64	13	1	0	0	0	0	13	1
1964-65	24	1	1	0	2	1	27	2
1965-66	20	2	1	0	2	1	23	3
	152	26	10	0	8	2	170	28

Sean O'Driscoll was given the nickname 'Noisey' by Les Strong because he was the quietest player in the team. A skilful midfielder with delicate and subtle touches, O'Driscoll was allowed to leave the Cottage for a paltry fee after showing great promise. He was born in Wolverhampton on 1 July 1953 of Irish parents. Fulham discovered O'Driscoll playing for Alvechurch and signed him in November 1979 for £12,000. He made his debut against Bristol Rovers in February 1980 and was soon a first-team regular. He played a leading role in Fulham's rise from the Third Division to the brink of the First Division in 1983. O'Driscoll toured South and Central America with the Republic of Ireland in May 1982. He made his debut against Chile in Santiago and then played before 60,000 spectators against Brazil in Uberaba but finished on the wrong end of a seven-goal thrashing. After losing his form, O'Driscoll went to Bournemouth on loan in February 1983, signing permanently three months later for only £6,000. He won an Associate Members Cup-winners' medal in 1984 and was a regular in the Cherries team which won the Third Division title in 1986-7, ironically clinching promotion in a victory at the Cottage.

	LEAGUE		FA CUP		FL CUP		TOTAL	
	App	Gls	App	Gls	App	Gls	App	Gls
1979-80	8/2	1	0	0	0	0	8/2	1
1980-81	39/3	2	6	0	1	0	46/3	2
1981-82	42	7	2	0	5	0	49	7
1982-83	42	3	3	0	4	0	49	3
1983-84	10/2	0	0/1	0	2/1	0	12/4	0
	141/7	13	11/1	0	12/1	0	164/9	13

SEAN O'DRISCOLL

A Fulham stalwart for most of the inter-war period, Len Oliver was one of the few men to be capped for England whilst playing in the Third Division. Born locally on 1 August 1905 to parents who were both Fulham supporters, Oliver played for Fulham Schools and Alma Athletic before joining Isthmian League amateurs Tufnell Park in 1920. Four years later he became Andy Ducat's first signing for Fulham and within weeks was in the first team. He became an automatic choice at half-back, missing only 23 games in ten seasons, 14 of which were the result of one bad injury in 1929-30. For seven seasons he was captain and he served under six managers. He was capped against Belgium in Brussels in May 1929, was reserve against Scotland in 1931 and went on the Canadian Tour of 1931. With Bert Barrett and either Jock McNabb or Syd Gibbons, he formed a formidable half-back line, which was the backbone of the 1932 promotion side. He lost his place when Jimmy Hogan became manager, but was held in such esteem by chairman John Dean that his future at the Cottage seemed assured. It was, therefore, something of a surprise when he left under a cloud in 1937. He coached Cliftonville until the outbreak of the war, during which he became a physical training instructor. After the war, he moved to Letchworth and coached Arlesey Town, and died at his home at the age of 62 in August 1967.

LEN OLIVER

	LEAGUE		FA CUP		TOTAL	
	App	Gls	App	Gls	App	Gls
1924-25	38	0	2	0	40	0
1925-26	41	0	5	0	46	0
1926-27	42	0	2	0	44	0
1927-28	41	0	1	0	42	0
1928-29	42	1	3	0	45	1
1929-30	28	0	3	0	31	0
1930-31	40	1	4	0	44	1
1931-32	39	0	4	0	43	0
1932-33	42	0	1	0	43	0
1933-34	40	0	2	0	42	0
1934-35	13	0	1	0	14	0
	406	2	28	0	434	2

Frank Osborne's career is unique in the history of Fulham. He was a player (the first Fulham player to be capped for England), director and then team, general or secretary-manager. Born in Wynberg, South Africa, on 14 October 1896, he came to England in 1911 and joined Bromley in 1919. He signed for Fulham in November 1921, and scored on his debut the same month, a 4-1 win at Sheffield Wednesday. He began at centre-forward but switched to outside-right, which better suited his graceful style and frail frame. He was capped, at centre-forward, against Ireland at West Brom in October 1922, but 15 months and one England cap later, he was transferred to Spurs. He spent seven and a half seasons at White Hart Lane, making 210 appearances and scoring 79 goals: he also won two more England caps, and scored a hat-trick in a 5-3 win over Belgium in Antwerp. His brother Reg was also an England international, and a full-back with Leicester. In June 1931 he moved on to Southampton, where he played 16 games before retiring in 1933. Osborne returned to London to work as a sales representative for Fulham chairman John Dean's blinds company, and in March 1935 accepted an invitation from his employer to serve on the Fulham board. This marked the start of the next phase of his Fulham career, which was to last 30 years. *(See Fulham Managers)*

FRANK OSBORNE

	LEAGUE		FA CUP		TOTAL	
	App	Gls	App	Gls	App	Gls
1921-22	22	8	2	0	24	8
1922-23	28	10	1	0	29	10
1923-24	17	0	0	0	17	0
	67	18	3	0	70	18

Paul Parker is a very talented central defender or full-back who always seems to have more time than most other players. He was described by Malcolm Macdonald as the best defender at the club when he broke into the first team. Parker's family origins are in Jamaica, but he was born in West Ham on 4 April 1964 and has lived most of his life in Dagenham. He played in the same team as Dean Coney and Steve Tapley as a lad and also represented Essex and Havering Schools before signing for Fulham as an apprentice in May 1980. Parker was still an apprentice when he made his debut against Reading in April 1981 and did not sign professional forms for another year. He gained England Youth honours in 1981 and has eight Under-21 caps. Parker scored a rare goal on his Under-21 debut against Finland at Southampton. A naturally-gifted player, he compensates for a lack of inches with tremendous speed and astute reading of the game. He is a fine defender who at times seems a bit lost when going forward. Parker achieved his ambition of First Division football when he moved to Queen's Park Rangers in the 1987 close season, which should increase his chances of full international honours.

PAUL PARKER

	LEAGUE		FA CUP		FL CUP		TOTAL	
	App	Gls	App	Gls	App	Gls	App	Gls
1980-81	1	0	0	0	0	0	1	0
1981-82	2/3	0	0	0	0	0	2/3	0
1982-83	6/11	0	3	0	2	0	11/11	0
1983-84	34	0	2	0	4	0	40	0
1984-85	36	0	1	0	3	0	40	0
1985-86	30	0	1	0	3	0	34	0
1986-87	31	2	4	0	4	1	39	3
	140/14	2	11	0	16	1	167/14	3

Pearce was a popular player who formed a fine goalscoring partnership with Tim Coleman just before World War One. He was born in Stratford East in 1889 and attended Park School with Harold Halse. This school also produced other players who reached Football League status, such as Ted Fenton, Jack Townrow, George Barber, Jim Barrett and finally Bert Barrett, who also played for Fulham. Pearce played for Wanstead, Ilford and Leytonstone, winning nine medals and Essex and London cups, before signing for Fulham in April 1911. He had been an amateur international trialist whilst with Leytonstone. Pearce created a new goalscoring record when he scored 21 League goals in his first season at the club, including three hat-tricks. He played in a full international trial for The South v England in 1912 at Craven Cottage. The war virtually finished Pearce's League career. He played occasionally for the Lilliewhites during the war but cannot be traced in peacetime.

HERBERT PEARCE

	LEAGUE		FA CUP		TOTAL	
	App	Gls	App	Gls	App	Gls
1911-12	34	21	4	1	38	22
1912-13	24	10	0	0	24	10
1913-14	26	13	1	0	27	13
1914-15	6	1	2	0	8	1
	90	45	7	0	97	45

Nobody can boast a longer unbroken period of service to Fulham than Frank Penn. As a player and trainer he spent 50 years at the Cottage. Born in Edmonton on 5 April 1896, he joined Fulham in 1915, and his early years were spent in the makeshift wartime competitions. He was, however, sufficently impressive to get a trial for England in the Victory international series in 1919. He went straight into the League side on the resumption of competitive football and for 12 seasons was an automatic choice on the left wing. Penn was ideally built for a winger, 5ft 8in tall, weighing just over 11st, and he was quick off the mark, with the ability to hit accurate centres whilst in full flight. He survived the upheavals of the 1920s at the Cottage but lost his place in 1931-2 to Jack Finch. His career total of appearances is the third highest in Fulham's history, after Haynes and Lowe. Whilst a player, Penn qualified as a physiotherapist and in 1939 took over from Bill 'Doc' Voisey as first-team trainer, a position he held until his retirement in the 1965 close season. In 1947, he was selected as the England team trainer. His retirement was short, for his health deteriorated rapidly. Penn's death on 19 December 1966 at the age of 70, marked the close of an important chapter in Fulham's history.

	LEAGUE		FA CUP		TOTAL	
	App	Gls	App	Gls	App	Gls
1919-20	23	1	0	0	23	1
1920-21	36	2	5	0	41	2
1921-22	23	0	0	0	23	0
1922-23	42	1	1	0	43	1
1923-24	36	2	3	0	39	2
1924-25	40	2	2	0	42	2
1925-26	27	5	5	1	32	6
1926-27	41	7	2	0	43	7
1927-28	40	3	1	0	41	3
1928-29	42	10	3	1	45	11
1929-30	38	6	5	3	43	9
1930-31	30	6	3	2	33	8
1931-32	9	0	2	0	11	0
1932-33	0	0	0	0	0	0
1933-34	1	0	0	0	1	0
	428	45	32	7	460	52

FRANK PENN

129

Eddie Perry was a go-getting, dashing centre-forward who always had an eye for goal. He was born in Rhymney on 19 January 1909 and attended the local school where he had a trial for Wales Schoolboys. He left school to become a mining engineer and gained some local fame as violinist and vocalist. Whilst playing for Welsh League side Rhymney, he got a chance to play for Merthyr Town against Bournemouth in a Cup tie. The opposition was so impressed they signed him after the game. Perry went to Thames FC in 1930 and was top goalscorer that season with 16 goals. Fulham saw his potential and obtained his signature in the summer of 1931. Perry spent much time in the reserves and still treasures the Football Combination runners-up medal he won in 1932-3. He had a long first-team run in 1935-6 and played in Fulham's Cup run to the semi-final, scoring four goals against Blackpool in the fourth round. Perry had much success at Doncaster Rovers, whom he joined in November 1936. He won three Welsh caps in 1938 and a wartime cap in 1940. Perry joined Fulham's coaching staff in 1946 and was team manager briefly in 1948. He managed Southend in the 1950s, and now lives in retirement in Kent.

	LEAGUE		FA CUP		TOTAL	
	App	Gls	App	Gls	App	Gls
1931-32	3	1	0	0	3	1
1932-33	1	1	0	0	1	1
1933-34	1	0	0	0	1	0
1934-35	19	15	0	0	19	15
1935-36	28	13	5	4	33	17
1936-37	10	6	0	0	10	6
	62	36	5	4	67	40

EDDIE PERRY

GERRY PEYTON

Goalkeeper Gerry Peyton possesses a fine positional sense and makes difficult saves look easy with his anticipation and handling skills. He was born in Birmingham on 20 May 1956 and as a youngster joined Aston Villa. Peyton never impressed at Villa Park and moved to non-League Atherstone. Burnley saw his potential and signed him in May 1975. Peyton made his League debut against Liverpool at Turf Moor and kept a clean sheet. He had lost his first-team place when Fulham signed him in December 1976 after an injury to regular 'keeper Peter Mellor. The £35,000 transfer fee was money well spent, as Peyton was to give Fulham excellent service over the next ten years. He was called up by Don Revie to join the England Under-21 side in 1977 but he chose to play for the Republic of Ireland, his parents' birthplace. Peyton has 21 caps to date. After earning a testimonial in 1986, he moved to Bournemouth on a free transfer. He ranks behind only Reynolds and Macedo in appearances made by goalkeepers for Fulham.

	LEAGUE		FA CUP		FL CUP		TOTAL	
	App	Gls	App	Gls	App	Gls	App	Gls
1976-77	23	0	2	0	0	0	25	0
1977-78	42	0	1	0	2	0	45	0
1978-79	40	0	3	0	2	0	45	0
1979-80	31	0	2	0	2	0	35	0
1980-81	28	0	6	0	2	0	36	0
1981-82	44	0	2	0	7	0	53	0
1982-83	42	0	3	0	4	0	49	0
1983-84	27	0	2	0	2	0	31	0
1984-85	32	0	0	0	3	0	35	0
1985-86	36	0	1	0	4	0	41	0
	345	0	22	0	28	0	395	0

A clever, scheming inside-forward, Johnny Price was a key figure in the Fulham sides of the early 1930s. Born in Mhow in India in the early years of the century, he signed for Fulham from Woking in 1928, having won three England Amateur caps. He went straight into the first team, and held his place for seven years. The highlight of his career was winning the Third Division title in 1931-2. Price also won some representative honours. He toured South Africa with the FA in 1929 and later played for The Rest in an England trial match, eventually being selected as reserve. An old-fashioned inside-forward, Price's style was likened by contemporaries to Alex James, specialising in feeding fast wingers or creating chances for the front men. In addition to football, Price was well-known in the world of greyhound racing, and owned several successful dogs. A loyal club man, he was a regular target of First Division clubs, but he never wanted to leave Fulham. Price was unlucky with injuries during his career, and a persistent hip injury ended his career prematurely in 1937, after a brief spell with Port Vale. When he retired, he returned to his previous employment, working for Fulham chairman, John Dean. He later worked in the accountancy department of an engineering factory at Colnbrook, and in the 1960s returned to the Cottage as assistant-secretary. He had also coached amateurs Wimbledon and Yiewsley with some success. Johnny Price died peacefully at his home in Southsea, at the age of 84, in June 1987.

JOHNNY PRICE

	LEAGUE		FA CUP		TOTAL	
	App	Gls	App	Gls	App	Gls
1928-29	29	13	3	1	32	14
1929-30	25	9	4	1	29	10
1930-31	19	6	1	1	20	7
1931-32	31	4	5	1	36	5
1932-33	30	6	1	0	31	6
1933-34	26	4	0	0	26	4
1934-35	23	4	1	0	24	4
1935-36	4	2	0	0	4	2
1936-37	2	1	0	0	2	1
	189	49	15	4	204	53

BILL PROUSE

	LEAGUE		FA CUP		TOTAL	
	App	Gls	App	Gls	App	Gls
1924-25	33	16	2	0	35	16
1925-26	24	8	3	1	27	9
1926-27	20	7	2	0	22	7
	77	31	7	1	84	32

A goalscoring inside-forward who played for Fulham in the 1920s, Bill Prouse was born in Birmingham on 23 March 1900. He was playing for Redditch Town when Rochdale discovered him in 1922. Prouse was soon among the goals for the Third Division North side. In season 1923-4 he scored 14 goals in 40 League appearances and this is what probably attracted Fulham to obtain his signature in the summer of 1924. Prouse scored 16 goals in his first season at the Cottage but goals were a little more difficult to come by after that. He shot one hat-trick for Fulham, against Crystal Palace in December 1924. Prouse started his Fulham career as an inside-right but later played in the other inside berth. Fulham were generally struggling in Prouse's spell at the club and after losing his place to Johnny Tonner, he moved out of League football with Wellington Town in the summer of 1927. His last game had been in a disastrous 7-1 defeat at Port Vale in April 1927.

131

A tireless midfield dynamo, Len Quested was an influential figure in Fulham's early post-war seasons and his transfer proved costly to manager Bill Dodgin. Born in Folkestone on 9 January 1925, he won schoolboy honours for Folkestone and Kent Schools, and then went on to the town's Southern League club. Quested signed as an amateur for Fulham in 1940-1, but after a few games, active service with the navy took him away for four years. On his demob in 1946, he signed professional terms for Fulham, and came into the side towards the end of the 1946-7 season. Originally an inside-forward, he was converted to wing-half, where he played alongside Taylor and Beasley. This was the backbone of the 1949 Second Division Championship side, and Quested's tireless running and effervescent play was a nice counter to Beasley's slower, more thoughtful approach. He was an ungainly figure on the field, tall and thin, with a short back-and-sides haircut and prominent front teeth. He made a great impression in the First Division, winning an England 'B' Cap against Holland in February 1950. Then, in October 1951, when the team was struggling near the foot of the table, Quested went to Huddersfield in exchange for Jeff Taylor. The move upset the supporters, who never forgave the manager. Quested played 220 League games for Huddersfield in six years, but in the summer of 1957, he emigrated to Australia. In the early 1980s, he was a director of an Australian League club of which his son was the star player.

LEN QUESTED

	LEAGUE		FA CUP		TOTAL	
	App	Gls	App	Gls	App	Gls
1946-47	6	0	0	0	6	0
1947-48	36	0	5	1	41	1
1948-49	39	1	1	0	40	1
1949-50	42	1	2	0	44	1
1950-51	39	4	5	0	44	4
1951-52	13	0	0	0	13	0
	175	6	13	1	188	7

Although losing four seasons to World War One, Arthur Reynolds still holds the Fulham record for most appearances by a goalkeeper. He was born on 30 June 1889 and began playing with his home-town club Dartford, where he spent four seasons and helped them win the Kent League and Dartford League titles. He joined Fulham in the early months of 1910, and within weeks was in the first team. Reynolds went on to make 100 consecutive League and Cup appearances before he missed a game, and held his place for 15 years. Just before the war, League Champions Blackburn, made an offer for Reynolds which Fulham rejected. At about the same time, October 1914, he won his only representative honour, playing for the Football League against the Southern League. Reynolds was an unorthodox goalkeeper using every part of his body to stop the ball: his legs were as effective as his hands, and it was by design not accident that they were used to keep his goal intact. Another feature of his play was the cry of 'R-iii-ght' whenever he wanted the ball, which could be heard at the other end of the ground. He left Fulham for Orient in 1925, but played in only two reserve games before retiring. He was the first Fulham player to play in 300 League games and 400 League and Cup games. Reynolds continued to support Fulham right up to his death on 14 March 1970.

ARTHUR REYNOLDS

	LEAGUE		FA CUP		TOTAL	
	App	Gls	App	Gls	App	Gls
1909-10	2	0	0	0	2	0
1910-11	38	0	1	0	39	0
1911-12	38	0	4	0	42	0
1912-13	36	0	1	0	37	0
1913-14	30	0	1	0	31	0
1914-15	19	0	0	0	19	0
1919-20	38	0	1	0	39	0
1920-21	40	0	5	0	45	0
1921-22	42	0	3	0	45	0
1922-23	42	0	1	0	43	0
1923-24	41	0	3	0	44	0
1924-25	33	0	1	0	34	0
	399	0	21	0	420	0

Quick on the ball and fast down the wing, Bill Richards was the first Fulham player to win a Welsh cap. He was born in Abercynaid, Wales in 1905, and worked down the pits after leaving school. Richards joined Wolves with his brother around 1927 from Welsh football and made 30 appearances before moving to Coventry City in 1929. Coventry were a Second Division club when he joined them but they plunged into the Third Division and Richards must have been relieved when Fulham signed him in the summer of 1931 for £100. His manager at Coventry, James McIntyre, brought him to the Cottage. Fulham won the Third Division Southern Section Championship in his first season at the Cottage, and amongst his goals was a hat-trick against Thames. Richards gained his one and only cap against Northern Ireland in December 1932. Thereafter, first-team opportunities were limited by the signing of John Arnold and Richards was transferred to Brighton in the summer of 1935. His final move was to Bristol Rovers in 1937 where he made only three appearances. Richards died in Wolverhampton on 30 September 1956.

BILL RICHARDS

	LEAGUE		FA CUP		TOTAL	
	App	Gls	App	Gls	App	Gls
1931-32	33	8	5	1	38	9
1932-33	29	6	1	0	30	6
1933-34	14	0	0	0	14	0
1934-35	0	0	0	0	0	0
	76	14	6	1	82	15

England manager, Bobby Robson, spent almost 11 of his 17 playing seasons with Fulham, and also cut his managerial teeth at the Cottage. Robson was born at Sacriston, County Durham, on 18 February 1933. He had a brief spell as an amateur with Middlesbrough, but was playing for another local side, Langley Park Juniors, when Fulham's Bill Dodgin pipped Newcastle for his signature. In May 1950, he left his coal-mining job to join Fulham for the first time. He established himself at inside-right in 1951-2, alongside Jezzard and Haynes. In March 1956, however, Vic Buckingham signed him for West Brom for £25,000 and in his seven years at The Hawthorns he played in 240 League games, scoring 61 goals. He was also converted to wing-half and renewed his partnership with Haynes, but for England. They were the two midfield dictators in manager Winterbottom's 4-2-4 formation. Robson won 20 England caps. Like Haynes, he lost his international place after the 1962 World Cup, but he again linked with the Maestro when he went back to Fulham. He played for five more First Division seasons, bringing an air of calm authority to a shaky defence. Robson retired in May 1967 and crossed the Atlantic to manage Vancouver Royals, but within six months was back at Fulham, as manager in succession to Vic Buckingham. Sadly he lasted less than 10 months, sacked for failing to arrest instantly a deep-seated malaise. He, of course, proved his managerial abilities at Ipswich before succeeding his former colleague Ron Greenwood as England manager in 1982. (See *Fulham Managers*).

BOBBY ROBSON

	LEAGUE		FA CUP		FL CUP		TOTAL	
	App	Gls	App	Gls	App	Gls	App	Gls
1950-51	1	0	0	0	0	0	1	0
1951-52	16	3	0	0	0	0	16	3
1952-53	35	19	1	0	0	0	36	19
1953-54	33	13	1	1	0	0	34	14
1954-55	42	23	1	0	0	0	43	23
1955-56	25	10	2	0	0	0	27	10
1962-63	34	1	2	1	2	0	38	2
1963-64	39	1	2	0	1	0	42	1
1964-65	42	1	2	0	3	1	47	2
1965-66	36	6	0	0	3	0	39	6
1966-67	41	0	3	0	3	0	47	0
	344	77	14	2	12	1	370	80

A goalscoring phenomenon, Rooke's contribution to Fulham would have been greater but for World War Two. He was born at Guildford on 11 December 1911, and showed his prowess early when he once scored 17 goals for his school team in a match against a Pick of Guildford. When he left school, he lied about his age and joined Stoke City, but could not settle and came back to London and signed professional for Crystal Palace in 1933. Rooke failed to establish himself at Selhurst Park and moved to Fulham in November 1936. His impact was immediate: he scored a hat-trick on his debut against West Ham, got three more trebles that season and was top scorer. He was in fact top scorer for all his 11 seasons at Fulham, seven of which were during the war when he got 212 goals in 199 games. Amongst his other records are ten hat-tricks and, against Bury in a Cup tie in January 1939, he scored all the goals in a 6-0 win. Rookie was an unmistakable figure on the pitch, with his bandy legs, shirt sleeves flapping and black, wavy hair on top of a craggy face dominated by a Roman nose. He was lethal with either foot, the most clinical and ruthless finisher of his day, and deserved more than his one wartime international cap. In December 1946, when he was Fulham's leading scorer, he was transferred to Arsenal for £1,000 and two players. Although 33 years old, he took the First Division by storm. Rooke helped save the Gunners from relegation, whilst in 1947-8, his 33 goals, the best haul in the League, contributed significantly to Arsenal's Championship win. After 93 games and 67 goals, he left Highbury and went back to Palace as player-manager. Another 26 goals in 46 appearances followed before he left in 1951. His final club was non-League Bedford. Rooke died of lung cancer in July 1985, at the age of 73.

RONNIE ROOKE

	LEAGUE		FA CUP		TOTAL	
	App	Gls	App	Gls	App	Gls
1936-37	22	19	0	0	22	19
1937-38	27	17	1	0	28	17
1938-39	38	20	2	6	40	26
1945-46	0	0	2	2	2	2
1946-47	18	13	0	0	18	13
	105	69	5	8	110	77

Harry Ross was a formidable defender who was rarely beaten by an opposing winger and won fame as an excellent penalty and free-kick exponent. Born in Brechin, Scotland, in 1881, Ross played for local clubs Harp FC and Brechin before moving South to join Burnley in 1900. He was a first-team regular after 1901 and played a total of 105 League games, scoring three goals, for the Lancashire club. Harry Bradshaw signed Ross in the summer of 1904. Southern League clubs did not have to pay Football League clubs' transfer fees in those days but when Fulham entered the League in 1907 they had to pay Burnley £229.10s (£229-50p) for his services. Ross won two Southern League Championship medals in Fulham's formidable defence and scored six goals in 1906-07. He played in a Scottish international trial in this period. Like Billy Morrison, he was dropped after a disastrous defeat by Glossop at the beginning of season 1908-09. Ross was transferred to St Mirren in November 1908 and later emigrated to the USA.

HARRY ROSS

	F LEAGUE		STHRN LGE		FA CUP		TOTAL	
	App	Gls	App	Gls	App	Gls	App	Gls
1909-10	0	0	29	2	7	1	36	3
1905-06	0	0	33	1	2	0	35	1
1906-07	0	0	36	6	4	0	40	6
1907-08	28	2	0	0	6	2	34	4
1908-09	1	1	0	0	0	0	1	1
	29	3	98	9	19	3	146	15

A tall and powerful centre-forward, Arthur Rowley had a lethal left-foot shot. He is the highest aggregate goalscorer in Football League history. When he retired in 1965, he had amassed 433 goals in 619 League games. Arthur, however, played in the shadow of his more famous brother, Jack, of Manchester United and England. He was born in Wolverhampton on 21 April 1926 and joined Wolves as an amateur during the war. He signed for West Brom on professional forms, making his League debut in 1946. Rowley became the missing link in Fulham's 1948-9 Second Division Championship side after joining the club in exchange for Ernie Shepherd in December 1948. He scored 19 goals in 22 appearances that season. Rowley moved to Leicester City in July 1950 for £12,000 and won another Division Two medal in 1953-4 and gained England 'B' and Football League honours. He was transferred to Shrewsbury in June 1958, later becoming manager. In the late 1960s he also managed Southend United. Rowley's goal tally was: WBA (4 goals), Fulham (26), Leicester (251) and Shrewsbury (152), but only 51 goals were scored in the First Division.

	LEAGUE		FA CUP		TOTAL	
	App	Gls	App	Gls	App	Gls
1948-49	22	19	1	0	23	19
1949-50	34	7	2	0	36	7
	56	26	3	0	59	26

ARTHUR ROWLEY

HARRY RUSSELL

Harry Russell was born in Chalk near Gravesend around 1888. When he was ten-years-old, he joined the Army as a bandboy with the 4th Lancashire Fusiliers. He represented The Army and his country at hockey, a game he learned to play whilst serving in India. Russell had lived in that country for five years prior to joining Fulham in February 1913. He walked into the office at Craven Cottage and asked for a trial and was signed immediately afterwards. Russell made his debut in a 3-2 home victory over Birmingham the following month. His best season at the Cottage was 1913-14 when he played 38 League and Cup games in a formidable half-back line with Alf Marshall and Jimmy Torrance. Russell could fill any position in the defence, appearing for Fulham as a full-back, wing-half and centre-half. After World War One, Harry's first-team appearances became more rare and in the close season of 1925 he left the club for Sheppey United after 12 years of service to Fulham.

	LEAGUE		FA CUP		TOTAL	
	App	Gls	App	Gls	App	Gls
1912-13	4	0	0	0	4	0
1913-14	37	1	1	0	38	1
1914-15	35	6	2	0	37	6
1919-20	31	0	0	0	31	0
1920-21	11	0	1	0	12	0
1921-22	17	0	0	0	17	0
1922-23	2	0	0	0	2	0
1923-24	0	0	0	0	0	0
1924-25	2	0	0	0	2	0
	139	7	4	0	143	7

Peter Scott is a ball-winning midfielder who also possesses fine passing ability. He was born in Notting Hill on 1 October 1963. His father played for Queen's Park Rangers as a youngster and later spent many seasons with Slough Town. It was while watching his father play that Scott decided he would like to be a professional footballer. He represented Slough and Berkshire Schools and had a trial with the England Schoolboy side. After a week's trial at Old Trafford, Fulham stepped in quickly to sign him. Scott became an apprentice in May 1980 and signed professional in September 1981. The following month he made his debut at Huddersfield in a 1-0 defeat. With the departure of Sean O'Driscoll to Bournemouth, he gained a regular first-team place. On his day, he is a potential match-winner, but has suffered from a lack of consistency. This is perhaps due to an unfortunate series of injuries which seemed to strike as he reached his best form.

Rated by contempories as the finest full-back of his generation, Jimmy Sharp was probably Fulham's outstanding pre-World War One player. Born on 11 October 1880 at Alyth in Perthshire, his early career was with East Craigie, but in 1899 he signed professional with Dundee. He won his first Scottish cap, in 1904, and played twice for the Scottish League before coming South to Fulham in 1904. Just 12 months later, Sharp was signed by Phil Kelso at Arsenal where he spent the next three years, playing in 102 League games. In April 1908, he went back to Scotland, to Rangers, but stayed only nine months before signing for Kelso again, but this time for Fulham. The fee of £1,000 equalled the existing transfer record. In his second spell at the Cottage, he made 108 appearances and won another international cap, in 1909, against Wales. His build gave no indication of his skill: he was only 5ft 6in tall but weighed 13st and was as slow as a shire horse. His great asset was his instinctive positional play and marvellous anticipation. He left Fulham again in November 1912, to try his luck in the United States but within months he was back in West London, playing 61 games for Chelsea before World War One. He officially retired during the war and went to Fulham as trainer in 1919, but when inside-left Harold Crockford missed the bus to an away game at Bury in April 1920, Sharp had to play. At the age of 40, he scored his only goal in first-class football. He left the Cottage for the last time in 1926, and went with Jimmy Torrance to Walsall, where he stayed for three years. In 1929, he spent 12 months as Cliftonville's trainer, before leaving football for good. He lived for the rest of his life in the Fulham Palace Road, working in the building industry. Sharp died, aged 69 on 18 November 1949.

PETER SCOTT

	LEAGUE		FA CUP		FL CUP		TOTAL	
	App	Gls	App	Gls	App	Gls	App	Gls
1981-82	1	0	0	0	0	0	1	0
1982-83	0	0	0	0	0/1	0	0/1	0
1983-84	31/4	4	2	0	2	1	35/4	5
1984-85	17/2	1	1	0	1/1	0	19/3	1
1985-86	32	5	1	0	4	0	37	5
1986-87	30	6	1	0	4	3	35	9
	111/6	16	5	0	11/2	4	127/8	20

	F LEAGUE		STHRN LGE		FA CUP		TOTAL	
	App	Gls	App	Gls	App	Gls	App	Gls
1904-05	0	0	17	0	1	0	18	0
1908-09	15	0	0	0	2	0	17	0
1909-10	28	0	0	0	3	0	31	0
1910-11	18	0	0	0	1	0	19	0
1911-12	25	0	0	0	4	0	29	0
1912-13	11	0	0	0	0	0	11	0
1919-20	1	1	0	0	0	0	1	1
	98	1	17	0	11	0	126	1

JIMMY SHARP

One of the supreme individual talents of his generation, Danny Shea was also one of football's natural wanderers. Born in Wapping in London on 6 November 1887, he played for Manor Park Albion before joining Southern League West Ham in 1907. His 110 goals in 169 games attracted many League clubs, and First Division Blackburn paid a world record £2,000 to take him to Ewood Park. In his first season, he won a League Championship medal, scoring 27 goals, and played twice for both England and the Football League. During World War One, he guested for Fulham amongst other clubs, but he was back at Rovers in 1919-20: in all he scored 64 goals in 108 games for Blackburn. In 1920, he had a six-month sojourn back at West Ham, but in December 1920, the 33-year-old Shea joined Fulham. He soon demonstrated that he had plenty of football left in him, and was a favourite of the supporters. Shea had a roly-poly appearance but also a superb football brain, and his dribbling and shooting delighted crowds. After leaving Fulham in 1923, he spent two years at Coventry and then 18 months with Orient. By the time he left League football, he had made 323 appearances, scoring 110 goals. Shea later worked in the docks of London's East End and he died, aged 73, on Christmas Day, 1960.

DANNY SHEA

	LEAGUE		FA CUP		TOTAL	
	App	Gls	App	Gls	App	Gls
1920-21	23	4	3	0	26	4
1921-22	38	11	3	1	41	12
1922-23	39	8	1	0	40	8
	100	23	7	1	107	24

LESLIE SKENE

Leslie Skene made up for his lack of inches (5ft 8½in) by his keen vision, sure hands, pluck and intelligent forecasting of events. He was born in Larbert, Scotland on 22 August 1882 and took up football seriously when studying to be a doctor at Edinburgh University. He played for Stenhousemuir before joining the famous Scottish amateur club, Queen's Park, in 1901. Skene spent six seasons at Hampden Park and won a Scottish international cap against Wales in March 1904 in a 1-1 draw at Dundee. He moved south to join Fulham on their entry into the Football League in 1907 and gave some brilliant displays in the FA Cup run of 1908. Unfortunately he conceded six goals in the semi-final defeat by Newcastle United. Skene moved to Glentoran in 1910 and Fulham were unable to get a transfer fee since he had moved out of the Football League. Skene represented the Irish League during his spell at The Oval. He later became a medical officer in a mental hospital on the Isle of Man.

	LEAGUE		FA CUP		TOTAL	
	App	Gls	App	Gls	App	Gls
1907-08	36	0	6	0	42	0
1908-09	27	0	0	0	27	0
1909-10	25	0	0	0	25	0
	88	0	6	0	94	0

Alan Slough was a utility man who played in most positions for Fulham but is best remembered as a hard-working midfield player. He was born in Luton on 24 September 1947 and joined Luton Town as a professional in May 1965. Under the managership of Alec Stock, Slough spent eight years at Kenilworth Road, winning a Fourth Division Championship medal in 1967-8. Slough joined Fulham for £45,000 at the same time as Viv Busby in August 1973, and again teamed up with Alec Stock. He played a prominent role in Fulham's run to a first Wembley appearance in 1975 and was made the Fulham captain in 1976 after Alan Mullery's retirement. Slough was transferred to Peterborough United for £25,000 in July 1977 where he became player-coach and once scored a hat-trick of penalties against Chester. He moved to Millwall in a similar capacity in 1981 and Torquay in August 1982. A year later, Slough moved into non-League football at Weymouth and has also coached at Yeovil and Minehead in recent years.

ALAN SLOUGH

	LEAGUE		FA CUP		FL CUP		TOTAL	
	App	Gls	App	Gls	App	Gls	App	Gls
1973-74	33	2	3	0	4	0	40	2
1974-75	39	2	12	2	3	1	54	5
1975-76	40	5	1	0	3	0	44	5
1976-77	42	4	2	0	5	1	49	5
	154	13	18	2	15	2	187	17

JAMES SMITH

James Smith was described in the Fulham programme of the time as 'a stylish lad who has all his wits at work to assist a speedy control of the ball, and is a dainty, forceful and effective footballer'. He was born in Preston around 1886 and attended the same school as Harry Lee, another Fulham winger. In 1903, he joined Bury and made 21 League appearances before being released in 1906. He drifted into non-League football with Stalybridge Rovers and later Accrington Stanley. Fulham discovered him playing for Chorley in March 1909 where he had scored 38 goals after joining the club the previous September. Smith was soon using his speed and accurate crosses to good effect in the Fulham first-team, where he performed regularly up to the outbreak of the World War One. He formed a fine right-wing partnership with Wattie White and later Tim Coleman. Smith was never a regular goalscorer but finished the 1910-11 season as leading scorer with 11 goals and scored the winning goal in the first-ever League meeting with Chelsea in December 1910.

	LEAGUE		FA CUP		TOTAL	
	App	Gls	App	Gls	App	Gls
1908-09	4	0	0	0	4	0
1909-10	26	2	3	0	29	2
1910-11	37	11	1	0	38	11
1911-12	30	3	4	0	34	3
1912-13	29	1	1	0	30	1
1913-14	32	1	1	0	33	1
1914-15	24	1	2	0	26	1
	182	19	12	0	194	19

A tenacious player, who, although small in stature (5ft 4½in) had plenty of spirit and determination. Trevor Smith was born in West Stanley in County Durham on 8 September 1910. He joined South Moors in the Durham Junior League as a youngster and won two championship medals. Smith became a semi-professional with Anfield Plain in 1930 and also worked as a telephone operator. Charlton Athletic spotted his potential and signed him on professional forms in 1933. He moved to Fulham in March 1935 for a £1,000 fee, making his debut as a right-winger. With the arrival of Bert Worsley from Leeds, he switched to the inside berth. These two struck up an instant understanding and were to prove a great combination, especially in Fulham's FA Cup run to the semi-final in 1936. In January 1938, Smith was on the move again, to Crystal Palace for a £2,500 fee. He returned to the Cottage briefly as a guest in the war and by 1946 was playing for Yeovil and Colchester United. Smith returned to League football with Watford in June 1947 but retired the following year. He became the manager of Wingate in June 1949.

	LEAGUE		FA CUP		TOTAL	
	App	Gls	App	Gls	App	Gls
1934-35	5	1	0	0	5	1
1935-36	36	9	6	2	42	11
1936-37	38	9	1	0	39	9
1937-38	14	0	0	0	14	0
	93	19	7	2	100	21

TREVOR SMITH

JOE STAPLETON

Joe Stapleton was reluctant to leave his sales job to become a professional. Eventually Fulham beat off a number of clubs to secure his signature in August 1952. Born in Marylebone of Irish parents on 27 June 1928, Stapleton attended schools in the Southall area. He did not play the game seriously until he joined Jubilee Park Boys Club in Southall as a right-half. Stapleton signed for Southall FC whilst doing his National Service, where he served in Egypt in the RASC. He joined Hayes on his return but after a few games moved to Uxbridge in the Corinthian League, where he won the Corinthian Memorial Shield. After signing for Fulham at the age of 24, Stapleton impressed everybody with his performances in the reserves and was soon promoted to the first team. Establishing himself as a right-half he later moved to centre-half in an emergency. Then, a serious ankle injury halted his career. Initially, Stapleton retired from playing but he later signed for Cambridge City in 1961.

	LEAGUE		FA CUP		TOTAL	
	App	Gls	App	Gls	App	Gls
1954-55	4	0	0	0	4	0
1955-56	18	0	0	0	18	0
1956-57	24	2	0	0	24	2
1957-58	32	0	5	0	37	0
1958-59	16	0	2	0	18	0
1959-60	3	0	0	0	3	0
	97	2	7	0	104	2

139

A flexible player who during his career actually played in every position except goalkeeper, Alex Steele represented Ireland as an amateur and as a professional. He was born in Belfast on 19 March 1899 and first played for Barnville and Dunmurray in Belfast district leagues. From Dunmurray, he joined Glenavon in the Irish Senior League and was then signed by Charlton Athletic in 1921: they had just been admitted to the Football League. In his five seasons at The Valley, Steele made 146 League and Cup appearances for the Valiants. He moved to Swansea Town in July 1926, but when manager Joe Bradshaw became Fulham's manager, Steele came with him to the Cottage for a £500 fee. He played mainly at left-half in his three seasons at Stevenage Road. Steele played four times for Northern Ireland, twice as a Fulham player in 1929. He made his international debut against Wales in February 1926 as an inside-right. Steele retired in 1930 and returned to Ireland to run a newsagent's shop in Whitehead, near Belfast Lock, but maintained his football connections by scouting for Blackpool. Steele was last heard of in 1956 living in Rayleigh, Essex and working as an audit clerk in the City.

ALEX STEELE

	LEAGUE		FA CUP		TOTAL	
	App	Gls	App	Gls	App	Gls
1927-28	25	0	0	0	25	0
1928-29	21	0	3	0	24	0
1929-30	4	0	1	0	5	0
	50	0	4	0	54	0

One of the most famous Fulham names, Arthur Stevens was only the third player to score a century of goals for the club, a remarkable performance for a winger. Battersea-born, on 13 January 1921, he began with local boys' sides before joining Isthmian League amateurs Wimbledon as a 16-year-old. Stevens was briefly on Brentford's groundstaff, but this ended with the outbreak of war. He continued as an amateur, with Sutton, until 1941 when Fulham were a man short and he was given a chance. He signed professional in 1943, but the war took him overseas: his group in the Artillery gave machine-gun support to the company led by Fulham's (Major) Jim Tompkins on the D-Day landings, the action in which Tompkins was killed. Stevens became a regular on his demob, and for 12 years was an automatic choice. With his peculiar running style, he could centre accurately at top speed, or cut in for a shot at goal. He nearly moved to Chelsea, in part-exchange for Tommy Lawton, in 1949, but Stevens rejected the move. He was a regular in the Fulham teams which won the Second Division title in 1949 and which got to the FA Cup semi-final in 1958. He holds the club record for goals in the Cup, 14 in 27 matches. In 1958-9, he lost his place to Graham Leggat but remained on the coaching staff until Vic Buckingham's arrival in January 1965.

ARTHUR STEVENS

	LEAGUE		FA CUP		TOTAL	
	App	Gls	App	Gls	App	Gls
1946-47	16	5	0	0	16	5
1947-48	23	11	5	4	28	15
1948-49	42	12	1	0	43	12
1949-50	39	5	2	0	41	5
1950-51	42	11	5	1	47	12
1951-52	39	7	1	0	40	7
1952-53	36	13	0	0	36	13
1953-54	32	10	3	1	35	11
1954-55	22	8	1	1	23	9
1955-56	30	9	0	0	30	9
1956-57	40	15	2	2	42	17
1957-58	22	4	7	5	29	9
1958-59	3	0	0	0	3	0
	386	110	27	14	413	124

Les Strong never allowed the serious business of football to interfere with his obvious enjoyment of the game. He was born in Streatham on 3 July 1953 and was on Crystal Palace's books as a schoolboy. After a trial, Strong joined Fulham as an apprentice in February 1970 and became a professional in June the following year. He made his debut as a winger, a position he occupied in his first season, but reverted to full-back in 1973. Strong played in every game in season 1974-5 and helped Fulham to their first Wembley Final, but injury struck just before the match and he lost his chance of a Cup medal. Later, the FA struck a special medal for him as compensation. Strong was probably playing the best football of his career at this time. Encouraged by Bobby Moore, he missed only four League games between 1976 and 1982 and was the only player to play throughout Bobby Campbell's period as manager. He skippered Fulham to promotion in season 1981-2, in his last full season at the club. After a loan period with Brentford in September 1982, Strong signed for Crystal Palace in the summer of 1983, and also played one game for Rochdale in October 1984. After retirement he became catering manager at Fulham in 1985.

	LEAGUE		FA CUP		FL CUP		TOTAL	
	App	Gls	App	Gls	App	Gls	App	Gls
1972-73	18/2	2	0	0	0	0	18/2	2
1973-74	17/1	0	3	0	0	0	20/1	0
1974-75	40	0	11	0	3	0	54	0
1975-76	36	0	0	0	3	0	39	0
1976-77	42	0	2	0	5	0	49	0
1977-78	41	1	1	0	2	0	44	1
1978-79	41	1	3	0	2	0	46	1
1979-80	41	0	1	0	2	0	44	0
1980-81	45	1	5	0	2	1	52	2
1981-82	46	0	2	0	7	0	55	0
1982-83	3	0	0	0	0	0	3	0
	370/3	5	28	0	26	1	424/3	6

LES STRONG

BOB SUART

A strong, plucky player, Bob Suart was a good header of the ball but sometimes a little untidy in his play. He was not tall for a centre-half but was a good, honest trier who was not always appreciated by the crowd. Suart could never be accused of playing badly, and yet in the finer touches of the game, he showed extremes of form, sometimes kicking and placing like a master, while at other times he was wild and inaccurate. He was born in Stockport around 1885 and joined the local professional club in 1903. He made 110 League and Cup appearances for County in his five seasons at the club. Fulham obtained his signature in March 1908 and he made his debut against Wolves the following month. His only honour at the Cottage was a London Challenge Cup-winners' medal in season 1909-10 when Fulham beat Spurs 4-1 in the Final. Suart moved on to Burslem Port Vale in August 1911 who were at that time a non-League club. He had been converted to left-half at the Cottage after criticism of his performances as a pivot.

	LEAGUE		FA CUP		TOTAL	
	App	Gls	App	Gls	App	Gls
1907-08	6	1	0	0	6	1
1908-09	35	0	1	0	3	0
1909-10	33	0	3	0	36	0
1910-11	23	0	1	0	24	0
	97	1	5	0	102	1

Arguably Fulham's best-ever centre-half, Jim Taylor was the club's first player to win a full England cap in the post-war era. Born on 5 November 1917, at Cowley in Middlesex, he went to the Cottage in March 1938, signed as an inside-forward from Hillingdon British Legion club. World War Two, in which Taylor served in the Navy, delayed his introduction to first-class football. He was 28 when he made his debut in August 1946, by which time he had been converted to wing-half. For the next seven seasons, only injuries kept him out of the side. On Christmas Day 1947, he replaced the injured Watson at centre-half, and thereafter made the position his own. With Quested and Beasley, he formed the backbone of the Second Division Championship team and was one of the few Fulham players to play consistently well in Division One between 1949 and 1952. After playing for the Football League in March 1948, Taylor was selected to tour Canada in 1950 with the FA and was in the ill-fated England party at the World Cup Finals that year, although he did not play. His caps came in the Festival of Britain matches in 1951 against Argentina and Portugal. Taylor's style resembled Neil Franklin, his competitor for the England position: both were quick in the tackle, had sound positional play and good distribution, although Taylor may have been weaker in the air. He left Fulham for Loftus Road in the 1953 close season, but after one season and 41 League games, he took over as player-manager of Tunbridge Wells. In 1959, managed Yiewsley before leaving football.

	LEAGUE		FA CUP		TOTAL	
	App	Gls	App	Gls	App	Gls
1945-46	0	0	2	0	2	0
1946-47	42	3	1	0	43	3
1947-48	36	2	5	0	41	2
1948-49	42	0	1	0	43	0
1949-50	35	0	2	0	37	0
1950-51	37	0	4	0	41	0
1951-52	33	0	1	0	34	0
1952-53	36	0	1	0	37	0
	261	5	17	0	278	5

JIM TAYLOR

A speedy, direct winger who scored goals regularly, Jimmy Temple never captured the form he showed at Fulham after leaving the Cottage. He was born in Scarborough on 16 September 1904, and played local football and worked as a fitter until joining Fulham in 1926. He followed his uncle George, who had played for Hull City between 1907 and 1914, into professional soccer. Temple made his debut in a five-goal defeat at Darlington in January 1927 and often struggled to find his form in a poor side. After Fulham's relegation to the Third Division South in 1928, Temple started to score regularly. He finished as the club's leading scorer in 1928-9 with 29 League and Cup goals. The following season, he hit his one and only hat-trick at Torquay in a 4-2 victory. Sunderland were on the look-out for a good-quality winger and paid a large fee and exchanged Albert Wood for his services in the summer of 1931. Temple was probably out of his depth in the First Division at Roker Park and moved on to Gateshead two years later after only 31 games. Things did not improve much at the Redheugh and Temple left senior soccer in 1934. He was killed on active service during World War Two.

	LEAGUE		FA CUP		TOTAL	
	App	Gls	App	Gls	App	Gls
1926-27	18	2	0	0	18	2
1927-28	24	7	0	0	24	7
1928-29	42	26	3	3	45	29
1929-30	39	14	5	0	44	14
1930-31	33	9	4	0	37	9
	156	58	12	3	168	61

JIMMY TEMPLE

Bob Thomas, born in Stepney on 2 August 1919, was Fulham's top scorer in the Second Division Championship season. Although he had played schoolboy football including representing London Boys, he took a job as a copy-boy at the *Daily Express* when he left school. He played as an amateur, with Romford, Hayes and Golders Green in the Athenian League, until 1939, when he joined Brentford's groundstaff. The war saw him serve in the Navy, although he did guest on occasion for Fulham. On his demob, he travelled west, to Plymouth, where his brother Dave was centreforward. Bob's 17 goals in 41 League games for Argyle impressed Jack Peart sufficiently to pay £4,000 to bring him to the Cottage in the 1947 close season. He was an inside-forward, relying on stealth and pace rather than strength to get into scoring positions. He needed a more conventional centre-forward off whom he could feed, and he found an ideal partner in Arthur Rowley in his second season at the Cottage. Thomas' 23 goals in 40 League outings in 1948-9 was four more than Rowley's and his own best-ever for a season. He found the going tougher in the top flight, but still managed 25 goals from 1949 to 1951. Thomas left the Cottage in 1952 and had three years with Crystal Palace, when he scored 31 goals in 96 games. In 1955, he went to Tunbridge Wells, who were managed by Jim Taylor, and went back to work in Fleet Street. Now retired, Thomas is still a frequent and welcome visitor to the Cottage.

BOB THOMAS

| | LEAGUE | | FA CUP | | TOTAL | |
	App	Gls	App	Gls	App	Gls
1947-48	36	5	5	1	41	6
1948-49	40	23	1	0	41	23
1949-50	42	10	2	1	44	11
1950-51	37	14	1	0	38	14
1951-52	12	3	0	0	12	3
	167	55	9	2	176	57

SID THOMAS

Sid Thomas possessed intricate ball skills. He often flattered to deceive however, as he wasted the opportunities he created with his deft touches and fine ballskills. He was born in Machynleth, Wales, on 12 November 1919. He joined Fulham from Welsh League club Treharris in 1938 but had to wait eight years for his debut, against Spurs in November 1946, after a handful of wartime appearances. Thomas won four Welsh caps in all. His international debut against England at Cardiff in October 1947 resulted in a three-goal defeat. In his next international Wales beat Scotland 2-1 at Hampden Park. Thomas was never a regular at the Cottage and was transferred to Bristol City in June 1950 for a £9,000 fee. After only 13 games, however, he was taken seriously ill with tuberculosis and was forced to give up the game. Thereafter followed a long dispute between the two clubs over the transfer fee paid. City eventually paid up in full.

| | LEAGUE | | FA CUP | | TOTAL | |
	App	Gls	App	Gls	App	Gls
1946-47	9	1	0	0	9	1
1947-48	31	2	4	0	35	2
1948-49	14	0	0	0	14	0
1949-50	3	1	0	0	3	1
	57	4	4	0	61	4

Fred Threlfall played with the great Billy Meredith during his six seasons at Maine Road, usually on the opposite wing to the 'Welsh Wizard'. He was a left-winger who possessed grace, speed and a deft touch but was a little inconsistent in his play. Fred, however, almost made the England side, playing in two trial games, firstly, for the Professionals v Amateurs in January 1906 and then for the South v North a year later. Born in Preston in 1880, Threlfall joined Manchester City around 1899 and played in 74 League and Cup games before moving to Craven Cottage in the close season of 1905. Threlfall had gained a Second Division Championship medal in 1902-03 for City when he had scored seven goals in 25 League games. To this, he added two Southern League Championship medals for Fulham between 1905-07 and played in Fulham's FA Cup run to the semi-final in 1908. After losing his first-team place at Fulham, Threlfall moved to Leicester Fosse in the summer of 1909 where he had two good seasons. He later enjoyed playing bowls and was a local champion.

	F LEAGUE		STHRN LGE		FA CUP		TOTAL	
	App	Gls	App	Gls	App	Gls	App	Gls
1905-06	0	0	34	6	2	0	36	6
1906-07	0	0	30	7	4	1	34	8
1907-08	27	4	0	0	4	1	31	5
1908-09	6	0	0	0	0	0	6	0
	33	4	64	13	10	2	107	19

FRED THRELFALL

JIMMY TOMPKINS

	LEAGUE		FA CUP		TOTAL	
	App	Gls	App	Gls	App	Gls
1933-34	4	0	0	0	4	0
1934-35	1	0	0	0	1	0
1935-36	29	0	6	0	35	0
1936-37	35	0	1	0	36	0
1937-38	42	1	1	0	43	1
1938-39	42	4	2	0	44	4
	153	5	10	0	163	5

One of the most heroic and tragic figures to play for Fulham, Jimmy Tompkins was a fine left-half. He was born in Edmonton, just before World War One, but grew up in Battersea where he played his schoolboy football. Whilst still at school, he joined Isthmian League Woking. He was then offered a place on Arsenal's groundstaff, at the same time as Fulham had signed him as an amateur. After lengthy discussions between managers McIntyre and Chapman, he became a Fulham player in March 1932. He was hardly an overnight sensation, probably because he was played at centre-half. His somewhat lightweight frame was better suited to wing-half, and he made the breakthrough in the 1936 semi-final team. From then until World War Two, the number-six slot was his, and his style was characterised by tight marking, fierce tackling and good distribution. He was cool and stylish, mature beyond his years, and always the epitome of fairness. When war come he saw action early because of his earlier experience with the Territorial Army. By 1944, he was a major, but was killed on 'D'Day. His wife was to die months later, and their only son also lost his life in the army in the 1950s.
NB.In 1984, a young student visited Craven Cottage seeking any information on his grandfather, who he thought might have once played for Fulham: it was Tompkins' grandson who had no idea of Jimmy's background.

Small and acrobatic, Alf Tootill, nicknamed 'The Birdcatcher', was described as an intelligent goalkeeper with a safe pair of hands. He was born in Ramsbottom on 12 November 1908 and joined his local club, United, who played in the Bury Amateur League. He quickly attracted the attention of Accrington Stanley and signed for them in September 1927. After 18 months of Third Division football, he moved to Wolves and soon established himself as the first-choice 'keeper. He was ever-present when Wolves won the Second Division Championship in season 1931-2 but struggled a little in First Division football. Fulham signed Tootill in November 1932 for a £1,000 fee and he missed only four games in the next four and a half seasons. He was by no means a bad cricketer and during the summer played for Ramsbottom in the Lancashire League. The highlight of his Fulham career was helping the side to the FA Cup semi-final in 1936. He moved to Crystal Palace in the summer of 1938 and appeared regularly in wartime soccer until he retired in 1945. He had made 372 League appearances and played 144 wartime games for Palace.

	LEAGUE		FA CUP		TOTAL	
	App	Gls	App	Gls	App	Gls
1932-33	23	0	1	0	24	0
1933-34	40	0	2	0	42	0
1934-35	42	0	1	0	43	0
1935-36	41	0	6	0	47	0
1936-37	41	0	1	0	42	0
1937-38	16	0	0	0	16	0
	203	0	11	0	214	0

ALF TOOTILL

The Scottish influence was strong at the Cottage 70-80 years ago, and one of the most famous Fulham Scots was Jimmy Torrance. A marvellous one-club man whose appearances total would have been higher but for World War One, he served the club well in many positions. Born in Coatbridge in 1889, Torrance joined Fulham as a 22-year-old in 1910-11, having gained experience north of the border with the Rob Roy and Ashfield clubs. In his early years, he was an inside or centre-forward, and found his first-team chances limited. When he switched to wing-half in 1913-14, however, he won a regular place, which he held for a dozen years. He had a curious build, since he was a bit on the short side, and seemed all body and no legs. He was, however, a wing-half in the true Scottish tradition, and when he switched to the centre, he was able to maintain his attacking instincts because of the old offside law. He was clearly past his best when he left Fulham in the summer of 1926, to become player-manager of Walsall, taking trainer Jimmy Sharp with him. He stayed only two seasons at Fellows Park, and left football for good. He then worked for a telephone company. Torrance was unlucky off the field, having an unhappy marriage and a son, his only child, dying in his teens. Jimmy, himself, also died prematurely, in July 1949, of lung cancer before he was 60, a sad end for one of the great Fulham names.

JIMMY TORRANCE

	LEAGUE		FA CUP		TOTAL	
	App	Gls	App	Gls	App	Gls
1910-11	12	1	0	0	12	1
1911-12	17	5	0	0	17	5
1912-13	18	6	1	0	19	6
1913-14	13	0	1	0	14	0
1914-15	36	4	2	0	38	4
1919-20	36	2	1	0	37	2
1920-21	42	3	5	0	47	3
1921-22	39	4	3	0	42	4
1922-23	38	4	1	0	39	4
1923-24	40	3	3	0	43	3
1924-25	38	3	2	0	40	3
1925-26	7	0	0	0	7	0
	336	35	19	0	355	35

Born in Sunderland in the 1890s, Travers was christened Bernard but prefered to be known as Barney. One of Fulham's most dashing and popular centre-forwards, his career was ruined when he was implicated in a bribery scandal after an important promotion tussle at South Shields in March 1922. Travers joined local club Sunderland West End and moved to Sunderland in World War One. Ever-present in season 1919-20, Travers scored 19 goals, helping Sunderland to fifth position in the First Division. He joined Fulham for a record £3,000 fee in February 1921 and was soon scoring regularly. Fulham looked on the brink of achieving success when the bribery scandal led to Travers being banned for life. He tried to make a comeback in Spanish football but when the authorities learned of the ban he was soon prevented from playing. Travers ran a fruit and veg stall in the Sunderland area and remained unembittered over a situation where he was the one that was caught, but the people who put up the money for the bribe were never brought to justice. Travers died in July 1949 in his home town.

BARNEY TRAVERS

| | LEAGUE | | FA CUP | | TOTAL | |
	App	Gls	App	Gls	App	Gls
1920-21	16	11	0	0	16	11
1921-22	30	17	3	1	33	18
	46	28	3	1	49	29

HUGH TURNER

Rather small for a goalkeeper, Hugh Turner was described by the *Topical Times* as 'a smart 'keeper who had inspired days when he could not be rivalled, as well as fine agility and anticipation'. Born in Wigan, Turner's first club was Felling Colliery in Darlington who he joined in the summer of 1924. His next move was to High Fell who played in the Northern Alliance, and it was from here that he joined Huddersfield Town. Turner gave the Terriers great service, making 363 League appearances over the next 11 seasons. He gained England caps against France and Belguim in May 1931, replacing the injured Harry Hibbs, and represented the Football League v The Irish League at Blackpool in 1931. Turner also gained an FA Cup runners-up medal in 1930 when Huddersfield lost to Arsenal 2-0. After only one appearance for Town in 1936-7, he moved to Fulham at the end of that season to replace Alf Tootill. He was ever-present in Fulham's last full season (1938-9) before World War Two.

| | LEAGUE | | FA CUP | | TOTAL | |
	App	Gls	App	Gls	App	Gls
1937-38	26	0	1	0	27	0
1938-39	42	0	2	0	44	0
	68	0	3	0	71	0

146

Willie Walker beat off the competition for the outside-left spot from Bert Lipsham and Fred Mouncher in Fulham's early League years. An instant success after his arrival from Darlington soccer, Walker gave Fulham great service during his 12 years at the club. Born in Durham around 1891, he spent much of his formative years playing soccer for various sides in Darlington. He played for Darlington FC, Darlington Albion and finally Darlington St Augustine from where he joined Fulham with Alf Marshall in September 1909. Walker was given his chance in the first team very soon afterwards, making some impressive performances. The only blot on his Fulham career was his sending-off against Bradford in February 1913 for retaliation. He was probably the first player sent off whilst playing for Fulham. Walker moved to Lincoln City in the close season of 1921 where he stayed for three seasons, rarely making the first team after season 1921-2. Walker won four gold medals before coming to the Cottage and won a London Challenge Cup-winners' medal in 1909-10 with Fulham.

	LEAGUE		FA CUP		TOTAL	
	App	Gls	App	Gls	App	Gls
1909-10	17	5	0	0	17	5
1910-11	29	3	0	0	29	3
1911-12	24	3	3	0	27	3
1912-13	32	10	1	0	33	10
1913-14	24	2	1	0	25	2
1914-15	15	0	2	1	17	1
1919-20	25	2	1	0	26	2
1920-21	2	0	0	0	2	0
	168	25	8	1	176	26

WILLIE WALKER

MALCOLM WEBSTER

At times, goalkeeper Malcolm Webster, 'the Sergeant Major', was spectacular but he was generally weak on crosses, although his game improved playing behind a tall Cambridge defence. Webster won a Fourth Division Championship medal in 1976-7 when he was ever-present, and a runners-up position the following season which brought Second Division football to the Abbey Stadium for the first time. Webster was born in Rossington, Yorkshire on 12 November 1950. He started his career at Arsenal where he won England Youth honours, and he made his debut in a local derby against Spurs in September 1969. Webster joined Fulham, initially on loan, in December 1969, and permanently the following May for £10,000. He started well at the Cottage, helping Fulham to promotion in 1971 but lost his place to Peter Mellor after some poor performances the following season. Webster moved to Southend United in January 1974 for a £7,000 fee where he made 108 appearances before his final move to Cambridge in September 1976. He retired in 1984 after 286 appearances for United to become the youth team coach and was made assistant-manager in 1986.

	LEAGUE		FA CUP		FL CUP		TOTAL	
	App	Gls	App	Gls	App	Gls	App	Gls
1969-70	26	0	0	0	0	0	26	0
1970-71	35	0	0	0	3	0	38	0
1971-72	29	0	3	0	2	0	34	0
1972-73	0	0	0	0	0	0	0	0
1973-74	4	0	0	0	2	0	6	0
	94	0	3	0	7	0	104	0

A small, skilful ball-player, Walter White was equally at home at wing-half or inside-forward. He was better known as 'Wattie' and was born in the same Scottish village as the Goldie brothers, on 15 May 1882. White joined his local side Hurlford Thistle and moved to Bolton Wanderers in 1902. He played in their FA Cup Final appearance in 1904 when they lost to Manchester City 1-0. White won two Scottish caps against England, in 1907 and 1908, and was probably unlucky not to gain more honours. He played 217 League and Cup games for Wanderers, scoring 94 goals, before a move to Everton in December 1908. They almost won the Championship in his first season at the club. His next move was to Fulham in October 1910, initially playing at inside-left but later mainly as a wing-half. He remained at the Cottage for 13 years, although his appearances after World War One were only occasional. He made his last appearance at Bury in February 1923 at the age of 40 and retired the following summer. White remained in the Fulham area and was living at Danehurst Street when he died on 8 July 1950. His daughter is still a resident at the house and a regular Fulham supporter.

	LEAGUE		FA CUP		TOTAL	
	App	Gls	App	Gls	App	Gls
1910-11	31	3	1	0	32	3
1911-12	37	0	4	0	41	0
1912-13	31	2	1	0	32	2
1913-14	36	3	1	0	37	3
1914-15	33	4	2	1	35	5
1919-20	16	3	0	0	16	3
1920-21	6	0	3	0	9	0
1921-22	0	0	0	0	0	0
1922-23	1	0	0	0	1	0
	191	15	12	1	203	16

WALTER 'WATTIE' WHITE

Robert Wilson started his career as a right-back but was later converted into an attacking midfield player who had an appetite for scoring goals. One of a large family, he was born in Parsons Green on 5 June 1961. Wilson represented West London and Inner London Schools and joined Fulham as an associate schoolboy. He signed apprentice forms in July 1977 and as a full professional in June 1979. Making his debut at Blackburn Rovers in the FA Cup in January 1980, he was soon a regular member of the first team. Although lacking pace, his strengths in midfield were his tackling, the timing of runs into the penalty-area to score vital goals and orchestrating clever one-touch moves. A serious gas accident at his new home was a setback for Wilson and his wife but both fortunately fully recovered. With the selling of many talented players at the club which took place at this time, Wilson was allowed to leave for Millwall in August 1985 for a fee of £57,500. He was the leading scorer in his only season at The Den. After a disagreement with the management, Wilson moved to Luton Town a year later for £40,000, teaming up once again with Ray Harford.

	LEAGUE		FA CUP		FL CUP		TOTAL	
	App	Gls	App	Gls	App	Gls	App	Gls
1979-80	2	0	2	0	0	0	4	0
1980-81	31/4	4	0/1	0	0/1	0	31/6	4
1981-82	42/1	5	2	0	7	3	51/1	8
1982-83	40	11	3	0	2	0	45	11
1983-84	14/2	3	0	0	4	0	18/2	3
1984-85	39	11	0	0	3	0	42	11
	168/7	34	7/1	0	16/1	3	191/9	37

ROBERT WILSON

The hard man of the side, Viv Woodward was a versatile player who had some clever tricks up his sleeve. Like so many other young players of his time, his career was wrecked by the war when he lost virtually seven seasons. One of six boys, he was born in Troedyrchiw in Wales on 20 May 1914 and joined his local club who played in the Welsh League. He gained Welsh Schoolboy honours before a move to Folkestone where he won three county trophies in his two and a half seasons at the club. After being spotted by director, Frank Osborne, Woodward joined Fulham in January 1936 and made his debut at Leicester City two months later, on the right wing. He played mainly at inside-right during his time at the Cottage. Woodward's proudest moment was representing Wales in a wartime international. His brother Laurie played for Bournemouth after the war. Viv moved to Millwall in February 1950 and he retired the following year. He remains a regular visitor to the Cottage.

	LEAGUE		FA CUP		TOTAL	
	App	Gls	App	Gls	App	Gls
1935-36	2	0	0	0	2	0
1936-37	13	5	1	0	14	5
1937-38	33	15	0	0	33	15
1938-39	34	4	0	0	34	4
1945-46	0	0	2	0	2	0
1946-47	10	0	0	0	10	0
	92	24	3	0	95	24

VIV WOODWARD

TED WORRALL

A solid right-back, Ted Worrall took over from Ted Charlton just after World War One. He was born John Edwin Worrall in Buxton on 2 October 1891, but was better known as Ted. He joined Sheffield Wednesday in 1910 and played 103 League games for them before the Football League was suspended in 1915. Worrall came south after the war to find work and was given a free transfer so that he could join Fulham. He made his debut against West Ham in November 1919 and was soon forming a fine full-back partnership with Alec Chaplin. After losing his place to Tom Fleming, Worrall moved to Aberdare Athletic in 1923 who were then a League club. After 50 appearances for the Welsh club he moved to another now defunct club, New Brighton, in the summer of 1923. He was ever-present in the next two seasons at Wallasey before a final move to Southport. He was again ever-present with the seaside club. He left League football in 1929 and died in Chesterfield on 24 September 1980 at the age of 88. Worrall was a cousin of the legendary goalkeeper, Sam Hardy.

	LEAGUE		FA CUP		TOTAL	
	App	Gls	App	Gls	App	Gls
1919-20	20	0	0	0	20	0
1920-21	38	0	5	0	43	0
1921-22	25	0	3	0	28	0
1922-23	5	0	0	0	5	0
	88	0	8	0	96	0

149

This skilful, speedy winger became a firm favourite with the crowd and established an excellent right-wing partnership with Trevor Smith. He was born in Stockport on 20 September 1911, and his first club was Altrincham. Worsley joined Bolton Wanderers as an amateur but was released to join Cheshire League club Manchester North End. He stayed three seasons before transferring to Leeds United as an amateur in August 1933, signing as a professional the following January. He played only three games for the Elland Road outfit before moving to Fulham in June 1935. He played in their fine FA Cup run to the semi-final in his first season at the club. Never a regular because of injuries, he averaged about 25 games a season for the Cottagers. Worsley also appeared at inside-right later in his Fulham career, which was virtually ended with the outbreak of war. He did, however, make a surprise one-game comeback for Fulham at Derby County in August 1945. Worsley died at Denton on 25 June 1971, aged 59.

BERT WORSLEY

	LEAGUE		FA CUP		TOTAL	
	App	Gls	App	Gls	App	Gls
1935-36	29	9	4	1	33	10
1936-37	23	2	0	0	23	2
1937-38	19	1	0	0	19	1
1938-39	35	4	2	0	37	4
	106	16	6	1	112	17

Dashing centre-forward Eddie Perry scores Fulham's goal in the 1-1 draw with Bury at Craven Cottage in October 1936.

Millwall goalkeeper Alex Stepney is beaten by Johnny Key's header in the 3-3 draw between Fulham and the Lions in the FA Cup game at Craven Cottage in January 1965.

151

Fulham Players Who's Who

The qualification for inclusion in this biographical section is that a player should have made at least one first-team appearance for Fulham in a Football League, Southern League, FA Cup or League Cup match between 1903 and 1987, but not including the war seasons, 1915-19 and 1939-46. Surnames are given first, followed by Christian names where known. Nicknames appear in inverted commas. Playing positions have become less precise since the start of the 1970s, when central defenders, midfielders and strikers took over the more traditional positions of right-half, inside-left, etc.

In the career details of individual players, clubs have been given the title they held when the transfer took place. This is followed by the month and year, if known, when the player signed for that club. Transfer fees are given in brackets. Prior to 1939, such fees are generally accurate; since the war, however, fees have usually been taken from newspaper sources. Birth and death details, where known, are given. The abbreviation 'cs' means close season.

Note: Some 150 of Fulham's best-known players are excluded from this section and are to be found in the section 'Fulham Stars A-Z'.

ABEL, Samuel, (1933-4) Centre-forward.
Born: Neston, 30 December 1908. Played for Accrington Stanley 1930; Chesterfield March 1931; Fulham cs 1933 (£500); QPR cs 1934-46 (£400); also guested for Fulham in the war. Abel's time at Fulham was dogged by injury. He arrived at the Cottage as a promising young striker having scored 57 goals in 96 League games for his previous clubs. On moving to QPR, he was converted to full-back, playing in over 200 League, Cup and wartime games for the West London club.
10FL 1g.

ACHAMPONG, Kenneth, (1983-7) Forward.
Born: Kilburn, 26 June 1966. Joined Fulham as an apprentice August 1983 and signed professional June 1984. Very skilful forward who on his day can be a match winner. Nicknamed 'Pongo' by his team mates, Achampong does not score as many goals as he might. Forced to play up front because of a lack of strikers at the club but prefers midfield.
40/5FL 6g, 1FA, 4LC

AIMER, George, (1923-5) Left-back or half-back.
Born: Dundee, 27 October 1898. Died: 1935. Played for Dundee Hibs; Fulham cs 1923; Third Lanark 1925. Aimer played equally well at left-back or half-back during his spell at Fulham but was unable to obtain a regular first-team place. Spent most of his career in Scottish football.
16FL, 1FA

ALLEN, Albert Robert, (1934-7) Outside-left.
Born: Bromley by Bow, 11 October 1916. Played for Clapton Orient as an amateur 1933; Fulham 1934; Doncaster Rovers cs 1937; QPR cs 1938; Brentford in war; Northampton Town 1946; Colchester United 1947-51. Allen won England Schoolboy honours prior to joining Clapton Orient. His first-team appearances at Fulham were limited by the presence of Johnny Arnold. Found his greatest success at Doncaster Rovers and Colchester United where he was involved in a fine FA Cup run during their Southern League days.
11FL

ALLEN, Ralph Slack Littlewood, (1928-30) Inside-right.
Born: Newburn, 30 June 1906. Died: Blyth, 9 May

1981. Played for Wombwell; Sheffield Wednesday on trial; Dipton United; Fulham cs 1928; Brentford March 1931 (£275); Charlton Athletic October 1934 (£650); Reading June 1936; Northampton Town October 1936; Torquay United November 1938-9. Allen still holds Charlton's goalscoring record for a season with 32 goals in only 28 games in their Third Division Championship season of 1934-5. Worked down the pits when with Dipton. Later was a prolific scorer for Brentford reserves, scoring 101 goals in two seasons. His brother Jack played for Brentford and Sheffield Wednesday.
16FL 8g

ANDERSON, Edward, (1903-04) Outside-left.
Woolwich Arsenal circa 1901; Fulham 1903-04; QPR 1906-08. A fast and skilful winger, Anderson spent two seasons at Woolwich prior to coming to the Cottage. His spell in the first team was brief losing his place to Hugh McQueen. Found himself included in the general clear-out of players by new manager Harry Bradshaw in 1904.
6SL

AVEY, Frederick, (1928-32) Centre-forward.
Born: London. Played for Leyton (amateur); Fulham April 1928; Torquay United cs 1932. Fred won a winners medal with Leyton in the 1928 FA Amateur Cup Final victory over Cockfield. Scored 16 goals in his first full season at the Cottage, including two hat-tricks. In later seasons, he lost his form completely. Played Second XI cricket for Essex.
62FL 28g, 6FA 1g

AXCELL, A. Charlie, (1903-05) Utility player.
Born: Leigh on Sea, 1882. Played for Leigh Ramblers; Fulham as an amateur in 1903, signed professional January 1904; Burton United cs 1905; Stoke December 1906; Southend United 1907-09. Axcell was a jack of all trades, filling in where there were injuries, playing in most defensive and attacking positions. He had worked as a fisherman at Leigh-on-Sea prior to joining Fulham. His travels eventually took him home to Southend United.
17SL 4g, 1FA

152

AYRES, Harry, (1946-50) Centre-forward.
Born: Redcar, 10 March 1920. Played for Clapton; Fulham July 1946; Gillingham June 1950-54. Ayres was a free-scoring centre-forward in Fulham's reserves but was unable to find the same form in the League side. He lacked the killer instinct in the box. Skilful and enthusiastic, he found his best position of wing-half when he moved to Gillingham.
38FL 8g, 5FA 3g

BAILLIE J., (1930-31) Wing-half.
Born: Hamilton. Played for Derry Celtic and possibly Cardiff City; Fulham cs 1930. Baillie managed only two appearances for Fulham because Len Oliver so rarely missed a match through injury. Made his debut in a 6-2 victory over Bristol Rovers at the Cottage in November 1930.
2FL

BANKS, William, (1919-21) Inside-forward.
Born: Cramlington, Northumberland. Played for Ashington; Liverpool 1913; to Fulham, December 1919. Banks played only spasmodically in the Liverpool first team and missed out on a Cup Final appearance for the Reds in 1914. Formed a fine right-wing partnership with Billy McDonald just after the war for Fulham. He eventually lost his place to Danny Shea.
40FL 12g, 3FA

BANTON, Geoffrey, (1978-82) Centre-half.
Born: Ashton-under-Lyme, 16 March 1957. Played for Bolton Wanderers as apprentice professional; Plymouth Argyle May 1975; Fulham July 1978; Dunstable 1984. Served his apprenticeship at Bolton but was discarded before making the first team. Never good enough to establish himself at either Plymouth or Fulham as his positional sense and reading of the game often let him down. High spot of his period at the Cottage was scoring two goals at Upton Park in a surprise 3-2 victory over West Ham in March 1980.
37FL 3g, 6FA, 2LC

BARNETT, Gary, (1984-) Midfield.
Born: Stratford-upon-Avon, 11 March 1963. Played for Coventry City as an apprentice; Oxford United July 1982 (Free); Wimbledon February 1983 (on loan); Fulham December 1984 (on loan); signed permanently Sept 1985 (£20,000). A busy, mobile forward whose lack of weight often inhibits his effectiveness. Played 99 games for Oxford in his four-year spell at the Manor Ground. He matured greatly when he signed permanently for Fulham and finished 1986-7 as the second-highest scorer.
76/4FL 16g, 6FA 1g, 8LC 2g

BATTY, Laurence William, (1984-) Goalkeeper.
Born: Westminster, 15 February 1964. Played for Farense (Portugal) February 1981-3; Maidenhead United; (on loan); Fulham signed professional cs 1984. Known as 'George' to everybody at the club, Batty spent most of his teenage years in Portugal. Signed professional at 17 with Portuguese Second Division club, Farense, where he stayed three seasons. After being loaned to Maidenhead United for a season by Fulham, Batty returned to the Cottage and made his debut against Grimsby Town in September 1984.
4FL

BELFITT, Rodney M., (1974) Centre-forward.
Born: Doncaster, 30 October 1945. Played for Retford Town; Leeds United July 1963; Ipswich November 1971; Everton November 1972; Sunderland October 1973; Fulham Novmber 1974 (on loan); Huddersfield Town February 1975. A member of Leeds squad during their great years and, although not a regular, he appeared in their Fairs Cup-winning side of 1968 and came on as substitute against Arsenal in the 1968 League Cup Final victory. Did not score as many goals as would be expected for a forward. His spell at Fulham was brief and not particularly successful.
6FL 1g

BELL, Mark Dickson, (1904-07) Outside-right.
Born: Edinburgh, 1881. Played for Roseberry Junior Club; St Bernard's (Edinburgh); Hearts October 1900; Southampton May 1902; Hearts April 1903; Fulham cs 1904; Clapton Orient cs 1907; Leyton 1910-12. Bell was a fine sprinter who used his speed to great effect on the right wing. Joined Hearts around 1900 and won a Scottish cap against Wales in a 1-1 draw at Wrexham in March 1901, and a Scottish Cup winners' medal in Hearts' fine 4-3 win over Celtic the following month. Bell joined Fulham in the summer of 1904, one of many Scottish players signed by new manager Harry Bradshaw at that time. Later played as a right-half for Clapton Orient and Leyton, for whom he made a combined total of 133 appearances between 1907-12. Reappeared briefly for Fulham in wartime soccer. Later emigrated to Australia.
59SL 4g, 3FA

BELLAMY, James T., (1914-15) Outside-right.
Born: Barking, 1885. Played for Reading 1903; Woolwich Arsenal 1904; Dundee 1906; Portsmouth 1907; Norwich City 1908; Dundee 1908; Motherwell 1911; Burnley 1912 (£1,000); Fulham cs 1914; Southend United 1919-20. Jim was a tricky, fast and skilful winger. A much-travelled player, he once commanded a £1,000 fee when moving from Motherwell to Burnley in 1912. However he was never a big success in England, reserving his best performances for the Scottish League. Played in Dundee's Cup-winning side of 1910 when they beat Clyde in a second replay.
17FL 1g

BERRY, Arthur, (1909-10) Outside-right.
Born: Liverpool, 3 January 1888. Died: Liverpool, 15 March 1953. Played for Denstone School; Wadham College (Oxford) and Oxford University; Fulham September 1909; Everton 1910; Wrexham 1911; Liverpool 1912; Oxford City 1913. A direct winger with few frills, he was one of the best amateurs of his time. Berry studied Law at Oxford and was capped for England whilst still attending university in 1909. As he was not available every week, he lost his place to James Smith and moved to Everton in 1910, playing some of his best football at Goodison. Berry played regularly for Oxford City and appeared in their 1913 Amateur Cup Final side which lost 1-0 to South Bank. Retired in 1913 to concentrate on his legal career. His father was a director of Liverpool and chairman from 1904-09. He gained 32 England Amateur caps including two Olympic gold medals in 1908 and 1912.
12FL

BERTRAM, George, (1919-21), Inside-forward.
Born: Brandon, County Durham, 15 January 1896.
Died: 1963. Played for Durham City; Fulham December
1919; Brentford cs 1921; South Shields and Middlesbrough during World War One. Played at inside-
forward and on the right wing during his spell at
Fulham. Played ten games for Brentford scoring two
goals in season 1921-2.
15FL 2g

BEVAN, Frederick Edward, (1907) Centre-forward.
Born: Hackney, summer 1880. Played for Millwall
Athletic May 1899; Manchester City April 1900; Reading
cs 1903; Queen' Park Rangers cs 1904; Bury cs 1906;
Fulham August 1907; Derby County November 1907;
Clapton Orient cs 1909; Retired 1913; Coach at Clapton
Orient from 1920-3. An ideal centre-forward, bold,
strong and fast with a terrific shot. Scored 119 goals in
his 320 Football League games but netted only one for
Fulham. Left the Cottage in mysterious circumstances
after a disastrous six-goal defeat at Barnsley. His best
season was 1904-05 when he scored 18 goals for QPR.
5FL 1g

BEWLEY, David G., (1946-53) Utility player.
Born: Bournemouth, 22 September 1920. Played for
Wolves as an amateur; Poole Town; Bournemouth;
Gravesend United; Fulham 1945; Reading March 1950;
Fulham again November 1950; Watford May 1953-6.
Scored his only goal for Fulham at Luton Town in
March 1948 in a 3-0 victory. Bewley won England
Schoolboy honours before joining Wolves. His most
successful period was at Watford where he made 113
appearances for the Hornets.
17FL 1g, 1FA

BIGGAR, Frederick William, (1903-04) Goalkeeper.
Born: Blaydon-on-Tyne, 1877. Died: 11 July 1935.
Played for Sheffield United 1899; West Ham United cs
1902; Fulham cs 1903; Watford cs 1904; Rochdale cs
1910-15. Reserve to Jack Fryer at Fulham and Billy

'Fatty' Foulke at Sheffield United. It was only at
Watford and Rochdale that Biggar was first-choice
'keeper. He played 217 Southern League games for
Watford, being ever present from 1906-09.
6SL, 3FA

BINKS, Sidney, (1928-30) Centre-half.
Born: Bishop Auckland, 1899. Played for Portsmouth;
Southend United cs 1928; Fulham March 1929; Chesterfield cs 1930-2. Binks had a lengthy spell in the Fulham
first team during season 1929-30 when Jock McNab
was injured. This included an experimental appearance
at centre-forward against his former club, Southend.
Binks helped Chesterfield to the Third Division North
Championship in 1931, playing 29 games, but was not
good enough for Second Division football.
27FL, 2FA

BIRD, Sidney, (1928-32) Left-back.
Born: Lemington-on-Tyne. Played for Scotswood FC;
Fulham cs 1928 (£250); Walsall cs 1932-5. Orthodox
back who lacked that extra ability to sustain a first-
team spot at the Cottage. Bird had an extended run at
left-back in season 1930-31 when he played 24 League
and Cup games for Fulham. Found more success at
Walsall and was ever-present in season 1932-3.
43FL, 3FA

BOLAND, Charles, (1922-3) Inside-left.
Born: Kilmarnock, 5 October 1895. Died: February
1969. Played for Queen of the South; Fulham March
1922. Boland scored on his debut at Barnsley in March
1922. One of many Scottish inside-forwards to play for
Fulham over the years but unable to make the grade at
the Cottage.
3FL 1g

BOLAND, George 'Dicky', (1929-31) Outside-left.
Born: Marley Hill, 6 October 1902. Died: Durham
North, summer 1977. Played for White-le-Head; Hartlepools United 1925; Reading 1928; Fulham cs 1929;
Gateshead cs 1931; Crewe Alexandra cs 1934-5. Boland
won honours in the North Eastern League with White-
le-Head prior to joining Hartlepools. Small and fast, he
lacked the ability to play at the highest level. Enjoyed
his most sucessful periods with United and Gateshead
where he played almost 100 games.
6FL

BOOT, Leonard George W., (1925-6) Goalkeeper.
Born: West Bromwich, 4 November 1899. Played for
Huddersfield Town circa 1923; Fulham cs 1925; Bradford
City cs 1926; Nottingham Forest cs 1927-8. Boot had a
handful of games in Huddersfield's first team during
their Championship seasons from 1923-5. He was never
the first-choice 'keeper at any of his clubs. Understudy
to Arthur Reynolds and then Ernie Beecham at the
Cottage.
9FL

BORLAND, William, (1910-11) Centre-half.
Born: Darvel, Scotland 1890. Played for Darvel Juniors;
Fulham 1910. Borland played three games for Fulham
over Easter 1911 when Fred Mavin was injured. Joined
the Cottagers from his home-town club where he had
also represented his county. After one season at the
Cottage he disappeared from the League scene.
3FL

BOWERING, Ernest George, (1912-13) Left-half.
Born: Wandsworth, 30 March 1891. Died 23 November 1961 at Tonbridge. Played for Tottenham Thursday; Tottenham Hotspur circa 1911; Fulham 1912; Merthyr FC cs 1913. Signed by Spurs from local football, Bowering made seven appearances in their First Division side in season 1911-12. Played only once for Fulham, in April 1913 in a 3-1 victory over Lincoln.
1FL

BOWIE, Jimmy D., (1951-2) Inside-forward.
Born: Aberdeen, 9 August 1924. Played for Park Vale (Aberdeen); Chelsea 1944; Fulham January 1951; Brentford March 1952; Watford July 1952; Bedford Town 1956; Fulham 1957; March Town cs 1958; Wisbech Town December 1959. Bowie was a typical Scottish inside-forward, a bundle of energy with a fiery temperament. In 1944, he played at Wembley in a wartime Cup Final between Chelsea and Charlton. He came to Fulham in exchange for Wally Hinshelwood. Later scored 39 goals in 124 appearances in four seasons at Watford.
33FL 7g, 4FA

BOYD, Gordon, (1978-9) Midfield.
Born: Glasgow, 27 March 1958. Played for Glasgow United; Eastercraig; Glasgow Rangers 1977; Fulham cs 1978; Glasgow Rangers again cs 1979; Barnsley June 1980; Scunthorpe United cs 1981-2. Boyd won Scottish Schoolboy and Youth international honours as a youngster. A hard working midfield player who made up in effort what he lacked in skill. Never played in Rangers' first team.
1/2FL, 0/1LC

BRADLEY, Robert, (1929-30) Full-back.
Born: Washington, 20 September 1906. Died: Carlisle, 18 February 1934. Played for Bishop Auckland; Newcastle United March 1927 (£100); Fulham May 1929 (£175); Tunbridge Wells Rangers cs 1930; Carlisle United circa 1932 until his death, when he was only 27 years old. A well-built full-back whose career only blossomed after joining Carlisle for whom he played 70 games until his untimely death.
6FL

BRADSHAW, Joseph, (1906-09) Outside-right.
Born: Lancashire, circa 1880. Played for Fulham 1904-09; Chelsea 1909-10; Southend United player-manager 1910-15. Bradshaw was an average winger who had a few outings while his father was manager at Fulham. His managerial career, which took in Southend, Swansea, Fulham and Bristol City, lasted longer and was more successful. (See *Fulham Managers*).
3SL, 3FL

BRADSHAW, Will, (1904-05) Outside-right.
Played for Woolwich Arsenal circa 1902; Fulham cs 1904; Burton United cs 1905; Fulham reserves briefly in 1909; Ton Pentre December 1909. Bradshaw arrived from Arsenal at the same time as Joe Bradshaw and may have been related. A skilful winger who had few opportunities to shine at the Cottage. He played 69 games scoring 13 goals in two seasons at Burton United before they were voted out of the Football League and replaced by Fulham in 1907. Moved to Canada in 1910, after playing for a season at Ton Pentre, who at that time played in the Southern League Second Division.
5SL 2g

BRATHWAITE, John Roderick, (1984-7) Striker.
Born: Isleworth, 19 December 1965. Played for Fulham (professional July 1984). On monthly contracts from July 1985-May 1986, then signed full professional again. Won four England Schoolboy caps before signing for Fulham. Made his debut at Bradford City (Odsal) in April 1986. A skilful forward who, if he was able to score more often, would find a regular first-team spot.
7/5FL 2g

BROOKS, John, (1924-5) Right-back.
Born: Stockton, 13 March 1904, Died: Stockton, 30 March 1973. Played for Stillington St Johns; Fulham cs 1924; Darlington cs 1926; Nelson March 1928; York City cs 1929-32. Brooks was awarded a gold medal when he gave blood to help save the life of trainer Elijah Morse who lost an arm in a car crash *en route* to a reserve match. Found more success in Third Division soccer, playing 36 games for Darlington in 1927-8 and was ever-present for York City in season 1930-31.
9FL

BROOKS, Leonard Walter, (1935-7) Goalkeeper.
Born: Manningtree, Essex 1913. Played for Fleet (Aldershot League); Fulham as an amateur cs 1935; Bournemouth cs 1937-9. Brooks was reserve goalkeeper to Alf Tootill at Fulham after his arrival from Fleet in 1935. Played regularly for Bournemouth until they closed down for the duration of the war.
2FL

BROWN, (1922-3) Centre-forward.
Little-known forward who made only one appearance, in a 2-1 defeat at Bradford City in December 1922.
1FL

155

BROWN, Michael, (1961-5) Inside-forward.
Born: Slough, 11 April 1944. Joined Fulham as an apprentice September 1961 and signed professional April 1962; Millwall February 1965; Luton Town July 1967; Colchester United October 1968-9 (£3,000); Wealdstone; Maidstone United; Tonbridge; Hillingdon Borough. Brown was unable to establish himself in the Fulham team and moved down a couple of divisions to join Millwall where he found more regular first-team football. Played 122 League games scoring 25 goals for his four League clubs before spending many years in non-League football.
4FL, 1LC 1g

BROWN, Robert H., (1960-61) Centre-forward.
Born: Streatham, 2 May 1940. Played for Barnet; Fulham October 1960 as an amateur; Watford November 1961 as a professional; Northampton Town December 1963; Cardiff City October 1966-7. Bobby Brown made a name for himself in amateur football with Barnet. He won 14 England Amateur caps, some whilst a Fulham player, and scored two goals in Barnet's FA Amateur Cup Final defeat by Crook Town in 1959. On target regularly for all his League clubs, scoring 60 in only 137 Football League appearances.
8FL 4g

BROWN, Thomas Frank, (1926-7) Right-back.
Born: Darlington. Played for Percy Main; Newcastle United; Fulham cs 1926; Charlton Athletic June 1927. Tommy Brown had a run in the Fulham first team during 1926-7. He made no Football League appearances with his other clubs. Moved to Charlton with Tommy Wolfe.
11FL, 2FA

BROWN, William, (1929-30) Inside-forward.
Born: Fence Houses near Chester-le-Street, 22 August 1899. Played for Hetton FC (Durham); West Ham United 1920; Chelsea March 1924; Fulham cs 1929-30. Brown won his one England cap against Belgium in 1924 when he scored in a 2-2 draw in Antwerp. He played in the first Wembley Final for West Ham but ended up on the losing side, although he helped the Hammers to promotion to the First Division the same season. Surprisingly, he played only 116 League games altogether for West Ham, Chelsea and Fulham.
2FL

BUCHANAN, Peter Symington, (1946-7) Outside-right.
Born: Glasgow, 13 October 1915. Played for Wishaw Juniors; Chelsea February 1936; Fulham 1945; Brentford August 1947; Headington United 1949. Orginally came south to join Chelsea in 1933 but was so homesick was sent back to Scotland. Buchanan was a very skilful winger who gained one Scottish cap against Czechoslovakia in 1938. His career was affected by the war but he often played as a guest for Fulham. He eventually signed permanently for the club, but played only in the first post-war season.
20FL 1g, 1FA

BUCKLEY, Ambrose, (1933-9) Left-back.
Born: Brinsley (Notts), 31 January 1909. Died: 2 September 1968 in Manchester. Played for the Army 1927-33; Fulham May 1933-43; Doncaster Rovers during wartime; Stockport County 1946-7. Buckley represented the Army 14 times and played in the Army Cup Final three years running for Sherwood Foresters before signing professional forms for Fulham in 1933. A fearless defender who was still not good enough to dislodge Mike Keeping from the first team.
6FL

BURNS, Robert, (1909-11) Inside-forward.
Born: Scotland. Played for the Army, 1903; Salisbury City; Heart of Midlothian 1908; Fulham January 1910-11. Burns came to the Cottage with a big reputation but was never a great success, finding himself in and out of the first team. Scored a hat-trick against Stockport in March 1911. He also scored four goals for Hearts in a Scottish First Division game. Played for the Army for five seasons and assisted Salisbury City when possible, before signing for Hearts.
18FL 7g

BURNS, Thomas, (1910-13) Full-back.
Born: Fulham circa 1891. Died: Wandsworth, August 1921. Played for Clapham; Shaftesbury Athletic; Tooting Graveney; Fulham cs 1910; retired through injury in 1913. Burns was signed from local parks football and beginning to shape up to being a fine full-back when injury cruelly ended his career in his early 20s. He was 30 when he died in an accident at Wandsworth Gasworks.
35FL, 1FA

BURVILL, Glen, (1986) Midfield.
Born: Canning Town, 26 October 1962. Played for West Ham United 1980; Aldershot August 1983; Reading March 1985; Fulham on loan March 1986; Aldershot cs 1986. Burvill had a brief period at Fulham on loan near the end of season 1985-6. A left-sided midfield player, he showed a lot of skill but not enough application. He made 16 appearances for Reading in their Third Division Championship season of 1985-6 but was released at the end of that season.
9FL 2g

BYRNE, Johnny J., (1968-9) Centre-forward.
Born: West Horsley, Surrey, 13 May 1939. Played for Effingham School; Epsom Town; Guildford City Youth; Surrey Youth and County; Crystal Palace May 1956; West Ham United March 1962 (£58,000); Crystal Palace February 1967 (£45,000); Fulham March 1968 (£25,000); Durban City (South Africa) June 1969, as manager August 1972; Hellenic (Cape Town) Manager 1973. Johnny won 11 full caps, seven Under-23 caps, Youth and Schoolboy honours for England and represented the Football League three times. He also

156

won an FA Cup winners' medal in 1964 and a League Cup runners-up medal in 1966, both with West Ham. 'Budgie' was one of the finest centre-forwards of his time. Converted to half-back during his spell at Fulham when he was past his best.
16/3FL 2g

CÆSAR, William Cecil, (1926) Centre-half.
Born: Battersea, 25 November 1889. Played for Dulwich Hamlet; Fulham April 1926; Harwich and Parkeston; Walsall 1928; Brentford 1929; Hayes; Leyton; Civil Service November 1931. Bill Cæsar was a famous amateur centre-half of the 1920s who occasionally turned out for Football League clubs during an injury crisis. He won two England Amateur international caps and played in the 1931 FA Amateur Cup Final for Hayes. Played one game for Somerset at cricket in 1923 and had to wait 24 years for his next county championship game, for Surrey in 1946. He was a good medium-pace bowler.
1FL

CAMP, Stephen, (1975-7) Forward.
Born: Manchester, 8 February 1954. Played for Leatherhead; Fulham September 1975; Peterborough United August 1977; Leatherhead 1978. Came late into professional football after studying for an accountancy degree at Manchester University. Made only a handful of appearances in his spell at the Cottage. After seven appearances for Peterborough, Camp spent many seasons playing for Leatherhead.
4/1FL

CANNON, George F., (1914-15) Centre-forward.
Born: Hammersmith. Played for Tooting FC; Fulham cs 1914; Brentford 1919-20. Cannon's career was hampered by World War One. He played only a handful of games during the hostilities and did not find much success at Brentford after the war.
6FL 5g

CARLTON, David G., (1968-73) Midfield.
Born: London, 24 November 1952. Played for West Ham United's youth team; Fulham apprentice August 1968, signed professional January 1970; Northampton Town October 1973; Brentford October 1976; Northampton Town September 1980-2. Spent much of his career in lower division football. Rather unfairly compared with Johnny Haynes when signed as a professional. Whilst not making the grade at the Cottage, Carlton went on to play over 300 games for Brentford and Northampton and proved a steady Third Division footballer.
5/4FL, 2LC

CARR, Clifford Paul, (1980-87) Left-back or midfield.
Born: Clapton, 19 June 1964. Played for East and Inner London Schools; joined Fulham as an apprentice June 1980, signed professional June 1982. Carr won England Under-21 international honours against Finland in October 1984. He progressed through Fulham's youth scheme as captain, playing in a left-sided midfield role but was converted to full-back after a few games in the first team. Made Fulham's captain after the departure of Ray Lewington to Sheffield United in the summer of 1985. Carr was transferred to Stoke City in July 1987.
136/9FL 14g, 4FA, 13LC 2g

CARTER, Robert, (1907-08) Outside-right.
Born: Sunderland. Died: Sunderland, 1927. Played for Burslem Port Vale 1904; Stockport County 1907; Fulham March 1908; Southampton March 1909-10. Father of the great Raich Carter, he had a very good goal ratio to appearances but was allowed to leave for Southampton. He scored 23 goals in 83 games for Port Vale between 1904-07. Had pluck, enterprise and was as slippery as an eel. Would shoot for goal at every opportunity.
10FL 7g

CHAMPION, Percy Arthur, (1913-14) Outside-left.
Born: Lewes, 1887. Played for Fulham 1913-14. A left-winger who played only two first-team games, the first at Nottingham Forest in April 1913 and the second and last at home to Glossop in January 1914.
2FL

CHENHALL, John C., (1953-8) Right-back.
Born: Bristol, 23 July 1927. Played for Arsenal 1945; Fulham July 1953; Guildford City cs 1958. A big, beefy full-back affectionately known as 'Garth' during his time at the Cottage. He played only 16 games during his eight-year stay at Highbury prior to joining Fulham but was ever-present in his first season at the Cottage.
91FL, 4FA

CLEMENT, David T., (1980-81) Right-back.
Born: Battersea, 2 February 1948. Died: Putney, 31 March 1982. Played for Queen's Park Rangers July 1965; Bolton Wanderers June 1979; (£165,000) Fulham October 1980; Wimbledon October 1981. Dave Clement met a tragic end, committing suicide through depression after breaking his leg playing for Wimbledon. He lived for football and his career had been one of great success. Clement played over 400 games for Rangers whom he helped to runners-up in Division One in 1976. As well as winning Youth international caps, he was capped five times for England at full level.
17/1FL, 2FA

CLIFFORD, R., (1911-12) Left-half.
Born: Scotland. Played for Trabbock FC; Bolton Wanderers circa 1903; Everton November 1908; Fulham October 1911-12. Followed the same path to Fulham as Wattie White. Played at right-half for Bolton in the 1904 FA Cup Final defeat against Manchester City at the old Crystal Palace arena. Played at left-back and left-half for Fulham. Appeared 141 times for Bolton between 1903-08.
8FL

CLUTTERBUCK, Henry James, (1904-05) Goalkeeper.
Born: Wheatenhurst near Gloucester. Died: 19 December 1948. Played for Hereford Thistle; Small Heath cs 1897; Queen's Park Rangers May 1899; Grimsby Town May 1901; Chesterfield cs 1902; New Brompton cs 1903; Fulham cs 1904; retired cs 1905. Clutterbuck was first-choice 'keeper at Small Heath, Queen's Park Rangers, Chesterfield and New Brompton but only deputy to Jack Fryer at Fulham. A sound, cool and clever custodian who played almost 200 games between 1897 and 1905. Served Hereford along with the famous Sharp brothers, one of whom, Jack, later represented England at both soccer and cricket.
3SL

COATES, Walter Albert, (1919-21) Outside-right.
Born: Burnhope. Played for Fulham 1919; Leadgate Park; Leeds United 1921; Newport County 1925-6; Hartlepools United 1928-9. Won a Second Division Championship medal with Leeds United in season 1923-4 when he appeared 18 times. Played only two games for Fulham in September 1919 without really making his mark. After a successful season at Newport County, Coates moved out of League football for two years.
2FL

COLLINS, Kenneth, (1952-61) Left-back.
Born: Pontypridd, 11 October 1933. Played for Ynysybwl; Fulham May 1952; Bexleyheath 1961. A fine club man who performed consistently, mainly for Fulham reserves for nine seasons. Won many honours as a youngster including Welsh Youth international caps in 1952 and also represented Wales and Great Britain Boys' Clubs. Played two games in Cardiff City's 'A' team before deciding to sign for Fulham.
32FL, 1FA

COLVILLE, H., (1903-04) Right-half.
Played for Glossop North End 1898; Fulham 1903-04. After 105 games for Glossop between 1898 and 1902, Colville was unable to get in the first team for 1902-03 season and decided to try his luck at the Cottage. At the end of his initial season, he was one of the many victims of new manager Harry Bradshaw's mass clear-out of players.
6SL

CONNOR, Maurice Joseph, (1903-04) Centre-forward.
Born: Lochee, Ireland, July 1880. Died: August 1934. Played for Queen's Gordon Highlanders; Glentoran; West Bromwich Albion 1897; Walsall 1899; Bristol City 1901; Woolwich Arsenal 1902; Brentford 1902; New Brompton cs 1903; Fulham October 1903; Glentoran cs 1904. Connor was Fulham's first international when he represented Ireland against England in March 1904. He won two more caps whilst with Brentford. Connor did

not like to settle in one place for any length of time. He proved very successful in Cup games for Fulham but could not establish himself in the Southern League side.
12SL 1g, 8FA 7g

CONWAY, John, (1971-5) Outside-right.
Born: Dublin, 11 July 1951. Played for Bohemians (Ireland); Fulham August 1971 (£2,000); Winterthur (Switzerland) cs 1975. Conway was unlucky with injuries during his spell at Fulham and just when he seemed to be establishing himself he was sidelined. Similar in style to his more successful brother Jim. He married a German woman and moved to Switzerland.
30/8FL 6g, 3FA 1g, 4LC

COQUET, Ernest, (1913-15) Left-back.
Born: Durston-upon-Tyne, 6 January 1883. Died: Gateshead, 26 October 1946. Played for Sunderland 1905; Reading 1907; Tottenham Hotspur March 1908; Burslem Port Vale cs 1911; Fulham January 1913-15. Well-built full-back who was anything but polished, but wonderfully effective. He won a reputation in London soccer with Spurs, for whom he played 83 games between 1907-11. Played non-League football for Port Vale before signing for Fulham.
47FA, 2FA

CORNER, Brian, (1977-81) Midfield.
Born: Glasgow, 6 January 1961. Played for Celtic Boys club; Joined Fulham August 1977 as an apprentice, signed professional January 1979; moved back to Scotland May 1981. Corner won Scottish Schoolboy international honours before joining Fulham. A left-sided midfielder who had three outings in Fulham's first team before returning to Scotland and obscurity.
1/2FL

COTTINGTON, Brian Anthony, (1981-7) Right-back.
Born: Hammersmith, 14 February 1965. West London Schools; joined Fulham as an apprentice June 1981 and signed professional February 1983. Cottington won Republic of Ireland Youth international honours through having Irish parents. He was ever-present at full-back during season 1985-6 and was one of Fulham's more dependable performers in a disappointing season. His dogged determination and enthusiasm have helped him turn in some excellent displays.
67/6FL 1g, 1/2FA, 8/1LC

COX, George junior, (1936-7) Centre-forward.
Born: Warnham, Surrey, 23 August 1911. Died: Burgess Hill, 30 March 1985. Played for Arsenal December 1933; Fulham May 1936; Luton Town March 1937-8. Sussex cricketer 1931-60. Cox won more fame as a cricketer than a footballer where, like his father, he played for Sussex, scoring 22,944 runs, including 50 centuries. Most of his football career was spent in reserve-team football where he won many London Challenge Cup and London Combination medals with Arsenal. Renowned as a fine after-dinner speaker in his capacity as President of Sussex's Cricket Society.
5FL 3g, 1FA

COX, William Charles, (1929-30) Centre-half.
Born: West Ham, 31 July 1905. Died: West Ham, 19 November 1978. Played for Glico Works (West Ham); Ilford; West Ham United circa 1927-32; Fulham and West Ham during season 1929-30; Southend United cs 1932. Mystery surrounds Cox's appearances for Fulham as he also seems to have been a West Ham player at the same time.
5FL

CRANFIELD, Harold R., (1937-47) Outside-left.
Born: Chesterton, 1918. Played for Cambridge Town; Fulham 1937; Bristol Rovers June 1947-8. Due to the war, Cranfield had to wait nine years for his League debut for Fulham. His one and only appearance came in a 3-2 home victory against Millwall in October 1946.
1FL

CROCKFORD, Harold Arthur, (1917-21) Inside-forward.
Born: Derby, 25 September 1893. Died: Tunbridge Wells, December 1983. Played for Fulham 1917; Exeter City cs 1922; Port Vale cs 1923; Chesterfield October 1923; Gillingham March 1925; Accrington Stanley cs 1925; Walsall November 1925; Darlington cs 1926; Norwich City cs 1927-8. Crockford was unable to settle down in any one place. During 1925 alone, he played for three different clubs. A regular goalscorer with all his clubs, scoring 87 Football League goals altogether. Later in life he was a bookmaker at Stamford Bridge for many years and revisited the Cottage for Wilf Nixon's 100th birthday celebrations in 1982.
26FL 9g

CRONIN, Thomas P., (1950-56) Inside-forward.
Born: Richmond, Surrey, 17 December 1932. Played for East Sheen Athletic; Fulham September 1950; Reading June 1956-7. At the Cottage at the same time as Bobby Robson and Johnny Haynes, Cronin had few opportunities to break into the first team. Played 30 games for Reading before becoming a successful businessman.
2FL

CROSS, Roger G., (1971-3) Centre-forward.
Born: East Ham, 20 October 1948. Played for West Ham United July 1964; Orient (on loan) October 1968; Brentford March 1970; Fulham September 1971 (£30,000); Brentford December 1972 (£12,000); Millwall January 1977 as player-coach. A bustling centre-forward who found success with lower division clubs but not with West Ham or Fulham. Although he had a very powerful left-foot shot, Cross did not hit the target enough during his stay at the Cottage and was allowed to return to Griffin Park at a reduced fee. A dog-breeder, he exhibited at Cruft's.
39/1FL 8g, 3FA 2g, 3LC

CROSSLEY, F., (1912-13) Outside-left.
Born: 1894. Played for Elswick St Andrews; Birtley; Newburn; Fulham 1912-13. Signed from Newcastle area football, this little-known winger played only one game for Fulham, against Blackpool in January 1913.
1FL

CROSSTHWAITE, Herbert, (1907-09) Goalkeeper.
Born: Preston, 4 April 1887. Played for Blackpool; Fulham cs 1907 (£15); Exeter City May 1909; Birmingham cs 1910-14; Stoke 1919-20; A splendidly equipped goalkeeper, young, keen and determined. Reserve to Leslie Skene at Fulham, he found more success with Exeter and Birmingham. A cousin of H.Crossthwaite who played for Stockport County before the war, he joined Birmingham City police in 1910 as a constable and rose to the rank of inspector by 1925. Took part in professional walking races.
2FL

CUNNINGHAM, Hugh, (1966-8) Midfield.
Born: Kirkintilloch, Scotland, 5 April 1947. Played for Glasgow Celtic; Fulham May 1966-8. Cunningham did not appear in Celtic's first team and made only the briefest appearance for Fulham when he came on as substitute for the second half against Leicester City in January 1967. A hard-working wing-half who lacked that extra skill to make the grade.
0/1FL

159

CURTIS, John Joseph, (1913-14) Outside-right.
Born: Southbank, 13 December 1888. Died: Wimbledon, 1955. Played for South Bank St Peters; South Bank; Sunderland 1907; Gainsborough Trinity 1908; Tottenham Hotspur April 1909; Fulham cs 1913; Brentford cs 1914. Much was expected of Curtis after his successes at Gainsborough and Spurs. However, this speedy little winger lost his place after only two first-team outings, never to re-appear. In 1910 he played in an international trial match at Anfield.
2FL

DARVILL, Harvey Arthur, (1921-4) Inside Left.
Born: Watford, spring 1896. Died: Watford, 26 November 1924. Played for Ilford 1919; Fulham cs 1921. Darvill died four days after bursting a blood vessel during a match against Coventry City in November 1924. Very promising player who at one time managed to keep Frank Penn out of the side.
68FL 10g, 6FA

DAVIDSON, Alexander, (1903) Centre-forward.
Born: Beith, Scotland, 1879. Played for Third Lanark; Brighton United 1898; Glossop North End December 1899; Manchester City March 1900; Reading cs 1901; West Ham United cs 1902; Luton Town 1903; Fulham August 1903; New Brompton October 1903-04. Another much-travelled forward who stayed at Fulham for only one month, probably the shortest spell of any player at the club. Moved to New Brompton in exchange for Joe Connor. Davidson was a fringe player with all of his clubs but scored nine goals in 21 games for Reading in season 1901-02.
1SL, 1FA

DAVIDSON, Roger, (1970-71) Right-half.
Born: Islington, 27 October 1948. Played for Arsenal November 1965; Portsmouth June 1969; Fulham August 1970; Lincoln City October 1971; Aldershot February 1972. Davidson represented Middlesex, London and England Schools. A hard-tackling wing-half who made two first-team appearances whilst at Fulham and failed to prosper elsewhere.
1FL, 0/1LC

DAY, Clive A., (1977-83) Midfield.
Born: Orsett, 27 January 1961. Played for Fulham, signed apprentice July 1977; professional August 1978; Mansfield Town (on loan) September 1982; Aldershot August 1983-5; Grays Athletic in 1986. Won England Youth international honours in his early days at the Cottage. He was unable to establish himself in any set position but was a good utility player in the reserves. Made 73 appearances for Aldershot at left-back after leaving Fulham.
2/8FL, 0/1FA

DEAR, Brian C., (1969) Centre-forward.
Born: Plaistow, 18 September 1943. Played for West Ham United November 1960; Brighton March 1967 (on loan); Fulham February 1969 (£20,000); Millwall July 1969 (£20,000); Woodford Town; West Ham United October 1970; Retired 1971. Won England Schoolboy international honours and with West Ham won a European Cup-winners' Cup medal in 1965 and a League Cup runners-up medal in 1966. The highlight of his career was scoring five goals in 20 minutes for West Ham against West Brom in 1966. Dear finished as

Fulham's leading scorer in season 1968-9 with six goals in only 13 games. Weight problems ended his career at only 27.
13FL 7g

DENNISON, Robert Smith, (1935-9) Utility player.
Born: Ambleside, 6 March 1912. Played for Radcliffe United; Newcastle United May 1929; Nottingham Forest May 1934; Fulham June 1935-9; Joined Northampton as a player in the war; appointed manager March 1948; Middlesbrough manager July 1954 — January 1963; Hereford United 1963; Coventry City chief scout December 1967, assistant manager December 1968; retired in 1978 and became a part-time scout. One of a family of ten, he started his career at Newcastle as an inside-forward but was later converted to a grim, determined centre-half. Stayed with Northampton for 15 years as player and manager. Discovered Brian Clough when manager of Middlesbrough and also brought Peter Taylor to Ayresome Park.
31FL, 3FA

DEVAN, Charlie F., (1927-8) Inside-left.
Born: Girvan, Scotland. Played for Morton; South Shields cs 1924; Grimsby Town June 1925; Fulham May 1927. Devan joined Fulham with wing partner Frank McKenna. He was a stocky player, equally effective on right or left. Played 32 games during Grimsby's Third Division North Championship season of 1925-6.
7FL 2g

DIAPER, Albert, (1933-5) Half-back.
Born: Woolston near Southampton, 11 February 1909. Played for Cowes (IOW); Arsenal July 1928; Luton Town cs 1932; Fulham cs 1933; Charlton Athletic cs 1935; Aldershot cs 1936-9. Whilst with Cowes, Diaper was employed as an oarsman in the summer. After years of reserve-team football, he finally won a regular place in the Aldershot side. A cousin of Tom Parker of Arsenal.
3FL

DIGWEED, Perry M., (1976-81) Goalkeeper.
Born: London, 26 October 1959. Played for Fulham September 1976; Brighton January 1981 (£150,000); WBA (on loan) October 1983; Charlton Athletic (on loan) January 1985. Perry won England Youth and Under-21 international honours. He was allowed to

leave the Cottage as Fulham had a surplus of goalkeepers in 1981. Brighton paid what was an enormous fee for a goalkeeper with only 15 first-team games to his name. Discovered by Fulham playing in parks football and working on a fruit and veg stall in a local market.
15FL

DIXON, William A., (1909-11) Outside-left.
Born: Newcastle-upon-Tyne, circa 1888. Played for Willington Athletic; Crowbrook Villa; Newcastle City; Fulham March 1910; Plymouth Argyle December 1911; Barrow cs 1921. Dixon was a professional sprinter before going to the Cottage from Newcastle football but made only one appearance, at West Brom in March 1910. He then moved to Plymouth and played 162 games (31 goals) for Argyle helping them win the Southern League Championship in 1912-13.
1FL

DODDS, James, (1935-6) Centre-forward.
Born: Belfast 1914. Played for Linfield; Fulham 1935; Gillingham May 1936-7. Dodds' stay in English football was brief. He played only one game for Fulham, at West Ham in April 1936, before a short period at Gillingham. Won Irish Schools and Junior international honours.
1FL

DOHERTY, John M., (1954-62) Centre-forward.
Born: Stoneleigh, 26 April 1936. Played for Chelsea (amateur); Fulham signed professional September 1954; South Coast United (Australia) July 1962; Aldershot January 1965. A deep-lying and skilful centre-forward who at one time looked like becoming one of Fulham's best-ever frontmen. However, he lost confidence when he did not score often enough and emigrated to Australia. Returned three years later, became a successful accountant and still lives in the Stoneleigh area.
49FL 7g, 2FA 1g

DONNELLAN, Leo, (1985-7) Midfield.
Born: Brent, 19 January 1965. Played for Chelsea 1982; Orient (on loan) December 1984; Fulham cs 1985. Won Republic of Ireland Under-21 international honours whilst with Chelsea when he came on as substitute against England in March 1985. Busy, ball-winning mifielder.
46/7FL 4g, 5FA, 0/1LC

DOWDEN, William W., (1929-30) Centre-forward.
Born: London, 1902. Played for Wimbledon; Fulham cs 1929 as an amateur. Nicknamed 'the Doc', he was famous in amateur football circles and played for and managed Wimbledon for many years in their Isthmian League days. He won many medals in amateur football and appeared in Wimbledon's FA Amateur Cup Final side of 1933 when they lost 2-1 to Bishop Auckland.
1FL

DOWIE, John, (1972-7) Midfield.
Born: Hamilton, 12 December 1955. Played for Glasgow Rangers; Fulham signed apprentice May 1972, signed professional May 1973; Glasgow Celtic November 1977 (£20,000); Doncaster Rovers July 1979; Clyde 1981. Recently playing soccer in Sydney, Australia. A fine passer of the ball, he showed much promise as a youngster but was probably too tall and slow to be effective. He won Scottish Youth international honours

and helped them to the semi-final of the 'Little World Cup' in 1974. One of the few players to play for both Rangers and Celtic.
32/5FL 2g, 8/3FA 1g, 2LC

DOYLE, Francis, (1923-5) Inside-left.
Born: Glasgow, 20 November 1901. Played for Rutherglen Glencairn; Airdrieonians; Fulham cs 1923; Celtic March 1926. Went to the Cottage with a reputation built up from helping Airdrie to runners-up in the Scottish First Division the previous season. After two seasons in London, he returned to Scottish football.
30FL 9g, 1FA

DRAKE, Robert James, (1961-8) Right-back.
Born: Southgate, 7 September 1943. Played for Chelsea 1959; Fulham December 1961; Nuneaton Borough cs 1968; Hastings United cs 1969-81 as player and manager. Son of Fulham Life President, Ted Drake, Bobby Drake made occasional First Division appearances because of injuries to other players. He spent 12 years with Hastings United as player and manager. Rather slow, he struggled against the speedier wingers.
15FL

DREYER, John, (1986) Left-back.
Born: Alnwick, 11 June 1963. Played for Wallingford Town; Oxford United; Fulham (on loan) March 1986. Played briefly on loan at the end of 1985-6. Equally effective in midfield or full-back. He scored a memorable goal at Brighton from a free kick.
12FL 2g

DUCAT, Andrew, (1921-4) Wing-half.
Born: Brixton, 16 February 1886. Died: Lord's Cricket Ground, London, 23 July 1942. Played for Brewery Road School and Compton House School, Southend; Westcliffe Athletic; Southend Athletic; Woolwich Arsenal February 1905; Aston Villa June 1912 (£1,500); Fulham May 1921; retired cs 1924; Fulham manager 1924-26 and then reinstated as an amateur for Corinthian Casuals cs 1926. After an illustrious career with Arsenal and Villa, where he won six England caps and a Cup-winners' medal, Ducat finished his playing days with Fulham and succeeded Phil Kelso as manager. A stylish half-back and a favourite with supporters, Ducat's brief spell as manager was unhappy. He was also a Test cricketer, and died whilst batting at Lord's. (See *Fulham Managers*).
64FL, 5FA

161

DUDLEY, John O.C., (1930-32) Centre-half.
Born: Forest Gate, 1910. Played for Great Eastern
Railway (Romford); Fulham cs 1930-32 as an amateur.
Occasionally played for Fulham Reserves prior to
joining the club permanently. Spent most of his career
in amateur soccer.
14FL, 2FA

DUNCAN, David, (1911-12) Outside-left.
Born: County Antrim, Ireland, 1891. Played for Glasgow
St Anthony; Bellshill Athletic; Albion Rovers; Fulham
cs 1911; Woolwich Arsenal cs 1912-13. One of many
Scottish players signed by Fulham in the early decades
of this century. Stayed one season at the Cottage before
moving to Plumstead where he played three games. For
Fulham he appeared at inside-left as well as on the
wing.
9FL

DYER, Reginald E., (1925-30) Right-back.
Born: Bristol, 18 April 1900. Played for Bristol City
circa 1922; Fulham cs 1925; Tunbridge Wells Rangers
cs 1930. Reg was a solid, orthodox full-back who won
Division Three South Championship honours at Bristol
City in 1922-3. He played 48 Football League games for
City in all. Moved to Tunbridge with Robert Bradley.
98FL, 5FA

DYSON, Terence Kent, (1965-7) Outside-left.
Born: Malton, 29 November 1934. Played for Scar-
borough; Tottenham Hotspur April 1955; Fulham
June 1965; Colchester United August 1968; Guildford
City July 1970; Kings Lynn; Wealdstone manager 1974-5;
Borehamwood manager 1983-4; Kingsbury Town
Manager August 1985. Son of a famous jockey. Although
only 5ft 4in tall, he played in Spurs' double-winning
side of 1961 and had his greatest game in their 5-1
victory over Atletico Madrid in the 1963 European
Cup-winners' Cup Final when he scored two goals. His
career was in decline by the time manager Vic Buckingham
signed him for Fulham. Still busy in non-League
soccer.
21/2FL 3g, 1FA, 4LC 3g

EASSON, James Ferrier, (1939) Inside-left.
Born: Brechin, 3 January 1906. Died: Birmingham 20
May 1983. Played for Grange FC (Arbroath); Carnoustie
Panmuir; East Craigie (Dundee); Portsmouth 1928;
Fulham March 1939. Easson was a typically dazzling
Scottish inside-forward who got among the goals. He
scored 108 in 314 appearances for Pompey from 1928-39.
Won three Scottish caps and played in the 1934 FA Cup
Final when Portsmouth lost 2-1 to Manchester City.
3FL

EDELSTON, Joseph, (1920-25) Wing-half.
Born: Appleby Bridge, near Wigan. 27 April 1891.
Died: London, 10 March 1970. Played for St Helen's
Recreation; Hull City March 1913; Manchester City
June 1920; Fulham November 1920. After retiring, was
coach and assistant-caretaker manager at Fulham
(1925-37) and manager and scout for Brentford, Reading
and Leyton Orient. One of the most influential figures
at the Cottage in the inter-war period, Edelston spent
his final playing years with Fulham in the early 1920s.
He completed an impressive half-back line of over-30s,
with Ducat and Torrance. Unspectacular but solid as a
player, he went on to make a great contribution as
coach and, on two occasions, as caretaker-manager.
(See *Fulham Managers*).
67FL, 4FA

EDELSTON, Maurice, (1935-8) Inside-left.
Born: Hull, 27 April 1918. Died: 30 January 1976.
Played for Fulham 1935; Brentford 1938; Reading May
1939; Northampton Town July 1952. Played in Britain's
1936 Olympic team and won nine Amateur caps and
five wartime caps. He gave Reading and Northampton
great service during and after the war. In the 1960s he
became famous as a BBC radio football commentator.
His father, Joe, was a former Fulham player and
assistant manager.
3FL

EDGLEY, Frank, (1905-07) Centre-forward.
Born: Crewe, 1881. Played for Crewe Alexandra;
Sheffield United 1903; Fulham cs 1905; Reading October
1906; Hartlepools United 1909. Edgley had a terrific
shot and used his weight to good effect. His favourite
trick was charging goalkeeper and ball into the net. He
found most success at Reading.
15SL 6g

EDWARDS, David J., (1952-64) Wing-half.
Born: Treharris, 10 December 1934. Played for Treharris;
Fulham May 1952; moved to Australia June 1964.
Edwards had to be patient during his 12 seasons at the
Cottage and made only 41 appearances. He appeared at
wing-half and on the wing. His brother played for
Yeovil and Cambridge Town.
38FL, 2FA, 1LC

EDWARDS, Walter, 'Tommy', (1946-8) Outside-left.
Born: Llanelli, Wales, 13 February 1923. Played for
Workington; Fulham August 1946; Southend United
March 1948; Leicester City December 1948; Walsall
May 1952-3. Rarely found first-team football at any of
his clubs and made only three League appearances in
four seasons with Leicester. Moved to Southend with
Cyril Grant in March 1948.
2FL, 1FA

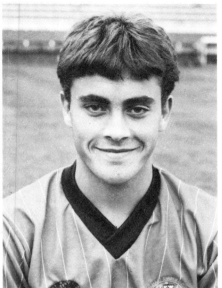

ELKINS, Gary, (1982-7) Full-back.
Born: Wallingford, 4 May 1966. Joined Fulham as an apprentice August 1982; signed professional October 1983. Elkins won 11 England Youth caps in 1984. Nicknamed 'Erko' by his team mates, he is a fine defender with an effective tackle. His career was seriously affected by a broken leg sustained in February 1986.
42/1FL, 0/1FA, 2LC

ELLIOTT, Frank F.G., (1954-6) Goalkeeper.
Born: Merthyr Tydfil, 23 July 1929. Played for Merthyr Tydfil; Swansea Town September 1949; Stoke City December 1952; Fulham March 1954; Mansfield Town July 1956-8. Signed as a stop-gap during an injury crisis. Elliott won a Welsh Cup winners' medal during his early career at Merthyr. Followed Charlie Mitten to Mansfield in 1956.
25FL, 1FA

ELLIOTT, Sidney D., (1927-8) Centre-forward.
Born: Sunderland. Played for Durham City circa 1926; Fulham cs 1927; Chelsea May 1928 (£3,600); Bristol City cs 1930; Notts County March 1932; Bradford City cs 1934; Rochdale cs 1935-6. Picked up for a small fee from Third Division Durham City, Elliott became top-scorer with 26 goals in his first and only season at the Cottage. Chelsea paid a record £3,600 for his signature in the close season of 1928. Not a great success at Stamford Bridge, but overall scored 90 Football League goals in 232 appearances for his seven clubs.
42FL 26g, 1FA

EVANS, Oswald, (1946-7) Goalkeeper.
Born: Llanelli, Wales, 2 September 1915. Played for Milford Haven; Fulham February 1946. Reputed to have weighed 20st. Played one Football League game, the first after the war when Fulham lost 7-2 at Bury.

Played some wartime games the previous season.
1FL

FABIAN, Aubrey Howard, (1934-5) Outside-right.
Born: Barnet, 20 March 1909. Died: Cranbrook, 6 September 1984. Played for Highgate School; Casuals and Corinthian Casuals 1928-46; Cambridge University 1929-31; Derby County 1932-3; Sutton United; Fulham December 1934—February 1935. Fabian had a colourful career in football and journalism. He was captain of the Cambridge University side, helped Derby to the FA Cup semi-final in 1933 and played for Casuals in their FA Amateur Cup victory of 1936. A schoolmaster at Highgate School and later contributed to *The Times*, *Daily Telegraph* and *FA News*. It was said of his play that he 'opened the game out wonderfully and was a very accurate passer of the ball'.
3FL

FARNFIELD, G.S., (1904) Outside-left.
Played for Cambridge University; Clapton; Fulham. One of five brothers who won Cambridge Blues and played for Clapton and one of whom, Eric, also played for Fulham during the war. Three of the brothers guested for Fulham in a Southern League game against West Ham in April 1904.
1SL

FARNFIELD, H.V., (1904) Inside-left.
Played for Corinthians; Clapton; Fulham; Cambridge University; New Crusaders. Played in the 1905 FA Amateur Cup Final for Clapton and won an England Amateur international cap in 1914. One of the leading lights of the New Crusaders Football Club. Later became a priest.
1SL

FARNFIELD, P.H., (1904) Centre-half.
Played for South Woodford; Woodford Clapton; Cambridge University; New Crusaders; Fulham. Played in the FA Amateur Cup Final of 1905 for Clapton against West Hartlepool (lost 3-2) with two of his brothers, P.H. and A.J. Won an England Amateur cap against France in 1907 and represented the Amateurs against Professionals at Craven Cottage in 1906.
1SL

FERGUSON, Robert L., (1925-6 and 1927-8) Outside-left.
Born: Stewarton, Ayrshire. Played for Stewarton; Fulham cs 1925; Coventry City September 1926; Fulham cs 1927 (£50). Signed twice for Fulham, from Stewarton and then Coventry. Had a successful season at City, playing 41 games and scoring four goals before returning to the Cottage. He scored the winning goal at Notts County in April 1928, thus preventing Fulham losing all their away games that season.
21FL 5g, 2FA

FISHENDEN, Paul, (1986) Forward.
Born: Hillingdon, 2 August 1963. Played for Wimbledon 1981; Napier City Rovers (New Zealand) 1981 (on loan); Karpola (Finland) 1982 (on loan); Fulham January 1986 (on loan). Orient (on loan) 1986. Played on loan for Fulham in early 1986 when it was thought that Dean Coney was going to be transferred to Portsmouth. His ball best season for the Dons was 1985-6 when he scored ten goals in 20 League games.
3FL

FISHER, Albert, (1903-04) Inside-left.
Played for Glasgow Celtic; Aston Villa; Fulham cs
1903; Bristol City cs 1904; Brighton cs 1905 and
possibly Manchester City cs 1906; Bradford cs 1907-08.
Fisher played in Fulham's first Southern League Division
One game and was then dropped. Played in four FA
Cup ties when the reserves represented Fulham in the
early qualifying rounds. Scored 13 goals for Bristol City
in 1904-05.
1SL, 4FA 2g

FISHER, George S., (1954-5) Right-back.
Born: Bermondsey, 19 June 1925. Played for Millwall
1942; Fulham November 1954; Colchester United
September 1955-9. Still scouting for Millwall in 1976.
Reliable and consistent full-back who played in a
wartime Wembley Final for Millwall in 1945. He played
almost 300 League games for Millwall and 163 for
Colchester after a brief spell at Fulham.
8FL

FITCHETT, Jack, (1905-07) Right-half.
Born: Manchester 1880. Played for Bolton Wanderers
1897; Manchester United 1902; Southampton 1903;
Plymouth Argyle cs 1903; Manchester United cs 1904;
Manchester City 1905; Fulham cs 1905-07. Past his best
by the time he joined Fulham from Manchester City.
Fitchett had represented the Football League three
times and played in an unofficial international against
Germany in 1901. After leaving football he became an
actor touring with the Karno Theatrical Company.
2SL, 1FA

**FITCHIE, Thomas Tindal, (1904-07 and 1912-13)
Inside-forward.**
Born: Edinburgh, 11 December 1881. Died: 17 October
1947. Played for West Norwood 1902-09; Woolwich
Arsenal 1901-05; Queens Park 1905-08; Fulham 1904-07;
Woolwich Arsenal 1908-09; Glossop 1909-12; Fulham
again October 1912-13. As an amateur, he tended to be
on the books of two or three clubs at the same time.
Described as 'the Prince of Dribblers', he remained an
amateur throughout his career due to business
commitments. Fitchie played only in Western League
matches for Fulham between 1904-07. Won four full
Scottish caps between 1905-07 whilst playing for Queen's
Park.
8FL 2g

FLANAGAN, John R. 'Pat', (1909-11) Inside-forward.
Born: Preston, circa 1891. Played for Verity's; Stourbridge; Norwich City 1907; Fulham cs 1909; Woolwich
Arsenal January 1911-15. Known as 'Little Jack',
probably because of his small stature, Flanagan, a
diminutive, scheming inside-forward, played regularly
for Norwich and Arsenal but could not establish
himself at Fulham.
11FL 1g, 1FA

FLETCHER, Harry Handley, (1903-05) Inside-right.
Born: Birmingham, 17 June 1873. Died: 30 November
1923. Played for Albion Swifts (Birmingham); Grimsby
Town 1892; Notts County March 1898; Grimsby Town
September 1900; Fulham cs 1903; Brentford November
1904; Grimsby Town October 1905-09, reserve trainer
for two years from August 1908. 'Ginger' Fletcher had
three spells with Grimsby Town, winning a Second
Division Championship medal in 1901. Fast, tricky, a

master of the intricate dribble and very versatile, he
played in an international trial in 1896 and won
Football league representative honours in 1899. He was
instrumental in helping Fulham to the first round
proper for the first time in 1904.
40SL 14g, 7FA 5g

FOLEY, Stephen, (1983-4) Midfield.
Born: Kirkdale, Liverpool, 4 October 1962. Played for
Liverpool signed professional September 1980; Fulham
(on loan) December 1983; Sheffield United August 1985.
Never made the first
team at Liverpool. Had a short spell at Fulham on loan
from the Reds during which he made his Football
League debut. Found greater success at Grimsby and
Sheffield United. He won three Central League
Championship medals at Liverpool.
2/1FL

FORBES, Alex R., (1957-8) Right-half.
Born: Dundee, 21 January 1925. Played for Dundee
North End; Sheffied United war; Arsenal February
1948; Leyton Orient August 1956; Fulham September
1957; Guildford City cs 1958. Originally a centre-
forward, converted to wing-half after joining Sheffield
United for a £40 fee. Red-haired, like his Arsenal
partner, Archie Macaulay, he was solidly built and a
firm tackler. Soon won Scottish international recognition
and was capped 14 times in all. Played in two FA Cup
Finals for Arsenal in 1950 and 1952 obtaining both
winners' and losers' medals. His weaknesses were a
sharp temper and an inclination to over-elaborate when
the situation called for a quick pass.
4FL

FORREST, Samuel, (1912-15) Centre-half.
Born: Paisley, December 1890. Played for Westmarch
1909; Petershill (Glasgow) 1911; Fulham cs 1912;
Reading November 1913; Fulham again cs 1914. One of
many discoveries in Scottish football at this time.
Manager Phil Kelso's scouts found Forrest playing in
Glasgow junior football. Spent nine months at Reading
before rejoining Fulham.
8FL

FRASER, John, (1969-76) Right-back.
Born: White City, 12 July 1953. Joined Fulham as an

164

apprentice 1969, signed professional June 1971; Brentford July 1976; Oxford City 1979. Played in Fulham's FA Cup Final side in 1975 because of injury to Les Strong just before the Final. A rather 'old-fashioned' full-back, short on pace but firm in the tackle. He left first-class football when only 26 to join Oxford City, then managed by Bobby Moore.
55/1FL 1g, 8FA, 2LC

FREEMAN, Walter, (1906-09) Inside-forward.
Born: Handsworth. Played for Lowestoft; Aston Villa; Fulham February 1906; Birmingham September 1909-11. Walter won a Southern League Championship medal with Fulham in 1906-07. His brother Bert played centre-forward for England, Everton and Burnley. Freeman had plenty of dash, strength and enthusiasm and could dribble and shoot in exemplary style. An electrician by trade.
21FL 9g, 35SL 12g, 6FA 3g

FRIEND, Barry N., (1973-4) Winger.
Born: Wandsworth, 13 October 1951. Played for Fulham's juniors and reserves 1967-70; Leatherhead 1970; Fulham as a professional October 1973; Leatherhead cs 1976; Slough; Carshalton Athletic. An orthodox winger who had two spells at Fulham. It was in the second period that he played three games in the first team. Spent much of his career in the Isthmian League.
2/1FL

GAGE, Larry Albert, (1948-50) Goalkeeper.
Born: London, 20 September 1922. Played for Walthamstow Avenue in the war; Fulham 1945; Aldershot July 1946; Canada 1947; Fulham August 1948; Gillingham June 1950-51. A former paratrooper, Gage began the 1948-9 season as fourth choice goalkeeper. An injury to Doug Flack on Easter Monday 1949, plunged Gage into the first team. In his three League games, Fulham won twice and drew once and the five points clinched the Second Division title.
3FL

GARNISH, Thomas Frederick, (1925-6) Outside-right.
Born: Wandsworth, 1900. Played for Wandsworth Town FC; Brentford 1923; Fulham cs 1925-26. Garnish spent two seasons at Griffin Park making 43 appearances for the Bees and scoring five goals from the right wing. Made just one appearance in Fulham's first team at South Shields in October 1925 in a resounding 5-2 defeat.
1FL

GARVEY, W.G., (1913-14) Left-half.
Born: London. Played for Metrogas FC; Fulham March 1913. Garvey was signed from local club Metrogas with William Taylor. Taylor stayed at the Cottage for eight years but Garvey stayed just one season. He managed only two appearances, at Blackpool and Huddersfield, in season 1913-14.
2FL

GAVIGAN, Peter, (1920-25) Outside-right.
Born: Glasgow, 11 December 1897. Died: Dundee, 2 March 1977. Played for Vale of Clyde; Fulham December 1920; Clapton Orient cs 1925; St Johnstone July 1927; Dundee; Dundee United. A Scottish winger who loved to take on a full-back, he was only 5ft 7½in but well-built. Being unable to hold a regular place in the

Fulham side, he moved on to Clapton Orient in 1925 where he made 61 appearances before returning to Scottish football.
71FL 1g, 6FA

GAYLE, Howard, (1980) Outside-right.
Born: Liverpool, 18 May 1958. Played for Liverpool November 1977; Fulham January — April 1980 (on loan); Newcastle United December 1982 (on loan); Birmingham City January 1983 (£100,000); Sunderland August 1984 (£70,000). Howard appeared in the European Cup semi final for Liverpool against Bayern Munich but otherwise had few opportunities at Anfield. When at Fulham, he played as a direct right-sided winger. Later in his career, Gayle gained a reputation as a hot-headed player and was accused by Sunderland manager, Lawrie McMenemy, of being a trouble-maker and given free transfer in summer 1986.
14FL

GIBSON, Harry, (1952-5) Right-half.
Born: Newcastle, 17 April 1930. Played for Spennymoor United; Fulham November 1952; King's Lynn cs 1955; Aldershot August 1956-7. Played one game for Fulham, at Plymouth in October 1954. After a season in the Southern League with King's Lynn, Gibson signed for Aldershot but appeared in only three games for the Shots.
1FL

GILCHRIST, John S., (1969-70) Full-back.
Born: Wishaw, Scotland, 5 September 1939. Played for Airdrie 1957; Millwall March 1961; Fulham July 1969; Colchester United July 1970. Joined Fulham in an exchange deal which took Brian Dear and Brendon Mullen to Millwall. He was a gritty, determined full-back who fitted in well with the Lions image in the 1960s. Played over 300 games for Millwall, helping them from the Fourth to the Second Division. Recently, his life has been threatened by a serious kidney illness and is now dependent on dialysis machine. Gilchrist won Scotland Schoolboy international honours as a youngster.
20/3FL 1g, 1FA, 3LC

165

GILROY, Joe, (1967-8) Inside-forward.
Born: Glasgow, 19 October 1941. Played for Montrose;
Queen's Park 1959; Clyde 1960; Fulham October 1967
(£20,000); Dundee September 1968 (£20,000); Highlands
Park (South Africa) 1973; Queen's Park (coach) 1979;
Brisbane Lions (Australia) coach. Gilroy was a part-
timer and schoolteacher when Fulham signed him from
Clyde in 1967. He put in some useful performances at
the Cottage but returned to Scottish football after just
11 months. He was troubled with injuries in his period
at the Cottage. After retiring, he coached in Iceland,
South Africa and Australia.
23/1FL 8g, 2FA 1g, 2LC 2g

GOLDIE, John 'Jock', (1908-11) Left-half.
Born: Hurlford, Scotland 1891. Played for Hurlford
Thistle; Fulham September 1908; Glossop July 1911;
Bury cs 1912-20; possibly Accrington Stanley 1921;
Kilmarnock 1922. Banned from football in 1923. A
similar player to his brother Billy but a little slower. A
good tackler and effective passer of the ball, Jock was a
regular performer for both Glossop and Bury. He was
banned for life from football in 1923 over a fixed game
between Bury and Coventry City which took place
three years earlier.
31FL, 2FA

GOODLASS, Ronald, (1980-82) Outside-left.
Born: Liverpool, 6 September 1953. Played for Everton
1969; NAC Breda (Holland) October 1977; Den Haag
(Holland) 1979; Fulham September 1980 (£30,000);
Scunthorpe United March 1982; Hong Kong cs 1982;
Tranmere Rovers November 1983; Barrow cs 1984.
Ronnie played in the same England Schoolboys side as
Chris Guthrie and joined Everton from school. He won
a League Cup runners-up medal in 1977 but his
appearances were generally rare. After a spell in Dutch
soccer, Goodlass signed for Fulham, but had lost much
of his speed.
21/1FL 2g, 5FA

GORE, Shaun Michael, (1986-7) Centre-half.
Born: Newham, 21 September 1968. Joined Fulham via
YTS Scheme July 1985 and signed professional May
1986. Made his debut when only 17 years old, straight
from the youth team. Very tall (6ft 4in) and commanding
central defender who should have a bright future.
12FL 1FA, 2LC

GRAHAM, Robert, (1904-05) Inside-right.
Born: Scotland. Played for Third Lanark; Fulham cs
1904; Third Lanark cs 1905. Graham was a highly
regarded and intelligent inside-forward who stayed one
season in English football, with Fulham. He won a
Scottish Cup runners-up medal in 1906 when Third
Lanark lost to Hearts 0-1.
23SL, 8FA 1g

GRANT, Cyril, (1946-8) Left-half.
Born: Wath upon Dearne, 10 July 1920. Played for
Mexborough FC; Lincoln City, signed in war; Arsenal
July 1946; Fulham December 1946; Southend United
March 1948-54. Signed with Dave Nelson from Arsenal
in exchange for Ronnie Rooke in 1946. Neither were
adequate substitutes for his loss. Joined Fulham as a
wing half but at Southend was converted to centre
forward scoring 62 goals in 174 games using his speed
and thrust.
14FL 4g, 1FA

GRAY, Archibald 'Baldie', (1912-14) Right-back.
Born: Govan, Scotland, 1883. Played for Hibernian;
Woolwich Arsenal cs 1904; Fulham April 1912 (£250).
An ashen-faced man, thin-lipped and as tense and eager
as a terrier, Gray learned his trade in Scottish football
with Hibernian. He won a Scottish Cup-winners' medal
with Hibs against Celtic in 1902, winning 1-0 in the
Final. Gray also gained one Scottish international cap
against Ireland in 1903 and represented the Scottish
League against the Irish League. He moved to Plumstead
in the summer of 1904 and struck up a fine partnership
with Jimmy Sharp who later played for Fulham. He
appeared in 183 League games for Arsenal before
joining Fulham in 1912. Also represented the Football
League whilst at Arsenal.
24FL, 1FA

GRAY, Peter 'Paddy', 1903-05) Centre-half.
Born: Glasgow. Played for Yoker Athletic; Partick
Thistle; Liverpool cs 1897; Grimsby Town May 1898;
Fulham cs 1903; Leyton cs 1905; Burton United June
1906-07. The brains of the defence, Gray was a great
strategist who worked out openings for the inside
forwards. Helped to establish Fulham as the leading
club in the South. Prior to joining Fulham, Paddy was a
regular performer for Grimsby Town, playing 121
games.
43SL 1g, 9FA

GREEN, Ellis, (1903-04) Right-half.
Played for Preston NE 1899; Brentford 1902; Fulham
cs 1903. Started his career at Preston, playing on the
wing, but was converted to wing-half at Brentford.
Soon lost his place to Harry Robotham after joining
Fulham from The Bees.
9SL, 4FA 1g

GREENAWAY, Brian J., (1974-82) Outside-right.
Born: London, 26 September 1957. Joined Fulham as

an apprentice April 1974, signed professional June 1975; Apoel (Cyprus) cs 1982; Wealdstone cs 1984. Greenaway was an industrious and wholehearted winger who progressed through the juniors. After eight seasons at the Cottage and being unable to gain regular first-team place, he tried his luck in Cyprus playing for Apoel (Nicosia). This period included playing in the European Cup in 1983. He helped Wealdstone to the non-League double in season 1984-5 of the FA Trophy at Wembley and the Alliance League championship.
68/17FL 8g, 7FA 1g, 2LC

GREENWOOD, Ron, (1955-7) Centre-half.
Born: Burnley, 11 November 1921. Played for Chelsea and Belfast Celtic in the war; Bradford 1946; Brentford March 1949; Chelsea October 1952; Fulham February 1955; coached Oxford University for three years and Walthamstowe Avenue for two years; Eastbourne United manager 1957; England Youth team manager; Arsenal assistant manager 1959; England Under-23 coach for two years; West Ham United manager April 1961; England manager 1976-July 1982; Brighton director November 1983. A stylish, unflappable centre-half who had his best playing days at Brentford and Chelsea. Gained an England 'B' cap in 1949 against Holland. He also won a League Championship medal with Chelsea in 1954-5. Won an enormous reputation as a manager for his tactical genius and knowledge of the game. Greenwood gained many honours with West Ham and had much success as the England manager.
42FL

GREGORY, Robert James, (1925-8) Left-back.
Born: Croydon, 26 August 1902. Died: London, 6 October 1973. Played for Fulham 1924; Norwich City cs 1928; Cricket for Essex and Surrey. Gregory was more renowned as a Surrey cricketer than a footballer and was on Surrey's books at the same time as Percy Fender and Andy Ducat, two other Fulham footballers. Bob's best season at the Cottage was 1926-7 when he played 27 games after Albert Barrett was injured. Never played in the Norwich first team.
37FL, 1FA

GREW, Mark Stuart, (1985) Goalkeeper.
Born: Bilston, 15 February 1958. Played for West Bromwich Albion June 1976; Wigan Athletic (on loan) December 1978; Notts County (on loan) March 1979; Leicester City July 1983; Oldham Athletic (on loan) October 1983; Ipswich Town March 1984; Fulham (on loan) September 1985; West Bromwich Albion (on loan) January 1986; Derby County (on loan) March 1986. Played in two semi-finals for West Brom in season 1981-2 in the FA Cup and League Cup. Known as the 'Lone Ranger' as he has so far played on loan for six clubs.
4FL

GRIFFITHS, Lew H., (1930-31) Centre-forward.
Born: Tonypandy, Wales. Played for Bristol Rovers 1925-26; Torquay United 1927; Crystal Palace cs 1928; Fulham cs 1930. One of many Welsh players to play for Bristol Rovers over the years. Crystal Palace bought him from Torquay after some impressive goalscoring for the Devon club and he scored 19 goals in his first season at Selhurst Park. Played just two games for Fulham in September 1930.
2FL

GUTHRIE, Christopher William, (1978-9) Centre-forward.
Born: Dilston, 7 September 1953. Played for Newcastle United December 1970; Southend United November 1972 (£10,000); Sheffield United, May 1975 (£100,000); Swindon Town July 1977 (£25,000); Fulham September 1978 (£65,000); Millwall February 1980 (£100,000); Willem II (Holland) 1982; retired through injury 1982. Guthrie was an excellent header of the ball who scored some spectacular goals during his spell at Fulham. Made his debut for Newcastle against Manchester United before 52,500 people. Found most success with lower division clubs. Had to retire through injury after joining Millwall. This led to a protracted court battle over the transfer-fee payments.
49/1FL 15g, 3FA, 2LC

HADDLETON, Arthur, (1932-3) Centre-forawrd.
Born: Manchester. Played for Southampton circa 1930; Fulham cs 1932; Swindon Town cs 1933; Walsall cs 1934-5. A little unlucky not to get a better chance at Fulham but Frank Newton kept him out of the side. Did not have much luck at Swindon or Walsall either.
4FL 4g

HALL, Joseph E., (1951-6) Inside-forward.
Born: Durham, 10 April 1934. Played for Sherburn Village; Newcastle United 'A' team; Fulham October 1951-6. Hall must be one of Fulham's unluckiest players. Shortly after making his debut at Sheffield Wednesday, in April 1956, he had to retire through injury due to a stomach complaint. Played for the Army during his National Service.
1FL

HALL, W., (1917-21) Inside-left.
Joined Fulham cs 1917. Hall made his debut in a London Combination match with West Ham United in September 1917 at right-half. When he played his final match against Blackburn in an FA Cup match he had been converted to inside-forward.
10FL 3g, 2FA

HAMILTON, John 'Jock', (1903-04) Centre-half.
Born: Ayr, 1872. Played for Ayr United; Wolves 1894-5; Loughborough 1896-97; Bristol City cs 1897; Gainsborough Trinity cs 1900; Watford April 1901; Wellingborough cs 1902; Fulham cs 1903, then trainer until 1910. Tough-tackling, dominant centre-half who ended his playing career at Fulham. First found fame at Bristol City and later played in the Football League for Gainsborough. A very popular trainer and much liked by the players.
12SL, 1FA

HAMILTON, Robert Cumming, (1906-07) Centre-forward.
Born: Elgin, 13 May 1877. Died: May 1948. Played for Glasgow Rangers; Fulham cs 1906; Glasgow Rangers cs 1907; Dundee 1910; Buckie Thistle circa 1914. Stylish centre-forward whose play was not appreciated by the Fulham crowd when he first joined the club from Rangers. Hamilton won many honours in Scottish football including 11 Scottish caps between 1899 and 1911; three Scottish Cup-winners' medals in 1898, 1903 and 1905; a runners-up medal in 1899; and four League Championship medals between 1899 and 1902. Spent one season at the Cottage but won a Southern League Championshiop medal. In the 1930s, Hamilton became the Lord Provost of Elgin, the town in which he was born.
28SL 11g, 4FA

HARRIS, George T., (1926-28) Left-back.
Born: High Wycombe. Played for Wycombe Wanderers; Southend United 1921; Notts County 1922; Queen's Park Rangers cs 1924; Fulham cs 1926-8. Scored his one and only League goal in his last appearance for Fulham at Clapton Orient in November 1927. Harris' best season was 1924-5 when he appeared for Queen's Park Rangers 25 times.
8FL 1g

HARRIS, Joshua 'Jack', (1925-6) Outside-right.
Born: Glasgow, 5 April 1891. Played for Glasgow Ashfield; Burnley 1910; City cs 1912; Leeds Bristol United July 1922; Fulham October 1925; retired 1928. This veteran winger joined Fulham when 34 years old. He was signed at the same time as Albert Pape after a

poor start to season 1925-6. Played 428 games scoring 46 goals for his four League clubs, including 204 appearances for Bristol City.
42FL 2g, 5FA

HARWOOD, Alfred, (1903-04) Utility player.
Born: Bishop Auckland, 16 May 1881. Played for Crook Town; Bishop Auckland; Fulham cs 1903; Leeds City May 1905; West Ham United cs 1907-09. Played at right-back in two FA Amateur Cup Finals, for Crook Town in 1901 and Bishop Auckland in 1902, as well as winning Northern League representative honours. Played at full-back, right-half and centre-forward during his spell at Craven Cottage. Mainly a reserve at Leeds City and West Ham. Lost his amateur status at Fulham when the League decided that as Harwood was employed as assistant secretary he was therefore a professional.
14SL 2g, 4FA

HATTER, Steve, (1975-83) Central defender.
Born: London, 21 October 1958. Joined Fulham as an apprentice in August 1975, signed professional May 1976; Exeter City (on loan) October 1982; Wimbledon (on loan) December 1982, permanently February 1983 (£6,000); Southend United (on loan) January 1985, permanently March 1985; Maidstone United cs 1986. A natural left-footer who was good in the air but kept out of the side by Tony Gale. Helped Wimbledon from the Fourth to the Second Division winning a Fourth Division Championship medal in season 1982-3.
25/1FL 1g, 5FA, 0/1LC

HAWORTH, Robert, (1904-06) Right-half.
Born: Blackburn. Played for Blackburn Rovers 1898; Fulham cs 1904; Brentford cs 1906-07. Appeared for Blackburn 116 times in his six seasons at Ewood Park, winning three Lancashire Cup medals from 1900-02. A regular for Fulham during season 1904-05. Lost his place to the more cultured Arthur Collins and so moved on to Brentford.
32SL, 9FA

HEALEY, William R., (1952-5) Right-back.
Born: Liverpool, 22 May 1926. Played for Chorley; Arsenal May 1949; Fulham December 1952; Hartlepools United August 1955-6. Another of the 'one game club', Bill made his debut at Bury shortly after joining the club from Arsenal where he never made the first team. Played at full-back, centre-half and wing-half for the reserves before leaving for Hartlepools for whom he made six appearances. When Healey was signed from Arsenal, Bill Dodgin moved in the other direction as part of an exchange deal, arranged by his father, Bill Dodgin (Senior).
1FL

HEARD, L.H., (1923-4) Inside-right.
Born: London. Played for Southall; Fulham cs 1923. Signed from Isthmian League club Southall and played for Fulham as an amateur. Scored on his debut for Fulham against South Shields and went on to play 19 games in his only season at the Cottage.
19FL 3g

HEBDEN, Jack T., (1927-9) Right-back.
Born: Castleford, 12 November 1900. Played for Rochdale in the war; Bradford City 1919; West Ham United 1921; Fulham December 1927 (£850); Thames Association

August 1929; Clapton Orient 1932; Halifax Town 1933. Well-built, orthodox full-back who joined Fulham from West Ham with full-back partner George Horler for £850. Played 110 games for the Hammers in six seasons, his best season being 1926-7 when he appeared 39 times. Not a success at Fulham and moved on to newly-formed Thames in the Southern League.
23FL, 1FA

HEGAZI, Hassan 'Heggy', (1911) Inside-forward.
Born: Egypt. Played for Cambridge University; Fulham as an amateur October 1911; Dulwich Hamlet. 'Heggy' played only one game for Fulham and scored and then refused to play again. He did not wish to sign for Fulham permanently and preferred to remain with Dulwich Hamlet. Although an Egyptian, he went to school in England and won his Cambridge Blue whilst attending St Catherine's College. Won a London cap and badge in 1912.
1FL 1g

HENDERSON, Samuel Joplin, (1929-30) Left-half.
Born: Willington. Played for South Shields July 1923; Portsmouth cs 1928; Chelsea 1929; Fulham cs 1929; Tunbridge Wells Rangers 1930. A tall and slim wing-half who played 23 games in season 1929-30 as a replacement for the injuried Len Oliver. Had previously made 13 appearances for South Shields but appeared only for Chelsea and Portsmouth reserves.
18FL, 5FA

HESFORD, Iain, (1985) Goalkeeper.
Born: Noola, Kenya, 4 March 1960. Played for Blackpool August 1977; Sheffield Wednesday August 1983; Fulham (on loan) January 1985; Notts County (on loan) December 1985; Sunderland August 1986 (£80,000). Hesford was virtually ever-present in his six seasons at Bloomfield Road but was unable to get in the first team at Hillsborough. Lawrie McMenemy resurrected his career when signing him for Sunderland. Hesford won England Youth and Under-21 honours and represented England when they won the European Under-21 Championships in 1983. Hesford's father, Bob, kept goal for Huddersfield and his brother played Rugby Union for England.
3FL

HEWKINS, Kenneth, (1955-62) Goalkeeper.
Born: Pretoria, South Africa, 30 October 1929. Played

for Clyde; Fulham November 1955; retired through injury 1962. One of the most injury-prone players due to his strong, brave and fearless goalkeeping. Played in Clyde's surprise 1-0 Scottish Cup Final victory over Celtic in 1955 prior to moving to Craven Cottage. Ken took the penalties for the reserves and one day hit one with such force it rebounded off the crossbar to the opposing centre-forward standing on the half-way line who scored with ease.
38FL, 2FA

HICKIE, William, (1931-2) Left-back.
Born: Larkhill, Lanarkshire, 9 December 1902. Died: 27 April 1957. Played for Aberdare Athletic 1924-6; Aberdeen; Newport County 1930; Fulham cs 1931; Aldershot cs 1932-3. This well built, Scottish full-back played for Aberdare in their Football League days in the early 1920s. After a period in Scottish football, Hickie returned to Wales and Newport County playing 23 games in season 1930-31. Started the following season as Fulham's regular left-back but lost his place to new signing Joe Birch.
9FL

HICKS, James, (1985-7) Centre-half.
Born: Ipswich, 16 September 1960. Played for Newmarket; Soham Town Rangers; Warwick University; Exeter City 1983; Oxford United 1984; Fulham August 1985. Hicks is a late developer in the game. Began his career in the Eastern Counties but decided to go to university as his career did not seem to be progressing. Improved enormously as a footballer over the next few years and finally played for Exeter City as a non-contract player whilst teaching at St Luke's College, Exeter. Hicks has good ball skills for such a large man.
30FL 1g, 1LC

HIGGINS, Dennis, (1935-9) Outside-right.
Born: Leek, Staffs. Died in 1942 on active service. Joined Fulham in 1935, in the face of stiff competition from Aston Villa. Gained early experience with Leek Alexandra and Tamworth before coming to the Cottage. Short and red-haired, Higgins was a direct winger who had taken over from Jack Finch in the second half of the 1938-9 season. Scored a hat-trick at Bradford in January 1939.
30FL 12g, 2FA

HILES, Ernest, (1934-48) Right-half.
Born: Little Birch, Hereford, 1 September 1913. Died: 1976. Played for Hereford Town 1932; Fulham 1934, left the club in 1948. Although Hiles stayed with the club until 1948, he did not play in the first team after the war. An honest, hardworking half-back who also played in a number of other positions for Fulham.
49FL

HIND, William, (1907-08) Right-half.
Played for Wellington Athletic; Fulham cs 1907; Clapton Orient cs 1908, assistant trainer 1920-26. Hind could play at full-back or half-back. A compact player who rarely thrilled but was an essential ingredient of the side. Stayed at Clapton for 18 seasons after leaving the Cottage, playing over 200 games for the 'O's' and after retirement taking on the post of assistant trainer.
3FL

169

HINDMARSH, James, (1906-07) Inside-left.
Born: Whitburn near Sunderland. Played for Whitburn
FC; Sunderland 1905; Fulham cs 1906 (£20); Watford
cs 1907; Plymouth Argyle cs 1908; Stockport County cs
1910; Manchester City cs 1913. Tall inside-forward who
found his greatest success after leaving Fulham. Signed
for £20 from Sunderland where, as at Fulham, he made
just one appearance. Was converted to wing-half with
Stockport and played First Division soccer at Maine
Road.
1SL

HINSHELWOOD, Wally A., (1946-53) Outside-right.
Born: London, 27 October 1929. Played for Sutton
United; Fulham October 1946; Chelsea January 1951;
Fulham April 1951; Reading December 1952; Bristol
City February 1956; Millwall June 1960; Newport
County November 1961-2; Deal Town 1964. Hinshelwood
was involved in a player-exchange deal with Jimmy
Bowie when moving to Chelsea. He stayed just three
months at Stamford Bridge. Later played over a 100
games for both Reading and Bristol City where he was
captain and represented the Third Division South. His
two sons, Paul and Martin, played for Crystal Palace.
19FL 1g

HOARE, Gordon Rahere, (1919-20) Inside-forward.
Born: 18 April 1884. Died: 27 October 1973. Played for
Woolwich Arsenal 1907; Glossop 1909; Woolwich
Arsenal 1910; Glossop cs 1912; Arsenal and Northfleet
1914; Fulham in war and December 1919. Also played
for West Norwood, Bromley and Queens Park (1914).
Hoare won a gold medal in the 1912 Olympic Games
scoring two of the goals in England's 4-2 victory over
Denmark in the Final. Like Tom Fitchie, he played as
an amateur and for many of the same clubs. A prolific
scorer for Fulham as a wartime guest, Hoare also
played briefly in season 1919-20.
2FL, 1FA 1g

HODDY, Kevin Raymond, (1984-7) Midfield.
Born: Havering, Essex, 6 January 1968. Havering
School; Fulham as YTS non-contract player July 1984,
signed apprentice January 1985. Young midfield player
with a bright future. An astute, clever player and is a
fine and perceptive passer of the ball. Scored some
memorable goals in reserve team football with his
powerful right foot.
11/4FL 1g, 4FA, 2LC

HOGAN, James, (1905-08) Inside-forward.
Born: Nelson, Lancashire, 16 October 1883. Died: 30
January 1974. Played for Nelson; Rochdale, Burnley;
Bolton Wanderers; Swindon Town; Fulham (1905-08);
then coached extensively in Europe before returning to
England. Never more than a competent inside-forward,
the much-travelled Hogan made a modest contribution
to Fulham as a player, but he claimed he learned a great
deal at the Cottage which served him well in his
coaching and managerial career. In the inter-war
period, he established himself in Europe as one of the
foremost coaches in football, although his return to
Fulham as manager in 1934 was even less glorious than
his time as a player. (See *Fulham Managers*).
4FL, 16SL, 6g 1FA

HOLMES, J.T., (1904-05) Outside-left.
Born: 1880. Played for Sheffield Brunswick; Sheffield

United; Fulham 1904; Southern United 1905; Fulham
again 1906; Tunbridge Wells Rangers in 1909. United
signed Holmes from local soccer. He never made their
first team and played just once for Fulham against
Swindon Town in April 1905 scoring one of the goals in
a 3-0 victory. Almost got sent off when returning to the
Cottage with Tunbridge Wells for a reserve game in
1909.
1SL 1g

HORLER, George Henry, (1927-8) Left-back.
Born: Coleford, near Bath, 10 February 1895. Died: 16
March 1967. Played for Frome Town; Reading 1914;
West Ham cs 1922; Fulham December 1927. Aldershot
cs 1928. Horler ran a chicken farm whilst playing for
Reading, for whom he played 87 times. Signed by
Fulham with Jack Hebden, neither being particularly
successful and, were nicknamed by the crowd 'Elsie and
Doris Waters.'
8FL, 1FA

HORNE, Stanley F., (1969-73) Right-half.
Born: Clanfield, near Oxford, 17 December 1944.
Played for Aston Villa December 1961; Manchester
City September 1965; Fulham February 1969 (£20,000);
Chester August 1973 (£2,000); Rochdale December
1973-4. Stan Horne was made captain on signing for
Fulham in an attempt to avoid relegation for the second
season in succession in 1969. A hardworking grafter
who lacked skill but made up for this with effort.
73/6FL, 2FA, 5/1LC

HORNE, W.G., (1906-07) Goalkeeper.
Played for Plymouth Argyle 1903; Fulham cs 1906;
Plymouth Argyle cs 1907-15. A well-known figure in
Plymouth football. Spent 11 seasons at Home Park
playing 197 games for the Pilgrims. Spent one season at
Fulham as deputy to Jack Fryer but being unable to
dislodge him, Horne returned to his first love.
2SL

HORTON, G., (1910-11) Centre-forward.
Joined Fulham in 1910 and made only one appearance
against Lincoln City at Craven Cottage in a goalless
draw in April 1911. Was not a success.
1FL

HOUGHTON, Jack, (1913-21) Left-back.
Born: Wallsend on Tyne 1888. Died: August 1950.
Played for Wallsend Park Villa 1907; Wallsend Elm
Villa 1908; Hull City May 1910; Fulham cs 1913 (175)
and possibly Walsall 1921-3. Also played for Norwich
City in the war. Houghton often appeared at centre-half
with Hull City but full-back was his position at Fulham.
He could kick with either foot and therefore assumed
both full-back positions.
63FL, 1FA

HOUGHTON, John H., (1919-20) Centre-half.
Played for Glasgow Rangers; Fulham November 1919-20;
Wigan Borough 1921. Not to be confused with Jack
Houghton who played at the club at the same time. A
centre-half from Rangers' reserves who played only two
games for Fulham.
2FL

HOWE, Ernest J., (1973-7) Centre-half.
Born: Chiswick, 15 February 1953. Played for Crystal

Palace as an apprentice; Croydon Amateurs; Hounslow; Fulham, October 1973; Queen's Park Rangers December 1977 (£50,000); Portsmouth June 1982-4. Good in the air and on the ground, Howe's career was resurrected after failing to make the grade with Palace, when Fulham signed him from Hounslow. Scored some memorable goals for Fulham at set pieces. One of the first players to have his fee set by a tribunal after moving to Queen's Park Rangers. The £50,000 paid was way below Fulham's estimation of his worth.
68/2FL 10g, 3FA 1g, 8/2LC 1g

HOWFIELD, Robert M., (1963-5) Centre-forward/outside-left.
Born: Manchester, 3 December 1936. Played for Bushey United; Watford September 1957; Crewe Alexandra July 1959; Aldershot October 1959; Watford July 1962; Fulham November 1963 (£6,000); Aldershot August 1965; New York Jets 1966. Howfield played in two periods for Watford and Aldershot during his career. Although possessing a powerful shot, he lacked the ability to be a regular in the First Division. Found most success in the USA, where he kicked goals for the American Football team the New York Jets.
26FL 9g, 4FA 1g, 1LC

HOYLAND, Walter, (1926-8) Inside-forward.
Born: Sheffield, 1903. Played for Sheffield United 1920; Fulham March 1927. Played 20 games for United during his five seasons at the club. His best season at the Cottage was 1927-8 when Hoyland appeared in 18 League and Cup games.
22FL 4g, 1FA

HUBBARD, Archibald 'Ranji', (1907) Inside-forward.
Born: Leicester 1884. Died 1967. Played for St Andrews (Leicester); Leicester Fosse May 1903; Fulham May 1907; Watford 1908; Norwich City May 1909; Grimsby Town November 1910; Lincoln City cs 1912; Leicester Imperial September 1913. Described on signing for the club as a young player of the brightest promise, clever, dashing, and a superb shot. However he never fulfilled that promise at Fulham and he was quickly transferred to Watford after a disastrous six-goal defeat at Barnsley.
5FL 1g

HUDSON, Albert G., (1946-7) Inside-forward.
Born: Swansea, 17 June 1920. Played for Caeru; signed for Fulham in the war. A Welsh inside-forward who played only one League game at West Bromwich Albion in November 1946 where Fulham lost 6-1. Served in India for five years during the war.
1FL

HUGHES, James A., (1946-7) Left-back/half-back.
Born: Leeds, 28 August 1918. Joined Fulham September 1946; Margate April 1949. Spent three seasons at the Cottage playing mainly for the reserves at either left-back or half-back. Made his Fulham debut in the same match as Mark Radcliffe at Coventry in December 1946.
1FL

HUNT, Fergus, (1903-05) Inside-right.
Born: 1876. Played for Darwen circa 1895; Woolwich Arsenal cs 1897; West Ham United cs 1900; Woolwich Arsenal cs 1902; Fulham cs 1903; Burton United cs 1905-07. Hunt was a prolific scorer until coming to the

Cottage when he scored only three goals in 23 games. In total he scored 100 goals in 256 appearances from 1895-1907 and was leading scorer two seasons running for Woolwich Arsenal between 1897-9. Well-known to London fans, as he also assisted West Ham.
21SL 3g, 2FA

JAMES, Tyrone S., (1975-8) Right-back.
Born: Paddington, 19 September 1956. Played for West Ham United Juniors; joined Fulham as an apprentice in November 1973, signing professional September 1974; Plymouth Argyle March 1978 (£20,000); Torquay United March 1983; Liskeard in 1984. James had a very impressive debut at Luton in front of the television cameras. Fulham's first black player, Tyrone was a cultured, graceful defender who moved on to Plymouth where he made 90 appearances. Last heard of playing in the Western League for Liskeard.
18/2FL, 0/1FA

JINKS, James T., (1948-50) Centre-forward.
Born: Camberwell, 19 August 1916. Played for Millwall circa 1938; Fulham August 1948; Luton Town March 1950; Aldershot September 1951-2. Jinks's best years were lost to the war. He appeared at Wembley for Millwall in a wartime final in 1945, finishing on the losing side. A prolific goalscorer in wartime soccer. Scored on his debut for Fulham but was unable to establish himself and fared little better at Luton and Aldershot.
11FL 3g

JOHNSON, Michael, (1958-62) Left-winger.
Born: York, 4 October 1933. Played for Newcastle United, April 1951; Brighton December 1955; Gloucester City circa 1956; Fulham August 1958; Doncaster Rovers July 1962; Barrow March 1963. Scored two goals on his debut against Charlton in December 1958. It was thought that he only used his right foot to stand on but scored a cracking right-foot drive for the first goal. Mainly a reserve during his four seasons at the Cottage. Signed from Gloucester City of the Southern League after unsuccessful spells at Newcastle and Brighton.
23FL 6g, 4FA 1g

171

JOHNSON, Reg J., (1926-8) Right-half.
Born: Cradley Heath. Played for Cradley Heath; Fulham cs 1926; Swindon Town cs 1929-30. Reg appeared at centre-half on his debut in a five-goal defeat at Darlington. Scored his only goal for Fulham at Barnsley in his last game in another large defeat, this time by 8-4. Played only 11 games for Swindon.
4FL 1g

JOHNSTON, George, (1970-72) Inside-forward.
Born: Glasgow, 21 March 1947. Played for Cardiff City May 1964; Arsenal March 1967; Birmingham City May 1969; Walsall (on loan) September 1970; Fulham October 1970 (£6,000); Hereford United August 1972; Newport County September 1973. Johnson possessed natural ability and had an eye for goal but unfortunately he lacked the essential speed for a striker. Played First Division football for Arsenal and scored some vital goals for Fulham in the promotion season of 1970-71.
33/6FL 12g, 1/1FA 1g, 0/1LC

JOHNSTON H., (1935-6) Outside-right.
Born: Dundee. Little-known Scottish winger who played three games for Fulham. Scored on his debut in a 5-1 victory over Bradford City in September 1935.
4FL 1g

JONES, Allan W., (1958-61) Inside-right.
Born: Paddington, 19 September 1940. Played for Fulham April 1958; Dover cs 1961. Scored on his debut with his first kick of the game after 35 seconds against Bolton Wanderers in February 1960. A prolific goalscorer in Fulham reserve and 'A' teams but did not have that extra ability to become a regular first-teamer.
7FL 3g, 1FA

JONES, Cliff W., (1968-70) Outside-left.
Born: Swansea, 7 February 1935. Played for Swansea Town May 1952; Tottenham Hotspur February 1958 (£35,000); Fulham October 1968 (£5,000); King's Lynn, July 1970; Wealdstone. Cliff, the son of Welsh international Ivor Jones, was one of the greatest wingers of his time. He possessed great speed, could cross the ball with pin-point accuracy and knew how to score goals. Jones won 59 caps for Wales and even represented the Football League on one occasion. Played in Spurs' great double-winning side of 1960-61 and won two other FA Cup medals (1962 and 1967) as well as a European Cup-winners' Cup medal in 1963. Helped

Wales get to the quarter-finals of the World Cup in 1958 when they lost 1-0 to Brazil. Jones was still playing in his late thirties.
23/2FL 2g, 1LC

JONES, Johnny, M., (1947-50) Inside-left.
Born: Dafen, Wales. Played for Larne (Northern Ireland); Fulham, January 1947; Millwall, March 1950; Dover cs 1952. Not to be confused with Jimmy Jones who was signed from Belfast Celtic but never allowed to play for Fulham. Johnny made his debut at West Ham in December 1947. Later scored seven goals in 27 appearances for Millwall. Joined Surrey's groundstaff at The Oval in 1948.
1FL

JONES, Michael K., (1964-5) Right-back.
Born: Berkhamstead, 8 January 1945. Played for Fulham 1961, signed professional January 1963; Chelsea December 1964; Orient February 1966; Charlton Athletic December 1971-3. Jones made one appearance for Fulham in a disastrous 3-1 defeat against Reading in the League Cup in October 1964. Did not find recognition until his arrival at Brisbane Road playing well over 200 games for the 'O's'.
1LC

JOY, Bernard, (1933-4) Centre-half.
Born: Fulham, 29 October 1911. Died: Kenton, 18 July 1984. Played for London University; Corinthians; Southend United cs 1931; Fulham 1933; Arsenal May 1935; also played for Casuals 1931-48. Joy did not sign permanently for Fulham and they lost an emerging star when Arsenal signed him in 1935. He was the last amateur to be capped in a full international, against Belgium in 1936. He also skippered the Great Britain side in the 1936 Olympics. Joy won a League Championship medal with Arsenal in season 1937-8, an FA Amateur Cup-winners' medal with Casuals in 1936 and 11 wartime international caps. For many years he worked as a journalist with the *Evening Standard* and *Sunday Express*.
1FL

JUMP, Stewart, (1977) Left-back.
Born: Campsell, 27 January 1952. Played for Stoke City July 1969; Crystal Palace December 1973 (£70,000); Fulham (on loan) January 1977; New York Cosmos; left Crystal Palace March 1978. Jump played three games for Fulham whilst on loan from Crystal Palace. Spent his winters in England and summers in the USA. He played for Team America against England in May 1976 in the same side as Pelé.
3FL

KEEBLE, A.G., (1929-30) Centre-forward.
Could possibly be Arthur George Keeble born in Marylebone 1908. Played for Barking Town in 1928; Leyton; Fulham 1929-30 as an amateur. Keeble was well-known in East London amateur football circles. Played his one and only game in a 5-4 victory over Merthyr Town in February 1930. He failed to impress that day.
1FL

KEEN, Walter James, (1931-2) Right-half.
Born: Loudwater, Bucks, spring 1904. Died: New Cross, 6 May 1968. Played for Wycombe Wanderers;

Millwall Athletic June 1925; Fulham cs 1930; Clapton Orient cs 1932-5. An uncle of Queen's Park Rangers player Mike Keen who was also a right-half. Walter gave Millwall many years of sterling service despite rarely being in the first team. He managed only one appearance for Fulham, in a shock 0-0 home draw with Yeovil and Petters United in the FA Cup. Later played 53 games for Orient. He was still living on Millwall's doorstep when he died in 1968, in Camplin Street.
1FA

KELLY, Tim, (1930-32) Inside-right.
Born: Belfast. Played for RAF 1924; Fulham cs 1930-32; Vauxhall Motors' manager after the war; FA Coaching Panel 1951; Luton Town 1952-56 coach and assistant manager; Bedford Town manager 1956. Tim won two Irish Amateur international caps and represented the RAF from whom he joined Fulham. Made one appearance at Walsall in February 1931. After the war he went into football management and coaching. His son Terry played for Luton Town in the 1950s.
1FL

KENNEDY, Samuel, (1924-6) Centre-half/centre-forward.
Born: Platts Common, 1896. Died: 9 December 1963. Played for Denaby United; Nelson January 1924; Fulham cs 1924; Barnsley October 1926; Mexborough March 1927. Kennedy played 21 Football League games in his career. Performed as a pivot in defence and attack whilst at the Cottage. His one and only goal came at South Shields in October 1925 when Fulham went down 5-2.
6FL 1g

KERRIGAN, Donald M., (1968-9) Inside-forward.
Born: Seamill, Scotland, 7 May 1941. Played for Johnstone Burgh; St Mirren; Aberdeen October 1963; Hearts cs 1965; Dunfermline; Fulham February 1968; Lincoln City March 1969. Kerrigan won Scottish Schoolboy and Youth honours as a youngster and appeared in the Scottish Cup Final for St Mirren in 1962 when they lost 2-0 to Rangers. Made his Fulham debut in the club's last First Divison match in May 1968 at Everton. Past his best by the time he arrived at the Cottage.
4/2FL 1g, 1LC

KERRINS, Wayne Michael, (1984-7) Left-back.
Born: Southend, 5 August 1965. Joined Fulham as an apprentice, June 1981; signed professional August 1983; Port Vale on loan March 1985. A naturally left-footed player who joined Fulham as a winger but was converted to left-back. His father played for Queen's Park Rangers and Southend. Had a brief spell on loan to Port Vale for whom he played 11 games.
40/8FL 1g, 4FA, 4LC

KERSLAKE, Michael, (1974-8) Left-back.
Born: London, 27 February 1958. Joined Fulham as an apprentice cs 1974, signed professional October 1975; Brighton June 1978-80. Looked a fine prospect when he made his debut aged 17 against Orient in October 1975 and England Youth honours soon followed. Kerslake never developed as anticipated and drifted off to Brighton where he again did not make the grade. His brother David plays for Queen's Park Rangers.
1/2FL

KINGABY, Herbert C. 'Rabbit', (1906-07) Outside-right.
Played for Clapton Orient 1903; Aston Villa March 1906; Fulham cs 1906; Leyton cs 1907-10; Peterborough City October 1910; Croydon Common 1914-15. Nicknamed the 'Rabbit' because of his speed, Kingaby was a fast and nippy winger. Scored Clapton Orient's first-ever League goal in September 1905. He was later involved in a long drawn-out court case over his transfer to Aston Villa. Kingaby claimed a percentage of his transfer fee to which he said he was entitled but Villa disagreed. The case had taken six years to come to court when the court ruled in Villa's favour in 1912.
33SL 4g

KINGSLEY, Alfred John 'Scotty', (1922-3) Outside-right.
Born: Barbados, 1892. Died: Plumstead, 14 April 1967. Played for Vanburgh Park FC; Blackheath St Johns; Charlton Athletic November 1912; Fulham January 1922; Millwall Athletic September 1923; retired injured 1925; made a comeback with Sittingbourne June 1928; Sheppey United July 1931. Although born in Barbados, Kingsley was very much a Londoner. He remained on Millwall's books in 1925 even though he had officially retired through injury. Had plenty of competition for the right-wing berth during his spell at Fulham. Made a comeback in the Kent League with Sittingbourne after three years out through injury in 1928.
29FL 2g, 2FA

KIRBY, Conyers, (1905-07) Outside-right.
Born: Birmingham 1884. Played for Army Medical Corps; Fulham 1905; Birmingham 1906; Blackpool cs 1907; Kidderminster; Willenhall Pickwick 1911-12; Fulham reserves 1913; then moved to Spain. A fine sprinter who was 100-yard champion whilst in the Army. Played only seven games for Fulham, Birmingham and Blackpool. When he moved to Spain, he became a referee.
4SL

KIRKWOOD, Joseph, (1910) Right-back.
Born: Pinxton 1887. Played for Pinxton; Sutton Town (Notts); Chesterfield; Fulham cs 1910; Millwall Athletic November 1910-15. Played one game during his brief stay at the Cottage against Leeds City in October 1910. Soon established himself as the Lions' regular full-back and made 121 appearances up until war ended the Football League programme.
1FL

KITCHEN, Peter M., (1979-80) Centre-forward.
Born: Mexborough, 16 February 1952. Played for
Doncaster Rovers, July 1970; Ipswich Town (on loan)
1974; Orient July 1977 (£30,000); Fulham February
1979 (£150,000); Cardiff City, August 1980 (£100,000);
Happy Valley (Hong Kong) 1982; Orient December
1982-4; Chester City March 1985; Dagenham April
1985. Peter won England Schoolboy international
honours prior to joining Doncaster Rovers. Scored 89
goals in 228 appearances for Rovers before joining
Orient whom he helped to the FA Cup semi-final in
1978. Signed by Bobby Campbell for a record fee, but
was never given a proper opportunity to establish
himself in the Fulham side. A natural goalscorer who
scored 194 League and Cup goals during his career.
21/3FL 6g

LAFFERTY, H., (1923-5) Half-back.
Born: Glasgow. Played for Bellshill Athletic; Fulham cs
1923-5; Arsenal cs 1925. Signed from Glasgow junior
club Bellshill Athletic who had a fine reputation for
producing many quality players. Lafferty played four
times during his two seasons at the Cottage.
4FL

LAMBERT, Jack, (1933-5) Centre-forward.
Born: Greasbrough near Rotherham, 22 May 1902.
Died: Tottenham, 7 December 1940. Played for The
Army; Sheffield Wednesday on trial; Rotherham County
1923; Leeds United; Doncaster Rovers 1924; Arsenal
December 1926 (£2,000); Fulham October 1933 (£2,500);
Margate cs 1935; Arsenal juniors coach. Big and raw-
boned Lambert had speed, stamina and pluck in
abundance but lacked ball-control and the finer points
of the game. Although not always a regular at Arsenal,
he was a prolific scorer with 95 goals in 146 matches
between 1927-33. Over-the-hill by the time he arrived at
Fulham, he had lost much of his pace. Won a League
Championship medal in 1930-31 with Arsenal scoring
34 goals and a FA Cup-winners' medal in 1930 and
runners-up medal in 1932.
34FL 4g, 2FA 1

LANGLEY, Richard, (1986-7) Right-back.
Born: 20 June 1965. Played for Gillingham Juniors;

Dulwich Hamlet 1983; Corinthian Casuals; Fulham as
a non-contract player in November 1986. Made a
surprise debut in the last game of the 1986-7 season, at
Mansfield Town, after only a handful of reserve games.
After failing to make any impression at Gillingham,
Langley moved to Dulwich Hamlet where he played
regularly. He joined Casuals where his brother had
played for a number of years. Langley is hoping to be
signed on a full contract at the Cottage.
1FL

LARGE, Frank, (1968-9) Centre-forward.
Born: Leeds, 26 January 1940. Played for Halifax
Town, June 1959; Queen Park Rangers June 1962;
Northampton Town March 1963; Swindon Town March
1964; Carlisle United September 1964; Oldham Athletic
December 1965; Northampton Town December 1966;
Leicester City November 1967; Fulham June 1968;
Northampton Town August 1969; Chesterfield November
1972-4. Scored goals freely at every club except Fulham.
It took him 908 minutes to score his first goal for
Fulham. The harder he tried the less likely it looked as if
he would succeed. Played for Northampton in three
seperate periods. Large scored 209 League goals in his
569 appearances in the Football League from 1958-74.
20/4FL 3g, 2FA, 2LC

LAWRENCE, Everard T., (1903-04) Outside-left.
Played for Kettering 1900; Northampton cs 1901;
Woolwich Arsenal cs 1902; Fulham cs 1903; Glossop
1904-05. Played for Northampton at the same time as
Ted Turner and Tim Coleman, both of whom later
joined Fulham. Had a season at Plumstead with
Woolwich Arsenal when they just missed out on
promotion to Division One in 1902-03. Helped to
establish Fulham in their first season in Division One of
the Southern League.
18SL 2g, 7FA 1g

LAWS, Thomas, (1913-14) Left-back.
Born: Summerstown, 1890. Died: Wimbledon, 1981.
Played for De Nevers Rubber Mills FC; Summerstown;
Fulham 1913-14; Morton and Clydebank after the war.
Laws was the first Fulham player to join up at the
beginning of World War One. Only 5ft 5in tall, he
formed a humourous-looking partnership in Fulham's
reserves with British heavyweight boxing champion,
'Bombardier' Billy Wells, who was massively built and
well over six feet tall.
6FL

LAWSON, Thomas, (1928-31) Wing-half.
Born: Bolden, circa 1906. Played for Newcastle United;
Bolden Colliery; Fulham cs 1928; West Ham United cs
1931; Aldershot cs 1932; Newport County 1934-5.
Versatile wing-half who could play at right or left-half.
Lawson's best season at the Cottage was 1928-9 when
he appeared 25 times in League and Cup games.
Appeared regularly for Aldershot in their initial two
seasons in the Football League.
29FL 2g, 3FA

LEE, Harry, (1907-15) Outside-right.
Born: Preston, 1888. Played for Moor Parts FC
(Preston); Leyland FC; St Helens Recreation; Fulham
1907; Reading November 1909; Fulham cs 1912-15;
Gillingham 1919-20. Lee was a strong, robust and
forceful player who was only 5ft 7in tall but weighed

over 12 stone. He failed to establish himself in the Fulham side in his first spell with the club. After winning a Southern League Second Division Championship medal with Reading he returned to Fulham. He scored regularly until the outbreak of war, having been converted to centre forward for much of season 1914-15.
65FL 32g

LEE, Trevor Carl, (1985) Centre-forward.
Born: London, 3 July 1954. Played for Fulham as an apprentice 1970-72; Epsom and Ewell 1972-75; Millwall October 1975; Colchester United October 1975 (£15,000); Gillingham January 1981 (£90,000); Orient (on loan) October 1982; Bournemouth November 1982 (£5,000); Cardiff City, December 1983; Northampton Town cs 1984; Fulham March 1985. Lee failed to make the grade as a youngster at Fulham. Moved to Epsom and Ewell and after playing in the FA Vase Final at Wembley he was signed along with Phil Walker by Millwall. After a number of moves, Lee found himself back at Fulham as a non-contract player and his career had gone full circle when he made his Fulham debut and last appearance of his career in March 1985.
1FL

LEIGH, Thomas 'Ginger', (1907-10) Full-back.
Born: Hollins, near Bury, circa 1888. Played for Haslington FC; Oldham Athletic; Fulham cs 1907; Queen's Park Rangers cs 1910-11. An energetic full-back described as dandy, bold, vigorous, and very fast. 'Ginger' could kick a ball far and low. Regarded as a great prospect but never quite made it at either Fulham or Queen's Park Rangers.
6FL

LENNIE, William, (1904-05) Outside-left.
Born: Glasgow, 26 January 1882. Played for Glasgow Rangers, Queen's Park 1902; Dundee; Fulham cs 1904; Aberdeen cs 1905; playing for Falkirk in 1914. A Scottish international, Lennie gained his caps after he left the Cottage in 1908, playing against Wales and Ireland. A small tricky winger who gained much fame at Aberdeen. Never performed as well with Fulham but played a major part in the run to the quarter-finals of the FA Cup in 1905.
18SL 3g, 9FA 1g

LEWIN, Ronald Dennis (1946-50) Right-back.
Born: Edmonton, 21 June 1920. Played for Bradford City in the war; Fulham, June 1946; Gillingham June 1950-54; Skeid (Norway) as coach; Chelmsford City manager 1962; Wellington Town manager 1963; Everton assistant coach 1963; Newcastle United coach, August 1966-68; Walsall manager cs 1969-February 1970; Newcastle United assistant manager cs 1974-July 1976; spells in Kuwait, Greece and Iceland; Brandon United coach 1981. An accomplished full-back who played intermittently for Fulham. Played almost 200 games for Gillingham before taking off on a long and varied coaching and management career which took him all over Europe and to all levels of football in this country. Lewin is a fully qualified FA Coach.
41FL, 1FA

LILLEY, Thomas, (1930-31) Right-back.
Born: New Herrington. Played for Hartlepools United cs 1924; Sunderland cs 1927; St Mirren; Fulham cs 1930 (£250). Very tall for a full-back and perhaps a little slow

because of this. Lilley played his football in all four Divisions of the Football League including brief spells in the First Division with Sunderland. Found most success at Hartlepools where he was ever-present during season 1925-6.
7FL, 1FA

LINDSAY, Archie, (1907-11) Full-back.
Born: Scotland, circa 1885. Played for Glencairne; Parkhead A; Renton; Reading cs 1905; Fulham cs 1907; Dundee January 1911. Lindsay partnered England international Herbert Smith during his two years at Reading. A sturdily-built back who cleared well and promptly. Reliable rather than dynamic, Lindsay gave Fulham fine service during their early spell in the Football League. Returned to Scottish football with Dundee in 1911.
78FL 1g, 6FA

LINFOOT, Frederick, (1924-6) Outside-left.
Born: Whitley Bay. Played for Leeds City 1919; Lincoln City October 1919; Chelsea May 1920; Fulham March 1924-26. Linfoot was with Leeds City when they were wound up by the Football League for illegal payments to players. Immediately got fixed up with Lincoln City and was a regular until his transfer to Chelsea the following summer. He made 41 appearances for the Blues in four seasons at the Bridge.
41FL 4g

LITTLEWORT, Harry Charles, (1909) Centre-half.
Born: Cosford, 1882. Died: Edmonton, 21 November 1934. Played for West Norwood 1905-10; Crystal Palace 1906; Fulham 1909; Glossop 1910-14. Littlewort was an amateur throughout his career but would have been a better player with full-time training. An elegant and masterly player who preferred West Norwood to any other club until moving north to play for Glossop. Littlewort won 10 England Amateur international caps including a gold medal in the 1912 Olympic games. When his playing career ended he became a cricket and football sportswriter and was working on the *News Chronicle* when he died in 1934.
4FL

LLOYD, Clifford, (1943-50) Left-back.
Born: Ellesmere Port, 14 November 1916. Played for
Brymbo; Liverpool 1935; Wrexham 1938; Fulham
December 1943; Margate player-manager 1949; Bristol
Rovers May 1950; Wrexham manager for a brief spell;
PFA Management Committee 1950-53, Secretary 1953-81.
Lloyd played on the wing and at inside-forward for
Wrexham before World War Two. He joined Fulham
as a guest in 1943, and permanently in 1946. More
famous as the secretary of the Professional Footballers
Association where he was involved in two famous
battles. Firstly, the abolition of the maximum wage
which was fought out alongside Fulham inside-forward
Jimmy Hill and secondly the George Eastham case
when the player was in dispute with Newcastle manager
Charlie Mitten. Another Fulham connection was Ernie
Clay who offered Eastham a job while his dispute
lasted.
2FL, 2FA

LLOYD, David, (1899-1904) Inside-right.
Born: East London, 1874. Played for Brentford; Thames
Ironworks; Fulham cs 1899. Lloyd won London Senior
Cup-winners' honours with Brentford in 1898 and a
Southern League Second Division Championship medal
with Fulham in season 1902-03. A fine inside-forward
who was converted to centre-half in the latter part of his
career. Even played in goal on one occasion for
Fulham. Fought in the Boer War armed forces between
1901-02.
38SL 19g, 11FA 5g

LONDON, George, (1923-4) Full-back.
Played for Barking FC: Fulham cs 1923; Clapton
Orient on trial in September 1925 but not signed.
London played as an amateur with Barking prior to
signing professional forms for Fulham. Had a short run
in the first team from October to December 1923 when
he partnered Alec Chaplin at full-back.
7FL

LOVELL, Mark A., (1978-9) Midfield.
Born: London, 20 January 1961. Joined Fulham as an
apprentice 1977, signed professional August 1978; later
played briefly for Woking. Lovell, a busy little midfield
player, looked to have a bright career at Fulham after
winning England Youth international honours in 1977.
It is rumoured that he just walked out of the club thus
ending a promising career abruptly.
4/2FL

LOWE, Harry, (1927-8) Centre-half.
Born: Northwich, 1890. Died: Camden Town, 15 July
1966. Played for Brighton 1913; Tottenham Hotspur cs
1914; Fulham cs 1927; later a coach with Spurs. Lowe
had a difficult early life, being adopted when very
young. Played 65 League games in his 13 years at Spurs.
Past his best by the time he arrived at Fulham.
3FL

LOWE, Reginald, (1950-53) Left-back.
Born: Halesowen, 15 December 1926. Played for
Finchley during World War Two; Aston Villa 1946;
Fulham May 1950 (£3,000); retired through injury in
1953. Lowe had an excellent understanding on the field
with his brother Eddie. When Eddie lost his place in the
Villa side, Reg moved with him to Fulham. Injury
ended his career in 1953. A testimonial match was

granted, played against the club, Luton Town, where he
sustained his injury. Once scored with a header from 60
yards in a reserve match. Is currently running the local
post office at Stanmore in Hampshire.
66FL 6FA

MACAULAY, Archie R., (1950-52) Right-half.
Born: Falkirk, 30 July 1915. Played for Camelon;
Sawyer; Glasgow Rangers 1933; West Ham United
1937 (£7,500); Brentford October 1946; Arsenal July
1947; Fulham cs 1950 (£10,000); Guildford City 1952 as
player-manager; Dundee manager 1955; Norwich City
manager 1956; West Bromwich Albion manager 1961;
Brighton manager 1963. Originally a forward, Macaulay
became a right-half in the classic mould. As a centre-
forward he once scored six goals for West Ham but
developed as a wing-half during World War Two. Won
honours galore with Rangers, including three Scottish
Championship medals, and was capped for Scotland on
seven occasions, also representing Great Britain against
the Rest of Europe in 1947. Macaulay helped Arsenal to
the League Championship in 1948 with another 'red-
head', Alex Forbes, who later also played for Fulham.
After retirement Macaulay found much fame in
management.
48FL 4g, 4FA

McCORMICK, James, (1946-7) Inside-forward.
Born: Rotherham, 26 April 1912. Died: Marbella
(Spain), 3 January 1968. Played for Rotherham United
1930; Chesterfield cs 1932; Tottenham Hotspur March
1933; Fulham and Spurs during World War Two;
Fulham May 1946; Lincoln City August 1947; Crystal
Palace, February 1949; also Lincoln City trainer and
York City manager. McCormick was employed in the
local steelworks when signed by Rotherham in 1930. A
goalscoring inside-forward, McCormick enjoyed much
success at Spurs playing 137 games and scoring 26 goals

176

before World War Two interrupted his career. He died whilst on holiday in Spain in a car crash.
9FL 2g, 1FA

McCOURT, John, (1908-09) Inside-forward.
Played for Hibernian; Glasgow Celtic; Fulham cs 1908; Croydon Common cs 1909-10. McCourt played a simple ball-passing game and was able to beat players effortlessly with his natural abilities. However, much of his career was spent in reserve-team football. McCourt remained a school teacher throughout his career and was appointed headmaster at Laycock Street School, Islington in December 1927.
2FL

McCREE, James, (1925-6) Outside-right.
Played for London Caledonians and also assisted Brentford 1924-5; Fulham 1925-6; Watford 1926-7. Tricky little winger, who, although a London Caledonian player first, occasionally helped out League clubs. Jimmy won England Amateur international honours and appeared in London Caledonian's FA Amateur Cup-winning side of 1923. Rejoined Callies in November 1929 after a spell of working in Darlington.
2FL

McCURDY, Colin, (1977-8) Centre-forward.
Born: Belfast, 18 July 1954. Played for Larne (Northern) Ireland); Fulham November 1977 (£20,000); Philadelphia Fury (NASL); Linfield April 1979. Well-built and a little slow, McCurdy played one game for Fulham, at Southampton in November 1977. Given a free transfer to play soccer in the United States and later returned to Irish Soccer with Linfield. Won international recognition when he represented Northern Ireland against Australia in 1980.
1FL

McDERMOTT, Brian, (1983) Midfield.
Born: Slough, 8 April 1961. Played for Arsenal, February 1979; Fulham (on loan) March 1983; Oxford United December 1984 (£25,000). Usually a midfield player but played as a striker during his loan period at the Cottage. Made 18 appearances in Oxford United's Second Division Championship team of season 1984-5.
0/3FL

McDONALD, Hugh Laughlan, (1913-14) Goalkeeper.
Born: Kilwinning, Ayrshire, 1884. Died: 27 August 1920. Played for Woolwich Arsenal 1905; Brighton 1906; Woolwich Arsenal cs 1908; Oldham Athletic cs 1910; Bradford November 1911; Fulham November 1913; Bristol Rovers February 1914. Signed by Fulham when Arthur Reynolds was badly injured in November 1913. McDonald was first choice at most of his other clubs and made a grand total of 224 League appearances from 1905-14.
8FL

MACDONALD, Malcolm, (1968-9) Centre-forward.
Born: Fulham, 7 January 1950. Played for Sloane Grammar School; Tonbridge, Fulham August 1968; Luton Town July 1969; Newcastle United May 1971; Arsenal July 1976; retired through injury cs 1979, returning to Fulham as the marketing executive and then manager (1980-84). A local boy who was not given a proper chance at the Cottage, Macdonald went on to become one of the most dynamic strikers of the 1970s.

His 191 in 339 games was as good a record as any in the League. When injury ended his career in 1979, he returned to Fulham and enjoyed a successful three and a half years as manager. (See *Fulham Managers*).
10/3FL 5g

McDONALD, William W., (1919-23) Outside-right.
Born: Quebec, Co Durham, 1892. Played for Craghead United (Durham); Hull City February 1912; Fulham cs 1919; Durham City cs 1923-4. A winger of great speed and ability who could centre with pinpoint accuracy. McDonald formed an excellent right-wing partnership at Fulham with Billy Banks just after World War One. A short, but sturdy wing-man, McDonald played 150 League games between 1911-25.
75FL 2g, 4FA 1g

McGIBBON, Douglas, (1947-8) Centre-forward.
Born: Netley near Southampton, 24 February 1919. Played for Southampton 1939; Swindon Town 1945 as a guest; Fulham January 1947 (£8,000); Bournemouth September 1948; Lovells Athletic 1950. One of only two players to score a hat-trick on their Fulham debuts, the other being Ronnie Rooke in 1936. Once scored six goals in a wartime game for Southampton against Chelsea. McGibbon's father played for Southampton in 1910. He felt that he never got the service he needed at Fulham and jumped at the chance to join Bournemouth where he scored 65 goals in 103 League games.
42FL 18g

McINTOSH, William, (1911-12) Outside-left.
Born: Glasgow 1890. Played for Rutherglen Glencairn FC; Ardrossan Winton Rovers; Fulham cs 1911. McIntosh won Scottish Junior international honours in 1910. Small, nimble winger who stayed just one season at the Cottage.
6FL, 1FA

177

McINTYRE, Edward, (1906-07) Right-half.
Born: Newcastle. Played for Allendale Park; Newcastle United, May 1900; Fulham May 1906; Plymouth Argyle cs 1907; Portsmouth cs 1909. McIntyre won a benefit at Newcastle for club loyalty but had mainly been a reserve. Played five games for Fulham before joining Plymouth. It was here that McIntyre was involved in a nasty case which led to him being charged with occasioning actual bodily harm. Returning from an away game at Derby on 25 March 1909, he and trainer Nicholas Wallis became involved in a row over a game of cards. Wallis shouted obscenities and became very argumentative, provoking McIntyre into hitting him and breaking his jaw. Wallis eventually died of heart failure. The jury acquitted McIntyre and no evidence was offered on a manslaughter charge. However, this incident ruined McIntyre's football career.
5SL

McINTYRE, Johnny McGregor, (1917-20) Inside-forward.
Born: Glasgow, 4 January 1895. Died: Blackpool, February 1974. Played for Partick Thistle; Fulham February 1917; Sheffield Wednesday March 1920; Blackburn Rovers January 1922; Blackpool January 1928. Joined Fulham during World War One and was a regular until he left the club after a row with manager Kelso over being caught out after curfew. McIntyre became a regular scorer at Wednesday and Blackburn, once scoring four goals in five minutes for Rovers against Everton during season 1922-3. He scored 85 goals in a total of 274 League appearances between 1919 and 1928.
26FL 9g, 1FA

McKAY, J., (1923-4) Centre-forward.
Born: Custom House, London. Played for Custom House; Fulham February 1923; Clapton Orient cs 1924-26. McKay made 16 appearances in the first team during his 16 months at the Cottage and scored five goals. Later played eight games for Clapton Orient in two seasons at Homerton where he was in competition for the centre-forward berth with Johnny Tonner, later to join Fulham.
16FL 5g

McKENNA, Francis Charles, (1927-8) Inside-left.
Born: Wallsend, 9 December 1902. Played for Swan Hunter (Tyneside); Spennymoor United; Wallsend FC; Grimsby Town, May 1922; Fulham cs 1927; Norwich City cs 1928 (£250); Newport County cs 1929-30; Walker Celtic; Wrexham cs 1932-33. McKenna joined Fulham with wing-partner Charlie Devan from Grimsby Town. He could play anywhere in the forward-line and, although slimly built, he was a gritty performer with a fair amount of speed and skill. Won a Third Division North Championship medal with Grimsby in the 1925-6 season when he scored 14 goals in 40 appearances. McKenna was Norwich City's top scorer with 18 goals after leaving Fulham in 1928 for a £250 fee.
25FL 10g, 1FA

McKENNA, Thomas, (1924-6) Goalkeeper.
Born: Stewarton, Ayrshire, 27 September 1900. Played for Dalry Thistle; Fulham March 1925; South Shields August 1926; Charlton Athletic cs 1927; Merthyr Town cs 1928, player manager from November 1928; Southend United cs 1929; Portadown cs 1930. Reserve 'keeper to Ernie Beecham who arrived in League Football quite late in life. Played a total of 102 League games for his five clubs. Rather surprisingly appointed Merthyr Town manager in November 1928 but did not stay very long as they finished 20th in the Third Division South that season.
10FL

McLAUGHLIN, Patrick, (1909-10) Centre-forward.
Born: 1888. Played for South Shields Adelaide; Fulham October 1909. Signed from Newcastle League club South Shields Adelaide by manager Phil Kelso, this small, slimly-built centre-forward was given few opportunities to establish himself at the Cottage. A vigorous and determined player.
2FL 1g

McQUEEN, Hugh, (1903-04) Inside-left.
Born: Harthill, Scotland, 1 October 1873. Played for Leith Athletic 1890; Liverpool 1893; Derby County July 1895; Queen's Park Rangers cs 1901; Gainsborough Trinity cs 1902; Fulham cs 1903; trainer from cs 1904, later Norwich City's trainer. McQueen spent much of his career playing on the left wing where his speed and the pinpoint accuracy of his crosses helped him gain a fine reputation at Liverpool and Derby. Won a Second Division Championship medal in 1893-4 with the Reds and played in Derby's beaten side in the 1898 FA Cup Final against Nottingham Forest. Appeared for Derby in 168 League and Cup games. Played mainly at inside-left for Fulham and after retirement stayed on as trainer for a couple of seasons.
10SL, 4FA 1g

MAHONEY, Anthony Joseph, (1976-82) Centre-forward.
Born: Barking, 26 September 1959. Joined Fulham as an apprentice April 1976, signed professional August 1977; Northampton (on loan) October 1981; Brentford August 1982; Crystal Palace cs 1984-85; Grays Athletic 1986. Lanky striker who never fulfilled his early

promise. Won England Youth international honours in 1977 and was still an apprentice when he made his debut as a 17 year old. Unable to find the net regularly for Fulham he moved to Brentford and was a sensation until he broke his leg in a Cup game. Never able to control his temper, he was sent off on a number of occasions during his career.
53/6FL 10g, 5FA 2g, 4LC 1g

MALCOLM, George, (1909-10) Inside-forward.
Born: Stockton, circa 1890. Played for Thornaby St Marks; Thornaby St Patricks; Darlington St Augustine; Woolwich Arsenal September 1909 on trial but not signed; Fulham February 1910; Plymouth Argyle December 1910; Darlington 1913; Durham City 1926-27. Signed from Darlington St Augustine, but did not stay as long at the Cottage as Alf Marshall and Willie Walker who were also signed from this club. Malcolm played nine games in Plymouth's Southern League Championship season of 1912-13 but it was at Darlington that he found most success as a half-back, rarely missing a game in their first four seasons in the Football League. A strong and keen player.
4FL 1g

MALPASS, Samuel T., (1939-47) Full-back.
Born: Consett, 12 September 1918. Died: September 1983. Played for Huddersfield Town circa 1937; Fulham cs 1939; Watford January 1947-48. Malpass did not make his Football League debut until he was 28 years old, much of his career being lost to World War Two. Made 41 appearances for Watford at full-back after leaving the Cottage.
2FL

MANSLEY, Alan, (1970) Outside-left.
Born: Liverpool, 31 August 1946. Played for Skelmersdale United; Blackpool June 1967; Brentford January 1968; Fulham (on loan) December 1970; Notts County March 1971; Lincoln City, December 1971-2. Mansley played only one game for Fulham, on loan from Brentford, against Swansea City in December 1970. An orthodox winger, he played 95 League games for the Bees scoring 24 goals in his three seasons at Griffin Park.
1FL

MARGERRISON, John, (1975-9) Midfield.
Born: Bushey, 20 October 1955. Played for Hertfordshire Schools; Tottenham Hotspur December 1972; Fulham, July 1975; Orient July 1979; (£65,000); Kansas City Comets (NASL) summer 1982; Wealdstone January 1983; Borehamwood; Barnet cs 1984. A talented, skilful midfielder who scored some memorable goals for Fulham. Fell out with manager Bobby Campbell because of his lack of consistency. As a youngster John had been an England Schoolboy international trialist and also won an FA Youth Cup-winners' medal with Spurs in 1974. Still playing well for Conference League side Barnet.
63/8FL 9g, 3/1FA 2g, 4LC

MARINELLO, Peter, (1978-80) Outside-right.
Born: Edinburgh, 20 February 1950. Played for Hibernian; Arsenal January 1970 (£100,000), Portsmouth, July 1973; Motherwell, December 1975; Fulham, December 1978 (£30,000); Phoenix Inferno (USA) 1980; Hearts October 1981-82 (£25,000). Marinello was having his

second spell in London when he joined Fulham. In January 1970 Arsenal had signed him for a club record fee of £100,000, coming to Highbury with a reputation as a fast, ball-playing winger. After failing to live up to his reputation he moved to Portsmouth where he made 110 appearances. Marinello won Scotland Under-23 honours whilst at Arsenal. He was an instant sensation at Fulham, however, opposition full-backs soon found ways of stopping Marinello playing to his highest potential.
25/2FL 1g, 3FA, 2LC

MARRABLE, Sidney Albert, (1920-21) Centre-half.
Born: Mile End, 25 April 1895. Died: Ilford, 13 April 1973. Played for Leytonstone; Fulham April 1920 as an amateur; Leytonstone. Still playing for Leytonstone in 1932 as an inside-left. Tall, dominant centre-half, Marrable played eight games during his brief spell at the Cottage.
8FL

MARSHALL, John, (1980-) Midfield.
Born: Balham, 18 August 1964. Joined Fulham as an apprentice, June 1980, signed professional August 1982. Fast developing into a speedy, right-sided, midfield player, Marshall would have been called a winger two decades ago but his all-round abilities have meant that he has played in nearly every position at Fulham. He is a good tackler, dribbler and perceptive passer of the ball. His speed is more than a match for most Third Division defenders.
121/7FL 8g, 7FA 2g, 13LC 1g

MARTIN, George, (1916-25) Left-half/Inside-left.
Born: Plumstead. Joined Fulham in 1916, left the club in the close season of 1925. In his first season at the club, Martin scored 15 goals in 13 games from the inside-left position. Gradually developed into a wing-half who made 50 appearances in his six seasons at the Cottage.
48FL, 2FA

MASON, Thomas J.R., (1977-81) Left-back.
Born: Fulham, 19 June 1960. Joined Fulham as an
apprentice 1977, signed professional January 1978;
Brighton, May 1981; Seattle Sounders (NASL); Tarague
(New Zealand) in 1983. Orthodox and methodical full-
back who won England Youth international honours.
Played seven games for Fulham before moving to
Brighton where he never made the first team. Has spent
many years playing in New Zealand football and gained
international honours for that country in 1986.
Occasionally plays for Fulham's reserves when on
holiday in England.
6FL, 1FA

MASON, William Sidney, (1928-33) Goalkeeper.
Born: Earlsfield, 31 October 1908. Played for Wimbledon;
Fulham September 1928, signed professional November
1928, Queen's Park Rangers May 1933-43 also played
as a guest for Fulham in 1940. Strongly-built and
muscular 'keeper, Mason was one of five players in the
1928-9 side who graduated through the Isthmian League.
He had an extended run in the first team after Ernie
Beecham had received a terrible injury in November
1928. Mason won a London Challenge Cup-winners'
medal and helped the reserves to runners-up position in
1932-3. First choice for much of his ten seasons at
Rangers playing 154 League games and 91 wartime
games. Became a policeman on his retirement from the
game.
35FL, 3FA

MAUGHAN, William, (1914-15) Right-half.
Born: West Stanley, 1895. Played for Stanley Juniors;
Easington Colliery, Fulham February 1914-15. Tenacious
wing-half who made a name for himself in season 1914-15
with some fine, determined displays in the first team.
21FL 1g, 2FA

MAY, Hugh, (1903-04) Inside-left.
Born: Dykehead, Lanark. Played for Glasgow Rangers;
Derby County July 1902; Fulham cs 1903-04. May had
six games for Derby County at centre-forward in
October and November of 1902. However, he could not
find the net and was dropped. Joined Fulham as an
inside-left but after ten games found himself back in the
reserves. One of many players allowed to leave the club
in the summer of 1904 as manager Harry Bradshaw
rebuilt the team.
8SL 2g, 2FA

MAYBANK, Edward G., (1975-7 and 1979-80) Forward.
Born: Lambeth, 11 October 1956. Played for South
London boys; Chelsea February 1974; Fulham (on
loan) November 1976, permanently March 1977 (£65,000);
Brighton November 1977 (£237,000); Fulham, December
1979 (£150,000); PSV Eindhoven (Holland) August
1980 (£250,000); retired through injury 1981. A great
favourite with the Fulham crowd, Maybank had two
spells at Craven Cottage. Manager Bobby Campbell
made plenty of money for Fulham out of Maybank's
transfer fees. Never a great success at Brighton despite
costing so much money. Formed a fine partnership with
John Mitchell as supplier of chances. Not so successful
when used as an out-and-out striker. Had to retire
through a knee injury after moving to Holland.
46FL 17g, 2FA, 2LC 2g

MAYES, Kenneth W., (1935-7) Inside-forward.
Born: Wickford, Essex. Played for Southend United
1931-32; Barking; Fulham 1935-37. After a season at
Southend where he played five games, Mayes moved
into non-League football with Barking. He made a
comeback in the Football League with Fulham and
appeared twice in the first team. His brother Arnold
played for Chelsea as a wing-half for a number of
seasons.
2FL

MEADE, Thomas George, (1900-04) Centre-forward.
Born: Plumstead, 14 May 1877. Played for Royal
Arsenal 1894, Tottenham Hotspur cs 1897; Fulham
December 1900-04. One of Fulham's most popular
players in their early Southern League days. A fine
pivot and explosive goalscorer, Meade was the leading
goalscorer from 1901 to 1903 when he scored 77 first-
team goals and picked up two Southern League Second
Division Championship medals on the way. He had his
up and downs at Spurs and Arsenal.
42SL 29g, 12FA 15g

MEALAND, Barry Kenneth, (1959-68) Right-back.
Born: Carshalton, 24 January 1943. Played for Surrey
schools; joined Fulham 1959, signed professional October
1961; Rotherham United August 1968-70 (£7,000).
Mealand may have become a professional golfer before
he joined Fulham but chose football instead. Developing
into a fine full-back when a broken leg at Highbury in
1965 seriously set back his career. Never quite the same
player afterwards. With Fulham's relegation from
Division One in 1968, Mealand was allowed to move to
Rotherham for whom he made 45 appearances.
28/1FL, 3FA, 3LC

MEESON, Arthur William, (1928-9) Goalkeeper.
Born: Headington, 1904. Played for Oxford City;
Arsenal 1927; Fulham December 1928 (£175); Lincoln
City cs 1929-32. Meeson won an England amateur cap
against Scotland in 1928. Being unable to get into
Arsenal's first team he moved to Fulham but appeared
just once in the first team in a disastrous performance
against Southend in March 1928. Fulham led 2-0 at the
interval but Meeson let in four second-half goals and
Fulham lost a vital match. Played 12 times for Lincoln
City.
1FL

180

METCHICK, David J., (1961-5) Inside-forward.
Born: Derby, 14 August 1943. Played for West Ham United Juniors; Fulham August 1961; Leyton Orient December 1964; Peterborough United March 1967; Queen's Park Rangers August 1968; Arsenal September 1970; Atlanta (USA); Brentford September 1973; Hendon 1975. A highly-promising youngster, Metchick won England Youth caps and had a flair for scoring goals. Too small for a striking role and playing out of position on the wing, he lost his confidence and was allowed to leave for Leyton Orient. Thereafter he wandered from one club to another, playing 220 League games and scoring 35 goals in total.
47FL 9g, 4FA 1g, 5LC 3g

MIERCZNIKOWSKI WL 'Micky', (1903-04) Outside-left.
Born: Paddington, 1877. Played for Pemberton, North County; Portsmouth (amateur) 1900; West Ham United (amateur) 1902; Fulham (amateur) December 1903; Southern United 1904; Clapton; Leyton 1906-07. Mierznikowski's family were East European refugees. Nicknamed 'Micky' for obvious reasons, he made only the odd appearances for his clubs, including just two for Fulham, at Wellingborough and Spurs at the turn of the year in 1903.
2SL

MILLER, Charles, (1914-15) Outside-right.
Played for Cambuslang Rangers; Fulham March 1915. Signed from Scottish Football as a talented right-winger, Miller stayed two months at the Cottage before going off to war.
6FL

MILLER, John W., (1938-47) Outside-left.
Born: London. Played for Dulwich Hamlet; signed for Fulham as an amateur cs 1937; Margate 1947. Miller played four games as a replacement for the injured John Arnold before war interrupted his career. Turned out occasionally for Fulham in wartime games when on leave from the army. Did not play for the first team after the hostilities. Miller was stationed in Scotland and assisted Ayr United on a number of occasions.
4FL

MILLINGTON, Ben, (1908-09) Inside-forward.
Born: Lincoln, circa 1892. Played for Lincoln South End; Fulham November 1908-09 Strong and quick with a good shot, Millington played regularly for Fulham's reserves but made just one appearance in the first team near the end of season 1908-09. A cousin of Charlie Millington.
1FL

MILLINGTON, Charles, (1907-09) Inside-forward.
Born: Lincoln, 25 April 1884. Played for Grantham; Ripley; Aston Villa 1905; Fulham October 1907; Birmingham cs 1909-12. Adaptable forward who was quick and strong despite being small. Scored four goals in a match with Glossop in November 1907 but could not be described as a prolific scorer. Scored 42 goals in 176 League games for Aston Villa, Fulham and Birmingham. Probably played his best soccer at the latter club.
57FL 18g, 6FA 3g

MOLLOY, Peter, (1931-3) Centre-half.
Born: Rossendale, April 1911. Played for Fulham cs

1931; Bristol Rovers cs 1933; Cardiff City January 1934; Queen's Park Rangers cs 1935; Stockport County cs 1936; Carlisle United cs 1937; Bradford City cs 1938 to 1943. Not very tall for a centre-half (5ft 10in) but Molloy was always effective in that position. Played mainly a reserve team role until he joined Carlisle in 1937 when he had his best season, making 33 appearances. Played his last game in a wartime game for Bradford City in 1943.
4FL

MORELINE, David J., (1968-74) Left-back.
Born: Dagenham, 2 December 1950. Played for Fulham as an apprentice in 1967, signed professional January 1968; Reading June 1974-81. Progressing through Fulham's youth scheme, Moreline was a competent full-back who also played some games in midfield in 1970. He once had the misfortune to be carried off after injuring himself in a pre-match kick-about against Hull City in September 1972. Moved on to Elm Park in 1974, where he made 166 appearances in seven seasons before retiring to become a postman in 1981.
63/7FL, 3/1FA, 7/1LC

MORRIS, David Harry 'Abe', (1920-21) Centre-forward.
Born: London, 25 November 1900. Died: USA, 20 December 1985. Played for Vicar of Wakefield FC; Fulham 1919; Brentford cs 1921; Millwall Athletic February 1923; Swansea Town cs 1925; Swindon Town cs 1926; Clapton Orient cs 1933; Cheltenham Town September 1934. Morris' family came to England as Jewish refugees from Eastern Europe. A promising forward, Harry fell foul of the Fulham management. Told to find another club after an incident at a Cardiff hotel where he was dubbed the 'Cardiff Casanova'. Unfortunately Fulham lost a great forward as Morris became a prolific scorer. In season 1922-3 he was top scorer for both Brentford and Millwall and later scored 214 goals for Swindon in 261 appearances. He scored 287 League goals in all before joining the diplomatic service after retiring from the game. Died in the USA in 1985.
6FL 2g, 1FA 1g

181

MORTON, Alan, (1970-71) Forward.
Born: Erith, 13 April 1950. Played for Woking; Crystal
Palace November 1967; Stockport County August 1969
(on loan): Nuneaton Borough 1970; Fulham August
1970; Wimbledon cs 1971; Maidstone United; Ashford
Town; Woking; Kingstonian; Wokingham Town; Epsom
and Ewell. Morton did the rounds of non-League
football after leaving Fulham in 1971. Scored in his one
and only League game for Fulham against Halifax in
November 1970. He also appeared in three League Cup
ties. Big, direct forward who scored plenty of goals in
non-League soccer.
1FL 1g, 2/1LC

MOSELEY, Robert A., (1926-7) Inside-forward.
Born: Lewisham. Joined Fulham in 1926. Little-known
Londoner who made his debut at Wolves in April 1926.
Played his second and last game at Blackpool ten
months later.
2FL

MOSS, Robert Stephen, (1966-8) Inside-forward.
Born: Kenton, 15 February 1949. Joined Fulham cs
1964, signed professional February 1966; Peterborough
United July 1969; Wealdstone 1972. Pint-sized player
who stood 5ft 5in tall and weighed only 8st 13lb. Very
few people who saw Moss' last-minute winning goal
against Everton in September 1967 will ever forget it.
He scored with a thunderous header from Fred Callaghan's
cross. After two seasons of relegation, Moss was given a
free transfer and he moved to Peterborough. He scored
16 goals in 103 games for the Posh before moving to
Wealdstone.
8/1FL 3g, 1LC

MOUNCHER, Frederick W., (1907-11) Outside-left.
Born: Southampton, circa 1884. Played for Cambridge;
Southampton 1903; Fulham November 1907; retired
1911. Mouncher won Southern League Championship
honours in his first season at The Dell. He scored 16

goals in 105 appearances for Southampton before being
transferred to Fulham with fellow forward Fred Harrison.
Played in an international trial game at Manchester in
January 1908 but his career was soon blighted by ill
health and he eventually had to retire because of
consumption in 1911. One of Fulham's fastest players, a
typically direct winger of his time. Mouncher was
converted to left-half near the end of his career.
43FL 10g, 9FA 1g

MULLEN, Brendan G.J., (1968-9) Forward.
Born: Coleraine, 20 Janaury 1950. Played for Coleraine
Fulham, February 1968; Millwall July 1969; Coleraine
1970. Mullen made a sensational debut in an FA Cup
tie at Roker Park. Fulham were bottom of the Second
Division and Sunderland were riding high in the First.
Mullen scored twice in a shock 4-1 victory. After
becoming homesick at Millwall he returned to Irish
soccer, playing in Coleraine's Irish Cup-winning side of
1972. Mullen won a Northern Ireland Under-23 cap
whilst at the Cottage against Italy and won Irish Youth
caps as a youngster.
2/2FL, 1FA 2g

MURPHY, Jerry, (1929-31) Inside-forward.
Born: Dowlais, Wales. Played for Merthyr Town 1925;
Cardiff City February 1927; Fulham cs 1929 (£125);
Crystal Palace cs 1931-32. Murphy, a diminutive,
scheming inside-forward arrived at the Cottage for a fee
of £125 from Cardiff City. He had made only one
appearance at Ninian Park in two seasons. Had previously
played for Merthyr Town who were at that time a Third
Division club.
13FL 2g

MURRAY, Allen Ferguson, (1931-4) Left-half.
Born: Darwen, circa 1912. Played for Rochdale 1927;
Darwen; Fulham cs 1931; Bristol Rovers cs 1935.
Murray had to wait three years for his Fulham debut at
Bradford City in March 1934. It also proved to be his
last game. His best season was 1935-6 when he played
13 games for Bristol Rovers.
1FL

MURRAY, Ivan H., (1968-9) Right-half.
Born: Ballymoney, Northern Ireland, 29 May 1944.
Played for Coleraine 1961; Fulham February 1968;
Coleraine May 1969; Ballymena United March 1979.
Spent seven years with Coleraine before signing for
Fulham. A part-time footballer in Ireland, Murray was
also employed as a driver for Coleraine University.
Made his first-team debut in Fulham's last home match
in Division One in May 1968. Released at the end of
season 1968-9 whereupon he returned to Coleraine.
Won an Irish Cup-winners' medal in 1972.
4/1FL

NASH, H., (1919-20) Outside-right.
Born: Sheffield. Joined Fulham in August 1919. Made
his debut against South Shields the same month.
Played three games for Fulham on the right wing.
Possibly later played for Cardiff City and Merthyr
Town.
3FL

NELSON, David, (1946-7) Inside-forward.
Born: Douglas Water, Scotland, 3 February 1918.
Played for Douglas Water FC; St Bernards (Edinburgh);

182

Arsenal cs 1936; Fulham December 1946; Brentford August 1947; Queen's Park Rangers February 1950; Crystal Palace March 1952; Ashford Town player-manager 1954. Started his professional career with Scottish Second Division club, St Bernards, and after moving to Arsenal played regularly throughout World War Two. Came to Fulham with Cyril Grant in a deal which took Ronnie Rooke to Highbury. Never settled in at Fulham and moved on to Brentford where he played over 100 games. A versatile player who was equally at home at half-back or inside-forward.
23FL 2g 1FA

NEWCOMBE, Len 'Bernie', (1948-55) Outside-left.
Born: Swansea, 28 February 1931. Signed professional for Fulham May 1948; Brentford April 1956-58. Newcombe had few chances at Fulham due to the fact that he was in competition for the left-wing berth with Charlie Mitten and Tosh Chamberlain. An orthodox winger who would try one hundred per cent but lacked the skills. Moved to Griffin Park in 1956 playing 84 games and scoring ten goals for the Bees. Scouting for Fulham in the mid 1970s.
23FL 3g

NICHOLL, James, (1914-18) Inside-left.
Born: Consett. Played for Dipton United; Spen Black; Allendale Park; Fulham 1915. Joined Fulham in 1915 as inside-left. Later played some wartime games at left-half. Scored his only goal for Fulham in a London Combination match in March 1916 when Clapton Orient were defeated 4-0.
3FL

NICHOLS, Brian Albert, (1963-8) Left-back.
Born: Dagenham, 30 May 1945. Played for Fulham as an apprentice in 1961, signed professional July 1963; Millwall July 1968 (£4,000); Romford cs 1969; Ashford Town; retired through illness in 1970; Grays Athletic manager, Ford United coach; Fulham as youth team coach cs 1982. Played at left-back in Fulham's 'Great Escape' season of 1965-6. Gradually lost his place to Fred Callaghan. Scored his only goal against Wolves in August 1967 with a 30-yard shot which took a deflection off a defender. Once had the misfortune to be substituted

through injury after only two minutes at Southampton. After moving into the Southern League, yellow jaundice prematurely ended his career at 25. Moved back to Fulham in 1982 as youth-team coach.
50/1FL 1g, 1/1FA, 4LC

NIDD, George Frederick, (1903-04) Left-back.
Born: Boston, Lincs, 1869. Died: 1956. Played for Preston NE 1893; Everton 1893; Southport Central; Stalybridge Rovers 1896; Lincoln City 1897; Grimsby Town 1898; Watford cs 1900; Brentford cs 1902; Fulham cs 1903-04. Sturdy and powerful full-back, Nidd never gained much success until joining Grimsby in 1899. Appeared regularly for Watford and Brentford as well. Played three FA Cup games for Fulham in 1903-04, but was really a reserve as they represented Fulham in the qualifying rounds of the Cup that season.
3FA

NIXON, Wilfred, (1909-21) Goalkeeper.
Born: Gateshead, 22 October 1882. Died: 8 April 1985. Played for Wallsend Park Villa, Newburn FC; Fulham 1909, retired 1921. Nixon lived until he was 102 years old and Fulham invited him back to the Cottage for a special celebration on his 100th birthday. As a 'keeper he had a safe pair of hands and keen eyes. Did not make his Football League debut until he was 30. He had obviously lied about his age when he signed for Fulham, because the club programme stated that he was 25 at the time.
27FL, 2FA

OAKES, Keith B., (1986) Centre-half.
Born: Bedworth, 3 July 1956. Played for Bedworth Peterborough United signed professional July 1973; Newport County, September 1978 (£15,000); Gillingham, August 1984; Fulham September 1986 (£15,000). Started his career at Peterborough but did not find regular first-team football until joining Newport County. Played 232 League games scoring 27 goals before signing for Gillingham. Reliable defender who carried out his duties efficently and methodically.
41FL 3g, 4FA 1g

O'CONNOR, Turlough, (1966-8) Centre-forward.
Born: Athlone, Republic of Ireland, 22 July 1946. Played for Athlone Town; Limerick United; Bohemians; Fulham May 1966; Dundalk June 1968; Bohemians; Athlone Town manager in 1983. O'Connor won a Republic of Ireland cap whilst at the Cottage and won seven in all. Scored the winning goal in a surprise World Cup victory in Czechoslovakia in 1968. Although top scorer for the reserves in his two seasons at Fulham, he played just one League match, at Sheffield Wednesday in September 1967. Also won Irish Amateur international honours. One of eight children of an Irish Army tuba-player.
1FL

O'DONNELL, Rudolph Peter, (1909-10) Goalkeeper.
Born: Madras, India. Played for the Army; Shepherd's Bush; Hanwell; Reading 1908; Fulham (on loan) December 1909. A fine all-round sportsman, he remained an amateur throughout his career. Won Middlesex County honours and was unlucky not to gain Amateur international honours. O'Donnell was a fine musician who also worked as a bandmaster with the Army.
3FL

O'LEARY, Daniel, (1969-70) Inside-forward.
Born: Cork, Republic of Ireland, 11 January 1951.
Played for Millwall, May 1968; Fulham July 1969.
O'Leary's only Football League appearance was as
substitute for Fulham at Bristol Rovers in September
1969. Came to Fulham with John Gilchrist in a deal
which took Brian Dear and Brendan Mullen to Millwall.
Won four Republic of Ireland Youth international caps
at Millwall.
0/1FL

ORR, William, (1903-04) Right-back.
Born: 1875 Died: December 1912. Played for Preston
NE 1894-97; Glossop NE 1899; Manchester City cs
1901; Fulham cs 1903; Glossop cs 1904; Watford cs
1906. Regular full-back in Fulham's first season as a
limited company. Gained plenty of Football League
experience with his previous clubs, Preston, Glossop
and Manchester City. Played in 13 out of 34 games for
Manchester City in season 1902-03 when they won the
Second Division Championship. Was only 37 years old
when he died in 1912.
26SL, 7FA

O'SULLIVAN, Peter A., (1981-3) Midfield.
Born: Colwyn Bay, 4 March 1951. Played for Manchester
United March 1968; Brighton April 1970; San Diego
(USA) 1979, Brighton 1980; Fulham cs 1981; Charlton
Athletic (on loan) October 1982; Reading (on loan)
November 1982; Aldershot August 1983; Maidstone
United February 1984, Crawley Town cs 1984; Worthing
1985. O'Sullivan won Welsh caps at full, Under-23 and
Schoolboy levels. Being unable to make the grade at
Old Trafford, O'Sullivan joined Brighton and gave
them great service, playing 433 games and scoring 38
goals between 1970 and 1981. Joined Fulham on a free
transfer and was almost ever-present in their promotion
season of 1981-2.
45/1FL 1g, 2FA, 7LC

OVEREND, A., (1912-13) Outside-right.
Played for Fulham 1912-13. A right-winger who played
just three games for Fulham. His debut was against
Bury in January 1913.
3FL

PACKMAN, Frederick W., (1924-6) Outside-right.
Born: Birmingham, 1901. Played for Barnet; Fulham cs
1924; Watford cs 1926-27. Packman played five games
each for Fulham and Watford. Signed from Athenian
League side Barnet for a small fee. Made his Fulham
debut at Clapton Orient in a 3-0 defeat in December
1924.
5FL

PAPE, Albert Arthur, (1925-7) Centre-forward.
Born: Wath-on-Dearne, summer 1897. Died: Doncaster,
18 November 1955. Played for Wath Athletic; Bolton-
on-Dearne; Rotherham County; 1919; Notts County cs
1923; Clapton Orient cs 1924; Manchester United
February 1925; Fulham October 1925; Rhyl Athletic cs
1927; Darwen; Hartlepools United cs 1929; Halifax
Town cs 1930-31. Involved in one of the strangest
transfers, Pape travelled with Clapton Orient to play
Manchester United as an Orient player but was transferred
to United before the game and scored one of their goals
in a 4-2 victory. He was unable to play League football
between 1927 and 1929 as Fulham held his registration
and no club would match Fulham's asking price.
Finally released in 1929. Scored 103 goals in his 266
Football League games.
42FL 12g, 6FA 4g

**PAPWORTH, Jack Martin, (1919-24) Centre-half/
centre-forward.**
Born: Deptford, 8 November 1895. Played for Fulham
1919; Watford December 1924-26. Made his debut as a
centre-half but by 1923 Jack had been converted to
centre-forward and scored ten goals in 19 games in
season 1923-4. Moved to Watford in December 1924
and carried on his goalscoring ways for the Hornets.
39FL 16g, 2FA

PARMENTER, Terence Leslie, (1963-9) Outside-left.
Born: Romford, 21 October 1947. Joined Fulham as an
apprentice in 1963, signed professional November
1964; Orient February 1969; Gillingham August 1971
to 1973. Parmenter, an orthodox winger, played
occasionally, usually when Les Barrett was injured. A
hot-headed player who was sent off twice in his Fulham
career. Converted to full-back at Gillingham but he left
League football at the age of 25.
18/1FL 1g, 1/1FA, 1LC

PARSONAGE, George, (1908-09) Centre-half.
Born: Darwen, 1880. Played for Blackburn Rovers;
Brentford cs 1903; Fulham cs 1908; Banned from
football cs 1909. A fine, positive player who supplied
his inside-forwards with a stream of good passes.
Appeared in two international trial matches in 1905 but
never gained a full cap. Played 176 games for Brentford
before transferring to Fulham. Sadly, he was banned
for life in 1909 after asking for a £50 signing-on fee to
join Chesterfield. The maximum was £10. The Chesterfield
board reported him and even though he said it had been
a joke and a large petition was presented, his ban could
not be prevented.
23FL 3g, 1FA

PAVITT, William E., (1946-53) Right-back.
Born: West Ham, 30 June 1920. Signed for Fulham as a
professional August 1946; Southend United May 1953;
Tunbridge Wells 1955. Pavitt was spotted playing on
the right wing for his RAF Flight team at Debden by his

own PTI, Ronnie Rooke. He either played at centre-half or full-back for Fulham and stood 6ft 2in tall. After a spell at Southend United, for whom he made 80 appearances, Pavitt joined Jim Taylor at Tunbridge Wells. Employed by the Post Office on retirement from soccer.
50FL 1g, 2FA

PEARSON, Mark 'Pancho', (1965-8) Inside-forward.
Born: Ridgeway, Derbyshire, 28 October 1939. Played for Manchester United May 1957; Sheffield Wednesday October 1963; Fulham May 1965; Halifax Town, March 1968. Pearson won England Schoolboy and Youth international honours as a youngster. Joined Manchester United but gained a bad reputation with his 'teddy boy' image, which got him into trouble with the referees. After the tragedy of Munich he featured in United's gallant fight to stay in the top flight, Wednesday manager Vic Buckingham signed him for £20,000 and his progress was checked when he twice broke a leg. Signed again by Buckingham in 1965, but this time for Fulham, he scored a vital goal at Leeds in April 1966 to help save Fulham from relegation.
53/5FL 7g, 1/1FA, 6LC

PENTECOST, Michael Eric, (1966-73) Right-back.
Born: Hounslow, 13 April 1948. Played for Crystal Palace Juniors; Sutton United; Fulham August 1966; Durban City (South Africa) January 1973. Signed from Sutton United as a midfield player and made his debut against Blackpool in April 1967 in this position. Bobby Robson converted Pentecost to full-back where he played unspectacularly and efficiently. A broken leg in December 1968 meant a long absence from the first team but he soon re-established himself on his return to fitness. Decided to emigrate to South Africa in January 1973. His elder brother Alan went to Oxford University where he won a Blue at soccer and basketball.
81/6FL, 1FA, 7LC

PETERS, Frank, (1931-3) Outside-right.
Born: Birmingham, 26 February 1910. Played for Wellington St George; Charlton Athletic 1930; Fulham March 1932; Swindon Town cs 1933; Bristol City cs 1936-39. Peters scored in his only game for Fulham, at Norwich in March 1932. After leaving the Cottage he made over 100 appearances for both Swindon and Bristol City. A regular scorer at Swindon with 44 goals in three seasons.
1FL 1g

PETERS, Gary D., (1979-82) Right-back.
Born: Carshalton, 3 August 1954. Played for Aldershot 1970-72 as an apprentice; Guildford City 1972-75; Reading, May 1975; Fulham August 1979 (£40,000); Wimbledon July 1982; Aldershot cs 1984; Reading February 1985. Peters holds three Divisional Championship medals, 1978-9 Fourth Division (Reading), 1982-3 Fourth Division (Wimbledon) and 1985-6 Third Division (Reading). Failed to make the grade as a youngster but Reading resurrected his career when they signed him from Southern League club Guildford City. Peters played 179 games for the Elm Park club before his move to Fulham. Although basically a defender, he appeared as a striker for a brief period for Fulham, under the direction of manager Malcolm Macdonald.
57/7FL 2g, 4FA, 4LC

PHILLIPSON, T., (1904-05) Inside-left.
Played for Bishop Aukland; Fulham cs 1904. Phillipson played only one game for Fulham at Reading in March 1905, in a 0-0 draw. Signed from the same club as Alfred Harwood.
1SL

PIKE, Christopher, (1985) Forward.
Born: Cardiff, 19 October 1961. Played for Maesteg; Barry Town; Fulham on trial April 1984, signed professional February 1985; Cardiff City (on loan) December 1986. Discovered in Welsh League football, this tall, lanky striker made his debut against Sheffield United in September 1985. Scored five goals in 32 appearances for the first team in his first season at the club.
32/7FL 4g, 3/1LC 1g

PIKE, Theophilus 'Tot', (1926-7) Outside-right.
Born: Sunderland, 25 March 1907. Died: Bury St Edmonds, 26 October 1967. Played for Sunderland Wednesday; Fulham cs 1925; Bournemouth cs 1927; Birmingham 1928; Southend United cs 1930; Norwich City cs 1933-35. Pike played three games for Fulham in his one season at the Cottage. Found most success at Southend where he scored 18 goals in 66 appearances. Mainly a reserve at his other clubs. His hobbies were golf and playing the piano.
3FL

PILKINGTON, Frederick Albert, (1924-7) Utility.
Born: Camberwell, 22 April 1901. Died: October 1986. Played for Dulwich Hamlet 1916-24; Fulham February 1924; Sheppey United cs 1927; Cricket for Surrey. Played at right-back for Dulwich Hamlet in their 1920 FA Amateur Cup victory over Tufnell Park. His partner was Leslie Bowker who also played for Fulham and was later Fulham's club president. Appeared at full-back, wing-half and inside-forward for Fulham. Scored Fulham's goal at Stockport in February 1925 on his debut, which was lost 4-1. Played one county championship game for Surrey in 1926. He was a fine bowler and reasonable tail-end batsman.
4FL 1g

PINKNEY, Alan J., (1973) Inside-forward.
Born: Battersea, 1 January 1947. Played for Corinthian Casuals 1965; St Luke's College, Exeter; Middlesex Wanderers; Exeter City as an amateur 1967; Crystal Palace July 1969-73; Fulham (on loan) January 1973. As an amateur Pinkney toured the Far East with Middlesex Wanderers. Like Jim Hicks, Pinkney was teaching at St Luke's College when he played for Exeter City. Played well during his loan spell at Fulham but was not signed permanently. Alan had been a Fulham fan as a boy and had a trial at the Cottage when 16. Scored one of the goals which beat Pelé's Santos in a friendly in March 1973.
11/1FL

PITTS, Harold, (1934-48) Right-back.
Born: Leyton, 1915. Played for London Boys; Islington Corinthians; Fulham cs 1934-48. Spotted by Fulham playing for London Boys at the Cottage and signed after the game. Played the odd game before the war and was still on Fulham's books up to 1948. Played his last first-team game in a wartime match in season 1942-3.
9FL

PORTER, William, (1902-04) Outside-right.
Played for London Caledonians; Fulham February 1902; Chelsea cs 1905-07. Porter would turn out occasionally for Fulham and Chelsea, but the London Caledonians were his first love. As an amateur he could pick and choose who he played for. Appeared regularly for Fulham before they moved up to Division One of the Southern League. Played twice for Chelsea in their first two seasons in the Football League.
8SL 3g, 4FA

PRATT, Thomas Peet, (1904-05) Centre-forward.
Born: Fleetwood, 28 August 1873, Died: Fleetwood, 1935. Played for Fleetwood Rangers; Grimsby Town cs 1895; Preston NE June 1896; Tottenham Hotspur, May 1899; Preston NE, May 1900; Woolwich Arsenal cs 1903; Fulham cs 1904; Blackpool cs 1905-06. Strongly built, forceful and fearless forward, Pratt was a splendid dribbler and possessed a fine shot. Won a Southern League Championship medal with Spurs in season 1899-1900 scoring 19 goals. Past his best by the time he arrived at the Cottage. A motor engineer by trade.
4SL

PROBERT, William H., (1925-7) Left-back.
Born: Worksop, 15 January 1893. Died: 1946. Played for Worksop; Portsmouth cs 1911; Southend United November 1913; Portsmouth cs 1914; Fulham cs 1925; retired cs 1927. A talented full-back who gave Portsmouth great service. Signed from his local club Worksop, Probert stayed 14 seasons at Fratton Park. Missed only nine games for Pompey between 1919 and 1924 and accumulated a total of 287 appearances for the South Coast club. He won a Southern League Championship medal in 1919-20 and a Third Division Championship medal in 1923-4. At the veteran stage when signed by Fulham. Had a brief spell at Southend in the early stages of his career who were then managed by Joe Bradshaw, later Fulham's manager when Probert was at the club. Became a publican when he left football.
16FL, 1FA

PROUD, Joseph, (1930-32) Outside-right.
Born: Dipton, Durham, 13 November 1905. Died: Woking, 28 June 1977. Played for Dipton; Spennymoor; Fulham 1930; Aldershot cs 1932 (£350); retired in 1941, rejoined Aldershot as trainer and various other jobs from 1956-74. Proud could play equally well on either wing. Small in build (5ft 6in, 10st 4lb) he tended to take a battering from the larger full-backs. Gave Aldershot great service, first as a player for nine seasons, then as trainer and general odd job man for another 18 years.
12FL 3g

PROUT, Richard S., (1908-10) Inside-forward.
Born: London, 1888. Played for Silverdale (Fulham); Fulham Amateurs; Tunbridge Wells Rangers; Fulham 1908; Stockport County cs 1910; Plymouth Argyle 1913. Versatile player who was equally effective at wing-half, inside or centre-forward. A fast, nimble and skilful player, Prout was unfortunate not to be given more chances at Fulham. Moved to Stockport and was a sensation in his first season scoring 16 goals in 35 games. However, after the death of his brother, playing in a local parks side, Prout's career seemed to decline.
7FL, 1FA

RADCLIFFE, Mark, (1946-8) Goalkeeper.
Born: Hyde, 26 October 1919. Played for Oldham Athletic; Fulham 1946; Witton Albion; Rochdale November 1952. A tall, well-built 'keeper who had the odd game in the Fulham goal. Played 88 wartime games for Oldham before signing for Fulham. Drifted out of League soccer after leaving the Cottage but made a brief, one-game comeback for Rochdale in 1952.
11FL, 2FA

RAMPLING, Dennis W., (1942-8) Outside-right.
Born: Gainsborough, 25 November 1923. Played for Fulham 1942; Worcester City (on loan) September 1946; Bournemouth July 1948; Brentford May 1949. Rampling, like so many others, had his early soccer career interrupted by the war. Turned out occasionally for Fulham in wartime games. His opportunities after the war were few because of his Royal Air Force responsibilities as a PT instructor.
2FL, 2FA 1g

REDWOOD, George E., (1910-11) Left-back.
Born: London, circa 1887. Played for Enfield Town; Fourth Battalion, Royal Fusiliers Regiment; Fulham, March 1910; West Ham United, April 1911-12. Powerful full-back, equally clever on either wing, tackled intrepidly and unerringly and possessed sound judgement. Made

only seven appearances for Fulham before moving to West Ham with Fred Harrison. Played ten games for the Hammers' first team before being given a free transfer at the end of season 1911-12.
7FL

REEVES, John Charles, (1979-85) Midfield.
Born: Hackney, 8 July 1963. Played for Hackney and London Schools, joined Fulham as an apprentice in July 1979, signed professional June 1981; Colchester United August 1985. A hard-working left-sided midfielder who possessed a fine shot. Kept out of the side by Ray Houghton and hampered by breaking both arms in season 1983-4. Found regular first-team football at Colchester.
9/5FL, 2FA, 1LC

REGAN, Edward Gerard Patrick, (1929-30) Half-back.
Born: Chester, 27 December 1900. Died: Runcorn, Autumn 1973. Played for Crichton Athletic; Wrexham cs 1921; Manchester Central cs 1928; Fulham cs 1929 to 1930. Regan played only one game for Fulham against Northampton in September 1929. He had gained much experience at Wrexham. In his seven seasons at the Racecourse Ground he played 188 League games.
1FL

REID, George H., (1923-4) Centre-forward.
Born: Belfast. Played for Walsall 1921; Cardiff City 1923; Fulham December 1923; Stockport County cs 1924-25. Reid won an Irish international cap against Scotland whilst playing for Cardiff City in March 1923. Ireland lost 1-0 in Belfast. Played only three games for Fulham during his short stay at the club. Never a regular at Cardiff but played the occasional First Division game for the Ninian Park club.
2FL, 1FA

REID, Joseph E., (1930-31) Full-back.
Born: Hebburn-on-Tyne. Played for Manchester City 1919; Stockport County cs 1920; Boston circa 1926; Newport County cs 1928; Fulham cs 1930-31. Orthodox full-back who won Third Division North Championship honours with Stockport County in 1921-2. Began his career with Manchester City but established himself at Stockport where he made 145 appearances. After two seasons out of League football, Reid made a comeback with Newport in 1928. He had few chances of regular first-team football when he joined Fulham, playing only seven games.
7FL

RICHARDS, Richard W., (1924-5) Inside-left.
Born: Glyncorrwg, Glamorgan. Died: Manchester, 27 January 1934. Played for Wolves 1914; West Ham United cs 1922; Fulham cs 1924; Mold cs 1925. Dicky Richards played in the same Welsh international side as the great Billy Meredith. Helped Wales to a rare Home Championship victory in season 1923-4 and scored one of the goals which beat England 2-1 in March 1920. Played for West Ham in the first Wembley FA Cup Final in 1923, the famous 'White Horse' Final, when about 200,000 people entered the stadium to watch the match. Surprisingly left Fulham for Mold in summer 1925 while seemingly still at the top of his profession.
21FL 2g, 2FA 1g

RICHARDSON, John P., (1969-73) Central-defender.
Born: Ashington, 5 February 1949. Played for Millwall 1965 as an apprentice; Brentford August 1966; Fulham August 1969 (£12,000); Aldershot July 1973-76; Napier City (New Zealand); Wokingham Town; Addlestone; Aylesbury United; Hayes. Essentially a central-defender but Richardson played the odd game at centre-forward. Scored a memorable goal against Bristol Rovers in December 1969 with a superb diving header. As a youngster John was allowed to leave Millwall at the end of his apprenticeship and sign professional for Brentford instead. Broke his leg in his first season at Griffin Park but went on to make 85 appearances for the Bees before joining Fulham.
61/10FL 6g, 4FA, 5LC 1g

RICKETT, Horace F.J., (1945-6) Goalkeeper.
Born: Orsett, 3 January 1912. Played for Chelmsford; Clapton Orient; Fulham (as a guest) February 1945; Reading June 1946-47. Rickett played in the two Cup ties against Charlton Athletic in season 1945-46 and also made 25 wartime appearances. Officially a Chelmsford player but played regularly for Clapton Orient from 1943 to 1945. Moved to Reading in 1946 where he made his Football League debut at the age of 34.
2FA

RIDDELL, James Harold, (1923-6) Left-half.
Born: Dumbarton, 6 February 1894. Played for Bellevue Hearts; Glasgow Ashfield; Glasgow Rangers May 1912; St Mirren; Millwall Athletic cs 1920; Fulham December 1923; Wigan Borough October 1925-29. If Riddell is alive today he has probably changed his name by deed poll. Never a regular with Fulham but had gained much experience in Scottish football and with Millwall where he made 105 appearances in three and a half seasons. Moved to Wigan Borough with Tom Fleming.
37FL, 5FA

ROBERTS, David Frazer, (1965-71) Centre-half.
Born: Southampton, 26 November 1949. Played for St
Albans Juniors; signed as an apprentice for Fulham
May 1965, signed professional September 1967; Oxford
United, February 1971 (£4,000); Hull City, February
1975 (£60,000); Cardiff City August 1978 (£30,000);
retired through injury 1980, made a comeback at
Kettering Town 1981; Tsun Wan (Hong Kong); Bath
City; Trowbridge Town. Roberts had the misfortune to
score an own-goal on his debut for Fulham. Allowed to
move to Oxford for a small fee and proved a very good
signing. Dave won Welsh Under-23 and full international
honours including 18 full games between 1973 and 1978.
Small for a central defender but became an economical
and highly-proficient player.
21/1FL, 3LC

ROBOTHAM, Harold, (1903-05) Right-half.
Born: Heath Town nr Wolverhampton, 1881. Played
for Wolves Post Office FC., Redshaw Albion (Leeds);
Ossett; Hunslet; Wolves 1901; Fulham cs 1903; Brentford
October 1905; Glossop cs 1906; New Brompton cs 1907-08.
Hard-working half-back who enjoyed a varied career at
all levels of football. Finally lost his place at Fulham to
the more experienced Billy Goldie. Found regular first-
team football at Brentford, Glossop and New Brompton.
34SL, 5FA 1g

RONSON, Brian, (1953-6) Goalkeeper.
Born: Durham, 7 August 1935. Played for Fulham
March 1953; Southend United August 1956; Norwich
City August 1959; Peterborough United July 1961-63.
Made his debut shortly after being signed as a replace-
ment for the injured Ian Black who had broken his arm.
Lasted two games and was then replaced by Frank
Elliott. Does not seem to have played again for Fulham
after this but remained on the books until transferred to
Southend. Played 30 games for Southend and 50 for
Peterborough.
2FL

ROSENIOR, Leroy, (1982-5) Centre-forward.
Born: Clapton, 24 March 1964. Signed professional for
Fulham August 1982; Queen's Park Rangers, September
1985 (£100,000); Fulham May 1987. Bustling striker
who often lacked finesse in his play but was sometimes
very effective. Good in the air and fast on the ground,
Rosenior won England Under-19 and Schoolboy honours.
His parents were from Sierra Leone and his full name is
Degraft-Rosenior. Transferred to neighbours Queen's
Park Rangers but, although he was substitute in Rangers'
League Cup Final appearance in 1986 when they lost
3-0 to Oxford, his chances in the first team were limited.
53/1FL 15g, 3FA

ROSIER, Bertie Leonard, (1928-30) Right-back.
Born: Hanwell, 21 March 1893. Played for Southall;
Brentford 1914; Clapton Orient March 1923; Southend
United cs 1927; Fulham cs 1928-30. Spent 17 months as
a PoW in World War One. Returned to Brentford and
helped them win the London Combination Championship in season 1918-19. Never scored a goal in his
337 Football League appearances however, he rarely
crossed the half-way line. A reliable full-back who
rendered all his clubs good service.
52FL, 5FA

ROUNCE, George Alfred, (1933-5) Centre-forward.
Born: Grays, Essex, autumn 1905. Died: Victoria
Park, 2 October 1936. Played for Uxbridge Town;
Queen's Park Rangers cs 1928; Fulham March 1933
(£450), Bristol Rovers cs 1935 (£150). Never played for
Bristol Rovers as he was struck down with tuberculosis
shortly after signing for them. Died at the early age of
31 a year later. Rounce scored 55 goals in 171 League
appearances for Rangers before signing for Fulham.
Unable to establish himself at the Cottage. A direct
forward with a hard shot.
12FL 1g

RYAN, John Gilbert, (1965-9) Right-back.
Born: Lewisham, 20 July 1947. Played for Tonbridge;
Maidstone United; Arsenal October 1964; Fulham July
1965; Luton Town July 1969; Norwich City August
1976 (£60,000) Seattle Sounders 1979; Sheffield United
September 1980 (£70,000); Manchester City January
1982; Stockport County August 1983; Chester City
September 1983; Cambridge United player-manager
January 1984-85. Joined Fulham as an inside-forward
but was converted to a defender. Surprisingly given a
free transfer and his move to Luton Town proved very
benificial for himself and that club. The only honour
that Ryan won was a Fourth Division Championship
medal with Sheffield United in season 1981-2. Played
266 times for Luton and over 100 games for Norwich.
Had a brief and unsuccessful period as manager of
Cambridge United.
42/5FL 1g, 4FA, 4LC

SALVAGE, Barry J., (1968-9) Outside-left.
Born: Bristol, 21 February 1947. Died: Eastbourne, 14
October 1986. Played for Eastbourne United; Fulham
September 1967; Millwall March 1969; Queen's Park
Rangers February 1971; Brentford February 1973;
Millwall August 1975-77; St Louis Stars (USA) 1977;
Hastings United. Died in 1986 of a heart attack whilst
on a charity run in Eastbourne at the early age of 39. A
tall orthodox left-footed winger, Salvage made his
Fulham debut in their last months as a First Division
club in April 1968. Found more success at Brentford
and Millwall where he found regular first-team football.
7FL

SCRIVENS, Steve, (1974-80) Outside-left.
Born: London, 11 March 1957. Signed as an apprentice
for Fulham in 1974, professional March 1975; Brentford
(on loan) December 1976; Woking cs 1980; Dorking
Town 1985. Old-fashioned winger, who liked to take
players on and centre for the tall strikers. Scored his
only goal for Fulham from the penalty spot at West
Brom in April 1976. Played five games for Brentford in
a loan period but was not signed permanently. Appeared
for Woking for a number of years where he represented
the FA and played in some memorable Cup runs with
Les Barrett. Wingers had become obsolete during
Scrivens' period in top-class football.
3/1FL

SCULLION, James P., (1926-7) Centre-forward.
Born: Holytown, Lanark. Played for Workington;
Fulham August 1926; Stockport County cs 1927;
Crewe Alexandra cs 1928; Wigan Borough cs 1930;
Stockport County May 1931; Mossley cs 1932. Scullion
played for Fulham only once, against Nottingham
Forest in August 1926 shortly after signing from
Workington. Enjoyed better fortune at Stockport,
Crewe and Wigan. His best season was 1929-30 with
Crewe, where he scored 29 goals in 37 appearances.
Played for Wigan Borough in their last full season as a
League club.
1FL

SEALY, Anthony, (1983-4) Forward.
Born: London, 7 May 1959. Played for Southampton
May 1977; Crystal Palace March 1979; Port Vale (on
loan) February 1980; Queen's Park Rangers March
1981; Port Vale (on loan) February 1982; Fulham
December 1983 (£80,000); Leicester City September
1985 (£60,000); Bournemouth (on loan) March 1987.
Sealy spent much of his period at Fulham on the injury
list. Appeared as substitute for Southampton in the
1979 League Cup Final against Nottingham Forest. His
best season was at Queen's Park Rangers, whom he
helped achieve promotion to the First Division in
season 1982-3 with 16 goals. Very muscular player who
has a natural knack for scoring goals.
22/3FL 11g

SEYMOUR, Ian, (1966-72) Goalkeeper.
Born: Edenbridge, 17 March 1948. Played for Tonbridge;
Fulham August 1966 (£1,250); Brighton (on loan)
February 1971; retired through injury 1972. Made his
debut at Old Trafford in front of 60,000 people. A
spectacular 'keeper on his day, but at other times he was
liable to make simple errors. Unfortunate to play for
Fulham during one of the most difficult periods in their
history. In a London Challenge Cup game, against
Enfield in 1970, he broke his leg diving bravely at an
attacker's feet. Eventually had to give up the game as a
result of this injury.
64FL, 2FA, 9LC

SHEPHERD, Ernest, (1936-48) Outside-left.
Born: Wombwell, 14 August 1919. Played for Bradford
Rovers; Fulham signed professional in 1936; West
Brom December 1948; Hull City March 1949; Queen's
Park Rangers August 1950 Hastings United cs 1956;
Bradford trainer; Southend United trainer, assistant-
manager and manager from April 1967 to 1972; Orient
trainer-coach 1973-76; Coaching in Dubai in the 1980s.
Made his debut against Luton in the last game before
war was declared in August 1939. Appeared for
Huddersfield and Bradford City in the war. A workman-
like winger, Shepherd played in three promotion teams
in season 1948-9, Fulham, West Bromwich Albion and
Hull City. Played well over 200 games for Queen's Park
Rangers in the early 1950s.
72FL 13g, 4FA

SHRUBB, Paul, (1970-75) Right-back.
Born: Guildford, 1 August 1955. Joined Fulham as an
apprentice September 1970, signed professional August
1972; Hellenic (South Africa) May 1975; Brentford
March 1977; Aldershot August 1982. Usually played at
full-back for Fulham reserves but made his debut as a
central-defender against Luton Town in March 1973
when only 17-years-old. This proved to be his only
game for Fulham. Shrubb was converted to a midfield
player at Griffin Park and has played over 350 games
since leaving the Cottage with the Bees and the Shots.
1FL

SIMONS, H.T., (1914) Inside-forward.
Born: Clapton, 1890. Played for Halifax; Leyton 1909;
Sheffield United 1910; Merthyr Town cs 1912; Brentford
cs 1913; Fulham cs 1914; Queen's Park Rangers
November 1914-15. Simons stayed only three months
at the Cottage before moving up the road to Queen's
Park Rangers. Had a brief spell in the First Division
with Sheffield United but spent much of his career
playing in the Southern League.
9FL 4g

SKINNER, Justin, (1986-7) Midfield.
Born: London, 30 January 1969. Signed as an apprentice
for Fulham in the summer of 1985, signed professional
November 1986. Skinner is a talented midfield player
who should develop into a fine passer of the ball. He
made his debut against Southend United in the
Freight/Rover Trophy in January 1987, in what was
essentially a reserve team. His full debut was at the
Cottage against Rotherham United the following month.
Skinner's father played in senior non-League soccer.
1/1FL

189

SLADE, Donald, (1914-20) Inside-forward.
Born: Southampton, 1890. Played for Southampton circa 1910; Lincoln City 1912; Arsenal 1913; Fulham cs 1914; Dundee cs 1920. Slade signed for his home-town club, Southampton, but after making the first team on just three occasions he decided to try his luck at Lincoln City. Never found regular first-team football at any of his clubs, including Fulham, and moved to Scottish football with Dundee in 1920.
17FL 4g

SMITH, Gary Neil, (1985) Defender.
Born: Harlow, 3 December 1968. Joined Fulham as a non-contract player in July 1985, signed professional September 1986. Tough-tackling, hard young player who sometimes let his enthusiasm get the better of him. Made his debut as substitute in the last game of season 1985-6 at Oldham.
0/1FL

SMITH, J.D., (1922-3) Centre-forward.
Played for Port Vale cs 1922; Fulham December 1922-23. Smith joined Fulham from Port Vale just before his debut against Notts County on Boxing Day 1922. Had scored two goals for Port Vale in seven appearances that season prior to coming to the Cottage.
5FL

SMITH, Jack R., (1926-8) Centre-forward.
Born: Bristol. Played for Victoria Albion (Bristol); Bristol City circa 1921; Plymouth Argyle 1924; Aberdare Athletic cs 1924; Fulham October 1926; Rochdale cs 1928; Wrexham 1929-30. Known as 'Smasher' whilst at Bristol City, his home-town club. His best season was at Third Division club Aberdare Athletic in 1925-6 when he scored 24 goals. Bought by Fulham to solve their goalscoring problem but he lost his touch at the Cottage. Not to be confused with J.R.Smith of Bolton and Bury.
34FL 9g

SMITH, Norman L., (1948-57) Right-half.
Born: Carshalton, 2 July 1928. Played for Wimbledon

1945; Bishop Auckland; Fulham July 1948; Tunbridge Wells. Began his career with Wimbledon in the Isthmian League, National Service took Smith to Catterick and he played for Bishop Auckland for a couple of seasons. Played in their FA Amateur Cup semi-final defeat against Leytonstone. A part-timer at Fulham, he was also employed as a part-time book-keeper. Nowadays Smith is a fully-qualified accountant. Useful player to have around as he could fill any half-back position.
60FL, 3FA

SOAR, T. Albert, (1903-04) Outside-left.
Born: Heanor, Derbyshire, 20 May 1881. Played for Nottingham Forest; Alfreton Town 1898; Newark Town 1899; Derby County (£150) 1902; Fulham cs 1903; Watford cs 1906-08. Every pass, touch, tap and shot spoke eloquently of Soar's ability. He was a real artiste and renowned as a skilful and tricky winger. Soar never made Forest's first team before moving into non-League soccer. Derby County spotted his talent and signed him for £150 in 1902 from Newark Town. Fulham proved a more successful port of call. He made an immediate impact, finishing as the second-highest goalscorer with 6 goals in 1903-04. Very popular with the crowd, Soar was one of the few players to escape manager Harry Bradshaw's purge in 1904. Later scored 3 goals in 34 League and Cup games for Watford.
71SL 6g, 15FA

SPACKMAN, Frederick, (1899-1904) Inside-left.
Born: Sharncliffe, 1878. Played for Wandsworth; Queen's Park Rangers; Fulham November 1899. Joined Fulham with his brother Harry from Queen's Park Rangers. Fred was never a regular in the side but played at left-half, inside-left and on the left wing during his four-and-a-half seasons at the Cottage. Brother Harry was a full-back who stayed with Fulham until 1902. Fred won a Southern League Second Division Championship medal in season 1902-03.
26SL 6g, 8FA

SPARKE, Cecil Frederick, (1927-8) Inside-left.
Born: London. Died: 1969. Joined Fulham from local football May 1927; Bristol City 1930-31; Tottenham Hotspur 1931 but played mainly for nursery-club Northfleet; Folkestone 1932; Crystal Palace cs 1933. The only Football League games played by Sparke were the two he played for Fulham at Preston and West Brom in season 1927-8. Appeared at left-half, inside and outside-left for Fulham reserves. Enjoyed most success in the Kent League with Northfleet and Folkestone. Unable to make much of an impression at his Football League clubs.
2FL

SPINK, Thomas William, (1910-12) Outside-right.
Born: Dipton nr Newcastle, 13 November 1887. Died: 6 August 1966. Played for Craghead United 1908; Fulham November 1910; Rochdale cs 1912; Grimsby Town May 1914-22; assisted West Stanley during World War One; Worksop Town 1922. Spink won many prizes as a sprinter. Never made much of an impression at Craven Cottage but was rated as one of Grimsy Town's finest wingers. Small in build, he beat defenders with his speed and tricky footwork and supplied the forwards with a fine supply of pinpoint crosses. Still playing for Worksop when 40 years old.
10FL 1g

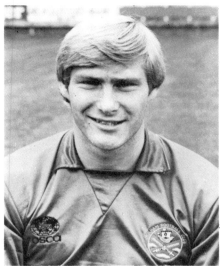

STANNARD, James David, (1980-85) Goalkeeper.
Born: Harold Hill, 6 October 1962. Played for Ford
United; Fulham signed professional June 1980; Southend
United (on loan) September 1984 and March 1985;
Charlton Athletic (on loan) February 1985; Southend
United cs 1985 (£12,000); Fulham June 1987. When
Stannard made his debut against Swindon in January
1981, he stepped straight from the juniors to the first
team. Large, well-built but agile 'keeper, Stannard had
a battle to oust Gerry Peyton out of the first-choice
goalkeeping spot. On his day he could be a brilliant
goalie but on another he would make silly mistakes.
Performed well for Southend United and was re-signed
by Fulham in the 1987 close season.
41FL, 1FA, 3LC

STEGGLES, Kevin P., (1986) Defender.
Born: Ditchingham, Norfolk, 19 March 1961. Joined
Ipswich as an apprentice in 1977, signed professional
December 1978; Southend United (on loan) February
1984; Fulham (on loan) August 1986; West Bromwich
Albion 1987. Played three games for Fulham on loan
from Ipswich Town at the beginning of season 1986-7.
Returned home after Fulham signed Keith Oakes from
Gillingham. Never a regular first-teamer at Portman
Road, Kevin had a loan period at Southend in 1984 and
finally moved on to West Brom in 1987.
3FL, 3LC

STEPHENSON, Alan C., (1971-2) Centre-half.
Born: Cheshunt, 26 September 1944. Played for Crystal
Palace February 1962; West Ham United March 1968
(£80,000); Fulham (on loan) October 1971 — January
1972; Portsmouth May 1972-74 (£32,000). In Bobby
Moore's biography, written by Jeff Powell, he accused
West Ham manager Ron Greenwood of ruining
Stephenson as a player when he signed him for West
Ham. Alan looked a highly-gifted player at Crystal
Palace where he won England Under-23 honours. Cost
West Ham a large fee but was never a big success at

Upton Park. Fulham seemed likely to sign him after a
lengthy and productive loan period but he moved to
Portsmouth instead.
10FL

STEPHENSON, Roy, (1903-04) Right-back.
Played for Chesham Generals; Fulham 1903; Southern
United cs 1904. Stephenson appeared only once for
Fulham in a 2-2 draw with Portsmouth at the Cottage.
Moved to Southern United, a leading semi-professional
club of the time.
1SL

STEWART, Andrew, (1913-14) Inside-left.
Played for Fulham 1913-14. Played three games in the
Fulham's first team near the end of season 1913-14. Not
to be confused with Tommy Stewart who was at the
club during the same period. Made his debut in a fine
three-goals victory at Grimsby Town in March 1914.
3FL

STEWART, Thomas, (1913-14) Half-back.
Born: Renfrew, Scotland, circa 1891. Played for
Cambuslang Rangers; Rutherglen-Glencairn; Fulham
1913-14. Came from the same club as William McIntosh,
Rutherglen-Glencairn. Stewart won a Scottish Junior
international cap against Ireland and represented the
Glasgow League on two occasions. Retired through
injury in 1914.
12FL

STOKES, Alfred F., (1959-60) Inside-forward.
Born: Hackney, 3 October 1932. Played for Clapton;
Tottenham Hotspur February 1953; Fulham July 1959
(£10,000); Watford April 1961; Guildford City 1962;
Later emigrated to Australia. Although never a regular
at White Hart Lane, Stokes won an England Under-23
cap against Denmark in 1956 and represented the
Football League versus the Scottish League. Scored 40
goals in 65 appearances for Spurs before signing for
Fulham for a large fee. Not a success at the Cottage and
moved to Watford. Never realised his early promise.
15FL 6g

STOREY, G.C., (1904) Centre-forward.
Played for Bury circa 1902; Luton Town cs 1903;
Fulham March 1904. Storey played three games for
First Division Bury before signing for Luton Town,
scoring four goals in 15 appearances for the Hatters.
Was unable to find the net in his three games for
Fulham.
3SL

STOREY, Peter Edwin, (1977-8) Right-half.
Born: Farnham, 7 September 1945. Played for Arsenal
as an apprentice in May 1961; signed professional October
1962; Fulham March 1977 (£10,000); retired November
1977. Storey won 19 England caps under the managership
of Alf Ramsey. He also represented the Football
League and played for England Schoolboys in 1961.
Had a highly successful career at Arsenal where he won
many honours including the League and Cup double in
1971, League Cup runners-up medals in 1968 and 1969,
and a European Fairs Cup-winners' medal in 1970.
Very aggressive defender who was not popular with
some of his fellow professionals due to some dubious
tactics on the pitch.
17FL, 2LC

STRATTON, Reginald M., (1959-60) Outside-left.
Born: Farnborough, 10 July 1939. Played for Woking 1955; Fulham August 1959; Colchester United June 1965; Vancouver Royals cs 1968. Stratton gained England Youth and Amateur international honours. Won an FA Amateur Cup-winners' medal in 1958 when Woking beat Ilford 3-0 before a 71,000 crowd at Wembley. Stratton scored one of the goals. Scored only one Football League goal for Fulham in 21 appearances, the winner in a 1-0 victory against Liverpool in March 1964. Later scored 50 goals in 112 appearances for Colchester.
21FL 1g, 3FA 2g

SULLIVAN, Brian A.J. 'Doc', Inside-forward.
Born: Edmonton, 30 December 1941. Died: 1985. Joined Fulham in 1958, signed professional May 1959. 'Doc' scored on his debut for Fulham at Blackpool in January 1960. Great things were expected of Sullivan as he had won England Schoolboy and Youth international honours. However, he played only one other game for Fulham then disappeared from the football scene.
2FL 1g

SUMMERS, John Henry, (1947-50) Centre-forward.
Born: Hammersmith, 10 September 1927. Died: London, 2 June 1962. Joined Fulham in 1944, signed professional February 1947; Norwich City June 1950; Millwall May 1954; Charlton Athletic November 1956-61 (£5,000). Scored five goals for Charlton Athletic against Huddersfield Town in a famous 7-6 victory in December 1957, when the Valiants came back from being 1-5 down and with only ten men. This was Summers' second five-goal spree for Charlton. A wholehearted player who loved to score goals, Summers played for Hexham whilst on National Service in Northumberland. Played a total of 338 games scoring 173 goals during his career but played only four for Fulham. Died of cancer at the early age of 34.
4FL

SYMES, Ernest H.C., (1917-23) Right-half/winger.
Born: Acton. Played for Fulham March 1917; Aberdare Athletic cs 1923; Queen's Park Rangers 1924-26. Symes made his debut in a London Combination match at Chelsea in March 1918 as a wing-half. Was later converted to a right winger. Moved on to Welsh club Aberdare Athletic in 1923 playing 31 games in their Third Division side that season. Returned to West London with Queen's Park Rangers in 1925 for whom he appeared 26 times. Played in the same side as Ted Worrall and Harry Walker at Aberdare.
6FL

TANNAHILL, Robert, (1901-04) Outside-right.
Born: Kilmarnock, 1872. Played for Kilmarnock, Bolton Wanderers 1893; Tottenham Hotspur cs 1897; Millwall cs 1898; Chesterfield (on loan) 1899; Fulham cs 1901; Grays United cs 1904. Gifted Scottish winger who found fame at Bolton Wanderers. Played in their FA Cup Final appearance in 1894 when they lost to Notts County 4-1. Nearly made it to the Final again in 1896, losing in the semi-final. Moved south to Spurs in 1898 then on to Millwall from where he joined Fulham in 1901. A regular on Fulham's right wing until 1903.
27SL 13g, 14FA 5g

TAPLEY, Steve, (1980-85) Centre-half/right-back.
Born: Camberwell, 3 October 1963. Joined Fulham as an apprentice in May 1980; signed professional October 1981; Rochdale (on loan) March 1985; Wealdstone August 1985. Captain of the Fulham youth team which produced the likes of Paul Parker, John Marshall, Brian Cottington, Dean Coney and Jeff Hopkins, and at that time looked the best prospect. However, Tapley did not develop as much as anticipated. Played twice for Fulham and in his final game at Shrewsbury in January 1985, he scored for both sides. Found his best position at Wealdstone as a right-back.
2FL 1g

TARGETT, Alfred Nicholas, (1935-7) Left-half.
Born: Southampton, 14 January 1916. Died: 1983. Played for Bournemouth Gasworks; Southampton 1932; Fulham September 1935. Played as an amateur for Southampton but signed professional with Fulham. Never made the first team whilst at The Dell and played only one for Fulham at Chesterfield in January 1936. Targett won England Schoolboy international honours.
1FL

TAYLOR, Jeffrey N., (1951-4) Inside-right).
Born: Huddersfield, 20 September 1930. Joined Huddersfield in 1945, signed professional September 1949; Fulham, November 1951; Brentford August 1954-56. Taylor did not sign professional until he was 19 as he was in the RAF. He went also to the University College of London at this time, studying for a BA Honours degree in Geography and later gained a Diploma in teaching. Enjoyed opera singing, later turning professional and appearing regularly at Covent Garden. Scored two hat-tricks whilst at Fulham but was kept out of the side by Bobby Robson. Scored a total of 76 goals in 195 games for his three League clubs. His brother played cricket for Yorkshire and soccer for Huddersfield Town.
33FL 14g, 2FA 4g

TAYLOR, John Henry, (1957) Outside-right.
Born: Tyton-on-Tyne, 6 October 1935. Played for Crawcrook; Newcastle United, November 1952; Fulham

(on loan) February-November 1957; Chelmsford City
June 1960. Geordie winger who played four games for
Fulham in his ten-month stay on loan from Newcastle.
Played only 28 games scoring five goals, in his seven
and a half seasons at St James' Park. Joined Fulham as
he was doing his National Service in the London area.
4FL

TAYLOR, William, (1912-21) Inside-forward.
Born: Millwall, 1895. Played for Tower Hamlets;
Metrogas; Fulham 1913-21. Would shoot at
every opportunity being famous for his snap shooting.
Joined Fulham with W.G.Garvey from Metrogas.
Unfortunately Taylor hit his peak form in the war years
where he scored prolifically when able to get away from
his other duties.
49FL 9g, 2FA 2g

TEALE, Richard, (1976-7) Goalkeeper.
Born: Millam, 27 February 1952. Played for Walton
and Hersham United; Slough Town; Queen's Park
Rangers July 1973; Fulham August 1976; Wimbledon
August 1977; Slough Town cs 1978; Staines Town;
Carshalton Athletic. Won an FA Amateur Cup-winners'
medal when Walton beat Slough Town 1-0 in the 1973
Final at Wembley. Signed professional with Queen's
Park Rangers in 1973 but made only one first-team
appearance. Joined Fulham as deputy to Gerry Peyton
staying just one season before signing for Wimbledon
who had just joined the Football League.
5FL

TEMPEST, Dale Michael, (1980-84) Forward.
Born: Leeds, 30 December 1963. Played for Fulham as
an apprentice, January 1980; signed professional
December 1980; Huddersfield Town August 1983
(£15,000); Gillingham (on loan) March 1986; Lokeren
(Belgium) August 1986. Dale is at his best in the six-
yard box and has that knack of being in the right place
at the right time. Established himself in Fulham's side at
the beginning of season 1983-4 but a bad injury cost him
his place. Moved to Huddersfield, scoring 16 goals in
his first season. Currently, Dale is a success in Belgium
Football with Lokeren.
25/9FL 6g, 1LC 1g

TEMPLETON, Robert Bryson, (1913-15) Outside-left.
Born: Kilmarnock, 22 June 1879. Died: 2 November
1919. Played for Kilmarnock 1896; Hibernian; Aston
Villa 1899; Newcastle United February 1903 (£400);
Woolwich Arsenal November 1904 (£375); Glasgow
Celtic May 1906 (£250); Kilmarnock October 1907;
Fulham cs 1913; Kilmarnock April 1915. Temperamental
and erratic but on his day was one of the greatest
players of his time. Unhappily, due to his waywardness
and irresponsibility, Templeton never fully realised the
possibilities of his superb ball control and tactical
genius. It was said (by Phil Kelso) that one of his
body-swerves caused the 1902 Ibrox Disaster, unbalancing
the watching crowd. He won 11 English caps altogether
but missed out on many more honours. Won a Scottish
League Championship and Cup-winners' medal with
Celtic in 1907. Templeton was never a regular first-
teamer at the Cottage.
32FL

THOMAS, Andrew, (1982-3) Forward.
Born: Oxford, 16 December 1962. Joined Oxford
United 1978, signed professional December 1980; Fulham
(on loan) November 1982; Derby County (on loan),
February 1983; Newcastle United September 1985.
Thomas won popularity almost instantaneously whilst
on loan at Fulham and scored two goals in his four
appearances. Sadly, Fulham could not afford Oxford's
asking price and this probably blocked their progress to
the First Division that season. Broke his leg in January
1984 and was unable to perform in Oxford's side for some
time. Found a new lease of life at Newcastle in 1986.
3/1FL 2g

THOMAS, Glen Andrew, (1984-) Left-back.
Born: Hackney, 6 October 1967. Joined Fulham via the
YTS Scheme in August 1984, signed as an apprentice
October 1984, signed professional October 1985. Started
his Fulham career as a central-defender but has played
at left-back. A good passer of the ball, Thomas is a
perceptive defender who tackles with aplomb, and
reads a game well. Made his debut in the Full Members
Cup at Shrewsbury in October 1986 as a substitute.
1FL

THOMAS, L., (1922-3) Inside-left.
Played only one game for Fulham at inside-left in a
one-goal victory at Bury in February 1923. Played as an
amateur for Bromley.
1FL

THOMAS, W. Louis 'Low', (1905-06) Inside-left.
Played for Fulham Amateurs; Fulham 1905; Clapton
Orient 1906-07. Signed from local football, 'Low' made
only one appearance for Fulham at Reading in November
1905. Moved to Homerton in 1906 and made five
appearances scoring one goal for the 'Os'.
1SL

THOMPSON, E.W., (1915) Left-back.
Born: Prudhoe. Played for Fulham for one game in
February 1915 against Grimsby Town in a 2-1 victory at
the Cottage. Signed from Spen Black in 1915..
1FL

THOMPSON, Frederick, (1905-06) Goalkeeper.
Born: South Hetton, Durham 1876. Died: Oswaldtwistle, 13 January 1958. Played for Sunderland 1895; Bury 1896; Bolton Wanderers cs 1902; Luton Town cs 1903; Portsmouth cs 1904; Fulham cs 1905; Norwich City cs 1906; Clapton Orient cs 1908; Hartlepools United 1909. Thompson won an FA Cup-winners' medal with Bury in 1900 when they beat Southampton 4-0 at the Crystal Palace. Thompson also played in an international trial game for the North versus the South in March 1899. The game ended in an exciting 4-4 draw. Thompson was deputy to Jack Fryer at Fulham. A much-travelled player, Thompson made 191 League appearances in a career which lasted from 1895 to 1909.
4SL, 1FA

THOMPSON, James William, (1930-31) Centre-forward.
Born: West Ham, 19 April 1898. Died: Epsom, August 1984. Played for Custom House; Charlton Athletic (Amateur) August 1921; Wimbledon September 1921; Millwall Athletic, signed professional December 1921; Coventry City June 1923; Clapton Orient August 1924; 1924; Luton Town July 1925; Chelsea cs 1927; Norwich City cs 1929; Sunderland May 1930; Fulham October 1930 (£300); Hull City October 1931; Tunbridge Wells Rangers January 1932; Dartford manager 1939; later a scout for Chelsea and Southampton. Started his career as a left winger but was converted to centre-forward. Found most success at Luton, Chelsea Hull and Norwich, scored 25 goals in 29 games for Chelsea in season 1927-8. Believed to be the man who discovered Jimmy Greaves whilst a Chelsea scout.
4FL 2g, 1FA

THOMPSON, W., (1906-07) Outside-left.
Played for Gainsborough Trinity 1902; Fulham cs 1906; Gainsborough Trinity cs 1907-09. Hartlepools United 1909. Described as 'a game lad of the robust type, recking no odds to great for him and is a thorough worker who always does his best'. Gained most success with Second Division Gainsborough Trinity playing 155 games and scoring two goals in his two spells at the Lincolnshire club. Played at Hartlepools with Frank Edgley.
7SL 2g

THORPE, Harry, (1904-07) Left-back.
Born: Barrow Hill, Derbyshire, 1880. Died: Leicester, 9 September 1908. Played for Chesterfield Town 1900; Woolwich Arsenal cs 1903; Fulham 1904; Leicester Fosse cs 1907. Thorpe was a daring full-back who swooped down on opposing forwards with matchless judgement. Brisk and dashing, Thorpe was a fine sportsman who played with the right attitude. He made up a very successful defensive trio with Jack Fryer and Harry Ross which won Southern League Championship medals in 1906 and 1907 for Fulham. Started his playing career with local club Chesterfield where he also appeared for the local cricket club. Thorpe died from a lung infection shortly after joining Leicester Fosse.
71SL, 10FA

TILFORD, Arthur, (1932-4) Left-back.
Born: Ilkeston, 14 May 1903. Played for Nottingham Forest 1924; Blackpool cs 1926; Coventry City 1929; Fulham February 1932 (£750); Southampton February 1932; Fulham cs 1933; Walsall cs 1934-35. Followed

manager James McIntyre from Coventry City in 1932. Just managed to qualify for a Third Division South Championship medal in 1931-2 with 14 appearances. He had already played 27 games for Coventry that season. Had two spells at Fulham, each side of a short period at The Dell.
41FL, 1FA

TONNER, Johnny, (1926-7) Inside-left.
Born: Holytown, Lanark, 20 February 1898. Played in Fife junior football; Clapton Orient September 1919; Fulham cs 1926; Crystal Palace May 1927; Thames Association cs 1928. Orient groundsman in the 1950s. One of three brother's signed by Orient from Scottish junior football. Johnny played 140 games, scoring 34 goals for Orient before moving to Fulham. He stayed just one season at the Cottage scoring 13 goals. Later joined newly-formed Thames in the Southern League from Crystal Palace.
28FL 13g, 2FA 2g

TOWNSEND, Martin V., (1963-4) Goalkeeper.
Born: Romford, 15 June 1946. Played for Fulham as an apprentice 1963; Guildford City cs 1964. Townsend, as a 17-year-old apprentice, was plunged into First Division action in September 1963 as Tony Macedo and Dave Underwood, the first and second-choice 'keepers were injured. Made his debut at Turf Moor against Burnley. Was never signed as a professional by the club. Lives in the Gidea Park area today.
2FL, 1LC

TRANTER, Wilfred, (1969-72) Full-back.
Born: Pendlebury, Manchester, 5 March 1945. Played for Manchester United April 1962; Brighton May 1966; Baltimore Bays 1968; Fulham January 1969-72. Failed to make the grade at Manchester United. After making only one appearance he moved to Brighton. A solid defender, Tranter played as pivot or full-back at The Goldstone. Enjoyed his season in the States before signing for Fulham at the same time as Stan Horne and Brian Dear. Tranter played mainly in the reserves at the Cottage. A qualified coach.
20/3FL, 0/1FA, 1LC

TUCKETT, Ernest W., (1938-43) Centre-forward.
Born: Guisborough, 1914. Died: during World War two on active service. Played for Scarborough; Arsenal

194

cs 1932; Bradford City February 1937; Fulham April 1938-43. Tuckett played only one League game for Fulham at Chesterfield in April 1939 and five wartime appearances. Being unable to break into the Arsenal team very often he moved to Bradford City but his first season at Valley Parade ended in relegation to the Third Division North.
1FL

TURNER, Edward, (1903-04) Left-back.
Born: Skerton, Lancashire 1879. Played for Everton; Royal Artillery (Portsmouth) 1898; Portsmouth 1899; Northampton 1901; Portsmouth 1902; Fulham cs 1903; Luton Town cs 1904-05 and possibly Brighton 1905-09. Known as 'Old Hookey', Turner played for Royal Artillery (Portsmouth) for one season, and when they disbanded in 1899 he transferred his allegiance to Portsmouth. A solid, naturally left-footed played, he played regularly in Fulham's first season as a limited company in season 1903-04.
29SL, 6FA

TUTTHILL, George R., (1899-1904) Left-half.
Born: Southwold, Suffolk, 1879. Played for Loughborough Town 1898; Wellingborough 1899; Fulham April 1899-cs 1904. Fulham's regular left-half for four years. An inspirational player whose enthusiam and tenacity rubbed off on the other players. Rarely missed a match but was suspended by the club for a month in October 1901 for a minor breach of discipline. Played 27 Football League games for Loughborough and Wellingborough when still a teenager. Tutthill once failed to turn up at a game at Chesham until the 70th minute. Fulham were 2-0 down but scored six goals in the remaining 20 minutes, Tutthill scoring two of them to win 6-2.
65SL 11g, 14FA 1g

UNDERWOOD, Dave E., (1963-5) Goalkeeper.
Born: London, 15 March 1928. Played for Queen's Park Rangers December 1949; Watford February 1952; Liverpool December 1953; Watford June 1956; Dartford; Watford April 1960; Fulham cs 1963, Dunstable cs 1965; Dartford; Hastings United manager 1967; Barnet chairman during the 1970s. Played for Watford in three separate periods, appearing 175 times in all. Underwood had been given a free transfer by Watford in the summer of 1963 when Fulham manager Bedford Jezzard rang to ask him if he would like to join the Cottagers as stand-in for Tony Macedo. He jumped at the chance to play First Division football again.
18FL, 1LC

VAUGHAN, John, (1986) Goalkeeper.
Born: Isleworth, 26 June 1964. Played for West Ham United 1981; Charlton Athletic (on loan) April 1985; Bristol Rovers (on loan) September 1985; Wrexham (on loan) October 1985; Bristol City (on loan) March 1986; Fulham August 1986 (£12,500). After a shaky start at Fulham, which included letting in ten goals at Anfield, Vaughan settled down and built up his confidence to produce some fine performances. Signed as a replacement for the departing Gerry Peyton. Vaughan won an FA Youth Cup-winners' medal and two Southern Junior Floodlit Cup medals at Upton Park but was unable to break into the League side.
44FL, 4FA, 4LC

WALKER, J. Harry, (1920-21) Right-half.
Born: Wirksworth. Died: 1934. Played for Clay Cross, Derby County May 1910; Notts County June 1920; Fulham March 1921; Reading cs 1921; Aberdare Athletic cs 1923; Bournemouth 1924. Walker occupied both half-back and inside-forward positions during his ten years at Derby County making 84 League appearances. After a brief spell at Meadow Lane, Walker signed for Fulham but stayed only three months. Appearing only at right-half for Fulham. Later played 62 games for Reading.
8FL

WALLBANKS, Harry 'Choppy', (1939-48) Right-half.
Born: Chopwell, Newcastle, 27 July 1921. Played for Fulham 1939; Southend United October 1949; Workington August 1952-53. Worked as a miner during the war in his native North-East. Played only three wartime games for Fulham and made his League debut in 1946. Choppy had four other brothers who played League football — Jack (Portsmouth) Fred (West Ham), Jim (Reading), Horace (Luton Town). Later made 39 appearances for Southend and 26 for Workington where he scored nine goals.
33FL 1g, 4FA

WALTERS, Charlie, (1926-8) Centre-half.
Born: Sandford-on-Thames, 1 April 1897. Died: Bath, 13 May 1971. Played for Oxford City; Tottenham Hotspur 1919; Fulham October 1926; Mansfield Town cs 1928. A spoiler centre-half who had great speed on the turn and fine powers of recovery, but was not always sufficiently constructive. However, he knew his limitations and did not attempt what he could not accomplish. Won an FA Cup-winners' medal with Spurs in 1921 when he marked George Edmonds (later of Fulham) out of the game and beat Wolves 1-0 at Stamford Bridge. Played 126 League games for Spurs between 1919 and 1926. Past his best at Fulham.
18FL, 2FA

195

WARBOYS, Alan, (1977) Centre-forward.
Born: Goldthorpe near Rotherham, 18 April 1949.
Played for Doncaster Rovers April 1967; Sheffield
Wednesday May 1968 (£12,000); Cardiff City December
1970 (£42,000); Sheffield United September 1972 (£20,000
+ players); Bristol Rovers March 1973 (£35,000); Fulham
February 1977 (£25,000); Hull City September 1977
(£20,000); Doncaster Rovers July 1979; retired October
1982. Burly centre-forward who scored 136 League
goals in 483 appearances between 1967 and 1982. Hit
three goals in the first nine minutes for Cardiff against
Carlisle in March 1971. Formed a properous 'Smash
and Grab' partnership with Bruce Bannister at Bristol
Rovers.
19FL 2g, 2FA

WARBURTON, Arthur, (1934-8) Right-half.
Born: Whitefield near Bury, 10 September 1908. Died:
Bury, 21 April 1978. Played for Sedgley Park, Manchester
United cs 1929; Burnley December 1933; Nelson cs
1934; Fulham October 1934; Queen's Park Rangers cs
1938-39. Hard-working player with boundless energy
and enthusiasm. Warburton joined Manchester United
from local soccer and scored ten goals in 35 appearances.
After a period at Burnley he moved to Nelson when he
could not agree terms with the club. Warburton was not
out of League football for long when Fulham matched
his terms. Not a regular at the Cottage but put in some
useful performances.
46FL 6g, 1FA

WARD, Felix, (1907-08) Outside-right.
Played for Seaham Harbour; Fulham cs 1907; Clapton
Orient cs 1908 and possibly Southend United 1910-11.
Extremely fast winger who drifted through the opposition
with easy skill and centred neatly. Ward was only 5ft 5in
tall and weighed 10st. Appeared in 33 League games for
Clapton Orient in season 1908-09 but only four for
Fulham.
4FL

WARDROPE, William, (1904-06) Centre-forward.
Born: Wishaw, 1876. Played for Dalziel Rovers;
Motherwell (Amateur); Linthouse; Newcastle United
May 1895; Middlesbrough May 1900; Third Lanark
1902; Fulham cs 1904; Swindon Town player-manager
cs 1906; Hamilton September 1907. Wardrope won
Scottish Junior international honours and represented
the Scottish League in 1903. Was on the small side for a
centre-forward, only 5ft 6in. Scored 65 goals for
Newcastle and Middlesbrough before coming to the
Cottage. Top scorer in his two seasons at Fulham.
Stayed only one season at Swindon as player-manager
before moving to the USA and later Canada.
59SL 29g, 11FA 3g

WATERSON, Frederick, (1903-09) Right-half.
Born: Burton upon Trent 1880. Played for Burton
Swifts 1896; Burton United cs 1901; Fulham cs 1903;
Doncaster Rovers cs 1909. A great club man and
captain of the reserves, Waterson was rewarded with a
benefit match against Woolwich Arsenal Reserves on
Boxing Day 1908. Played 164 games for the Burton
clubs before signing for Fulham. An adaptable player,
Waterson won many medals with the reserve side which
won the London League on a number of occasions.
2FL, 6SL, 6FA

WATKINS, Ernest Thomas, (1930-31) Centre-forward.
Born: Finchley, 3 April 1898. Died: Finchley, 10
October 1976. Played for Birmingham circa 1922;
Southend United, February 1924; Brentford January
1926; Millwall, February 1930; Fulham August 1930;
Gillingham August 1931; Charlton Athletic, November
1931; retired through injury 1932. Much-travelled
striker who gained most fame at Brentford. Scored 54
goals in 118 League games for the Bees between 1925
and 1929. Stayed only one season at the Cottage scoring
ten goals in 17 games. An injury playing for Charlton
against Millwall in February 1932 effectively ending his
career.
17FL 10g, 3FA 2g

WATSON, John F. 'Jack', (1946-8) Left-half.
Born: Hamilton, 31 December 1917. Played for Douglas
Junior Club; Bury 1938; Fulham August 1946; Real
Madrid player-coach cs 1948; Crystal Palace July 1949
to 1951. Joined Fulham as a wartime guest in 1943 but
also appeared for Bury throughout the war. Made just
six appearances for the Gigg Lane club before war
broke out in 1939. Fulham's regular centre-half in the
first two seasons after the war. Watson played for and
coached Real Madrid for a season before ending his
career at Crystal Palace.
71FL 2g, 1FA 1g

WATSON, Trevor P., (1956-64) Left-half/outside-right.
Born: Great Yarmouth, 26 September 1938. Joined
Fulham in 1954, signed professional July 1956; Hillingdon
Borough April 1964. Watson had to be patient in his ten
years at the Cottage as he appeared in the first team on
only 17 occasions, playing as a left-half and right-
winger. He moved to Southern League Hillingdon
Borough in 1964 where he played for a number of
seasons.
17FL 1g

WEBB, Harold, (1930-33) Left-half.
Born: Fulham. Played for Park Royal; Walthamstow
Avenue; Fulham 1930; Exeter City March 1933; Coventry
City cs 1935, Newport County cs 1936; Bristol Rovers
cs 1938. Mainly a reserve at Fulham. Gained a London
Challenge Cup-winners' medal in 1932. Moved to
Exeter City with Frank Wrightson, playing 70 appea-
rances for the Grecians. He moved from Exeter to the
Midlands with Coventry but was unable to find regular
first-team football. Later played 54 games for Newport.
7FL 1g

WEIR, Jimmy, (1957-60) Outside-left.
Born: Glasgow, 12 April 1939. Played for Clydebank
Juniors; Fulham July 1957; York City June 1960;
Mansfield Town September 1962; Luton Town August
1963; Tranmere Rovers July 1964-65. Signed from
Clydebank Juniors with Bill Clarkson who never made
the first team. Weir made his debut at Ipswich in
September 1957 but played only two more games for
Fulham. Found regular first-team action at York City
scoring 38 goals in 82 games before brief spells at
Mansfield, Luton and Tranmere.
3FL

WEIR, John 'Jock', (1912-13) Centre-forward.
Played for Bellshill Athletic; Fulham 1912; Swansea
Town cs 1913-19; Reading 1919-20. Made only one
appearance for Fulham in a 1-0 home defeat against
Grimsby Town in January 1913. One of many top-class
players produced by Scottish junior club Bellshill
Athletic. Joined Swansea who were then playing in the
Welsh League but joined the Southern League in 1919.
Scored two goals in 13 appearances for Reading in 1920
in a brief spell at Elm Park.
1FL

WENT, Paul F., (1972-3) Centre-half.
Born: Bromley-by-Bow, 12 October 1949. Played for
Leyton Orient as an apprentice August 1965; signed
professional October 1966; Charlton Athletic June
1967 (£25,000); Fulham July 1972 (£80,000); Portsmouth,
December 1973 (£155,000); Cardiff City October 1976;
Orient September 1979; retired 1981; Orient as a coach,
manager September 1981; Went was manager of Orient
for just 19 days when former Sunderland boss Ken
Knighton was appointed in his place. Paul won England
Schoolboy and Youth honours and much was expected
when he signed for Leyton Orient. Later gave Charlton
good service before signing for Fulham. Sold to
Portsmouth for £155,000 to ease Fulham's financial
problems. A fine, commanding central-defender.
58FL 3g, 1FA, 8LC 2g

WHALLEY, Frederick Harold, (1924-5) Goalkeeper.
Born: Salford, 9 October 1898. Died: Eccles, 25 April
1976. Played for the Army; Preston NE June 1919;
Grimsby Town cs 1920; Leeds United May 1921;
Fulham March 1924 — cs 1925. Enlisted in the North
Lancashire regiment when only 15-years-old and saw
active service in France. A reserve at Preston and
Fulham but found regular first-team football at Grimsby
and Leeds where he was ever-present in season 1922-3.
Became a policeman on retirement from football.
8FL, 1FA

WHEATCROFT, Frederick George, (1906-07) Inside-left.
Born: Alfreton, 1882. Died: France, November 1917 on
active service. Played for Alfreton Town; Derby County
1903; Swindon Town 1905; Fulham March 1906;
Derby County February 1907; Reading cs 1908; Swindon
Town cs 1909-15. Remained an amateur throughout his
career as his main occupation was teaching. Discovered
by Derby in local football. Won three Southern League
Championship medals, in season 1906-07 with Fulham
and in 1910-11 and 1913-14 with Swindon Town.
Played 218 games scoring 82 goals in his two spells with
Swindon and guested for Fulham in World War One.
Wheatcroft won one England Amateur cap against
Ireland in 1907. Died serving his country in the trenches
of France.
25SL 8g, 4FA

WHITE, Henry A., (1925-6) Centre-forward.
Born: Watford, 17 April 1892. Died: Barrow Gurney
Somerset, 27 November 1972. Played for Brentford
during World War One; Arsenal 1919; Blackpool 1923;
Fulham cs 1925; Walsall February 1926; Nelson March
1927; Thames Association 1929. Played for the South
versus the North in an international trial game in April
1919. Very successful at Arsenal and Blackpool but did
not have a happy time at Craven Cottage. Found his
goal touch again at Walsall and Nelson. White also
excelled at cricket and appeared in eight County
Championship games for Warwickshire as an off-break
bowler. Son of Harry White, who was ground superin-
tendent at Lord's, he became Charterhouse School
coach in April 1924.
7FL 1g, 1FA 1g

WILKES, Albert, (1907-09) Right-half.
Born: Birmingham 1875. Died: 9 December 1936.
Played for Oldbury Town; Walsall 1896; Aston Villa cs
1898; Fulham cs 1907; Chesterfield Town April 1909. A
tough-tackling player with a high capacity for work.
Wilkes won five England caps in 1901-02. Gained a
League Championship medal in season 1899-1900 with
Aston Villa for whom he played a total of 142 games
before moving to Chesterfield. Past his best by the time
he arrived at Fulham. Retired in July 1909 to concentrate
on his very successful photographic business. Was a
Villa director from 1934 to his death in 1936.
16FL 1g

WILLIAMSON, Brian W., (1968-9) Goalkeeper.
Born: Blyth, 6 October 1939. Played for Seaton Delaval;
Gateshead October 1958; Crewe Alexandra July 1960;
Leeds United December 1962; Nottingham Forest
February 1966; Leicester City (on loan) August 1967;
Fulham December 1968 (£10,000); retired September
1969. Reserve to Gary Sprake at Leeds and Peter
Grummitt at Nottingham Forest, Williamson was with
Gateshead when they were surprisingly voted out of the
Football League in 1960. He joined Fulham expecting
regular first-team football, when this did not materialise
he decided to retire and became a security officer.
12FL, 2FA

WILSON, Thomas F., (1950-57) Right-back.
Born: Southampton, 3 July 1930. Played for Southampton (Amateur) 1947; Fulham August 1950; Brentford July 1957-61. Wilson caught pleurisy in his early days at the Cottage and was unable to play for 16 months. With the emergence of George Cohen, Wilson moved on to Brentford where he was made captain. Retired in 1961 after 148 appearances for the Bees. Wilson qualified as a chartered surveyor whilst at Fulham. In 1987 is the chairman of a large company in the City.
45FL, 4FA

WINSHIP, T. 'Wee', (1913) Outside-left.
Born: Wallsend. Played for Woolwich Arsenal 1910; Fulham March 1913; Arsenal May 1913; Darlington 1919-26. Winship played briefly for Fulham in 1913, possibly on loan from Arsenal. Known as 'Wee' because he was only 5ft 3in tall. Appeared 56 times for Arsenal scoring seven goals before World War One. Was a regular for Darlington afterwards and won a Third Division North Championship medal in 1924-5.
2FL

WOLFE, Thomas Henry, (1924-7) Half-back/inside-forward.
Born: Barry Dock, Wales, 7 March 1900. Died: Edgware, 23 March 1954. Played for Swansea Town; Sheffield Wednesday cs 1922; Coventry City cs 1923; Southend United June 1924; Fulham March 1925; Charlton Athletic June 1927; Bristol Rovers May 1929 — January 1930. Wolfe gained Welsh Amateur international honours as an amateur with Swansea Town. Did not make his Football League debut until he joined Coventry in 1923. Wolfe made his debut for Fulham at centre-forward but started the 1926-7 season as regular left-half but eventually lost his place to Charlie Walters. He moved to Charlton with full-back Tommy Brown.
27FL 1g

WOOD, Albert, (1931-5) Inside-right.
Born: Seaham Harbour. Played for Seaham Harbour; Sunderland 1927; Fulham cs 1931; Crewe Alexandra 1935; Tranmere Rovers cs 1936; New Brighton cs 1937 to 1939. Came to Fulham in part exchange for Jimmy Temple. Played the occasional game when Jim Hammond was injured. His best season was at Crewe in 1935-6

when he was ever-present and scored 14 goals. Wood had one good season in the First Division with Sunderland in 1929-30.
21FL 9g, 2FA

WOOD, Arthur Basil, (1911-15) Inside-forward.
Born: Southampton, 8 May 1890. Died: Merton, 17 January 1977. Played for St Mary's Athletic; Eastleigh Athletic; Fulham April 1911; Gillingham 1919; Newport County cs 1922; Queen's Park Rangers cs 1923-25. Wood had the misfortune to play four seasons out of five for the club which came bottom in its League. Gillingham came bottom of the Southern League in 1920 and Gillingham, Newport and Queen's Park Rangers came bottom of the Third Division South in seasons 1920-21, 1922-3, 1923-4 respectively. Finally retired from playing at the age of 37, due to a knee injury. Told amusing stories of 'training sessions' at the Green Man, Putney Hill with his fellow players.
21FL 1g

WOOD, L., (1924-5) Inside-left.
Born: Wednesbury. Played for Stourbridge Town; Fulham cs 1923-24. Wood made his debut against Crystal Palace in December 1924 after arriving from Stourbridge in the summer. Played three other games for Fulham scoring two goals, including one in a fine 3-1 win at Middlesbrough.
4FL 2g

WOOD, William, (1905-06) Inside-right.
Born: Middleton, 1878. Played for Bury circa 1898; Fulham cs 1905; Norwich City February 1906; Leyton cs 1907-08. Wood gained two FA Cup-winners' medals with Bury in 1900 and 1903, scoring goals in both games. Scored 61 goals in 188 League appearances for Bury before joining Fulham. Wood also represented the Football League in a 9-0 victory over the Irish League in 1901. Surprisingly, Wood was not a success at Fulham but did well at Norwich and Leyton.
9SL 2g, 2FA

WRIGHTSON, Frank Lawrence, (1931-3) Inside-forward.
Born: Shildon, County Durham, 9 January 1906. Died: circa 1979. Played for Ferryhill; Darlington 1928; Manchester City April 1930; Fulham March 1932 (£1,200); Exeter City March 1933; Chester cs 1935-39. One of soccer's wanderers, Wrightson was working as a blacksmith when signed by Darlington. Soon caught the attention of First Division Manchester City due to his goalscoring exploits. Signed by Fulham for a large fee to help their push for the Third Division South Championship. Wrightson gained most success at Chester where he scored 26 goals in 1935-6 and 32 in season 1936-7. Hit the net 121 times in 227 League games in total.
18FL 5g, 1FA

WYLLIE, David, (1908-09) Centre-forward.
Born: circa 1883. Played for Renfrew Victoria; St Mirren; Fulham December 1908. Cost Fulham a lot of money when signed from St Mirren but proved a flop as he was unable to adapt to English football. He had won a Scottish Cup runners-up medal when St Mirren lost 5-1 to Celtic in 1908. Signed as a centre-forward but probably had his best games at centre-half for Fulham.
6FL

Fulham 2   Manchester United 1

FULHAM'S first Football League season saw them chasing promotion from Division Two and a fine FA Cup run which reached its peak when they met Manchester United in the quarter-finals.

Not since Spurs won the Cup in 1901, had London seen such wild enthusiasm at a football match. People swarmed to Craven Cottage to see United who, with the great Billy Meredith in their line-up and the famous half-back line of Duckworth, Roberts and Bell, were First Division leaders and on their way to the League title.

Fulham began well and only a fine tackle by Burgess robbed Harrison after United full-back Stacey had miskicked. It was only a temporary let-off for the Manchester club, however, and in the 12th minute Burgess took too long over his clearance and Harrison charged down the kick. It cannoned off his body and past Moger — a lucky goal perhaps, but one that Fulham deserved, nonetheless.

In the latter period of the first half United's brilliant half-backs and clever forwards gave them the edge and Skene was forced to make two fine saves, first from Sandy Turnbull, then from Bannister, before Sandy Turnbull headed down Meredith's centre to the feet of Jimmy Turnbull for him to equalise early in the second half.

The Londoners were now called upon to show great character and they responded magnificently. In the 65th minute Harrison got the ball just outside the United penalty area and took advantage of a hesitant defence to score with a low shot.

United's heads dropped and Fulham deserved their place in the semi-final, although there they crashed 6-0 to Newcastle, the outstanding team of the Edwardian era.

Fulham: Skene; Ross, Lindsay, Collins, Morrison, Goldie, Millington, Dalrymple, Harrison, Fraser, Mouncher.
Manchester United: Moger; Stacey, Burgess, Duckworth, Roberts, Bell, Meredith, Bannister, J.Turnbull, A.Turnbull, Wall.

Attendance: 41,000   *Referee: Mr T.Kirkham (Burslem)*

In September 1981, a Fulham supporter named Milligan died, aged 99, in an old people's home. He had been an artist and amongst his possessions were two paintings he had done at the time of the 1908 Fulham-Manchester United FA Cup match. The one shown here depicts Harrison's winning goal.

Left-winger Willie Walker had a hand in all three Fulham goals.

Match to Remember 2　　　　3 February 1912

Fulham 3　Liverpool 0

THE first meeting between Fulham and Liverpool would not be remembered with pleasure by anyone from the Anfield club. The occasion was a second round FA Cup match at Craven Cottage and Liverpool, despite fielding such players as goalkeeper Sam Hardy and full-back Eph Longworth — giants of their day — were never in the hunt.

Fulham were still a Second Division side and Liverpool had been in the First Division throughout the Londoners' brief League career. Yet reputations counted for little as Fulham's dash and purpose, particularly on the wings, won the day handsomely.

The goals were all superbly executed and Fulham were 1-0 ahead at half-time through a splendid effort involving Walker, Pearce and Coleman. It was Pearce who ran on to Walker's speculative through-ball before laying on the chance for Coleman. Hardy came rushing out but Coleman placed the ball just wide of the goalkeeper who, although he got a finger to it, could not stop it.

A spectacular diving header by Pearce drove Walker's corner into the net for Fulham's second goal and then Coleman, who had just missed one good chance, netted the third. He met Walker's centre and drove it 'obliquely across Hardy and into the side of the network'.

There was no doubt that Fulham deserved their victory. Left-back Sharp and centre-half Mavin were the pick of the defence, 'although Marshall did good work as a spoiler'; and whilst Coleman scored twice, and Walker was involved in all three goals, it was Pearce who was the pick of the forwards.

Fulham defeated Northampton in the next round before falling to West Brom in the quarter-finals.

Fulham: Reynolds; Charlton, Sharp, Marshall, Mavin, White, Smith, Coleman, Pearce, Brown, Walker.
Liverpool: Hardy; Longworth, Pursell, Lowe, Harrop, Robinson, Parkinson, Uren, McDonald, Bovill, Stewart.

Attendance: 30,000　　　　　　　　　　　*Referee: Mr R.Pook (Portsmouth)*

Fulham 1   Everton 0

FIRST Division Everton have fallen three times to Second Division Fulham in the FA Cup. The first occasion ranks as Fulham's most famous victory of the 1920s and the day belonged to a young goalkeeper called Ernie Beecham, who started the season in Fulham's third team.

On a freezing cold Thursday afternoon, at snow-covered Craven Cottage, young Beecham defied the might of Dixie Dean and his colleagues to help Fulham win their third round replay before a 40,000 crowd. For good measure Fulham beat Liverpool, and Notts County, before falling to Manchester United in the quarter-final.

Even the snow, which fell heavily throughout the greater part of the match, and darkness, which made it difficult for the spectators to see the ball in the closing minutes, could not spoil the day for Fulham's wildly enthusiastic supporters.

According to one local newspaper, 'Fulham won, but they were lucky'. The report went on: 'Their only goal, which was scored by White 17 minutes into the second-half, had an element of fluke. Time after time, Everton had the home defence hopelessly beaten, only for a goal shot to fail by inches'.

It should be said, however, that Fulham were handicapped by an injury to left-back Chaplin throughout the second-half. Although he remained on the pitch until 15 minutes from the end, he was limping painfully at outside-left.

The real hero, though was Beecham: 'He is not yet 19 years of age, but he showed both a coolness and a judgement that many a man of twice his experience might be proud to possess. He was here, there and everywhere. He leapt high to save, he dived wide and low to save. One of his best clearances came in the last minute. A number of spectators rushed over the ground and carried him to the entrance to the dressing rooms. He deserved it.'

Fulham: Beecham; Dyer, Chaplin, Oliver, McNabb, Barrett, Harris, Craig, Edmonds, White, Penn.
Everton: Hardy; Raitt, McDonald, Peacock, Bain, Virr, Chedgzoy, Irvine, Dean, O'Donnell, Troup.

Attendance: 40,000   *Referee: Mr F. W. Warriss (Birmingham)*

Fulham players and officials enjoy a seaside break at Brighton before meeting Everton in the Cup. Standing (left to right): George Uttley (trainer), Andy Ducat (manager), Tom Pearks (director), Teddy Craig, an unidentified reporter, and Bill Prouse. Seated: Albert Barrett, Frank Penn, Jock McNab, Ernie Beecham, Albert Pape, Len Oliver, Alec Chaplin, Reg Dyer.

Fulham, champions of the Third Division South. This is the team which won the club's first major honour. Back row (left to right): Oliver, Gibbon, Iceton, Birch, Penn. Front: Richards, Hammond, Newton, Price, Finch, Gibbons.

Match to Remember 4   30 April 1932

Fulham 3   Bristol Rovers 2

AFTER four seasons in Division Three South, Fulham were desperate to regain their Second Division status and with it, their first title. Victory over Bristol Rovers clinched both ambitions but not before the Eastville club had given Fulham some anxious moments.

Indeed, until an injury to Rovers' left-back, Pickering, sent him limping on to the right wing for the remainder of the match, it seemed that Fulham might have to endure Third Division football for at least another season.

Rovers, lying in the lower reaches of the table, shocked an over-anxious Fulham by taking the lead in the 22nd minute when Cook scored following a corner.

Then came the injury to Pickering and Fulham began to settle down against a hastily re-organised Bristol side. With the wind behind them in the second half, Fulham brought Calvert to several smart saves before Finch equalised following a corner.

The goalkeeper had appeared to be completely unsighted and the stroke of good fortune lifted Fulham's spirits. In an inspired period they made sure of the game with two goals in two minutes, through Barrett, who headed home a corner, and then Hammond, whose headed goal came following a lofted free-kick.

Young Ronnie Dix, later to play for England, went close for Bristol before Pickering, who could hardly raise a gallop, caught Iceton napping with a low drive which curled out of the goalkeeper's arms and over the line.

By now, however, the result was beyond doubt and the Fulham management must have been supremely confident because at the final whistle a flag was hoisted over Craven Cottage. On it was the inscription: 'Fulham, Champions Division III, 1931-32'.

Fulham: Iceton; Tilford, Birch, Oliver, Gibbons, Barrett, Richards, Wrightson, Newton, Hammond, Finch.
Bristol Rovers: Calvert; Russell, Pickering, Stoddart, Blake, Townrow, Routledge, Dix, Cook, Hill, Oakton.

Attendance: 21,000

Fulham 2　Tottenham Hotspur 2

THIS match between the teams second and fifth in Division Two attracted a then record crowd of more than 43,000 to Craven Cottage. They were rewarded with a thrilling encounter which contained enough drama and good football to satisfy most football fans for a season.

Fulham were clearly the superior team in the opening stages with outside-left Finch tormenting Spurs' full-back Felton. The Cottagers stormed into a two-goal lead in the first 25 minutes, through Richards and Newton.

The turning point of the match, however, came just before the interval when Fulham spurned the chance to go 3-0 ahead. Rowe brought down Finch, but Newton's penalty-kick, although fiercely struck, went straight at Tottenham goalkeeper, Nicholls.

The ball knocked the 'keeper unconscious but he had the consolation of keeping it out of his net — and when he finally regained his feet, Nicholls went on to have a magnificent game.

Even the fact that Spurs lost their brilliant inside-left Greenfield, who broke a leg in a collision with Birch, did not prevent them from pulling back both goals, through Hunt, in an enthralling second half.

Although Fulham had undoubtedly failed to capitalise on a splendid first-half performance, there was also no doubt that both teams had served up one of the best-ever London derby games and, for once, a match between high-riding teams had fully lived up to expectations.

Fulham: Tootill; Birch, Tilford, Oliver, Gibbons, Barrett, Richards, Hammond, Newton, Price, Finch.
Tottenham Hotspur: Nicholls; Felton, Whatley, Colquoun, Rowe, Meads, Howe, O'Callaghan, Hunt, Greenfield, Evans.

Attendance: 43,407　　　　　　　　　*Referee: Mr W.P.Harper (Worcester)*

Left-back Arthur Tilford (left), who had just won a Third Division Championship medal with Fulham, was kept busy as Spurs launched their fight-back. Four months later Tilford joined Southampton but by the close season was a Fulham player once more. Joe Birch, Fulham's other full-back, was involved in the incident in which Greenfield broke a leg.

Match programme for the visit of Southampton.

Syd Gibbons was the hero of the day as he switched from the hub of the defence to spearhead the attack and scored three goals in 20 minutes to earn a draw.

Match to Remember 6   3 November 1934

Fulham 3   Southampton 3

ON the face of it the visit of Southampton to Craven Cottage was a run-of-the-mill Second Division encounter, yet it turned out to be one Fulham's most thrilling games of the 1930s. It was also the only time that a defender has scored a hat-trick for Fulham — and none of his goals were from the penalty spot or free-kicks.

The match belonged to Syd Gibbons, Fulham's dynamic centre-half for more than a decade, who retrieved an apparantly lost cause virtually single-handed.

Saints stormed into a three-goal lead in the first hour, despite having three defenders carried off the field. They took a deserved lead after 27 minutes through Horton. Then Ward left the pitch with a wrenched knee, and within a minute of each other, both McIlwane and Sillett collapsed with head injuries from different collisions.

All three were back for the second half, Ward limping at outside-right and McIlwane and Sillett with their heads bandaged. Ward had a hand in Southampton's second goal, scored by Luckett, and McIlwane got the third to put the game seemingly beyond Fulham's reach.

But that was where Gibbons took over. He took matters into his own hands, turned himself into an 'extra centre-forward' and scored three goals in 20 minutes to cap a comeback of epic proportions.

His first goal was a header from Arnold's centre; the other two came from 'headlong rushes which he led and it was his foot on both occasions which applied the touch needed to put the ball past the stubborn Scriven'. Four minutes later the referee ended one of Fulham's most famous games.

Fulham: Tootill; Birch, Hindson, Clarke, Gibbons, Barrett, Finch, Hammond, Newton, Price, Arnold.
Southampton: Scriven; Adams, Sillett, Ward, McIlwane, Luckett, Tully, Brewis, Horton, Holt, Fishlock.

Attendance: 18,000   *Referee: Mr C.P. West (Brighton)*

Fulham 3   Derby County 0

FULHAM reached the FA Cup semi-finals for the second time after a superb win over First Division Derby County, whose team included six internationals.

Fulham had shown their worth long before Derby were disorganised by a shoulder injury to right-back Ted Udall, who finished the game at outside-right. Even when Derby were at full-strength in the first 30 minutes, Fulham should have gone in front.

First Hammond missed with the goal at his mercy from ten yards out; then Perry's header was brilliantly saved one-handed by Kirby who tipped it from under his bar.

England forward Sammy Crooks brought a fine save from Tootill at the start of the second half, but Fulham soon took the lead.

It came through a great goal from Arnold six minutes after the interval. Smith began it with a forward pass to Finch and the winger 'hopped like a bird between Barker and Collin' before crossing for Arnold to head home.

Twenty minutes later Barrett fired a left-foot shot past the motionless Kirby following Arnold's corner. Another corner from Arnold one minute later found Smith who netted Fulham's third.

One report said: 'There was no finer player afield than Gibbons. The huge Fulham defender overshadowed Barker. He combined the third-back game with many fine dribbles upfield.'

Barrett and Tompkins were the stars of a splendid defensive performance and the forward honours went to Smith, the 'mighty atom' according to the report.

It was the best of Fulham's four Cup wins that season, but in the semi-final Sheffield United denied them a first Wembley appearance.

Fulham: Tootill; Hindson, Keeping, Barrett, Gibbons, Tompkins, Finch, Smith, Perry, Hammond, Arnold.
Derby County: Kirby; Udall, Collin, Nicholas, Barker, Keen, Crooks, Napier, Bowers, Ramage, Duncan.

Attendance: 37,151   *Referee: Mr E.C.Carnwell (Staffordshire)*

Fulham's 1936 FA Cup semi-final squad. Back row (left to right): Mr Peart (manager), Barrett, Gibbons, Hindson, Tootill, Keeping, Tompkins, Hammond, Mr Dean (chairman), Mr Pearks (director). Front: Worsley, Smith, Perry, Finch, Arnold, Voisey (trainer).

Newspaper cutting shows the crowd at the Putney End spilling on to the pitch.

Match to Remember 8   8 October 1938

Fulham 2   Millwall 1

'CRUSH barriers folding like paper, wooden supports cracking and splintering, a horde of small boys invading the pitch and reaching the half-way line each time Fulham scored, a free-fight in the crowd....Imagine a saucer full of nearly 50,000 worms and you get some idea of the wriggling, squirming crowd that roared without stopping....'

That was how one newspaper described the visit of Millwall to Craven Cottage for this London 'derby' just a week after Premier Neville Chamberlain returned from his 'peace in our time' trip to Munich. The mood of the people was one of enormous relief after being told that war had been averted and that was reflected in many ways, not least in the attendances at football matches.

Even so, the 'gate' at the Cottage was quite astonishing. It was the biggest Football League attendance of the day, and is Fulham's record crowd for any home match — a record which will, of course, now never be beaten.

The huge crowd saw an exciting game. Millwall took their first-half lead through an own-goal when Keeping headed Barker's 'whip-lash centre' past Turner. The Lions might have gone in at half-time even further ahead but for fine defensive work by the Fulham rearguard.

In the second half Fulham hit back with everything and, following a free-kick from Arnold, Woodward 'did a William Tell' header about which there was no argument. A minute earlier one of the crush barriers had given way and people were still 'extricating themselves from the swirling mob' when Woodward's goal went in. From that moment it was all Fulham and Evans settled the issue with a close-range shot.

Fulham: Turner; Bacuzzi, Keeping, Evans, Hiles, Tompkins, Finch, Worsley, Rooke, Woodward, Arnold.
Millwall: Pearson; E.Smith, Dudley, Lea, Chiverton, Forsyth, Rawlings, Richardson, Walsh, Barker, J.R.Smith.

Attendance: 49,335   *Referee: Mr G.Dutton (Warwick)*

Three stars of Fulham's great win over Everton, pictured at a re-union 35 years later. Left to right: Joe Bacuzzi, Jim Taylor and Bob Thomas, scorer of the winning goal.

Match to Remember 9   14 February 1948

Everton 0   Fulham 1

FULHAM'S victory over Everton in this FA Cup fifth-round replay was more emphatic than the 1-0 scoreline suggests. The Cottagers swept aside the Merseysiders and were worth more than the lone goal, scored by Bob Thomas 17 minutes from the end.

And what a superb goal it was. Thomas cleverly balanced himself to meet Stevens's through-ball at just the right moment and shot past Ted Sagar to ensure Fulham's place in the quarter-finals.

Fulham's great hero, though, was centre-half Taylor who rallied his colleagues to such an extent that the Merseysiders were allowed only two shots at goal all afternoon.

Despite suffering a head injury early in the game, Taylor tackled, kicked and headed away at the heart of the Fulham defence, reducing Everton to also-rans.

Sagar had already prevented Fulham taking the lead when he produced a superb save to beat out Thomas's header, but he could do nothing about the inside-right's effort late in the game.

Everton's chances had come to nought when first Bacuzzi headed off the line, then Hinton turned a long shot against the bar and over. Thereafter, it was all Fulham, who could even afford to miss a penalty when Freeman shot wide after Watson had handled.

Everton: Sager; Saunders, Dugdale, Farrell, Humphreys, Watson, Grant, Boyes, Dodds, Fielding, Eglington.
Fulham: Hinton; Freeman, Bacuzzi, Quested, Taylor, Beasley, S.Thomas, R.Thomas, Stevens, Ayres, Bewley.

Att: 71,587   *Referee: Mr R.Leafe (Nottingham)*

Fulham 2   West Ham United 0

WHEN West Ham visited Craven Cottage for the final match of the 1948-9 season, Fulham were already practically assured of First Division football and only a huge defeat by the Hammers could cost them promotion.

What was still at stake, however, was the Second Division Championship and Fulham went into the game desperate to extend their remarkable end-of-season run which had already seen them take 19 points from their previous 12 games.

One newspaper commented that Fulham were 'scared stiffer than waxworks dummies' before the game; and two directors who had bought champagne to lead the after-match celebrations, hid it in a neighbouring house until the result was in no doubt.

But Fulham need not have worried. Team-work and a rare fighting spirit had brought them to the threshold of Division One and it served them well on this day too. Add to all that the fact that manager Frank Osborne had made an inspired signing by bringing 22-year-old Arthur Rowley from West Brom and you have the recipe for their success.

It was Rowley who opened the scoring in the 32nd minute, swivelling on Thomas' pass to hit a screaming 20-yard drive just underneath the Hammers' bar. It scraped the paintwork and crashed down over the line.

In the 76th minute, Rowley made it 2-0, and then Gage, Fulham's former third-team goalkeeper, made a superb save, somehow holding on to a powerful header from Robinson.

At the final whistle, thousands of Fulham supporters raced on to the pitch and some carried Rowley off shoulder-high as a banner was unfolded. It read: 'Fulham for ever — Division One'.

Fulham: Gage; Freeman, Bacuzzi, Quested, Taylor, Beasley, Stevens, R.Thomas, Rowley, Jezzard, McDonald.
West Ham United: Taylor; Devlin, Ford, Corbett, Walker, Moroney, Woodgate, Parsons, Robinson, McGowan, Bainbridge.

Attendance: 40,000   *Referee: Mr H.Hartley (Chelmsford)*

Arthur Rowley opens the scoring for Fulham against West Ham.

Fulham 4   Newcastle United 5

'TOSH' Chamberlain, playing in his first FA Cup match, scored a hat-trick in what many older supporters still regard as the finest match ever seen at Craven Cottage.

Chamberlain might have had a fourth but the 'goal' was disallowed on the signal of a young linesman called Jack Taylor, who was to one day referee a World Cup Final.

Despite his hat-trick, Chamberlain still finished on the losing side and it was Cup-holders Newcastle's number-11, Bobby Mitchell, who had the final say and denied Fulham a place in the fifth round.

Yet Fulham themselves had already staged a remarkable fight-back, leading 4-3 after being 3-0 down when Newcastle hit three goals in a ten-minute spell in the first-half.

First Milburn smashed the ball into the roof of the Fulham net after 16 minutes following Mitchell's corner. Four minutes later, following another Mitchell corner, Stokoe's shot went in off Wilson; and five minutes after that Casey ended a mesmerising Mitchell-Stokoe-Mitchell-Milburn move by sliding through the mud to hit a left-foot shot into the Fulham net.

But now it was Fulham's turn to grasp the game. With Johnny Haynes at his inspired best, the Cottagers surged forward. Chamberlain pulled a goal back after 39 minutes and completed his hat-trick with goals in the 68th and 70th minutes.

It was Chamberlain who laid on a goal for Hill in the 73rd minute — their third in five minutes — and a remarkable victory looked imminent.

But 12 minutes from the end Ian Black went to gather Mitchell's cross, only for United's Keeble to bundle him over the line. With eight minutes remaining, Davies, Casey and Mitchell combined and the 'flu-ridden Keeble netted the winner to seal a remarkable game.

Fulham: Black; Wilson, Lawler, Smith, Brice, Lowe, Hill, Robson, Jezzard, Haynes, Chamberlain.
Newcastle United: Simpson; Woollard, McMichael, Stokoe, Paterson, Casey, Milburn, Davies, Keeble, Curry, Mitchell.

Attendance: 39,200   *Referee: Mr J.Mitchell (Lancashire)*

Chamberlain (11) makes the score 3-2 with his second goal. Other Fulham players are Bobby Robson (left) and Bedford Jezzard.

Jimmy Hill shoots past Harry Gregg to put Fulham 2-1 ahead.

Match to Remember 12   22 March 1958

Fulham 2   Manchester United 2

UNDER normal circumstances the British love for the underdog would have won Second Division Fulham many casual supporters when they met mighty Manchester United in the FA Cup semi-final at Villa Park.

But this occasion was different, for United were struggling to rebuild in the aftermath of the Munich air crash. On emotional grounds alone there were few people outside London who wanted anything but a United victory.

They were no doubt pleased when, after only 12 minutes, Taylor and Crowther combined and Bobby Charlton crashed a great shot past Tony Macedo.

In the next minute, however, Fulham were level. Langley moved up to beat the United defence with a beautiful lob and there was Stevens to flick the ball past Gregg from a few yards out.

Dwight then wasted a glorious opportunity but, with Johnny Haynes breaking up United attacks and then sending fellow forwards away, it was not long before Fulham went into the lead.

Haynes began the move in the 38th minute and Lawler and Dwight carried it on for Hill to hold off Cope before shooting past the advancing Gregg. It was a great goal.

Soon afterwards Langley was carried off injured and, with Fulham down to ten men, Charlton smashed home the equaliser.

In the second half, with Langley limping on the left wing, Fulham still looked the more imaginative in attack but, there were no more goals.

In the replay at Highbury, some uncharacteristic mistakes by Macedo helped United to a 5-3 win but, despite those eight goals, it was the Villa Park encounter that will go down as one of the most thrilling of all Cup semi-finals.

Fulham: Macedo; Cohen, Langley, Bentley, Stapleton, Lawler, Dwight, Hill, Stevens, Haynes, Chamberlain.
Manchester United: Gregg; Foulkes, Greaves, Goodwin, Cope, Crowther, Webster, Taylor, Dawson, Pearson, Charlton.

Attendance: 69,745   *Referee: Mr C.W.Kingston (Newport, Mon.)*

Fulham 6   Sheffield Wednesday 2

FULHAM'S return to the First Division after a seven-year absence was virtually clinched with this emphatic victory over promotion rivals, Sheffield Wednesday, on Good Friday morning.

But for one man in particular the game proved a personal triumph. Inside-right Jimmy Hill had been without a goal for 11 months and cat-calls and chants of 'Go home Hill' had turned his season into a nightmare.

Hill had also fallen out with the club, having disagreements with chairman Tommy Trinder, and being 'dropped' from the first team by manager Bedford Jezzard in practice matches.

Before this vital match, Trinder and Hill met and cleared the air but with 16 minutes remaining, and Fulham hanging on precariously to a 3-2 lead through Leggat, Langley and Cook, Hill was still looking for a goal.

The crowd were still barracking him and, finally, skipper Johnny Haynes turned to a section of Hill's critics and demanded, "Give him a break, can't you?"

A newspaper reporter takes up the story: 'With just 16 minutes left, Hill got that break from a right-wing corner by outside-left Chamberlain. All you could see was a black and white flash as Hill soared to head the ball.

'Hill went wild, and so did Fulham. Jimmy was hugged, thumped and buried under a crowing crowd of players....When Hill headed the fifth and sixth goals in the 78th and 88th minutes, Trinder gagged away to the fans below.

' "This was Jimmy's day, the stinker that became a blinder, the humiliation that ended in glory." '

Fulham: Macedo; Cohen, Langley, Mullery, Bentley, Lowe, Leggat, Hill, Cook, Haynes, Chamberlain.
Sheffield Wednesday: Pinner; Staniforth, Curtis, McAnearney, Swan, Kay, Wilkinson, Fantham, Shiner, Froggatt, Finney.

Attendance: 39,377   *Referee: Mr K.Stokes (Newark)*

Jimmy Hill answered his critics in fine style.

*Programme cover for the promotion clash
with rivals Sheffield Wednesday.*

211

Official Programme . . .

THE FOOTBALL ASSOCIATION CHALLENGE CUP

SEMI-FINAL TIE

BURNLEY v. FULHAM

VILLA PARK, BIRMINGHAM
SATURDAY, MARCH 31st, 1962
KICK-OFF 3·0 p.m.

Price - - - - *SIXPENCE*
ISSUED BY ASTON VILLA F.C.

Johnny Haynes had a superb game.

Cover of the 1962 semi-final programme.

Match to Remember 14   31 March 1962

Fulham 1   Burnley 1

WHEN this Cup tie was settled by a replay, Fulham set the unenviable record of playing in more semi-finals than any other club without ever reaching the FA Cup Final.

As in the 1958 semi-final against Manchester United, few people doubted that Fulham were the better side in the first game, but they could not press home their advantage. The Cup run did spark off an ultimately successful fight against relegation and there was genuine disappointment that a 'double' was not achieved.

As one reporter commented: 'If Bedford Jezzard, Tommy Trinder, Johnny Haynes and the faithful supporters echoed the well-known boxing adage, "We wuz robbed", as Fulham tramped away from Villa Park, they would be no more than speaking the truth about 1962's surprise Cup contenders'.

Burnley, who were to finish League Championship runners-up that season, fell behind to a Graham Leggat goal. John Connelly equalised, but it was only thanks to goalkeeper Adam Blacklaw that Burnley lived to fight again.

Fulham, prompted by wing-halves Mullery and Lowe, and inside-forward genius, Johnny Haynes, were in charge for the whole game and centre-forward Maurice Cook had a fine match.

Cook had recently signed a two-year contract after having earlier made it clear that he wanted to leave Fulham. His performance at Villa Park underlined Fulham's wisdom in persuading him to stay.

Fulham: Macedo; Cohen, Langley, Mullery, Dodgin, Lowe, Leggat, Henderson, Cook, Haynes, O'Connell.
Burnley: Blacklaw; Angus, Elder, Adamson, Cummings, Miller, Connelly, McIlroy, Pointer, Robson, Harris.

Attendance: 59,989   *Referee: Mr W.Clements (West Bromwich)*

Fulham 10   Ipswich Town 1

GRAHAM Leggat equalled the First Division's fastest hat-trick when he netted three goals in as many minutes to send Ipswich Town sliding to defeat in this Boxing Day fixture.

Once before Fulham had scored ten goals, in 1931 when they beat Torquay 10-2 in a Third Division South match, but this was the Cottagers' record margin of victory, a record which still stands.

According to one reporter: 'It was misty murder in the mind, torment by timetable to the accompaniment of clicking stop-watches and rustling record books. But it was not a match because it takes two to make one.

'Maurice Cook missed an easy goal in the 12th minute, scored a difficult one by hurling himself to a cross in the 16th, and the dam burst. After the next four and a half minutes Ipswich were 4-0 down. Fulham centre-forward Leggat tapped in a rebound from the bar, spun in a second by a post and flashed in a third from 25 yards.'

Ipswich goalkeeper Roy Bailey palmed in a corner from Bobby Howfield after 43 minutes before Gerry Baker made it 5-1 in the dying seconds of the first half.

Strangely, Macedo seemed busier than Bailey in the second half, yet Fulham still managed another five goals. Howfield (47 and 71 minutes) completed his own hat-trick in between which Robson had notched Fulham's seventh. With two minutes remaining, Fulham reached double figures through Mullery and, appropriately, Leggat.

Eighteen months earlier, Ipswich had won the League Championship under Alf Ramsey and only two days after the crushing defeat at the Cottage they gained some revenge with a 4-2 win at Portman Road.

Fulham: Macedo; Cohen, Langley, Mullery, Keetch, Robson, Key, Cook, Leggat, Haynes, Howfield.
Ipswich Town: Bailey; Davies, Compton, Baxter, Bolton, Dougan, Broadfoot, Moran, Baker, Phillips, Blackwood.

Attendance: 19,374   *Referee: Mr P.Bye (Bedford)*

Fulham's high-scoring forward, Graham Leggat (left), set a First Division record with a hat-trick in three minutes. Maurice Cook (above) missed an easy chance, then scored a spectacular goal to open the floodgates.

Steve Earle (right) completes his hat-trick and Fulham are safe. Graham Leggat is the other Fulham player.

Match to Remember 16   23 April 1966

Northampton Town   2 Fulham 4

FULHAM'S First Division life between 1959 and 1968 was characterised by some breathtaking escapes from relegation. The most thrilling was in 1965-6 when, with 13 games left, Fulham had only 15 points and were five adrift of 20th-placed Northampton.

The arrival of a new coach, Dave Sexton, sparked off a remarkable revival and by the time Fulham visited the County Ground it was clear that whoever won the match would stay up, whilst the losers would go down. Not suprisingly, the game attracted a record crowd to the County Ground.

They saw Northampton sweep ahead after 13 minutes through George Hudson, but six minutes later Fulham were level with a brilliant goal from Bobby Robson. He took Mark Pearson's return pass and flighted his shot just inside the right-hand post.

It was Robson's mistake which allowed Northampton to regain the lead after 29 minutes. The right-half failed to clear Walden's cross and Kiernan smashed the ball home from outside the penalty area.

After 65 minutes Fulham drew level again. From one of Cohen's rare excursions up the wing, Steve Earle slipped the ball home to set up a frantic last effort from the side desperate for survival.

There were two minutes left when Leggat floated over a cross, pulling the ball back from the by-line, and there was Earle, ten yards out, to place his header beautifully into the net.

The final goal was quite amazing. With practically every Northampton outfield player in the Fulham penalty area, Earle and Leggat stood unmarked ten yards inside their own half. Haynes cleared the ball and Earle had a clear run before dribbling around Coe to complete his hat-trick and ensure Fulham's survival for another year.

Northampton Town: Coe; Mackin, Everitt, Kurila, Branston, Kiernan, Walden, Moore, Hudson, Martin, Lines.
Fulham: McClelland; Cohen, Nichols, Robson, Dempsey, Brown, Earle, Clarke, Haynes, Pearson, Leggat.

Attendance: 24,523   *Referee: Mr J.Taylor (Wolverhampton)*

214

Halifax Town 0   Fulham 8

STEVE Earle equalled a club record — and Fulham themselves set a new one — with this eight-goal hammering of Halifax Town in a Third Division match at The Shay.

Earle's five goals joined Jimmy Hill's five at Doncaster in March 1958 as the best performance by a Fulham player on an opponent's ground; and the result still stands as the Cottagers' biggest away win. Two players, Fred Harrison and Bedford Jezzard, have scored five for Fulham in a home League game.

On the face of it, the game promised to be a difficult one, for Halifax were defending an unbeaten home League record that season. Fulham, however, would have crushed most Third Division teams that night and they cashed in on some shocking defending — and atrocious finishing — by the Yorkshire club.

Four of the goals came from long balls down the middle which Halifax simply failed to clear, and two more were the direct result of mistakes by Halifax left-back Andy Burgin.

There was a hint of good fortune about Fulham's first goal. After 12 minutes a clearance from Shawcross hit the referee before rebounding to Horne, who crossed for Earle to score.

Thirty minutes into the first half Fulham had made sure of both points with goals from Barry Lloyd and, again, Earle. To their credit, Halifax were still playing some attractive football, but three minutes from the interval they went 4-0 down when Jimmy Conway scored from a penalty.

In a 20-minute spell in the second half, Fulham hit four more. Earle found the net three times, Conway once, and poor Halifax were utterly devastated.

Halifax Town: Smith; Wallace, Burgin, Lennard, Pickering, Robertson, Flower, Hill, Lawther, Shawcross, McCarthy.
Fulham: Seymour; Brown, Callaghan, Horne, Matthewson, Richardson, Conway, Lloyd, Earle, Haynes (Roberts), Barrett.

Attendance: 5,809   *Referee: Mr D.Laing (Preston)*

Jimmy Conway (left) and Steve Earle (right) who between them got seven of Fulham's eight goals. In 1969-70 both men scored 20 goals, the last time two Fulham players managed this many in the same season.

Viv Busby drives home Fulham's winning goal.

Match to Remember 18   15 February 1975

Everton 1   Fulham 2

WHEN Fulham reached the 1975 FA Cup Final, they ended a semi-final 'jinx' which stretched back to 1908. Fulham also played a remarkable 12 FA Cup ties that season, and the pick of the bunch was this fifth-round game against Everton, then top of Division One.

The Goodison Park thriller came only four days after the end of a four-match marathon against Nottingham Forest, and Bobby Moore, who led England to World Cup triumph, and Alan Mullery, winner of UEFA Cup and FA Cup medals with Spurs, each rated this victory amongst their greatest memories.

Everton were FA Cup favourites and on target for a League and Cup double; Fulham were billed as 'the plodders' from the lower reaches of the Second Division. But in Moore and Mullery, Fulham had, as one critic put it, 'two men in key positions with more accumulated experience at the most demanding level than the whole Everton team together'.

The writer continued: 'They run these days on 33-year-old legs, Mullery faster than Moore, but both with intelligent economy. What really mattered was that these are men who respond to the sound of brave bugles and tunes of glory'.

Fulham's Busby was credited with both his side's goals. The first came from point-blank range, tapped in after Conway's slide to meet Barrett's cross at the near post had 'disrupted Kenyon and Davies'.

Early in the second half, Kenyon headed home a well-placed corner from Jones and for a while it seemed that Fulham had lost their chance.

But with five minutes to play, Conway pulled the ball back from the by-line and there was Busby, who had time to turn before hammering home the winner.

Everton: Davies; Bernard, Seargeant, Clements, Kenyon, Hurst, Jones, Dobson, Lyons, Latchford(Telfer), Pearson.
Fulham: Mellor; Cutbush, Strong, Mullery, Lacy, Moore, Dowie(Lloyd), Conway, Busby, Slough, Barrett.

Attendance: 45,233   *Referee: Mr C.Thomas (Treorchy)*

216

Fulham 1 Lincoln City 1

FULHAM won promotion to Division Two in the most dramatic fashion when they met Lincoln in the final match of the season. The game had been postponed from its original December date and now Fulham needed at least a draw to go up, whilst victory would probably give them the Third Division title.

The issue was further fuelled by the fact that Lincoln needed victory to gain promotion. Some 20,000 fans packed Craven Cottage and were treated to an evening of tension and drama.

For almost an hour of this absorbing match Lincoln had outfought and outplayed their opponents and Fulham could see Second Division football slipping from their grasp.

In the 57th minute, however, the Sincil Bank club were dealt two devastating blows. First their hard-tackling defender, Steve Thompson, was ordered off for a foul on Dean Coney. Thompson had already been booked in the first half and as he trudged to the dressing-rooms, Tony Gale floated over the free-kick for Roger Brown to head Fulham into the lead.

Lincoln's misery was eased in the 72nd minute when Dave Carr scrambled home an equaliser from Phil Turner's corner, but their ten men could do no more in a heart-stopping climax as Fulham held on.

At the final whistle of a match which had seen five players booked — amongst them Fulham's Wilson and Hopkins — thousands of delighted Fulham fans swarmed on to the pitch to carry off their heroes.

Manager Malcolm Macdonald said, "We didn't play much football tonight but we've produced the goods over a 46-match programme and that's what matters most." The fans agreed wholeheartedly.

Fulham: Peyton; Hopkins, Strong(Tempest), O'Driscoll, Brown, Gale, Davies, Wilson, Coney, O'Sullivan, Lewington.
Lincoln City: Felgate; Carr, Neale, Cockerill, Peake, Thompson, Shipley, Turner, Hobson, Cunningham, Hibberd(Gilbert).

Attendance: 20,398   *Referee: Mr E.Read (Bristol)*

Jubilant Fulham players celebrate promotion on the balcony of Craven Cottage.

217

Gordon Davies (left) whose two goals rocked Newcastle. His first goal was runner-up in BBC-TV's 'Goal of the Season' competition. Dean Coney (right) scored Fulham's second and it was his shot which led to Davies' second goal.

Match to Remember 20   16 October 1982

Newcastle United 1   Fulham 4

FULHAM played some exhilarating football when they returned to Division Two in 1982-3 and hopes of promotion straight through to the First Division were dashed only on the final day of the season, in a highly controversial match at Derby.

Earlier in the campaign, as Fulham became one of the pace-setters, they went to St James' Park and destroyed Newcastle United with some superb football. It was Malcolm Macdonald's first visit to Gallowgate as a manager and the atmosphere was charged with emotion.

Fulham swept to a 3-0 lead inside the first 37 minutes. Davies hit the first goal with a first-time effort after only ten minutes; Dean Coney made it two; and Ray Houghton put the game beyond Newcastle's reach when he lobbed a 25-yarder past goalkeeper Carr.

The only sour notes on an otherwise memorable day were two highly debateable penalty awards to Newcastle. Both of them involved challenges on Kevin Keegan, and Macdonald said afterwards, "Any team three goals down will try and win these awards."

The former England captain slammed the first spot kick past Gerry Peyton to give Newcastle a glimmer of hope but Peyton, playing the game of his life, dived full length to save the second.

When Carr failed to hold a fierce shot from Coney, Davies reacted quicker than anyone to force the ball over the line and Fulham's day was complete.

Newcastle manager, Arthur Cox, admitted, "We were too arrogant. In fact, our players thought Fulham should not have been on the same field."

Newcastle United: Carr; Anderson, Saunders, Martin, Clarke, Carney, Keegan, Todd(Wharton), Varadi, McDermott, McCreery.
Fulham: Peyton; Hopkins, Lock(Tempest), O'Driscoll, Brown, Gale, Davies, Wilson, Coney, Houghton, Lewington.

Attendance: 29,647   *Referee: Mr A.Robinson (Radcliffe)*

218

FULHAM IN THE SOUTHERN LEAGUE

FULHAM'S entry to the Southern League was a significant step in the transition from park team to League club. In 1896, the year they moved to Craven Cottage, Fulham had joined the London League. After two seasons, the club committee sought a higher standard of football, and an application to the Southern League was successful in 1898. After a poor start to their debut season, Fulham made the decision to turn professional in December 1898 and, as a result of the turnover caused by this change of status, 40 players were used in only 22 games in 1898-9.

Crowds for these early Southern League games were usually between 1,000 and 3,000 (although 8,000 attended the local 'derby' against Shepherd's Bush at Wormholt Farm over Easter 1899). Fulham were known at this time as The Reds, but changed colours to the familiar black and white strip in 1903. The Cottage site then comprised mudheap terraces from the Central Line excavations, a rickety wooden stand and access through waterlogged farm tracks.

Progress was slow and unspectacular. Fulham won the Second Division title twice from 1901 to 1903, but lost the Test Matches for entry to the higher division. By 1902-03 there were only six clubs in the Second Division and Fulham rejoined the London League to ensure a sufficient number of fixtures. The club also played its first match against foreign opposition when, over Easter 1903, Rotterdam Sparta were beaten 3-2 at the Cottage.

The defeats in the play-offs seemed likely to condemn Fulham to obscurity, but they were advised that if they could raise a first-class team by 30 May 1903, they would be admitted to the First Division of the Southern League. The response was immediate: a limited liability company was formed and many new players were signed, most with League experience. When the votes were counted, Plymouth had 33, Fulham 22, and Watford missed out with only 13.

The Southern League Division One was the Edwardian equivalent of the Third Division (the Football League comprised only two divisions at this time). This stimulated interest in Fulham and attendances rose substantially. An estimated 163,000 saw the 17 home matches in 1903-04, an average of 9,500. By 1906-07, this average had risen to 16,000. The next critical move was the appointment of the experienced Harry Bradshaw as manager in April 1904. At the close of the following season, the ground was redeveloped, with the building of Archibald Leitch's Stevenage Road stand and the re-building of the Cottage. The growing crowds had put an enormous strain on the existing facilities and Leitch's redesigned stadium remained virtually unchanged until the 1960s.

Success came quickly to Bradshaw. Fulham finished sixth in 1904-05, but reached the FA Cup quarter-finals, losing to the eventual winners, Aston Villa, before a 47,000 crowd. In the next season, the club won the Southern League championship, and retained it the following year. New attendance records were quickly set: the 25,000 that saw the visit of Spurs in September 1905 was exceeded when 30,000 turned up for the visit of Portsmouth a year later. The second title was clinched by a superb run in the second half of the season, when Fulham took 22 points out of a possible 26, including a 3-0 win in the penultimate game, over nearest rivals Southampton.

This second championship prompted an application to join the Football League. After considerable lobbying by chairman Henry Norris and director George Allen, Fulham got 25 votes, equal highest with Lincoln, in the poll for three places in the Second Division. In the summer of 1907, therefore, Fulham were ready to take their place amongst football's elite.

Fulham's Wardrope and Fraser watch as a Brentford defender clears at Griffin Park in October 1903.

FULHAM FOOTBALL CLUB. (A.Team.)
Winners of London League and Second Division Southern League Championship   Season 1904-1905.

STUTTARD. HAMILTON.(trainer) GRAY. CLUTTERBUCK.   SHARP. WATERSON. MR.BARTER.(Director) WALKER
(Trainer)   AXCELL   HUNT.   SHELLEY.   HOLMES. ROWBOTHAM. MORRISON. MR.BRADSHAW.(Groundman
        J.BRADSHAW.   W.BRADSHAW.   HARWOOD.   (Manager)

Fulham playing staff pictured in 1904-05 with the Southern League Second Division and London League trophies. Back row (left to right): Stuttard (trainer), Hamilton (trainer), Gray, Clutterbuck, Sharp, Waterson, Mr Barter (director), Walker (groundsman). Middle row: Axcell, Hunt, Shelley, Holmes, Rowbotham, Morrison, Mr Bradshaw (manager). Front row: J.Bradshaw, W.Bradshaw, Harwood.

Action around the Fulham goal in the third round (the quarter final) of the FA Cup against Aston Villa at Villa Park in March 1905. Villa won 5-0 and went on to win the Cup.

The Fulham team in 1908-09. Back row (left to right): J.Hamilton (trainer), L.Skene, B.Dalrymple, A.Lindsay, F.Harrison, R.Suart. Middle row: J.E.Norris, Mr Watts (director), Mr E.D.Evans (director), Mr W.Hall (chairman), Mr H.G.Norris, Mr J.Dean (director), G.Parsonage, H.Bradshaw (secretary). Front row: F.Mouncher, F.Threlfall, J.Fryer, A.Collins (captain), H.Brown. On ground: E.Charlton, C.Millington.

1898-99

1	Sep	10	(a)	Maidenhead	W 3-0	Alexander 2, Ives
2		17	(h)	Brentford	L 1-4	Alexander
3	Oct	1	(a)	Uxbridge	L 1-2	Freeman
4		22	(a)	Chesham T	L 1-2	Freeman
5	Nov	12	(h)	Maidenhead	D 2-2	Brown, Craney
6	Dec	3	(a)	Thames Iron	L 1-2	Freeman
7		10	(h)	St Albans	D 2-2	Craney 2
8		17	(h)	Wycombe W	W 3-1	Sherran 2, Hobart
9	Jan	14	(a)	Southall	L 0-2	
10		21	(h)	Uxbridge	D 1-1	Stapley
11		28	(a)	Watford	L 3-6	Sherran 2, Pask
12	Feb	4	(h)	Wolv'ton&LNWR	L 1-3	Sherran
13		11	(h)	Shepherd's Bush	W 3-2	Sherran, Hobart, Mayes
14		26	(a)	Brentford	L 1-2	Hopkinson
15	Mar	4	(a)	St Albans	L 1-3	Hopkinson
16		18	(h)	Chesham T	W 2-1	Hopkinson 2
17		22	(h)	Watford	W 2-0	Robertson, Hopkinson
18		25	(a)	Wolv'ton&LNWR	D 2-2	Sherran, Hopkinson
19		31	(a)	Shepherd's Bush	L 0-1	
20	Apr	8	(h)	Thames Iron	L 0-1	
21		12	(a)	Wycombe W	L 1-4	Sherran
22		29	(h)	Southall	W 5-1	Hopkinson 3, Sherran, Bowden

P	W	D	L	F	A	W	D	L	F	A	Pts	Pos	Div	
22	5	3	3	22	18	1	1	9	14	26	16	10th	SL2	Appearances
														Goals

FA Amateur Cup

1Q	Oct	15	(h)	2nd Cold'm Gds	W 4-0	Freeman, Brown 2, Mandry
2Q		29	(a)	3rd Grenadiers	W 8-1	Brown 2, Craney 2, Pask, Robertson, Freeman, opp own goal
3Q	Nov	19	(a)	Hammersmith A	L 0-1	

Appearances
Goals

London Senior Cup

1	Oct	8	(a)	Civil Service	W 5-0	Freeman, Brown 2
2	Nov	5	(h)	Old St Mark's	L 0-1	

Appearances
Goals

Fulham pictured in 1898, the earliest known team photograph of the Cottagers. Unfortunately, no record was kept of the players' identities.

Football appearances grid (shirt numbers by player and match):

Maile AJ	Robert SW	Aylott SJ	Johnson H	Taylor J	Bowden J	Alexander	Freeman EH	Ives WG	Craney W	Robertson	Woodham WA	Simpson RW	Maile T	Surmon A	Craig W	Ballantyne	Mandry J	Pask J	Bull	Holley	Brown J	Dawson	Sherran G	Lewis	Love W	Hobart	Waite	Curling HS	Tutthill G	Stapley	Mackie	Rose	Mayes A	Humphries P	Walker D	Hopkinson F	Hounsell R	Turrill	#
1	2	3	4	5	6	7	8	9	10	11																													1
1		3	4	5	6	7	8	9	10	11			2																										2
1		3		5	6	7	8		10	11	2				4		9																						3
1		4		5			8		10	11		2	3				6	7			9																		4
1		4			6		8		10	11		2	3			5		7			9																		5
1		4			6		8					2	3			5		7	10	11		9																	6
1		4			6		8		10	11		2	3			5		7					9																7
1		4			6							2	3	5									9	7	8	10	11												8
		4		5								2						7					10		9	8		1	11	6	3								9
		4		5	6								2					7					10			8		1		11	3	9							10
1				5	6								2					7					10			8				4	3		9	11					11
1				5	6								2					4					10			8					3		9	11	7				12
1		4		5									2					9					10			7				6	3		8		11				13
1				5	6								2					7					10							4	3			8	11	9			14
1				5	6								2					7					10			8					3			4	11	9			15
1		4		5	6								2					7					10			8				11	3					9			16
1				5	6								2					7					10						11	4	3					9	8		17
1		4		5	6								2					7					10							11	3					9	8		18
1		4		5									2					7					10							6	3				11	9	8		19
1				5	6													7					10				2			4	3					9	8	11	20
1				5	6													7					10			8				4	3					9		11	21
1		4		5	6													7					10			8				2	3					9			22
20	**1**	**15**	**2**	**18**	**19**	**3**	**7**	**2**	**6**	**7**	**1**	**6**	**16**	**1**	**1**	**3**	**2**	**17**	**1**	**1**	**2**	**1**	**16**	**1**	**2**	**9**	**1**	**2**	**3**	**12**	**14**	**1**	**3**	**5**	**5**	**9**	**4**	**2**	
			1	3	3	1	3	1				1						1					1							9	2					9			

Qualifying rounds:

Maile AJ	Robert SW	Aylott SJ	Johnson H	Taylor J	Bowden J	Alexander	Freeman EH	Ives WG	Craney W	Robertson	Woodham WA	Simpson RW	Maile T	Surmon A	Craig W	Ballantyne	Mandry J	Pask J	Bull	Holley	Brown J	Dawson	Sherran G	...	
1		4		5	6		8		10			2	3				11	7					9		1Q
1		4			6		8		10	11		2	3			5		7					9		2Q
1		4			6		8		10	11		2	3			5		7					9		3Q
3		3		1	3		3		3	2		3	3			2	1	3					3		
		2		2	1		1		1			1	1					4							

London Senior Cup:

Maile AJ	...	Aylott SJ	...	Taylor J	Bowden J	...	Freeman EH	...	Craney W	...	Simpson RW	Maile T	...	Craig W	Ballantyne	Mandry J	Pask J	...	Sherran G	...	
1		4		5	6		8		10			3		11		11	7		9		1
1		4			6				10		2	3		11	5		7		9		2
2		2	1	2			1		2		1	2		1	1		1	2	2		
		3																2			

W. Reed played number 11 in Match 22; L. Cheshire played number 2 in round one, London Senior Cup; H. Shrimpton played number 8 in round two, London Senior Cup.

1899-1900

1	Sep	2	(h)	Southall	W	3-0	Sherran, Lloyd 2
2		16	(h)	Maidenhead	W	4-1	Hopkinson 3, Sherran
3	Oct	7	(a)	Dartford ·	W	2-1	Read, Lloyd
4		21	(a)	Wolv'ton&LNWR	L	3-4	Lloyd 2, Tutthill
5	Nov	4	(a)	Brentford	D	3-3	Lloyd, Tutthill, Powell
6		11	(h)	Dartford	W	4-3	Reed 3, Lloyd
7	Dec	2	(h)	Chesham T*	D	1-1	Lloyd
8		30	(h)	Brentford	W	5-0	Lloyd, Powell 2, Reed, Johnson
9	Jan	6	(a)	Watford	L	1-2	Reed
10		13	(h)	Shepherd's Bush	W	2-0	Johnson 2
11		20	(h)	Wolv'ton&LNWR	L	0-1	
12		27	(a)	Maidenhead	D	1-1	F.Spackman
13	Feb	17	(h)	Grays U	W	3-1	Ambrose, Reed 2
14	Mar	3	(h)	Watford	L	0-1	
15		10	(a)	Chesham T	L	0-1	
16		24	(a)	Southall	W	4-1	Tutthill, Newlands, Johnson, Lloyd
17	Apr	7	(a)	Grays U	D	0-0	
18		13	(a)	Shepherd's Bush	L	0-1	
19		14	(h)	Wycombe W	W	2-1	Ives, Lloyd
20		25	(a)	Wycombe W	W	6-0	Ives 2, Lloyd 2, Frewin, Anderson

P	W	D	L	F	A	W	D	L	F	A	Pts	Pos	Div		Appearances
20	7	1	2	24	9	3	3	4	20	14	24	2nd	SL2		Goals

*Abandoned after 80 minutes but never replayed. The result stood.

Test Match

	Apr	30	(n)	Thames Iron	L	1-5	Lloyd (Played at Tottenham)

			Appearances
			Goals

FA Cup

1Q	Sep	30	(a)	Queen's Park R	L	0-3	

			Appearances
			Goals

Maile	Howland	Morton	Stubbs	Taylor	Tutthill	Johnson	Lloyd	Hopkinson	Sherran	Reed	Curling	Spackman H	Pask	Aylott	Bowden	Powell	Drury	Angus	Janes	Spackman F	Head	McMorran	Davis	Charratt	Anderson	Ambrose	Frewin	Ives	Windust	Newlands	Newbiggin	Humphries	#
1	2	3	4	5	6	7	8	9	10	11																							1
1	3	2	4	5	6	7	8	9	10	11																							2
		3	4	5	6	7	8	9	10	11	1	2																					3
		3	4	5	6		8			9	1	2	7	10	11																		4
		3	4	5	6	7	8			10	1	2				9	11																5
1		3	4	5	6	7	8			11		2				9		10															6
1		3	4	5	6		8			11		2				9			7	10													7
		3	4	5	6	7	8			11						9				10	1	2											8
		3	4	5	6	7	8			11		2				9				10	1												9
		3	4	5	6	7	8			11		2				9				10	1												10
		3	4	5	6	7	8			11		2				9				10	1												11
		3	4	5	6	7	8					2				9				11	1	10											12
		3	4	5	6	7	8			11		2								10	1						9						13
		3	4	5	6	7	8			11		2								10	1						9						14
		3	2	4	5	6	7	8		11											1						9		10				15
		3	4	5	6	7	8			11											1	2					9			10			16
		3	4	5	6	7	8														1						9			10	11	2	17
		3	4	5	6	7	8														1					10		9			11	2	18
		3	4	5	6	7	8														1					10		9			11	2	19
				5	6		8														1	2	3	4	7	10		9			11		20
4	14	8	19	20	20	17	20	3	3	15	3	11	1	1	1	8	1	1	1	8	13	4	1	1	1	3	5	3	1	2	4	3	
		3	4	12	3	2	8									3								1	1	1	3				1			

Maile	Howland	Morton	Stubbs	Taylor	Tutthill	Johnson	Lloyd	Hopkinson	Sherran	Reed	Curling	Spackman H	Pask	Aylott	Bowden	Powell	Drury	Angus	Janes	Spackman F	Head	McMorran	Davis	Charratt	Anderson	Ambrose	Frewin	Ives	Windust	Newlands	Newbiggin	Humphries	T
		3	4	5	6	7	8														1							9	11			10	2	T
	1		1	1	1	1	1														1							1	1			1	1	
							1																											

Maile	Howland	Morton	Stubbs	Taylor	Tutthill	Johnson	Lloyd	Hopkinson	Sherran	Reed	Curling	Spackman H	Pask	Aylott	Bowden	Powell	Drury	Angus	Janes	Spackman F	Head	McMorran	Davis	Charratt	Anderson	Ambrose	Frewin	Ives	Windust	Newlands	Newbiggin	Humphries	1Q
1		3	4	5	6	7	8	9	10	11		2																					1Q
1		1	1	1	1	1	1	1	1	1		1																					

1900-01

1	Sep	8	(a)	Southall	L	0-1	
2		29	(h)	Brentford	L	1-2	Opp own goal
3	Oct	6	(a)	Maidenhead	W	3-2	Robertson, Lloyd, Anderson
4	Nov	17	(a)	Chesham T	L	1-3	Lloyd
5	Dec	8	(a)	Grays U	L	0-1	
6		26	(h)	Shepherd's Bush	L	0-3	
7	Feb	9	(a)	Sheppey U	L	0-2	
8		16	(h)	Grays U	L	0-2	
9		23	(h)	Chesham T	W	5-2	Meade 2, Taylor, F.Spackman, McKay
10	Mar	2	(a)	Brentford	L	1-5	Tutthill
11		16	(h)	Wycombe W	W	5-0	Levy, Meade, McKay, F.Spackman, Ferne
12		30	(h)	Sheppey U	W	3-0	F.Spackman, Meade, Ferne
13	Apr	5	(a)	Shepherd's Bush	W	3-0	F.Spackman, Meade, opp own goal
14		9	(h)	Southall	W	3-1	Miller 2, Levy
15		18	(h)	Maidenhead	W	9-0	Meade 3, Ferne 3, F.Spackman, McKay, Tutthill
16		29	(a)	Wycombe W	W	3-2	Stone, Holmes, Lloyd

P	W	D	L	F	A	W	D	L	F	A	Pts	Pos	Div		Appearances
16	5	0	3	26	10	3	0	5	11	16	16	5th	SL2		Goals

FA Cup

3Q	Nov	3	(a)	Queen's Park R	L	0-7

Appearances

Goals

226

Head J	Steven	Englefield	Stubbs R	Taylor J	Tutthill G	Johnson W	Lloyd D	Levy	Holmes	Howland C	Molyneux	Spackman F	Anderson H	Robertson WA	McMorran	Miller J	Gray A	Spackman H	Stone O	Mckay K	Meade T	Turner R	Ferne	Underwood T	Nobbs	
1	2	3	4	5	6	7	8	9	10	11																1
1	2	3	4	5	6	7	8	10	11		9															2
1	2	3		5	6		8	10			9	4	7	11												3
1		3		5	6		8	10				11	7		2	4	9									4
1		3		5	6		8	10			9					4	7	2	11							5
1		3		5	6			10								4		2		9	8	11	7			6
1		3		5	6			7								4		2		8	9	10	11			7
1		3·		5	6			11			7					4		2		8	9	10				8
1		3		5	6			7				10				4				8	9	2	11			9
1		3		5	6			7				10				4				8	9	2	11			10
1		3		5	6			7				10				4				8	9	2	11			11
1		3		5	6			7				10				4				8	9	2	11			12
1				5	6			7				10				4	2			8	9	3	11			13
1				5	6		3	7								9			11	8		2	10	4		14
				5	6		1			7		10				4	2			8	9	3	11			15
1				5	6		8	7	9								2		10			3	11	4		16
15	3	12	2	16	16	2	8	15	4	1	4	8	2	1	1	12	2	7	3	9	9	11	10	2	1	
	1	2		3	2	1		5	1	1		2							1	3	8		5			

Head J	Steven	Englefield	Stubbs R	Taylor J	Tutthill G	Johnson W	Lloyd D	Levy	Holmes	Howland C	Molyneux	Spackman F	Anderson H	Robertson WA	McMorran	Miller J	Gray A		
1	2	3	4	5	6		8	10				7	11			9			3Q
1	1	1	1	1	1		1	1				1	1			1			

1901-02

1	Sep	14	(h)	Southall	W	2-1	Meade 2
2		28	(h)	Grays U	L	0-2	
3	Oct	12	(h)	Maidenhead	W	5-2	Meade, McKay, Tannahill 2, McNee
4		19	(a)	Wycombe W	W	2-1	McKay 2
5	Nov	30	(a)	Brighton & HR	L	0-2	
6	Dec	21	(h)	West Hampstead	W	4-2	Tannahill 2, Meade, Slaughter
7		26	(h)	Shepherd's Bush	W	3-1	McKay 2, Stone
8	Jan	11	(a)	Grays U	L	1-6	Tannahill
9	Feb	22	(a)	Chesham T	W	5-2	F.Dwight, McKay, Meade 2, Sherran
10	Mar	8	(a)	Maidenhead	W	2-1	Meade 2
11		22	(h)	Brighton & HR	W	2-1	Meade, opp own goal
12		28	(a)	Shepherd's Bush	W	2-0	Tannahill, Tutthill
13		29	(h)	Chesham T	W	8-0	McKay 3, Hopkinson 2, Tutthill, Reed 2
14	Apr	5	(a)	Southall	W	5-0	Meade 4, Sherran
15		12	(h)	Wycombe W	W	8-0	Sherran 2, Porter 2, McKay 3, Tannahill
16		19	(a)	West Hampstead	W	2-0	Sherran, Tannahill

P	W	D	L	F	A	W	D	L	F	A	Pts	Pos	Div		
														Appearances	
16	7	0	1	32	9	6	0	2	19	12	26	1st	SL2	Goals	

Test Match

	Apr	30	(n)	Swindon T	L	1-3	Meade (Played at Reading)

Appearances

Goals

FA Cup

P	Sep	21	(a)	Chiswick	W	3-2	McKay, Tannahill, Meade
1Q	Oct	5	(a)	Crouch End V	L	2-4	Tannahill, Meade

Appearances

Goals

228

Team appearance / line-up chart (position numbers by player and match).

Head J	Graham J	Dwight C	Miller J	Tutthill G	Spackman F	Tannahill R	Mckay K	Meade T	McNee J	Dwight F	Spackman H	Underwood T	Lacey W	Pickett	Slaughter	Stone O	Sherran G	Porter W	Rance C	Reed W	Hopkinson F	#
1	2	3	4	5	6	7	8	9	10	11												1
1	6	3	4	5		7	8	9	11	10	2											2
1	6	3	4			7	8	9	10		2	5				11						3
		3	4			7	8	9	10		2		5	6		11		1				4
		3	4		6	7	8	9			2		5			10	11	1				5
1		3	4		6	7	8	9			2		5			10	11					6
1		3	4		6	7	8	9			2		5			10	11					7
1		3	2		6	7	8	9					5			10	11					8
1	2	3	4		6	7	8	9					5			11	10					9
1		3	4		6	7	8	9			2		5			10						10
1	2	3	4			7	8	9					5		6	10	11					11
1	2	3	4		6	7	8	9					5			10	11					12
1	2		4	6			8			11			5			10		7	9			13
1	2	3	4		6	7	8	9					5			10	11					14
1	2	3	4		6	7	8	9					5			10	11					15
1	2	3	4		6	7	8	9					5			10	11					16
14	10	16	16	13	1	15	16	15	4	3	7	1	13	1	4	9	7	5	2	1	1	
			1			9	13	14	1	1					1	1	5	2		2	2	

Head J	Graham J	Dwight C	Miller J	Tutthill G	Spackman F	Tannahill R	Mckay K	Meade T	McNee J	Dwight F	Spackman H	Underwood T	Lacey W	Pickett	Slaughter	Stone O	Sherran G	Porter W	Rance C	Reed W	Hopkinson F	T
1	2	3	4	6		7	8	9					5			10	11					T
1	1	1	1	1	1	1	1	1					1			1	1					
									1													

Head J	Graham J	Dwight C	Miller J	Tutthill G	Spackman F	Tannahill R	Mckay K	Meade T	McNee J	Dwight F	Spackman H	Underwood T	Lacey W	Pickett	Slaughter	Stone O	Sherran G	Porter W	Rance C	Reed W	Hopkinson F	P
1		3	4	5	6	7	8	9	10	11	2											P
1	5	3	4			7	8	9	10		2				6	11						1
2	1	2	2	1	1	2	2	2	2	1	2				1	1						
					2	1	2															

229

1902-03

1	Oct	11	(h)	Brighton & HA	W	1-0	Tannahill	
2		25	(h)	Wycombe W	W	5-0	Tutthill, Meade 2, Hopkinson 2	
3	Dec	13	(a)	Southall	W	2-0	Hopkinson, Meade	
4		20	(h)	Chesham T	W	6-0	Meade 2, Hopkinson 2, Porter, Tutthill	
5	Jan	31	(a)	Brighton & HA	L	1-3	Lloyd	
6	Mar	2	(a)	Chesham T	W	6-2	Tutthill 2, Sherran 2, Hopkinson, Tannahill	
7	Apr	4	(h)	Southall	W	4-0	Dwight, Lloyd, Tannahill, opp own goal	
8		11	(h)	Grays U	W	1-0	Tutthill	
9		14	(a)	Wycombe W	D	0-0		
10		22	(a)	Grays U	L	1-2	Tannahill	

P	W	D	L	F	A	W	D	L	F	A	Pts	Pos	Div			Appearances
10	5	0	0	17	0		2	1	2	10	7	15	1st	SL2		Goals

Test Match

	Apr	27	(n)	Brentford	L	2-7	Meade, Lloyd (Played at Shepherd's Bush)	3,000

Appearances

Goals

FA Cup

P	Sep	20	(h)	Civil Service*	W	2-0	Meade, Lloyd	
1Q	Oct	4	(h)	Crouch End V	W	4-0	Tutthill, Meade, Porter 2	
2Q		18	(h)	Willesden T*	D	0-0		
R		23	(h)	Willesden T	W	5-0	Meade 3, Lloyd, Dwight	
3Q	Nov	1	(a)	Watford	D	1-1	Meade	
R		6	(h)	Watford	W	3-0	Meade 2, Sherran	
4Q		15	(h)	Luton Ams	W	4-1	Lloyd, Meade, Tannahill, Hopkinson	
5Q		29	(a)	Luton T	L	1-5	Cowan	

Appearances

*Fulham drawn away but tie played at Craven Cottage.

Goals

Head J	Graham J	Dwight C	Spackman F	Lloyd D	Tuthill G	Tannahill R	Cowan	Meade T	Hopkinson F	Sherran G	Lacey W	Charratt R	Porter W	Hilsdon G	Easter	Brown A	Stone O	
1	2	3	4	5	6	7	8	9	10	11								1
1	2	3	11	5	6	7	8	9	10		4							2
1	2	3			6	7	8	9	10	11	5	4						3
1	2	3	4			6	7	10	9	8	5		11					4
1	2	3	11	5	6	7		10	8		4			9				5
1	2			5	6	7		8	10		4			9	11	3		6
1		3	11	5	6	7		8	2	10	4			9				7
1	2	3	11	5	6	7		10		8	4			9				8
1	2	3	11	5	6	7		9	8		4			10				9
1	2	3	11	5	6	7		9	8	10	4							10
10	9	9	8	8	10	10	3	9	9	7	9	1	1	4	1	1	1	
	1		2	5	4			5	6	2				1				

Head J	Graham J	Dwight C	Spackman F	Lloyd D	Tuthill G	Tannahill R	Cowan	Meade T	Hopkinson F	Sherran G	Lacey W		
1	2	3	11	5	6	7		9	8	10	4		T
1	1	1	1	1	1	1		1	1	1	1		
		1						1					

Head J	Graham J	Dwight C	Spackman F	Lloyd D	Tuthill G	Tannahill R	Cowan	Meade T	Hopkinson F	Sherran G	Lacey W	Charratt R	Porter W	
1	2	3		8	6	7		9		10	5	4	11	P
1	2	3	4		6	7	8	9	10		5		11	1Q
1	2	3	11	5	6	7	4	9	10	8				2Q
1	2	3		5	6	7	8	9	10		4		11	R
1	2	3	11	5	6	7	8	10	9		4			3Q
1	2	3		5	6	7	8	10	9	11	4			R
1	2	3	4	5	6	7	8	10	9	11				4Q
1	2	3	4		6	7	8	10	9		5		11	5Q
8	8	8	5	6	8	8	7	8	7	4	6	1	4	
	1		3	1	1	1		9	1	1			2	

231

1903-04

1	Sep	5	(h)	Tottenham H	D	0-0		14,000
2		12	(a)	Luton T	D	0-0		3,000
3		19	(h)	New Brompton	W	1-0	Lawrence	7,000
4		26	(a)	Kettering T	L	0-1		2,000
5	Oct	3	(h)	Southampton	D	2-2	Hogan, May	17,583
6		10	(a)	Swindon T	D	2-2	Soar, Lawrence	4,000
7		17	(a)	Millwall A	W	2-1	Fletcher, May	8,000
8		24	(h)	Queen's Park R	D	2-2	Soar, Fletcher	15,135
9	Nov	7	(h)	Reading	L	0-1		12,000
10		11	(a)	Plymouth A	L	0-1		4,000
11		21	(h)	Bristol R	L	0-1		8,000
12	Dec	26	(a)	Brentford	D	1-1	Soar	15,000
13		28	(a)	West Ham U	L	0-2		2,000
14		30	(a)	Wellingborough	W	3-2	Axcell, Hunt, Fletcher	3,000
15	Jan	2	(a)	Tottenham H	L	0-1		12,000
16		9	(h)	Luton T	W	1-0	Fletcher	17,000
17		16	(a)	New Brompton	D	0-0		4,000
18		27	(h)	Kettering T	W	4-1	Axcell 2, Gray, Fletcher	1,200
19		30	(a)	Southampton	L	0-2		3,000
20	Feb	13	(h)	Millwall A	L	1-2	Fletcher	9,500
21		20	(a)	Queen's Park R	D	1-1	Fletcher	12,000
22		24	(a)	Brighton & HA	L	1-2	Connor	3,000
23		27	(h)	Plymouth A	W	1-0	Meade	13,000
24	Mar	5	(a)	Reading	L	0-3		4,000
25		12	(h)	Wellingborough	W	2-0	Axcell, Soar	9,000
26		19	(a)	Bristol R	L	0-1		3,000
27		21	(a)	Northampton T	L	1-2	Soar	2,000
28		26	(h)	Brighton & HA	W	3-0	Fletcher 3	8,000
29	Apr	2	(a)	Portsmouth	D	0-0		8,000
30		5	(h)	Swindon T	L	1-2	Fletcher	4,000
31		9	(h)	Northampton T	W	2-0	Soar, Fletcher	9,000
32		16	(h)	Brentford	D	0-0		12,500
33		18	(h)	Portsmouth	D	2-2	Hunt 2	3,000
34		23	(h)	West Ham U	D	1-1	Fletcher	7,000

P	W	D	L	F	A	W	D	L	F	A	Pts	Pos	Div		Appearances
34	7	6	4	23	14	2	6	9	11	22	30	11th	SL1		Goals

FA Cup

1Q	Sep	19	(h)	Hampstead	W	3-0	Lloyd 2, Meade	Unknown
2Q	Oct	3	(a)	Crouch End V	W	5-0	Meade 3, Fisher, Tannahill	Unknown
3Q		17	(h)	Civil Service	D	3-3	Green, Connor, Tannahill	5,000
R		22	(a)	Civil Service	W	3-0	Fisher, Connor, Fletcher	2,000
4Q		31	(a)	Queen's Park R	D	1-1	Fletcher	20,000
R	Nov	4	(h)	Queen's Park R	W	3-1	Fletcher, McQueen, Connor	10,000
5Q		14	(h)	West Norwood	W	4-0	Connor 3, Fletcher	5,000
6Q		28	(h)	Luton T	W	3-1	Connor, Lawrence, Robotham	10,000
7Q	Dec	12	(a)	West Ham U	W	1-0	Fletcher	14,000
1	Feb	6	(a)	Woolwich A	L	0-1		15,000

Appearances

Goals

Fryer	Orr	Turner	Green	Hamilton	Robotham	Fletcher	May	Davidson	Fisher	Lawrence	Soar	Meade	Hunt	Biggar	Gray	Hogan	Connor	McQueen	Waterson	Colville	Porter	Axcell	Miercnikowski	Goldie	Harwood	Anderson	Storey	Stephenson	Farnfield PH	Farnfield HV	Farnfield GS	Nidd	Tannahill	Tutthill	Lloyd	Spackman	#
1	2	3	4	5	6	7	8	9	10	11																											1
1	2	3	4	5	6		8			11	7	9	10																								2
	2	3	4	5	6		8		10	11	7				9	1																					3
	2	3	4	5	6		8		10	11	7				9	1																					4
1	2	3		4	6		8		10	11	7				5		9																				5
1	2	3		4	6		8		10	11	7				5		9																				6
1	2	3		4	6		8		10	11	7	9			5																						7
1	2	3		4	6		8		10	11	7				5		9																				8
	2	3	4	5	6		8			11	7			1			9	10																			9
1	2	3		4	6		8			11	7				5		9	10																			10
1	2	3			6		8			11	7	10			5		9		4																		11
1	2	3	6				8			11	7			9	5		10					4															12
1	2	3			6		8			11				9	5		10					4	7														13
1	2	3	6	5			8				7	9										4		10	11												14
1	2	3	6				8				7	9			5							4		10	11												15
1	2	3			6		8			11	7				5		9					4		10													16
	2	3					8			11	7			1	5		9					4		10	6												17
1		3		4			8				7	9			5							10		6	2	11											18
1		3		4			8			11	7				5		9					10		6	2												19
1	2	3		4			8				7				5		10					9		6		11											20
1				2			4	10			7	9	8		5									6	3	11											21
1				2			4	10			7		8		5		9							6	3	11											22
1	2	3		4			10				7	9	8		5									6		11											23
1	2	3		4			8				7	9			5									6		11	10										24
1	2			4							7		8		5		11					10		6	3		9										25
1	2			4							7		8		5		11					10		6	3		9										26
1	2			4			8				7	9			5		11					10		6	3												27
	2			4			8				7	9	1	5			11					10		6	3												28
1	2	3		4			8				7	9			5		11					10		6													29
1		3	4				8				7	9			5		11					10		6	2												30
1		3					8		10		7				5		9		4			11		6	2												31
1	2	3		4			8				7	9			5		10					11		6													32
				4	7		8			11			8	1	5		10	3				9		6			2										33
1		3		4			8				7	9										6	2								5	10	11					34
28	26	29	9	12	27	31	8	1	1	18	31	7	19	6	27	2	12	10	3	6	1	16	2	18	11	6	3	1	1	1	1	1					
							13	2				2	6	1	3		1	1	1			4															

Fryer	Orr	Turner	Green	Hamilton	Robotham	Fletcher	May	Davidson	Fisher	Lawrence	Soar	Meade	Hunt	Biggar	Gray	Hogan	Connor	McQueen	Waterson	Colville	Porter	Axcell	Miercnikowski	Goldie	Harwood	Anderson	Storey	Stephenson	Farnfield PH	Farnfield HV	Farnfield GS	Nidd	Tannahill	Tutthill	Lloyd	Spackman	#
								9	10			8		1	5							4		2									3	7	6	11	1Q
			5						10			9	8	1								4		2									3	7	6	11	2Q
			5						10				8	1			9	11	4					2									3	7	6		3Q
1	2		4				8		10	11					5		9							3										7	6		R
1	2	3			4	6	8			11	7				5		9																				4Q
1	2	3	4			6	8			11	7				5		9	10																			R
1	2	3					8	9		11	7				5		10		4						6												5Q
1	2	3			6		8			11	7				5		9	10	4																		6Q
1	2	3					8			11	7				5		9	10	4						6												7Q
1	2	3				4	8			11	7				5		9					10		6													1R
7	7	6	4	1	4	7	2	1	4	7	6	2	2	3	8		8	4	6			1		1	4								3	4	3	3	2
			1		1	5			2	1		4					7	1																2	2			

1904-05

						Result		Scorers	Attendance
1	Sep	3	(a)	Tottenham H		W	1-0	Wardrope	20,000
2		10	(h)	Luton T		D	0-0		15,000
3		17	(a)	Swindon T		L	1-2	Bell	5,000
4		24	(h)	New Brompton		D	1-1	Morrison	15,000
5	Oct	1	(a)	Wellingborough		L	1-2	Fletcher	2,000
6		8	(h)	Southampton		D	0-0		20,000
7		15	(h)	Brighton & HA		W	1-0	Goldie	12,000
8		22	(a)	Watford		L	1-2	Bell	5,800
9		29	(h)	Plymouth A		D	0-0		16,000
10	Nov	5	(a)	West Ham U		D	0-0		8,000
11		12	(h)	Reading		W	2-0	Wardrope 2	20,000
12		19	(a)	Bristol R		L	1-4	Bell	5,000
13	Dec	3	(a)	Portsmouth		L	0-1		7,000
14		17	(a)	Queen's Park R		L	0-2		14,000
15		24	(h)	Millwall A		W	2-1	Lennie, Wardrope	20,000
16		31	(h)	Tottenham H		W	1-0	Wardrope	19,000
17	Jan	7	(a)	Luton T		L	0-6		5,000
18		21	(a)	New Brompton		L	0-3		6,000
19		28	(h)	Wellingborough		W	12-0	Fraser 5, Wardrope 3, Goldie 2, Lennie, Morrison	12,000
20	Feb	11	(a)	Brighton & HA		W	4-1	W.Bradshaw, Harwood 2, Bell	5,000
22		22	(h)	Watford		W	2-1	Lennie, Wardrope	2,000
22		25	(a)	Plymouth A		D	1-1	Wardrope	10,000
23	Mar	11	(a)	Reading		D	0-0		3,000
24		18	(h)	Bristol R		D	0-0		11,000
25		23	(a)	Northampton T		D	0-0		2,000
26		25	(h)	Northampton T		W	4-1	Wardrope, Ross, Bell, Bradshaw	8,000
27	Apr	1	(h)	Portsmouth		W	2-0	Fraser 2	12,000
28		3	(h)	Swindon T		W	3-0	Ross, Wardrope, Holmes	2,000
29		8	(a)	Brentford		D	1-1	Wardrope	10,000
30		15	(a)	Queen's Park R		L	1-2	Wardrope	12,000
31		17	(h)	West Ham U		L	0-3		2,000
32		22	(a)	Millwall A		W	2-0	Goldie, Wardrope	7,000
33		24	(a)	Southampton		W	1-0	Wardrope	10,000
34		29	(h)	Brentford		W	1-0	Fraser	12,000

P	W	D	L	F	A	W	D	L	F	A	Pts	Pos	Div		Appearances
34	10	5	2	32	9	4	5	8	14	25	38	6th	SL1		Goals

FA Cup

6Q	Dec	10	(h)	Luton T		W	4-0	Wardrope, Lennie, Ross, Fraser	16,000
7Q	Jan	14	(a)	Manchester U		D	2-2	Fraser, Wardrope	17,000
R		18	(h)	Manchester U		D	0-0		20,000
2R		23	(n)	Manchester U*		W	1-0	Graham	8,000
1	Feb	4	(h)	Reading		D	0-0		30,000
R		8	(a)	Reading		D	0-0		13,500
2R		13	(n)	Reading†		W	1-0	Fraser	22,000
2		18	(h)	Nottingham F		W	1-0	Wardrope	18,000
3	Mar	4	(a)	Aston Villa		L	0-5		47,000

*Played at Villa Park, Birmingham
†Played at White Hart Lane

Appearances
Goals

Fryer	Ross	Sharp	Howarth	Gray	Goldie	Soar	Fletcher	Wardrope	Graham	Bell	Morrison	Pratt	Robotham	Clutterbuck	Lennie	Hunt	Fraser	Bradshaw W	Thorpe	Bradshaw J	Harwood	Waterson	Axcell	Phillipson	Holmes	
1	2	3	4	5	6	7	8	9	10	11																1
1	2	3	4	5	6	7	8	9	10	11																2
1	2	3	4	5	6	7	8	9	10	11																3
1	2	3	4		6		7	9	10	11	5	8														4
1	2	3		5		7	8		10	11	4	9	6													5
	2	3	4			7	8		10		5	9	6	1	11											6
1	2	3	4		6	7	8	9	10		5				11											7
	2	3	4		6	7			10	9	5			1	11	8										8
1	2	3	4	5	6	7	8		10	11	9															9
1	2	3	4		6	7			10	8	11	5					9		3							10
1	2		4		6	7			10	8	11	5					9		3							11
1	2		4		6	7			10	8	11	5					9		3							12
1	2			4	5	6			8						11		9	7	3	10						13
1	2		4		6	7			10	8					11		9		3							14
1	2		4	5	6	7			10	8					11		9		3							15
1	2		4	5	6	7			10	8					11		9		3							16
1	2		4	5	6	7			10	8	11						9		3							17
1			4	5	6	7			10	8	11	2					9		3							18
1		3	4		6	7			10	8	5				11		9		2							19
1		3		5						11		6			8		7	10	9	2	4					20
1		3	4	5	6	7			10	8					11		9		2							21
1	2	3	4	5	6	7			10	8	9				11											22
1	2	3	4	5	6	7				8					11		9					10				23
1	2		4		6			8		11	5							7	3	10	9					24
1	2		4		6				10	8	5				11		9	7	3							25
1	2		4		6				10	8	5		4		11		9	7	3							26
1	2	3			6	7			10	8	9	5	4											11		28
1	2		4		6	7			10	8	5				11		9		3							29
1	2		4		6	7			10	8	5				11		9		3							30
		3	4		6	7			10	8	11	5		1			9		2							31
1	2		4		6				10	8	11	5					9		3							32
1	2		4		6	7			10	8	5				11		9		3							33
1	2		4		6	7			10	8	5				11		9		3							34
31	29	18	30	16	31	26	9	27	23	27	20	4	5	3	18	2	21	5	18	3	3	1	1	1	1	
	2			4		1		16	5	2					3		8	2		2				1		

Fryer	Ross	Sharp	Howarth	Gray	Goldie	Soar	Fletcher	Wardrope	Graham	Bell	Morrison	Pratt	Robotham	Clutterbuck	Lennie	Hunt	Fraser	Bradshaw W	Thorpe	Bradshaw J	Harwood	Waterson	Axcell	Phillipson	Holmes	
1	2		4	5	6	7			10	8					11		9		3							6Q
1	2		4		6	7			10	8	5				11		9		3							7Q
1		3			6	7			10	8	5		4		11		9		2							R
1	2		4		6	7			10	8	5				11		9		3							2R
1	2		4		6	7			10	8	5				11		9		3							1
1	2		4		6	7			10	8	5				11		9		3							R
1	2		4		6	7			10	8	5				11		9		3							2R
1	2		4		6	7			10		8	5			11		9		3							2
1	2		4		6	7			10	8	5				11		9		3							QF
8	6	1	8	1	8	8		8	7	1	7		1		8		3	3		2				1		
	1								3	1							1		3							

235

1905-06

1	Sep	2	(h)	Portsmouth	D	0-0		20,000
2		9	(a)	Swindon T	W	4-1	Edgley, Wardrope, Wood, Threlfall	6,000
3		16	(h)	Millwall A	D	1-1	Threlfall	20,000
4		23	(a)	Luton T	W	1-0	Edgley	9,000
5		30	(h)	Tottenham H	D	0-0		25,000
6	Oct	7	(a)	Brentford	W	2-0	Fraser, Threlfall	12,000
7		14	(h)	Norwich C	W	2-1	Threlfall 2	15,000
8		21	(a)	Plymouth A	D	0-0		12,000
9		28	(h)	Southampton	D	1-1	Morrison	25,000
10	Nov	4	(a)	Reading	L	0-1		5,000
11		11	(h)	Watford	D	0-0		10,000
12		18	(a)	Brighton & HA	W	2-1	Threlfall, Wardrope	5,000
13		25	(h)	West Ham U	W	1-0	Opp own goal	15,000
14	Dec	2	(a)	Northampton T	W	3-1	Edgley 2, Morrison	3,000
15		9	(a)	Queen's Park R	W	3-1	Wardrope 2, Edgley	12,000
16		16	(h)	Bristol R	W	1-0	Wardrope	16,000
17		23	(a)	New Brompton	W	3-0	Fraser, Wardrope 2	4,000
18		30	(a)	Portsmouth	L	0-1		8,000
19	Jan	6	(h)	Swindon T	D	1-1	Fraser	5,000
20		20	(a)	Millwall A	D	1-1	Wardrope	8,000
21		27	(h)	Luton T	W	3-0	Morrison, Fraser, Wood	14,000
22	Feb	10	(h)	Brentford	W	2-0	Wardrope, Fraser	10,000
23		12	(a)	Tottenham H	W	1-0	Fraser	20,000
24		17	(a)	Norwich C	D	0-0		9,000
25		24	(h)	Plymouth A	W	3-1	Freeman, Wardrope, Bell	15,000
26	Mar	3	(a)	Southampton	L	1-2	Wardrope	8,000
27		10	(h)	Reading	D	0-0		20,000
28		17	(a)	Watford	D	0-0		5,000
29		24	(h)	Brighton & HA	W	2-0	Wardrope, Wheatcroft	9,000
30		31	(a)	West Ham U	D	0-0		12,000
31	Apr	7	(h)	Northampton T	W	3-1	Wardrope, Fraser, Wheatcroft	15,000
32		14	(h)	Queen's Park R	W	1-0	Fraser	20,000
33		21	(a)	Bristol R	W	1-0	Freeman	6,000
34		25	(h)	New Brompton	W	1-0	Ross	3,000

P	W	D	L	F	A	W	D	L	F	A	Pts	Pos	Div	
34	10	7	0	22	6	9	5	3	22	9	50	1st	SLI	Appearances
														Goals

FA Cup

1	Jan	13	(h)	Queen's Park R	W	1-0	Collins	27,000
2	Feb	3	(h)	Nottingham F	L	1-3	Fraser	31,000

Appearances

Goals

Squad appearance and scoring grid.

Fryer	Ross	Thorpe	Haworth	Morrison	Goldie	Soar	Wood	Edgley	Wardrope	Threlfall	Collins	Robotham	Fraser	Bell	Kirby	Waterson	Hogan	Thomas	Thompson	Fitchett	Freeman	Wheatcroft	#
1	2	3	4	5	6	7	8	9	10	11													1
1	2	3	4	5	6	7	8	9	10	11													2
1	2	3	4		6	7	8	9	10	11	5												3
1	2	3		5	6	7	8	9	10	11		4											4
1	2	3		5	6	7	8	9	10	11	4												5
1	2	3		5	6	7			10	11	4		9	8									6
1	2	3		5	6	7			10	11	4		9	8									7
1	2	3		5	6	7			10	11	4		9	8									8
1	2	3		5	6				10	11	4		9	8	7								9
1		3		5	6			9		11	4				7	2	8	10					10
1	2	3		5	6				10	11	4		9	7			8						11
	2	3		5	6		8	9	10	11	4			7						1			12
	2	3		5	6	7		9	10	11	4			8						1			13
1	2	3		5	6			9	10	11	4			7			8						14
	2	3		5	6			9	10	11	4		8	7						1			15
	2	3		5	6	7			10	11	4		9	8						1			16
1	2	3		5	6		8		10	11	4		9	7									17
1	2	3		5	6				10	11	4		9	7			8						18
1	2	3		5	6				10	11	4		9	7			8						19
1	2	3		5	6		8		10	11	4		9	7									20
1	2	3		5	6		8		10	11	4		9	7									21
1	2			5	6	7			10	11	4		9	8					3		-		22
1	2			5	6	7				11	4		10	8					3			9	23
1	2	3		5	6	7				11	4		10	8								9	24
1	2	3		5	6				10	11	4		9	7							8		25
1	2	3		5	6				10	11	4		9	7							8		26
1	2	3		5	6	7			10	11	4										8	9	27
1	2	3		5	6				10	11	4			7							8	9	28
1	2	3		5	6			9	10	11	4			7							8	9	29
1	2	3		5	6			9	10	11	4				7						8		30
1	2	3		5	6				10	11	4		9	7							8		31
1	2	3		5	6				10	11	4		9	7							8		32
1	2	3		5	6				10	11	4		9	7						8			33
1	2	3		5	6				10	11	4		9	7						8			34
30	33	32	3	33	34	14	9	12	31	34	31	1	21	26	3	1	5	1	4	2	8	6	
	1		3			2	5	13	6					8	1						2	2	

Fryer	Ross	Thorpe	Haworth	Morrison	Goldie	Soar	Wood	Edgley	Wardrope	Threlfall	Collins	Robotham	Fraser	Bell	Kirby	Waterson	Hogan	Thomas	Thompson	Fitchett	Freeman	Wheatcroft	#
1	2	3		5	6		8		10	11	4		9	7									1
	2			5	6		8		10	11	4		9	7					1	3			2
1	2	1	2	2	2		2		2	2	2		2	2					1	1			
																			1	1			

1906-07

1	Sep	1	(a)	Norwich C	D	0-0		8,000
2		8	(h)	Luton T	D	0-0		20,000
3		15	(a)	Crystal P	W	3-0	Wheatcroft, Hamilton, Thompson	8,000
4		22	(h)	Brentford	W	1-0	Ross	20,000
5		24	(a)	Tottenham H	L	1-5	Ross	15,000
6		29	(a)	Millwall A	D	2-2	Hamilton, Kingaby	12,000
7	Oct	3	(a)	Swindon T	D	2-2	Wheatcroft, Hamilton	2,000
8		6	(h)	Leyton	W	3-1	Ross, Edgley, Thompson	13,000
9		13	(a)	Portsmouth	D	0-0		14,000
10		20	(h)	New Brompton	W	2-1	Wheatcroft, Fraser	17,000
11		27	(a)	Plymouth A	D	1-1	Fraser	10,000
12		29	(h)	Tottenham H	W	2-1	Threlfall, Freeman	20,000
13	Nov	3	(h)	Brighton & HA	W	2-0	Fraser, Ross	16,000
14		10	(a)	Reading	W	1-0	Wheatcroft	8,000
15		17	(h)	Watford	D	0-0		10,000
16		24	(a)	Northampton T	W	4-0	Freeman 2, Wheatcroft 2	3,000
17	Dec	1	(h)	Queen's Park R	D	1-1	Morrison	21,000
18		8	(h)	Bristol R	W	3-0	Hamilton, Threlfall 2	10,000
19		15	(a)	Southampton	W	2-1	Freeman, Hamilton	10,000
20		22	(h)	West Ham U	L	1-4	Hamilton	12,000
21		29	(h)	Norwich C	D	1-1	Hogan	12,000
22	Jan	5	(a)	Luton T	L	0-2		7,000
23		19	(h)	Crystal P	W	2-1	Hamilton, Goldie	12,000
24		26	(a)	Brentford	L	0-1		15,000
25	Feb	9	(a)	Leyton	D	1-1	Wheatcroft	6,000
26		16	(h)	Portsmouth	W	2-0	Hamilton, Kingaby	30,000
27		23	(a)	New Brompton	D	1-1	Threlfall	6,000
28	Mar	2	(h)	Plymouth A	W	2-0	Threlfall, Freeman	16,000
29		9	(a)	Brighton & HA	D	0-0		10,000
30		16	(h)	Reading	W	2-1	Hogan, Morrison	17,000
31		23	(a)	Watford	W	1-0	Freeman	8,000
32		29	(h)	Swindon T	W	4-0	Threlfall 2, Freeman 2	14,000
33		30	(h)	Northampton T	W	30-1	Hamilton, Ross, Hogan	10,000
34	Apr	2	(h)	Millwall A	D	0-0		12,000
35		6	(a)	Queen's Park R	W	2-0	Freeman, Hogan	14,000
36		13	(a)	Bristol R	W	2-0	Hogan, Kingaby	8,000
37		20	(h)	Southampton	W	3-0	Hamilton, Freeman, Ross	16,000
38		27	(a)	West Ham U	L	1-4	Hamilton	10,000

P	W	D	L	F	A	W	D	L	F	A	Pts	Pos	Div	
38	13	5	1	34	12	7	8	4	24	20	53	1st	SL1	Appearances
														Goals

FA Cup

1	Jan	12	(a)	Stockport C*	D	0-0		30,000
R		16	(h)	Stockport C	W	2-1	Freeman, Threlfall	10,000
2	Feb	2	(h)	Crystal P	D	0-0		30,000
R		6	(a)	Crystal P	L	0-1		20,000

*Played at Craven Cottage.

Appearances
Goals

Fryer	Ross	Thorpe	Waterson	Morrison	Goldie	Bell	Edgley	Hamilton	Wheatcroft	Threlfall	Collins	Kingaby	Fraser	Thompson	McIntyre	Freeman	Charlton	Hogan	Horne	Hindmarsh	
1	2	3	4	5	6	7	8	9	10	11											1
1	2	3		5	6	7	8	9	10	11	4										2
1	2	3		5	6			9	10	11	4	7	8								3
1	2	3		5	6			9	10		4	7	8	11							4
1	2	3		5	6	7		9			4		8	11			10				5
1	2	3		5	6			9	10	11		7	8		4						6
1	2	3		5	6	7		9	10		4		8	11							7
1	2	3		5	6		9		10		4	7	8	11							8
1	2	3		5	6			9	10			7	8	11	4						9
1	2			5	6				10		4	7	9	11		8					10
1	2			5	6			9		11	4	7	10			8	3				11
1	2			5	6				9	11	4	7	10			8	3				12
1	2			5	6				10	11	4	7	9			8	3				13
1	2			5	6				10	11	4	7	9			8	3				14
1	2			5	6				10	11	4	7	9			8	3				15
1	2			5	6				10	11	4	7	9			8	3				16
1	2			5	6			9	10	11	4	7				8	3				17
1	2	3		5	6			9		11		7	10		4	8					18
1	2			5	6			9		11		7	10		4	8	3				19
1	2			5	6			9			4	7	10	11		8	3				20
1	2	3		5	6	8				11	4	7				9		10			21
1		3		5	6			9		11	4	7				8	2	10			22
1	2			5	6			9		11	4	7	10			8	3				23
1	2			5	6	11			10			7	9		4	8	3				24
1	2			5	6			9	8	11	4	7	10				3				25
1	2			5	6			9		11	4	7	10			8	3				26
1	2			5	6			9		11	4	7	10			8	3				27
1	2			5	6			9		11	4	7	10			8	3				28
1	2			5	6			9		11	4	7	10			8	3				29
	2			5	6			9		11	4		10			8	3	7	1		30
1	2			5	6			9		11	4	7	10			8	3				31
1	2			5	6			9		11	4	7	10			8	3				32
1	2	3		5	6			9		11	4	7				8		10			33
1	2	3		5	6			9		11	4	7				8		10			34
1	2	3		5	6			9		11	4	7				8		10			35
1	2	3		5	6			9		11	4	7				8		10			36
1	2	3		5	6			9		11	4	7				8		10			37
	2	3		5	6			9		11	4	7				8		10	1		38
36	37	19	1	38	38	6	3	29	17	30	32	33	27	7	5	28	20	9	2	1	
	6			2	1	1		11	7	7			3	3	2	10	5				

Fryer	Ross	Thorpe	Waterson	Morrison	Goldie	Bell	Edgley	Hamilton	Wheatcroft	Threlfall	Collins	Kingaby	Fraser	Thompson	McIntyre	Freeman	Charlton	Hogan	Horne	Hindmarsh	
1	2			5	6			9	10	11	4	7				8	3				1
1	2			5	6			9	10	11	4	7				8	3				R
1	2			5	6			9	10	11	4	7				8	3				2
1	2			5	6			9	10	11	4	7				8	3				R
4	4			4	4			4	4	4	4	4				4	4				
										1						1					

239

Fulham in the Football League 1907-08 to 1986-87

	P	W	D	L	F	A	W	D	L	F	A	Pts	Pos
			HOME					*AWAY*					

<table>
<tr><th></th><th>P</th><th>W</th><th>D</th><th>L</th><th>F</th><th>A</th><th>W</th><th>D</th><th>L</th><th>F</th><th>A</th><th>Pts</th><th>Pos</th></tr>
<tr><td colspan="14" align="center">DIVISION TWO</td></tr>
<tr><td>1907-08</td><td>38</td><td>12</td><td>2</td><td>5</td><td>50</td><td>14</td><td>10</td><td>3</td><td>6</td><td>32</td><td>35</td><td>49</td><td>4th</td></tr>
<tr><td>1908-09</td><td>38</td><td>8</td><td>4</td><td>7</td><td>39</td><td>26</td><td>5</td><td>7</td><td>7</td><td>19</td><td>22</td><td>37</td><td>10th</td></tr>
<tr><td>1909-10</td><td>38</td><td>9</td><td>7</td><td>3</td><td>28</td><td>13</td><td>5</td><td>6</td><td>8</td><td>23</td><td>30</td><td>41</td><td>7th</td></tr>
<tr><td>1910-11</td><td>38</td><td>12</td><td>3</td><td>4</td><td>35</td><td>15</td><td>3</td><td>4</td><td>12</td><td>17</td><td>33</td><td>37</td><td>10th</td></tr>
<tr><td>1911-12</td><td>38</td><td>10</td><td>3</td><td>6</td><td>42</td><td>24</td><td>6</td><td>4</td><td>9</td><td>24</td><td>34</td><td>39</td><td>8th</td></tr>
<tr><td>1912-13</td><td>38</td><td>13</td><td>5</td><td>1</td><td>47</td><td>16</td><td>4</td><td>0</td><td>15</td><td>18</td><td>39</td><td>39</td><td>9th</td></tr>
<tr><td>1913-14</td><td>38</td><td>10</td><td>3</td><td>6</td><td>31</td><td>20</td><td>6</td><td>3</td><td>10</td><td>15</td><td>23</td><td>38</td><td>11th</td></tr>
<tr><td>1914-15</td><td>38</td><td>12</td><td>0</td><td>7</td><td>35</td><td>20</td><td>3</td><td>7</td><td>9</td><td>18</td><td>27</td><td>37</td><td>12th</td></tr>
<tr><td>1919-20</td><td>42</td><td>11</td><td>6</td><td>4</td><td>36</td><td>18</td><td>8</td><td>3</td><td>10</td><td>25</td><td>32</td><td>47</td><td>6th</td></tr>
<tr><td>1920-21</td><td>42</td><td>14</td><td>4</td><td>3</td><td>33</td><td>12</td><td>2</td><td>6</td><td>13</td><td>10</td><td>35</td><td>42</td><td>9th</td></tr>
<tr><td>1921-22</td><td>42</td><td>14</td><td>5</td><td>2</td><td>41</td><td>8</td><td>4</td><td>4</td><td>13</td><td>16</td><td>30</td><td>45</td><td>7th</td></tr>
<tr><td>1922-23</td><td>42</td><td>10</td><td>7</td><td>4</td><td>29</td><td>12</td><td>6</td><td>5</td><td>10</td><td>14</td><td>20</td><td>44</td><td>10th</td></tr>
<tr><td>1923-24</td><td>42</td><td>9</td><td>8</td><td>4</td><td>30</td><td>20</td><td>1</td><td>6</td><td>14</td><td>15</td><td>36</td><td>34</td><td>20th</td></tr>
<tr><td>1924-25</td><td>42</td><td>11</td><td>6</td><td>4</td><td>26</td><td>15</td><td>4</td><td>4</td><td>13</td><td>15</td><td>41</td><td>40</td><td>12th</td></tr>
<tr><td>1925-26</td><td>42</td><td>8</td><td>6</td><td>7</td><td>32</td><td>29</td><td>3</td><td>6</td><td>12</td><td>14</td><td>48</td><td>34</td><td>19th</td></tr>
<tr><td>1926-27</td><td>42</td><td>11</td><td>4</td><td>6</td><td>39</td><td>31</td><td>2</td><td>4</td><td>15</td><td>19</td><td>61</td><td>34</td><td>18th</td></tr>
<tr><td>1927-28</td><td>42</td><td>12</td><td>7</td><td>2</td><td>46</td><td>22</td><td>1</td><td>0</td><td>20</td><td>22</td><td>67</td><td>33</td><td>21st</td></tr>
<tr><td colspan="14" align="center">DIVISION THREE (SOUTH)</td></tr>
<tr><td>1928-29</td><td>42</td><td>14</td><td>3</td><td>4</td><td>60</td><td>31</td><td>7</td><td>7</td><td>7</td><td>41</td><td>40</td><td>52</td><td>5th</td></tr>
<tr><td>1929-30</td><td>42</td><td>12</td><td>6</td><td>3</td><td>54</td><td>33</td><td>6</td><td>5</td><td>10</td><td>33</td><td>50</td><td>47</td><td>7th</td></tr>
<tr><td>1930-31</td><td>42</td><td>15</td><td>3</td><td>3</td><td>49</td><td>21</td><td>3</td><td>4</td><td>14</td><td>28</td><td>54</td><td>43</td><td>9th</td></tr>
<tr><td>1931-32</td><td>42</td><td>15</td><td>3</td><td>3</td><td>72</td><td>27</td><td>9</td><td>6</td><td>6</td><td>39</td><td>35</td><td>57</td><td>1st</td></tr>
<tr><td colspan="14" align="center">DIVISION TWO</td></tr>
<tr><td>1932-33</td><td>42</td><td>12</td><td>5</td><td>4</td><td>46</td><td>31</td><td>8</td><td>5</td><td>8</td><td>32</td><td>34</td><td>50</td><td>3rd</td></tr>
<tr><td>1933-34</td><td>42</td><td>13</td><td>3</td><td>5</td><td>29</td><td>17</td><td>2</td><td>4</td><td>15</td><td>19</td><td>50</td><td>37</td><td>16th</td></tr>
<tr><td>1934-35</td><td>42</td><td>15</td><td>3</td><td>3</td><td>62</td><td>26</td><td>2</td><td>9</td><td>10</td><td>14</td><td>30</td><td>46</td><td>7th</td></tr>
<tr><td>1935-36</td><td>42</td><td>11</td><td>6</td><td>4</td><td>58</td><td>24</td><td>4</td><td>8</td><td>9</td><td>18</td><td>28</td><td>44</td><td>9th</td></tr>
<tr><td>1936-37</td><td>42</td><td>11</td><td>5</td><td>5</td><td>43</td><td>24</td><td>4</td><td>8</td><td>9</td><td>28</td><td>37</td><td>43</td><td>11th</td></tr>
<tr><td>1937-38</td><td>42</td><td>10</td><td>7</td><td>4</td><td>44</td><td>23</td><td>6</td><td>4</td><td>11</td><td>17</td><td>34</td><td>43</td><td>8th</td></tr>
<tr><td>1938-39</td><td>42</td><td>12</td><td>5</td><td>4</td><td>35</td><td>20</td><td>5</td><td>5</td><td>11</td><td>26</td><td>35</td><td>44</td><td>12th</td></tr>
<tr><td>1946-47</td><td>42</td><td>12</td><td>4</td><td>5</td><td>40</td><td>25</td><td>3</td><td>5</td><td>13</td><td>23</td><td>49</td><td>39</td><td>15th</td></tr>
<tr><td>1947-48</td><td>42</td><td>6</td><td>9</td><td>6</td><td>24</td><td>19</td><td>9</td><td>1</td><td>11</td><td>23</td><td>27</td><td>40</td><td>11th</td></tr>
<tr><td>1948-49</td><td>42</td><td>16</td><td>4</td><td>1</td><td>52</td><td>14</td><td>8</td><td>5</td><td>8</td><td>25</td><td>23</td><td>57</td><td>1st</td></tr>
<tr><td colspan="14" align="center">DIVISION ONE</td></tr>
<tr><td>1949-50</td><td>42</td><td>8</td><td>6</td><td>7</td><td>24</td><td>19</td><td>2</td><td>8</td><td>11</td><td>17</td><td>35</td><td>34</td><td>17th</td></tr>
<tr><td>1950-51</td><td>42</td><td>8</td><td>5</td><td>8</td><td>35</td><td>37</td><td>5</td><td>6</td><td>10</td><td>17</td><td>31</td><td>37</td><td>18th</td></tr>
<tr><td>1951-52</td><td>42</td><td>5</td><td>7</td><td>9</td><td>38</td><td>31</td><td>3</td><td>4</td><td>14</td><td>20</td><td>46</td><td>27</td><td>22nd</td></tr>
<tr><td colspan="14" align="center">DIVISION TWO</td></tr>
<tr><td>1952-53</td><td>42</td><td>14</td><td>1</td><td>6</td><td>52</td><td>28</td><td>3</td><td>9</td><td>9</td><td>29</td><td>43</td><td>44</td><td>8th</td></tr>
<tr><td>1953-54</td><td>42</td><td>12</td><td>3</td><td>6</td><td>62</td><td>39</td><td>5</td><td>7</td><td>9</td><td>36</td><td>46</td><td>44</td><td>8th</td></tr>
<tr><td>1954-55</td><td>42</td><td>10</td><td>5</td><td>6</td><td>46</td><td>29</td><td>4</td><td>6</td><td>11</td><td>30</td><td>50</td><td>39</td><td>14th</td></tr>
<tr><td>1955-56</td><td>42</td><td>15</td><td>2</td><td>4</td><td>59</td><td>27</td><td>5</td><td>4</td><td>12</td><td>30</td><td>52</td><td>46</td><td>9th</td></tr>
<tr><td>1956-57</td><td>42</td><td>13</td><td>1</td><td>7</td><td>53</td><td>32</td><td>6</td><td>3</td><td>12</td><td>31</td><td>44</td><td>42</td><td>11th</td></tr>
<tr><td>1957-58</td><td>42</td><td>13</td><td>5</td><td>3</td><td>53</td><td>24</td><td>7</td><td>7</td><td>7</td><td>44</td><td>35</td><td>52</td><td>5th</td></tr>
<tr><td>1958-59</td><td>42</td><td>18</td><td>1</td><td>2</td><td>65</td><td>26</td><td>9</td><td>5</td><td>7</td><td>31</td><td>35</td><td>60</td><td>2nd</td></tr>
<tr><td colspan="14" align="center">DIVISION ONE</td></tr>
<tr><td>1959-60</td><td>42</td><td>12</td><td>4</td><td>5</td><td>42</td><td>28</td><td>5</td><td>6</td><td>10</td><td>31</td><td>52</td><td>44</td><td>10th</td></tr>
</table>

			HOME						AWAY				
	P	W	D	L	F	A	W	D	L	F	A	Pts	Pos
1960-61	42	8	8	5	39	39	6	0	15	33	56	36	17th
1961-62	42	8	3	10	38	34	5	4	12	28	40	33	20th
1962-63	42	8	6	7	28	30	6	4	11	22	41	38	16th
1963-64	42	11	8	2	45	23	2	5	14	13	42	39	15th
1964-65	42	10	5	6	44	32	1	7	13	16	46	34	20th
1965-66	42	9	4	8	34	37	5	3	13	33	48	35	20th
1966-67	42	8	7	6	49	34	3	5	13	22	49	34	18th
1967-68	42	6	4	11	27	41	4	3	14	29	57	27	22nd

DIVISION TWO

	P	W	D	L	F	A	W	D	L	F	A	Pts	Pos
1968-69	42	6	7	8	20	28	1	4	16	20	53	25	22nd

DIVISION THREE

	P	W	D	L	F	A	W	D	L	F	A	Pts	Pos
1969-70	46	12	9	2	43	26	8	6	9	38	29	55	4th
1970-71	46	15	6	2	39	12	9	6	8	29	29	60	2nd

DIVISION TWO

	P	W	D	L	F	A	W	D	L	F	A	Pts	Pos
1971-72	42	10	7	4	29	20	2	3	16	16	48	34	20th
1972-73	42	11	6	4	32	16	5	6	10	26	33	44	9th
1973-74	42	11	4	6	26	20	5	6	10	13	23	42	13th
1974-75	42	9	8	4	29	17	4	8	9	15	22	42	9th
1975-76	42	9	8	4	27	14	4	6	11	18	33	40	12th
1976-77	42	9	7	5	39	25	2	6	13	15	36	35	17th
1977-78	42	9	8	4	32	19	5	5	11	17	30	41	10th
1978-79	42	10	7	4	35	19	3	8	10	15	28	41	10th
1979-80	42	6	4	11	19	28	5	3	13	23	46	29	20th

DIVISION THREE

	P	W	D	L	F	A	W	D	L	F	A	Pts	Pos
1980-81	46	8	7	8	28	29	7	6	10	29	35	43	13th
1981-82	46	12	9	2	44	22	9	6	8	33	29	78	3rd

DIVISION TWO

	P	W	D	L	F	A	W	D	L	F	A	Pts	Pos
1982-83	42	13	5	3	36	20	7	4	10	28	27	69	4th
1983-84	42	9	6	6	35	24	6	6	9	25	29	57	11th
1984-85	42	13	3	5	35	26	6	5	10	33	38	65	9th
1985-86	42	8	3	10	29	32	2	3	16	16	37	36	22nd

DIVISION THREE

	P	W	D	L	F	A	W	D	L	F	A	Pts	Pos
1986-87	46	8	8	7	35	41	4	9	10	24	36	53	18th

CONSOLIDATED COMPETITIVE RECORD 1907-1987

		Home					Away				
	P	W	D	L	F	A	W	D	L	F	A
Division One	504	101	67	84	443	385	47	55	150	281	543
Division Two	1984	532	232	228	1865	1051	220	240	532	1052	1748
Division Three	398	111	54	34	424	242	62	55	82	294	337
Total League	2886	744	353	346	2732	1678	329	350	764	1627	2628
FA Cup	198	43	22	28	157	107	32	27	46	126	174
League Cup	89	24	13	7	84	37	12	12	21	54	76
TOTALS	**3173**	**811**	**388**	**381**	**2973**	**1822**	**373**	**389**	**831**	**1807**	**2878**

1907-08

1	Sep	3	(h)	Hull C	L	0-1		8,000
2		7	(a)	Derby C	W	1-0	Freeman	8,000
3		14	(h)	Lincoln C	W	6-1	Threlfall 2, Hubbard, Freeman, Bevan, Dalrymple	20,000
4		21	(h)	Grimsby T	L	0-1		20,000
5		28	(a)	Barnsley	L	0-6		7,000
6	Oct	5	(h)	Chesterfield	W	5-0	Dalrymple 2, Millington 2, Fraser	15,000
7		12	(a)	Burnley	W	1-0	Dalrymple	8,000
8		16	(a)	Lincoln C	W	4-2	Dalrymple 3, Millington	3,000
9		19	(h)	Oldham A	L	1-2	Fraser	30,000
10		26	(a)	Clapton O	W	1-0	Dalrymple	15,000
11	Nov	2	(h)	Leeds C	W	2-0	Fraser, Threlfall	20,000
12		9	(a)	Wolves	L	0-2		10,000
13		16	(h)	Gainsborough T	W	6-0	Lee, Fraser, Millington, Dalrymple 3	15,000
14		23	(a)	Stockport C	L	0-2		8,000
15		30	(h)	Glossop NE	W	6-1	Millington 4, Harrison, Mouncher	13,000
16	Dec	7	(a)	Leicester F	W	3-2	Harrison 2, Threlfall	12,000
17		14	(h)	Blackpool	W	3-0	Millington, Mouncher, Wilkes	6,000
18		21	(a)	Stoke	L	1-6	Dalrymple	5,000
19		26	(a)	Bradford C	W	3-1	Millington, Harrison, Mouncher	10,000
20		28	(h)	West Brom A	D	1-1	Ross	20,000
21	Jan	1	(a)	Chesterfield	D	1-1	Millington	8,000
22		4	(h)	Derby C	D	0-0		25,000
23		18	(a)	Grimsby T	W	4-0	Harrison, Ross, Millington, Mouncher	5,000
24		25	(h)	Barnsley	W	2-0	Harrison, Mouncher	12,000
25	Feb	8	(h)	Burnley	W	2-1	Millington, Harrison	15,000
26		15	(a)	Oldham A	D	3-3	Harrison 2, Dalrymple	8,000
27		29	(a)	Leeds C	W	1-0	Dalrymple	10,000
28	Mar	14	(a)	Gainsborough T	D	3-3	Mouncher, Morrison, Fraser	5,000
29		18	(h)	Clapton O	W	4-0	Dalrymple 3, Harrison	10,000
30		21	(h)	Stockport C	L	0-1		20,000
31	Apr	1	(h)	Wolves	W	2-1	Suart, Dalrymple, Brown 2	10,000
32		4	(h)	Leicester F	W	5-1	Harrison, Dalrymple, Carter, Brown 2	30,000
33		11	(a)	Blackpool	L	1-2	Lipsham	4,000
34		17	(h)	Bradford C	L	0-2		40,000
35		18	(h)	Stoke	W	5-1	Brown 3, Carter 2	15,000
36		20	(a)	Hull C	W	2-1	Harrison, Carter	16,000
37		25	(a)	West Brom A	L	1-3	Carter	10,000
38		29	(a)	Glossop NE	W	2-1	Carter, opp own goal	500

P	W	D	L	F	A	W	D	L	F	A	Pts	Pos	Div		Appearances
38	12		2	5	50	14	10	3	6	32	35	49	4th	2	Goals

FA Cup

1	Jan	11	(a)	Luton T	W	8-3	Dalrymple 2, Harrison 2, Morrison, Millington 2, Ross	7,000
2	Feb	1	(a)	Norwich C*	W	2-1	Millington, Threlfall	19,000
3		22	(a)	Manchester C	D	1-1	Harrison	23,000
R		26	(h)	Manchester C	W	3-1	Ross, Harrison, Dalrymple	38,000
4	Mar	7	(h)	Manchester U	W	2-1	Harrison 2	41,000
SF		28	(n)	Newcastle U	L	0-6		50,000

*Fulham drawn away but the match was played at Craven Cottage.

Appearances

FA Cup semi-final played at Liverpool

Goals

Skene	Ross	Lindsay	Collins	Morrison	Goldie	Dalrymple	Freeman	Bevan	Hubbard	Threlfall	Wilkes	Fraser	Hogan	Millington C	Hind	Ward	Lee	Harrison	Mouncher	Charlton	Crossthwaite	Carter	Suart	Brown	Lipsham	Waterson	Bradshaw J	
1	2	3	4	5	6	7	8	9	10	11																		1
1	2	3	4	5	6	7	8	9	10	11																		2
1	2	3	4	5	6	7	8	9	10	11																		3
1	2	3	4	5	6	7	8	9	10	11																		4
1	2	3	5		6	7	8	9	10	11	4																	5
1		3	5	2	6	8				11	4	10	7	9														6
1		3	5	2	6	8				11	4	10	7	9														7
1		3	5	2	6	8				11	4	10	7	9														8
1		3	5	2	6	8				11	4	10	7	9														9
1		3	5	2	6	8				11		10		9	4	7												10
1		3	5	2	6	8				11	4	10		9		7												11
1		3	5	2	6	8				7	4	10		9			11											12
1		3	5	2	6	8				7	4	10		9			11											13
1		3	5	2	6	8				7	4			10				9	11									14
1	2		5		6	8				7	4			10				9	11	3								15
1	2		5		6	8				7	4			10				9	11	3								16
1	2		5		6	8				7	4			10				9	11	3								17
1	2		5		6	8				7	4			10				9	11	3								18
1	2	3	5		6	8				7	4			10				9	11									19
1	2	3	4	5	6	8				7				10				9	11			-						20
1	2	3	4	5	6	8				7				10				9	11									21
1	2	3	5		6	8				7	4			10				9	11									22
1	2		4	5	6	8				7				10				9	11	3								23
1	2	3	4	5	6	8				7				10				9	11									24
	2	3	4	5	6	8				7				10				9	11		1							25
1	2	3	4	5	6	8				7				10				9	11									26
1	2	3	4	5	6	8				7				10				9	11									27
1	2	3	4	5	6	8						10		7				9	11									28
1	2	3	5		6	8								10	4	7		9	11									29
1	2	3	5		6	8						10		9	4	7			11									30
1	2	3	5		6	8								10				9	11			7	4					31
1	2	3	5		6	8													9			7	4	10	11			32
1	2	3	5		6	8													9			7	4	10	11			33
1	2	3	4	5	6	8													9			7		10	11			34
1	2				6	8												9	11	3		7	5	10		4		35
1	2		4	5		8													9	3		7	6	10	11			36
1	2		4	5	6	8													9	3		7		10	11			37
	2		4	5														9	11	3	1	7	6	10			8	38
36	28	30	32	30	36	33	5	5	5	27	15	10	4	30	3	4	2	24	20	9	2	8	6	7	5	1	1	
	2		1			19	2	1	1	4	1	5		13			1	12	6			6	1	5	1			

Skene	Ross	Lindsay	Collins	Morrison	Goldie	Dalrymple	Freeman	Bevan	Hubbard	Threlfall	Wilkes	Fraser	Hogan	Millington C	Hind	Ward	Lee	Harrison	Mouncher	Charlton	Crossthwaite	Carter	Suart	Brown	Lipsham	Waterson	Bradshaw J	
1	2	3	4	5	6	8				7				10				9	11									1
1	2	3	4	5	6	8				7				10				9	11									2
1	2	3	4	5	6	8				7				10				9	11									3
1	2	3	4	5	6	8				7				10				9	11									R
1	2	3	4	5	6	8							10	7				9	11									4
1	2	3	4	5	6	8								10			7	9	11									SF
6	6	6	6	6	6	6				4			1	6			1	6	6									
	2		1			3								1				3	6									

Month End		Sep	Oct	Nov	Dec	Jan	Feb	Mar	Apr	Final
1907-08	Pld	5	10	15	20	24	27	30	38	38
	Pts	4	12	18	25	31	36	39	49	49
	Pos	15th	7th	5th	6th	5th	5th	8th	4th	4th

1908-09

1	Sep	2	(h)	Glossop NE	L	2-3	Carter, Ross	10,000
2		5	(h)	Stockport C	W	5-1	Harrison 5	25,000
3		12	(a)	West Brom A	D	1-1	Brown	20,000
4		19	(h)	Birmingham	D	1-1	Dalrymple	30,000
5		26	(a)	Gainsborough T	D	1-1	Harrison	20,000
6	Oct	3	(h)	Grimsby T	W	5-2	Brown 2, Harrison, Dalrymple, opp own goal	16,000
7		10	(a)	Bolton W	D	0-0		12,000
8		17	(a)	Burnley	W	3-1	Charlton, Harrison, Lipsham	7,000
9		24	(h)	Bradford	W	3-1	Dalrymple, Brown, Charlton	20,000
10		31	(a)	Wolves	W	1-0	Millington	10,000
11	Nov	7	(h)	Oldham A	W	3-2	Brown, Charlton, Harrison	25,000
12		14	(a)	Clapton O	D	1-1	Millington	15,000
13		21	(h)	Leeds C	L	0-1		25,000
14		28	(a)	Barnsley	W	2-1	Harrison, Brown	6,000
15	Dec	5	(h)	Tottenham H	L	2-3	Dalrymple, Lipsham	40,000
16		12	(a)	Hull C	L	0-2		8,000
17		19	(h)	Derby C	L	1-2	Lipsham	15,000
18		25	(h)	Chesterfield	D	0-0		15,000
19		26	(a)	Blackpool	L	0-2		5,000
20	Jan	1	(a)	Chesterfield	L	1-2	Millington	8,000
21		2	(a)	Stockport C	W	2-1	Freeman, Harrison	7,000
22		9	(h)	West Brom A	W	2-0	Dalrymple, Millington	25,000
23		23	(a)	Birmingham	W	3-1	Freeman 2, Parsonage	9,000
24		30	(h)	Gainsborough T	W	4-0	Freeman 2, Dalrymple, Millington	10,000
25	Feb	13	(h)	Bolton W	L	1-2	Freeman	18,000
26		27	(a)	Bradford	D	1-1	Parsonage	9,000
27	Mar	6	(h)	Wolves	D	1-1	Lee	6,000
28		13	(a)	Oldham A	L	0-1		15,000
29		20	(h)	Clapton O	L	1-2	Dalrymple	25,000
30		25	(a)	Grimsby T	D	2-2	Freeman 2	4,000
31		27	(a)	Leeds C	L	0-2		9,000
32		31	(h)	Burnley	W	3-0	Charlton, Dalrymple 2	8,000
33	Apr	3	(h)	Barnsley	D	2-2	Dalrymple, Harrison	16,000
34		9	(a)	Glossop NE	D	0-0		5,000
35		10	(a)	Tottenham H	L	0-1		25,000
36		12	(h)	Blackpool	W	3-0	Harrison, Dalrymple, Parsonage	10,000
37		17	(h)	Hull C	L	0-3		15,000
38		24	(a)	Derby C	L	1-2	Dalrymple	5,000

P	W	D	L	F	A	W	D	L	F	A	Pts	Pos	Div			
38	8	4	7	39	26	5	7	7	19	22	37	10th	2		Appearances	
															Goals	

FA Cup

1	Jan	16	(a)	Carlisle U*	W	4-1	Millington, Freeman 2, Collins	18,000
2	Feb	6	(a)	Tottenham H	L	0-1		33,100

*Played at Craven Cottage.

Appearances

Goals

Football appearances and goals grid, season 1908-09:

#	Skene	Ross	Charlton	Collins	Morrison	Wilkes	Carter	Dalrymple	Harrison	Millington C	Lipsham	Lindsay	Parsonage	Suart	Threlfall	Brown	Wyllie	Goldie J	Fryer	Millington B	Freeman	Leigh	Sharp	Mouncher	Lee	McCourt	Smith	Littlewort	Waterson	Bradshaw	#
1	1	2	3	4	5	6	7	8	9	10	11																				1
2	1		2	4				8	9		11	3	5	6	7	10															2
3	1		2	4					9	8	11	3	5	6	7	10															3
4	1		2	4				8	9		11	3	5	6	7	10															4
5	1		2	4				8	9		11	3	5	6	7	10															5
6	1		2	4				8	9		11	3	5	6	7	10															6
7	1		2	4				8	9	7	11	3	5	6		10															7
8	1		2	4				8	9	7	11	3	5	6		10															8
9	1		2	4				8	9	7	11	3	5	6		10															9
10	1		2	4				8	9	7	11	3	5	6		10															10
11	1		2	4				8	9	7	11	3	5	6		10															11
12	1		2	4				8	9	7	11	3	5	6		10															12
13	1		2	4				8	9	7	11	3	5	6		10															13
14	1		2	4				8	9	7	11	3	5	6		11															14
15	1		2	4				8	9		11	3	5	6	7	10															15
16	1		2	4			7	8	10		11	3	5	6			9														16
17	1		2	4				8	7	9	11	3		5		10		6													17
18			2	4				8	7	10	11	3	5	6			9		1												18
19	1		2	4					8	7	11	3	5	6		10	9														19
20			2					8	7	10	11			4			5	6	1			9	3								20
21				4				8	7	10	11	3		5				6	1			9	2								21
22			2	4				8	7	10				5				6	1			9		3	11						22
23			2	4					7	8			5			10		6	1			9		3	11						23
24			2	4				8	7	10	11			5				6	1			9		3							24
25			2	4				8	7	10	11		5	6					1			9		3							25
26			2	4						9			5	6		10			1			8		3	11	7					26
27				4						9	11	2	5			10			1			8		3	6	7					27
28	1			4							11	2	5				9					8		3	6	7	10				28
29				4				8	9		11	2	5						1					3	6	10	7				29
30	1			4				8	7		11	2	5							10	9			3	6						30
31	1			4				8		10	11	2	5								9			3	6		7				31
32	1	3						10	9	7	11	2		6					4			8				5					32
33	1		2	4				10	9	7	11			6								8		3		5					33
34											11	3	5			9	4	1				10	2		7			6	8		34
35	1		2	4				10	9	7	11			5								8		3	6						35
36	1			4				10	9	8	11	2	5	6										3		7					36
37	1			4				10			11	2	6				9							3		7		5	8		37
38	1							10		8	11	2	4								9			3	6		7	5			38
	27	1	28	34	1	1	2	31	31	27	35	29	22	35	6	19	7	8	11	1	16	3	15	10	5	2	4	4	1	2	
		1	4				1	12	13	5	3		3			6					8			1							

#	Skene	Ross	Charlton	Collins	Morrison	Wilkes	Carter	Dalrymple	Harrison	Millington C	Lipsham	Lindsay	Parsonage	Suart	Threlfall	Brown	Wyllie	Goldie J	Fryer	Millington B	Freeman	Leigh	Sharp	Mouncher	Lee	McCourt	Smith	Littlewort	Waterson	Bradshaw	#
1			2	4				8	7	10			5					6	1			9		3	11						1
2			2	4				8	7	10	11			5				6	1			9		3							2
			2	2				2	2	2	1		1	1				2	2			2		2	1						
													1									2									

Month End		Sep	Oct	Nov	Dec	Jan	Feb	Mar	Apr	Final
1908-09	Pld	5	10	14	19	24	26	32	38	38
	Pts	5	14	19	20	28	29	33	37	37
	Pos	10th	4th	3rd	7th	6th	7th	8th	10th	10th

1909-10

1	Sep	4	(a)	Stockport C	W	2-0	Harrison, Charlton	10,000
2		11	(h)	Glossop NE	W	2-0	Harrison, Collins	20,000
3		13	(h)	Blackpool	L	0-1		10,000
4		18	(a)	Birmingham	D	1-1	Brown	12,000
5		25	(h)	West Brom A	L	0-2		25,000
6	Oct	2	(a)	Oldham A	W	1-0	Harrison	11,000
7		4	(a)	Blackpool	D	1-1	Charlton	5,000
8		9	(h)	Barnsley	W	3-0	Harrison, Brown, Mavin	20,000
9		16	(h)	Bradford	W	3-1	Dalrymple 2, Lipsham	10,000
10		23	(a)	Burnley	L	0-2		3,000
11		30	(h)	Leeds C	W	5-1	Harrison 3, Brown 2	15,000
12	Nov	6	(a)	Wolves	D	1-1	Dalrymple	5,000
13		13	(h)	Gainsborough T	L	0-1		12,000
14		20	(a)	Grimsby T	W	2-0	McLaughlin, Brown	4,000
15		27	(h)	Manchester C	D	1-1	Walker	20,000
16	Dec	4	(a)	Leicester F	W	3-2	Dalrymple, Mavin, opp own goal	4,000
17		11	(h)	Lincoln C	D	1-1	Brown	10,000
18		18	(a)	Clapton O	D	0-0		10,000
19		25	(h)	Hull C	W	3-1	Walker 2, Harrison	25,000
20		27	(a)	Hull C	L	2-3	Brown, Dalrymple	15,000
21	Jan	1	(a)	Derby C	L	1-3	Brown	8,000
22		8	(h)	Stockport C	W	2-0	Harrison, Brown	10,000
23		22	(a)	Glossop NE	W	1-0	Dalrymple	4,000
24		29	(h)	Birmingham	D	0-0		10,000
25	Feb	12	(h)	Oldham A	D	1-1	Walker	12,000
26		24	(a)	Barnsley	L	1-2	Walker	4,000
27		26	(a)	Bradford	L	0-3		12,000
28	Mar	5	(h)	Burnley	W	2-1	Malcolm, Harrison	12,000
29		12	(a)	Leeds C	D	2-2	Harrison, Mouncher	5,000
30		19	(h)	Wolves	D	0-0		12,000
31		25	(h)	Derby C	D	0-0		20,000
32		26	(a)	Gainsborough T	L	0-2		3,000
33		29	(a)	West Brom A	L	2-3	Burns, Lindsay	15,000
34	Apr	2	(h)	Grimsby T	W	3-2	Smith, Harrison, Flanagan	10,000
35		9	(a)	Manchester C	L	1-3	Mouncher	20,000
36		16	(h)	Leicester F	W	2-0	Brown, Smith	14,000
37		23	(a)	Lincoln C	D	2-2	Harrison 2	4,000
38		30	(h)	Clapton O	D	0-0		12,000

P	W	D	L	F	A	W	D	L	F	A	Pts	Pos	Div	
35	9	7	3	28	13	5	6	8	23	30	41	7th	2	Appearances
														Goals

FA Cup

1	Jan	15	(a)	Chesterfield	D	0-0		9,000
R		19	(h)	Chesterfield	W	2-1	Dalrymple, Harrison	8,000
2	Feb	5	(a)	Newcastle U	L	0-4		35,846

Appearances

Goals

Appearance grid — season 1909-10

Skene	Charlton	Sharp	Collins	Mavin	Suart	Berry	Dalrymple	Harrison	Brown	Lipsham	Flanagan	Goldie	Smith	Walker	Lindsay	McLaughlin	O'Donnell	Prout	Burns	Fryer	Leigh	Malcolm	Marshall	Mouncher	Dixon	Reynolds	No.
1	2	3	4	5	6	7	8	9	10	11																	1
1	2	3	4	5	6	7	8	9	10	11																	2
1	2	3	4	5	6	7		9	10	11	8																3
1	2	3	4	5	6	7	8	9	10	11																	4
1	2	3	4	5	6	7	8	9	10	11																	5
1	2	3	4	5	6	7	8	9	10	11																	6
1	2	3	4	5			8	9	10				6	7	11												7
1	2	3	4	5		7	8	9	10	11			6														8
1	2	3	4	5	6	7	8	9	10	11																	9
1	2		4	5	6	7	8	9	10	11					3												10
1	2	3	4	5	6	7	8	9	10					11													11
1	2	3	4	5	6		8	9	10	11			7														12
1	2		4	5	6	7	8	9	10	11					3												13
1	2	3	4	5	6		8		10				7	11		9											14
1	2		4	5	6		8	9	10				7	11	3												15
1	2	3	4	5	6		8	9	10				7	11													16
1	2	3	4	5	6		8	9	10				7	11													17
1	2	3	4	5	6		8		10				7	11		9											18
1	2	3	4	5	6		8	9	10				7	11													19
	2	3	4	5	6		8	9	10				7	11			1										20
	2	3	4	5	6		8	9	10				7	11			1										21
	2	3	4	5	6	7		9	10	11							1	8									22
	2	3	4	5	6		8		10				7	11					9	1							23
	2	3	4	5	6		8		10	11			7						9	1							24
	2	3	4	5	6		8		10				7	11					9	1							25
	2		4	5	6		8		10				7	11					9	1	3						26
	2		4		6		8	9					7	11						1	3		10	5			27
1	2			5	6		8		10	11			7		3			4				9					28
1	2	3	4	5	6		8	9					7									10		11			29
1	2	3	4	5			8	9	10			6	7											11			30
1	2	3	4	5	6		8	9			10		7											11			31
1	2		4		5			9		11		6	7		3							10	8				32
1	2		4	5				9				6	7		3			8	10	1			11				33
	2			5				9		11	8	6	7		3			4	10	1							34
		3		5	4			9	10			6	7		2			8		1			11				35
	2	3	4	5				9	10		8	6	7	11											1		36
	2		4	5				9	10		8	6	7	11									3			1	37
	2	3	4	5				9	10		8	6	7	11												1	38
25	37	28	36	32	33	12	29	35	27	16	7	10	26	17	8	2	3	7	4	8	3	4	2	4	1	2	
	2	1	2						6	14	10	1	1	2	5	1	1			1			1	2			

Play-off / Test matches

Skene	Charlton	Sharp	Collins	Mavin	Suart	Berry	Dalrymple	Harrison	Brown	Lipsham	Flanagan	Goldie	Smith	Walker	Lindsay	McLaughlin	O'Donnell	Prout	Burns	Fryer	Leigh	Malcolm	Marshall	Mouncher	Dixon	Reynolds	No.
	2	3	4	5	6			9	10				7					8		1			11				1
	2	3	4	5	6		8	9		11	10		7							1							R
	2	3	4	5	6		8	9	10	11			7							1							2
	3	3	3	3	3		2	3	2	2	1		3					1		3			1				
									1	1																	

Month End		Sep	Oct	Nov	Dec	Jan	Feb	Mar	Apr	Final
1909-10	**Pld**	5	11	15	20	24	27	33	38	**38**
	Pts	5	14	18	24	29	30	35	41	**41**
	Pos	9th	5th	4th	6th	6th	6th	6th	7th	**7th**

1910-11

1	Sep	3	(h)	Birmingham	W	3-0	Smith 2, Mavin	25,000
2		10	(a)	West Brom A	L	1-2	Dalrymple	12,000
3		17	(h)	Hull C	L	0-1		20,000
4		24	(a)	Bolton W	L	0-2		6,000
5	Oct	1	(a)	Bradford	L	0-1		20,000
6		8	(h)	Burnley	W	3-0	Harrison, Torrance, Dalrymple	10,000
7		15	(a)	Gainsborough T	W	1-0	Smith	6,000
8		22	(h)	Leeds C	W	2-1	Harrison, Mavin	10,000
9		29	(a)	Stockport C	D	1-1	White	7,500
10	Nov	5	(h)	Derby C	W	3-1	Mavin, Brown 2	17,000
11		12	(a)	Barnsley	L	2-4	Walker, Smith	5,200
12		19	(h)	Leicester F	W	3-1	Smith, White, Mavin	15,000
13		26	(a)	Wolves	L	1-5	Smith	9,000
14	Dec	3	(h)	Chelsea	W	1-0	Smith	35,000
15		10	(a)	Clapton O	L	0-1		15,000
16		17	(h)	Blackpool	W	2-1	Harrison, Smith	14,000
17		24	(a)	Glossop NE	L	1-2	Mouncher	2,000
18		26	(h)	Huddersfield T	W	2-1	Harrison, White	20,000
19		31	(a)	Birmingham	D	1-1	Mavin	14,000
20	Jan	7	(h)	West Brom A	L	0-1		20,000
21		21	(a)	Hull C	D	0-0		10,000
22		28	(h)	Bolton W	W	2-0	Harrison, Mavin	18,000
23	Feb	11	(a)	Burnley	L	0-1		10,000
24		13	(h)	Bradford	W	4-0	Walker, Harrison, Smith 2	4,000
25		18	(h)	Gainsborough T	W	1-0	Spink	7,000
26		25	(a)	Leeds C	L	1-3	Mavin	5,000
27		28	(a)	Huddersfield T	W	2-1	White, Burns	4,000
28	Mar	4	(h)	Stockport C	W	6-2	Burns 3, Smith, Mavin, Harrison	8,000
29		15	(a)	Derby C	D	2-2	Harrison, Burns	2,000
30		18	(h)	Barnsley	L	0-2		8,000
31		25	(a)	Leicester F	L	2-3	Mavin, Brown	6,000
32	Apr	1	(h)	Wolves	L	0-1		10,000
33		8	(a)	Chelsea	L	0-2		50,000
34		14	(a)	Lincoln C	L	0-1		10,000
35		15	(h)	Clapton O	D	1-1	Charlton	16,000
36		17	(h)	Lincoln C	D	0-0		8,000
37		22	(a)	Blackpool	W	2-1	Brown, Mouncher	5,000
38		29	(h)	Glossop NE	D	2-2	Mavin, Burns	8,000

P	W	D	L	F	A	W	D	L	F	A	Pts	Pos	Div		
38	12	3	4	35	15	3	4	12	17	33	37	10th	2	Appearances	
														Goals	

FA Cup

1	Jan	14	(a)	West Brom A	L	1-4	Mouncher	18,034

Appearances

Goals

Player appearance and goalscoring grid — Season 1910-11

#	Reynolds	Charlton	Lindsay	Collins	Mavin	Goldie	Smith	Dalrymple	Harrison	Flanagan	Walker	Torrance	Suart	White	Kirkwood	Brown A	Sharp	Marshall	Mouncher	Burns R	Redwood	Spink	Borland	Burns T	Horton
1	1	2	3	4	5	6	7	8	9	10	11														
2	1	2	3	4	5	6	7	8	9	10	11														
3	1	2	3	4	5	6	7	8	9	10	11														
4	1	2	3	4	5	6	7	8		10	11	9													
5	1	2	3	4	5		7	9	8		11	10	6	.											
6	1	2	3	4	5		7		8		9	11	10	6											
7	1	2	3	4	5		7		9		11	10	6	8											
8	1		3	4	5		7		9		11	10	6	8		2									
9	1	2	3	4	5		7		9		11		6	8		10									
10	1	2	3	4	5		7		9		11		6	8		10									
11	1	2	3	4	5		7		9		11		6	8		10									
12	1	2		4	5		7		9		11		6	8		10	3								
13	1	2		4	5		7		9		11		6	8		10	3								
14	1	2		4	5		7		9		11		6	8		10	3								
15	1	2		4		6	7		9		11		5	8		10	3								
16	1	2		4	5		7		9				6	8		10	3		11						
17	1	2			5		7		9				6	8		10	3	4	11						
18	1	2		4	5		7		9				6	8		10	3		11						
19	1	2		4	5		7		9				6	8		10	3		11						
20	1	2			5	6	7		9				4	8		10	3		11						
21	1	2			5	6	7					10		8		3	4		11	9					
22	1	2		4	5		7					10	6	8		11			9	3					
23	1	2		4	5							10	6	8		11			9	3		7			
24	1	2		4	5		7				10	11	6	8					9	3					
25	1	2		4	5		7				10	11	6						9	3	8				
26	1	2		4	5	6	7				10	11		8					9	3					
27	1	2		4	5	6	7				10	11		8					9	3					
28	1	2		4	5		7				10	11	6	8					9	3					
29	1	2		4	5	6	7				10	11		8			3			9					
30	1	2		4	5	6	7				10	11		8			3			9					
31	1	2		4	5		7				11	10		9		3	6	8							
32	1	2		4	5		7				11	10	6	8		3				9					
33	1	2		4	5		7		9		11	10				3	6	8							
34	1	2		4			7				11	10		8		9	3	6					5		
35	1	2		4			7				11	10		8		9	6						5	3	
36	1	2		4			7				11	10		8			6						5	3	9
37	1	2			5		7					10	6	8		9	3	4	11						
38	1	2			5	6	7				11	10		8			3	4		9					
Apps	38	37	11	32	34	13	37	5	30	4	29	12	23	31	1	16	18	9	9	14	7	2	3	2	1
Goals		1					10		11		2	8		2	1		4		4	2	6		1		

Cup appearances:

Reynolds	Charlton	Lindsay	Collins	Mavin	Goldie	Smith	Dalrymple	Harrison	Flanagan	Walker	Torrance	Suart	White	Kirkwood	Brown A	Sharp	Marshall	Mouncher	Burns R	Redwood	Spink	Borland	Burns T	Horton
1	2		4	5		7					10	6	8		9	3		11						
1	1		1	1		1					1	1	1		1	1		1						
																		1						

Month End		Sep	Oct	Nov	Dec	Jan	Feb	Mar	Apr	Final
1910-11	**Pld**	4	9	13	19	22	27	31	38	**38**
	Pts	2	9	13	20	23	29	32	37	**37**
	Pos	18th	11th	11th	11th	11th	10th	9th	10th	**10th**

1911-12

1	Sep	2	(a)	Bristol C	L	0-1		8,000
2		9	(h)	Birmingham	W	2-1	Pearce 2	12,000
3		16	(a)	Huddersfield T	L	0-2		7,000
4		23	(h)	Blackpool	W	3-0	Pearce, Torrance, Smith	10,000
5		30	(a)	Glossop NE	D	1-1	Coleman	2,000
6	Dec	7	(h)	Hull C	L	0-1		10,000
7		14	(a)	Barnsley	D	2-2	Pearce, Mavin	8,000
8		21	(h)	Bradford	W	2-0	Coleman, Smith	20,000
9		28	(h)	Burnley	L	3-4	Torrance, Coleman, Mavin	16,000
10	Nov	4	(a)	Derby C	L	1-6	Pearce	10,000
11		11	(h)	Stockport C	W	3-1	Hegazi, Coleman, Collins	15,000
12		18	(a)	Leeds C	W	2-0	Coleman, Brown	8,000
13		25	(h)	Wolves	D	1-1	Pearce	10,000
14	Dec	2	(a)	Leicester F	W	5-2	Pearce 2, Coleman, Collins, Walker	8,000
15		9	(h)	Gainsborough T	W	7-1	Coleman 2, Mavin 2, Brown, Pearce 2	10,000
16		16	(a)	Grimsby T	L	0-1		5,000
17		23	(h)	Nottingham F	W	2-0	Collins, Pearce	10,000
18		25	(h)	Chelsea	L	0-1		41,761
19		26	(a)	Chelsea	L	0-1		35,000
20		30	(h)	Bristol C	W	2-1	Coleman 2	12,000
21	Jan	6	(a)	Birmingham	W	3-1	Walker 2, Mavin	7,000
22		20	(h)	Huddersfield T	W	3-1	Mavin, Pearce 2	10,000
23		27	(a)	Blackpool	L	1-3	Brown	4,000
24	Feb	10	(a)	Hull C	W	3-2	Torrance, Smith, Brown	10,000
25		17	(h)	Barnsley	D	2-2	Coleman, Mavin	15,000
26	Mar	2	(a)	Burnley	L	1-5	Pearce	16,000
27		16	(a)	Stockport C	L	1-2	Mavin	6,000
28		23	(h)	Leeds C	W	7-2	Pearce 3, Coleman 2, Mavin 2	5,000
29		27	(a)	Bradford	W	2-0	Torrance, Coleman	4,000
30		30	(a)	Wolves	D	0-0		8,000
31	Apr	1	(h)	Glossop NE	L	0-2		3,000
32		5	(h)	Clapton O	L	0-2		25,000
33		6	(h)	Leicester F	W	4-1	Pearce 3, Coleman	9,000
34		8	(a)	Clapton O	L	0-4		20,000
35		13	(a)	Gainsborough T	W	1-0	Torrance	3,000
36		15	(h)	Derby C	D	0-0		10,000
37		20	(h)	Grimsby T	L	1-3	Pearce	8,000
38		27	(a)	Nottingham F	D	1-1	Brown	3,000

P	W	D	L	F	A	W	D	L	F	A	Pts	Pos	Div		
38	10	3	6	42	24	6	4	9	24	34	39	8th	2		Appearances
															Goals

FA Cup

1	Jan	13	(h)	Burnley	W	2-1	Coleman, Brown	13,100
2	Feb	3	(h)	Liverpool	W	3-0	Coleman 2, Pearce	30,000
3		24	(h)	Northampton T	W	2-1	Brown 2	32,035
4	Mar	9	(a)	West Brom A	L	0-3		50,000

Appearances

Goals

Reynolds	Charlton	Sharp	Collins	Mavin	Marshall	Smith	Coleman	Pearce	White	Walker	Torrance	Burns	Duncan	McIntosh	Spink	Clifford	Brown	Hegazi	Gray	Wood	
1	2	3	4	5	6	7	8	9	10	11											1
1	2	3	4	5	6	7	8	9	10	11											2
1	2	3	4	5	6	7	8	9	10	11											3
1	2	3	4	5		7	8	9	6	11	10										4
1	2		4	5		7	8	9	6	11			3	10							5
1	2	3	4	5		7	8	9	6	11	10										6
1	2		4	5			8	9	6		10	3			11	7					7
1	2	3	4		5	7	8	9	6		10				11						8
1	2		4	5		7	8	9	6		10		3		11						9
1		2	5	4		7	8	9	6		10	11				3					10
1	2	3	4	5		7	8		6	11							10	9			11
1	2	3	4	5		7	8	9	6	11							10				12
1	2	3	4	5		7	8	9	6	11							10				13
1	2	3	4	5		7	8	9	6	11							10				14
1	2		4	5		7	8	9	6	11						3	10				15
1	2	3	4	5		7	8		6	11	9						10				16
1	2	3	4	5		7	8	9	6	11							10				17
1	2	3	4	5		7	8	9	6	11							10				18
1	2	3		5			8	9	6	11					7	4	10				19
1	2	3		5		7	8	9	6			11				4	10				20
1	2	3		5		7		9	6	11	8					4	10				21
1	2	3		5	4	7	8	9	6	11							10				22
1	2	3		5	4	7	8	9	6	11							10				23
1	2	3		5		7		9	6	11	8					4	10				24
1	2	3		5	4	7	8	9		11					6		10				25
1	2	3	4	5		7		9	6	11	8						10				26
1	2	3	4	5		7	8	9	6								10				27
1	2	3	4	5		7	8	9	6		11						10				28
1	2	3	4	5		7	8		6		9	11					10				29
1	2		4	5		7		9	6		8	3	11				10				30
1		3	4	5		7		9	6		8	2	11				10				31
1			4	5		8	9	6	11	10	3		7						2		32
1			4	5		8	9	6	11		3		7				10		2		33
1			4	5		9	6				3	11	7				10		2	8	34
1			4	5		9	6		10		3	11	7						2	8	35
1			4	5		7	8	9	6	11	3						10		2		36
1			5	4		8	9	6	10		3	11	7						2		37
1			4	5		7	8		6	10	3		11				9		2		38
38	29	25	30	37	9	31	31	34	37	24	17	11	9	6	7	8	25	1	7	2	
		3	10			3	15	21		3	5						5	1			

Reynolds	Charlton	Sharp	Collins	Mavin	Marshall	Smith	Coleman	Pearce	White	Walker	Torrance	Burns	Duncan	McIntosh	Spink	Clifford	Brown	Hegazi	Gray	Wood	
1	2	3		5	4	7	8	9	6	11							10				1
1	2	3		5	4	7	8	9	6	11							10				2
1	2	3		5	4	7	8	9	6	11							10				3
1	2	3		5	4	7	8	9	6			11					10				4
4	4	4		4	4	4	4	4	4	3			1				10				
		3	1										3								

Month End		Sep	Oct	Nov	Dec	Jan	Feb	Mar	Apr	Final
1911-12	Pld	5	9	13	20	23	25	30	38	38
	Pts	5	8	13	21	25	28	33	39	39
	Pos	12th	14th	9th	9th	9th	9th	8th	8th	8th

1912-13

1	Sep	7	(h)	Leeds C	W	4-0	Walker 2, Pearce, Coleman	20,000
2		9	(a)	Birmingham	L	1-2	Collins	7,000
3		14	(a)	Grimsby T	L	1-2	Torrance	8,000
4		16	(h)	Huddersfield T	W	2-0	Walker 2	12,000
5		21	(h)	Bury	W	3-1	Pearce 2, Collins	17,000
6		28	(a)	Blackpool	L	0-2		5,000
7	Oct	5	(a)	Barnsley	L	1-2	Mavin	7,000
8		12	(h)	Bradford	W	3-1	Pearce, Coleman, Collins	12,000
9		19	(a)	Wolves	L	1-2	Pearce	12,500
10		26	(h)	Leicester F	D	1-1	Pearce	6,000
11	Nov	2	(a)	Stockport C	L	0-1		5,000
12		9	(h)	Preston NE	W	3-1	Fitchie, Coleman, Walker	15,000
13		16	(a)	Burnley	L	0-5		13,000
14		23	(h)	Hull C	W	2-0	Walker, Coleman	12,000
15		30	(a)	Leicester F	L	0-1		9,000
16	Dec	7	(h)	Clapton O	D	1-1	Coleman	20,000
17		21	(h)	Nottingham F	D	0-0		10,000
18		25	(a)	Bristol C	L	1-2	Coleman	15,000
19		28	(a)	Leeds C	W	3-2	Torrance 2, Walker	10,000
20	Jan	2	(a)	Glossop NE	L	0-2		2,000
21		4	(h)	Grimsby T	L	0-1		7,000
22		18	(a)	Bury	L	0-1		5,000
23		25	(h)	Blackpool	W	4-2	Torrance 2, Fitchie, Coleman	7,000
24	Feb	8	(h)	Barnsley	D	1-1	Coleman	20,000
25		15	(a)	Bradford	W	3-2	Mavin, Lee, Pearce	8,000
26		22	(h)	Wolves	W	4-2	Coleman 3, Torrance	15,000
27	Mar	8	(h)	Stockport C	W	7-0	Pearce 3, Coleman 3, Lee	8,000
28		15	(a)	Preston NE	L	0-1		12,000
29		21	(a)	Lincoln C	L	0-3		5,000
30		22	(h)	Burnley	W	4-2	White, Walker, Smith, Coleman	25,000
31		24	(h)	Birmingham	W	3-2	Coleman, Lee 2	8,000
32		25	(a)	Huddersfield T	L	1-5	Lee	11,000
33		29	(a)	Hull C	W	1-0	White	4,000
34	Apr	5	(h)	Glossop NE	W	2-0	Lee, Walker	7,000
35		7	(h)	Bristol C	D	0-0		5,000
36		12	(a)	Clapton O	L	1-2	Coleman	14,000
37		19	(h)	Lincoln C	W	3-1	Coleman 2, Walker	9,000
38		26	(a)	Nottingham F	W	4-2	Lee 2, Coleman, Taylor	3,000

P	W	D	L	F	A	W	D	L	F	A	Pts	Pos	Div		Appearances
38	13	5	1	47	16	4	0	15	18	39	39	9th	2		Goals

FA Cup

1	Jan	11	(h)	Hull C		L	0-2		10,000
									Appearances
									Goals

Reynolds	Charlton	Sharp	Collins	Mavin	White	Smith	Coleman	Pearce	Torrance	Walker	Gray	Marshall	Burns	Wood	Forrest	Fitchie	Lee	Nixon	Weir	Overend	Coquet	Crossley	Winship	Russell	Stewart	Bowering	Taylor	Champion								
1	2	3	4	5	6	7	8	9	10	11																										1
1	2	3	4	5	6	7	8	9	10	11																										2
1		3	4	5	6	7	8	9	10	11	2																									3
1		3	4	5	6	7	8	9	10	11	2																									4
1	2	3	4	5		7	8	9	10	11		6																								5
1	2		4	5	6	7	8	9	10	11			3																							6
1	2			5	6	7		9	10	11			4	3	8																					7
1	2	3	5		6	7	10	9		11			4		8																					8
1	2	3	6			7	8	9	10	11			4		5																					9
1		3	4	5	6	7	8	9		11			2			10																				10
1	2	3	4	5	6	7	8	9								10	11																			11
1	2	3			6	7	8	9		11		4			5	10																				12
1	2	3			6		8	9		11		4			5	10	7																			13
1	2		4	5	6	7	8	9		11			3			10																				14
1	2		4	5	6	7	8	9		11			3			10																				15
1			4	5	6	7	8	9		11	2		3			10																				16
1			4	2	6	7	8	9	10	11			3		5																					17
			5	6	7	8	9	10	11	2	4	3						1																		18
			4	5	10	7	8		9	11	2	6	3					1																		19
1			4	5	10	7	8		9	11	2	6	3																							20
1	2		4	5	6	7	8		10	11			3						9																	21
1			4		10				9	11	2	6	3	8	5					7																22
1			4		6	7	8		9				3	5	10						2	11														23
1			4	5	6	7	8	9	10			3			11						2															24
1			4	5	6		8	9	10	11	3				7						2															25
1			4	5			8	9	10	11	3	6			7						2															26
1			4	5			8	9		11	3	6		10	7						2															27
1			4	5			8	9			3	6		10	7						2		11													28
1			4	5			8	9		11		6	3	10	7						2															29
1			4	5	10	7	8			11		6	3			9					2															30
1			4		10	7	8		11		6	3				9					2			5												31
1			4		10	7	8		11		6	3				9					2			5												32
1					10	7	8		11		6	3				9					2			5	4											33
1					10	7	8		11		6	3				9					2			5	4											34
1				5	10		8				3	6				9				7	2		11		4											35
1				5	10	7	8		11		6	3				9					2				4											36
1				5			8		11	3						9				7	2				4	6	10									37
1				5	6	7	8					3				9					2				4		10	11								38
36	13	11	28	28	31	29	36	24	18	32	13	21	22	6	6	8	17	2	1	3	16	1	2	4	6	1	2	1								
	3	2	2	1			20	10	6	10						2	8				1															

1			4	5	10	7	8		9	11	2	6	3																							1
1			1	1	1	1	1		1	1	1	1	1																							1

Month End		Sep	Oct	Nov	Dec	Jan	Feb	Mar	Apr	Final
1912-13	Pld	6	10	15	19	23	26	33	38	38
	Pts	6	9	13	17	19	24	32	39	39
	Pos	9th	12th	10th	14th	16th	12th	12th	9th	9th

253

1913-14

1	Sep	1	(h)	Bury	D	1-1	Mavin	6,000
2		6	(a)	Clapton O	L	0-1		16,000
3		13	(h)	Huddersfield T	W	1-0	Smith	25,000
4		20	(a)	Glossop NE	W	1-0	White	2,000
5		27	(h)	Lincoln C	W	4-0	Mavin, Lee 2, Coleman	14,000
6	Oct	4	(a)	Stockport C	W	3-1	Mavin, White, opp own goal	6,000
7		11	(h)	Blackpool	D	0-0		6,000
8		18	(a)	Bradford	L	0-1		12,000
9		25	(h)	Nottingham F	W	2-0	Pearce 2	15,000
10	Nov	1	(a)	Notts C	L	0-4		12,000
11		8	(h)	Woolwich A	W	6-1	Coleman 2, Pearce 2, Taylor, Walker	35,000
12		15	(a)	Leicester F	L	0-3		10,000
13		22	(h)	Grimsby T	D	2-2	Coleman, Collins	15,000
14		29	(a)	Wolves	L	0-1		12,000
15	Dec	6	(h)	Birmingham	W	1-0	Taylor	10,000
16		13	(a)	Hull C	D	1-1	Pearce	8,000
17		20	(h)	Bristol C	W	3-1	Pearce, Coleman 2	10,000
18		25	(a)	Leeds C	L	1-2	Taylor	30,000
19		26	(h)	Leeds C	L	0-1		26,000
20		27	(h)	Clapton O	W	2-0	Coleman, Taylor	25,000
21	Jan	1	(a)	Bury	L	0-1		12,000
22		3	(a)	Huddersfield T	L	1-3	Pearce	6,000
23		17	(h)	Glossop NE	W	2-1	Pearce, Coleman	9,000
24		24	(a)	Lincoln C	W	1-0	Lee	5,000
25	Feb	7	(h)	Stockport C	W	2-0	Lee, Walker	5,000
26		14	(a)	Blackpool	D	1-1	Coleman	5,000
27		21	(h)	Bradford	L	1-6	Pearce	8,000
28		28	(a)	Nottingham F	D	1-1	Pearce	6,000
29	Mar	7	(h)	Notts C	L	1-2	Pearce	18,000
30		14	(a)	Woolwich A	L	0-2		35,000
31		21	(h)	Leicester F	L	1-2	Coleman	6,000
32		28	(a)	Grimsby T	W	3-0	White, Pearce, Lee	8,000
33	Apr	4	(h)	Wolves	W	1-0	Pearce	12,000
34		10	(h)	Barnsley	L	1-2	Russell	25,000
35		11	(a)	Birmingham	W	1-0	Lee	20,000
36		13	(a)	Barnsley	L	0-1		10,000
37		18	(h)	Hull C	L	0-1		10,000
38		25	(a)	Bristol C	W	1-0	Wood	7,000

P	W	D	L	F	A	W	D	L	F	A	Pts	Pos	Div	
38	10	3	6	31	20	6	3	10	15	23	38	11th	2	Appearances
														Goals

FA Cup

1	Jan	10	(a)	Manchester C	L	0-3		25,000

Appearances

Goals

254

Player appearance grid (shirt numbers per match). Columns left-to-right: Reynolds, Coquet, Houghton, Stewart T, Mavin, White, Curtis, Coleman, Pearce, Lee, Templeton, Russell, Torrance, Marshall, Smith, Walker, Forrest, Charlton, Taylor, McDonald, Collins, Wood, Garvey, Champton, Maughan, Laws, Stewart A.

Reynolds	Coquet	Houghton	Stewart T	Mavin	White	Curtis	Coleman	Pearce	Lee	Templeton	Russell	Torrance	Marshall	Smith	Walker	Forrest	Charlton	Taylor	McDonald	Collins	Wood	Garvey	Champton	Maughan	Laws	Stewart A	#
1	2	3	4	5	6	7	8	9	10	11																	1
1	2	3	4	5	6	7	8	9			10	11															2
1	2	3		5	6		8	9			10		4	7	11												3
1	2	3		5	10		8		9		6		4	7	11												4
1	2	3		5	10		8		9		6		4	7	11												5
1	2	3		5	10		8		9		6	11		7		4											6
1	2	3	4	5	10		8		9		6	11		7													7
1		3	4	5	10		8	9			6			7	11			2									8
1		3	4	5	10		8	9			6			7	11			2									9
1	2	3	4		6		8	9			5			7	11			10									10
	2	3			6		8	9			5			7	11			10	1	4							11
	2	3			6		8	9			5			7	11			10	1	4							12
	2	3			6		8		9		5			7	11			10	1	4							13
	2	3			6			9			5			7	11			10	1	4	8						14
		3			6			9			5			7	11		2	10	1	4	8						15
		3			6			9			5		4	7	11		2	10	1		8						16
		3			6		8	9			5		4	7	11		2	10	1								17
		3			6		8	9	7		5		4		11		2	10	1								18
1		3			6		8	9			5		4	7	11		2	10									19
1		3			6		8	9			5		4	7	11		2	10									20
1		3			6			9		11	5	8	4	7			2	10									21
1		3						9		11	5	8	4	7			2	10					6				22
1		3			6		8	9			5		4	7			2	10				11					23
1		3			6		8		9		5		4	7	11		2	10									24
1		3			6		8		9		5		4	7	11		2	10									25
1		3					8	9			5		4	7	11		2	10				6					26
1		3			6		8	9			5		4	7	11		2	10									27
1		3			6		8	9			5		4	7	11		2	10									28
1		3			6		8	9			5		4	7	11		2	10									29
1		3			6		8	9			5		4	7	11		2	10									30
1		3			6		8	9			5			7	11		2	10						4			31
1		3			6			9	7	11	5	4					2				8					10	32
1		3			6			9	7	11	5	4					2				8					10	33
1		3			6		8	9	7	11	5	4					2									10	34
1		3			10			9		11	5	6		7			2				8				4		35
1		3			10			9		11	5	6		7			2				8				4		36
1		3			10			9		11	5	6		7			2				8				4		37
1		3			10			9		11	5	6		7			2				8				4		38
30	**12**	**38**	**6**	**9**	**36**	**2**	**27**	**26**	**16**	**10**	**37**	**13**	**18**	**32**	**24**	**1**	**24**	**22**	**8**	**5**	**9**	**2**	**1**	**1**	**6**	**3**	
				3	3		10	13	6		1			1	2			4		1	1						

Cup / additional appearances:

Reynolds	Coquet	Houghton	Stewart T	Mavin	White	Curtis	Coleman	Pearce	Lee	Templeton	Russell	Torrance	Marshall	Smith	Walker	Forrest	Charlton	Taylor	McDonald	Collins	Wood	Garvey	Champton	Maughan	Laws	Stewart A	#
1		3			6		8	9			5	10	4	7	11		2										1
1		1			1		1	1			1	1	1	1	1		1										

Month End		Sep	Oct	Nov	Dec	Jan	Feb	Mar	Apr	Final
1913-14	Pld	5	9	14	20	24	28	32	38	**38**
	Pts	7	12	15	22	26	30	32	38	**38**
	Pos	5th	3rd	9th	9th	8th	8th	9th	11th	**11th**

1914-15

1	Sep	2	(a)	Leeds C	W	1-0	Lee		6,000
2		5	(h)	Clapton O	W	4-0	Lee 2, Simons 2		12,000
3		9	(h)	Leeds C	W	1-0	Slade		5,000
4		12	(a)	Arsenal	L	0-3			10,000
5		19	(h)	Derby C	W	2-0	Russell, Lee		14,000
6		26	(a)	Lincoln C	L	1-3	Cannon		6,000
7	Oct	3	(h)	Birmingham	L	2-3	Cannon, Simons		12,000
8		10	(a)	Grimsby T	D	1-1	Opp own goal		8,000
9		17	(h)	Huddersfield T	L	2-3	Simons, Russell		10,000
10		24	(a)	Bristol C	D	0-0			7,000
11		31	(h)	Bury	W	6-3	White 2, Slade 2, Russell, Lee		8,000
12	Nov	7	(a)	Preston NE	L	1-2	Russell		9,000
13		14	(h)	Nottingham F	W	2-1	Lee, White		8,000
14		21	(a)	Leicester F	W	2-0	Lee 2		4,000
15		28	(h)	Barnsley	W	2-0	Russell, Lee		1,000
16	Dec	5	(a)	Glossop NE	L	0-1			1,000
17		12	(h)	Wolves	L	0-1			5,000
18		19	(a)	Blackpool	D	2-2	Pearce 2		2,000
19		26	(h)	Stockport C	W	1-0	Bellamy		5,000
20	Jan	2	(a)	Clapton O	L	1-2	Taylor		10,000
21		16	(h)	Arsenal	L	0-1			10,000
22		23	(a)	Derby C	D	1-1	Russell		6,000
23	Feb	13	(h)	Grimsby T	W	2-1	Cannon, Taylor		3,000
24		20	(a)	Huddersfield T	D	2-2	Torrance 2		6,000
25		27	(h)	Bristol C	L	1-2	Torrance		4,000
26	Mar	1	(a)	Birmingham	L	0-1			5,000
27		6	(a)	Bury	L	0-1			4,000
28		13	(h)	Preston NE	L	0-2			6,000
29		20	(a)	Nottingham F	D	2-2	Lee 2		5,000
30		27	(h)	Leicester F	W	1-0	Maughan		4,000
31		29	(h)	Lincoln C	W	3-1	Lee 3		1,800
32	Apr	2	(a)	Stockport C	W	2-0	Taylor, Torrance		4,000
33		3	(a)	Barnsley	D	2-2	Taylor, Lee		4,600
34		5	(a)	Hull C	L	0-2			8,000
35		6	(h)	Hull C	W	4-1	Slade, Lee, White, Smith		2,000
36		10	(h)	Glossop NE	W	2-0	Cannon 2		6,000
37		17	(a)	Wolves	L	0-2			8,000
38		24	(h)	Blackpool	L	0-1			5,000

P	W	D	L	F	A	W	D	L	F	A	Pts	Pos	Div		
38	12	0	7	35	20	3	7	9	18	27	37	12th	2		Appearances
															Goals

FA Cup

1	Jan	9	(a)	South Shields	W	2-1	Taylor, Walker		15,000
2		30	(h)	Southampton	L	2-3	Taylor, Pearce		8,898

Appearances

Goals

Reynolds	Charlton	Houghton	Torrance	Russell	White	Bellamy	Slade	Lee	Simons	Templeton	Forrest	Cannon	Pearce	Marshall	Smith	Gray	Coquet	Nixon	Wood	Taylor	Maughan	Walker	Thompson	Nicholl	Miller	#
1	2	3	4	5	6	7	8	9	10	11																1
1	2	3	4	5	6	7	8	9	10	11																2
1	2	3	4	5	6	7	8	9	10	11																3
1	2	3	4	5	6	7	8	9	10	11																4
1	2	3	4	5	6	7	8	9	10	11																5
1	2	3	4		6	7			10	11	5	8	9													6
1	2	3	5		6			9	10	11		8		4	7											7
1	2	5	6			4	8	7	10	11			9			3										8
1	2	3	6	5		4	8	7	10	11			9													9
1	2		6	5	10	4	8	9		11					7	3										10
1	2		6	5	10	4	8	9		11					7	3										11
1	2		6	5	10	4	8	9		11					7		3									12
1	2		6	5	10	4	8	9		11					7		3									13
	2		6	5	10	4		9		11					7		3	1	8							14
	2		6	5	10	4		9		11					7		3	1	8							15
	2		6	5	10	4				11					7		3	1	8	9						16
	2		6	5	10	7				11							3	1	8	9	4					17
	2		6	5	8					11			9		7	3		1		10	4					18
	2		6	5	8	4							9		7		3	1		10		11				19
	2		6	5	8								9		7		3	1		10	4	11				20
	2		6	5	8								9		7		3	1		10	4	11				21
	2		6	5	8			9		11					7		3	1		10	4					22
	2		6	5			8					9			7			1		10	4	11	3			23
1	2		9	5			8				6	7			3					10	4	11				24
1	2		9	5			8				6	7			3					10	4	11				25
1		2	9	5	6		8								7		3			10	4	11				26
1		2	9	5	6		8								7		3			10	4	11				27
1		2	6	5	8					11		9			7		3			4		10				28
	2		8	5	6			9		11					7		3	1		10	4					29
	2	3	8	5	6			9		11					7			1		10	4					30
	2	3	8	5	6			9										1		10	4	11			7	31
	2	3	8	5	6			9										1		10	4	11			7	32
	2	3	8	5	6			9										1		10	4	11			7	33
	2	3	8	5	6			9										1		10	4	11			7	34
	2	3		5	6		8	9							7			1		10	4			11		35
	2			5	6		8	9									3	1		10	4	11			7	36
	2		8	5	6			9									3	1		10	4	11			7	37
1	2		8	5	6			9							7		3			10	4	11				38
19	**34**	**19**	**36**	**35**	**33**	**17**	**17**	**25**	**9**	**22**	**1**	**6**	**6**	**3**	**24**	**4**	**19**	**19**	**4**	**20**	**21**	**15**	**1**	**3**	**6**	
			4	6	4	1	4	16	4			5	2		1					4	1					

Reynolds	Charlton	Houghton	Torrance	Russell	White	Bellamy	Slade	Lee	Simons	Templeton	Forrest	Cannon	Pearce	Marshall	Smith	Gray	Coquet	Nixon	Wood	Taylor	Maughan	Walker	Thompson	Nicholl	Miller	#
	2		6	5	8								9		7		3	1		10	4	11				1
	2		6	5	8								9		7		3	1		10	4	11				2
	2		2	2	2								2		2		2	2		2	2	2				
													1							2	1					

Month End		Sep	Oct	Nov	Dec	Jan	Feb	Mar	Apr	Final
1914-15	**Pld**	6	11	15	19	22	25	31	38	**38**
	Pts	8	12	18	21	22	25	30	37	**37**
	Pos	5th	7th	5th	10th	12th	12th	12th	12th	**12th**

1919-20

#					Result		Scorers											Att.
1	Aug	30	(h)	South Shields	W	1-0	McIntyre										20,000
2	Sep	4	(a)	Clapton O	W	1-0	Torrance										9,000
3		6	(a)	South Shields	L	0-2											18,000
4		13	(a)	Leicester C	L	2-3	Cock 2										12,000
5		15	(h)	Clapton O	W	2-1	Cock 2										9,000
6		20	(h)	Leicester C	W	5-0	Cock 3, McIntyre 2										16,000
7		29	(h)	Rotherham C	W	3-0	McIntyre, Cock 2										4,000
8	Oct	4	(a)	Bristol C	W	3-0	Cock 2, McIntyre										20,000
9		11	(a)	Coventry C	W	1-0	White										19,000
10		13	(h)	Bristol C	D	1-1	McDonald										9,000
11		18	(h)	Coventry C	D	0-0											20,000
12		25	(h)	Huddersfield T	D	2-2	Cock 2										18,000
13	Nov	1	(a)	Huddersfield T	L	0-3											2,000
14		8	(h)	Blackpool	L	1-2	White										14,000
15		15	(a)	Blackpool	D	1-1	Cock										6,000
16		22	(h)	West Ham U	L	1-2	White										19,000
17		29	(a)	West Ham U	W	1-0	McIntyre										23,000
18	Dec	6	(h)	Tottenham H	L	1-4	Cock										30,000
19		13	(a)	Tottenham H	L	0-4											40,000
20		25	(h)	Grimsby T	W	2-1	McIntyre, Walker										12,000
21		27	(a)	Rotherham C	D	1-1	Cock										5,000
22	Jan	1	(a)	Port Vale	W	4-3	Cock 2, (1 own goal), Banks										8,000
23		3	(h)	Stoke	D	0-0											12,000
24		17	(a)	Stoke	L	0-1											3,000
25		24	(h)	Wolves	D	1-1	Cock										12,000
26	Feb	7	(h)	Hull C	W	1-0	McIntyre										18,000
27		14	(a)	Hull C	L	0-2											10,000
28		21	(h)	Stockport C	W	4-1	Walker, Cock 2, Torrance										16,000
29		23	(a)	Wolves	L	1-2	McIntyre										10,000
30		28	(a)	Stockport C	L	1-2	Cock										4,000
31	Mar	6	(a)	Barnsley	L	1-4	Banks										6,000
32		13	(h)	Barnsley	D	1-1	Banks										16,000
33		20	(a)	Nottingham F	W	3-0	Banks 2, Bertram										6,000
34		27	(h)	Nottingham F	W	1-0	McDonald										12,000
35	Apr	2	(a)	Grimsby T	W	2-0	Crockford 2										10,000
36		3	(a)	Lincoln C	W	1-0	Crockford										9,000
37		5	(h)	Birmingham	L	1-2	Crockford										18,000
38		6	(a)	Birmingham	L	0-2											20,000
39		10	(h)	Lincoln C	W	3-0	Bertram, Banks, Crockford										13,000
40		17	(a)	Bury	D	2-2	Sharp, Cock										15,000
41		24	(h)	Bury	W	1-0	Crockford										15,000
42	May	1	(h)	Port Vale	W	4-0	Cock 2, Crockford, Penn										14,000

P	W	D	L	F	A	W	D	L	F	A	Pts	Pos	Div		Appearances
42	11	6	4	36	18	8	3	10	25	32	47	6th	2		Goals

FA Cup

1	Jan	10	(h)	Swindon T	L	1-2	Hoare		30,000

Appearances

Goals

> The oldest player to play in a first class match for Fulham was Scottish international Jimmy Sharp. He was 40 when he played inside-left against Bury at Gigg Lane in April 1920. When the regular inside-forward, Harold Crockford, missed the bus to the match, Sharp, who was the trainer and had retired before the war, was forced to play, and he scored the only goal of his League career in a 2-2 draw. The youngest player was Tony Mahoney, who was 17 years 1 month when he made his debut against Cardiff in November 1976.

Appearance and goalscorer grid — 1919‑20

Nixon	Charlton	Chaplin	Russell	Torrance	Bagge	Nash	McIntyre	Taylor	Martin	Penn	Walker	Marshall	Cock	Coates	Reynolds	McDonald	White	Bertram	Hall	Worrall	Houghton J	Houghton JH	Banks	Hoare GR	Papworth	Crockford	Sharp	Marrable	No.
1	2	3	4	5	6	7	8	9	10	11																			1
1	2	3	4	5	6	7	8		10	11	9																		2
1	2	3	4		6	7	8		10	11	9	5																	3
1	2	3	4		6		8		10	11		5	9	7															4
	2	3		5	6		8		10	11		4	9	7	1														5
	2	3	4	5			10			11		6	9		1	7	8												6
	2	3	4	5			10			11		6	9		1	7	8												7
	2	3	4	5			10			11		6	9		1	7	8												8
	2	3	4	5			10			11		6	9		1	7	8												9
	2	3	4	5			10			11		6	9		1	7	8												10
	2	3	4	5			10			11		6	9		1	7	8												11
	2	3	4	5			10			11		6	9		1	7	8												12
	2	3	6	5			10			11		4	9		1	7	8												13
	2	3	4	5			8			11		6	9		1	7		10											14
	2	3	5	4						11		6	9		1	7	8	10											15
		3		5						11		6	9		1	7	8	10	4	2									16
	10	3	4				8			11		6	9		1	7					2	5							17
		3	4				8			11		6	9		1	7		10			2	5							18
		3	5	4			8			11		6	9		1	7		10			2								19
	2		5	4			8			11		6	9		1	7		10			3								20
	2	3		5			6				11	4	9		1	7	8	10											21
		3		5			6				11	4	9		1	7		10		2			8						22
	2	3		5			6				11	4	9		1	7		10					8						23
		3		5			6				11	4	9		1	7				2			8	10					24
		3		5			6				11	4	9		1	7				2			8	10					25
		3	6	5			10				11	4	9		1	7				2			8						26
		3	6	5			10				11	4	9		1	7				2			8						27
		3	6	5			10				11	4	9		1	7				2			8						28
		3	6				10				11	4	9		1	7				2			8		5				29
		3	6				10				11	4	9		1	7				2			8		5				30
		3	4		6						11	10			1	7				2			8		5	9			31
		3	5	4	6						11		9		1	7				2			8			10			32
		3		5			6				11	4			1	7		10		2			8			9			33
		3		5			6				11	4			1	7		10		2			8			9			34
		3					6				11	4			1	7		10		2			8		5	9			35
		3	4				7					6			1	11	8			2			10		5	9			36
		3		5			6				11	4			1	7		10		2			8			9			37
		3	2				6				11	4	9		1	7				2			8		5	10			38
		3		5			6				11	4			1	7		10		2			8			9			39
		3					6				11	4	9		1	7	8			2					5	10			40
		3					6				11	4	9		1	7	8			2						10	5		41
		3		5			6				11	4	9		1	7	8			2						10			42
4	18	39	31	36	7	3	26	1	5	23	25	38	33	2	38	37	16	12	1	20	4	2	19	2	7	11	1	1	
		2					9				1	2	25			2	3	2					6			7	1		

FA Cup

Nixon	Charlton	Chaplin	Russell	Torrance	Bagge	Nash	McIntyre	Taylor	Martin	Penn	Walker	Marshall	Cock	Coates	Reynolds	McDonald	White	Bertram	Hall	Worrall	Houghton J	Houghton JH	Banks	Hoare GR	Papworth	Crockford	Sharp	Marrable	No.
	2	3		5			6				11	4	9		1	7							8	10					1
	1	1		1			1				1	1	1		1	1							1	1					
													1																

Month End		Sep	Oct	Nov	Dec	Jan	Feb	Mar	Apr	Final
1919-20	Pld	7	12	17	21	25	30	34	41	42
	Pts	10	17	20	23	27	31	36	45	47
	Pos	8th	4th	7th	11th	10th	10th	8th	6th	6th

1920-21

1	Aug	28	(h)	Wolves	W	2-0	Banks, Cock	25,000
2		30	(h)	Stockport C	W	3-1	Penn, Morris, Banks	10,000
3	Sep	4	(a)	Wolves	L	0-1		25,000
4		11	(h)	West Ham U	D	0-0		30,000
5		13	(a)	Stockport C	D	1-1	Crockford	8,000
6		18	(a)	West Ham U	L	0-2		20,000
7		25	(h)	Notts C	W	3-1	Banks 2, Crockford	20,000
8	Oct	2	(a)	Notts C	L	1-2	Banks	14,000
9		9	(h)	Cardiff C	L	0-3		28,000
10		16	(a)	Cardiff C	L	0-3		25,000
11		23	(a)	Leicester C	D	1-1	Torrance	20,000
12		30	(h)	Leicester C	D	1-1	Banks	20,000
13	Nov	6	(a)	Blackpool	L	0-1		8,000
14		13	(h)	Blackpool	L	1-2	Cock	8,000
15		20	(a)	Sheffield W	L	0-3		20,000
16		27	(h)	Sheffield W	W	2-0	Hall, Cock	8,000
17	Dec	4	(a)	Clapton O	L	0-3		22,000
18		11	(h)	Clapton O	W	1-0	Cock	25,000
19		18	(a)	Stoke	W	2-1	Cock, Hall	8,000
20		25	(a)	Leeds U	D	0-0		25,000
21		27	(h)	Leeds U	W	1-0	Hall	30,000
22	Jan	1	(h)	Stoke	L	1-3	Cock	10,000
23		15	(a)	Bury	D	1-1	Cock	10,000
24		22	(h)	Bury	D	0-0		19,000
25	Feb	5	(a)	Coventry C	W	2-0	Morris, Torrance	18,000
26		12	(a)	Bristol C	L	0-2		16,000
27		26	(a)	Barnsley	L	1-3	Cock	12,000
28		28	(h)	Bristol C	W	3-0	Travers 2, Shea	10,000
29	Mar	5	(h)	Barnsley	W	1-0	Cock	18,000
30		12	(a)	Nottingham F	L	1-5	Travers	9,000
31		14	(h)	Coventry C	W	2-0	Torrance, Penn	4,000
32		19	(h)	Nottingham F	W	2-1	Travers 2	15,000
33		25	(h)	Birmingham	W	5-0	Cock, Shea 2, Travers 2	40,000
34		26	(h)	Rotherham C	W	1-0	Travers	26,000
35		29	(a)	Birmingham	L	0-1		25,000
36	Apr	2	(a)	Rotherham C	L	0-2		12,000
37		9	(h)	Port Vale	W	1-0	Travers	20,000
38		16	(a)	Port Vale	D	0-0		10,000
39		23	(h)	South Shields	D	0-0		16,000
40		30	(a)	South Shields	L	0-3		16,000
41	May	2	(h)	Hull C	W	3-0	Travers 2, Shea	10,000
42		7	(a)	Hull C	D	0-0		8,000

P	W	D	L	F	A	W	D	L	F	A	Pts	Pos	Div		
42	14	4	3	33	12	2	6	13	10	35	42	9th	2		Appearances
															Goals

FA Cup

1	Jan	8	(a)	Blackburn R	D	1-1	Cock	45,000
R		13	(h)	Blackburn R	W	1-0	McDonald	23,219
2		29	(a)	Lincoln C	D	0-0		14,000
R	Feb	7	(h)	Lincoln C	W	1-0	Morris	18,000
3		19	(h)	Wolves	L	0-1		27,530

Appearances

Goals

#	Reynolds	Worrall	Chaplin	Bagge	Marrable	Torrance	McDonald	Banks	Cock	Crockford	Penn	Morris	Russell	Martin	Taylor	Houghton	Hall	Papworth	Walker W	Symes	White	Bertram	Edelston	Shea	Gavigan	Travers	Nixon	Walker JA
1	1	2	3	4	5	6	7	8	9	10	11																	
2	1	2	3	4	5	6	7	8		10	11	9																
3	1	2	3	4	5	6	7	8		10	11	9																
4	1	2	3	4	5	6	7	8	9	10	11																	
5	1	2	3	4	5	7		8	9		11		6				10											
6	1	2	3	4		6	7	8	9	10	11	5																
7	1	2	3	4	5	7		8	9		11		6				10											
8	1		3	4	5	7		8	9		11		6	10	2													
9	1		3	4	5	6	7	8	9		11			10	2													
10	1		3	4	5	6	7	8	9		11				2		10											
11	1	2	3	4	5	7		8	9		11		6				10											
12	1	2	3	4	5	7		8	9		11		6				10											
13	1	2	3	4	5			8	9	10	11		6			7												
14	1	2	3	4	5	6		8	9		11			10		7												
15	1	2	3	4	5	7		8	9	10	11					6												
16	1	2	3	4		7		8	9		11						10				5		6					
17	1	2	3	4		7			9		11						10				5		6	8				
18	1	2	3	4	5				9		11						10						6	8		7		
19	1	2	3	4	5				9		11						10						6	8		7		
20	1	2	3	4	5				9		11						10						6	8		7		
21	1	2	3	4	5				9		11						10						6	8		7		
22	1	2	3	4	5				9		11						10						6	8		7		
23	1	2	3	4	5	7		8	9		11						10						6					
24	1	2	3	4	5	7			9		11						10						6	8				
25	1	2	3	4	5			10	9		11												6	8		7		
26	1		3	4	5				9		11				2		10						6	8		7		
27	1	2		4	5				9		11											3	6	8	7	10		
28	1	2		4	5				10		11											3	6	8	7	9		
29	1	2	3	4	5				10		11												6	8	7	9		
30	1	2	3		5	7			10		11												6	8	9			4
31	1	2	3		5	7			10		11												6	8	9			4
32	1	2			5	7			10		11											3	6	8	9			4
33	1	2	3		5	7			10		11												6	8	9			4
34	1	2	3		5	7			10		11												6	8	9			4
35	1	2	3		5	7			10		11												6	8	9			4
36	1	2	3		5	7			10		11												6	8	9			4
37	1	2	3	4	5	7					11												6	8	9	10		
38		2	3	4	5	7			10		11												6	8	9		1	
39	1	2	3	4	5	7			10		11												6	8	9			
40		2	3	4	5	7			10		11												6	8	9		1	
41	1	2	3	4	5	7			10		11												6	8	9			
42	1	2	3	4	5	7			10		11												6	8	9			
Apps	40	38	39	35	7	42	27	21	29	15	36	6	11	3	4	2	9	1	2	2	6	3	25	23	10	16	2	8
Goals			3									6	10	2	2	2					3			4	11			

FA Cup line-ups:

Rd	Reynolds	Worrall	Chaplin	Bagge	Marrable	Torrance	McDonald	Banks	Cock	Crockford	Penn	Morris	Russell	Martin	Taylor	Houghton	Hall	Papworth	Walker W	Symes	White	Bertram	Edelston	Shea	Gavigan	Travers	Nixon	Walker JA
1	1	2	3	4	5	7			9		11						10						6	8				
R	1	2	3	4	5	7		8	9		11						10						6					
2	1	2	3	4	5	7			9		11						10						6	8				
R	1	2	3	4	5			10	9		11												6	8		7		
3	1	2	3	4	5				9		11						10						6	8		7		
Apps	5	5	5	5	5	3		2	4		5		1	1			2						3	4	3	2		
Goals									1								1									1		

Month End		Sep	Oct	Nov	Dec	Jan	Feb	Mar	Apr	Final
1920-21	Pld	7	12	16	21	24	28	35	40	**42**
	Pts	8	10	12	19	21	25	35	39	**42**
	Pos	9th	19th	19th	18th	19th	19th	9th	10th	**9th**

1921-22

1	Aug	27	(h)	Coventry C	W	5-0	Cock 2, Torrance, Travers, Shea	25,000
2		29	(a)	Leicester C	W	2-1	Shea, Cock	16,000
3	Sep	3	(a)	Coventry C	L	0-2		20,000
4		5	(h)	Leicester C	D	0-0		16,000
5		10	(a)	Hull C	L	1-2	Travers	8,000
6		17	(h)	Hull C	W	6-0	Travers 3, Shea, Cock 2	20,000
7		24	(a)	Notts C	L	0-3		17,000
8	Oct	1	(h)	Notts C	W	4-0	Travers 2, Shea, opp own goal	25,000
9		8	(a)	Crystal P	L	0-2		20,000
10		15	(h)	Crystal P	D	1-1	Travers	34,000
11		22	(h)	Rotherham C	W	4-0	Travers 2, Shea, Cock	23,500
12		29	(a)	Rotherham C	L	0-1		10,000
13	Nov	5	(a)	Sheffield W	W	4-1	Shea, Darvill, Travers, Osborne	16,000
14		12	(h)	Sheffield W	W	3-1	Travers 2, Osborne	25,000
15		19	(a)	Bradford	W	2-1	Osborne, Travers	9,000
16		26	(h)	Bradford	W	2-1	Shea, Travers	19,000
17	Dec	3	(a)	Blackpool	W	2-0	Torrance, opp own goal	10,000
18		10	(a)	Blackpool	W	1-0	Gavigan	30,000
19		17	(h)	Clapton O	W	2-0	Shea 2	25,000
20		24	(a)	Clapton O	L	2-4	Travers, Osborne	20,000
21		26	(h)	Stoke	W	2-1	Shea, Torrance	30,000
22		27	(a)	Stoke	L	0-3		15,000
23		31	(a)	Derby C	D	1-1	Travers	10,000
24	Jan	14	(h)	Derby C	D	2-2	Cock, Shea	18,000
25		21	(h)	Barnsley	D	0-0		15,000
26	Feb	4	(h)	Wolves	W	1-0	Darvill	10,000
27		11	(a)	Wolves	D	0-0		17,600
28		25	(a)	Nottingham F	D	0-0		16,000
29		28	(h)	Nottingham F	W	2-0	Kingsley, Cock	20,000
30	Mar	4	(h)	Bristol C	D	0-0		20,000
31		6	(a)	Barnsley	L	1-2	Boland	10,000
32		11	(a)	Bristol C	L	0-1		20,000
33		18	(a)	South Shields	L	0-1		10,000
34		25	(h)	South Shields	W	3-0	Osborne, Croal 2	20,000
35	Apr	1	(a)	Port Vale	D	1-1	Osborne	10,000
36		8	(h)	Port Vale	W	1-0	Torrance	15,000
37		14	(a)	Leeds U	L	0-2		20,000
38		15	(a)	West Ham U	L	0-1		25,000
39		17	(h)	Leeds U	L	0-1		20,000
40		22	(h)	West Ham U	W	2-0	Osborne 2	14,000
41		29	(a)	Bury	L	0-1		8,000
42	May	6	(h)	Bury	L	0-1		10,000

P	W	D	L	F	A	W	D	L	F	A	Pts	Pos	Div		
42	14	5	2	41	8	4	4	13	16	30	45	7th	2		Appearances
															Goals

FA Cup

1	Jan	7	(a)	Plymouth A	D	1-1	Travers	29,966
R		11	(h)	Plymouth A	W	1-0	Shea	28,373
2		28	(a)	Leicester C	L	0-2		30,020

Appearances

Goals

Appearance grid (shirt numbers by player and match)

	Reynolds	Worrall	Symes	Bagge	Torrance	Russell	Gavigan	Shea	Travers	Cock	Penn	Chaplin	Ducat	Edelston	Osborne	Darvill	McDonald	Martin	Kingsley	Fleming	Boland	Croal	#
	1	2	3	4	5	6	7	8	9	10	11												1
	1	2		4	5	6	7	8	9	10	11	3											2
	1	2			5	6	7	8	9	10	11	3	4										3
	1	2			5	6	7	8	9	10	11	3	4										4
	1	2		4	5		7	8	9	10	11	3		6									5
	1	2			5	6	7	8	9	10	11	3	4										6
	1	2			5	6	7	8	9	10	11	3	4										7
	1	2		6	5		7	8	9	10	11	3	4										8
	1	2		6	5		7	8	9	10	11	3	4										9
	1	2		6	5		7	8	9	10	11	3	4										10
	1	2		6	5		7	8	9	10	11	3	4										11
	1	2		6	5		7	8	9	10	11	3	4										12
	1	2		6	5		7	8	9			3	4		10	11							13
	1	2		6	5		7	8	9			3	4		10	11							14
	1	2		6	5		7	8	9			3	4		10								15
	1	2		6	5	4	7	8	9	11		3			10								16
	1	2		6	5	4	7	8	9			3			10	11							17
	1	2		6	5	4	7	8	9			3			10	11							18
	1	2		6	5	4	7	8	9			3			10	11							19
	1	2		6	5	4		8	9			3			10	11	7						20
	1	2		6	5	4	7	8	9			3			10	11							21
	1	2		6	5	4	7	8	9			3			10	11							22
	1	2		4	5		7	8	9			3			10	11		6					23
	1	2			5			8	9	10	11	3	4					6	7				24
	1	2		6	5			8	9	10		3	4			11			7				25
	1			6	5			8	9	10		3	4			11			7	2			26
	1			4	5			8	9	10		3				11		6	7	2			27
	1			4	5			8		10		3			9	11		6	7	2			28
	1				5			8		10		3	4		9	11		6	7	2			29
	1				5			8		10		3	4		9	11		6	7	2			30
	1			4	5			8	9			3				11		6	7	2		10	31
	1			6	5			8	9			3	4			11			7	2		10	32
	1				5			8	9			3	4			11		6	7	2		10	33
	1				5			8			11	3	4		9			6	7	2		10	34
	1				5			8			11	3	4		9			6	7	2		10	35
	1			6	5			8			11	3	4		9				7	2		10	36
	1			6	5						11	3	4		9				7	2	8	10	37
	1			6	5			8			11	3	4		9				7	2		10	38
	1			6	5			8	9		11	3	4				7			2		10	39
	1			4	5				9		11	3			8			6	7	2		10	40
	1			4	5				9		11	3			8			6	7	2		10	41
	1			4	5				9		11	3			8			6	7	2		10	42
Apps	42	25	1	31	39	17	22	38	30	23	23	41	25	1	22	19	2	13	18	17	2	11	
Goals					4			1	11	17	8				8	2			1		1	2	

Cup matches

	Reynolds	Worrall	Symes	Bagge	Torrance	Russell	Gavigan	Shea	Travers	Cock	Penn	Chaplin	Ducat	Edelston	Osborne	Darvill	McDonald	Martin	Kingsley	Fleming	Boland	Croal	
	1	2		4	5		7	8	9			3			10	11		6					1
	1	2		4	5		7	8	9	7		3			10	11		6					R
	1	2		6	5			8	9	10		3	4			11			7				2
Apps	3	3		3	3		1	3	3	2		3	1		2	3		2	1				
Goals								1	1														

Month End		Sep	Oct	Nov	Dec	Jan	Feb	Mar	Apr	Final
1921-22	**Pld**	7	12	16	23	25	29	34	41	**42**
	Pts	7	12	20	29	31	37	40	45	**45**
	Pos	7th	12th	3rd	3rd	3rd	4th	5th	5th	**7th**

1922-23

1	Aug	26	(a)	Port Vale	W 1-0	Shea		12,000
2		28	(h)	Wolves	W 2-0	Osborne 2		14,000
3	Sep	2	(h)	Port Vale	D 1-1	Shea		23,000
4		4	(a)	Wolves	D 0-0			12,000
5		9	(a)	Crystal P	D 0-0			12,000
6		16	(h)	Crystal P	W 2-1	Osborne 2		26,000
7		23	(a)	Hull C	L 0-1			8,000
8		30	(h)	Hull C	D 0-0			22,000
9	Oct	7	(a)	Sheffield W	L 0-1			15,000
10		14	(h)	Sheffield W	W 1-0	Torrance		25,000
11		21	(a)	Manchester U	D 1-1	Shea		20,000
12		28	(h)	Manchester U	D 0-0			20,000
13	Nov	4	(h)	Barnsley	L 0-1			19,000
14		11	(a)	Barnsley	W 1-0	Osborne		14,000
15		18	(h)	Blackpool	D 1-1	Papworth		16,000
16		25	(a)	Blackpool	L 0-3			10,000
17	Dec	9	(h)	Coventry C	W 4-0	Torrance 2, Osborne 2		16,000
18		11	(a)	Coventry C	L 0-1			5,000
19		16	(a)	Bradford C	L 1-2	Darvill		10,000
20		23	(h)	Bradford C	D 0-0			15,000
21		25	(a)	Notts C	L 0-1			14,000
22		26	(h)	Notts C	W 2-1	Darvill, Smith		25,000
23		30	(a)	Southampton	L 0-2			10,000
24	Jan	6	(h)	Southampton	D 1-1	Osborne		24,000
25		20	(a)	Derby C	L 0-2			11,000
26		27	(h)	Derby C	W 3-1	Papworth 2, Croal		18,000
27	Feb	10	(h)	Bury	W 3-0	Papworth 2, Osborne		12,000
28		14	(a)	Bury	W 1-0	Penn		6,000
29		17	(a)	Rotherham C	W 3-1	Kingsley, Shea, Papworth		9,000
30		24	(h)	Rotherham C	L 1-2	Croal		15,000
31	Mar	3	(a)	Clapton O	W 2-0	Osborne, Croal		22,000
32		10	(h)	Clapton O	D 0-0			22,000
33		17	(h)	Stockport C	W 3-0	Shea 3		16,000
34		24	(a)	Stockport C	W 2-0	McKay, Croal		9,000
35		30	(h)	Leicester C	W 2-0	Shea, McKay		25,000
36		31	(h)	Leeds U	W 3-0	Torrance, McKay 2		18,000
37	Apr	2	(a)	Leicester C	D 1-1	McKay		24,000
38		7	(a)	Leeds U	D 1-1	Darvill		10,000
39		14	(h)	West Ham U	L 0-2			35,000
40		21	(a)	West Ham U	L 0-1			20,000
41		28	(h)	South Shields	L 0-1			14,000
42	May	5	(a)	South Shields	L 0-2			6,000

P	W	D	L	F	A	W	D	L	F	A	Pts	Pos	Div		Appearances
42	10	7	4	29	12	6	5	10	14	20	44	10th	2		Goals

FA Cup

1	Jan	13	(a)	Leicester C	L 0-3		25,870

Appearances

Goals

264

Appearances & Goals Grid, 1922–23

No	Reynolds	Fleming	Chaplin	Bagge	Torrance	Martin	McDonald	Shea	Osborne	Darvill	Penn	Cock	Kingsley	Symes	Russell	Ducat	Croal	Worrall	Papworth	Gavigan	Brown	Smith	Edelston	Thomas	White	Boland	McKay
1	1	2	3	4	5	6	7	8	9	10	11																
2	1	2	3	4	5	6	7	8	9	10	11																
3	1	2	3	4	5	6	7	8	9	10	11																
4	1	2	3	4	5	6	7	8		10	11	9															
5	1	2	3	4	5	6	7	8	9	10	11																
6	1	2	3	4	5	6	7	8	9	10	11																
7	1	2	3	4	5	6		8	9	10	11		7														
8	1	2	3	4	5	6		8	9	10	11			7													
9	1	2	3	4		6		8	9		11			7	5		10										
10	1	2	3	6	5		7	8	9		11					4	10										
11	1	2	3	5	9	6		8		10	11			7		4											
12	1		3		5	6	7	8	9		11					4	10	2									
13	1		3		5	6	7	8	9		11					4	10	2									
14	1		3		5	6		8	10		11		7			4		2	9								
15	1		3		5	6		8	10		11		7			4		2	9								
16	1		3		5	6		8	10		11		7			4		2	9								
17	1	2	3		5	6		8	9	10	11					4				7							
18	1	2	3		5	6		8		10	11					4			9	7							
19	1	2	3		5	6		8		10	11					4				7	9						
20	1	2	3		5	6		8	9	10	11					4				7							
21	1	2	3	4	5	6				10	11		7						9							8	
22	1	2	3	4	5	6		8		10	11		7						9								
23	1	2	3	4	5	6		8		10	11		7						9								
24	1	2	3	4	5	6		8		10	11		7						9								
25	1	2	3	10	5	6		8	7		11					4			9								
26	1	2	3	4	5			8	7		11						10					9	6				
27	1	2	3	4	5			8	7		11						10					9	6				
28	1	2	3			6		8			11					4						9	5	7	10		
29	1	2	3	5				8			11		7			4	10					9	6				
30	1	2	3	5							11		7			4	10					8	6				
31	1	2	3	4	5			8	7		11						10						6				9
32	1	2	3	4	5			8			11						10			7			6				9
33	1	2	3	4	5			8			11						10			7			6				9
34	1	2	3	4	5			8	7		11						10						6				9
35	1	2	3	4	5			8	7		11						10						6				9
36	1	2	3	4	5			8	7		11						10						6				9
37	1	2		4	5			8	7		11				3		10						6				9
38	1	2	3	4	5			8		10	11		7										6				9
39	1	2	3	4	5			8	7		11						10						6				9
40	1	2	3	4				8	7		11			5			10						6				9
41	1	2	3	4	5			8	7		11						10						6				9
42	1	2	3	4	5			8			11		7				10						6				9
Tot	42	37	41	30	38	26	9	39	28	18	42	1	11	3	2	16	19	5	10	7	1	5	17	1	1	1	12
Gls				4				8	10	3	1		1				4		6				1				5

No	Reynolds	Fleming	Chaplin	Bagge	Torrance	Martin	McDonald	Shea	Osborne	Darvill	Penn	Cock	Kingsley	Symes	Russell	Ducat	Croal	Worrall	Papworth	Gavigan	Brown	Smith	Edelston	Thomas	White	Boland	McKay
1	1	2	3	6	5			8	9	10	11		7			4											
	1	1	1	1	1			1	1	1	1		1			1											

Month End		Sep	Oct	Nov	Dec	Jan	Feb	Mar	Apr	Final
1922-23	**Pld**	8	12	16	23	26	30	36	41	**42**
	Pts	10	14	17	22	25	31	42	44	**44**
	Pos	8th	6th	8th	13th	13th	10th	4th	10th	**10th**

1923-24

1	Aug	25	(h)	South Shields	L	2-3	Heard, Torrance	22,000
2		27	(a)	Bury	L	1-2	Penn	10,000
3	Sep	1	(a)	South Shields	L	0-1		14,000
4		3	(h)	Bury	L	0-2		14,000
5		8	(a)	Crystal P	D	1-1	Papworth	12,000
6		15	(h)	Crystal P	W	1-0	Doyle	18,000
7		22	(a)	Sheffield W	L	1-2	Doyle	12,000
8		29	(h)	Sheffield W	W	4-1	Doyle 3, Papworth	18,000
9	Oct	6	(a)	Coventry C	L	0-3		16,000
10		13	(h)	Coventry C	D	1-1	Papworth	10,000
11		20	(a)	Bristol C	W	1-0	Papworth	12,000
12		27	(h)	Bristol C	D	1-1	Papworth	12,000
13	Nov	3	(a)	Southampton	L	0-1		14,000
14		10	(h)	Southampton	W	3-2	Torrance, Doyle, Papworth	16,000
15		17	(h)	Derby C	W	3-2	Edmonds 2, Torrance	18,000
16		24	(a)	Derby C	D	3-3	Penn, Edmonds, Doyle	12,000
17	Dec	1	(h)	Blackpool	L	2-3	Doyle, Edmonds	16,000
18		8	(a)	Blackpool	L	0-3		10,000
19		15	(h)	Nelson	D	0-0		15,000
20		22	(a)	Nelson	D	1-1	Papworth	6,000
21		25	(h)	Hull C	D	1-1	Doyle	22,000
22		26	(a)	Hull C	L	2-4	Papworth 2	12,000
23		29	(h)	Oldham A	D	0-0		15,000
24	Jan	5	(a)	Oldham A	L	1-2	Papworth	12,000
25		19	(h)	Manchester U	W	3-1	Edmonds 3	12,000
26		26	(a)	Manchester U	D	0-0		25,000
27	Feb	9	(a)	Barnsley	L	1-2	Heard	6,000
28		16	(h)	Bradford C	D	1-1	Edmonds	15,000
29		23	(a)	Bradford C	L	0-1		15,000
30	Mar	1	(h)	Port Vale	D	0-0		15,000
31		8	(a)	Port Vale	L	1-3	Edmonds	10,000
32		10	(h)	Barnsley	W	3-0	Darvill, Edmonds 2	7,200
33		15	(a)	Leeds U	L	0-3		18,000
34		22	(h)	Leeds U	L	0-2		17,000
35		29	(a)	Leicester C	L	1-2	Chaplin	14,000
36	Apr	5	(h)	Leicester C	W	1-0	Edmonds	17,000
37		12	(h)	Clapton O	D	0-0		10,000
38		19	(a)	Clapton O	D	0-0		18,000
39		21	(h)	Stoke	W	3-0	Edmonds, Heard, Bagge	15,000
40		22	(a)	Stoke	D	0-0		6,000
41		26	(a)	Stockport C	L	1-2	Darvill	8,000
42	May	3	(h)	Stockport C	W	1-0	Linfoot	20,000

P	W	D	L	F	A	W	D	L	F	A	Pts	Pos	Div		Appearances
42	9	8	4	30	20	1	6	14	15	36	34	20th	2		Goals

FA Cup

1	Jan	12	(h)	Llanelly	W	2-0	Edmonds 2	14,000
2	Feb	2	(a)	Burnley	D	0-0		23,500
R		7	(h)	Burnley	L	0-1		31,000

Appearances

Goals

266

Football season player-appearance grid (1923–24).

Reynolds	Fleming	Chaplin	Bagge	Torrance	Edelston	Osborne	Heard	McKay	Doyle	Penn	Gavigan	Croal	Papworth	Darvill	Aimer	London	Ducat	Edmonds	Riddell	Reid	Lafferty	Linfoot	Whalley	Martin	#
1	2	3	4	5	6	7	8	9	10	11															1
1	2	3	4	5	6		8	9	10	11	7														2
1	2	3	4	5	6	7	8	9	10	11															3
1	2	3	4	5	6	9	8		10	11	7														4
1	2	3	4	5	6	7			10			8	9	11											5
1	2	3	4	5	6	7			10			8	9	11											6
1	2	3	4	5	6	7			10	11		8	9												7
1	2	3	4	5		7			10	11		8	9		6										8
1	2	3	4	5		7			10	11		8	9		6										9
1		3	6	5					10	11	7	8	9				2	4							10
1		3	6	5		7	8		10	11			9				2	4							11
1		3	6	5		7			10	11			9				2	4	8						12
1	2	3	6	5		7			10	11		8	9					4							13
1	2	3	6	5			8		10	11	7		9					4							14
1		3	6	5			8		10	11	7						2	4	9						15
1		3	6	5			8		10	11	7						2	4	9						16
1		3	6	5					10	11	7			8			2	4	9						17
1		3	6	5					10	11	7			8			2	4	9						18
1	2		6	5			8			11	7		10	3				4	9						19
1		3	6	4		7			10	11			8	9			2	5							20
1	2	3	6	5		7			10	11			8	9				4							21
1		3	6	4		7			10	11			8				2	5	9						22
1		3	6	4		7			10	11			8				2	5	9						23
1		3	6	4					10	11	7		8				2	5	9						24
1		3	6	4						11	7		9	10			2	8	5						25
1		3	6	4						11	7		9	10			2	8	5						26
1	2	3	4				8		10	11	7							9	5	6					27
1		3	6	4			8		10	11	7						2	9	5						28
1		3	6	4						11	7		9	10			2	8	5						29
1		3	6	4						11	7		9	10			2	8	5						30
1		3	8	5	6					11	7			10			2	9	4						31
1		3	8	5	6					11	7			10			2	9	4						32
1		3	8	5	6					11				10			2	9	4			7			33
1	2	3	6	5						11			8	10				9	4			7			34
	2	9	4	5	6					11	7			10				3	8				1		35
1	2		4	10	6		8			11			9					3	5			7			36
1	2	10	5	4			8			11			9			6		3				7			37
1	2	10	4	5	6		8			11			9					3				7			38
1	2		4	5	6		8		10	11			9					3				7			39
1	2		4	5	6		8	9		11				10				3				7			40
1	2		4	5	6		8			11	7		9	10				3							41
1	2		4	5	6		8			11			9	10				3				7			42
41	**23**	**36**	**40**	**40**	**20**	**17**	**19**	**4**	**25**	**36**	**25**	**6**	**19**	**19**	**11**	**7**	**23**	**23**	**15**	**2**	**1**	**8**	**1**	**1**	
		1	1	3			3		9	2			10	2				13				1			Goals

Reynolds	Fleming	Chaplin	Bagge	Torrance	Edelston	Osborne	Heard	McKay	Doyle	Penn	Gavigan	Croal	Papworth	Darvill	Aimer	London	Ducat	Edmonds	Riddell	Reid	Lafferty	Linfoot	Whalley	Martin	#
1		3	6	4					10	11	7						2	8	5	9					1
1		3	6	4						11	7		9	10			2	8	5						2
1		3	6	4						11	7		9	10			2	8	5						R
3		3	3	3			1		3	3			2	2			3	3	3	1					
																		2							

Month End		Sep	Oct	Nov	Dec	Jan	Feb	Mar	Apr	Final
1923-24	Pld	8	12	16	23	26	29	35	41	**42**
	Pts	5	9	14	18	21	22	25	32	**34**
	Pos	21th	19th	17th	20th	19th	20th	21st	20th	**20th**

1924-25

1	Aug	30	(a)	Bradford C	D 1-1	Prouse		19,000
2	Sep	6	(h)	South Shields	D 1-1	Darvill		20,000
3		8	(a)	Port Vale	W 1-0	Prouse		10,000
4		13	(a)	Derby C	L 1-5	Prouse		17,458
5		20	(h)	Blackpool	W 1-0	Darvill		22,000
6		27	(a)	Hull C	L 0-3			9,000
7	Oct	4	(h)	Portsmouth	D 0-0			25,000
8		11	(a)	Chelsea	D 0-0			45,000
9		18	(a)	Wolves	L 1-2	Richards		19,000
10		25	(h)	Stockport C	W 2-0	Torrance, Prouse		17,000
11	Nov	1	(a)	Manchester U	L 0-2			28,000
12		8	(h)	Leicester C	D 2-2	Prouse 2		18,000
13		15	(a)	Stoke	D 1-1	Darvill		9,000
14		22	(h)	Coventry C	W 2-0	Prouse 2		16,000
15		29	(a)	Oldham A	D 0-0			7,000
16	Dec	1	(h)	Middlesbrough	D 0-0			7,000
17		6	(h)	Sheffield W	W 2-1	Torrance 2		15,000
18		13	(a)	Clapton O	L 0-3			15,000
19		20	(h)	Crystal P	W 3-1	Prouse 3		18,000
20		26	(a)	Southampton	L 0-1			17,000
21		27	(h)	Bradford C	D 1-1	Richards		8,000
22	Jan	1	(a)	Middlesbrough	W 3-1	Wood 2, Craig		14,000
23		17	(h)	Derby C	L 0-2			25,000
24		24	(a)	Blackpool	L 1-4	Prouse		8,000
25	Feb	7	(a)	Portsmouth	L 0-3			18,000
26		9	(h)	Hull C	W 4-0	Linfoot, Penn, Edmonds, Prouse		10,000
27		14	(h)	Chelsea	L 1-2	Linfoot		30,000
28		21	(h)	Wolves	W 1-0	Prouse		20,000
29		25	(a)	South Shields	L 1-2	Prouse		5,000
30		28	(a)	Stockport C	L 1-4	Pilkington		10,000
31	Mar	7	(h)	Manchester U	W 1-0	Edmonds		16,000
32		14	(a)	Leicester C	L 0-4			22,000
33		21	(h)	Stoke	W 1-0	Penn		16,000
34		28	(a)	Coventry C	W 1-0	Prouse		13,000
35	Apr	4	(h)	Oldham A	W 1-0	Edmonds		12,000
36		10	(h)	Southampton	W 1-0	Edmonds		20,000
37		11	(a)	Sheffield W	L 1-3	Edmonds		18,000
38		13	(a)	Barnsley	L 0-1			11,000
39		14	(h)	Barnsley	L 1-2	Craig		5,000
40		18	(h)	Clapton O	L 0-2			16,000
41		25	(a)	Crystal P	W 2-1	Edmonds, Wolfe		10,000
42	May	2	(h)	Port Vale	D 1-1	Edmonds		10,000

P	W	D	L	F	A	W	D	L	F	A	Pts	Pos	Div	Appearances
42	11	6	4	26	15	4	4	13	15	41	40	12th	2	Goals

FA Cup

1	Jan	10	(a)	Swindon T	W 2-1	Edmonds, Richards	20,301
2	Feb	1	(a)	Cardiff C	L 0-1		20,000

Appearances

Goals

Appearance grid — season 1924-25 (shirt/position numbers by match). Player columns left to right; match number at far right.

Reynolds	Russell	Chaplin	Bagge	Torrance	Lafferty	Linfoot	Prouse	Edmonds	Darvill	Penn	Brooks	Oliver	Riddell	Aimer	Fleming	Richards	Gavigan	Kennedy	Papworth	Packham	Wood	Craig	McKenna	Whalley	Edelston	Pilkington	Wolfe	Doyle	No.
1	2	3	4	5	6	7	8	9	10	11																			1
1	2	3	4	5	6	7	8	9	10	11																			2
1		3	4	5	6	7	8	9	10	11	2																		3
1		3	6			7	8	9	10	11		4	5	2															4
1		3	6			7	8	9	10	11		4	5		2														5
1		3	6				8	9	10	11		4	5		2	7													6
1			6	5			8	9	10	11		4		3	2	7													7
1		3	6	5			9	8		11		4			2	10	7												8
1		3	6	5			8			11		4	9		2	10	7												9
1		3	6	5			8			11		4	9		2	10	7												10
1		3		5			8	10				4	6		2	11	7	9											11
1		3		5			8		9	11		4	6		2	10	7												12
1		3		5		7	8		9	11		4	6		2	10													13
1		3		5		7	8		9	11		4	6		2	10													14
1		3		5		7	8			11		4	6		2	10		9											15
1		3		5		7	8			11	2	4	6			10		9											16
1		3	8	5		7	9			11		4	6		2	10													17
1		3	8	5			9			11		4	6		2	10				7									18
1		3		5			8			11		4	6		2	10				7	9								19
1		3		5			8			11		4	6		2	10				7	9								20
1		3		5			8			11		4	6		2	10				7	9								21
1				5			8			11		4	6	3	2	7					9	10							22
1		3	4	5			8	9		11			6		2	7						10							23
1				5			8	9		11		4	6	3	2	7						10							24
				5			8	9		11		4	6	3	2	7						10		1					25
				5		7	8	9		11	3	4			2							10		1	6				26
				5		7	8	9		11	3	4			2							10		1	6				27
				5		7	8	9		11	3	4			2							10		1	6				28
1				5		7	8	9		11	3	4			2							10			6				29
1		3	6	5		7		9		11		4			2							10			8				30
		3	6	5		7	8	9		11		4			2							10		1					31
		3	6	5		7	8	9		11		4			2							10		1					32
		3	6	5		7	8			11		4			2							10		1	9				33
1		3	6	5		7	8			11		4			2							10			9				34
1		3	6	5		7	8	9		11	2	4			2							10							35
1		3	6	5		7		9		11	2	4			2							8					10		36
1		3	6	5		7		9		11	2	4			2							8					10		37
1		3	6			7		9				4			11	5										2	10	8	38
1		3	6	5		7		9		11		4			2	7						8				2	10		39
1		3	6	5				9		11		4			2	7						8				2	10		40
		3	6	5				9		11		4			2							8	1					10	41
		3	6	5		7		9		11		4			2							8	1					10	42
33	2	34	26	38	3	25	33	26	12	40	9	38	20	5	32	21	7	2	2	4	4	20	2	7	4	3	5	5	
			3			2	16	7	3	2					2						2	2				1	1		

FA Cup section:

Reynolds	Russell	Chaplin	Bagge	Torrance	Lafferty	Linfoot	Prouse	Edmonds	Darvill	Penn	Brooks	Oliver	Riddell	Aimer	Fleming	Richards	Gavigan	Kennedy	Papworth	Packham	Wood	Craig	McKenna	No.
1		3		5			8	9		11		4	6		2	7						10		1
				5			8	9		11		4	6	3	2	7						10	1	2
1	1	2		2			2	2		2		2	2	1	2	2						2	1	
				1											1									

Month End		Sep	Oct	Nov	Dec	Jan	Feb	Mar	Apr	Final
1924-25	Pld	6	10	15	21	24	30	34	41	42
	Pts	6	10	15	21	23	27	33	39	40
	Pos	15th	14th	13th	10th	14th	14th	10th	13th	12th

1925-26

1	Aug	29	(a)	Sheffield W	L	0-3				25,000
2		31	(h)	Swansea T	L	0-1				14,000
3	Sep	5	(h)	Stoke C	L	2-4	Edmonds, White			12,000
4		12	(a)	Oldham A	L	0-4				11,000
5		19	(h)	Stockport C	W	1-0	Edmonds			6,000
6		21	(a)	Swansea T	L	0-6				5,000
7		26	(a)	Chelsea	L	0-4				50,000
8	Oct	3	(a)	South Shields	L	2-5	Kennedy, Penn			9,000
9		5	(h)	Wolves	L	1-2	Penn			8,000
10		10	(h)	Preston NE	W	2-1	Pape 2			20,000
11		17	(h)	Clapton O	L	0-2				25,000
12		24	(a)	Barnsley	D	2-2	Prouse, Pape			7,000
13		31	(h)	Darlington	W	4-0	Pape 2, Ferguson 2			18,000
14	Nov	7	(a)	Hull C	L	0-1				7,000
15		14	(h)	Derby C	D	1-1	Harris			18,000
16		21	(a)	Nottingham F	D	2-2	Craig, Barrett			6,000
17		28	(h)	Southampton	D	1-1	Craig			18,000
18	Dec	5	(a)	Blackpool	L	0-2				8,000
19		12	(h)	Port Vale	D	3-3	Ferguson, Barrett, Craig			12,000
20		19	(a)	Bradford C	D	0-0				8,000
21		25	(h)	Middlesbrough	W	2-0				18,000
22		26	(a)	Middlesbrough	L	0-4	Pape, Penn			20,000
23	Jan	2	(h)	Sheffield W	W	3-0	Pape, McNabb, Penn			15,000
24		16	(a)	Stoke C	L	0-5				8,000
25		23	(a)	Oldham A	W	2-1	McNabb, Craig			15,000
26	Feb	6	(h)	Chelsea	L	0-3				42,968
27		9	(a)	Stockport C	W	2-1	Prouse 2			4,000
28		13	(h)	South Shields	W	2-1	Pape, McNabb			25,000
29		27	(a)	Clapton O	D	1-1	Craig			21,000
30	Mar	13	(a)	Darlington	W	2-1	Linfoot, Pape			7,000
31		20	(h)	Hull C	D	1-1	Pape			14,000
32		25	(a)	Preston NE	L	1-2	Pape			7,000
33		27	(a)	Derby C	L	1-3	Edmonds			12,000
34	Apr	2	(a)	Portsmouth	D	0-0				20,000
35		3	(h)	Nottingham F	L	0-2				16,000
36		5	(h)	Portsmouth	L	2-3	Prouse 2			13,200
37		10	(a)	Southampton	L	0-2				7,000
38		12	(a)	Wolves	D	0-0				10,000
39		17	(h)	Blackpool	D	1-1	Craig			10,000
40		19	(h)	Barnsley	D	2-2	Prouse 2			5,000
41		24	(a)	Port Vale	W	1-0	Prouse			8,000
42	May	1	(h)	Bradford C	W	2-0	Craig, Penn			18,000

P	W	D	L	F	A	W	D	L	F	A	Pts	Pos	Div	
														Appearances
42	8	6	7	32	29	3	6	12	14	48	34	19th	2	Goals

FA Cup

3	Jan	9	(a)	Everton	D	1-1	Craig		46,000
R		14	(h)	Everton	W	1-0	White		20,116
4		30	(h)	Liverpool	W	3-1	Pape 2, Penn		36,381
5	Feb	20	(a)	Notts C	W	1-0	Prouse		33,000
6	Mar	6	(h)	Manchester U	L	1-2	Pape		28,699

Appearances

Goals

Appearances and scorers grid (shirt numbers per match). Columns left-to-right: Boot, Fleming, Chaplin, Oliver, Torrance, Bagge, McCree, Prouse, White, Craig, Penn, Wolfe, Dyer, Edmonds, Packham, Riddell, Barrett, McKenna, Kennedy, Feguson, Garnish, Harris, Pape, Probert, McNabb, Beecham, Linfoot, Caesar, Moseley, Gregory; final column = match number.

Boot	Flem	Chap	Oliv	Torr	Bagge	McCr	Prou	White	Craig	Penn	Wolfe	Dyer	Edm	Pack	Ridd	Barr	McKe	Kenn	Fegu	Garn	Harr	Pape	Prob	McNa	Beec	Linf	Caes	Mose	Greg	#
1	2	3	4	5	6	7	8	9	10	11																				1
1	2	3	4	5	6	7	8	9		11	10																			2
1		3	4	5	6		8			11	10	2	9	7																3
		3	4				8	11	7	10		2	9		5	6	1													4
		3	8		4		7	10	11			2	9		5	6	1	·												5
		3	8		4		7	10				2	9			6	1	5	11											6
		3	5		4		8	10	7			2	9			6	1		11											7
		3	5	6	4		8	10	11			2					1		9	7										8
		3	5	6	4		8	9	7	11		2	10				1													9
		3	5	6			8			11						4	1				7	9	2							10
		3	4	5						11	10	2	8			6	1				7	9								11
1		3	6				8				10	2				4		11				7	9		5						12
1		3	6				8				10	2				4		11				7	9		5						13
1		3	6				8				10	2				4		11				7	9		5						14
1		3	6								10	2	8			4			11			7	9		5						15
1		3	4						8		10	2				6			11			7	9		5						16
1		3	4						10	8		2				6			11			7	9		5						17
		3	4						8		10	2				6			11			7	9		5	1					18
		3	4						8			2	10			6			11			7	9		5	1					19
		3	4						8		11	2	10			6						7	9		5	1					20
		3	4						8		11	2	10			6						7	9		5	1					21
			4						8		11	2	10			6						7	9	3	5	1					22
		3	4					10	8		11	2				6						7	9		5	1					23
			4					10	8		11	2	9			6						7		3	5	1					24
			4					10	8		11	2	10			6						7	9	3	5	1					25
			4					10	8				6			3			11			7	9	2	5	1					26
			4					10	8				6			3			11			7	9	2	5	1					27
			4					10	8		11	2				6						7	9	3	5	1					28
			4					10	8			2	6			3			11			7	9		5	1					29
		3	4						10	8		2	6									7	9		5	1	11				30
		3	4						10	8		2				6						7	9		5	1	11				31
			4					10	8			2	6			3			11			7			5	1					32
			4					10	8		11	2	9									7		3	5	1					33
		3	4						8		11		10			6							9	2	5	1	7				34
		3	4						8				10			6			11				9	2	5	1	7				35
		3	4		11				10	8						6							9	2	5	1	7				36
			4						10	8		2				6			11				9	3	5	1	7				37
			4						10			2				6			11		7	9	3		1		5	8		38
			4					10	8		11	2				6						7	9	3	5	1					39
		3	4						8		11	2	10			6			9						5	1	7				40
		10	4						8		11	2				6			9						5	1	7			3	41
			4					10	8		11	2				6			9		7	9		5	1				3	42
9	2	29	41	7	10	2	24	7	34	27	13	34	17	1	2	36	8	4	17	1	27	29	14	30	25	8	1	1	2	
							8	1	7	5			3			2			1	3		1	11		3		1				

Cup matches:

Boot	Flem	Chap	Oliv	Torr	Bagge	McCr	Prou	White	Craig	Penn	Wolfe	Dyer	Edm	Pack	Ridd	Barr	McKe	Kenn	Fegu	Garn	Harr	Pape	Prob	McNa	Beec	Linf	Caes	Mose	Greg	Rd
		3	4					10		8	11	2				6					7	9		5	1					3
		3	4					10	8	11		2	9			6					7			5	1					R
			4					10	8	11		2				6					7	9	3	5	1					4
			4					10	8	6		2				3			11		7	9		5	1					5
		3	4						8	6		2	10						11		7	9		2						6
		3	5					3	1	5	5	5	2			4			2		5	4	1	5	5					
								1	1	1	1											3								

Month End		Sep	Oct	Nov	Dec	Jan	Feb	Mar	Apr	Final
1925-26	**Pld**	7	13	17	22	25	29	33	41	**42**
	Pts	2	7	10	14	18	23	26	32	**34**
	Pos	22nd	21st	20th	21st	20th	19th	18th	19th	**19th**

271

1926-27

1	Aug	28	(a)	Manchester C	L	2-4	Tonner, McNabb	34,000
2		30	(h)	Nottingham F	W	2-1	Craig, Wolfe	15,000
3	Sep	4	(h)	Darlington	W	2-1	Harris, McNabb	20,000
4		11	(a)	Portsmouth	L	0-2		15,000
5		13	(h)	Barnsley	W	1-0	Tonner	10,000
6		18	(h)	Oldham A	D	1-1	Tonner	18,000
7		25	(a)	Chelsea	D	2-2	McNabb, Tonner	38,000
8	Oct	2	(a)	Grimsby T	L	0-2		14,000
9		7	(a)	Nottingham F	L	0-2		10,000
10		9	(h)	Blackpool	W	1-0	McNabb	17,000
11		16	(h)	South Shields	D	2-2	Opp own goal, Smith	18,000
12		23	(a)	Preston NE	D	2-2	Penn, Prouse	20,000
13		30	(h)	Bradford C	D	1-1	Smith	16,000
14	Nov	6	(a)	Southampton	L	1-4	Smith	9,000
15		13	(h)	Port Vale	W	6-2	McNabb 2, Prouse 2, Tonner, Smith	3,500
16		20	(a)	Middlesbrough	L	1-6	Tonner	12,000
17		27	(h)	Clapton O	W	2-0	Prouse, Tonner	19,000
18	Dec	4	(a)	Notts C	L	0-4		12,000
19		11	(h)	Wolves	W	4-1	Penn 2, Prouse, Craig	16,000
20		18	(a)	Hull C	L	0-2		10,000
21		25	(a)	Reading	L	0-2		15,000
22		27	(h)	Reading	L	1-2	McNabb	40,500
23		28	(a)	Barnsley	L	0-5		5,000
24	Jan	15	(h)	Manchester C	L	2-5	Penn, Craig	24,000
25		22	(a)	Darlington	L	0-5		8,000
26	Feb	5	(a)	Oldham A	W	3-2	Craig 2, Temple	11,000
27		12	(h)	Chelsea	L	1-2	Pape	32,000
28		19	(h)	Grimsby T	L	0-5		9,000
29		26	(a)	Blackpool	D	0-0		8,000
30	Mar	5	(a)	South Shields	D	1-1	Hoyland	6,000
31		12	(h)	Preston NE	L	0-1		20,000
32		14	(h)	Portsmouth	D	0-0		6,000
33		19	(a)	Bradford C	L	0-1		10,000
34		28	(h)	Southampton	W	3-0	Prouse 2, Penn	8,000
35	Apr	2	(a)	Port Vale	L	1-7	Smith	6,000
36		9	(h)	Middlesbrough	L	0-3		13,000
37		15	(h)	Swansea T	W	4-3	Tonner 2, Oliver, Penn	25,000
38		16	(a)	Clapton O	W	3-2	Tonner, Smith, Penn	20,000
39		18	(a)	Swansea T	L	2-4	Tonner 2	12,000
40		23	(h)	Notts C	W	3-0	Hoyland 2, Temple	12,000
41		30	(a)	Wolves	L	1-2	McNabb	8,000
42	May	7	(h)	Hull C	W	3-1	Smith, Tonner, McNabb	12,000

P	W	D	L	F	A	W	D	L	F	A	Pts	Pos	Div		Appearances
42	11	4	6	39	31	2	4	15	19	61	34	18th	2		Goals

FA Cup

3	Jan	8	(h)	Chesterfield	W	4-3	Tonner 2, Pape, Craig	16,571
4		29	(h)	Burnley	L	0-4		23,562

Appearances

Goals

Appearance and goalscoring grid (season 1926-27):

Beecham	Dyer	Barrett	Oliver	McNabb	Wolfe	Harris J	Craig	Pape	Tonner	Penn	Scullion	Prouse	Pike	Probert	Gregory	Walters	Smith	Brown	Johnson	Temple	Pilkington	Moseley	Harris G	Hoyland	No
1	2	3	4	5	6	7	8	9	10	11															1
1	2	3	4	5	6	7	8		10	11	9														2
1	2	3	4	5	6	7	10		9	11		8													3
1	2	3	4	5	6	7	8	9	10	11															4
1	2	3	4	5	6	7	8	9	10	11															5
1	2	3	4	5	6	7	10	9	8	11															6
1	2	3	4	5	6		10	9	8	11			7												7
1		3	4	5	6		10	9	8	11			7	2											8
1			4	5		11	10		8	6		9	7	2	3										9
1	2		4	5		7	10		8	11		9			3	6									10
1	2		4	5		7	10		8	11					3	6	9								11
1	2		4	6		7	10			11		8			3	5	9								12
1	2		4	6		7	10			11		8			3	5	9								13
1	2		4	6		7	11		10			8			3	5	9								14
1	2		4	6		7			10	11		8			3	5	9								15
1	2		4	6		7			10	11		8			3	5	9								16
1			4	5			7		10	11		8			3	6	9	2							17
1			4	5			7		10	11		8			3	6	9	2							18
1		6	4	10			7			11		8			3	5	9	2							19
1		6	4	5			7		10	11		8			3		9	2							20
1		6	4	5			7		10	11		8			3		9	2							21
1		6	4	10			7			11		8			3	5	9	2							22
1	3	6	4		10		7	9	8	11					5			2							23
1	2	3	4	5			7	9	10	11		8			6										24
1			4	11			9		6		10				3	8	2	5		7					25
1		6	4	5			8	9	10	11					3			2		7					26
1		6	4				8	9	10	11					3	5		2		7					27
1		6	4				8	9	10	11					3	5		2		7					28
1	2	3	4	5				9		11									10	7	6	8			29
1	2	6	4	5			8			11					3		9			7			3	10	30
1	2	6	4	5			8			11					3		9			7			3	10	31
1	2	6	4	5			8			11					3		9			7			3	10	32
1	2	6	4	5			8			11		10			3		9			7			3		33
1	2	6	4	5			8			11		10			3		9			7			3		34
1	2	3	4	5			8			11						6	9			7					35
1	2	6	4	5			8		10	11					3		9			7					36
1	2	6	4	5			8		10	11					3		9			7					37
1	2	6	4	5			8		10	11					3		9			7					38
1	2		4	5					10	11		8			3	6	9			7					39
1	2	6	4	5			8			11					3		9			7				10	40
1	2	6	4	5			8			11					3		9			7				10	41
1	2	6	4	5			8		10	11					3		9			7					42
42	30	30	42	38	9	15	37	13	28	41	1	20	3	2	25	17	27	11	1	18	1	1	5	5	
		1	9	1	1	5	1	13	7		7						7			2				3	

Cup grid:

Beecham	Dyer	Barrett	Oliver	McNabb	Wolfe	Harris J	Craig	Pape	Tonner	Penn	Scullion	Prouse	Pike	Probert	Gregory	Walters	Smith	Brown	Johnson	Temple	Pilkington	Moseley	Harris G	Hoyland	No
1		3	4	5			7	9	10	11		8			6		2								1
1		6	4				7	9	10	11		8			3	5	2								2
2		2	2	1			2	2	2	2		2			1	2	2								
							1	1	2																

Month End		Sep	Oct	Nov	Dec	Jan	Feb	Mar	Apr	Final
1926-27	Pld	7	13	17	23	25	29	34	41	**42**
	Pts	8	13	17	19	19	22	26	32	**34**
	Pos	15th	12th	12th	13th	16th	19th	19th	18th	**18th**

1927-28

1	Aug	27	(h)	Preston NE	D	2-2	Elliott 2	26,000
2		29	(a)	Nottingham F	L	0-7		13,000
3	Sep	3	(a)	Swansea T	L	1-2	Elliott	16,000
4		10	(h)	Chelsea	D	1-1	McKenna	40,000
5		15	(h)	Nottingham F	W	2-0	McKenna, Elliott	10,000
6		17	(h)	Barnsley	W	3-1	Elliott, Craig, Devan	18,000
7		24	(a)	Wolves	L	1-3	McKenna	11,500
8	Oct	1	(h)	Port Vale	W	4-0	Hoyland, McKenna, Elliott, McNabb	12,000
9		8	(a)	South Shields	L	1-2	Devan	7,000
10		15	(h)	Leeds U	D	1-1	Craig	18,000
11		22	(a)	Bristol C	L	0-3		10,000
12		29	(h)	West Brom A	W	3-1	Elliott 2, Temple	18,000
13	Nov	5	(a)	Clapton O	L	2-3	Elliott, Harris	16,000
14		12	(h)	Stoke C	L	1-5	Temple	15,000
15		19	(a)	Southampton	L	2-5	Elliott 2	5,000
16		26	(h)	Grimsby T	D	2-2	McKenna, Elliott	10,000
17	Dec	3	(a)	Oldham A	L	2-4	Elliott 2	10,000
18		10	(h)	Notts C	W	2-1	Elliott, Craig	15,000
19		17	(a)	Reading	L	1-2	McKenna	7,400
20		24	(h)	Blackpool	D	2-2	Penn, Elliott	16,000
21		27	(a)	Hull C	L	2-3	McNabb, McKenna	17,000
22		31	(a)	Preston NE	L	0-1		12,000
23	Jan	7	(h)	Swansea T	W	3-2	Elliott, McKenna, Craig	20,000
24		21	(a)	Chelsea	L	1-2	Elliott	45,000
25		28	(a)	Barnsley	L	4-8	Craig, Elliott 2, Johnson	5,000
26	Feb	4	(h)	Wolves	W	7-0	Elliott 3, McKenna, Craig, Temple 2	10,000
27		11	(a)	Port Vale	L	1-4	Penn	6,000
28		18	(h)	South Shields	W	2-0	Craig, Smith	18,000
29		25	(a)	Leeds U	L	1-2	Temple	14,000
30	Mar	3	(h)	Bristol C	W	5-0	Elliott 3, Craig, Temple	20,000
31		10	(a)	West Brom A	L	0-4		20,000
32		17	(h)	Clapton O	W	2-0	McKenna, Penn	18,000
33		24	(a)	Stoke C	L	1-5	Craig	10,000
34		26	(h)	Hull C	L	0-2		12,000
35		31	(h)	Southampton	W	1-0	Smith	8,000
36	Apr	6	(a)	Manchester C	L	1-2	McNabb	60,000
37		7	(a)	Grimsby T	L	0-1		12,000
38		9	(h)	Manchester C	D	1-1	Temple	27,000
39		14	(h)	Oldham A	D	1-1	Ferguson	16,000
40		21	(a)	Notts C	W	1-0	Ferguson	10,000
41		28	(h)	Reading	W	1-0	Craig	19,000
42	May	5	(a)	Blackpool	L	0-4		17,000

P	W	D	L	F	A	W	D	L	F	A	Pts	Pos	Div		Appearances
42	12	7	2	46	22	1	0	20	22	67	33	21st	2		Goals

FA Cup

3	Jan	15	(a)	Southport	L	0-3	8,000

Appearances

Goals

The record run of away defeats was close to the all-time Football League record (held by Nelson in 1931-2). Fulham lost the first 20 of their 21 away games in 1927-8, which, when added to the defeats in the last two matches of 1926-7, made 23 consecutive defeats. They also lost their only Cup-tie in 1927-8, which was away from home.

Football appearance and goalscoring grid, season 1927–28. Player shirt numbers are shown per match (rows 1–42).

Beecham	Barrett	Harris	Oliver	McNabb	Steele	Temple	Craig	Elliott	Hoyland	Penn	Dyer	Devan	McKenna	Lowe	Johnson	Gregory	Horler	Hebden	Sparke	Smith	Walters	Lawson	Ferguson	Avey	No.
1	2	3	4	5	6	7	8	9	10	11															1
1	2	3	4	5	6	7	8	9	10	11															2
1	3		4	5	6	7	8	9			2	11	10												3
1	3		4	5	6		10	9		11	2	7	8												4
1	3		4	5	6		10	9		11	2	7	8												5
1	3		4	5	6		10	9		11	2	7	8												6
1	3		4	5	6		10	9		11	2	7	8												7
1	3		4	5	6			9	10	11	2	7	8												8
1	3		4		6			9	10	11	2	7	8	5											9
1	3		4		6	7	10	9		11	2		8	5											10
1	3		4	5	6	7	10	9		11	2		8												11
1	3		4	5	6	7	10	9		11	2		8												12
1	3	2	4	5		7	10	9	8	11					6										13
1	3		4	5		7	10	9		11	2		8		6										14
1	3		4	5	6	7	9	10	11				8			2									15
1	3		4	5	6	7	9	10	11		2		8												16
1	3		4	5	6	7	9	10	11		2		8												17
1			4	5	6	7	9	10	11		2		8			3									18
1			4	5	6	7	9	10	11		2		8			3									19
1			4	5	6	7	9	10	11		2		8				3								20
1	6		4	5		7	9	10	11				8				3	2							21
1	6		4	5		7	9	10					8				3	2	11						22
1	6		4	5		7	9	10	11				8				3	2							23
1	6		4	5	8	7	9	10	11								3	2							24
1	6				8	7	9	10	11					5	4		3	2							25
1	6		4	5		7	8	9		11						3		2		10					26
1	6		4	5		7	8	9		11						3		2		10					27
1	6		4	5			8	9	7	11						3		2							28
1	6		4	5	10	7	8	9		11						3		2							29
1	6		4	5		7	8	9		11			10			3		2							30
1	4		6	5		7	8	9		11			10			3		2							31
1	6		4	5		7	8	9		11			10				3	2							32
1	6		4	5		7	8	9		11			10				3	2							33
1	6		4	5		7	8	9		11						3		2							34
1	3		4	5	6	7	8	10		11								2		9					35
1	3		4	5	6	7	8	10		11								2		9					36
1	3		4		6	7	8	10		11								2		9	5				37
1	3		4	5		7	8	10		11								2		9		6			38
1	3		4	5		7		9	10									2		8		6	11		39
1	3		8	5	4	7	10	9			6							2					11		40
1	3		4	5		7	10	9			6							2					11	8	41
1	3		4	5		7	10	9			6							2					11	8	42
42	**39**	**3**	**41**	**38**	**25**	**24**	**39**	**42**	**17**	**40**	**16**	**7**	**25**	**3**	**3**	**10**	**8**	**22**	**2**	**7**	**1**	**2**	**4**	**2**	
			1		3	7	10	26	1	3		2	10			1		2					2		

Cup appearances:

Beecham	Barrett	Harris	Oliver	McNabb	Steele	Temple	Craig	Elliott	Hoyland	Penn	Dyer	Devan	McKenna	Lowe	Johnson	Gregory	Horler	Hebden	Sparke	Smith	Walters	Lawson	Ferguson	Avey	No.
1	6		4	5		7	9	10	11				8				3	2							3
1	1		1	1		1	1	1	1				1				1	1							

Month End		Sep	Oct	Nov	Dec	Jan	Feb	Mar	Apr	Final
1927-28	**Pld**	7	12	16	22	25	29	35	41	**42**
	Pts	6	11	12	15	17	21	29	33	**33**
	Pos	15th	15th	17th	20th	20th	20th	20th	21st	**21st**

1928-29

1	Aug	25	(a)	Gillingham	D	2-2	Price, Avey	9,000
2	Sep	1	(h)	Plymouth A	W	5-2	Temple, Avey, Haley, Price, Penn	20,000
3		5	(a)	Crystal P	L	1-2	Temple	16,000
4		8	(a)	Bournemouth	L	0-1		7,000
5		10	(h)	Crystal P	D	2-2	Haley 2	10,000
6		15	(a)	Queen's Park R	L	1-2	Price	20,000
7		22	(h)	Bristol R	W	6-1	Avey 2, Price, Temple, Penn, McNabb	15,000
8		29	(a)	Watford	W	6-2	Price 3, Haley 2, Temple	12,000
9	Oct	6	(h)	Walsall	W	5-1	Temple, Oliver, Haley 2, Price	15,000
10		13	(a)	Newport C	D	3-3	Haley, Temple, Avey	8,000
11		20	(h)	Merthyr T	W	4-0	McNabb 2, Haley, Temple	18,000
12		27	(a)	Southend U	W	1-0	Temple	9,000
13	Nov	3	(h)	Exeter C	D	0-0		16,000
14		10	(a)	Brighton & HA	L	0-2		9,000
15		17	(h)	Norwich C	W	2-1	Temple, Price	18,000
16	Dec	1	(h)	Northampton T	W	2-1	Penn, Lawson	15,000
17		15	(h)	Luton T	W	4-2	McNabb, Temple 2, Penn	12,000
18		22	(a)	Brentford	W	2-1	Avey, Craig	15,000
19		25	(h)	Torquay U	W	2-1	Haley, McNabb	20,000
20		26	(a)	Torquay U	D	1-1	Penn	6,000
21		29	(h)	Gillingham	W	4-2	Temple, Haley, Avey 2	15,000
22	Jan	5	(a)	Plymouth A	L	2-4	Haley, Temple	15,000
23		12	(a)	Coventry C	W	2-1	Temple, Haley	15,000
24		19	(a)	Bournemouth	W	3-0	Haley 2, McNabb	15,000
25		26	(h)	Queen's Park R	W	5-0	Haley 2, Temple 2, Price	25,000
26	Feb	2	(a)	Bristol R	L	3-5	Craig, Temple 2	10,000
27		9	(h)	Watford	L	2-3	Haley, Price	20,000
28		16	(a)	Walsall	D	2-2	Temple, Price	6,000
29		23	(h)	Newport C	L	2-3	Allen, Temple	14,000
30	Mar	2	(a)	Merthyr T	L	1-4	Penn	4,000
31		9	(h)	Southend U	L	2-4	Hammond, Temple	20,000
32		16	(a)	Exeter C	W	4-1	Avey 3, Hammond	5,000
33		23	(h)	Brighton & HA	W	3-1	Penn, Avey, Hammond	20,000
34		29	(h)	Swindon T	W	2-0	Price, Penn	30,000
35		30	(a)	Norwich C	D	2-2	Hammond 2	9,000
36	Apr	1	(a)	Swindon T	W	2-1	Temple, Gibbon	7,000
37		6	(h)	Charlton A	L	2-5	Avey, Temple	30,000
38		13	(a)	Northampton T	D	3-3	Temple 2, Avey	10,000
39		17	(a)	Charlton A	D	0-0		15,000
40		20	(h)	Coventry C	D	2-2	Temple, Penn	15,000
41		27	(a)	Luton T	W	3-1	Penn, Haley, Avey	13,000
42	May	4	(h)	Brentford	W	1-0	Craig	18,000

P	W	D	L	F	A	W	D	L	F	A	Pts	Pos	Div		Appearances
42	14	3	4	60	31	7	7	7	41	40	52	5th	3S		Goals

FA Cup

1	Nov	24	(a)	Coventry C	W	4-1	Temple 2, Price, Penn	28,000
2	Dec	8	(h)	Luton T	D	0-0		19,000
R		13	(a)	Luton T	L	1-4	Temple	11,250

Appearances

Goals

Beecham	Barrett	Rosier	Oliver	McNabb	Steele	Temple	Avey	Haley	Price	Penn	Dyer	Craig	Lawson	Mason	Bird	Allen	Hammond	Meeson	Hebden	Gibbon	Binks	
1	2	3	4	5	6	7	8	9	10	11												1
1	2	3	4	5	6	7	9	8	10	11												2
1	2	3	4	5	6	7	9	8	10	11												3
1	2	3	4	5	6	7	8	9	10	11												4
1	3		4	5	6	7	9	8	10	11	2											5
1	3		4	5		7	9	8	10	6	2	11										6
1	2	3	4	5	6	7	9	8	10	11												7
1	3	2	4	5	6	7	9	8	10	11												8
1	3	2	4	5	6	7	8	9	10	11												9
1	3	2	4	5	6	7	8	9	10	11												10
1	3	2	4	5	6	7	9	8	10	11												11
1	2	3	4	5	6	7	8	9	10	11												12
1	2	3	4	5	6	7	9	8	10	11												13
	2	3	4	5		7	9	8	10	11			6	1								14
	4	2	5			7	9	8	10	11			6	1	3							15
	3	2	5	4		7	9	8	10	11			6	1								16
			4	5		7	9	8		11	2	10	6	1	3							17
			4	5		7	9	8		11	2	10	6	1	3							18
			4	5		7	9	8		11	2	10	6	1	3							19
				5	4	7	9	8		11	2	10	6	1	3							20
			4	5		7	9	8		11	2	10	6	1	3							21
			4	5		7	9	8		11	2	10	6	1	3							22
			4	5	6	7	9	8	10	11	2			1	3							23
			4	5		7	9	8	10	11	2		6	1	3							24
			4	5		7	9	8	10	11	2		6	1	3							25
			4	5		7	9		8	11	2	10	6	1	3							26
	3	2	4	5		7	10	9	8	11			6	1								27
	3	2	5		4	7		8	10	11			6	1		9						28
	6	2	4	5		7		8	10	11				1	3	9						29
	3	2	5		4	7	9	8		11			6	1			10					30
	3		4	5	6	7	8	9		11							10	1	2			31
	3		4			7	9		10	11			6	1			8			2	5	32
	3		4			7	9		8	11			6	1			10			2	5	33
	3		4			7		8	10	11			6	1			9			2	5	34
	3		4			7		8	10	11			6	1			9			2	5	35
	3		4		8	7			10	11	2		6	1						9	5	36
	3		4			7	9	8	10	11			6	1						2	5	37
	6		4	5	8	7	9			11	2	10		1	3							38
	6		4	5		7	9			11	2	8		1	3		10					39
	6		4	5		7	9			11	2	8		1	3		10					40
	6		4	5		7	9	8		11	2	10		1	3							41
	2		4	5		7	9		10	11		8	6	1	3							42
13	31	19	42	30	20	42	37	35	29	42	17	13	22	28	17	2	8	1	1	6	6	
			1	6			26	15	19	13	10		3	1			1	5		1		

Beecham	Barrett	Rosier	Oliver	McNabb	Steele	Temple	Avey	Haley	Price	Penn	Dyer	Craig	Lawson	Mason	Bird	Allen	Hammond	Meeson	Hebden	Gibbon	Binks	
	3	2	5		4	7	9	8	10	11			6	1								1
	3	2	5		6	7	9	8	10	11			4	1								2
		2	5	9	4	7		8	10	11			6	1	3							R
	2	3	3	1	3	3	2	3	3	3			3	3	1							
					3			1	1													

Month End		Sep	Oct	Nov	Dec	Jan	Feb	Mar	Apr	Final
1928-29	Pld	8	12	15	21	25	29	35	41	**42**
	Pts	8	15	18	29	35	36	43	50	**52**
	Pos	10th	4th	6th	1st	1st	3rd	5th	5th	**5th**

1929-30

1	Aug	31	(a)	Norwich C	W 4-0	Temple 2, Haley, Avey	15,000
2	Sep	2	(h)	Bournemouth	D 3-3	Price 2, Haley	15,000
3		7	(h)	Crystal P	L 1-2	Avey	22,000
4		11	(a)	Bournemouth	L 0-5		6,000
5		14	(a)	Gillingham	W 1-0	Avey	7,000
6		16	(a)	Queen's Park R	D 0-0		14,000
7		21	(h)	Northampton T	W 1-0	Avey	20,000
8		28	(a)	Exeter C	L 1-2	Avey	5,000
9	Oct	5	(h)	Southend U	D 2-2	Temple, Craig	22,005
10		12	(a)	Luton T	L 1-4	Allen	10,000
11		19	(h)	Brentford	W 2-0	Hammond, Allen	30,000
12		26	(a)	Clapton O	W 4-2	Hammond 3, Barrett	20,000
13	Nov	2	(h)	Coventry C	W 2-0	Price, Hammond	16,000
14		9	(a)	Watford	D 0-0		12,000
15		16	(h)	Newport C	W 2-1	Penn, Avey	3,000
16		23	(a)	Torquay U	W 4-2	Price, Temple 3	6,000
17	Dec	7	(a)	Plymouth A	L 1-3	Hammond	14,000
18		21	(a)	Brighton & HA	L 0-5		4,000
19		25	(h)	Bristol R	W 6-2	Haley 3, Penn 2, Price	16,000
20		26	(a)	Bristol R	L 1-4	Allen	15,000
21		28	(h)	Norwich C	D 3-3	Haley 3	16,000
22	Jan	1	(h)	Swindon T	W 4-1	Temple 2, Haley 2	10,000
23		4	(a)	Crystal P	L 3-4	Allen, Temple, Hammond	20,000
24		18	(h)	Gillingham	W 2-1	Haley, Craig	15,000
25	Feb	1	(h)	Exeter C	D 2-2	Hammond, Penn	10,000
26		3	(h)	Merthyr T	W 5-4	Temple 2, Haley, Lawson, Penn	7,000
27		8	(a)	Southend U	W 2-1	Hammond, Temple	6,000
28		15	(h)	Luton T	D 1-1	Allen	12,000
29		22	(a)	Brentford	L 1-5	Hammond	22,033
30	Mar	1	(h)	Clapton O	D 2-2	Temple, Allen	15,000
31		8	(a)	Coventry C	L 1-3	Hammond	12,000
32		13	(a)	Northampton T	L 1-3	Murphy	6,000
33		15	(h)	Watford	W 6-1	Haley 4, Cox, Price	10,000
34		22	(a)	Newport C	D 1-1	Penn	5,000
35		29	(h)	Torquay U	W 1-0	Price	10,000
36	Apr	5	(a)	Merthyr T	W 4-3	Haley 3, Hammond	2,000
37		12	(h)	Plymouth A	L 1-3	Hammond	20,000
38		19	(a)	Swindon T	D 1-1	Avey	3,000
39		21	(h)	Walsall	W 3-2	Hammond, Price, Avey	18,000
40		22	(a)	Walsall	D 2-2	Temple, Haley	6,000
41		26	(h)	Brighton & HA	W 5-1	Haley, Hammond 3, Price	11,000
42	May	3	(h)	Queen's Park R	L 0-2		20,000

P	W	D	L	F	A	W	D	L	F	A	Pts	Pos	Div	
42	12	6	3	54	33	6	5	10	33	50	47	7th	3S	Appearances
														Goals

FA Cup

1	Nov	30	(h)	Thames A	W 4-0	Penn, Avey, Barrett 2	13,994
2	Dec	14	(a)	Leyton	W 4-1	Penn 2, Barrett, Hammond	14,000
3	Jan	11	(h)	Bournemouth	D 1-1	Penn	21,806
R		15	(a)	Bournemouth	W 2-0	Haley, Barrett	12,381
4		25	(a)	Nottingham F	L 1-2	Haley	31,250

Appearances

Goals

Football appearance and goalscoring grid for the 1929–30 season.

Beecham	Rosier	Gibbon	Oliver	Binks	Henderson	Temple	Hammond	Haley	Price	Penn	Bradley	Barrett	Bird	McNabb	Cox	Mason	Murphy	Borland	Steele	Brown	Keeble	Avey	Regan	Craig	Allen	Lawson	
1	3	2	4			7		8	10	11		6		5								9					1
1	3	2	4			7		8	10	11		6			5							9					2
1	3	2	4			7		9	10	11		6		5					8								3
1	3		4			7	10	8		11		6		5													4
1	3	2	4			7	10	8		11		6		5								9					5
1	2	3				7	10	8		11		6		5								9	4				6
1	2	3	4			7		8		11		6		5								9	10				7
1	2	3	4	9		7		8		11		6		5									10				8
1	2	3	4	5		7	8		10	11		6												9			9
1	2	3	4	5		7	8		10	11						6								9			10
1	2	3	4	5		7	8		10	11		6												9			11
1	2	3	4	5		7	8		10	11		6												9			12
1	2	3	4	5		7	8		10	11		6												9			13
1	2	3	4	5		7	8		10	11		6												9			14
1	2	3	4	5		7	8		10	11		6										9					15
1	2	3	4	5		7	8		10	11		6										9					16
1	2	3		5	4	7	8		10	11		6										9					17
1	2	3		5	4	7	10	8		11		6										9					18
1	2	3		5	4		9	8	10	11		6										7					19
1	2			5	4		8	7		11		6					3						10	9			20
1	2			5	4		8	9	10	11		6					3						7				21
1	2			3	4	7		9	10	11		6	5											8			22
1	3		4	5	6	7	10			11		2											8	9			23
1		3	4		6	7	9			11		2		5		10							8				24
1		3		4	7	8	9			11		2		5		10									6		25
1		3		4	7		8			11		2		5		10		9							6		26
1	2	3		4	7	10	8			11		6		5									9				27
1	2	3		4	7	10	8			11		6		5									9				28
1	2	3	4		7	10	9			11		6		5								8					29
1	2			4	7	10	8			11	3	5	6									9					30
	2	3		4	7	9	8					5	6	1	10	11											31
	2			7	9				3			5	4	1	10	11	6	8									32
1	2		4	7	8	9	10	11			3	5	6														33
1	2	3	4		6	7	8	9	10	11		5															34
1	2	3	4	5	6	7	8	9	10	11																	35
1	2	3	4	5	6	7	8	9	10	11																	36
1		3	4	5		7	8	9	10	11	2	6															37
			4			7	8		10	6	2	3		5		1		11				9					38
			4			7	8		10	6	2	3		5		1		11				9					39
			8	5	4	7		9	10		2	3				1		11							6		40
			4	5		7	8	9	10		2	3				1		11							6		41
			4	5		7	10	8		11	2	3				1						9			6		42
35	33	29	28	21	18	39	31	30	25	38	6	34	3	22	5	7	5	6	4	2	1	14	1	7	12	5	
						14	17	21	9	6		1				1		2				8		2	6	1	

Beecham	Rosier	Gibbon	Oliver	Binks	Henderson	Temple	Hammond	Haley	Price	Penn	Bradley	Barrett	Bird	McNabb	Cox	Mason	Murphy	Borland	Steele	Brown	Keeble	Avey	Regan	Craig	Allen	Lawson	
1	2	3		5	4	7	8		10	11		6										9					1
1	2	3		5	4	7	8		10	11		6										9					2
1		2	4		6	7	10	9	8	11		3		5													3
1		2	4		6	7	10	9	8	11		3		9													R
1		2	4		6	7	10	9		11		3		5				8							6		4
5	2	5	3	2	5	5	5	3	4	5		5	3				1					2					
						1	2	1	3			4										1					

Month End		Sep	Oct	Nov	Dec	Jan	Feb	Mar	Apr	Final
1929-30	**Pld**	8	12	16	21	24	29	35	41	**42**
	Pts	8	13	20	23	27	33	39	47	**47**
	Pos	10th	10th	6th	9th	9th	8th	8th	6th	**7th**

1930-31

1	Aug	30	(h)	Watford	W	3-2	Penn, Haley, Allen		15,000
2	Sep	1	(h)	Coventry C	D	0-0			10,000
3		6	(a)	Notts C	L	1-6	Penn		10,000
4		8	(h)	Brentford	D	1-1	Haley		14,000
5		13	(h)	Clapton O	W	2-0	Hammond, Temple		10,000
6		17	(a)	Brentford	L	1-4	Opp own goal		15,000
7		20	(a)	Thames	D	0-0			7,000
8		27	(h)	Norwich C	W	1-0	Penn		18,000
9	Oct	4	(a)	Queen's Park R	W	2-0	Hammond, Avey		15,000
10		11	(h)	Walsall	W	5-2	Temple 2, Hammond, Avey, Penn		18,000
11		18	(a)	Crystal P	L	2-5	Temple, Barrett		27,000
12		25	(h)	Southend U	W	1-0	Barrett		8,000
13	Nov	1	(a)	Luton T	L	0-5			8,000
14		8	(h)	Bristol R	W	6-2	Avey 3, Price, Thompson, Temple		15,000
15		15	(a)	Newport C	W	3-1	Penn, Price, Hammond		5,000
16		22	(h)	Gillingham	D	1-1	Thompson		10,000
17	Dec	6	(h)	Brighton & HA	L	0-1			10,000
18		17	(a)	Torquay U	L	1-3	Hammond		4,000
19		20	(h)	Northampton T	W	4-2	Hammond 2, Watkins 2		12,000
20		25	(a)	Swindon T	L	1-4	Barrett		12,000
21		26	(h)	Swindon T	W	6-1	Watkins 2, Finch, Hammond, Temple, Haley		8,000
22		27	(a)	Watford	D	2-2	Haley, Dowden		7,000
23	Jan	3	(h)	Notts C	W	3-1	Watkins, Temple 2		12,000
24		14	(a)	Exeter C	L	2-3	Watkins, opp own goal		4,000
25		17	(a)	Clapton O	L	0-2			8,000
26		24	(h)	Thames	W	4-2	Hammond 3, Price		10,000
27		31	(a)	Norwich C	D	1-1	Hammond		10,000
28	Feb	7	(h)	Queen's Park R	L	0-2			22,000
29		14	(a)	Walsall	L	0-2			6,000
30		21	(h)	Crystal P	W	2-0	Haley, opp own goal		20,000
31		28	(a)	Southend U	W	4-2	Proud, Haley, Penn, Oliver		7,000
32	Mar	7	(h)	Luton T	W	2-1	Watkins 2		6,000
33		14	(a)	Bristol R	L	1-2	Barrett		8,000
34		21	(h)	Newport C	L	0-1			21,000
35		28	(a)	Gillingham	L	2-3	Haley 2		5,000
36	Apr	3	(h)	Bournemouth	W	1-0	Hammond		10,000
37		4	(h)	Exeter C	W	4-2	Haley 2, Barrett, Temple		15,000
38		6	(a)	Bournemouth	L	1-2	Murphy		4,000
39		11	(a)	Brighton & HA	D	1-1	Hammond		8,000
40		18	(h)	Torquay U	W	3-0	Watkins 2, Webb		8,000
41		25	(a)	Northampton T	L	2-4	Price 2		3,000
42	May	2	(a)	Coventry C	L	1-2	Price		6,000

P	W	D	L	F	A	W	D	L	F	A	Pts	Pos	Div	
42	15	3	3	49	21	3	4	14	28	54	43	9th	3S	Appearances
														Goals

FA Cup

1	Nov	30	(h)	Wimbledon	D	1-1	Price	13,305
R	Dec	3	(a)	Wimbledon	W	6-0	Penn 2, Gibbons 2, Watkins, Hammond	12,146
2		13	(h)	Halifax T	W	4-0	Haley 2, Watkins, Hammond	18,000
3	Jan	10	(h)	Portsmouth	L	0-2		27,516

Appearances

Goals

Football appearances and goals grid, season 1930-31.

Iceton	Gibbon	Lilley	Oliver	Gibbons	Barrett	Temple	Haley	Allen	Price	Penn	Beecham	Hammond	Murphy	Griffiths	Watkins	Reid	Dudley	Avey	Thompson	Baillie	Finch	Bird	Dowden	Proud	Kelly	Webb	No
1	2	3	4	5	6	7	8	9	10	11																	1
1	2	3	4	5	6	7	8	9	10	11																	2
	2	3	4	5	6	7	8			11	1	9	10														3
1	2	3	4	5	6	7	8		10	11		9															4
1	2	3	4	5	6	7			10	11		8		9													5
1	2	3	4	5	6	7				11		10		9	8												6
1	2		4		6	7				11		10			8	3	5	9									7
	2		4		6	7			10	11	1				8	3	5	9									8
1	2		4		6	7			10	11					8	3	5	9									9
1	2		4		6	7			10	11					8	3	5	9									10
1	2		4		6	7			10	11					8	3	5	9									11
1	2		4		6	7	9		10	11					8	3	5										12
1	2		4		6	7			10	11					8	3	5		9								13
1	2				3	7			10	6		8					5	11	9	4							14
1	2		4		3	7			10	6		8					5	11	9								15
1	2		4		3	7	8		10	6							5	11	9								16
1	2	3	4	10	6					11		8			9		5				7						17
1	2		4	5	6	7	8			11		10			9							3					18
1	2		4	5	6	7	8			11		10			9							3					19
	2		4	5	6	7	8				1	10			9						11	3					20
	2		4	5	6	7	8				1	10			9						11	3					21
	2		4	5	6	7	8				1	10									11	3	9				22
1	2		4	5	6	7	8					10			9						11	3					23
1	2		4	5	6	7			10			8			9						11	3					24
1	2		4	5	6		8					10			9						11	3		7			25
1	2		4	5	6		8		10			9			7						11	3					26
1	2		4	5	6	7	8		10			9									11	3					27
1	2		4	5	6	7	8		10			9									11	3					28
1	2		4	5	6	7			10			9			3						11					8	29
1	2		4	5	6		8			11		10			9							3		7			30
1	2		4	5	6		8			11		10						9				3		7			31
1	2		4	5	6		8			11		10			9							3		7			32
1	2		4	5	6	7	8			11		10			9							3					33
1	2		4	5	6	7	8			11		10			9							3					34
1	2			5	6	7	9		10			8								4	11	3					35
1	2		4	5	6	7	9		10			8									11	3					36
1	2		4	5	6	7	9		10			8									11	3					37
1	2		4	5	6		9			11		10	8								7	3					38
1	2		4	5	6		9			11		10	8								7	3					39
1	2		4	5		3		8				11	10				9				7					6	40
1	2		4	5	6		9		10	11											8	3		7		6	41
	2		4	5	3	7			10	11	1				8		9									6	42
36	42	7	40	32	42	33	28	2	19	30	6	36	8	2	17	7	11	9	4	2	18	22	1	5	1	2	
		1			5	9	10	1	6	6		14	1		10		5	2			1		1	1		1	

Iceton	Gibbon	Lilley	Oliver	Gibbons	Barrett	Temple	Haley	Allen	Price	Penn	Beecham	Hammond	Murphy	Griffiths	Watkins	Reid	Dudley	Avey	Thompson	Baillie	Finch	Bird	Dowden	Proud	Kelly	Webb	No
1	2		4		3	7			10	6		8					5	11	9								1
1	2	3	4	10	6	7				11		8					9	5									R
1	2		4	5	6	7	8			11		10			9							3					2
1	2		4	5	6	7	8					10			9						11	3					3
4	4	1	4	3	4	4	2		1	3		4			3		2	2	1			2					
				2			2		1	2		2			2			2									

Month End		Sep	Oct	Nov	Dec	Jan	Feb	Mar	Apr	Final
1930-31	Pld	8	12	16	22	27	31	35	41	42
	Pts	9	15	20	25	30	34	36	43	43
	Pos	10th	6th	7th	7th	7th	7th	11th	8th	9th

281

1931-32

1	Aug	29	(h)	Coventry C	W	5-3	Newton 2, Barrett, Hammond 2	20,000
2	Sep	2	(a)	Exeter C	W	3-0	Newton 3	7,000
3		5	(a)	Gillingham	L	1-2	Richards	5,000
4		7	(h)	Torquay U	W	10-2	Hammond 4, Newton 2, Price 2, Finch, Proud	8,000
5		12	(h)	Luton T	W	3-2	Hammond, Newton, Proud	10,000
6		16	(a)	Torquay U	W	3-2	Hammond, Newton, Finch	5,000
7		19	(a)	Cardiff C	W	3-0	Hammond 2, Newton	15,000
8		26	(h)	Northampton T	L	1-3	Newton	18,000
9	Oct	3	(a)	Reading	L	2-4	Newton 2	11,000
10		10	(h)	Southend U	D	1-1	Barrett	25,000
11		17	(h)	Clapton O	W	5-1	Hammond 2, Price, Newton, Barrett	18,000
12		24	(a)	Swindon T	D	2-2	Newton, Price	5,000
13		31	(h)	Norwich C	W	4-0	Hammond, Finch, Newton, Richards	17,000
14	Nov	7	(a)	Brighton & HA	W	3-2	Hammond, Newton 2	8,000
15		14	(h)	Mansfield T	W	2-1	Finch, Barrett	15,000
16		21	(a)	Watford	L	1-3	Newton	14,000
17	Dec	5	(a)	Bournemouth	W	3-0	Finch, Newton 2	5,000
18		19	(a)	Bristol R	W	2-2	Hammond 2	5,000
19		25	(a)	Brentford	D	0-0		26,731
20		26	(h)	Brentford	W	2-1	Richards, Perry	25,000
21		28	(h)	Queen's Park R	L	1-3	Newton	23,173
22	Jan	2	(a)	Coventry C	D	5-5	Newton 3, Hammond, Finch	8,000
23		16	(h)	Gillingham	L	0-2		15,000
24		18	(h)	Crystal P	W	4-0	Hammond, Newton 2, Richards	8,616
25		23	(a)	Luton T	W	3-1	Newton 3	6,000
26		30	(h)	Cardiff C	W	4-0	Hammond, Newton 2, Richards	15,000
27	Feb	6	(a)	Northampton T	W	1-0	Newton	6,000
28		13	(h)	Reading	D	3-3	Hammond 2, opp own goal	16,000
29		20	(a)	Southend U	L	1-4	Hammond	7,000
30		27	(a)	Clapton O	W	1-0	Newton	15,000
31	Mar	5	(h)	Swindon T	D	2-2	Newton, Wood	15,000
32		12	(a)	Norwich C	D	2-2	Finch, Peters	15,000
33		19	(h)	Brighton & HA	W	3-0	Finch, Hammond, Wrightson	20,000
34		25	(a)	Thames	D	0-0		5,000
35		26	(a)	Mansfield T	W	2-1	Wrightson, Richards	7,000
36		28	(h)	Thames	W	8-0	Hammond 3, Richards 2, Finch, Newton 2	20,000
37	Apr	2	(h)	Watford	W	5-0	Finch, Newton 2, Hammond 2	20,000
38		9	(a)	Crystal P	L	0-2		27,000
39		16	(h)	Bournemouth	W	3-0	Wrightson, Newton 2	15,000
40		23	(a)	Queen's Park R	L	1-3	Hammond	21,527
41		30	(h)	Bristol R	W	3-2	Finch, Barrett, Hammond	21,000
42	May	7	(h)	Exeter C	W	3-1	Hammond, Newton 2	16,000

P	W	D	L	F	A	W	D	L	F	A	Pts	Pos	Div		Appearances
42	15	3	3	72	27	9	6	6	39	35	57	1st	3S		Goals

FA Cup

1	Nov	28	(h)	Guildford	W	2-0	Hammond 2	12,000
2	Dec	5	(h)	Yeovil	D	0-0		15,146
R		17	(a)	Yeovil	W	5-2	Newton 3, Price, Richards	8,004
3	Jan	9	(a)	Watford	D	1-1	Newton	15,978
R		14	(h)	Watford	L	0-3		23,113

Appearances

Goals

Appearances 1931–32

Beecham	Gibbon	Hickie	Oliver	Gibbons	Barrett	Richards	Hammond	Newton	Price	Penn	Proud	Finch	Iceton	Birch	Webb	Bird	Dudley	Perry	Hindson	Molloy	Tilford	Wrightson	Wood	Peters	Keen	No.
1	2	3		5	6	7	8	9	10	11					4											1
1	2	3		5	6	7	8	9	10	11					4											2
1	2	3		5	6	7	8	9	10	11					4											3
1	2	3	4	5	6		8	9	10		7	11														4
1	2	3	4	5	6		8	9	10		7	11														5
1	2	3	4	5	6		8	9	10		7	11														6
1	2	3	4	5	6		8	9	10		7	11														7
1	2	3	4	5	6		8	9	10		7	11														8
1	2	3	4	5	6		8	9	10		7	11														9
	2		4	5	6		8	9	10		7	11	1	3												10
	2		4	5	6	7	8	9	10			11	1	3												11
	2		4	5	6	7	8	9	10			11	1	3												12
	2		4	5	6	7	8	9	10			11	1	3												13
	2		4	5	6	7	8	9	10			11	1	3												14
	2		4	5	6	7	8	9	10			11	1	3												15
	2		4	5	6	7	8	9	10			11	1		3											16
	2		4	5	6	7	8	9	10			11	1	3												17
	2			5		7	8	9	10	6		11	1	3			4									18
	2		4	5		7	8		10	6		11	1	3				9								19
	2		4	5		7	8		10	6		11	1	3				9								20
	2		4	5		7	8	9	10	6		11	1	3												21
	2		4	5		7	8	9	10	6		11	1	3												22
			4	5			8	9	10	11		7	1	3					6	2						23
			4	5		7	8	9	10			11	1	3					6	2						24
			4	5		7	8	9	10			11	1	3					6	2						25
			4	5		7	8	9	10			11	1	3					6	2						26
			4	5		7	8	9	10			11	1	3					6	2						27
			4	5		7	8	9	10			11	1	3					6	2						28
			4	5	6	7	8	9	10			11	1	2							3					29
			4	5	6	7	8	9	10			11	1	2							3					30
			4	5	6	7	8	9				11	1	2							3	10				31
			4	5	6		8		10			11	1	2				9			3			7		32
			4	5	6	7	8	9				11	1	2							3	8				33
			4	5	6	7	8	9				11	1	2							3	8				34
			4	5		7	8	9	10			11	1	2		6					3	8				35
			4	5	6	7	8	9	10			11	1	2							3	8				36
			4	5	6	7	8	9	10			11	1	2							3	8				37
			4	5	6	7	8	9	10			11	1	2							3	8				38
			4	5	6	7	8	9	10			11	1	2							3	8				39
			4	5	6	7	8	9	10			11	1	2							3	8				40
			4	5	6	7	8	9	10			11	1	2							3	8				41
			4	5	6	7	8	9	10			11	1	2							3	8				42
9	22	9	39	42	30	33	42	39	31	9	7	39	33	32	3	1	3	3	6	4	14	10	1	1		
							5	8	31	43	4		2	11						1		3	1	1		

Cup appearances

Beecham	Gibbon	Hickie	Oliver	Gibbons	Barrett	Richards	Hammond	Newton	Price	Penn	Proud	Finch	Iceton	Birch	Webb	Bird	Dudley	Perry	Hindson	Molloy	Tilford	Wrightson	Wood	Peters	Keen	
	2		4	5	6	7	8	9	10			11	1	3												1
	2			5	6	7	8	9	10			11	1	3								4				2
	2		4	5		7	8	9	10	6		11	1	3												R
	2		4	5	6	7	8	9	10			11	1	3												3
			4	5		7	8	9	10	6		11	1	3					2							R
	4		4	5	3	5	5	5	5	2		5	5	5	1				1			1				
								1	2	4	1															

Month End		Sep	Oct	Nov	Dec	Jan	Feb	Mar	Apr	Final
1931-32	Pld	8	13	16	21	26	30	36	41	**42**
	Pts	12	18	22	28	35	40	49	55	**57**
	Pos	3rd	3rd	3rd	2nd	2nd	1st	1st	1st	**1st**

283

1932-33

					Result	Scorers	Attendance
1	Aug	27	(a)	Bradford C	L 0-2		17,000
2	Sep	3	(h)	Swansea T	W 3-1	Haddleton 2, Hammond	17,000
3		5	(h)	Chesterfield	D 2-2	Finch, Gibbons	10,000
4		10	(a)	Notts C	W 2-1	Haddleton 2	12,000
5		17	(h)	Port Vale	D 1-1	Price	22,000
6		24	(a)	Millwall	L 1-2	Newton	28,000
7	Oct	1	(h)	Southampton	W 4-2	Newton 2, Hammond, Richards	15,000
8		8	(a)	Bury	D 1-1	Price	5,000
9		15	(h)	Lincoln C	W 3-2	Price, Newton 2	25,000
10		22	(a)	Burnley	D 3-3	Newton 2, Gibbons	5,000
11		29	(h)	Bradford	W 5-2	Newton 2, Richards, Price, Finch	18,000
12	Nov	5	(a)	Plymouth A	W 3-2	Newton 2, Finch	20,000
13		12	(h)	Oldham A	W 1-0	Newton	20,000
14		19	(a)	Manchester U	L 3-4	Price, Richards, Newton	35,000
15		26	(h)	Stoke C	L 1-3	Newton	30,000
16	Dec	3	(a)	Charlton A	W 2-1	Newton, Hammond	25,000
17		10	(h)	Tottenham H	D 2-2	Richards, Newton	43,407
18		17	(a)	Grimsby T	L 0-1		8,000
19		24	(h)	Nottingham F	L 0-1		22,000
20		26	(h)	West Ham U	W 4-2	Hammond 2, Wrightson, Barrett	30,000
21		27	(a)	West Ham U	D 1-1	Richards	40,000
22		31	(h)	Bradford C	W 1-0	Hammond	25,000
23	Jan	2	(a)	Chesterfield	L 2-3	Gibbons, Wrightson	10,376
24		7	(a)	Swansea T	L 0-3		8,000
25		21	(h)	Notts C	L 3-4	Hammond, Newton 2	15,000
26		28	(a)	Port Vale	W 2-1	Newton, Finch	5,000
27	Feb	4	(h)	Millwall	D 1-1	Newton	18,000
28		11	(a)	Southampton	D 2-2	Richards, Newton	9,000
29		18	(h)	Bury	D 3-3	Arnold, Barrett, Perry	22,000
30	Mar	8	(h)	Burnley	W 2-1	Wood, opp own goal	10,000
31		11	(a)	Bradford	W 4-1	Newton 2, Hammond, Arnold	12,000
32		18	(h)	Plymouth A	W 3-1	Arnold, Newton 2	25,000
33		25	(a)	Oldham A	W 3-1	Arnold 2, Hammond	12,000
34	Apr	1	(h)	Manchester U	W 3-1	Newton, Finch, Hammond	30,000
35		5	(a)	Lincoln C	L 0-3		6,000
36		8	(a)	Stoke C	W 1-0	Price	22,000
37		14	(h)	Preston NE	W 1-0	Arnold	28,000
38		15	(h)	Charlton A	W 3-1	Wood 2, Newton	20,000
39		17	(a)	Preston NE	W 2-1	Finch, Rounce	15,000
40		22	(a)	Tottenham H	D 0-0		46,750
41		29	(h)	Grimsby T	L 0-1		17,000
42	May	6	(a)	Nottingham F	L 0-1		4,000

P	W	D	L	F	A	W	D	L	F	A	Pts	Pos	Div	
42	12	5	4	46	31	8	5	8	32	34	50	3rd	2	Appearances
														Goals

FA Cup

					Result		Attendance
3	Jan	14	(a)	Chester	L 0-5		14,328
							Appearances
							Goals

284

Iceton	Birch	Tilford	Oliver	Gibbons	Barrett	Richards	Wrightson	Newton	Hammond	Finch	Haddleton	Price	Tootill	Webb	Gibbon	Hindson	Keeping	Perry	Arnold	Wood	Rounce	#
1	2	3	4	5	6	7	8	9	10	11												1
1	2	3	4	5	6	7			8	11	9	10										2
1	2	3	4	5	6	7			8	11	9	10										3
1	2	3	4	5	6	7			8	11	9	10										4
1	2	3	4	5	6	7			8	11	9	10										5
1	2	3	4	5	6	7		9	8	11		10										6
1	2	3	4	5	6	7		9	8	11		10										7
1	2	3	4	5	6	7		9	8	11		10										8
1	2	3	4	5	6	7		9	8	11		10										9
1	2	3	4	5	6	7		9	8	11		10										10
1	2	3	4	5	6	7		9	8	11		10										11
1	2	3	4	5	6	7		9	8	11		10										12
1	2	3	4	5	6	7		9	8	11		10										13
1	2	3	4	5	6	7		9	8	11		10										14
1	2	3	4	5	6	7	10	9	8	11												15
	2	3	4	5	6	7	8	9	10	11			1									16
	2	3	4	5	6	7		9	8	11		10	1									17
	2	3	4	5	6	7		9	8	11		10	1									18
	2	3	4	5	6	7		9	8	11		10	1									19
	2	3	4	5	6	7	9		8	11		10	1									20
	2	3	4	5	6	7	9		8	11		10	1									21
	2	3	4	5	6	7	9		8	11		10	1									22
	2		4	5	6	7	9		8	11		10	1	3								23
	2		4	5	6	7	9		8	11		10	1	3								24
	3		4	5	6	7		9	8	11		10	1		2							25
1	2		4	5	6	7		9	8	11		10					3					26
1	2		4	5	6	7		9	8	11		10					3					27
1	2		4	5	6	7		9	8	11		10					3					28
1	2		4	5	6				8	7		10					3	9	11			29
	2		4	5	6			9	8	7			1				3		11	10		30
	2		4	5	6			9	8	7			1				3		11	10		31
	2		4	5				9	8	7			1				3		11	6	10	32
	2		4	5	6			9	8	7			1			3			11	10		33
	2		4	5	6			9	8	7			1			3			11	10		34
	2		4	5	6			9		7		10	1			3			11		8	35
			4	5	6			9		7		10	1			2	3		11		8	36
			4	5	6			9		7		10	1			2	3		11		8	37
			4	5	6			9		7		10	1			2	3		11		8	38
			4	5	6			9	8	7			1			2	3		11	10		39
			4	5	6				8	7			1			2	3		11	9	10	40
			4	5	6			9	8	7			1			2	3		11	10		41
			4	5	6			9	8	7			1			2	3		11		10	42
19	35	22	42	42	41	29	8	31	38	42	4	30	23	2	1	10	14	1	13	8	7	
				3	2	6	2	27	10	6	4	6						1	6	3	1	

Iceton	Birch	Tilford	Oliver	Gibbons	Barrett	Richards	Wrightson	Newton	Hammond	Finch	Haddleton	Price	Tootill	Webb	Gibbon	Hindson	Keeping	Perry	Arnold	Wood	Rounce	#
	2	3	4	5	6	7	9		8	11		10	1									3
	1	1	1	1	1	1	1		1	1		1	1									

Month End		Sep	Oct	Nov	Dec	Jan	Feb	Mar	Apr	Final
1932-33	Pld	6	11	15	22	26	29	33	41	42
	Pts	6	14	18	26	28	31	39	50	50
	Pos	11th	7th	9th	6th	10th	10th	5th	3rd	3rd

1933-34

1	Aug	26	(h)	Port Vale	W	3-0	Finch, Newton 2	24,000
2		28	(h)	Blackpool	W	1-0	Price	15,000
3	Sep	2	(a)	Notts C	L	1-4	Arnold	17,000
4		4	(a)	Blackpool	L	3-4	Abel, Hammond, opp own goal	25,000
5		9	(h)	Swansea T	W	1-0	Arnold	20,000
6		16	(a)	Millwall	W	1-0	Hammond	35,000
7		23	(h)	Lincoln C	W	1-0	Price	15,000
8		30	(a)	Bury	D	3-3	Price, Hammond 2	8,000
9	Oct	7	(h)	Hull C	D	1-1	Finch	25,000
10		14	(a)	Burnley	L	1-2	Arnold	8,000
11		21	(h)	Brentford	D	1-1	Lambert	36,000
12		28	(a)	Bolton W	L	1-3	Lambert	15,000
13	Nov	4	(h)	Manchester U	L	0-2		20,000
14		11	(a)	Plymouth A	L	0-4		20,000
15		18	(h)	West Ham U	W	3-1	Price, Arnold, Hammond	18,000
16		25	(a)	Nottingham F	L	0-2		10,000
17	Dec	2	(h)	Grimsby T	W	1-0	Finch	14,000
18		9	(a)	Bradford	L	1-3	Finch	8,000
19		16	(h)	Preston NE	W	1-0	Wood	12,000
20		23	(a)	Oldham A	D	2-2	Wood, Hammond	5,000
21		25	(h)	Southampton	W	1-0	Lambert	18,000
22		26	(a)	Southampton	L	0-2		25,000
23		30	(a)	Port Vale	D	2-2	Hammond 2	7,000
24	Jan	6	(h)	Notts C	W	3-0	Wood 2, Finch	10,000
25		20	(a)	Swansea T	L	0-1		10,000
26		29	(h)	Millwall	W	2-0	Gibbons, Hammond	6,000
27	Feb	3	(a)	Lincoln C	L	0-5		7,000
28		10	(h)	Bury	W	2-1	Hammond, Barrett	22,000
29		17	(a)	Hull C	D	0-0		7,000
30		24	(h)	Burnley	D	1-1	Arnold	18,000
31	Mar	3	(a)	Brentford	W	2-1	Gibbons 2	29,000
32		10	(h)	Bolton W	L	0-2		18,983
33		17	(a)	Manchester U	L	0-1		15,000
34		24	(h)	Plymouth A	W	3-2	Hammond 2, Arnold	12,642
35		30	(h)	Bradford C	L	0-1		24,000
36		31	(a)	West Ham U	L	1-5	Finch	26,000
37	Apr	2	(a)	Bradford C	L	0-1		12,000
38		7	(h)	Nottingham F	W	3-1	Hammond 2, Lambert	10,000
39		14	(a)	Grimsby T	L	1-3	Hammond	12,000
40		21	(h)	Bradford	L	0-2		14,000
41		28	(a)	Preston NE	L	0-2		12,000
42	May	5	(h)	Oldham A	L	1-2	Finch	10,000

P	W	D	L	F	A	W	D	L	F	A	Pts	Pos	Div		Appearances
42	13	3	5	29	17	2	4	15	19	50	37	16th	2		Goals

FA Cup

3	Jan	13	(a)	Liverpool	D	1-1	Lambert	45,619
R		17	(h)	Liverpool	L	2-3	Hammond, Arnold	28,000

Appearances
Goals

Football appearances and goals grid — Season 1933-34

#	Tootill	Hindson	Keeping	Oliver	Gibbons	Barrett	Richards	Hammond	Newton	Price	Finch	Arnold	Tilford	Abel	Tompkins	Birch	Lambert	Rounce	Wood	Diaper	Iceton	Gibbon	Perry	Murray	Penn	Joy
1	1	2	3	4	5	6	7	8	9	10	11															
2	1	2	3	4	5	6	7	8	9	10	11															
3	1	2	3	4	5	6		8	9	10	7	11														
4	1	2		4	5	6		8		10	7	11	3	9												
5	1		3	4		6		8		10	7	11		9	5	2										
6	1		3	4	5	6		8	9	10	7	11				2										
7	1		3	4	5	6		8		10	7	11		9		2										
8	1		3	4	5	6		8		10	7	11		9		2										
9	1		3	4	5	6		8		10	7	11		9		2										
10	1		3	4	5	6		8		10	7	11				2	9									
11	1		3	4	5	6		8		10	7	11				2	9									
12	1		3	4	5	6		8			7	11				2	9	10								
13	1		3	4	5	6		8		10	7	11				2	9									
14	1		3	4	5	6	7	8		10		11				2	9									
15	1		3	4	5	6		8		10	7	11				2	9									
16	1		3	4	5	6		8		10	7	11				2	9									
17	1		3	4	5	6		8			7	11				2	9	10								
18	1		3	4	5	3		8		6	7	11				2	9	10								
19	1			4	5	6				10	7	11	3			2	9		8							
20	1				5	6				10	7	11	3			2	9		8	4						
21	1			4	5	6	7			10		11	3			2	9		8							
22	1			4		6	7			10		11	3		5	2	9		8							
23		3		4		6				10	11			7	5	2	9		8	1						
24	1	3		4	5	6				10	7	11				2	9		8							
25	1	3		4	5	6				10	11			7		2	9		8							
26	1	3		4	5	6				10	7	11				2	9		8							
27	1		3	4	5	6				10	7	11				2	9		8							
28	1	3		4	9	6				10	7	11		8	5	2										
29	1			4	5	6		8		10	7	11				3	9					2				
30	1			4	5	6		8		10	7	11				3	9					2				
31	1			4	5	6		8		10	7	11				3						2	9			
32	1	3		4	5	6		8			11			7				10				2	9			
33	1	3		4	5	6		8			7	11					9	10				2				
34	1	3		4	5	6	7	8		10		11					9					2				
35	1	3		4	5		7	8		10		11					9					2		6		
36	1	3		4			7	8		10	11				5		9					2			6	
37		3			5	6	7	8									9	10		4	1	2				
38	1	3		4	5	6	7			10	9	11					8					2				
39	1	3		4	5	6	7			10	9	11					8					2				
40	1	3		4	5	6	7			10	9	11					8					2				
41	1	3		4	5	10	7				9	11					8				6	2				
42	1	3		4	5	10	7	8			11											2	9			6
App	40	20	17	40	38	40	14	41	4	26	36	31	5	9	5	31	26	5	9	3	2	14	3	1	1	1
Gls			3	1						15	2	4	7	6		1	4		4							

FA Cup

Tootill	Hindson	Keeping	Oliver	Gibbons	Barrett	Richards	Hammond	Newton	Price	Finch	Arnold	Tilford	Abel	Tompkins	Birch	Lambert	Rounce	Wood	Diaper	Iceton	Gibbon	Perry	Murray	Penn	Joy	#
1		3	4	5	6				10		7	11				2	9		8								3
1	3		4	5	6				10		7	11				2	9		8								3
2	1	1	2	2	2				2		2	2				2	2		2								
									1		1					1										

Month End		Sep	Oct	Nov	Dec	Jan	Feb	Mar	Apr	Final
1933-34	Pld	8	12	16	23	26	30	36	41	42
	Pts	11	13	15	23	27	31	35	37	37
	Pos	3rd	10th	17th	12th	9th	10th	14th	16th	16th

287

1934-35

1	Aug	25	(h)	Plymouth A	W	3-0	Hammond 3	20,000
2		27	(h)	Brentford	D	2-2	Hammond, Gibbons	30,000
3	Sep	1	(a)	Norwich C	D	0-0		22,000
4		5	(a)	Brentford	L	0-1		25,000
5		8	(h)	Newcastle U	W	3-2	Finch, Hammond 2	22,000
6		15	(a)	West Ham U	L	1-2	Hammond	35,000
7		22	(h)	Blackpool	W	4-1	Hammond, Price, Clarke, Finch	10,000
8		29	(a)	Bury	L	0-2		5,000
9	Oct	6	(h)	Hull C	W	4-0	Gibbons, Hammond, opp own goal 2	20,000
10		13	(a)	Nottingham F	D	1-1	Price	14,000
11		20	(h)	Bradford C	W	3-1	Price, Arnold, Newton	21,000
12		27	(a)	Notts C	D	1-1	Newton	14,000
13	Nov	3	(h)	Southampton	D	3-3	Gibbons 3	18,000
14		10	(a)	Bolton W	L	0-4		20,000
15		17	(h)	Oldham A	W	3-1	Newton, Arnold 2	15,000
16		25	(a)	Burnley	L	1-3	Arnold	11,000
17	Dec	1	(h)	Swansea T	W	4-1	Newton 2, Hammond, Price	17,000
18		8	(a)	Manchester U	L	0-1		30,000
19		15	(h)	Port Vale	W	2-0	Finch, Arnold	10,000
20		22	(a)	Barnsley	L	0-2		3,000
21		25	(a)	Bradford	D	0-0		12,000
22		26	(h)	Bradford	D	2-2	Wood, Arnold	28,000
23		29	(a)	Plymouth A	L	1-3	Hammond	18,188
24	Jan	5	(h)	Norwich C	L	1-3	Hammond	15,000
25		19	(a)	Newcastle U	D	1-1	Perry	30,000
26		26	(h)	West Ham U	W	3-0	Finch, Perry 2	28,000
27	Feb	2	(a)	Blackpool	D	1-1	Hammond	10,000
28		9	(h)	Bury	L	1-2	Perry	15,000
29		16	(a)	Hull C	W	2-1	Finch 2	4,000
30		23	(h)	Nottingham F	W	2-1	Perry 2	16,000
31	Mar	2	(a)	Bradford C	D	0-0		8,000
32		9	(h)	Notts C	W	7-0	Perry 3, Arnold 2, Finch, Hammond	10,000
33		16	(a)	Southampton	D	1-1	Hammond	8,000
34		23	(h)	Bolton W	W	2-1	Hammond, Perry	23,000
35		30	(a)	Oldham A	L	1-2	Perry	5,000
36	Apr	6	(h)	Burnley	W	2-0	Smith, Hammond	15,000
37		13	(a)	Swansea T	L	0-2		7,000
38		19	(h)	Sheffield U	W	7-2	Hammond 4, Perry 2, Finch	14,000
39		20	(h)	Manchester U	W	3-1	Perry, Warburton, Hammond	10,000
40		22	(a)	Sheffield U	W	2-1	Warburton, opp own goal	15,000
41		27	(a)	Port Vale	D	1-1	Warburton	4,000
42	May	4	(h)	Barnsley	L	1-3	Perry	10,000

P	W	D	L	F	A	W	D	L	F	A	Pts	Pos	Div		Appearances
42	15	3	3	62	26	2	9	10	14	30	46	7th	2		Goals

FA Cup

3	Jan	12	(a)	Sunderland	L	2-3	Finch, Arnold	40,100

Appearances

Goals

Player appearance & goalscoring grid (shirt numbers by match). Columns left-to-right: Tootill, Birch, Keeping, Oliver, Gibbons, Barrett, Clarke, Lambert, Hammond, Price, Finch, Hiles, Arnold, Newton, Hindson, Perry, Fabian, Wood, Warburton, Smith, Allen, Buckley, Tompkins, Mayes.

Too	Bir	Kee	Oli	Gib	Bar	Cla	Lam	Ham	Pri	Fin	Hil	Arn	New	Hin	Per	Fab	Woo	War	Smi	All	Buc	Tom	May	#
1	2	3	4	5	6	7	8	9	10	11														1
1	2	3	4	5	6	7	8	9	10	11														2
1	2	3	4	5	6	7	8	9	10	11														3
1	2	3	4	5	6	7		8	10		9	11												4
1	2	3	4	5	6		8	9	10	7		11												5
1	2	3	4	5	6		8	9	10	7		11												6
1	2	3	4	5	6		8	9	10	7		11												7
1	2	3	4	5	6		8	9	10	7		11												8
1	2	3		5	6	4	7	8	10			11	9											9
1	2			5	6	4		8	10	7		11	9	3										10
1	2			5	6	4		8	10	7		11	9	3										11
1	2			5	6	4		8	10	7		11	9	3										12
1	2			5	6	4		8	10	7		11	9	3										13
1	2			5	6	4		8	10	7		11	9	3										14
1	2	3		5	6	4		8	10	7		11	9											15
1	2	3		5	6	4	8	10		7		11	9											16
1	2	3		5	6	4		8	10	7		11	9											17
1	2			5	6	4		8	10	7		11		3	9									18
1	2			5	6	4	9	8	10	7		11		3										19
1	2	3		5	6	4	9	8	10	7		11												20
1	2	3		5	6	4	8	9	10			11					7							21
1	2			5	6	4		9	10	7		11		3			8							22
1	2	3	4	5	6		8	9	10			11					7							23
1	2			5	6	4	8	7	10			11		3			9							24
1		3	4	5	6	7	8		10			11	2	9										25
1		3	4	5	6	7	8		10			11	2	9										26
1		3	4	5	6		8		10			11	2	9										27
1		3	4	5	6		8		10			11	2	9	7									28
1		3		5	6	4	8		10			11	2	9					7					29
1		3		5	6	4	8		10			11	2	9					7					30
1		3		5	6	4	8		10			11	2	9					7					31
1		3		5	6	4	8		10			11	2	9					7					32
1	2			5	6	4	8		10			11	3	9					7					33
1		3		5	6	4	8		10			11	3	9				7						34
1	2			5	6	4	8		10			11	3	9				7						35
1		3		5	6	4	8		10			11	2	9				7						36
1		3		5	6	4	8		10			11	2	9				7						37
1				5	6	4	8		10				2	9				7		11	3			38
1				5	6	4	8		10				2	9				7		11	3			39
1	2			5		4	8		10				3	9				7		11		6		40
1	2			5	6	4	8						3	9				7		11				41
1	2			5	6	4			10				3	9			8	7					11	42
42	**29**	**26**	**13**	**42**	**42**	**40**	**8**	**40**	**23**	**39**	**1**	**34**	**9**	**27**	**19**	**3**	**3**	**10**	**5**	**3**	**2**	**1**	**1**	
		5					1		22	4		8	8	5	15	1	3	1						

Cup section (3 ties):

Too	Bir	Kee	Oli	Gib	Bar	Cla	Lam	Ham	Pri	Fin	Hil	Arn												#
1	2	3	8	5	6	4		9	7	10		11												3
1	1	1	1	1	1	1		1	1	1		1												
									1	1														

Month End		Sep	Oct	Nov	Dec	Jan	Feb	Mar	Apr	Final
1934-35	Pld	8	12	16	23	26	30	35	41	**42**
	Pts	8	14	17	23	26	31	37	46	**46**
	Pos	10th	6th	8th	10th	10th	8th	8th	6th	**7th**

1935-36

1	Aug	31	(a)	Hull C	D	1-1	Perry	11,000
2	Sep	2	(h)	Nottingham F	W	6-0	Finch 2, Hammond 3, Smith	20,000
3		7	(h)	Barnsley	D	1-1	Perry	20,000
4		11	(a)	Nottingham F	D	1-1	Perry	12,000
5		14	(a)	Plymouth A	L	0-2		16,000
6		18	(h)	Burnley	D	2-2	Price, Hammond	15,000
7		21	(h)	Bradford C	W	5-1	Perry 3, Hammond, Johnstone	18,000
8		28	(a)	Newcastle U	L	2-6	Price, Hammond	26,000
9	Oct	5	(h)	Tottenham H	L	1-2	Perry	40,000
10		12	(a)	Manchester U	L	0-1		25,000
11		19	(h)	Norwich C	D	1-1	Arnold	15,000
12		26	(a)	Southampton	W	2-1	Finch, Worsley	12,000
13	Nov	2	(h)	Sheffield U	W	3-1	Perry, Worsley, Smith	13,000
14		9	(a)	Bradford	D	1-1	Finch	10,000
15		16	(h)	Leicester C	W	2-0	Hammond, Perry	12,000
16		23	(a)	Blackpool	D	1-1	Worsley	12,000
17		30	(h)	West Ham U	W	4-2	Smith, Perry, Finch 2	27,000
18	Dec	7	(a)	Bury	D	0-0		7,000
19		14	(h)	Doncaster R	L	1-3	Hammond	15,000
20		21	(a)	Swansea T	W	2-0	Smith, Arnold	6,000
21		25	(h)	Charlton A	D	0-0		25,000
22		26	(a)	Charlton A	L	1-2	Worsley	35,000
23		28	(h)	Hull C	W	3-0	Hammond 3	12,000
24	Jan	4	(a)	Barnsley	L	0-2		9,000
25		18	(h)	Plymouth A	D	2-2	Worsley, Gibbons	16,000
26	Feb	1	(h)	Newcastle U	W	3-1	Worsley, Smith, opp own goal	30,000
27		8	(a)	Tottenham H	D	2-2	Worsley 2	55,000
28		22	(a)	Norwich C	L	0-1		11,500
29	Mar	4	(h)	Bury	W	7-0	Keeping, Hammond 2, Arnold 2, Higgins, Smith	6,000
30		7	(a)	Leicester C	L	2-5	Smith 2	12,000
31		14	(h)	Bradford	W	4-1	Arnold, Perry, Hammond, Keeping	20,000
32		26	(a)	Sheffield U	W	1-0	Keeping	14,000
33		28	(h)	Blackpool	W	4-2	Hammond, Arnold, Finch 2	20,000
34	Apr	1	(h)	Manchester U	D	2-2	Finch 2	7,000
35		4	(a)	West Ham U	D	0-0		33,000
36		10	(a)	Port Vale	L	0-1		12,000
37		11	(h)	Southampton	L	0-2		15,000
38		13	(h)	Port Vale	W	7-0	Arnold 2, Perry, Smith, Worsley, opp own goal 2	9,000
39		18	(a)	Doncaster R	D	0-0		10,000
40		25	(h)	Swansea T	L	0-1		9,000
41		29	(a)	Bradford C	L	0-1		4,000
42	May	2	(a)	Burnley	W	2-0	Perry, Arnold	4,000

P	W	D	L	F	A	W	D	L	F	A	Pts	Pos	Div		
42	11	6	4	58	24	4	8	9	18	28	44	9th	2	Appearances	
														Goals	

FA Cup

3	Jan	11	(h)	Brighton & HA	W	2-1	Worsley, Hammond	29,328
4		25	(h)	Blackpool	W	5-2	Hammond, Perry 4	20,714
5	Feb	19	(a)	Chelsea	D	0-0		52,096
R		24	(h)	Chelsea	W	3-2	Smith, Hammond, Arnold	30,696
6		29	(h)	Derby C	W	3-0	Arnold, Barrett, Smith	37,151
SF	Mar	21	(n)	Sheffield U	L	1-2	Arnold	51,568

FA Cup semi-final played at Molineux.

Appearances

Goals

Tootill	Hindson	Keeping	Clarke	Gibbons	Barrett	Smith	Hammond	Perry	Finch	Allen	Price	Dennison	Johnston	Arnold	Tompkins	Warburton	Worsley	Birch	Higgins	Woodward	Edelston	Dodds	Pitts	Hiles	Mayes	Brooks	№
1	2	3	4	5	6	7	8	9	10	11																	1
1	2	3	4	5	6	7	8	9	10	11																	2
1	2	3	4	5	6	7	8	9	10					11													3
1	2	3	4	5	6	7	8	9	10	11																	4
1	2	3	4	5	6	7	8	9	10	11																	5
1	2	3	4	5	6		8	9		11	10		7														6
1	2	3	4	5			8	9	10	11		6	7														7
1	2	3	4	5			8	9	10			6	7	11													8
1	2	3	4	5	6		8	9	10				7	11													9
1	2	3		5			8	9	10			7		11	6	4											10
1	2	3	4			9	8		10					11	6	5	7										11
1	2	3	4	5			8	10						11	6		7										12
1	2	3	4	5			8	10	9					11	6		7										13
1	2	3	4	5			8	10	9					11	6		7										14
1	2	3	4	5			8	10	9					11	6		7										15
1	2	3	4	5			8	10	9					11	6		7										16
1	2	4	5	3			8	10	9					11	6		7										17
1	2	3	4	5			8	10	9					11			7										18
1	2	3	4	5	6	7		10	9					11			7										19
1	2	3		5	6		8	9	10					11		4	7										20
1	2	3		5	6		8	9	10					11		4	7										21
1	2	3		5			8	9	10					11	6	4	7										22
1		3		5			8	9	10					11	6	4	7			2							23
1	2	3		5			8	9	10					11	6	4	7										24
1	2	3		5			8	9	10					11	6	4	7										25
1	2	3	4	5			8	10	9	11					6		7										26
1	2	3	4	5			8	10	9	11					6		7										27
1		3	4	5			8	10	9	7				11	6					2							28
1		3	4				8	10	9	5				11					7	2							29
1		3	4	5			8		9					11	6				7	2	10						30
1	2	3	4	5			8	10	9					11	6		7										31
1	2	3	4	5			8	10	9					11	6		7										32
1	2	3	4	5			8	10	9					11	6		7										33
1	2	3	4	5			8	10	9					11	6		7										34
1	2	3	4	5			8	10						11	6		7					9					35
1	2	3	4	5			8	10	9					11	6		7										36
1		3	4	5			8	10	9					11	6		7	2									37
1			4				8	10	9					11	6		7	2					3	5			38
1							8	9						11	6	4	7	2					3		10		39
			4	5			8	10						11	6		7	2				9	3			1	40
1			4	5			8	10	9					11	6		7	2					3				41
1			4	5			8		9					11	6		7	2					3				42
41	**33**	**35**	**26**	**39**	**19**	**36**	**40**	**28**	**30**	**7**	**4**	**6**	**4**	**24**	**29**	**9**	**29**	**10**	**1**	**2**	**1**	**1**	**5**	**1**	**1**	**1**	
		3		1			9	15	13	10			2	1	9		9	1									

Tootill	Hindson	Keeping	Clarke	Gibbons	Barrett	Smith	Hammond	Perry	Finch	Allen	Price	Dennison	Johnston	Arnold	Tompkins	Warburton	Worsley	Birch	Higgins	Woodward	Edelston	Dodds	Pitts	Hiles	Mayes	Brooks	Rd
1	2	3		5			8	9	10					11	6	4	7										
1	2	3	4	5			8	10	9					11	6		7										3
1	2	3	4	5			8	10	9					11	6		7										R
1	2	3	4	5			8	10	9	7				11	6												4
1	2	3	4	5			8	10	9	7				11	6												5
1	2	3	4	5			8	10	9					11	6		7										
6	6	6	6	5			6	6	5	5				4	6	1	4										
							1	2	3					4	1		3										

Month End		Sep	Oct	Nov	Dec	Jan	Feb	Mar	Apr	Final
1935-36	**Pld**	8	12	17	23	25	28	33	41	**42**
	Pts	8	11	19	25	26	29	37	42	**44**
	Pos	11th	13th	8th	9th	10th	11th	8th	10th	**9th**

1936-37

1	Aug	29	(h)	Plymouth A	D	2-2	Smith, Price		22,000
2	Sep	5	(a)	Nottingham F	L	3-5	Cox 2, Keeping		12,000
3		7	(a)	Burnley	W	2-0	Smith, Arnold		10,000
4		12	(h)	Chesterfield	W	1-0	Perry		18,000
5		14	(a)	Coventry C	D	1-1	Worsley		18,000
6		19	(a)	Aston Villa	W	3-0	Perry 2, Arnold		50,000
7		21	(h)	Burnley	W	2-0	Perry, Arnold		14,000
8		26	(h)	Bradford C	L	0-1			18,000
9	Oct	3	(a)	Swansea T	L	0-3			12,000
10		10	(h)	Southampton	W	2-0	Worsley, Arnold		26,000
11		17	(a)	Blackburn R	W	2-0	Perry, Hammond		9,000
12		24	(h)	Bury	D	1-1	Perry		30,000
13		31	(a)	Leicester C	L	0-2			12,000
14	Nov	7	(h)	West Ham U	W	5-0	Rooke 3, Arnold, Hammond		20,000
15		14	(a)	Norwich C	L	0-3			12,838
16		21	(h)	Newcastle U	L	3-4	Smith, Keeping, Finch		23,508
17		28	(a)	Bradford	D	1-1	Hammond		10,000
18	Dec	5	(h)	Barnsley	W	1-0	Rooke		10,000
19		12	(a)	Sheffield U	L	0-2			20,000
20		19	(h)	Tottenham H	D	3-3	Hammond 2, Woodward		30,000
21		25	(h)	Blackpool	L	0-3			23,000
22		26	(a)	Plymouth A	W	3-0	Cox, Smith, Hammond		37,000
23		28	(a)	Blackpool	L	1-3	Smith		15,000
24	Jan	2	(h)	Nottingham F	W	5-2	Smith, Arnold, Woodward 2, opp own goal		10,000
25		9	(a)	Chesterfield	L	1-4	Woodward		10,000
26		23	(h)	Aston Villa	W	3-2	Rooke 3		16,000
27		30	(a)	Bradford C	D	1-1	Rooke		4,000
28	Feb	6	(h)	Swansea T	W	5-0	Rooke 2, Arnold, Warburton 2		16,000
29		13	(a)	Southampton	D	3-3	Rooke 3		14,317
30		20	(h)	Blackburn R	D	1-1	Hammond		18,000
31		27	(a)	Bury	D	1-1	Arnold		8,000
32	Mar	6	(h)	Leicester C	W	2-0	Woodward, Smith		18,000
33		13	(a)	West Ham U	D	3-3	Arnold 2, Rooke		35,000
34		20	(h)	Norwich C	L	2-3	Rooke, Smith		18,000
35		26	(a)	Doncaster R	L	1-2	Gibbons		14,000
36		27	(a)	Newcastle U	D	1-1	Smith		10,000
37		29	(h)	Doncaster R	W	1-0	Arnold		15,000
38	Apr	3	(h)	Bradford	D	0-0			15,000
39		10	(a)	Barnsley	L	0-1			9,000
40		17	(h)	Sheffield U	W	4-0	Rooke 3, Arnold		8,000
41		24	(a)	Tottenham H	D	1-1	Rooke		25,000
42	May	1	(h)	Coventry C	L	0-2			8,000

P	W	D	L	F	A	W	D	L	F	A	Pts	Pos	Div		Appearances
42	11	5	5	43	24	4	8	9	28	37	43	11th	2		Goals

FA Cup

3	Jan	16	(a)	Millwall	L	0-2			32,499

Appearances

Goals

292

1936-37 Appearances and Goals

Tootill	Hindson	Keeping	Clarke	Gibbons	Tompkins	Worsley	Smith	Finch	Price	Allen	Cox	Arnold	Barrett	Perry	Birch	Warburton	Pitts	Hammond	Rooke	Dennison	Woodward	Brooks	Bacuzzi	Targett	Higgins	No
1	2	3	4	5	6	7	8	9	10	11																1
1	2	3	4	5	6	7	8		10			9	11													2
1	2	3	4	5		7	8				10	9	11	6												3
1	2	3	4	5	6	7	8	10				11			9											4
1		3	4	5	6	7	8					11			9	2	10									5
1		3	4	5	6	7	8					11			9	2	10									6
1			4	5	6	7	8					11			9	2	10	3								7
1		3	4	5	6	7	8					11			9	2		10								8
1		3	4	5	6	7	8					11			9	2		10								9
1		3	4	5		7	8					11		6	9	2		10								10
1		3	4	5		7	8					11		6	9	2		10								11
1		3	4	5		7	8					11		6	9	2		10								12
1		3	4	5	6	7	8					11			9	2		10								13
1		3	4	5	6		8	7				11				2		10	9							14
1		3	4	5	6		8	7				11				2		10	9							15
1		3	4	5	6	7	8	10				11				2			9							16
1		3	4	5		7	8					11				2		10	9	6						17
1		3	4	5		7	8	11								2		10	9	6						18
1		3	4	5	6	7	8	10				11				2			9							19
1		3	4	5	6	7		10				11				2		8			9					20
1		3	4	5	6	7	10				11					2		8			9					21
1		3	4	5	6	7	11		9							2		10			8					22
1			5	6		7	11		9				4			2		10			8					23
			4	5		8			9		11					2		10				6	7		1	24
1			4	5		8	7				11							10	9				2	6		25
1		3	4	5	6	7	8					11				2		10	9							26
1		3	4	5	6	7	8					11				2		10	9							27
1		3	4	5	6	7	8					11				2		10	9							28
1		3	4	5	6	7						11				2		10	9		8					29
1		3	4	5	6	7						11				2		10	9		8					30
1		3	4	5	6	7						11				2		10	9		8					31
1		3	4	5	6		8					11				2		10	9		7					32
1		3	4	5	6		8					11				2		10	9		7					33
1		3	4	5			8					11				2		10	9	6	7					34
1		3	4	5	6		8					11				2		10	9		7					35
1		3	4	5	6		8	11								2		10	9		7					36
1		3	4	5	6	7	8					11				2		10	9							37
1		3	4	5	6	7	8					11				2		10	9							38
1			4	5	6	7	8	10				11							9	2	3					39
1		3	4	5	6	7						11				2		10	9		8					40
1		3	4	5	6	7	8					11				2		10	9							41
1		3	4	5	6		8	11								2		10	9					7		42
41	**4**	**40**	**39**	**42**	**35**	**23**	**38**	**21**	**2**	**1**	**5**	**36**	**4**	**10**	**35**	**18**	**3**	**21**	**22**	**4**	**13**	**1**	**2**	**1**	**1**	
	2		1				2	9	1	1		3			12	6	2	7	19		5					

Tootill	Hindson	Keeping	Clarke	Gibbons	Tompkins	Worsley	Smith	Finch	Price	Allen	Cox	Arnold	Barrett	Perry	Birch	Warburton	Pitts	Hammond	Rooke	Dennison	Woodward	Brooks	Bacuzzi	Targett	Higgins	No
1		3	4	5	6		8					9	11			2		10			7					1
1		1	1	1	1		1					1	1			1		1			1					

Month End		Sep	Oct	Nov	Dec	Jan	Feb	Mar	Apr	Final
1936-37	Pld	8	13	17	23	27	31	37	41	**42**
	Pts	10	15	18	23	28	33	39	43	**43**
	Pos	4th	7th	7th	10th	10th	8th	10th	10th	**11th**

293

1937-38

1	Aug	28	(a)	Plymouth A	L	0-4		24,500
2	Sep	2	(a)	Sheffield W	L	1-2	Rooke	18,000
3		4	(h)	Chesterfield	D	1-1	Woodward	18,000
4		6	(h)	Sheffield W	D	0-0		10,000
5		11	(a)	Swansea T	L	0-2		8,000
6		18	(h)	Norwich C	L	3-4	Woodward 2, Finch	20,000
7		20	(a)	Blackburn R	D	2-2	Woodward, Hammond	15,000
8		25	(a)	Aston Villa	L	0-2		40,000
9	Oct	2	(h)	Bradford	D	1-1	Woodward	20,000
10		9	(a)	West Ham U	D	0-0		35,400
11		16	(h)	Tottenham H	W	3-1	Rooke 2, Woodward	35,000
12		23	(a)	Sheffield U	L	1-2	Woodward	11,000
13		30	(h)	Manchester U	W	1-0	Woodward	18,000
14	Nov	6	(a)	Stockport C	L	0-2		15,000
15		13	(h)	Barnsley	D	0-0		15,000
16		20	(a)	Nottingham F	W	1-0	Hammond	11,000
17		27	(h)	Newcastle U	L	1-2	Warburton	14,000
18	Dec	4	(a)	Luton T	L	0-4		14,000
19		11	(h)	Coventry C	L	3-4	Hammond 3	15,000
20		25	(a)	Burnley	L	0-1		25,900
21		27	(h)	Burnley	W	2-1	O'Callaghan, Arnold	17,000
22	Jan	1	(h)	Plymouth A	L	2-3	Worsley, O'Callaghan	12,900
23		15	(a)	Chesterfield	W	2-0	Evans, O'Callaghan	6,000
24		22	(h)	Swansea T	W	8-1	Rooke 4, O'Callaghan, Finch 2, Hammond	18,000
25		29	(a)	Norwich C	W	2-1	Woodward 2	9,000
26	Feb	5	(h)	Aston Villa	D	1-1	Finch	39,265
27		12	(a)	Bury	L	2-4	Tompkins, Rooke	8,000
28		16	(a)	Bradford	W	2-1	Arnold, opp own goal	6,000
29		19	(h)	West Ham U	D	1-1	Arnold	23,000
30		26	(a)	Tottenham H	D	1-1	Rooke	35,000
31	Mar	5	(h)	Sheffield U	D	1-1	Woodward	22,000
32		12	(a)	Manchester U	L	0-1		35,000
33		19	(h)	Stockport C	W	2-0	Woodward, Arnold	18,000
34		26	(a)	Barnsley	D	0-0		10,000
35	Apr	2	(h)	Nottingham F	W	2-0	Arnold, Rooke	17,000
36		9	(a)	Newcastle U	W	2-1	Woodward, Arnold	12,000
37		15	(h)	Southampton	W	1-0	Arnold	16,000
38		16	(h)	Luton T	W	4-1	Woodward 2, Bacuzzi, Rooke	17,000
39		18	(a)	Southampton	L	0-4		15,000
40		23	(a)	Coventry C	W	1-0	Arnold	25,000
41		30	(h)	Bury	W	4-0	Rooke 3, Higgins	9,981
42	May	7	(h)	Blackburn R	W	3-1	Rooke 3	12,000

P	W	D	L	F	A	W	D	L	F	A	Pts	Pos	Div		Appearances
42	10	7	4	44	23	6	4	11	17	34	43	8th	2		Goals

FA Cup

3	Jan	8	(a)	Brentford	L	1-3	O'Callaghan	29,867

Appearances

Goals

Player appearance / goalscorer grid (shirt numbers shown per match):

#	Turner	Birch	Keeping	Evans	Gibbons	Tompkins	Worsley	Smith	Rooke	Hammond	Finch	Arnold	Woodward	Bacuzzi	Dennison	Higgins	Warburton	Clarke	Tootill	O'Callaghan	Hindson	Buckley	Hiles	Pitts	Edelston
1	1	2	3	4	5	6		8	9	10	7	11													
2	1	2	3	4	5	6	7	8	9	10		11													
3	1	2	3	4	5	6		7	9		10	11	8												
4	1		3	4	5	6	7	8	9		11		10	2											
5	1		3	4	5	6					11		9	2	10	7	8								
6	1		3	6		5	7		8		11		9	2				4							10
7			3		5	6	7	8		10	11		9	2				4	1						
8		2	3		5	6	7		8		11		9				10	4	1						
9		2	3	4	5	6			8	9	10	11	7						1						
10		2	3	4	5	6			8	9	11		7						1						10
11		2	3	4	5	6				9	7	11	8						1	10					
12		2	3	4	5	6				9	11		8			7			1	10					
13		2	3	4	5	6		8			7	11	9						1	10					
14		2	3		5	6	7	8			11		9					4	1	10					
15			3		5	6		8			7	11	9	2				4	1	10					
16					5	6	7		9	10	11	3				4			1	8	2				
17			3		5	6	7		9	10	11					4			1	8	2				
18			3		5	6	7		9	10	11					4			1	8	2				
19					5	6		8	9		7	11				4			1	10	2	3			
20		2			5	6	7	8	9		11					4			1	10		3			
21		2			5	6	7	8	9		11					4			1	10		3			
22		2	3		5	6	7	8	9		11					4			1	10					
23	1		3	4		6		9	8	7	11	6		2						10					
24	1		3	4		6		9	8		11		7	2	5					10					
25	1		3	4		6		9	8		11		7	2	5					10					
26	1		3	4		6		9	8		11		7	2	5					10					
27	1		3	4		6		9	8		11		7	2	5					10					
28	1		3	4		6		9			7	11	8	2	5					10					
29	1		3	4		6		9			7	11	8	2	5					10					
30	1		3	4	5	6		9			7	11	8	2						10					
31	1		3	4		6		9			7	11	8	2	5					10					
32	1		3	4		6		9			7	11	8	2	5					10					
33	1		3	4		6		9			7	11	8	2						10			5		
34	1		3	4		6	8		9		7	11	9	2						10			5		
35	1		3	4		6		9			7	11	8	2						10			5		
36	1		3	4		6	7	9	8		11	10	2										5		
37	1		3	4		6	7	9	8		11	10	2										5		
38	1		3	4		6	8	9			7	11	10	2									5		
39	1			4		6		9			7	11	10	2					8			5	3		
40	1		3	4		6	8	9			7	11	10	2									5		
41	1		3	4		6	8	9				11	10	2			7						5		
42	1		3	4		6	8	9			11		10	2			7						5		
Apps	26	13	37	31	22	42	19	14	27	19	34	30	33	26	9	4	9	5	16	26	4	3	10	1	2
Gls				1			1	1		17	6	4	8	15	1		1	1			4				

Additional match (appearances / goals):

	Turner	Birch	Keeping	Evans	Gibbons	Tompkins	Worsley	Smith	Rooke	Hammond	Finch	Arnold	Woodward	Bacuzzi	Dennison	Higgins	Warburton	Clarke	Tootill	O'Callaghan	Hindson	Buckley	Hiles	Pitts	Edelston
App	1		3	4		6		9	8	7	11			5						10	2				3
Gls	1		1	1		1		1	1	1				1						1	1				
														1											

Month End		Sep	Oct	Nov	Dec	Jan	Feb	Mar	Apr	Final
1937-38	Pld	8	13	17	21	25	30	34	41	**42**
	Pts	3	9	12	14	20	25	29	41	**43**
	Pos	22nd	20th	21st	21st	19th	17th	17th	9th	**8th**

295

1938-39

1	Aug	27	(h)	West Ham U	W	3-2	Finch, Arnold, Worsley	24,410
2		29	(a)	Bury	W	2-0	Arnold, Tomkins	11,000
3	Sep	3	(a)	Tranmere R	W	1-0	Woodward	13,000
4		5	(a)	Burnley	L	0-2		14,000
5		10	(h)	Chesterfield	W	2-0	Worsley, Rooke	23,000
6		12	(h)	Burnley	D	0-0		18,000
7		17	(a)	Swansea T	D	1-1	Rooke	5,000
8		24	(h)	Bradford	W	4-0	Rooke 2, Arnold, Finch	20,000
9	Oct	1	(a)	Manchester C	W	5-3	Rooke 4, Arnold	25,000
10		8	(h)	Millwall	W	2-1	Woodward, Evans	49,335
11		15	(a)	Tottenham H	L	0-1		47,689
12		22	(h)	Southampton	D	1-1	Evans	25,000
13		29	(a)	Plymouth A	D	0-0		27,000
14	Nov	5	(h)	Nottingham F	D	2-2	Keeping, Worsley	23,000
15		12	(a)	Newcastle U	L	1-2	Rooke	64,000
16		19	(h)	West Brom A	W	3-0	Arnold 2, Woodward	24,000
17		26	(a)	Norwich C	D	3-3	Tompkins 2, Rooke	10,000
18	Dec	3	(h)	Luton T	W	2-1	Higgins, Keeping	20,000
19		10	(a)	Coventry C	L	1-3	Evans	17,000
20		17	(h)	Sheffield U	L	1-2	Rooke	12,000
21		24	(a)	West Ham U	L	0-1		8,000
22		27	(a)	Sheffield W	L	1-5	Evans	40,000
23		31	(h)	Tranmere R	W	1-0	Rooke	11,897
24	Jan	23	(h)	Swansea T	W	1-0	Rooke	3,000
25		28	(a)	Bradford	W	5-1	Higgins 3, Rooke 2	8,602
26	Feb	4	(h)	Manchester C	W	2-1	Arnold, Rooke	24,366
27		11	(a)	Millwall	D	1-1	O'Callaghan	32,500
28		18	(h)	Tottenham H	W	1-0	O'Callaghan	26,172
29		25	(a)	Southampton	L	1-2	Higgins	10,000
30	Mar	4	(h)	Plymouth A	L	1-2	Rooke	7,092
31		11	(a)	Nottingham F	D	1-1	Higgins	9,306
32		18	(h)	Newcastle U	D	1-1	Woodward	19,941
33		25	(a)	West Brom A	L	0-3		20,000
34	Apr	1	(h)	Norwich C	W	2-0	Higgins 2	12,411
35		7	(h)	Blackburn R	L	2-3	Higgins, Rooke	28,000
36		8	(a)	Luton T	L	1-2	Woodward	17,000
37		10	(a)	Blackburn R	L	1-2	Higgins	25,000
38		15	(h)	Coventry C	W	1-0	Arnold	14,831
39		18	(h)	Sheffield W	D	2-2	Tompkins, Rooke	10,000
40		22	(a)	Sheffield U	L	0-2		28,000
41		24	(a)	Chesterfield	W	1-0	Rooke	10,000
42		29	(h)	Bury	L	1-2	Rooke	7,500

P	W	D	L	F	A	W	D	L	F	A	Pts	Pos	Div	
42	12	5	4	35	20	5	5	11	26	35	44	12th	2	Appearances
														Goals

FA Cup

3	Jan	7	(h)	Bury	W	6-0	Rooke 6	11,221
4		21	(a)	Chelsea	L	0-3		69,987

Appearances

Goals

Appearances / goals grid — Fulham 1938‑39

Turner	Bacuzzi	Keeping	Evans	Hiles	Tompkins	Finch	Worsley	Rooke	Woodward	Arnold	Higgins	Dennison	O'Callaghan	Buckley	Easson	Freeman	Miller	Clarke	Tuckett	
1	2	3	4	5	6	7	8	9	10	11										1
1	2	3	4	5	6	7	8	9	10	11										2
1	2	3	4	5	6	7	8	9	10	11										3
1	2	3	4	5	6	11	8	9	10		7									4
1	2	3	4		6	11	8	9	10			5	7							5
1	2	3	4		6	11	8	9	7			5	10							6
1	2	3	4	5	6	7	8	9	10	11										7
1	2	3	4	5	6	7	8	9	10	11										8
1	2	3	4	5	6	7	8	9	10	11										9
1	2	3	4	5	6	7	8	9	10	11										10
1	2	3	4	5	6	7	8	9	10	11										11
1	2	3	4	5	6	7	8	9	10	11										12
1	2	3	4	5	6	7	8	9	10	11										13
1	2	3	4	5	6		7	9	10	11				8						14
1	2	3	4	5	6	7	8	9		11	10									15
1	2		4	5	6		8	9	10	11	7	3								16
1	2		4	5	6		8	9	10	11	7	3								17
1	2	3	4	5	6		8	9	10	11	7									18
1	2		4	5	6	10	8		9	11	7	3								19
1	2		4	5	6	7	8	9	10	11		3								20
1	2	3	4	5	6	7		9	10	11				8						21
1	2	3	4	5	6	7			10	11		9	8							22
1	2		4		6	7	8	9	10	11		5	3							23
1	2	3	4		6		8	9		11	7	5	10							24
1	2	3	4	5	6		8	9		11	7		10							25
1	2	3	4	5	6		8	9		11	7		10							26
1	2	3	4	5	6		8	9		11	7		10							27
1	2	3	4	5	6		8	9		11	7		10							28
1	2	3	4	5	6		8	9		7	11		10							29
1	2	3	4	5	6		8	9		11	7		10							30
1	2	3	4	5	6			9	8	11	7				10					31
1	2		4	5	6	10		9	8	11	7				3					32
1	2	3	4	5	6	10		9	8	11	7									33
1	2	3	4	5	6		8	9	10		7						11			34
1	2	3	4	5	6			9	8		7					10	11			35
1	2	3	4	5	6		8		10		7	9					11			36
1	2	3	4	5	6		8		9		7				10		11			37
1	2	3	4	5	6		10	9	8	11	7									38
1	2	3	4	5	6		10	9	8	11	7									39
1	2	3	4	5	6		10	9	8	11	7									40
1	2	3			6		9	8	11	7		10						4	5	41
1	2	3		5	6		8	9	10	11	7							4		42
42	42	36	40	37	42	21	35	38	34	34	24	12	13	1	3	1	4	2	1	
	2	4			4	2	3	21	5	8	10		2							

Cup / supplementary matches:

Turner	Bacuzzi	Keeping	Evans	Hiles	Tompkins	Finch	Worsley	Rooke	Woodward	Arnold	Higgins	Dennison	O'Callaghan							
1	2	3	4		6		8	9		11	7	5	10							3
1	2	3	4		6		8	9		11	7	5	10							4
2	2	2	2		2		2	2		2	2	2	2							
								6												

Month End		Sep	Oct	Nov	Dec	Jan	Feb	Mar	Apr	Final
1938-39	Pld	8	13	17	23	25	29	33	42	42
	Pts	12	18	22	26	30	35	37	44	41
	Pos	2nd	1st	1st	8th	6th	5th	10th	12th	12th

1946-47

1	Aug	31	(a)	Bury	L	2-7	Rooke 2	12,000
2	Sep	2	(a)	West Ham U	L	2-3	Beasley, Rooke	27,000
3		7	(h)	Luton T	W	2-1	Shepherd, Rooke	30,000
4		9	(h)	West Ham U	W	3-2	Wallbanks, Rooke, Shepherd	19,913
5		14	(a)	Plymouth A	D	2-2	Beasley 2	25,000
6		16	(a)	Sheffield W	D	1-1	Rooke	21,000
7		21	(h)	Leicester C	W	4-2	Stevens, Shepherd, McCormick, Rooke	30,000
8		28	(a)	Chesterfield	D	1-1	Rooke	16,812
9	Oct	5	(h)	Millwall	W	3-2	Stevens, Rooke, Beasley	30,000
10		12	(a)	Bradford	W	2-1	Taylor, Watson	15,479
11		19	(h)	Barnsley	W	6-1	Rooke 2, Beasley 2, Shepherd, McCormick	37,000
12		26	(a)	Burnley	L	0-2		30,000
13	Nov	2	(h)	Tottenham H	D	1-1	Freeman	40,339
14		9	(a)	Swansea T	W	2-0	Rooke 2	31,000
15		16	(h)	Newcastle U	L	0-3		40,000
16		23	(a)	West Brom A	L	1-6	Thomas	18,000
17		30	(h)	Birmingham C	L	0-1		25,000
18	Dec	7	(a)	Coventry C	L	0-1		17,011
19		25	(a)	Newport C	L	2-4	Beasley, Taylor	14,727
20		26	(h)	Newport C	W	4-1	Nelson, Buchanan, Shepherd 2	25,000
21		28	(h)	Bury	W	2-0	Grant, Nelson	20,294
22	Jan	1	(a)	Manchester C	L	0-4		47,658
23		4	(a)	Luton T	L	0-2		20,000
24		18	(h)	Plymouth A	W	3-1	McGibbon 3	24,068
25	Mar	1	(h)	Manchester C	D	2-2	Ayres, Beasley	32,000
26		8	(a)	Tottenham H	D	1-1	Shepherd	27,700
27		15	(h)	Swansea T	W	3-0	Ayres 2, McGibbon	20,000
28		22	(a)	Newcastle U	W	3-1	Stevens 2, McGibbon	35,000
29		29	(h)	West Brom A	L	0-1		30,000
30	Apr	5	(a)	Birmingham C	L	1-2	McGibbon	30,000
31		7	(h)	Sheffield W	L	1-2	Freeman	26,500
32		12	(h)	Coventry C	W	2-0	Nelson, Stevens	16,660
33		19	(a)	Nottingham F	L	1-2	Ayres	20,233
34		26	(h)	Southampton	D	0-0		15,000
35	May	3	(a)	Barnsley	L	1-4	McGibbon	12,297
36		10	(h)	Chesterfield	W	2-1	Freeman, Taylor	10,260
37		17	(h)	Burnley	W	1-0	Beasley	32,000
38		24	(a)	Southampton	L	0-2		12,000
39		26	(h)	Nottingham F	D	1-1	Grant	10,000
40		31	(h)	Bradford	L	0-3		10,000
41	Jun	7	(a)	Leicester C	L	0-2		8,036
42		14	(a)	Millwall	D	1-1	McGibbon	12,000

P	W	D	L	F	A	W	D	L	F	A	Pts	Pos	Div		
42	12	4	5	40	25	3	5	13	23	49	39	15th	2	Appearances	
														Goals	

FA Cup

3	Jan	11	(h)	Birmingham C	L	1-2	Watson	30,000

Appearances	
Goals	

Appearance & goalscorer grid (1946‑47). Figures are the shirt numbers worn by each player in each League match (rows 1–42).

Evans	Freeman	Lloyd	Wallbanks	Watson	Taylor	Buchanan	Woodward	Rooke	Beasley	Shepherd	Hinton	Malpass	McCormick	Lewin	Stevens	Cranfield	Thomas	Hudson	Ratcliffe	Hughes	Nelson	Grant	McGibbon	Bacuzzi	Ayres	Quested	Bewley	Hinshelwood	Match
1	2	3	4	5	6	7	8	9	10	11																			1
	2	3	4	5	6	7	8	9	10	11	1																		2
	2		4	5	6	7	8	9	10	11	1	3																	3
	2		4	5	6	7		9	10	11	1	3	8																4
	2		4	5	6		8	9	10	11	1			3			7												5
	2		4	5	6	7		9	10	11	1		8	3															6
	2		4	5	6			9	10	11	1		8	3			7												7
	2		4	5	6			9	10	11	1		8	3			7												8
	2		4	5	6			9	10		1		8	3		11	7												9
	2		4	5	6			9	10	11	1		8	3			7												10
	2		4	5	6	7		9	10	11	1		8	3															11
	2		4	5	6	7		9	10	11	1		8	3															12
	2		4	5	6			9	10	11	1		8	3			7												13
	2		4	5	6		8	9	10	11	1			3			7												14
	2		4	5	6		8	9	10	11	1			3			7												15
	2		4	5	6			9	10	11	1			3			7	8											16
	2		4	5	6		8	9	10	11	1			3			7												17
	2			5	6		8	9	10	11				3			7		1	4									18
	2		4	5	6	7			10	11				3					1		8	9							19
	2		4	5	6	7			10	11				3					1		8	9							20
	2		4	5	6	7			10	11				3					1		8	9							21
	2		4	5	6	7			10	11				3					1		8	9							22
	2		4	5	6	7			10	11				3					1		8	9							23
	2		4	5	6	7			10	11				3					1		8	9							24
	2		4	5	6	7				11									1		8	9		3	10				25
	2		4	5	6					11					7				1		8		9	3	10				26
	2		4	5	6				10	11					7				1				9	3	8				27
	2		4	5	6				10	11	1				7								9	3	8				28
	2		4	5	6				10	11	1				7								9	3	8				29
	2		4	5	6				10	11	1				7								9	3	8				30
	2		4	5	6				10	11	1				7								9	3	8				31
	2		4	5	6				10	11	1				7								9	3	8				32
	2		4	5	6				10	11	1				7						8		9	3					33
	2		4	5	6				10	11	1				7								9	3	8				34
	2		4	5	6				10	11	1				7								9	3	8				35
	2		4	5	6		8			11	1				7								9	3	10				36
	2			5	6				10		1				7						8		9	3	4	11			37
	2			5	6				10		1				7						8		9	3	4	11			38
	2			5	6				10		1				7						8		9	3	4	11			39
	2		4	5	6				10		1				7								9	3	8	11			40
	2			5	6				10		1										8		9	3	4	11	7		41
	2			5	6				10		1										8		9	3	4	11		7	42
1	42	2	26	41	42	20	10	18	40	35	31	2	9	20	16	1	9	1	10	1	23	7	17	18	12	6	1	1	**Apps**
3		1	1	1	3	1		13	9	7			2		5		1				3	2	8		4				**Goals**

Supplementary block:

Evans	Freeman	Lloyd	Wallbanks	Watson	Taylor	Buchanan	Woodward	Rooke	Beasley	Shepherd	Hinton	Malpass	McCormick	Lewin	Stevens	Cranfield	Thomas	Hudson	Ratcliffe	Hughes	Nelson	Grant	McGibbon	Bacuzzi	Ayres	Quested	Bewley	Hinshelwood	
	2		4	5	6	7			10	11			8	3					1		9								3
	1		1	1	1	1			1	1			1	1					1		1								
					1																								

Month End	Sep	Oct	Nov	Dec	Jan	Feb	Mar	Apr	Final
1946‑47 Pld	8	12	17	21	24	24	29	34	**42**
Pts	9	15	18	22	24	24	30	33	**39**
Pos	8th	6th	10th	13th	14th	14th	12th	15th	**15th**

1947-48

1	Aug	23	(h)	Brentford	W	5-0	Beasley, R.Thomas, McGibbon 3		32,697
2		27	(a)	West Brom A	L	1-2	McGibbon		25,000
3		30	(a)	Leicester C	W	2-0	McGibbon 2		21,000
4	Sep	3	(h)	West Brom A	L	0-1			24,500
5		6	(h)	Leeds U	W	3-2	Beasley, S.Thomas, Shepherd		30,000
6		10	(a)	Barnsley	W	2-1	R.Thomas, Shepherd		15,000
7		13	(a)	Bury	L	0-1			14,483
8		17	(h)	Barnsley	L	0-1			17,000
9		20	(a)	Coventry C	L	2-5	Grant, Stevens		20,216
10		27	(h)	Newcastle U	W	3-0	Shepherd, S.Thomas, Grant		41,500
11	Oct	4	(a)	Birmingham C	L	1-3	Watson		40,000
12		11	(h)	Southampton	L	0-2			35,000
13		18	(a)	Doncaster R	W	1-0	Taylor		20,995
14		25	(h)	Notts F	D	0-0			22,000
15	Nov	1	(a)	Bradford	L	0-3			16,390
16		8	(h)	Cardiff C	W	4-1	R.Thomas, Beasley, Stevens 2		40,000
17		15	(a)	Sheffield W	L	0-2			35,000
18		22	(h)	Tottenham H	L	0-2			38,000
19		29	(a)	Millwall	W	2-1	Shepherd, R.Thomas		17,000
20	Dec	6	(h)	Chesterfield	D	0-0			9,818
21		13	(a)	West Ham U	L	0-3			25,000
22		20	(a)	Brentford	W	2-0	McGibbon, Taylor		23,880
23		25	(h)	Plymouth A	D	1-1	Shepherd		16,800
24		27	(a)	Plymouth A	L	2-3	Stevens, opp own goal		25,157
25	Jan	3	(h)	Leicester C	W	3-1	Stevens 2, Freeman		17,000
26		17	(a)	Leeds U	W	1-0	Stevens		29,500
27		31	(h)	Bury	D	1-1	Stevens		18,000
28	Feb	21	(h)	Birmingham C	D	1-1	Stevens		13,000
29	Mar	6	(h)	Doncaster R	D	0-0			15,000
30		13	(a)	Nottingham F	W	2-0	Stevens 2		20,866
31		20	(h)	Bradford	D	0-0			16,000
32		26	(a)	Luton T	W	3-0	McGibbon, Bewley, Ayres		18,033
33		27	(a)	Cardiff C	D	0-0			38,000
34		29	(h)	Luton T	D	1-1	McGibbon		20,000
35	Apr	3	(h)	Sheffield W	L	0-2			25,000
36		10	(a)	Tottenham H	W	2-0	McGibbon, Shepherd		32,490
37		14	(a)	Newcastle U	L	0-1			54,071
38		17	(h)	Millwall	W	1-0	R.Thomas		18,000
39		21	(a)	Southampton	L	0-1			15,280
40		24	(a)	Chesterfield	L	0-1			9,031
41		28	(h)	Coventry C	L	0-2			7,000
42	May	1	(h)	West Ham U	D	1-1	Ayres		20,000

P	W	D	L	F	A	W	D	L	F	A	Pts	Pos	Div		Appearances
42	6	9	6	24	19	9	1	11	23	27	40	11th	2		Goals

FA Cup

3	Jan	10	(h)	Doncaster R	W	2-0	Ayres, Stevens	16,162
4		24	(h)	Bristol R	W	5-2	Ayres 2, Stevens 3	20,000
5	Feb	7	(h)	Everton	D	1-1	Quested	37,500
R		14	(a)	Everton	W	1-0	R.Thomas	71,587
6		28	(h)	Blackpool	L	0-2		40,000

Appearances

Goals

Appearances & Goals — Season 1947-48

Hinton	Freeman	Bacuzzi	Quested	Watson	Taylor	Thomas S	Thomas R	McGibbon	Beasley	Shepherd	Grant	Stevens	Radcliffe	Lewin	Jones	Wallbanks	Ayres	Hinshelwood	Edwards	Bewley	Rampling	#
1	2	3	4	5	6	7	8	9	10	11												1
1	2	3	4	5	6	7	8	9	10	11												2
1	2	3	4	5	6	7	8	9	10	11												3
1	3	2	4	5	6	7	8	9	10	11												4
1	3	2	4	5	6	7	8	9	10	11												5
1	3	2	4	5	6	7	8	9	10	11												6
1	3	2	4	5	6	7	8	9	10	11												7
1	2	3	4	5	6	7	8	9	10	11												8
1	2	3	4	5	6		8		10	11		9	7									9
1	2	3	4	5	6	8			10	11		9	7									10
	2	3	4	5	6	8			10	11		9	7	1								11
1	2	3			5	6	8	10	4	11	9	7										12
1	2	3	4	5	6	8		9	10	11		7										13
1	2	3	4	5	6	8	9		10	11		7										14
1	2	3	4	5	6	8		9	10	11		7										15
1	2	3	4	5	6	7	8		10	11		9										16
1	2	3	4	5	6	7	8		10	11		9										17
1	2	3	4	5	6	7	8		10	11		9										18
1	2		4	5	6		8		10	11	9	7		3								19
1	2		4	5	6		8		10	11	9	7		3								20
1	2	3	4	5	6		8			11	9	7			10							21
1	2	3			5	6	8	9		11		7				4	10					22
1	2	3			5	6	8	9		11		7				4	10					23
1	2	3	8	5	6			9		11		7				4	10					24
1	2	3		5		7		6		11		9				4	10	8				25
1	2	3	4	5		7	8	6	10	11		9										26
1	2	3	4	5		7	8	10		11		9					6					27
1	2	3	4	5		7	8	9	10	11		6										28
1		3	4	5		7	8	6		11		9		2			10					29
1		3	4	5		7	8			11		9		2			10		6			30
1		3	4	5		7	8			11		9		2			10		6			31
1		3	4	5		7	8	9		11				2			10			6		32
1		3	4	5		7	8	9	6	11				2			10					33
1		3	4	5		7	8	9		11				2			10			6		34
1		3	4	5		7	8	9		11				2			10			6		35
1		3	4	5		7		9	10	11				2			8			6		36
1		3	8	5		7		9	10	11				2			4			6		37
1		3		5		7	8	9	10	11				2			4			6		38
1	2	3	4	5		7	8	9	6							11	10					39
1		3	4	5		7	8	9	10	11				2						6		40
1		3	4	5		6	8	9		11				2			10				7	41
1	2		4	5		6	8	9		11				3			10				7	42
41	30	39	36	30	36	31	36	25	36	35	7	23	1	15	1	7	17	2	2	10	2	
	1			1	2	2	5	10	3	6	2	11					2				1	

Cup matches

Hinton	Freeman	Bacuzzi	Quested	Watson	Taylor	Thomas S	Thomas R	McGibbon	Beasley	Shepherd	Grant	Stevens	Radcliffe	Lewin	Jones	Wallbanks	Ayres	Hinshelwood	Edwards	Bewley	Rampling	Rd
1	2	3	8	5		7	6	9								4	10	11				3
1	2	3	4	5		7	8	6		9							10					4
1	2	3	4	5		7	8	6	11	9							10					5
1	2	3	4	5		7	8	6		9							10	11				R
	2	3	4	5		7	8	6	11	9	1						10					6
4	5	5	5	5		5	4	5	5	1	1	5	1		1	1	5	1	1			
		1				1			4					3								

Month End	Sep	Oct	Nov	Dec	Jan	Feb	Mar	Apr	Final
1947-48 Pld	10	14	19	24	27	28	34	41	**42**
Pts	10	13	17	21	26	27	35	39	**40**
Pos	14th	13th	15th	14th	13th	15th	10th	11th	**11th**

1948-49

1	Aug	21	(a)	Grimsby T	W 3-2	Jinks, Ayres, R.Thomas	20,000
2		25	(h)	Barnsley	D 1-1	Stevens	25,000
3		28	(h)	Nottingham F	W 4-0	Jinks 2, Stevens 2	25,000
4	Sep	1	(a)	Barnsley	D 1-1	McDonald	17,788
5		4	(a)	Bury	L 0-2		18,687
6		8	(h)	Southampton	W 1-0	Stevens	25,000
7		11	(a)	Plymouth A	L 1-3	R.Thomas	25,322
8		15	(a)	Southampton	L 0-3		25,400
9		18	(h)	Blackburn R	D 1-1	Ayres	30,000
10		25	(a)	Cardiff C	L 1-2	McDonald	42,000
11	Oct	2	(h)	Queen's Park R	W 5-0	R.Thomas 2, Stevens 3	39,500
12		9	(h)	West Brom A	L 1-2	R.Thomas	32,500
13		16	(a)	Chesterfield	W 1-0	R.Thomas	16,488
14		23	(h)	Lincoln C	W 2-1	Stevens, McDonald	21,000
15		30	(a)	Sheffield W	W 2-1	R.Thomas, Jezzard	32,000
16	Nov	6	(h)	Coventry C	W 1-0	Jezzard	25,000
17		13	(a)	Leeds U	D 1-1	R.Thomas	26,500
18		20	(h)	Leicester C	W 1-0	R.Thomas	20,000
19	Dec	4	(h)	Tottenham H	D 1-1	Freeman	38,000
20		11	(a)	West Ham U	L 0-1		22,500
21		18	(h)	Grimsby T	W 3-1	McDonald, R.Thomas, Beasley	20,000
22		25	(a)	Bradford	D 1-1	Stevens	20,742
23		27	(h)	Bradford	W 2-0	McDonald 2	20,000
24	Jan	1	(a)	Nottingham F	W 2-0	Rowley, McDonald	16,176
25		15	(h)	Bury	W 7-2	Rowley 4, R.Thomas 2, McDonald	19,000
26		22	(h)	Plymouth A	W 6-1	Rowley 3, Stevens, R.Thomas, Jezzard	25,000
27	Feb	5	(a)	Blackburn R	L 0-1		22,500
28		19	(h)	Cardiff C	W 4-0	Jezzard, Stevens, R.Thomas 2	36,000
29		26	(a)	Queen's Park R	L 0-1		25,000
30	Mar	5	(a)	West Brom A	W 2-1	Quested, Rowley	25,000
31		12	(h)	Chesterfield	W 2-1	R.Thomas 2	30,220
32		19	(a)	Lincoln C	W 3-0	Jezzard, Rowley 2	13,199
33		26	(h)	Sheffield W	D 1-1	R.Thomas	35,000
34	Apr	2	(a)	Coventry C	L 0-1		25,000
35		6	(a)	Brentford	D 0-0		25,800
36		9	(h)	Leeds U	W 1-0	Rowley	30,000
37		15	(h)	Luton T	W 4-1	Rowley 2, Stevens, R.Thomas	35,000
38		16	(a)	Leicester C	W 3-0	Jezzard, R.Thomas, Rowley	35,592
39		18	(a)	Luton T	W 3-1	Rowley, McDonald, R.Thomas	20,125
40		23	(h)	Brentford	W 2-1	Rowley, R.Thomas	40,000
41		30	(a)	Tottenham H	D 1-1	R.Thomas	50,199
42	May	7	(h)	West Ham U	W 2-0	Rowley 2	40,000

P	W	D	L	F	A	W	D	L	F	A	Pts	Pos	Div		
														Appearances	
42	16	4	1	52	14	8	5	8	25	23	57	1st	2	Goals	

FA Cup

3	Jan	8	(h)	Walsall	L 0-1		32,000

Appearances

Goals

In the autumn of 1948, Fulham exchanged winger Ernie Shepherd for West Brom's Arthur Rowley. Later that season, Shepherd moved again, to Hull City. At the end of 1948-9, Fulham and West Brom won promotion from Division Two, and Hull City were champions of Division Three North.

302

Hinton	Freeman	Baccuzzi	Quested	Taylor	Beasley	Thomas R	Stevens	Jinks	Ayres	McDonald	Shepherd	Flack	Bewley	Thomas S	Jezzard	Rowley	Hinshelwood	Lewin	Gage	No.
1	2	3	4	5	6	8	7	9	10	11										1
1	2	3	4	5	6	8	7	9	10		11									2
1	2	3	4	5	6		8	9	10	11				7						3
1	2	3	4	5	6		8	9	10	11				7						4
1	2	3	4	5	6	8	7	9	10	11										5
1	2	3	4	5	6	8	7	9	10	11										6
1	2	3	4	5		8	7	9		10	11		6							7
1	2	3	4	5	6	8	7	9	10	11										8
1	2	3	4	5	6	8	7	9	10	11										9
1	2	3	4	5	6	8	9			11				7	10					10
	2	3	4	5	6	8	9			11		1		7	10					11
	2	3	4	5	6	8	9			11		1		7	10					12
	2	3	4	5		8	9			11		1	6	7	10					13
	2	3	4	5	6	8	9			11		1			10	7				14
	2	3	4	5	6	8	9			11		1		7	10					15
	2	3	4	5	6	8	9			11		1		7	10					16
	2	3	4	5	6	8	9			11		1		7	10					17
		3	4	5		8	9			11		1	6	7	10		2			18
	2	3		5	6	8	9			11		1	4	7	10					19
	3	2		5	4	8	9			11		1	6	7	10					20
	2		4	5	6	8	7			11		1			10	9	3			21
	2	3	4	5	6	8	7			11		1			10	9				22
	2	3	4	5	6	8	7			11		1			10	9				23
	2	3	4	5	6	8	7			11		1			10	9				24
	2	3	4	5	6	8	7			11		1			10	9				25
	2	3	4	5	6	8	7			11		1			10	9				26
	2	3	4	5	6	8	7			11		1			10	9				27
	2	3	4	5	6	8	7			11		1			10	9				28
	2	3	4	5	6	8	7			11		1			10	9				29
	2	3	4	5	6	8	7			11		1			10	9				30
	2	3	4	5	6	8	7			11		1			10	9				31
	2	3	4	5	6	8	7			11		1			10	9				32
	2	3	4	5	6	8	7			11		1			10	9				33
	2	3	4	5	6	8	7		10	11		1				9				34
	2	3	4	5	6	10	8			11		1		7		9				35
	2	3		5	6	10	8			11		1	4	7		9				36
		3	4	5	6	8	7			11		1			10	9		2		37
		3	4	5	6	8	7			11		1			10	9		2		38
		3	4	5	6	8	7			11		1			10	9		2		39
		3	4	5	6	8	7			11					10	9		2	1	40
	2	3	4	5	6	8	7			11					10	9			1	41
	2	3	4	5	6	8	7			11					10	9			1	42
10	37	41	39	42	39	40	42	9	9	41	2	29	6	14	30	22	1	6	3	
1		1			1		23	12	3	2		9			6	19				

Hinton	Freeman	Baccuzzi	Quested	Taylor	Beasley	Thomas R	Stevens	Jinks	Ayres	McDonald	Shepherd	Flack	Bewley	Thomas S	Jezzard	Rowley	Hinshelwood	Lewin	Gage	
	2	3	4	5	6	8	7			11		1			10	9				3
	1	1	1	1	1	1	1			1		1			1	1				

Month End		Sep	Oct	Nov	Dec	Jan	Feb	Mar	Apr	Final
1948-49	Pld	10	15	18	23	26	29	33	41	**42**
	Pts	9	17	22	28	34	36	43	55	**57**
	Pos	17th	6th	4th	4th	3rd	2nd	2nd	1st	**1st**

303

1949-50

1	Aug	20	(h)	Wolves	L	1-2	Bacuzzi	44,000
2		24	(a)	Huddersfield T	D	2-2	Rowley, R.Thomas	21,805
3		27	(a)	Aston Villa	L	1-3	Quested	45,000
4		31	(h)	Huddersfield T	W	4-1	Rowley 2, Jezzard, opp own goal	30,000
5	Sep	3	(h)	Charlton A	L	1-2	McDonald	40,000
6		7	(a)	Middlesbrough	W	2-1	R.Thomas 2	38,000
7		10	(a)	Manchester C	L	0-2		42,192
8		17	(h)	Chelsea	D	1-1	Freeman	44,000
9		24	(h)	Newcastle U	W	2-1	R.Thomas, Jezzard	40,000
10	Oct	1	(a)	Blackpool	D	0-0		32,000
11		9	(a)	Stoke C	W	2-0	R.Thomas, Jezzard	28,000
12		15	(h)	Burnley	W	1-0	Rowley	36,000
13		22	(a)	Sunderland	L	0-2		46,252
14		29	(h)	Liverpool	L	0-1		42,000
15	Nov	5	(a)	Arsenal	L	1-2	Jezzard	43,000
16		12	(h)	Bolton W	W	3-0	Jezzard, R.Thomas, Rowley	30,000
17		19	(a)	Birmingham C	D	1-1	Stevens	21,000
18		26	(h)	Derby C	D	0-0		38,000
19	Dec	3	(a)	West Brom A	L	1-4	Jezzard	35,000
20		10	(h)	Manchester U	W	1-0	Jezzard	38,000
21		17	(a)	Wolves	D	1-1	Rowley	30,000
22		24	(h)	Aston Villa	W	3-0	Rowley, McDonald 2	32,000
23		26	(a)	Everton	D	1-1	Stevens	54,726
24		27	(h)	Everton	D	0-0		34,999
25		31	(a)	Charlton A	L	1-2	McDonald	32,000
26	Jan	14	(h)	Manchester C	W	1-0	McDonald	30,000
27		21	(a)	Chelsea	D	0-0		51,660
28	Feb	4	(a)	Newcastle U	L	1-3	R.Thomas	40,000
29		18	(h)	Blackpool	W	1-0	R.Thomas	35,000
30		25	(h)	Stoke C	D	2-2	R.Thomas 2	30,000
31	Mar	4	(a)	Burnley	D	0-0		19,858
32		11	(h)	Birmingham C	D	0-0		25,000
33		18	(a)	Derby C	L	1-2	S.Thomas	18,975
34		25	(h)	Arsenal	D	2-2	Campbell, Stevens	40,000
35	Apr	1	(a)	Bolton W	L	1-2	Jezzard	25,000
36		7	(a)	Portsmouth	L	0-3		39,342
37		8	(h)	Sunderland	L	0-3		40,000
38		10	(h)	Portsmouth	L	0-1		25,000
39		15	(a)	Liverpool	D	1-1	Stevens	36,274
40		22	(h)	West Brom A	L	0-1		35,000
41		29	(a)	Manchester U	L	0-3		15,000
42	May	6	(h)	Middlesbrough	L	1-2	Stevens	25,000

P	W	D	L	F	A	W	D	L	F	A	Pts	Pos	Div		Appearances
42	8	6	7	24	19	2	8	11	17	35	34	17th	1		Goals

FA Cup

3	Jan	9	(a)	Charlton A	D	2-2	R.Thomas, Freeman	51,979
R		11	(h)	Charlton A	L	1-2	McDonald	41,600

Appearances

Goals

Flack	Freeman	Bacuzzi	Quested	Taylor	Beasley	Stevens	Thomas R	Rowley	Jezzard	McDonald	Kelly	Campbell	Thomas S	Summers	Lawler	Pavitt	Jinks	Hinshelwood	No.
1	2	3	4	5	6	7	8	9	10	11									1
1	2	3	4	5	6	7	8	9	10	11									2
1	2	3	4	5	6	7	8	9	10	11									3
1	2	3	4	5	6	7	8	9	10	11									4
1	2	3	4	5	6	7	8	9	10	11									5
1	2	3	4	5	6	7	8	9	10	11									6
1	2	3	4	5	6	7	8	9	10	11									7
	2	3	4	5	6	7	8	9	10	11	1								8
	2	3	4	5	6	7	8	9	10	11	1								9
	2	3	4	5	6	7	10	9	11		1			8					10
	2	3	4	5	6	7	10	9	11		1			8					11
	2	3	4	5	6	7	10	9	11		1			8					12
	2	3	4	5	6	7	10	9	11		1			8					13
	2	3	4	5	6	7	8	9	10		1	11							14
	2	3	4	5	6	8	11	9	10		1		7						15
	2	3	4	5	6	7	8	9	10		1	11							16
	2	3	4	5	6	7	8	9	10		1	11							17
	2	3	4	5	6	7	8	9	10		1	11							18
	2	3	4	5	6	7	8	9	10		1	11							19
	2	3	4	5	6	7	8	9	10	11	1								20
1	2	3	4	5	6	7	8	9	10	11									21
	2	3	4	5	6	7	8	9	10	11	1								22
	2	3	4	5	6	7	8	9	10	11	1								23
	2	3	4	5	6	7	8	9	10	11	1								24
	2	3	4	5		7	8	9	10	11	1				6				25
	2		4	5		7	8	9	10	11	1				6	3			26
1	2		4	5	6	7	8	9	10	11						3			27
1	2		4	5	6	7	8	9	10	11						3			28
1	2	3	4		6	7	8		10							5	9	11	29
1	2	3	4		6	7	8		10							5	9	11	30
	2	3	4		6	7	8		10		1	9				5		11	31
1	2	3	4		6	7	8		10			9				5		11	32
1	2	3	4		6		8		10			9	7			5		11	33
1	2	3	4		6	7	8		10			9				5		11	34
	2	3	4		6	7	8		10		1	9				5		11	35
	2	3	4	5	6	7	8		10		1	9						11	36
	3	4	5	6			10	9		11	1	8				2		7	37
1	2	3	4		6		10	9		11		8				5		7	38
	2	3	4		6	7	8	9	10	11	1					5			39
1	2	3	4		6	7	8	9	10	11						5			40
	2		4	5	6	7	8	9	10	11	1					3			41
	2	3	4	5	6	7	10	9		11	1		8						42
17	41	38	42	35	37	39	42	34	39	24	25	13	3	4	2	15	2	10	
	1	1	1			5	10	7	8	5			1	1					

Flack	Freeman	Bacuzzi	Quested	Taylor	Beasley	Stevens	Thomas R	Rowley	Jezzard	McDonald	Kelly	Campbell	Thomas S	Summers	Lawler	Pavitt	Jinks	Hinshelwood	
	2	3	4	5	6	7	8	9	10	11	1								3
	2		4	5	6	7	8	9	10	11	1					3			R
	2	1	2	2	2	2	2	2	2	2	2					1			
	1					1													

Month End		Sep	Oct	Nov	Dec	Jan	Feb	Mar	Apr	Final
1949-50	Pld	9	14	18	25	27	30	34	41	42
	Pts	8	13	17	24	27	30	33	34	34
	Pos	16th	16th	12th	13th	12th	12th	13th	17th	17th

305

1950-51

1	Aug	19	(a)	Manchester U	L	0-1		44,042
2		23	(h)	Charlton A	L	1-3	Stevens	32,000
3		26	(h)	Wolves	W	2-1	Stevens, Quested	35,000
4		30	(a)	Charlton A	D	0-0		30,000
5	Sep	2	(a)	Sunderland	W	1-0	Macaulay	42,080
6		4	(a)	Blackpool	L	0-4		30,000
7		9	(h)	Aston Villa	W	2-1	Jezzard, Thomas	40,000
8		13	(h)	Blackpool	D	2-2	Jezzard, Thomas	39,000
9		16	(a)	Derby C	L	2-3	Jezzard, opp own goal	25,329
10		23	(h)	Liverpool	W	2-1	Jezzard, Thomas	42,000
11		30	(a)	Portsmouth	L	0-1		32,082
12	Oct	7	(h)	Everton	L	1-5	Hinshelwood	34,700
13		14	(a)	Stoke C	D	1-1	Quested	30,000
14		21	(h)	Huddersfield T	D	1-1	Stevens	36,000
15		28	(a)	Middlesbrough	D	1-1	Jezzard	32,000
16	Nov	4	(h)	West Brom A	L	0-1		25,000
17		11	(a)	Newcastle U	W	2-1	Thomas, Stevens	58,000
18		18	(h)	Sheffield W	W	4-2	McDonald, Thomas 2, Macaulay	27,000
19		25	(a)	Arsenal	L	1-5	Thomas	45,450
20	Dec	2	(h)	Burnley	W	4-1	Thomas, Jezzard, Stevens, opp own goal	25,000
21		9	(a)	Chelsea	L	0-2		43,835
22		16	(h)	Manchester U	D	2-2	Stevens 2	25,000
23		23	(a)	Wolves	D	1-1	Stevens	30,000
24		25	(h)	Bolton W	L	0-1		25,000
25		26	(a)	Bolton W	W	1-0	Campbell	35,000
26		30	(h)	Sunderland	D	1-1	Brennan	35,000
27	Jan	13	(a)	Aston Villa	L	0-3		35,000
28		20	(h)	Derby C	L	3-5	Stevens, Brennan 2	32,000
29	Feb	3	(a)	Liverpool	L	0-2		33,330
30		28	(a)	Everton	L	0-1		19,904
31	Mar	3	(h)	Stoke C	W	2-0	Stevens, Bowie	35,000
32		10	(a)	Huddersfield T	W	2-1	Jezzard, Thomas	19,651
33		17	(h)	Middlesbrough	W	2-0	Bowie, Quested	30,000
34		23	(h)	Tottenham H	L	0-1		44,000
35		24	(a)	West Brom A	D	0-0		25,000
36		26	(a)	Tottenham H	L	1-2	Jezzard	51,862
37		31	(h)	Newcastle U	D	1-1	Campbell	30,000
38	Apr	7	(a)	Sheffield W	D	2-2	Thomas, Bowie	35,000
39		14	(h)	Arsenal	W	3-2	Quested, Thomas 2	35,000
40		21	(a)	Burnley	W	2-0	Thomas 2	18,997
41		28	(h)	Chelsea	L	1-2	Jezzard	30,000
42	May	2	(h)	Portsmouth	L	1-4	Stevens	24,000

P	W	D	L	F	A	W	D	L	F	A	Pts	Pos	Div	Appearances
42	8	5	8	35	37	5	6	10	17	31	37	18th	1	Goals

FA Cup

3	Jan	6	(h)	Sheffield W	W	1-0	Brennan	29,200
4		27	(a)	Millwall	W	1-0	Campbell	42,170
5	Feb	10	(a)	Chelsea	D	1-1	Campbell	69,434
R		14	(h)	Chelsea	W	3-0	Brennan 2, Stevens	29,946
6		24	(a)	Blackpool	L	0-1		32,000

Appearances

Goals

	Black	Freeman	Bacuzzi	Macaulay	Taylor	Lowe E	Stevens	Quested	Jezzard	Brennan	McDonald	Thomas R	Hinshelwood	Lowe R	Campbell	Pavitt	Lawler	Bowie	Robson	
	1	2	3	4	5	6	7	8	9	10	11									1
	1	2	3	4	5	6	7	8	9	10		11								2
	1	2	3	8	5	6	7	4	9	10		11								3
	1	2	3	8	5	6	7	4	9			10	11							4
	1	2		8	5	6	11	4	9			10		3	7					5
	1	2		8	5	6	11	4	9			10		3	7					6
	1	2		8	5	6	11	4	9			10		3	7					7
	1	2	3	8	5	6	11	4	9			10			7					8
	1	2	3	8	5	6	11	4	9			10			7					9
	1		3	8	5	6	11	4	9			10			7	2				10
	1		3	8	5	6	11	4	9	10					7	2				11
	1		3	8	5	6	11	4	9			10	7		2					12
	1	2		4	5	6	11	8	9			10	7		3					13
	1	2		4	5	6	11	7	9	10	8				3					14
	1	2	3	4	5	6	11	7	9	10	8									15
	1	2	3	4	5	6	11	7	9	10	8									16
	1	2	3	8	5	6	7	4		10	11	9								17
	1	2	3	8	5	6	7	4		10	11	9								18
	1		3	8	5	6	7	4		10	11	9				2				19
	1		2	8	5	6	7	4	11	10		9		3						20
	1		2	8	5	6	7	4	11	10		9		3						21
	1		2	8	5	6	7	4	11	10		9		3						22
	1		2	8	5	6	7	4	11	10		9		3						23
	1		2	8	5	6	7	4	11	10		9		3						24
	1		2	8		6	7			10		9		3	11	5	4			25
	1		2	8		6	7			10		9		3	11	5	4			26
	1		2	8			7	4		10		9		3	11	5	6			27
	1		2	8			7	4	9	10				3	11	5	6			28
	1		2	4		6	7		9	10				3	11	5		8		29
	1		2		5	6	7	4	10			9		3	11			8		30
	1		2		5	6	7	4	10			9		3	11			8		31
	1		2		5	6	7	4	10			9		3	11			8		32
	1		2		5	6	7	4	10			9		3	11			8		33
	1		2		5	6	7	4	10			9		3	11			8		34
	1		2		5	6	7	4	10			9		3	11			8		35
	1		2		5	6	7	4	10			9		3	11			8		36
	1		2		5	6	7	4	10			9		3	11			8		37
	1		2		5	6	7	4	11			9		3				8	10	38
	1		2		5	6	7	4	10			9		3	11			8		39
	1	2			5	6	7	4	10			9		3	11			8		40
	1	2			5	6	7	4	10			9		3	11			8		41
	1	2			5	6	7	4	10	11		9		3				8		42
	42	18	34	29	37	40	42	39	35	22	5	37	3	26	23	11	4	14	1	
				2				11	4	9	3	1	14	1		2			3	

	Black	Freeman	Bacuzzi	Macaulay	Taylor	Lowe E	Stevens	Quested	Jezzard	Brennan	McDonald	Thomas R	Hinshelwood	Lowe R	Campbell	Pavitt	Lawler	Bowie	Robson	
	1		2	8		6	7	4		10		9		3	11	5				3
	1		2	8	5	6	7	4	9	10				3	11					4
	1		2	10	5	6	7	4				9		3	11			8		5
	1		2		5	6	7	4	10			9		3	11			8		R
	1		2		5	6	7	4	10	9				3	11			8		6
	5		5	3	4	5	5	5	3	5		1		5	5	1		3		
									1						3			2		

Month End		Sep	Oct	Nov	Dec	Jan	Feb	Mar	Apr	Final
1950-51	**Pld**	11	15	19	26	28	30	37	41	**42**
	Pts	10	13	17	24	24	24	32	37	**37**
	Pos	15th	15th	15th	14th	16th	18th	16th	16th	**18th**

1951-52

1	Aug	18	(h)	Preston NE	L	2-3	Bowie, Jezzard	42,000
2		20	(a)	Tottenham H	L	0-1		48,780
3		25	(a)	Burnley	L	0-1		18,697
4		29	(h)	Tottenham H	L	1-2	Thomas	36,500
5	Sep	1	(h)	Charlton A	D	3-3	Stevens, Jezzard, McDonald	30,000
6		3	(a)	Stoke C	D	1-1	Newcombe	20,000
7		8	(a)	Chelsea	L	1-2	McDonald	47,537
8		12	(h)	Stoke C	W	5-0	Jezzard 2, Macaulay 2, Bowie	20,000
9		15	(a)	Middlesbrough	L	0-2		30,000
10		22	(h)	West Brom A	W	1-0	Bowie	30,000
11		29	(a)	Newcastle U	W	1-0	McDonald	55,531
12	Oct	6	(h)	Portsmouth	L	2-3	McDonald, Bowie	42,000
13		13	(a)	Liverpool	L	0-4		36,793
14		20	(h)	Blackpool	L	1-2	Brennan	40,000
15		27	(a)	Arsenal	L	3-4	Stevens 2, Brennan	54,178
16	Nov	3	(h)	Manchester C	L	1-2	Stevens	35,000
17		10	(a)	Derby C	L	0-5		20,549
18		17	(h)	Aston Villa	D	2-2	Pavitt, Brennan	16,000
19		24	(a)	Sunderland	D	2-2	Robson, Brennan	34,024
20	Dec	1	(h)	Wolves	D	2-2	Taylor (Jeff), Brennan	30,000
21		8	(a)	Huddersfield T	L	0-1		8,260
22		15	(a)	Preston NE	W	1-0	Lowe	26,000
23		22	(h)	Burnley	L	1-2	Campbell	20,000
24		25	(a)	Manchester U	L	2-3	Thomas 2	33,802
25		26	(h)	Manchester U	D	3-3	Lowe 2, Stevens	35,000
26		29	(a)	Charlton A	L	0-3		20,000
27	Jan	5	(a)	Chelsea	L	1-2	Jezzard	45,000
28		19	(h)	Middlesbrough	W	6-0	Mitten 2, Taylor (Jeff) 3, Jezzard	30,000
29		26	(a)	West Brom A	W	2-0	Taylor (Jeff), opp own goal	25,000
30	Feb	9	(h)	Newcastle U	D	1-1	Lowe	46,000
31		16	(a)	Portsmouth	L	0-4		36,765
32	Mar	1	(h)	Liverpool	D	1-1	Mitten	37,000
33		8	(a)	Blackpool	L	2-4	Mitten, Hill	18,600
34		15	(h)	Arsenal	D	0-0		46,000
35		22	(a)	Manchester C	D	1-1	Mitten	22,000
36	Apr	5	(a)	Aston Villa	L	1-4	Stevens	20,500
37		11	(h)	Bolton W	L	1-2	Mitten	38,000
38		12	(h)	Sunderland	L	0-1		30,000
39		14	(a)	Bolton W	L	1-2	Stevens	35,000
40		19	(a)	Wolves	D	2-2	Brennan, Robson	20,000
41		26	(h)	Huddersfield T	W	1-0	Jezzard	25,000
42	May	1	(h)	Derby C	W	3-0	Jezzard, Brennan, Robson	15,000

P	W	D	L	F	A	W	D	L	F	A	Pts	Pos	Div	
42	5	7	9	38	31	3	4	14	20	46	27	22nd	1	Appearances
														Goals

FA Cup

3	Jan	13	(h)	Birmingham C	L	0-1		26,000
								Appearances
								Goals

Appearance grid (shirt number worn by each player in each match). Empty cells indicate the player did not appear.

Black	Bacuzzi	Lowe R	Quested	Taylor Jim	Lowe E	Stevens	Bowie	Jezzard	Brennan	Campbell	Thomas	Newcombe	Pavitt	McDonald	Macaulay	Freeman	Robson	Flack	Taylor Jeff	Lawler	Dodgin	Mitten	Hill	Hinshelwood	#
1	2	3	4	5	6	7	8	9	10	11															1
1	2	3	4	5	6	7	8	9		11	10														2
1	2	3		4	6		8	9	10	7		11	5												3
1	2	3		4	6	8	10	9		7		11	5												4
1	2		4	5	6	7	8	10			11			3	9										5
1	2		4	5	6		8	10		7	11			3	9										6
1	2		4	5	6	7		10			11			3	9	8									7
1		3		4	6	7	10	9		11			5		8		2								8
1		3		4	6	7	10	9	8	11			5				2								9
1		3		4	6	7	10	9	8	11			5				2								10
1		3		4	6	7	8			11			5		10	9	2								11
1		3		4	6	7	8			11			5		10	9	2								12
1		3		4	6	7	8			11	9		5		10		2								13
1		3		4	6	7		9		11			5		10	8	2								14
		3		4	6	7	10	9		11			5		8		2	1							15
		3		4	6	7	10			11			5		8	9	2	1							16
	2	3		4	6	7	10		8	11			5			9		1							17
1	2	3		4	6	7		9	8	11			5		10										18
1	2	3	5	4	6	7		9	8	11					10										19
1		3		5	6	7		9				11			10	8	4			2					20
1		3		5	6	7		9				11			10	8	4			2					21
1	2			5	6	7		9	8								4		10		3	11			22
1	2			5	6	7		9	8						10		4				3	11			23
1	2			5	6	7		9	8								4		10		3	11			24
1	2			5	6	7	8	9									4		10		3	11			25
1		3		5	6	7	8	9									4		10	6	2	11			26
1	2			5	6	7		9	8						10		4				3	11			27
1		3		5	6	7	8	9									4		10		2	11			28
1		3		5	6	7	8	9									4		10		2	11			29
1		3		5	6	7	8	9									4		10		2	11			30
1		3		5	6	7	8	9									4		10		2	11			31
1		3		5	6	7	8	9									4		10		2	11			32
1		3		5	6	7		9									4		10		2	11	4		33
1		3		5	6	7		9									4		10		2	11	6		34
1		3		5	6	7		9		8									10		2	11	4		35
1		3		5	4	7		10		8							9				2	11	6		36
1		3		5	4	7		9	10	8											2	11	6		37
1		3		5	6		9	10						4	8						2	11		7	38
1		3			6	9	10				5			4	8						2	11		7	39
1		3		5		7		9	10					4	8				6		2	11			40
1		3		5		7		9	10						8				6		2	11	4		41
1		3		5	4	7		9	10						8				6		2	11			42
39	**26**	**22**	**13**	**33**	**39**	**39**	**20**	**27**	**19**	**25**	**12**	**5**	**19**	**5**	**19**	**10**	**16**	**3**	**21**	**5**	**21**	**16**	**6**	**2**	
			4	7	4	8	7	1	3	1	1		4	2	3		5			6	1				

Cup / additional match:

Black	Bacuzzi	Lowe R	Quested	Taylor Jim	Lowe E	Stevens	Bowie	Jezzard	Brennan	Campbell	Thomas	Newcombe	Pavitt	McDonald	Macaulay	Freeman	Robson	Flack	Taylor Jeff	Lawler	Dodgin	Mitten	Hill	Hinshelwood	#
1		3		5	6	7	8	9	10	11				4					2						3
1		1		1	1	1	1	1	1	1				1					1						

Month End		Sep	Oct	Nov	Dec	Jan	Feb	Mar	Apr	Final
1951-52	**Pld**	11	15	19	26	29	31	35	41	**42**
	Pts	8	8	10	14	18	19	22	25	**27**
	Pos	14th	21st	21st	21st	21st	21st	22nd	22nd	**22nd**

1952-53

1	Aug	23	(h)	Bury	W	2-0	Stevens, Robson	35,000
2		25	(a)	Leicester C	L	1-6	Black	25,000
3		30	(a)	Birmingham C	W	4-1	Robson 2, Brennan, Stevens	30,000
4	Sep	3	(h)	Leicester C	L	4-6	Stevens, Jezzard 2, Mitten	30,000
5		6	(h)	Luton T	W	2-0	Robson 2	29,000
6		11	(a)	Notts C	D	1-1	Robson	19,109
7		13	(a)	Leeds U	L	0-2		18,300
8		17	(h)	Notts C	W	6-0	Jezzard, Robson 2, Stevens 2, Brennan	15,000
9		20	(h)	Plymouth A	W	2-1	Jezzard 2	40,000
10		27	(a)	Rotherham U	L	0-1		16,500
11	Oct	4	(h)	Lincoln C	W	4-2	Stevens, Jezzard 2, Robson	26,000
12		11	(a)	Hull C	L	1-3	Robson	30,160
13		18	(h)	Blackburn R	W	2-1	Jezzard, Stevens	30,000
14		25	(a)	Nottingham F	W	1-0	Robson	20,029
15	Nov	1	(h)	Everton	W	3-0	Jezzard, Mitten, Stevens	30,000
16		8	(a)	Brentford	D	2-2	Jezzard, Robson	30,000
17		15	(h)	Doncaster R	L	1-3	Jezzard	20,000
18		22	(a)	Swansea T	D	1-1	Stevens	22,000
19		29	(h)	Huddersfield T	L	0-2		25,000
20	Dec	6	(a)	Sheffield U	L	1-2	Jezzard	29,845
21		13	(h)	Barnsley	W	3-1	Jezzard, Brennan, Mitten	15,000
22		20	(a)	Bury	D	1-1	Jezzard	6,089
23		26	(h)	Southampton	D	1-1	Stevens	15,000
24		27	(a)	Southampton	L	3-5	Jezzard 2, Taylor (Jeff)	21,935
25	Jan	3	(h)	Birmingham C	W	3-1	Jezzard 2, Robson	20,000
26		17	(a)	Luton T	L	0-2		21,409
27		24	(h)	Leeds U	W	2-1	Jezzard, Mitten	18,000
28		31	(a)	Doncaster R	D	0-0		12,000
29	Feb	7	(a)	Plymouth A	L	1-3	Mitten	21,199
30		18	(h)	Rotherham U	W	4-1	Jezzard 3, Stevens	10,000
31		21	(a)	Lincoln C	D	2-2	Jezzard 2	14,954
32		28	(h)	Hull C	W	2-1	Jezzard, Mitten	27,000
33	Mar	7	(a)	Blackburn R	D	2-2	Mitten, Jezzard	23,500
34		14	(h)	Nottingham F	L	0-1		25,100
35		25	(a)	Everton	D	3-3	Stevens, Jezzard 2	15,874
36		28	(h)	Brentford	W	5-0	Jezzard 2, Robson 2, Stevens	27,000
37	Apr	3	(a)	West Ham U	W	2-1	Jezzard 2	24,500
38		6	(h)	West Ham U	L	2-3	Haynes, Newcombe	22,000
39		11	(h)	Swansea T	W	3-1	Robson 2, Jezzard	27,500
40		18	(a)	Huddersfield T	L	2-4	Robson 2	23,871
41		25	(h)	Sheffield U	L	1-2	Jezzard	32,000
42		29	(a)	Barnsley	D	1-1	Jezzard	3,155

P	W	D	L	F	A	W	D	L	F	A	Pts	Pos	Div		
42	14	1	6	52	28	3	9	9	29	43	44	8th	2	Appearances	
														Goals	

FA Cup

3	Jan	14	(a)	Bolton W	L	1-3	Mitten

Appearances

Goals

310

	Black	Dodgin	Bacuzzi	Lowe E	Taylor Jim	Hill	Stevens	Robson	Jezzard	Brennan	Mitten	Lawler	Macaulay	Flack	Lowe R	Campbell	Wilson	Taylor Jeff	Healy	Haynes	Smith	Pavitt	Newcombe	Brice	
	1	2	3	4	5	6	7	8	9	10	11														1
	1	2		3	5		7	8	9	10	11	6	4												2
		2		3	5	4	7	8	9	10	11	6		1											3
		2		3	5	4	7	8	9	10	11	6		1											4
	1	2		3	5	4	7	8	9	10	11	6													5
	1	2		3	5	4	7	8	9	10	11	6													6
	1	2		3	5	4	7	8	9	10	11	6													7
	1	2		4	5		7	8	9	10	11	6			3										8
	1	2		4	5		7	8	9	10	11	6			3										9
	1	2		4	5			8	9	10	11	6			3	7									10
	1	2		4	5		7	8	9	10	11	6			3										11
	1	2		4	5		7	8	9	10	11	6			3										12
	1	5		4			7	8	9	10	11	6			3		2								13
	1	5		4			7	8	9	10	11	6			3		2								14
	1			4	5		7	8	9	10	11	6			3		2								15
	1			4	5		7	8	9	10	11	6			3		2								16
	1			4	5		7		9	10	11	6			3		2	8							17
	1			4	5	8	7		9	10	11	6			3		2								18
	1			4	5		7	8	9	10	11	6			3		2								19
	1	2		4	5	6	7	8	9	10	11				3										20
	1	2		4	5	6	7	8	9	10	11				3										21
	1	2		4	5	6	7	8	9	10	11							3							22
	1			4	5	6	7	8	9		11				3		2			10					23
	1			4	5	6	7		9	10	11				3		2	8							24
	1				5	6	7	8	9		11				3		2			10	4				25
				4	5	6	7	8	9	10	11			1	3							2			26
				4	5	6	7	8	9		11			1						10		2			27
				4	5	6	7	8	9		11	3		1						10		2			28
	1			4	5	6	7	8	9		11	3								10		2			29
	1	2			5	6	7	8	9			3								10	4		11		30
	1	2			5	6	7	8	9		11	3								10	4				31
	1	2			5	6	7	8	9		11	3								10	4		11		32
	1	2			5	6	7		9	8		3								10	4		11		33
	1	2			5	6	7	8	9		11	3								10	4				34
	1		3		5	6	7	8	9		11									10	4	2			35
	1			4	5	6	7	8	9		11	3						2		10					36
	1	2	4	5	6	7	8	9		11	3									10					37
	1	2	4	5	6		8	9		11	3									10			7		38
	1	2	4		6	7	8	9		11	3									10				5	39
	1	2	4		6	7	8	9		11	3									10				5	40
	1	2	4		6	7		9	8		11	3								10				5	41
	1	2	4		6	7		9	8		11	3								10				5	42
	37	14	15	36	36	30	36	35	42	32	40	33	1	5	18	1	11	2	1	18	7	5	3	4	
	1						13	19	35	3	7						1			1			1		

Cup:

	Black	Dodgin	Bacuzzi	Lowe E	Taylor Jim	Hill	Stevens	Robson	Jezzard	Brennan	Mitten	Lawler	Macaulay	Flack	Lowe R	Campbell	Wilson	Taylor Jeff	Healy	Haynes	Smith	Pavitt	Newcombe	Brice	
	1			3	5	6		8	9	7	11				2			10	4						3
	1			1	1	1		1	1	1	1				1			1	1						
									1																

Month End		Sep	Oct	Nov	Dec	Jan	Feb	Mar	Apr	Final
1952-53	Pld	10	14	19	24	28	32	36	41	**42**
	Pts	11	17	21	25	30	35	39	43	**44**
	Pos	7th	6th	9th	10th	10th	7th	6th	9th	**8th**

1953-54

#					Result	Scorers	Attendance
1	Aug	20	(h)	Bristol R	D 4-4	Robson 2, Stevens, Haynes	25,000
2		22	(h)	Stoke C	L 0-1		28,000
3		24	(a)	Leicester C	D 2-2	Haynes, Jezzard	19,950
4		29	(a)	Brentford	L 1-2	Mitten	21,600
5	Sep	2	(h)	Leicester C	D 1-1	Mitten	18,000
6		5	(a)	West Ham U	L 1-3	Jezzard	30,000
7		7	(a)	Rotherham U	L 2-3	Jezzard, Haynes	14,252
8		12	(h)	Leeds U	L 1-3	Taylor	27,000
9		16	(h)	Rotherham U	L 2-4	Taylor, Mitten	12,000
10		19	(a)	Birmingham C	D 2-2	Jezzard 2	22,000
11		26	(h)	Nottingham F	W 3-1	Jezzard 2, Robson	26,000
12	Oct	3	(a)	Luton T	W 2-1	Lowe, Jezzard	18,619
13		10	(h)	Derby C	W 5-2	Jezzard 4, Mitten	23,000
14		17	(a)	Blackburn R	L 1-5	Robson	25,700
15		24	(h)	Doncaster R	L 1-2	Hill	26,000
16		31	(a)	Bury	W 3-1	Jezzard 2, Robson	9,391
17	Nov	7	(h)	Oldham A	W 3-1	Mitten, Jezzard 2	21,000
18		14	(a)	Everton	D 2-2	Jezzard, Stevens	36,092
19		21	(h)	Hull C	W 5-1	Robson 2, Haynes 2, Jezzard	24,000
20		28	(a)	Notts C	D 0-0		20,000
21	Dec	5	(h)	Lincoln C	W 4-1	Robson, Jezzard 2, Haynes	20,000
22		12	(a)	Bristol R	L 1-2	Stevens	22,885
23		19	(a)	Stoke C	W 3-1	Mitten, Haynes, Robson	13,884
24		25	(h)	Plymouth A	W 3-1	Jezzard 3	18,000
25		26	(a)	Plymouth A	D 2-2	Jezzard, Mitten	14,000
26	Jan	2	(h)	Brentford	W 4-1	Robson, Hill, Stevens, Jezzard	23,500
27		16	(h)	West Ham U	L 3-4	Stevens, Jezzard, Haynes	30,000
28		23	(a)	Leeds U	W 2-1	Stevens, Jezzard	20,000
29	Feb	6	(h)	Birmingham C	W 5-2	Jezzard, Robson 2, Haynes, Stevens	21,500
30		13	(a)	Nottingham F	L 1-4	Jezzard	24,997
31		20	(h)	Luton T	W 5-1	Jezzard, Haynes 3, Taylor	28,000
32		27	(a)	Derby C	D 3-3	Jezzard, Taylor, Stevens	13,425
33	Mar	6	(h)	Blackburn R	L 2-3	Taylor 2	25,000
34		13	(a)	Doncaster R	D 2-2	Mitten, Taylor	10,025
35		20	(h)	Bury	W 3-0	Taylor, Jezzard 2	20,000
36		27	(a)	Hull C	L 1-2	Haynes	16,942
37	Apr	3	(h)	Notts C	W 4-3	Jezzard 2, Stevens, Mitten	20,000
38		10	(a)	Oldham A	W 3-2	Robson, Haynes 2	13,295
39		16	(a)	Swansea T	L 0-2		20,000
40		17	(h)	Everton	D 0-0		30,000
41		19	(h)	Swansea T	W 4-3	Jezzard 2, Stevens, opp own goal	19,000
42		24	(a)	Lincoln C	L 2-4	Haynes, Jezzard	11,754

P	W	D	L	F	A	W	D	L	F	A	Pts	Pos	Div	
42	12	3	6	62	39	5	7	9	36	46	44	8th	2	Appearances
														Goals

FA Cup

					Result	Scorers	Attendance
3	Jan	9	(a)	Grimsby T	D 5-5	Taylor 3, Stevens, Hill	14,764
R		18	(h)	Grimsby T	W 3-1	Taylor, Haynes 2	18,729
4		30	(a)	Leyton O	L 1-2	Robson	25,803
							Appearances
							Goals

Player appearances grid (shirt numbers by match):

Barton	Black	Brice	Chenhall	Cronin	Elliott	Haynes	Hill	Jezzard	Lawler	Lowe	Mitten	Newcombe	Robson	Ronson	Smith	Stevens	Taylor	#
1	5	2				10	4	9	3	6	11		8		7			1
1	5	2				10	4	9	3	6	11		8		7			2
1	5	2				10	6	9	3		11	7	8	4				3
1	5	2				10	4	9	3	6	11	7	8					4
1	5	2				10	6	9	3	4	11	7	8					5
1	5	2				10		9	3	6	11	7	8	4				6
1	5	2				10		9	3	6	11	7		4		8		7
1	5	2				10		9	3	6	11			4	7	8		8
1	5	2						9	3	6	11	7	8	4		10		9
1	5	2				10		9	3	6	11		8	4	7			10
1	5	2				10		9	3	6	11		8	4	7			11
1	5	2				10		9	3	6	11		8	4	7			12
1	5	2				10		9	3	6	11		3	4	7			13
1	5	2				10		9	3	6	11		8	4	7			14
1	5	2				10	4	9	3	6	11		8		7			15
1	5	2				10	4	9	3	6	11		8		7			16
1	5	2				10	4	9	3	6	11		8		7			17
1	5	2				10	4	9	3	6	11		8		7			18
1	5	2				10	4	9	3	6	11		8		7			19
1	5	2				10	4	9	3	6	11		8		7			20
1	5	2				10	4	9	3	6	11		8		7			21
1	5	2				10	4	9	3	6	11		8		7			22
1	5	2				10	4	9	3	6	11		8		7			23
1	5	2				10	4	9	3	6	11		8		7			24
1	5	2				10	4	9	3	6	11		8		7			25
1	5	2				10	4	9	3	6	11		8		7			26
1	5	2				10	4	9	3	6	11				7	8		27
1	5	2				10	4	9	3	6	11		8		7			28
1	5	2				10	6	9	3		11		8	4	7			29
1	5	2				10	6	9	3		11		8	4	7			30
1	5	2				10	4	9	3	6	11				7	8		31
1	5	2				10	4	9	3	6	11				7	8		32
	5	2				10	4	9	3	6	11			1	7	8		33
	5	2				10	4	9	3	6	11	7		1		8		34
	5	2			1	10	4	9	3	6	11	7				8		35
	5	2			1	10	4	9	3	6	11	7				8		36
	5	2	4		1	10	8	9	3	6	11				7			37
	5	2			1	10	4	9	3	6	11		8		7			38
	5	2			1	10	4	9	3	6	11		8		7			39
	5	2			1	10	4	9	3	6	11		8		7			40
	5	2			1	10	4	9	3	6	11		8		7			41
7	5	2			1	10	4	9	3	6	11		8		7			42
1	**32**	**42**	**42**	**1**	**8**	**41**	**33**	**42**	**42**	**39**	**41**	**9**	**33**	**2**	**12**	**32**	**10**	
						16	2	38		1	9		13		10	8		

FA Cup:

Barton	Black	Brice	Chenhall	Cronin	Elliott	Haynes	Hill	Jezzard	Lawler	Lowe	Mitten	Newcombe	Robson	Ronson	Smith	Stevens	Taylor	
1	5	2				10	4	9	3	6	11				7	8		3
1	5	2				10	4	9	3	6	11				7	8		R
1	5	2				10	4	9	3	6	11		8		7			4
3	**3**	**3**				**3**	**3**	**3**	**3**	**3**	**3**		**1**		**3**	**2**		
						2	1						1		1	4		

Month End		Sep	Oct	Nov	Dec	Jan	Feb	Mar	Apr	Final
1953-54	Pld	11	16	20	25	28	32	36	42	**42**
	Pts	6	12	18	25	29	34	37	44	**44**
	Pos	19th	16th	15th	10th	9th	9th	8th	8th	**8th**

1954-55

						Result	Scorers	Attendance
1	Aug	21	(h)	Blackburn R		W 5-1	Stevens, Jezzard, Mitten 2, Haynes	33,000
2		25	(a)	Derby C		W 4-3	Jezzard, Haynes 2, Robson	18,650
3		28	(a)	Bury		W 3-1	Jezzard, Stevens, Haynes	18,174
4	Sep	1	(h)	Derby C		W 2-0	Jezzard, Haynes	27,000
5		4	(a)	Swansea T		D 2-2	Robson, Jezzard	25,000
6		8	(h)	Doncaster R		W 5-2	Robson 2, Jezzard 2, Mitten	31,500
7		11	(h)	Notts C		W 3-1	Haynes, Jezzard, Mitten	27,000
8		15	(a)	Doncaster R		L 0-4		15,000
9		18	(a)	Liverpool		L 1-4	Robson	44,372
10		25	(h)	Bristol R		L 2-3	Jezzard 2	33,000
11	Oct	2	(a)	Plymouth A		L 2-3	Stevens, Robson	23,077
12		9	(h)	Birmingham C		W 2-1	Stevens, Robson	31,500
13		16	(a)	Ipswich T		W 4-2	Robson 2, Stevens, Jezzard	20,059
14		23	(h)	Luton T		W 3-1	Stevens 2, Robson	33,500
15		30	(a)	Rotherham U		W 3-2	Robson, Jezzard 2	19,000
16	Nov	6	(h)	Stoke C		D 2-2	Mitten, Stevens	32,000
17		13	(a)	Middlesbrough		L 2-4	Robson, Jezzard	23,000
18		20	(h)	Lincoln C		W 3-2	Chamberlain, Robson 2	22,500
19		27	(a)	Hull C		D 0-0		17,869
20	Dec	4	(h)	Nottingham F		D 1-1	Robson	20,000
21		11	(a)	Leeds U		D 1-1	Newcombe	30,500
22		18	(a)	Blackburn R		L 1-3	Haynes	25,600
23		25	(h)	Port Vale		W 3-1	Haynes, Robson, Jezzard	20,000
24		27	(a)	Port Vale		L 0-4		29,182
25	Jan	1	(h)	Bury		D 0-0		19,500
26	Feb	5	(h)	Liverpool		L 1-2	Brice	24,000
27		12	(a)	Bristol R		L 1-4	Jezzard	19,311
28		19	(h)	Plymouth A		L 2-3	Robson 2	12,000
29	Mar	5	(a)	Ipswich T		W 4-1	Jezzard, Barton, Hill, Robson	17,179
30		12	(a)	Luton T		L 0-3		17,966
31		19	(h)	Rotherham U		D 1-1	Jezzard	18,500
32		26	(a)	Stoke C		D 1-1	Mitten	7,000
33		30	(a)	Birmingham C		L 2-3	Robson, Dwight	7,000
34	Apr	2	(h)	Middlesbrough		L 1-2	Dwight	20,000
35		8	(a)	West Ham U		L 1-2	Jezzard	34,200
36		9	(a)	Lincoln C		D 2-2	Jezzard, Robson	12,357
37		11	(h)	West Ham U		D 0-0		22,500
38		16	(h)	Hull C		L 0-1		14,500
39		20	(h)	Swansea T		W 5-1	Robson, Jezzard 3, Barton	11,500
40		23	(a)	Nottingham F		L 0-2		9,871
41		27	(a)	Notts C		D 0-0		8,500
42		30	(h)	Leeds U		L 1-3	Robson	22,500

P	W	D	L	F	A	W	D	L	F	A	Pts	Pos	Div	
42	10	5	6	46	29	4	6	11	30	50	39	14th	2	Appearances
														Goals

FA Cup

3	Jan	8	(h)	Preston NE		L 2-3	Haynes, Stevens	24,766
								Appearances
								Goals

314

Player appearance grid (1954-55). Columns are players; cell values are shirt numbers worn; the right-hand column is the match number.

Bacuzzi	Barton	Black	Brice	Chamberlain	Chenhall	Cronin	Dwight	Elliott	Fisher	Gibson	Greenwood	Haynes	Hill	Jezzard	Lawler	Lowe	Mitten	Newcombe	Robson	Smith	Stapleton	Stevens	Wilson	No
		5			2		1					10	4	9	3	6	11		8			7		1
		5			2		1					10	4	9	3	6	11		8			7		2
		5			2		1					10	4	9	3	6	11		8			7		3
		5			2		1					10	4	9	3	6	11		8			7		4
		5			2		1					10	4	9	3	6	11		8			7		5
		5			2		1					10		9	3	6	11		8	4		7		6
		5			2		1					10		9	3	6	11		8	4		7		7
		5			2		1					10	4	9	3	6	11		8			7		8
		5			2		1					10	4	9	3	6	11		8			7		9
		5			2		1					10	6	9	3		11		8	4		7		10
					2	10	1			5			6	9	3		11		8	4		7		11
	1				2							10	5	9	3	6	11		8	4		7		12
	1	5			2							10	4	9	5	6	11		8			7		13
	1	5			2							10		9	3	6	11		8	4		7		14
	1	5			2							10		9	3	6	11		8	4		7		15
3	1	5			2							10		9		6	11		8	4		7		16
	1	5			2							10		9	3	6	11		8	4		7		17
	1	5	11						2			10		9	3	6		7	8	4				18
	1	5							2			10		9	3	6	11	7	8	4				19
	1	5							2			10		9	3	6	11	7	8					20
	1	5							2			10	4	9	3	6	11		8					21
	1	5			2							10	4	9	3	6	11	7	8					22
	1	5			2							10	4	9	3	6	11		8			7		23
		5			2		1					10	4	9	3	6	11		8			7		24
		5					1					10	4	9	3	6	11		8			7	2	25
		5						1	3			10	4	9		6	11		8			7	2	26
		5						1				10	4	9	3	6	11		8			7	2	27
	1	5	11						3			10		9		6		7	8	4			2	28
	7	1					9				5	10	4	9	3	6	11		8					29
	7	1					3		2		5	10	4	9		6	11		8					30
	7	1					3		2		5	10	4	9		6	11		8					31
	7	1									5	10	4	9	3	6	11		8					32
	7	1					9				5	10	4		3	6	11		8					33
	7	1	11				9				5	10	4		3	6			8					34
	7	1	11								5	10	4	9	3	6			8					35
	7	1	11								5	10	4	9	3	6			8					36
	7	1									5	10	4	9	3	6	11		8					37
	7	1	11								5	10	4	9	5	6			8					38
	7	1									5	10	4	9	3		11		8		6		2	39
	7	1									5	10	4	9	3		11		8		6		2	40
	7	1									5	10		9	3		11		8	4	6		2	41
	7	1									5	10		9	3		11		8	4	6		2	42
1	12	27	27	5	22	1	4	15	8	1	14	37	32	39	39	37	37	6	42	34	4	22	16	
	2			1	1				2			8	1	23			6	1	23			8		

Summary (additional) row:

Black	Dwight	Haynes	Hill	Jezzard	Lawler	Lowe	Mitten	Robson	Stevens	Wilson	No
5	1	10	4	9	3	6	11	8	7	2	3
	1		1	1	1	1	1	1	1		
			1						1	1	

Month End		Sep	Oct	Nov	Dec	Jan	Feb	Mar	Apr	Final
1954-55	Pld	10	15	19	24	25	28	33	42	42
	Pts	13	21	25	29	30	30	34	39	39
	Pos	7th	2nd	2nd	6th	8th	10th	11th	14th	14th

315

1955-56

1	Aug	20	(a)	Bury	W	5-1	Haynes 2, Jezzard 2, Stevens		13,566
2		24	(h)	Blackburn R	W	3-0	Stevens, Haynes, Jezzard		18,499
3		27	(h)	Barnsley	W	5-1	Jezzard 4, Robson		22,500
4		29	(a)	Blackburn R	L	0-1			24,600
5	Sep	3	(a)	Middlesbrough	D	1-1	Mitten		25,000
6		7	(h)	Notts C	D	1-1	Stevens		17,000
7		10	(h)	Bristol C	W	3-0	Haynes, Jezzard 2		26,847
8		15	(a)	Notts C	W	4-3	Haynes 3, Mitten		10,000
9		17	(a)	West Ham U	L	1-2	Jezzard		26,000
10		24	(h)	Port Vale	L	1-4	Mitten		26,500
11	Oct	1	(a)	Rotherham U	W	3-2	Robson, Jezzard 2		13,000
12		8	(h)	Hull C	W	5-0	Jezzard 5		21,117
13		15	(a)	Nottingham F	L	0-1			15,878
14		22	(h)	Leicester C	W	3-2	Robson 2, Jezzard		18,000
15		29	(a)	Doncaster R	L	2-4	Robson, Haynes		14,121
16	Nov	5	(h)	Bristol R	L	3-5	Jezzard 2, Stevens		31,500
17		12	(a)	Stoke C	W	2-1	Hill, Robson		18,942
18		19	(h)	Plymouth A	W	2-1	Jezzard, Mitten		23,000
19		26	(a)	Liverpool	L	0-7			34,955
20	Dec	3	(h)	Sheffield W	L	1-2	Hill		22,000
21		10	(a)	Lincoln C	L	1-6	Barton		11,635
22		17	(h)	Bury	W	3-1	Jezzard 2, Haynes		12,000
23		24	(a)	Barnsley	L	0-3			14,943
24		26	(h)	Swansea T	W	4-1	Haynes 2, Chamberlain, Jezzard		14,000
25		27	(a)	Swansea T	L	0-2			20,000
26		31	(h)	Middlesbrough	W	4-1	Hill, Chamberlain, Robson 2		19,000
27	Jan	14	(a)	Bristol C	L	1-2	Haynes		27,674
28		21	(h)	West Ham U	W	3-1	Chamberlain, Hill, Jezzard		25,000
29	Feb	4	(a)	Port Vale	L	1-2	Robson		13,304
30		11	(h)	Rotherham U	D	1-1	Haynes		9,000
31		18	(a)	Plymouth A	D	0-0			16,962
32	Mar	3	(a)	Leicester C	L	1-2	Robson		35,496
33		10	(h)	Lincoln C	W	3-0	Jezzard, Chamberlain, Haynes		19,500
34		17	(a)	Bristol R	D	2-2	Haynes, Stevens		21,836
35		24	(h)	Stoke C	W	2-0	Stevens, Chamberlain		16,000
36		30	(h)	Leeds U	L	1-2	Chamberlain		25,500
37		31	(a)	Hull C	D	2-2	Haynes 2		12,683
38	Apr	2	(a)	Leeds U	L	1-6	Haynes		20,000
39		7	(h)	Liverpool	W	3-1	Dwight 3		16,000
40		14	(a)	Sheffield W	W	3-2	Stevens, Dwight, Chamberlain		27,439
41		21	(h)	Doncaster R	W	4-0	Chamberlain 3, Stevens		18,000
42	May	2	(h)	Nottingham F	W	4-3	Stevens, Dwight, Jezzard, Chamberlain		10,000

P	W	D	L	F	A	W	D	L	F	A	Pts	Pos	Div	
42	15	2	4	59	27	5	4	12	30	52	46	9th	2	Appearances
														Goals

FA Cup

3	Jan	7	(a)	Notts C	W	1-0	Haynes		21,500
4		28	(h)	Newcastle U	L	4-5	Chamberlain 3, Hill		39,200
									Appearances
									Goals

Player appearance grid, Season 1955-56. Player columns (left to right): Black, Hewkins, Elliott, Chenhall, Wilson, Lawler, Bacuzzi, Stapleton, Collins, Smith, Hill, Greenwood, Brice, Lowe, Stevens, Barton, Robson, Haynes, Dwight, Jezzard, Hall, Mitten, Chamberlain. Final column = match number.

Bla	Hew	Ell	Che	Wil	Law	Bac	Sta	Col	Smi	Hil	Gre	Bri	Low	Ste	Bar	Rob	Hay	Dwi	Jez	Hal	Mit	Cha	#
1			2	3	4					5			6	7		8	10	9			11		1
1			2	3	4					5			6	7		8	10	9			11		2
1			2	3	4					5			6	7		8	10	9			11		3
1			2	3	4					5			6	7		8	10	9			11		4
1			2	3	4					5			6	9	7	8	10				11		5
1			2	3	4					5			6	9	7	8	10				11		6
1			2	3	4					5			6	7		8	10		9		11		7
1			2	3	4				8	5			6	7			10		9		11		8
1			2	3	4				8	5			6		7		10		9		11		9
1			2	3	4					5			6	7		8	10		9		11		10
1			2	3	4					5			6	7		8	10		9		11		11
1			2	3	4				6	5				7		8	10		9		11		12
1			2	3	4				6	5				7		8	10		9		11		13
1			2	3	4				6	5				7		8	10		9		11		14
1			2	3					4	5			6	7		8	10		9		11		15
1			2	3					4	5			6	7		8	10		9		11		16
	1		2	3	4				10	5			6	7		8			9		11		17
	1		2	3					4	5			6	7		8	10		9		11		18
	1		2	3					4	5			6	7		8	10		9			11	19
		1	2	3	4				10	5			6			7	8		9		11		20
		1	2	3					4	5			6		7	8	10		9		11		21
1					2		3	4	8	5			6	7			10		9			11	22
1					2		3	4	8	5			6				10		9			11	23
1					2		3	4	8	5			6	7			10		9			11	24
1					2		3	4	8	5			6	7			10		9			11	25
1					2		3	4	7	5			6			8	10		9			11	26
1					2		3	4	7	5			6			8	10		9		11		27
1					2		3	4	8	5			6	7			10		9			11	28
1					2		3		7	5			6			8	10		9			11	29
1					2		3		7	5			6			8	10		9			11	30
1					2		3		7	5			6			8	10		9			11	31
1					2		3				4	7	5	6		8	10		9			11	32
1					2		3				4	8	5	6	7		10		9			11	33
1					2		3				4	2	5	6	7		10		9			11	34
1				2							4	6	5	6	7		10		9			11	35
1				2							4	8	5	6	7		10		9			11	36
1					2						4	8	5	6	7		10		9			11	37
1					2						4	8	5	6	7		10		9			11	38
1					2	3					4	8	5	6	7		10		9			11	39
	1				2	3					4	8	5	6	7		10	9				11	40
	1			3		2					4		5	6	7	10	8	9				11	41
	1			3		2					4		5	6	7	10	8	9				11	42
34	**6**	**2**	**21**	**16**	**37**	**1**	**18**	**7**	**21**	**31**	**28**	**14**	**39**	**30**	**7**	**25**	**40**	**4**	**38**	**1**	**21**	**21**	
											4		9	1		10	18	5	27		4	11	

FA Cup:

Bla	Hew	Ell	Che	Wil	Law	Bac	Sta	Col	Smi	Hil	Gre	Bri	Low	Ste	Bar	Rob	Hay	Dwi	Jez	Hal	Mit	Cha	#
1			2	3						4		7	5	6		8	10		9		11		3
1			2	3						4		7	5	6		8	10		9			11	4
2			2	2						2		2	2	2		2	2		2		1	1	
												1					1		3				

Month End	Sep	Oct	Nov	Dec	Jan	Feb	Mar	Apr	Final
1955-56 Pld	10	15	19	26	28	31	37	41	**42**
Pts	12	18	22	28	30	32	38	44	**46**
Pos	2nd	3rd	5th	10th	10th	11th	12th	12th	**9th**

1956-57

1	Aug	18	(h)	West Ham U	L 1-4	Dwight	26,000
2		20	(a)	Sheffield U	L 2-5	Stapleton, Dwight	25,000
3		25	(a)	Nottingham F	L 1-3	Dwight	21,344
4		29	(h)	Sheffield U	L 1-2	Dwight	8,500
5	Sep	1	(h)	Huddersfield T	W 1-0	Dwight	18,000
6		4	(a)	Bristol C	W 3-0	Dwight, Chamberlain, Stevens	22,432
7		8	(h)	Swansea T	W 7-3	Dwight 3, Chamberlain, Stevens 2, opp own goal	25,000
8		12	(h)	Bristol C	W 2-1	Chamberlain, Hill	15,019
9		15	(a)	Lincoln C	L 0-1		11,476
10		22	(h)	Rotherham U	W 3-1	Bentley, Chamberlain, Stevens	31,080
11		29	(a)	Port Vale	L 1-2	Stevens	21,273
12	Oct	6	(a)	Bury	W 1-0	Dwight	11,853
13		13	(h)	Grimsby T	W 3-1	Stevens 3	32,000
14		20	(a)	Liverpool	L 3-4	Chamberlain 2, Haynes	36,735
15		27	(h)	Stoke C	W 1-0	Stevens	30,000
16	Nov	3	(a)	Middlesbrough	L 1-3	Hill	30,000
17		10	(h)	Leicester C	D 2-2	Bentley 2	33,700
18		17	(a)	Bristol R	L 0-4		24,658
19		24	(h)	Notts C	W 5-1	Dwight 3, Stevens 2	16,000
20	Dec	1	(a)	Doncaster R	L 0-4		13,143
21		8	(h)	Leyton O	W 3-1	Dwight, Haynes 2	27,000
22		15	(a)	West Ham U	L 1-2	Bentley	18,250
23		22	(h)	Nottingham F	L 0-1		13,000
24		25	(a)	Blackburn R	L 0-2		23,900
25		26	(h)	Blackburn R	W 7-2	Chamberlain 3, Dwight 2, Bentley 2	8,000
26		29	(a)	Huddersfield T	D 1-1	Dwight	16,503
27	Jan	12	(a)	Swansea T	W 5-4	Dwight 3, Chamberlain 2	16,000
28		19	(h)	Lincoln C	L 0-1		17,500
29	Feb	2	(a)	Rotherham U	L 3-4	Opp own goal, Bentley, Dwight	10,391
30		9	(h)	Port Vale	W 6-3	Bentley 3, Dwight 3	14,300
31		16	(h)	Bury	L 1-3	Haynes	26,000
32		23	(a)	Grimsby T	L 1-3	Watson	13,006
33	Mar	2	(h)	Liverpool	L 1-2	Dwight	26,500
34		9	(a)	Stoke C	W 2-0	Bentley 2	24,756
35		16	(h)	Middlesbrough	L 1-2	Chamberlain	20,500
36		23	(a)	Leicester C	W 3-1	Bentley, Hill, Langley	36,450
37		30	(h)	Bristol R	W 3-2	Chamberlain, Hill, Stapleton	22,000
38	Apr	6	(a)	Notts C	D 0-0		17,121
39		13	(h)	Doncaster R	W 3-0	Hill, Stevens, Bentley	15,000
40		19	(h)	Barnsley	W 2-0	Stevens, Chamberlain	17,000
41		20	(a)	Leyton O	W 2-0	Stevens 2	16,436
42		22	(a)	Barnsley	D 1-1	Chamberlain	8,410

P	W	D	L	F	A	W	D	L	F	A	Pts	Pos	Div		
42	13	1	7	53	32	6	3	12	31	44	42	11th	2	Appearances	
														Goals	

FA Cup

3	Jan	5	(a)	Ipswich T	W 3-2	Stevens 2, Dwight	22,210
4		26	(a)	Blackpool	L 2-6	Lowe, Bentley	26,248

Appearances

Goals

Black	Chenhall	Lawler	Smith	Lampe	Lowe	Stevens	Stapleton	Dwight	Haynes	Chamberlain	Barton	Hill	Collins	Doherty	Bentley	Edwards	Wilson	Hewkins	Watson	Langley	Cohen	#
1	2	3	4	5	6	7	8	9	10	11												1
1	2	3	4	5	10	8	6	9		11		7										2
1	2	3	4	5	6	7	8	10		11		9										3
1		3		5	6	7	4	9	10	11		8	2									4
1		3		5	6	7	4	9	10			8	2	11								5
1		3		5	6	7	4	9	10	11		8	2									6
1		3		5	6	7	4	9	10	11		8	2									7
1		3		5	6	7	4	9	10	11		8	2									8
1		3		5	6	7	4	9		11		8	2	10								9
1		3		5	6	7	4	9		11		8	2		10							10
1		3	4	5		7				11		8	2	10	9	6						11
1		3	4	5	6	7		9		11		8	2	10								12
1		3		5	6	7		9	10	11		4	2		8							13
1		3		5	6	7	4		10	11		8	2		9							14
1		3		5	6	7	4		10	11		8	2		9							15
1		3		5	6	7	4		10	11		8	2		9							16
1		3		5	6	7		9	10	11		4			8	2						17
1		3		5	6	7		9		11		4		10	8	2						18
1		3		5	6	7		9	10	11		4	2		8							19
1		3		5	6	7	4	9		11		10	2		8							20
1		3		5	6	7		9	10	11		4	2		8							21
1		3		5	6	7		9	10	11		4	2		8							22
1		3		5	6	7		9		11		4	2	8	10							23
1		3		5	6	7		9	10	11		4	2		8							24
1		3		5	6	7		9	10	11		4	2		8							25
1		3		5	6	7		9	10	11		4	2		8							26
1	2	3		5	6	7		9	10	11		4			8							27
1	2	3		5	6	7		9	10	11		4			8							28
		3		5	6	7		9	10	11		4	2		8			1				29
		3		5	6	7	2	9	10	11		4			8			1				30
		2		5	6	7		9	10	11		4			8			1		3		31
		2			5			9	10	11		4			8		6	1	7	3		32
				5	6	11		9	10			4			8		1	7		3	2	33
1		2		5	6	11	4	7	10			8			9					3		34
1		2		5	6		4	7	10	11		8			9					3		35
1		2		5	6	7	4		10	11		8			9					3		36
1		2		5	6	7	4		10	11		8			9					3		37
1		2		5	6	7	4		10	11		8			9					3		38
1		2		5	6	7	4		10	11		8			9					3		39
1		2		5	6	7	4	9	10	11					8					3		40
1		2		5	6	7	4	9	10	11					8					3		41
1		2		5	6	7	4	9	10	11					8					3		42
37	5	41	5	40	42	40	24	34	33	39	1	37	22	6	32	2	2	5	2	12	1	
							15	2	25	4		15	5		14			1	1			

Black	Chenhall	Lawler	Smith	Lampe	Lowe	Stevens	Stapleton	Dwight	Haynes	Chamberlain	Barton	Hill	Collins	Doherty	Bentley	Edwards	Wilson	Hewkins	Watson	Langley	Cohen	#
1	2	3		5	6	7		9	10	11		4			8							3
1		3		5	6	7		9	10	11		4	2		8							4
2	1	2		2	2	2		2	2	2		2	1		2							
								1	2			1			1							

Month End		Sep	Oct	Nov	Dec	Jan	Feb	Mar	Apr	Final
1956-57	Pld	11	15	19	26	28	32	37	42	**42**
	Pts	10	16	19	24	26	28	34	42	**42**
	Pos	11th	9th	12th	12th	14th	16th	14th	11th	**11th**

319

1957-58

1	Aug	24	(h)	Derby C	W	2-0	Haynes, Dwight	27,000
2		29	(a)	Notts C	W	5-1	Dwight 2, Haynes, Chamberlain 2	17,516
3		31	(a)	Swansea T	D	4-4	Dwight 2, Hill, Bentley	24,000
4	Sep	4	(h)	Notts C	W	1-0	Dwight	14,600
5		7	(h)	Liverpool	D	2-2	Chamberlain, Haynes	33,000
6		11	(a)	Ipswich T	D	1-1	Langley	19,648
7		14	(h)	Barnsley	D	1-1	Haynes	25,000
8		18	(h)	Ipswich T	D	0-0		16,200
9		21	(a)	West Ham U	L	2-3	Dwight, Bentley	24,000
10		28	(h)	Sheffield U	W	6-3	Dwight 4, Bentley, Stevens	26,200
11	Oct	5	(a)	Blackburn R	D	1-1	Stevens	25,600
12		12	(a)	Middlesbrough	L	0-2		30,000
13		19	(h)	Leyton O	W	3-1	Dwight, Hill, Bentley	30,000
14		26	(a)	Charlton A	D	2-2	Stevens, Langley	29,664
15	Nov	2	(h)	Doncaster R	W	4-1	Opp own goal, Hill, Haynes, Stevens	21,500
16		9	(a)	Rotherham U	L	1-3	Bentley	8,565
17		16	(h)	Huddersfield T	W	2-1	Haynes 2	18,000
18		23	(a)	Grimsby T	L	1-3	Barton	15,102
19		30	(h)	Stoke C	L	3-4	Dwight, Bentley, Hill	20,000
20	Dec	7	(a)	Bristol C	W	5-0	Dwight 2, Haynes, Hill, Chamberlain	16,746
21		14	(h)	Cardiff C	W	2-0	Hill, opp own goal	17,000
22		21	(a)	Derby C	D	3-3	Dwight 2, Bentley	21,994
23		25	(a)	Lincoln C	W	1-0	Dwight	8,028
24		26	(h)	Lincoln C	W	4-1	Haynes 2, Chamberlain, Hill	19,100
25		28	(h)	Swansea T	W	2-0	Doherty, Haynes	25,000
26	Jan	11	(a)	Liverpool	L	1-2	Chamberlain	51,701
27		18	(a)	Barnsley	L	0-1		14,263
28	Feb	1	(h)	West Ham U	D	2-2	Haynes, Langley	42,289
29		22	(h)	Grimsby T	W	6-0	Dwight 2, Haynes, Hill, Cook, Chamberlain	22,000
30	Mar	8	(h)	Charlton A	W	3-1	Haynes, Hill, Chamberlain	33,000
31		13	(a)	Leyton O	W	3-1	Dwight, Cook, Lowe	12,407
32		15	(a)	Doncaster R	W	6-1	Cook, Hill 5	14,000
33		29	(a)	Huddersfield T	W	3-0	Haynes, Cook, Chamberlain	19,215
34	Apr	4	(a)	Bristol R	D	2-2	Hill, Dwight	31,109
35		7	(h)	Bristol R	W	3-0	Chamberlain, Langley, Cook	31,300
36		12	(a)	Stoke C	W	2-1	Chamberlain, Cook	18,918
37		19	(h)	Bristol C	L	3-4	Cook, Barton 2	27,200
38		21	(h)	Middlesbrough	L	0-1		26,000
39		23	(h)	Blackburn R	D	1-1	Chamberlain	32,157
40		26	(a)	Cardiff C	L	0-3		10,000
41		28	(a)	Sheffield U	D	1-1	Hill	16,403
42	May	1	(h)	Rotherham U	W	3-1	Chamberlain, Cook 2	7,700

P	W	D	L	F	A	W	D	L	F	A	Pts	Pos	Div		
42	13	5	3	53	24	7	7	7	44	35	52	5th	2	Appearances	
														Goals	

FA Cup

3	Jan	4	(h)	Yeovil	W	4-0	Hill 2, Key, Doherty	29,820
4		25	(h)	Charlton A	D	1-1	Hill	39,586
R		29	(a)	Charlton A	W	2-0	Bentley, Stevens	43,097
5	Feb	15	(a)	West Ham U	W	3-2	Dwight, Hill, Haynes	37,500
6	Mar	1	(h)	Bristol R	W	3-1	Hill, Stevens 2	42,000
SF		22	(n)	Manchester U	D	2-2	Stevens, Hill	69,745
R		26	(n)	Manchester U	L	3-5	Dwight, Stevens Chamberlain	32,800

FA Cup semi-final played at Villa Park, Birmingham, replay at Highbury.   Appearances

Goals

> *Fulham's record for consecutive Football League victories is seven, covering the last game of 1957-8 and the first six of 1958-9.*

Player appearance and goalscoring grid (Fulham 1957-58). Columns are shirt numbers worn; the final column is the match number.

Black	Lawler	Langley	Edwards	Stapleton	Lowe	Stevens	Bentley	Dwight	Haynes	Chamberlain	Hill	Weir	Taylor	Lampe	Watson	Hewkins	Doherty	Cohen	Barton	Macedo	Forbes	Cook	Chenhall	Collins	Key	#
1	2	3	4	5	6	7	8	9	10	11																1
1	2	3	4	5	6		9	7	10	11	8															2
1	2	3	4	5	6		9	7	10	11	8															3
1	2	3	4	5	6		9	7	10	11	8															4
1	2	3	4	5	6		9	7	10	11	8															5
1	2	3	4	5	6	7	8	9	10			11														6
1	2	3	4	5	6		8	7	10			11	9													7
1	2	3	4	5	6		9	7	10		8	11														8
1	2	3	6	4		11	10	9	8					5	7											9
	2	3		4		11	8	9	10				7	5		1						6				10
	2	3	4			11	6	9	10		8		7	5		1										11
1	2	3	4	5	6	11	9		10		8		7													12
1	2	3	4	5	6	11	9	7			8						10									13
1	2	3	4	5	6	11	9	7	10		8															14
1	2	3	4	5	6	11	9	7	10		8															15
1	2	3	4		6	11	9	7	10		8			5												16
1		3		5	6	11	4	9	10		8							2	7							17
		3		5	6	11	4	9	10		8					1		2	7							18
		3		5	6	11	4	9	10		8					1		2	7							19
		3			6		4	9	10	11	8			5				2	7	1						20
		3			6		4	9	10	11	8			5				2	7	1						21
		3			6		4	9	10	11	8			5				2	7	1						22
		3			6	11	4	9	10		8			5				2	7	1						23
		3			6	7	4		10	11	8			5			9	2		1						24
		3			6	7	4		10	11	8			5			9	2		1						25
		3			6	7	4		10	11	8			5			9	2		1						26
		3			6	7	9			11	8			5			10	2		1	4					27
	6	3	4	5				7	10	11	8							2		1		9				28
	6	3	4	5				7	10	11	8							2		1		9				29
	6	3	4	5				7	10	11	8							2		1		9				30
	6	3	4	5				7	10	11	8							2		1		9				31
	6	3	4	5				7	10	11	8							2		1		9				32
	6	3	4	5				7	10	11	8							2		1		9				33
	6	3	4	5				7	10	11	8							2		1		9				34
	6	3	4	5				7	10	11	8							2		1		9				35
		3		5	6				10	11	8							2	7	1	4	9				36
				5	6	7			10	11								2	8	1	4	9	3			37
		3		5	6		4		10	11	8							2	7	1		9				38
	6			5			4	7	10	11								2	7	1		9		3		39
	6	3	4	5				7	10	11	8							2	7	1		9				40
	6	3	4	5				7	10	11	8							2		1		9				41
	6		4	5				7	10	11								2	8	1		9		3		42
15	**25**	**38**	**18**	**32**	**35**	**22**	**31**	**30**	**38**	**27**	**37**	**3**	**4**	**13**	**1**	**4**	**5**	**26**	**13**	**23**	**4**	**15**	**1**	**2**		
	4					1	4	7	22	15	13	16						1	3			9				

FA Cup matches (right-hand column shows round):

Black	Lawler	Langley	Edwards	Stapleton	Lowe	Stevens	Bentley	Dwight	Haynes	Chamberlain	Hill	Weir	Taylor	Lampe	Watson	Hewkins	Doherty	Cohen	Barton	Macedo	Forbes	Cook	Chenhall	Collins	Key	Rd
		3			6	7	4		10		8			5			9	2		1				11		3
	6	3		5		7	4	9	10	11	8							2		1						4
	6	3				7	4	9	10	11	8			5				2		1						R
	6	3		5		9	4	7	10	11	8							2		1						5
	6	3		5		9	4	7	10	11	8							2		1						6
	6	3		5		9	4	7	10	11	8							2		1						7
	6	3		5		9	4	7	10	11	8							2		1						R
	6	7		5	1	7	7	6	7	6	7		2				1	7		7			1			
				5	1	2	1	1	6				1					1					1			

Month End		Sep	Oct	Nov	Dec	Jan	Feb	Mar	Apr	Final
1957-58	**Pld**	10	14	19	25	27	29	33	41	**42**
	Pts	13	17	21	32	32	35	43	50	**52**
	Pos	3rd	5th	5th	1st	5th	6th	4th	6th	**5th**

1958-59

1	Aug	23	(h)	Stoke C	W	6-1	Cook 3, Haynes, Leggat, Chamberlain	31,854
2		27	(a)	Sunderland	W	2-1	Leggat, Chamberlain	37,772
3		30	(a)	Swansea T	W	2-1	Haynes, Leggat	23,000
4	Sep	3	(h)	Sunderland	W	6-2	Haynes 3, Chamberlain, Leggat, Langley	27,000
5		6	(h)	Ipswich T	W	3-2	Haynes, Cook, Leggat	34,000
6		10	(a)	Lincoln C	W	4-2	Leggat 2, Chamberlain, Haynes	13,092
7		13	(a)	Bristol R	D	0-0		30,076
8		17	(h)	Lincoln C	W	4-2	Haynes 4	21,000
9		20	(h)	Derby C	W	4-2	Haynes 2, Langley, Cook	32,000
10		27	(a)	Leyton O	W	2-0	Chamberlain, Cook	24,681
11	Oct	4	(h)	Scunthorpe U	D	1-1	Leggat	25,000
12		11	(a)	Grimsby T	D	2-2	Langley, Chamberlain	18,000
13		18	(h)	Liverpool	L	0-1		32,000
14		25	(a)	Middlesbrough	W	3-2	Leggat 3	31,763
15	Nov	1	(h)	Sheffield U	W	4-2	Key, Haynes, Cook, Leggat	32,500
16		8	(a)	Bristol C	D	1-1	Haynes	32,092
17		15	(h)	Cardiff C	W	2-1	Cook, Chamberlain	24,500
18		22	(a)	Huddersfield T	L	1-2	Key	19,778
19		29	(h)	Barnsley	W	5-2	Opp own goal, Leggat 2, Doherty, Cook	19,000
20	Dec	6	(a)	Rotherham U	L	0-4		7,638
21		13	(h)	Charlton A	W	2-1	Johnson 2	19,000
22		20	(a)	Stoke C	L	1-4	Barton	18,457
23		26	(h)	Brighton & HA	W	3-1	Johnson, Cohen, Langley	29,000
24		27	(a)	Brighton & HA	L	0-3		36,747
25	Jan	3	(h)	Swansea T	L	1-2	Cook	28,100
26		17	(a)	Ipswich T	W	2-1	Cook, Haynes	16,056
27		31	(h)	Bristol R	W	1-0	Cook	24,100
28	Feb	7	(a)	Derby C	L	0-2		21,678
29		14	(h)	Leyton O	W	5-2	Leggat, Doherty, Haynes 3	20,700
30		21	(a)	Scunthorpe U	W	2-1	Langley, Haynes	9,500
31		28	(h)	Bristol C	W	1-0	Leggat	27,000
32	Mar	7	(a)	Liverpool	D	0-0		43,926
33		14	(h)	Middlesbrough	W	3-2	Leggat, Haynes, Barton	27,200
34		21	(a)	Sheffield U	L	0-2		17,832
35		27	(h)	Sheffield W	W	6-2	Leggat, Langley, Cook, Hill 3	40,000
36		28	(a)	Grimsby T	W	3-0	Haynes, Leggat, Langley	25,500
37		30	(a)	Sheffield W	D	2-2	Cook 2	32,170
38	Apr	4	(a)	Cardiff C	W	2-1	Leggat, Haynes	30,000
39		11	(h)	Huddersfield T	W	1-0	Cook	24,000
40		18	(a)	Barnsley	W	4-2	Hill, Cook, Leggat, opp own goal	7,964
41		23	(a)	Charlton A	L	1-2	Hill	22,129
42		25	(h)	Rotherham U	W	4-0	Haynes 3, Hill	18,300

P	W	D	L	F	A	W	D	L	F	A	Pts	Pos	Div	
42	18	1	2	65	26	9	5	7	31	35	60	2nd	2	Appearances
														Goals

FA Cup

3	Jan	10	(h)	Peterborough U	D	0-0		31,908
R		24	(a)	Peterborough U	W	1-0	Johnson	21,400
4		28	(a)	Birmingham C	D	1-1	Hill	42,677
R	Feb	4	(h)	Birmingham C	L	2-3	Leggat, Hill	27,521

Appearances

Goals

The longest winning sequence of home matches is 12 which covered the last eight games of 1958-9 and the first four of 1959-60.

Appearance and goalscoring grid — Season 1958-59

Barton	Bentley	Chamberlain	Cohen	Collins	Cook	Doherty	Edwards	Haynes	Hewkins	Hill	Johnson	Key	Lampe	Langley	Lawler	Lowe	Leggat	Macedo	Mullery	O'Connell	Stapleton	Stevens	No.
	4	11	2		9			10		8				3		6	7	1			5		1
	4	11	2		9			10		8				3		6	7	1			5		2
	4	11	2		9			10		8				3		6	7	1			5		3
		11	2		9			10		8				3	4	6	7	1			5		4
		11	2		9			10		8				3	4	6	7	1			5		5
		11	2		9			10		8				3	4	6	7	1			5		6
	4	11	2		9			10		8				3		6	7	1			5		7
	4	11	2		9			10		8				3		6	7	1			5		8
	4	11	2		9			10		8				3	6		7	1			5		9
	4	11	2		9			10						3	6			1			5	7	10
	4	11	2		9					8				3	6		7	1			5	10	11
	4	11	2		9	8		10						3	6		7	1			5		12
8	4		2		9			10			7			3	6			1			5	11	13
8	5		2		9			10				11		3	6	4	7	1					14
8	5		2		9			10				11		3	4	6	7	1					15
	5		2		9			10		8	7			3	4	6	11	1					16
		11	2		9	10			8				5	3	6	4	7	1					17
	5	11	2		9	10			8		7			3	6	4		1					18
	5	11	2		9	10			8					3	6	4	7	1					19
		11	2		9	10			8					3	6	4	7	1			5		20
7	5		2		9	10			8	11				3	6	4		1					21
7	5		2		9	10				11				3	6	4		1		8			22
8	5		2		9			10		11				3	6	4	7	1					23
8	5		2		9			10		11				3	6	4	7	1					24
	5		2		9			10	8	11				3	6	4	7	1					25
			2		9			10	8	11				3	6	4	7	1			5		26
	4		2		9		1	8		11				3	6	7					5		27
8	5		2	3	9			10	1					11	6	4	7						28
7	5		2				9	10	1	8				3	6	11			4				29
8					7	9	6	10	1				5	3	2		11		4				30
8	5		2		9	7		10	1					3	6		11		4				31
7	5		2		9			10		8				3	6		11	1	4				32
7	5		2		9			10		8				3		6	11	1	4				33
7	5		2		9			10		8				3		6	11	1	4				34
	5	11	2		9			10		8				3		6	7	1	4				35
	5	11	2		9			10		8				3	6		7	1	4				36
	5	11	2		9			10		8				3	6		7	1	4				37
	5	11	2		9			10		8				3		6	7	1	4				38
7	5	11	2		9	10				8				3		6		1	4				39
	5	11	2		9			10		8				3		6	7	1	4				40
	5	11	2		9			10		8				3		6	7	1	4				41
	5	11	2		9			10		8				3		6	7	1	4				42
15	35	24	41	1	41	11	1	34	5	32	6	6	2	40	29	32	36	37	14	1	16	3	
2		7	1		17	2		26		6	3	2		7			21						

Cup matches

Barton	Bentley	Chamberlain	Cohen	Collins	Cook	Doherty	Edwards	Haynes	Hewkins	Hill	Johnson	Key	Lampe	Langley	Lawler	Lowe	Leggat	Macedo	Mullery	O'Connell	Stapleton	Stevens	Rd
	5		2		9			10		8	11			3	6	4	7	1					3
	5		2		9			10		8	11			3	6	4	7	1					R
	4		2		9			10		8	11			3	6	7		1			5		4
	4		2		9		1	8			11			3	6	7					5		R
	4		4		4	1	4	3	1		2	4	4	4	4	3		2					
					2	1												1					

Month End		Sep	Oct	Nov	Dec	Jan	Feb	Mar	Apr	Final
1958-59	Pld	10	14	19	24	27	31	37	42	**42**
	Pts	19	23	30	34	38	44	52	60	**60**
	Pos	1st	2nd	1st	2nd	2nd	2nd	1st	2nd	**2nd**

323

1959-60

1	Aug	22	(a)	Blackburn R	L	0-4		30,800
2		26	(h)	Manchester C	W	5-2	Haynes 2, Leggat 2, Mullery	27,000
3		29	(h)	Blackpool	W	1-0	Leggat	42,600
4	Sep	2	(a)	Manchester C	L	1-3	Stokes	26,000
5		5	(a)	Everton	D	0-0		31,000
6		9	(h)	Wolves	W	3-1	Doherty, Cook, Stokes	32,500
7		12	(h)	Luton T	W	4-2	Leggat 2, Hill, Doherty	30,100
8		16	(a)	Wolves	L	0-9		41,600
9		19	(a)	Bolton W	L	2-3	Cook 2	24,634
10		26	(h)	Chelsea	L	1-3	Chamberlain	41,500
11	Oct	3	(h)	Nottingham F	W	3-1	Stokes 2, Cook	29,700
12		10	(a)	West Brom A	W	4-2	Chamberlain 2, Cook, Stokes	20,000
13		17	(h)	Newcastle U	W	4-3	Key, Cook, Hill, Haynes	37,200
14		24	(a)	Birmingham C	W	4-2	Cook 2, Key, Langley	26,698
15		31	(h)	West Ham U	W	1-0	Stokes	44,695
16	Nov	7	(a)	Manchester U	D	3-3	Leggat 3	44,063
17		14	(h)	Preston NE	L	1-2	Haynes	26,432
18		21	(a)	Leicester C	W	1-0	Chamberlain	24,165
19		28	(h)	Burnley	W	1-0	Hill	29,342
20	Dec	5	(a)	Leeds U	W	4-1	Leggat 2, Chamberlain, Haynes	18,500
21		12	(h)	Tottenham H	D	1-1	Hill	37,000
22		19	(h)	Blackburn R	L	0-1		17,398
23		26	(a)	Sheffield W	D	1-1	Leggat	50,240
24		28	(h)	Sheffield W	L	1-2	Langley	36,856
25	Jan	2	(a)	Blackpool	L	1-3	Sullivan	17,030
26		16	(h)	Everton	W	2-0	Haynes, Mullery	21,226
27		23	(a)	Luton T	L	1-4	Hill	17,876
28	Feb	6	(h)	Bolton W	D	1-1	Jones	24,743
29		13	(a)	Chelsea	L	2-4	Haynes, Bentley	38,087
30		20	(a)	Nottingham F	D	2-2	Key, Leggat	23,057
31		27	(h)	Leeds U	W	5-0	Leggat 4, Langley	23,335
32	Mar	5	(a)	Newcastle U	L	1-3	Bentley	33,840
33		12	(h)	Birmingham C	D	2-2	Leggat 2	25,100
34		19	(a)	Tottenham H	D	1-1	Haynes	52,150
35		26	(h)	Manchester U	L	0-5		38,250
36	Apr	2	(a)	Preston NE	L	1-4	Haynes	15,007
37		9	(h)	Leicester C	D	1-1	Johnson	18,664
38		15	(a)	Arsenal	L	0-2		37,873
39		16	(a)	West Ham U	W	2-1	Chamberlain, O'Connell	24,083
40		18	(h)	Arsenal	W	3-0	Key, Jones, O'Connell	31,058
41		23	(h)	West Brom A	W	2-1	Jones, Haynes	23,631
42		30	(a)	Burnley	D	0-0		29,856

P	W	D	L	F	A	W	D	L	F	A	Pts	Pos	Div	
42	12	4	5	42	28	5	6	10	31	52	44	10th	1	Appearances
														Goals

FA Cup

3	Jan	9	(h)	Hull C	W	5-0	Leggat 2; Chamberlain, Cook, Hill	22,000
4		30	(a)	Leicester C	L	1-2	Opp own goal	31,000

Appearances

Goals

324

Bentley	Chamberlain	Cohen	Cook	Doherty	Haynes	Hewkins	Hill	Johnson	Jones	Lampe	Langley	Lawler	Leggat	Lowe	Key	Macedo	Mullery	O'Connell	Stapleton	Stokes	Stratton	Sullivan	
5	11	2	6	9	10		8				3		7			1	4						1
5	11	2		9	10		8				3	6	7			1	4						2
5	11	2		9	10		8				3	6	7			1	4						3
5	11	2	10	9							3	6	7			1	4			8			4
5	11	2		9	10						3	6	7			1	4			8			5
5		2		9	10				11		3	6	7			1	4			8			6
5		2		9			8		11		3	6	7			1	4			10			7
		2		9			8		11		3	6	7			1	4		5	10			8
		2	10	9			8		11	5	3			6	7	1	4						9
	11	2	10	9			8			5	3		7	6		1	4						10
5	11	2	10				8				3			6	7	1	4			9			11
5	11	2	10				8				3			6	7	1	4			9			12
5	11	2	9		10		8				3			6	7	1	4						13
5	11	2	9		10		8				3			6	7	1	4						14
5	11	2	9		10						3			6	7	1	4			8			15
5	11	2			10		8				3		9	6	7	1	4						16
5	11	2			10		8				3		9	6	7	1	4						17
	11	2			10		8			5	3		7	6		1	4			9			18
	11	2			10		8			5	3		9	6	7	1	4						19
	11	2			10		8			5	3		9	6	7	1	4						20
	11	2			10		8			5	3		9	6	7	1	4						21
	11	2	9		10		8			5	3	4	7	6		1							22
	11	2			10		8			5	3		7	6		1	4			9			23
		2			10		8				3		11	6	7	1	4		5	9			24
5	11	2	9				8				3		7	6		1	4				10		25
5	11	2	9		10		8				3		7	6		1	4						26
5	11	2		9	10	1					3		7	6			4						27
5	11	2		7	10	1		9			3			6			4			8			28
5		2			10			9			3	4	7	6		1				8		11	29
		2			10			9		5	3	6	11	4	7	1				8			30
		2	8		10			9		5	3	6	11	4	7	1							31
9		2	8		10					5	3	4	11	6	7	1							32
		2	8		10			9			3	4	11	6	7	1			5				33
9		2			10		8			5	3		11	6	7	1	4						34
9		2			10		8			5	3		11	7	6	1	4						35
5		2	9	10		1					3		11	6	7		4			8			36
5		2	9				11				3			6	7	1	4	10		8			37
5		2			10		11				3		9	6	7	1	4	8					38
9	11	2			10					5	3	6			7	1	4	8					39
5	11	2			10			9			3			6	7	1	4	8					40
5	11	2			10			9			3			6	7	1	4	8					41
5	11	2	9		10						3			6	7	1	4	8					42
29	27	42	17	15	31	3	25	6	7	14	42	16	28	33	25	39	36	6	3	15	1	2	
2	6		8	2	10		5	1	3		3		18		4		2	2		6		1	

Bentley	Chamberlain	Cohen	Cook	Doherty	Haynes	Hewkins	Hill	Johnson	Jones	Lampe	Langley	Lawler	Leggat	Lowe	Key	Macedo	Mullery	O'Connell	Stapleton	Stokes	Stratton	Sullivan	
5	11	2	9		10		8				3		7	6		1	4						3
5	11	2	9	8	10						3		7	6		1	4						4
2	2	2	2	1	2		1				2		2	2		2	2						
1		1			1								2										

Month End		Sep	Oct	Nov	Dec	Jan	Feb	Mar	Apr	Final
1959-60	Pld	10	15	19	24	27	31	35	42	**42**
	Pts	9	19	24	28	30	34	36	44	**44**
	Pos	15th	6th	5th	8th	7th	9th	11th	10th	**10th**

1960-61

1	Aug	20	(h)	Cardiff C	D	2-2	Leggat, Haynes	30,275
2		24	(a)	Newcastle U	L	2-7	Key, Doherty	22,370
3		27	(a)	West Brom A	W	4-2	Leggat 2, Cook, Haynes	20,470
4		31	(h)	Newcastle U	W	4-3	Key 2, Haynes 2	21,361
5	Sep	3	(h)	Birmingham C	W	2-1	O'Connell, Cook	19,297
6		10	(a)	Sheffield W	L	0-2		27,842
7		14	(h)	Nottingham F	W	1-0	Leggat	13,470
8		17	(h)	Chelsea	W	3-2	Leggat, O'Connell, Haynes	37,376
9		21	(a)	Nottingham F	L	2-4	Cook, O'Connell	14,959
10		24	(h)	Preston NE	W	2-0	Langley, Cook	23,595
11	Oct	1	(a)	Burnley	L	0-5		19,808
12		8	(a)	Blackpool	W	5-2	Cook 2, Langley, O'Connell, Leggat	20,323
13		15	(h)	Everton	L	2-3	Key, Langley	30,306
14		22	(a)	Bolton W	W	3-0	Leggat 3	19,816
15		29	(h)	West Ham U	D	1-1	Leggat	20,806
16	Nov	5	(a)	Tottenham H	L	1-5	Leggat	56,210
17		12	(h)	Leicester C	W	4-2	Leggat 3, Key	16,617
18		19	(a)	Aston Villa	L	1-2	Leggat	32,000
19		26	(h)	Wolves	L	1-3	Haynes	25,905
20	Dec	3	(a)	Blackburn R	L	1-5	O'Connell	12,900
21		10	(h)	Manchester U	D	4-4	Brown 2, Mullery, O'Connell	23,635
22		17	(a)	Cardiff C	L	0-2		20,000
23		24	(a)	Manchester C	L	2-3	Leggat, Cook	18,467
24		26	(h)	Manchester C	W	1-0	Chamberlain	20,121
25		31	(h)	West Brom A	L	1-2	Haynes	18,080
26	Jan	14	(a)	Birmingham C	L	0-1		23,805
27		21	(h)	Sheffield U	L	1-6	O'Connell	17,920
28	Feb	4	(a)	Chelsea	L	1-2	Leggat	39,186
29		11	(a)	Preston NE	L	0-2		8,692
30		22	(h)	Burnley	L	0-1		13,006
31		25	(h)	Blackpool	W	4-3	Cook, Hill, Johnson, Leggat	19,432
32	Mar	4	(a)	Everton	L	0-1		36,000
33		11	(h)	Bolton W	D	2-2	Johnson, Leggat	19,000
34		18	(a)	West Ham U	W	2-1	Cook, Langley	18,000
35		25	(h)	Tottenham H	D	0-0		38,000
36		31	(h)	Arsenal	D	2-2	Haynes 2	24,000
37	Apr	1	(a)	Manchester U	L	1-3	O'Connell	24,000
38		3	(a)	Arsenal	L	2-4	Langley, Leggat	20,142
39		8	(h)	Aston Villa	D	1-1	Leggat	23,000
40		15	(a)	Leicester C	W	2-1	O'Connell, Leggat	31,000
41		22	(h)	Blackburn R	D	1-1	Leggat	17,000
42		29	(a)	Wolves	W	4-2	Cook 3, O'Connell	25,000

P	W	D	L	F	A	W	D	L	F	A	Pts	Pos	Div		Appearances
42	8	8	5	39	39	6	0	12	33	56	36	17th	1		Goals

FA Cup

3	Jan	7	(a)	Newcastle U	L	0-5		36,037

	Appearances
	Goals

League Cup

1	Sep	26	(a)	Bristol R	L	1-2	Cook	20,022

	Appearances
	Goals

326

Fulham appearance & goalscoring grid, season 1960-61. Players (columns, left to right): Macedo, Cohen, Langley, Mullery, Lampe, Bentley, Leggat, O'Connell, Hill, Haynes, Key, Doherty, Cook, Lowe, Hewkins, Brown R, Chamberlain, Watson, Lawler, Brown S, Johnson, Dodgin, Edwards.

Mac	Coh	Lan	Mul	Lam	Ben	Leg	OCo	Hil	Hay	Key	Doh	Coo	Low	Hew	BrR	Cha	Wat	Law	BrS	Joh	Dod	Edw	#
1	2	3	4	5	6	7	8	9	10	11													1
1	2	3	4	5	6		11	8	10	7	9												2
1	2	3	4	5	6		11	8	10	7		9											3
1	2	3	4	5		11	8		10	7		9	6										4
1	2	3	4	5		11	8		10	7		9	6										5
1	2	3	4			11	8		10	7	9	6	5										6
1	2	3	4	5		11	8		10	7		9	6										7
1	2	3	4	5		11	8		10	7		9	6										8
1	2	3	4		5	11	8		10	7		9	6										9
1	2	3	4		5	11	8		10	7		9	6										10
	2	3		5		11	8		10	7		9	6	1		4							11
	2	3	4	5			11	8	10	7		9	6	1									12
	2	3	4	5		11		8	10	7		9	6	1									13
	2	3	4	5		11		8	10	7				1		9						6	14
1	2	3	4	5		11		8	10	7		9										6	15
1	2	3	4	5		11		8	10	7		9										6	16
1		3		5			10	8	6	7		9	4			11					2		17
1	2	3		5			10	8	6	7		9	4			11							18
1	2	3		5			10	8	6	7		9	4			11							19
	2	3	4	5		11		8	10	7			6	1		9							20
	2	3	4	5		7	8		10	11				1		9						6	21
	2	3	4				8		10	11			5	1		9	7					6	22
	2	3	4			9	8		10				5	1		11	7					6	23
	2	3	4			9	8		10				5	1		11	7					6	24
	2	3	4			9	8		10				5	1		11	7					6	25
1	2	11	4				8		10	7		9	5				3					6	26
1	2	11	4				8			7		9	5				3	10				6	27
1	2	3	4			11		8	10	7		9	5									6	28
1	2	3	4			7		8	10			9	5			11						6	29
1	2	3	4	5				8	10			9	6			11	7						30
1	2	3	4	5		7		8	10			9	6			11							31
1	2	3	4	5		9		8	10				6			11	7						32
1	2	3	4					8	10	7		9	5			11	6						33
1	2	3	4					8	10			9	6			11	7			5			34
1	2	3	4			7		8	10			9	6			11				5			35
1	2	3	4			7		8	10			9	6			11				5			36
1	2	3						8	10			9	6			11	7	4		5			37
1	2	3	4			7		8	10			9	6			11				5			38
	2	3	4			7		8	10			9		1		11				5	6		39
1	2	3	4					8	10	7		9	6			11				5			40
1	2	3	4			9		8	10	7			6			11				5			41
1	2	3	4					8	10	7		9	6			11				5			42
31	**41**	**42**	**37**	**11**	**15**	**36**	**26**	**13**	**39**	**28**	**4**	**32**	**34**	**11**	**5**	**11**	**8**	**7**	**1**	**9**	**9**	**12**	
	5	1							23	10	1	9	5	1		12				2	1	2	

Cup / additional sub-grids (below main table):

Mac	Coh	Lan	Mul	Lam	Ben	Leg	OCo	Hil	Hay	Key	Doh	Coo	Low	Hew	BrR	Cha	Wat	Law	BrS	Joh	Dod	Edw	Gm
	2	3	4					8		10	7		9	5	1		11					6	3
	1	1	1					1		1	1		1	1	1		1					1	

Mac	Coh	Lan	Mul	Lam	Ben	Leg	OCo	Hil	Hay	Key	Doh	Coo	Low	Hew	BrR	Cha	Wat	Law	BrS	Joh	Dod	Edw	Gm
	2	3		5			8		10	7		9	6	1		11						4	1
	1	1		1			1		1	1		1	1	1		1						1	
												1											

Month End		Sep	Oct	Nov	Dec	Jan	Feb	Mar	Apr	Final
1960-61	**Pld**	10	15	19	25	27	31	36	42	**42**
	Pts	13	18	20	23	23	25	30	36	**36**
	Pos	7th	6th	12th	10th	12th	16th	17th	17th	**17th**

1961-62

1	Aug	19	(a)	Birmingham C	L 1-2	O'Connell		25,371
2		23	(h)	Manchester C	L 3-4	O'Connell, Langley, Mullery		16,175
3		26	(h)	Everton	W 2-1	Cook, Doherty		23,039
4		30	(a)	Manchester C	L 1-2	Brown		36,775
5	Sep	2	(a)	Chelsea	D 0-0			37,988
6		6	(h)	Bolton W	D 2-2	Brown, opp own goal		12,639
7		9	(a)	Sheffield W	D 1-1	Metchick		35,733
8		16	(h)	Leicester C	W 2-1	Leggat, Chamberlain		19,831
9		20	(a)	Bolton W	W 3-2	Mullery 2, O'Connell		16,748
10		23	(a)	Ipswich T	W 4-2	Cook, Cohen, Haynes, O'Connell		23,050
11		30	(h)	Burnley	L 3-5	Cook 2, Leggat		30,665
12	Oct	7	(h)	Aston Villa	W 3-1	Leggat, Cook, Metchick		22,229
13		14	(a)	Nottingham F	D 1-1	Leggat		21,761
14		21	(h)	West Ham U	W 2-0	Mullery, Leggat		26,540
15		28	(a)	Sheffield U	D 2-2	Cook, Mullery		19,601
16	Nov	4	(h)	Cardiff C	L 0-1			20,007
17		11	(a)	Tottenham H	L 2-4	Leggat, Haynes		35,662
18		18	(h)	Blackpool	L 0-1			18,592
19		25	(a)	Blackburn R	W 2-0	Cook, opp own goal		12,800
20	Dec	2	(h)	Wolves	L 0-1			22,109
21		9	(a)	Manchester U	L 0-3			22,479
22		16	(h)	Birmingham C	L 0-1			12,630
23		23	(a)	Everton	L 0-3			30,261
24		26	(a)	Arsenal	L 0-1			32,969
25	Jan	13	(h)	Chelsea	L 3-4	Leggat, Chamberlain, Lowe		35,640
26		20	(h)	Sheffield W	L 0-2			19,966
27	Feb	3	(a)	Leicester C	L 1-4	Haynes		20,272
28		10	(h)	Ipswich T	L 1-2	Mullery		25,309
29		20	(a)	Burnley	L 1-2	Henderson		25,700
30		24	(a)	Aston Villa	L 0-2			25,000
31	Mar	3	(h)	Nottingham F	D 1-1	Henderson		18,419
32		17	(h)	Sheffield U	W 5-2	Cook 3, Leggat, Lowe		22,711
33		23	(a)	Cardiff C	W 3-0	Cook, Henderson, Leggat		18,000
34	Apr	7	(a)	Blackpool	L 1-2	Haynes		10,641
35		11	(h)	Arsenal	W 5-2	Cook 2, Leggat, Henderson, O'Connell		26,517
36		14	(h)	Blackburn R	W 2-0	O'Connell, Cook		20,012
37		17	(h)	Tottenham H	D 1-1	O'Connell		43,355
38		21	(a)	Wolves	W 3-1	Leggat 2, O'Connell		21,027
39		23	(h)	West Brom A	L 1-2	Haynes		29,322
40		24	(a)	West Brom A	L 0-2			23,200
41		28	(h)	Manchester U	W 2-0	Cook, Leggat		40,113
42		30	(a)	West Ham U	L 2-4	Langley, Henderson		24,837

P	W	D	L	F	A	W	D	L	F	A	Pts	Pos	Div		Appearances
42	8	3	10	38	34	5	4	12	28	40	33	20th	1		Goals

FA Cup

3	Jan	6	(h)	Hartlepools U	W 3-1	Cook 2, Key		18,044
4		27	(h)	Walsall	D 2-2	Cook, Henderson		30,030
R		30	(a)	Walsall	W 2-0	Lowe, Metchick		24,045
5	Feb	17	(h)	Port Vale	W 1-0	Langley		29,559
6	Mar	10	(h)	Blackburn R	D 2-2	Haynes, opp own goal		29,997
R		14	(a)	Blackburn R	W 1-0	Cook		34,000
SF		31	(n)	Burnley	D 1-1	Leggat		59,989
R	Apr	9	(n)	Burnley	L 1-2	Langley		35,000

FA Cup semi-final played at Villa Park, replay at Filbert Street, Leicester.

Appearances
Goals

League Cup

1	Sep	13	(h)	Sheffield U	D 1-1	M.Brown		5,517
R		25	(a)	Sheffield U	L 0-4			8,820

Appearances
Goals

Month End		Sep	Oct	Nov	Dec	Jan	Feb	Mar	Apr	Final
1961-62	**Pld**	11	15	19	24	26	30	33	42	**42**
	Pts	11	17	19	19	19	19	24	33	**33**
	Pos	8th	5th	9th	20th	21st	22nd	22nd	20th	**20th**

Brown M	Brown R	Chamberlain	Cohen	Cook	Dodgin	Doherty	Edwards	Haynes	Hawkins	Henderson	Johnson	Kay	Lampe	Langley	Lawler	Leggat	Lowe	Macedo	Mullery	Metchick	Mealand	O'Connell	Keetch	
		11	2		5	9		10						3		7	6	1	4			8		1
		11	2	9	5			10			7			3			6	1	4			8		2
			2	7	5	9		10		11				3			6	1	4			8		3
	9		2	7	5		8	10						3			6	1	4	11				4
	9		2	7	5		8	10						3			6	1	4	11				5
	9	11	2	7	5			10						3			6	1	4			8		6
7		11	2	9	5			10						3			6	1	4			8		7
		11	2	9	5			10						3		7	6	1	4			8		8
		11	2	9	5			10						3		7	6	1	4			8		9
		11	2	9	5			10			7			3			6	1	4			8		10
		11	2	9	5			10						3		7	6	1	4			8		11
				9	5			10						3		7	6	1	4	11	2	8		12
10			2	9	5									3		7	6	1	4	11		8		13
		11	2	9	5			10						3		7	6	1	4	8				14
		11	2	9	5			10						3		7	6	1	4	8				15
		11	2	9	5			10						3		7	6	1	4			8		16
		11	2	9	5			10						3		7	6	1	4			8		17
			2		5	9		10						3		7	6	1	4	11		8		18
			2	9	5			10				7		3			6	1	4	11		8		19
			2	9	5			10						3		7	6	1	4	11		8		20
			2	9	5	6			1			7		3		8			4	11		10		21
			2	9	5			10	1			7		3		8	6		4	11				22
			2	9	5			10				7				8	6	1	4	11	3			23
			2		5			10				7				9	6	1	4	11	3	8		24
		11	2		5			10	1	9		7				8	6		4	3				25
		11	2					10		9		7	5			8	6		4	3				26
			2			6		10		9		7	5		1				4	11	3	8		27
			2	7	5			10	1	9						8	6		4	11	3			28
			2	7		9		8					5	3			6	1	4	11		10		29
			2	7		9		10				8	5	3			6	1	4	11				30
			2			9		10		8			5	3		7	6	1	4	11				31
			2	9	5			10		8				3		7	6	1	4			11		32
			2	9	5			10		8				3		7	6	1	4			11		33
			2	9	5			10		8				3		7	6	1	4			11		34
			2	9	5					8				3		7	6	1	4			11		35
			2	9	5					8				3		7	6	1	4	10		11		36
			2	9	5			10		8				3		7	6	1	4			11		37
			2	9	5			10		8				3		7	6	1	4			11		38
			2	9	5		4	10		8				3		7	6	1				11		39
			2	9	5		4	10		8				3		7	6	1				11		40
			2	9	5			10		8				3		7	6	1	4			11		41
			2	9	5			10		8				3		7	6	1	4			11		42
2	3	14	41	35	37	8	4	38	4	18	2	9	5	35	1	31	40	38	40	19	7	31		
2	2	1		15			1			5		5	2			13	2		6	2		8		

Brown M	Brown R	Chamberlain	Cohen	Cook	Dodgin	Doherty	Edwards	Haynes	Hawkins	Henderson	Johnson	Kay	Lampe	Langley	Lawler	Leggat	Lowe	Macedo	Mullery	Metchick	Mealand	O'Connell	Keetch	
			2	9	5		4			11		7				8	6	1			3	10		3
			2	9				10		11			5			7	6	1	4		3	8		4
			2	7				10		9			5			8	6	1	4	11	3			R
			2	7						9			5	3		8	6	1	4	11		10		5
			2	9	5			10		8				3		7	6	1	4			11		6
			2	9	5			10		8				3		7	6	1	4			11		R
			2	9	5			10		8				3		7	6	1	4			11		SF
			2	9	5			10		8				3		7	6	1	4			11		R
			8	8	5		1	6		7		1	1	3		5	8	8	8	7	2	3	7	
				4				1		1			1	2			1		1			1		

Brown M	Brown R	Chamberlain	Cohen	Cook	Dodgin	Doherty	Edwards	Haynes	Hawkins	Henderson	Johnson	Kay	Lampe	Langley	Lawler	Leggat	Lowe	Macedo	Mullery	Metchick	Mealand	O'Connell	Keetch	
7		11	2	9				10						3			6	1	4			8	5	1
		11	2	9	5							7		3			6	1	4	10		8		R
1		2	2	2	1			1				1		2			2	2	2	2		1	1	
1																								

In 1961-2, Fulham recorded their worst series of home defeats, losing seven in a row.

329

1962-63

1	Aug	18	(h)	Leicester C	W	2-1	Leggat 2	27,064
2		22	(a)	Sheffield U	L	0-2		19,890
3		25	(a)	Bolton W	L	0-1		16,601
4		29	(h)	Sheffield U	D	2-2	Cook 2	15,735
5	Sep	1	(h)	Everton	W	1-0	Brown	30,592
6		8	(a)	West Brom A	L	1-6	Henderson	19,300
7		12	(a)	Sheffield W	L	0-1		21,062
8		15	(h)	Arsenal	L	1-3	Mullery	31,442
9		19	(h)	Sheffield W	W	4-1	Brown, Cook 3	22,635
10		22	(a)	Birmingham C	L	1-4	Langley	20,477
11		29	(h)	Leyton O	L	0-2		26,505
12	Oct	6	(a)	Nottingham F	L	1-3	Langley	23,254
13		13	(h)	Ipswich T	D	1-1	Brown	22,966
14		20	(a)	Blackpool	D	0-0		17,115
15		27	(h)	Blackburn R	D	0-0		18,098
16	Nov	3	(a)	Aston Villa	W	2-1	Henderson, Brown	28,000
17		10	(h)	Tottenham H	L	0-2		39,961
18		17	(a)	West Ham U	D	2-2	Leggat, Langley	17,668
19		24	(h)	Manchester C	L	2-4	Brown, Leggat	17,871
20	Dec	1	(a)	Liverpool	L	1-2	Langley	38,267
21		8	(h)	Wolves	L	0-5		17,454
22		15	(a)	Leicester C	W	3-2	Leggat, Brown, Cook	18,840
23		26	(h)	Manchester U	L	0-1		23,928
24	Feb	16	(a)	Leyton O	D	1-1	Cook	17,132
25		23	(h)	Nottingham F	W	3-1	Robson, Key, opp own goal	15,780
26	Mar	2	(a)	Ipswich T	W	1-0	Leggat	18,225
27		9	(h)	Blackpool	W	2-0	Leggat, Cook	8,954
28		16	(a)	Blackburn R	W	1-0	Cook	10,000
29		23	(h)	Aston Villa	W	1-0	Marsh	22,500
30		29	(a)	Manchester C	W	3-2	Cook 2, O'Connell	12,789
31	Apr	1	(a)	Manchester U	W	2-0	O'Connell, Leggat	28,124
32		6	(h)	West Ham U	W	2-0	Cook, Key	26,861
33		12	(a)	Burnley	L	0-4		22,905
34		13	(a)	Tottenham H	D	1-1	Leggat	15,951
35		15	(h)	Burnley	D	1-1	Key	25,869
36		20	(h)	Liverpool	D	0-0		18,894
37		27	(a)	Wolves	L	1-2	Cook	18,984
38	May	1	(h)	Bolton W	W	2-1	Leggat, Brown	10,900
39		4	(h)	Birmingham C	D	3-3	Cook, opp own goal 2	20,279
40		11	(a)	Everton	L	1-4	Key	60,578
41		14	(a)	Arsenal	L	0-3		17,389
42		18	(h)	West Brom A	L	1-2	Cook	17,481

P	W	D	L	F	A	W	D	L	F	A	Pts	Pos	Div	
42	8	6	7	28	30	6	4	11	22	41	38	16th	1	Appearances
														Goals

FA Cup

3	Feb	4	(a)	West Ham U	D	0-0		21,000
R		20	(h)	West Ham U	L	1-2	Robson	20,644
								Appearances
								Goals

League Cup

2	Sep	26	(h)	Bournemouth	W	4-0	Key 2, Brown, Henderson	7,022
3	Oct	17	(a)	Hull C	W	2-1	Key, Metchick	20,308
4	Nov	14	(a)	Norwich C	L	0-1		17,551
								Appearances
								Goals

Month End		Sep	Oct	Nov	Dec	Jan	Feb	Mar	Apr	Final
1962-63	**Pld**	11	15	19	23	23	25	30	37	**42**
	Pts	7	10	13	15	15	18	28	35	**38**
	Pos	21st	20th	21st	21st	21st	21st	11th	12th	**16th**

Appearance / line-up grid (shirt numbers by player and match).

Brown M	Brown S	Chamberlain	Cohen	Cook	Dodgin	Haynes	Henderson	Key	Keetch	Lampe	Langley	Leggat	Lowe	Macedo	Marsh	Mealand	Metchick	Mullery	O'Connell	Robson	Stratton	Watson	#
		2		5	10	9					3	7	6	1				4	11	8			1
		2		5	10	9					3	7	6	1				4	11	8			2
		2	9	5		8					3	7	6	1			10	4	11				3
	9	2	8	5		10					3	7	6	1			11	4					4
	9	2	8	5		10					3	7	6	1			11	4					5
8	9	2	4	5		10					3	7	6	1			11						6
	9	2	8	5		10	7				3		6	1			11					4	7
	9		7	5		10					3		6	1	2		11	4		8			8
	9	11	8	5	10		7				3			1			2	4		6			9
	9	11	8	5	10		7				3			1			2	4		6			10
	9	11	8	5	10		7	2			3			1				4		6			11
	9	2	8	5	10		7				3			1				4	11	6			12
	9	2	8	5	10						3	7	6	1				4	11				13
	9	2	8	5	10						3	7	6	1				4	11				14
	9	2		5	10						3	7	6	1		8		4	11				15
	9	2		5	10						3	7	6	1				4	11	8			16
	9	2			10				5		3	7	6	1				4	11	8			17
	9	2			10				5		3	7	6	1		8			11	4			18
	9	2			10				5		3	7	6	1		8			11	4			19
	9	2	8		10						3	7	5	1				4	11	6			20
	9	2	8		10						3	7	5	1				4	11	6			21
	9	2	8						5		3	7	6	1				4		10	11		22
	9	2	8						5		3	7		1				4		10	11	6	23
	9	2	8		10				5		3	7		1				4		6	11		24
		2	9		10		7				3	8	5	1				4	11	6			25
		2	9		10		7				3	8	5	1				4	11	6			26
		2	9		10	7					3	8	5	1				4	11	6			27
		2	9		10	7					3	8	5	1				4	11	6			28
		2	9			7					3	8	5	1	10			4	11	6			29
	10	2	9			7					3	8	5	1				4	11	6			30
	10	2	9			7	5				3	8		1				4	11	6			31
	10	2	9			7					3	8	5	1				4	11	6			32
	10	2	9			7					3	8	5	1				4	11	6			33
	10	2	9			7	5				3	8		1				4	11	6			34
	10	2	9			7	5				3	8		1				4	11	6			35
	10	2	9			7	5				3	8		1				4	11	6			36
	10	2	9			7	5				3	8		1				4	11	6			37
	10	2	9			7	5				3	8		1				4	11	6			38
	10	2	9			7					3	8	5	1				4	11	6			39
	8	2	9		10	7	5				3			1				4	11	6			40
	8	2	9		10	7					3		5	1				4	11	6			41
7	8	2	9		10						3			1				4	11	6			42
2	34	3	38	35	16	8	23	22	12	3	42	33	28	42	1	3	9	38	31	34	3	2	
	7		15				2	4			4	10				1			1	2	1		

Brown M	Brown S	Chamberlain	Cohen	Cook	Dodgin	Haynes	Henderson	Key	Keetch	Lampe	Langley	Leggat	Lowe	Macedo	Marsh	Mealand	Metchick	Mullery	O'Connell	Robson	Stratton	Watson	#
	9	2	8		10						3	7	5	1				4		6	11		3
	9	2	8		10	7					3		5	1		11		4		6			R
	2		2	2			2	1			2	1	2	2		1		2		2	1		
																			1				

Brown M	Brown S	Chamberlain	Cohen	Cook	Dodgin	Haynes	Henderson	Key	Keetch	Lampe	Langley	Leggat	Lowe	Macedo	Marsh	Mealand	Metchick	Mullery	O'Connell	Robson	Stratton	Watson	#
	9	11		8	5		10	7	2		3			1				4		6			2
	9			8	5			7	2		3		6	1		10		4	11				3
	9	2			10				5		3	7	6	1		8			11	4			4
	3	1	1	2	2		2	2	2	1		3	1	2	3			2	2	2	2		
	1			1	3								1						1				

1963-64

1	Aug	24	(a)	Everton	L 0-3				49,520
2		28	(h)	Sheffield W	W 2-0	Mullery, Haynes			20,875
3		31	(h)	Birmingham C	W 2-1	Chamberlain 2			21,260
4	Sep	4	(a)	Sheffield W	L 0-3				22,045
5		7	(a)	West Brom A	L 0-3				18,000
6		10	(a)	Burnley	L 1-4	Leggat			19,369
7		14	(h)	Arsenal	L 1-4	Leggat			34,910
8		18	(h)	Burnley	W 2-1	Haynes, Leggat			16,281
9		21	(a)	Leicester C	W 1-0	Marsh			26,548
10		28	(h)	Bolton W	W 3-1	Cook, Haynes, Langley			17,345
11		30	(a)	Blackpool	L 0-1				12,508
12	Oct	5	(a)	Blackburn R	L 0-2				13,700
13		12	(h)	Nottingham F	L 0-0				23,551
14		19	(a)	Stoke C	D 1-1	Leggat			24,464
15		26	(h)	Chelsea	L 0-1				32,949
16	Nov	2	(a)	Tottenham H	L 0-1				41,818
17		9	(h)	Aston Villa	W 2-0	Cohen, Key			15,060
18		16	(a)	Liverpool	L 0-2				38,478
19		23	(h)	Sheffield U	W 3-1	Cook, Leggat, Howfield			22,046
20		30	(a)	West Ham U	D 1-1	Leggat			23,175
21	Dec	7	(h)	Wolves	W 4-1	Haynes, Cook, Key, Leggat			19,305
22		14	(h)	Everton	D 2-2	Keetch, Cook			17,760
23		21	(a)	Birmingham C	D 0-0				13,902
24		26	(h)	Ipswich T	W 10-1	Leggat 4, Howfield 3, Cook, Mullery, Robson			19,374
25		28	(a)	Ipswich T	L 2-4	Leggat, Key			15,808
26	Jan	11	(h)	West Brom A	D 1-1	Mullery			16,398
27		18	(a)	Arsenal	D 2-2	Howfield, Haynes			35,895
28	Feb	1	(h)	Leicester C	W 2-1	Metchick, Key			17,583
29		8	(a)	Bolton W	L 1-2	Howfield			9,503
30		19	(h)	Blackburn R	D 1-1	Key			11,165
31		22	(a)	Nottingham F	L 0-2				14,755
32		29	(h)	Blackpool	D 1-1	Earle			12,199
33	Mar	7	(a)	Chelsea	W 2-1	O'Connell, Earle			26,249
34		14	(h)	Liverpool	W 1-0	Stratton			14,022
35		21	(a)	Aston Villa	D 2-2	Leggat 2			11,436
36		27	(h)	Manchester U	D 2-2	Earle, Haynes			41,769
37		28	(h)	Tottenham H	D 1-1	Haynes			30,388
38		30	(a)	Manchester U	L 0-3				42,279
39	Apr	4	(a)	Sheffield U	L 0-1				15,153
40		11	(h)	West Ham U	W 2-0	Keetch, Haynes			22,020
41		18	(a)	Wolves	L 0-4				16,438
42		25	(h)	Stoke C	D 3-3	Earle 2, Leggat			15,748

P	W	D	L	F	A	W	D	L	F	A	Pts	Pos	Div	
42	11	8	2	45	23	2	5	14	13	42	39	15th	1	Appearances
														Goals

FA Cup

3	Jan	4	(h)	Luton T	W 4-1	Mullery, Leggat, Cook, Howfield	18,089
4		25	(a)	Blackburn R	L 0-2		24,314
							Appearances
							Goals

League Cup

2	Sep	25	(a)	Colchester U	L 3-5	Metchick 2, Key	7,772
							Appearances
							Goals

332

Appearances & goals chart — Season 1963-64

Brown S	Callaghan	Chamberlain	Cohen	Cook	Dodgin	Drake	Earle	Edwards	Haynes	Henderson	Howfield	Keetch	Key	Langley	Leggat	Macedo	Marsh	Mealand	Metchick	Mullery	O'Connell	Robson	Stratton	Townsend	Underwood	Watson		No.
8		11	2	9	5				10					3	7	1				4		6						1
8		11	2	9	5				10					3	7					4		6			1			2
8		11	2	9	5				10					3	7					4		6			1			3
8		11	2	9	5				10					3	7					4		6			1			4
		11	2	9	5				10					3	7				8	4		6			1			5
9		11	2		5				10					3	7				8	4		6			1			6
		11	2	9	5				10					3	7				8	4		6			1			7
			2	9					10		11	5		3	7				8	4		6			1			8
			2	9					10		11	5		3	7				8	4		6			1			9
8			2	9					10		11	5		3	7					4		6			1			10
8			2	9					10			5		3	7					4		6	11		1			11
8			2	9					10			5		3	7					4		6	11		1			12
8			2	9					10			5		3	7					4		6	11		1			13
8			2	9					10		11	5		3	7					4		6			1			14
8			2	9					10		11	5		3	7					4		6			1			15
8		11	2	9					10			5		3	7					4		6			1			16
9		11	2						10			5		3	7				8	4		6			1			17
9			2						10		11	5		3	7	1			8	4		6						18
			2	9			8		10		11	5		3	7	1				4		6						19
			2	9		3	8		10		11	5			7	1				4		6						20
			2	9		3	8		10		11	5			7	1				4		6						21
			2	9		3	8		10		11	5			7	1				4		6						22
			2	9		3	8		10		11	5			7	1				4		6						23
			2	9			8		10		11	5		3	7	1				4		6						24
			2	9			8		10		11	5		3	7	1				4		6						25
			2	9			8		10		11	5		3	7	1				4		6						26
			2	9		3	8		10		11	5			7	1				4		6	9					27
			2					9	11	5	7	3				1			8	4	10	6						28
			2				10	9	7	5		3				1			8	4	11	6						29
			2				10	9	11	5	7	3				1			8	4		6						30
			2				10	9	11	5		3		8		1	7			4		6						31
			2				7		10			5				3	8	1		4	11	6	9					32
			2				7		10			5				3	8	1		4	11	6	9					33
			2				7		10			5				3	8	1		4	11	6	9					34
	6		2				7	4	10			5				3	8	1			11		9					35
	6		2				7		10			5				3	8	1			11	4	9					36
	6		2	8			7		10			5				3		1			11	4	9					37
4	6		2	8		3	7		10												11	5	9	1				38
	6		2	8		3	7					5					1		10		11	4	9					39
	6						7		10			5				3	9	1	2	8	11	4						40
	6		2				7		10			5				3	9	1		8	11	4						41
	6		2				7		10			5				3	9	1		8	11	4						42
15	**8**	**7**	**41**	**29**	**7**	**7**	**12**	**1**	**40**	**4**	**14**	**38**	**27**	**31**	**25**	**24**	**4**	**1**	**8**	**34**	**13**	**39**	**11**	**2**	**16**	**4**		
	2	1	5				5		8			6	2	5	1	15			1		1	3	1	1	1			

Brown S	Callaghan	Chamberlain	Cohen	Cook	Dodgin	Drake	Earle	Edwards	Haynes	Henderson	Howfield	Keetch	Key	Langley	Leggat	Macedo	Marsh	Mealand	Metchick	Mullery	O'Connell	Robson	Stratton	Townsend	Underwood	Watson		No.
			2	8					10			11	5		7	3	9	1			4		6					3
			2	8					10			11	5			3	9	1		7	4		6					4
			2	2					2			2	2	1	2	2	2			1	2		2					
			1									1				1	'				1							

Brown S	Callaghan	Chamberlain	Cohen	Cook	Dodgin	Drake	Earle	Edwards	Haynes	Henderson	Howfield	Keetch	Key	Langley	Leggat	Macedo	Marsh	Mealand	Metchick	Mullery	O'Connell	Robson	Stratton	Townsend	Underwood	Watson		No.
			2	9					10			5		7	3	11			8	4		6		1				2
			1	1					1			1		1	1	1			1	1		1		1				
																1			2									

Month End		Sep	Oct	Nov	Dec	Jan	Feb	Mar	Apr	Final
1963-64	**Pld**	11	15	20	25	27	32	38	42	**42**
	Pts	10	12	17	23	25	29	36	39	**39**
	Pos	17th	19th	18th	15th	14th	16th	15th	15th	**15th**

333

1964-65

1	Aug	22	(h)	West Ham U	L	1-2	Metchick	31,688
2		26	(a)	Birmingham C	D	2-2	Metchick, Langley	20,678
3		29	(a)	West Brom A	D	2-2	Metchick, Cohen	18,712
4	Sep	2	(h)	Birmingham C	W	3-1	Metchick 3	13,100
5		5	(h)	Manchester U	W	2-1	Haynes, opp own goal	36,291
6		9	(a)	Sheffield U	D	1-1	Marsh	20,379
7		12	(a)	Chelsea	L	0-1		41,472
8		16	(h)	Sheffield U	L	1-2	Marsh	12,615
9		19	(a)	Nottingham F	W	3-2	Langley, Marsh 2	22,307
10		26	(h)	Stoke C	L	1-4	Marsh	15,177
11		30	(a)	Leeds U	D	2-2	Leggat, Marsh	31,260
12	Oct	5	(a)	Tottenham H	L	0-3		31,208
13		10	(h)	Leicester C	W	5-2	Marsh 2, Leggat 2, O'Connell	14,300
14		17	(a)	Sunderland	D	0-0		38,297
15		24	(h)	Wolves	W	2-0	Marsh, Cohen	14,671
16		31	(a)	Aston Villa	L	0-2		15,000
17	Nov	7	(h)	Liverpool	D	1-1	Haynes	18,637
18		14	(a)	Sheffield W	D	1-1	Earle	18,027
19		21	(h)	Blackpool	D	3-3	Earle, Chamberlain, Howfield	16,587
20		28	(a)	Blackburn R	L	0-2		12,434
21	Dec	5	(h)	Arsenal	L	3-4	Marsh, Brown, Cook	13,784
22		12	(a)	West Ham U	L	0-2		21,985
23		19	(h)	West Brom A	W	3-1	Marsh, Howfield, Haynes	10,390
24		26	(a)	Burnley	L	0-4		15,700
25		28	(h)	Burnley	L	0-1		10,162
26	Jan	16	(h)	Chelsea	L	1-2	Cook	26,400
27		23	(h)	Nottingham F	W	4-1	Howfield, Cook, Marsh, Key	15,827
28	Feb	6	(a)	Stoke C	L	1-3	Marsh	28,585
29		13	(h)	Tottenham H	W	4-1	Key 2, Cook, Marsh	27,708
30		20	(a)	Arsenal	L	0-2		22,101
31		24	(a)	Leicester C	L	1-5	Haynes	16,760
32		27	(h)	Sunderland	W	1-0	Cook	18,861
33	Mar	13	(h)	Leeds U	D	2-2	Langley, Cook	24,704
34		15	(a)	Manchester U	L	1-4	Marsh	45,402
35		20	(a)	Liverpool	L	2-3	Marsh, Cook	28,465
36		27	(h)	Sheffield W	W	2-0	Leggat, Cook	12,146
37		30	(a)	Wolves	D	0-0		20,000
38	Apr	3	(a)	Blackpool	L	0-3		11,972
39		9	(h)	Blackburn R	W	3-2	Robson, Haynes, Marsh	11,653
40		16	(a)	Everton	L	0-2		38,537
41		19	(h)	Everton	D	1-1	Key	13,323
42		24	(h)	Aston Villa	D	1-1	Langley	13,494

P	W	D	L	F	A	W	D	L	F	A	Pts	Pos	Div	Appearances
42	10	5	6	44	32	1	7	13	16	46	34	20th	1	Goals

FA Cup

3	Jan	9	(h)	Millwall	D	3-3	Key, Stratton 2	21,315
R		11	(a)	Millwall	L	0-2		35,000

Appearances

Goals

League Cup

2	Sep	23	(h)	Oxford U	W	2-0	Key, O'Connell	8,334
3	Oct	14	(a)	Reading	D	1-1	Cook	13,873
R		19	(h)	Reading	L	1-3	Robson	5,270

Appearances

Goals

Brown	Cohen	Callaghan	Cook	Chamberlain	Dempsey	Drake	Earle	Haynes	Howfield	Keetch	Key	Leggat	Langley	Metchick	Macedo	Marsh	Mealand	O'Connell	Parmenter	Robson	Stratton	Underwood	Jones	No.
	2	6					7	10		5		9	3	8	1			11		4				1
	2	6						10		5	7		3	8	1	9		11		4				2
10	2	6								5	7		3	8	1	9		11		4				3
	2	6						10		5	7		3	8	1	9		11		4				4
	2	6						10		5	7		3	8	1	9		11		4				5
	2	6						10		5	7		3	8	1	9		11		4				6
	2	6						10		5	7		3	8	1	9		11		4				7
	2	6						10		5	7		3	8	1	9		11		4				8
6	2							10		5	7		3	8		9		11		4		1		9
8	2	6						10		5	7		3			9		11		4		1		10
6	2							10		5	7		3	8	1	9		11		4				11
6	2							10		5	7		3	8	1	9		11		4				12
6	2	8						10		5	7		3		1	9		11		4				13
6	2	8						10		5	7		3		1	9		11		4				14
6	2	8						10		5	7		3		1	9		11		4				15
8	2	6						10		5	7		3		1	9		11		4				16
6	2		11				7	10	8	5			3		1	9				4				17
6	2		11				7	10	8	5			3		1	9				4				18
6	2		11				7	10	8	5			3		1	9				4				19
6	2		7	11		3			8	5					1	9		10		4				20
6	2		7	11					8	5			3		1	9		10		4				21
6		8	11					10		5	7		3		1	9	2			4				22
6	2	8	11					10		5	7		3		1	9				4				23
6	2		11					10		5	7		3		1	9		8		4				24
6	2							10	11	5	7		3		1	9		8		4				25
6	2	9		5				10	11		7		3		1	8				4				26
6	2	9		5				10	11		7		3		1	8				4				27
4	2			5				10	11		7	9	3		1	8				6				28
4	2	9		5				10			7	11	3		1	8				6				29
4	2							10		5	7	11	3		1	8				6	9			30
4	2							10		5	7	11	3		1	8				6	9			31
6	2	9						10		5	7		3		1	8				4	11			32
6	2	9						10		5	7		3		1	8				4	11			33
6	2	9						10		5	7	11	3		1	8				4				34
6	2	9						10		5	7		3		1	8			11	4				35
6	2	9						10		5	7	11	3		1	8				4				36
6	2	9						10		5	7	11	3		1	8				4	9			37
6	2	9						10		5	7	11	3		1	8				4	9			38
6		5	9					10			7		3		1	8	2	11		4				39
6	2							10		5	7	9	3		1	8		11		4				40
6	2	9						10		5	7		3		1	8		11		4				41
4	2	9						10		5	7		3		1	8		11		6				42
35	40	12	17	8	4	1	4	39	12	37	26	17	41	11	40	41	2	24	1	42	6	2		
1	2		8	1			2	5	3		4	4	4	6				17		1		1		

Brown	Cohen	Callaghan	Cook	Chamberlain	Dempsey	Drake	Earle	Haynes	Howfield	Keetch	Key	Leggat	Langley	Metchick	Macedo	Marsh	Mealand	O'Connell	Parmenter	Robson	Stratton	Underwood	Jones	
6	2							10	8	5	7		3		1			11		4	9			3
6	2		11	5				10			7		3		1	8				4	9			R
2	2		1	1				2	1	1	2		2		2	1		1		2	2			
											1													

Brown	Cohen	Callaghan	Cook	Chamberlain	Dempsey	Drake	Earle	Haynes	Howfield	Keetch	Key	Leggat	Langley	Metchick	Macedo	Marsh	Mealand	O'Connell	Parmenter	Robson	Stratton	Underwood	Jones	
8	2	6						10		5	7		3			9		11		4		1		2
10	2	6	8							5	7		3		1	9		11		4				3
6		9						10	11	5	7		3		1		2			4		8		R
3	2	2	2					2	1	3	1	2	3		2	2	1	2		3		1	1	
			1								1							1		1				

Month End	Sep	Oct	Nov	Dec	Jan	Feb	Mar	Apr	Final
1964-65 Pld	11	16	20	25	27	32	37	42	**42**
Pts	10	15	18	20	22	26	30	34	**34**
Pos	16th	14th	15th	18th	18th	17th	19th	20th	**20th**

335

1965-66

1	Aug	21	(a)	Blackpool	D	2-2	Key, Haynes	15,280
2		25	(h)	Blackburn R	W	5-2	Brown 2, Key 2, Dyson	14,880
3		28	(h)	Chelsea	L	0-3		34,097
4	Sep	1	(a)	Blackburn R	L	2-3	Brown, O'Connell	10,497
5		4	(h)	Tottenham H	L	0-2		28,178
6		8	(h)	Sheffield U	D	0-0		9,785
7		11	(a)	Liverpool	L	1-2	Key	46,382
8		15	(a)	Sheffield U	L	0-2		17,967
9		18	(h)	Aston Villa	L	3-6	Leggat 3	12,634
10		25	(a)	Sunderland	D	2-2	O'Connell, Robson	39,292
11	Oct	2	(h)	West Ham U	W	3-0	Haynes, Leggat, opp own goal	22,310
12		9	(a)	Arsenal	L	1-2	Dyson	32,318
13		16	(h)	Everton	W	3-2	Dempsey, Dyson, Pearson	18,110
14		23	(a)	Manchester U	L	1-4	Dempsey	32,716
15		30	(h)	Newcastle U	W	2-0	Key, Leggat	19,226
16	Nov	6	(a)	West Brom A	L	2-6	Leggat, Robson	20,170
17		13	(h)	Nottingham F	D	1-1	Marsh	13,863
18		20	(a)	Sheffield W	L	0-1		16,030
19		27	(h)	Northampton T	L	1-4	Haynes	11,339
20	Dec	4	(a)	Stoke C	L	2-3	Marsh 2	14,871
21		11	(h)	Burnley	L	2-5	Haynes, Pearson	12,092
22		18	(a)	Everton	L	0-2		20,670
23		28	(a)	Leicester C	L	0-5		20,164
24	Jan	1	(h)	Arsenal	W	1-0	Leggat	25,801
25		8	(a)	Burnley	L	0-1		17,200
26		15	(h)	Manchester U	L	0-1		33,018
27		29	(h)	Blackpool	D	0-0		12,093
28	Feb	5	(a)	Chelsea	L	1-2	Leggat	35,438
29		19	(a)	Tottenham H	L	3-4	Earle, Leggat, Barrett	31,719
30		26	(h)	Liverpool	W	2-0	Earle 2	31,616
31	Mar	12	(a)	Aston Villa	W	5-2	Earle 2, Leggat 2, Barrett	13,829
32		19	(h)	Sunderland	W	3-0	Earle, Leggat, opp own goal	20,918
33		26	(a)	West Ham U	W	3-1	Earle, Leggat, Barrett	18,997
34	Apr	2	(h)	West Brom A	W	2-1	Haynes 2	20,426
35		8	(h)	Leeds U	L	1-3	Robson	38,960
36		12	(a)	Leeds U	W	1-0	Pearson	33,968
37		16	(h)	Sheffield U	W	4-2	Barrett, Earle, Leggat, Robson	20,980
38		18	(h)	Leicester C	L	0-4		18,014
39		23	(a)	Northampton T	W	4-2	Earle 3, Robson	24,532
40		26	(a)	Nottingham F	W	2-1	Leggat, Pearson	19,618
41		30	(h)	Stoke C	D	1-1	Clarke	25,491
42	May	7	(a)	Newcastle U	D	1-1	Robson	18,810

P	W	D	L	F	A	W	D	L	F	A	Pts	Pos	Div	
42	9	4	8	34	37	5	3	13	33	48	35	20th	1	Appearances
														Sub Appearances
														Goals

FA Cup

3	Jan	22	(a)	Sheffield U	L	1-3	Dempsey	18,009

Appearances

Sub Appearances

Goals

League Cup

2	Sep	22	(a)	Wrexham	W	2-1	O'Connell, Dyson	12,001
3	Oct	13	(h)	Northampton T	W	5-0	Dempsey 3, Dyson 2	7,834
4	Nov	3	(h)	Aston Villa	D	1-1	Haynes	10,083
R		8	(a)	Aston Villa	L	0-2		18,536

Appearances

Sub Appearances

Goals

Month End		Sep	Oct	Nov	Dec	Jan	Feb	Mar	Apr	Final
1965-66	**Pld**	10	15	19	23	27	30	33	41	**42**
	Pts	5	11	12	12	15	17	23	34	**35**
	Pos	20th	18th	22nd	22nd	22nd	22nd	21st	19th	**20th**

Football appearances and goals grid (shirt numbers by player and match).

Barrett	Brown	Callaghan	Clarke	Cohen	Dempsey	Drake	Dyson	Earle	Haynes	Keetch	Key	Leggat	Macedo	Marsh	McClelland	Mealand	Nichols	O'Connell	Parmenter	Pearson	Robson	Ryan	#
	4			2			11		10	5	7	9	1		3			8			6		1
	4			2			11		10	5	7	12	1	9	3			8			6		2
	4			2			11		10*	5	7	12	1	9	3			8			6		3
	4			2			11			5	7	10	1	9	3			8			6		4
	4	10		2	5		11			3	7		1	9				8			6		5
	4			2	5		11			3	7	9	1	8				10			6		6
	4			2	5		11			3	7	9	1	8				10			6		7
	4			2	5		11		10	3	7		1	9				8		6	6		8
	4			2	5		11		10	3	7	9	1					8			6		9
	6			2	5		11		10		7	9	1		3			8		4			10
					5		11		10	6	7	9	1		3	2		8		4			11
				2	5		11		10	6	7		1	9	3*			8	12	4			12
				2	9		11		10	5	7		1	8			3			4	6		13
				2	9		11		10	5	7		1	8			3			4	6		14
				2	9		11		10	5	7	8	1				3			4	6		15
	4			2	9		11		10	5	7	8	1				3				6		16
	4	6		2	5		11		8		7	1	9			3	10						17
	4	6		2	5		11		8		7	1	9			3	10						18
	4	6		2	9		12		10	5	7	1*	8			3	11						19
	4	6		2	5				9		7	8	1			3			10				20
		6		2	5				10		7	9	1			3	8	11	4				21
	6			2	5		11		8		7	9	1			3			10	4		22
	4			2	5		11		8		7	9	1				3		10	6		23
	6			2	5			10	4	7	9		1				3	11	8				24
	6			2	5		11	10	4		7	1					3		9	8			25
	6			2	5			10	8	7	9	1				3	11		4			26
8	9	6		2	5			7						1			3	11	10	4*	12	27
8	9	6		2	5						7		1			3	11	10	4		28
8	6			2	5			7	9		11		1			3		10	4		29
11	6			2	5			7	9		8		1			3		10	4		30
11	6			2	5			7	9		8		1			3		10	4		31
11	6			2	5			7	9		8		1			3		10	4		32
11	6			2	5			7	9		8		1			3		10	4		33
11	6				5			7	9		8		1			3	2	10	4		34
11	6		12	2	5			7	9*		8		1			3		10	4		35
11	6	9		2	5			7			8		1			3		10	4		36
11	6	9		2	5			7			8		1			3		10	4		37
11	6	9		2	5			7			8		1			3		10	4		38
	6	8		2	5			7	9		11		1			3		10	4		39
12	4	8		2	5			7	9*		11		1			3		10	6		40
12	4	8	2*		5			7	9		11		1			3		10	6		41
	4	10	9		5	2		7	8		11		1			3			6		42
12	36	9	7	39	38	1	21	15	33	19	20	32	21	17	21	7	27	20	6	24	36	1	
2		1		1		1							1							1		1	
4	3		1	2			3	11	6		5	15					2			4	6		

Barrett	Brown	Callaghan	Clarke	Cohen	Dempsey	Drake	Dyson	Earle	Haynes	Keetch	Key	Leggat	Macedo	Marsh	McClelland	Mealand	Nichols	O'Connell	Parmenter	Pearson	Robson	Ryan	#
	6			2	5		11		8	4	9		7	1			3			10			3
	1			1	1		1		1	1	1		1	1			1			1			
					1																		

Barrett	Brown	Callaghan	Clarke	Cohen	Dempsey	Drake	Dyson	Earle	Haynes	Keetch	Key	Leggat	Macedo	Marsh	McClelland	Mealand	Nichols	O'Connell	Parmenter	Pearson	Robson	Ryan	#
	4			2	5		11		10		7	9	1		3			8			6		2
				2	9		11		10	5	7		1	8			3			4	6		3
				2	9		11		10	5	7	8	1				3			4	6		4
	6	4			5		11		3	2	7	9		1			3	10					R
2	1		3	4	4		4		4	3	4	3	3	1	1		3	2		2	3		
					3		3		1									1						

337

1966-67

1	Aug	20	(h)	Everton	L	0-1		21,634
2		23	(a)	Burnley	L	0-3		18,340
3		27	(a)	Stoke C	W	2-1	Leggat, Clarke	26,333
4		29	(h)	Burnley	D	0-0		15,027
5	Sep	3	(h)	Sheffield U	L	0-1		14,887
6		6	(a)	Nottingham F	L	1-2	Earle	22,125
7		10	(a)	West Brom A	L	1-5	Earle	18,000
8		17	(h)	Leeds U	D	2-2	Leggat, Earle	19,915
9		24	(a)	Newcastle U	D	1-1	Earle	20,330
10	Oct	1	(h)	Tottenham H	L	3-4	Clarke, Earle, Leggat	28,628
11		8	(a)	Liverpool	D	2-2	Clarke 2	44,025
12		15	(h)	West Ham U	W	4-2	Clarke 2, Earle, opp own goal	34,826
13		22	(a)	Sheffield W	D	1-1	Haynes	20,044
14		29	(h)	Chelsea	L	1-3	Barrett	43,149
15	Nov	5	(a)	West Ham U	L	1-6	Callaghan	22,260
16		12	(h)	Aston Villa	W	5-1	Clarke 2, Conway, Pearson, Parmenter	16,072
17		19	(a)	Arsenal	L	0-1		25,755
18		26	(h)	Manchester C	W	4-1	Clarke 2, Haynes, Cohen	14,570
19	Dec	3	(a)	Blackpool	W	1-0	Earle	13,518
20		10	(h)	Southampton	W	3-1	Clarke 2, Conway	19,874
21		17	(a)	Everton	L	2-3	Clarke, Barrett	31,396
22		26	(a)	Leicester C	W	2-0	Callaghan, Barrett	26,936
23		27	(h)	Leicester C	W	4-2	Leggat 3, Haynes	25,174
24		31	(h)	Stoke C	W	4-1	Leggat 2, Clarke, opp own goal	24,851
25	Jan	7	(a)	Sheffield U	L	0-4		15,008
26		14	(h)	West Brom A	D	2-2	Callaghan, Barrett	20,680
27		21	(a)	Leeds U	L	1-3	Barrett	32,015
28	Feb	4	(h)	Newcastle U	W	5-1	Clarke 3, Haynes, Earle	21,612
29		11	(a)	Tottenham H	L	2-4	Haynes, Clarke	43,961
30		25	(h)	Liverpool	D	2-2	Barrett, opp own goal	37,481
31	Mar	4	(a)	Chelsea	D	0-0		46,784
32		18	(h)	Sheffield U	L	1-2	Barrett	21,771
33		25	(a)	Southampton	L	2-4	Earle, Clarke	27,945
34		27	(h)	Manchester U	D	2-2	Clarke, Barrett	47,290
35		28	(a)	Manchester U	L	1-2	Earle	51,673
36	Apr	1	(h)	Sunderland	W	3-1	Clarke, Pearson, Earle	22,724
37		8	(a)	Aston Villa	D	1-1	Haynes	13,714
38		19	(h)	Arsenal	D	0-0		27,490
39		22	(a)	Manchester C	L	0-3		22,752
40		29	(h)	Blackpool	D	2-2	Clarke 2	14,867
41	May	6	(a)	Sunderland	L	1-3	Conway	18,604
42		13	(h)	Nottingham F	L	2-3	Clarke, Earle	20,417

P	W	D	L	F	A	W	D	L	F	A	Pts	Pos	Div		
42	8	7	6	49	34	3	5	13	22	49	34	18th	1	Appearances	
														Sub Appearances	
														Goals	

FA Cup

3	Jan	28	(a)	Bradford	W	3-1	Clarke 2, Haynes	14,710
4	Feb	18	(h)	Sheffield U	D	1-1	Clarke	32,659
R	Mar	1	(a)	Sheffield U	L	1-3	Callaghan	33,279

Appearances

Sub Appearances

Goals

League Cup

2	Sep	13	(h)	Crystal P	W	2-0	Leggat 2	9,906
3	Oct	5	(h)	Wolves	W	5-0	Clarke 2, Barrett, Earle, Conway	14,321
4		26	(a)	Blackpool	L	2-4	Callaghan, Parmenter	15,349

Appearances

Sub Appearances

Goals

Month End		Sep	Oct	Nov	Dec	Jan	Feb	Mar	Apr	Final
1966-67	**Pld**	9	14	18	24	27	30	35	40	**42**
	Pts	5	9	13	23	24	27	29	34	**34**
	Pos	20th	20th	18th	14th	16th	16th	16th	18th	**18th**

338

Barrett	Brown	Callaghan	Clarke	Cohen	Conway	Dempsey	Drake	Earle	Haynes	Leggat	Macedo	McClelland	Nichols	Parmenter	Pentecost	Pearson	Robson	Seymour	Dyson	
11	6		9	2		5		7		8		1	3			10	4			1
	6		8	2		5		7	9	11		1	3			10	4			2
	6		8	2		5		7	9	11	1		3			10	4			3
	6		8	2		5		7	9	11	1		3			10	4			4
	4		8	2		5		7	9	11	1		3			10	6			5
9	4	12	8	2		5		7		11	1	3*				10	6			6
9	6	3	8	2		5		7		11	1					10	4			7
	4	5	10	2		3		9	7	11	1					8	6			8
	4	5	10	2		3		9	7	11	1					8	6			9
	4	5	10	2		3		9	7	11	1					8	6			10
11	8	5	10	2	6	3		9	7		1						4			11
11	8	5	10	2	6	3		9	7		1						4			12
11	8	5	10			3	2	9	7*	6	1					12	4			13
11	7	8	10	2		3		9			1	5				6	4			14
11	6	5	10	2	8	3		9	7		1						4			15
9		5	10	2	6	3			7		1			11		8	4			16
9	8	5	10	2	6	3		7			1			11			4			17
11	8	5	10	2	6	3		9	7		1						4			18
11	8	5	10	2	6	3		9	7		1						4			19
11	8	5	10	2	6	3		9	7	12	1						4*			20
11	8	4	10	2	6	3		9	7		1		5				4			21
11	8	5	10	2*	6	3		9	7	12	1						4			22
11	8	5	10		6	3	2		7	9	1						4			23
11	8	5	10		6	3	2		7	9	1						4			24
11	8	5	10		6	3	2	9	7		1						4			25
11	8	5	10	2	6	3		9	7		1						4			26
11	8	5	10	2	6	3		9*	7		1					12	4			27
11	8	5	10	2	6	3		9	7		1						4			28
11	8	5	10	2	6	3		9	7			1					4			29
11	5		10	2	6	3		9	7		1					8	4			30
11	5		10	2	6	3		9	7		1					8	4			31
11	6	5	10	2	7	3		9			1					8	4			32
11	8	5	10	2	6	3			7		1					9	4			33
11	8	5	10	2	6	3		12	7							9*	4	1		34
11*	8	5	10	2	6	3		12	7		1					9	4			35
	8	5	10	2	6	3		11	7		1					9	4			36
	9	5	10	2	6	3		11	7		1					8*	4	12		37
11	8	5	10		6	3		9	7		1		2				4			38
11		5	10		6	3		9	7		1		2		8		4			39
11	8	5	10	2	6	3		9	7		1						4			40
11	8	5	10	2	6	3		9	7		1						4			41
11	8	5	10		6	3	2	9	7		1						4			42
33	40	34	42	35	30	42	5	36	36	13	33	8	10	2	1	20	41	1		
		1						2		2						2		1		
8		3	24	1	3			12	6	8					1	2				

Barrett	Brown	Callaghan	Clarke	Cohen	Conway	Dempsey	Drake	Earle	Haynes	Leggat	Macedo	McClelland	Nichols	Parmenter	Pentecost	Pearson	Robson	Seymour	Dyson	
11	8	5	10	2	6	3		9	7		1					12	4			3
11	8	5	10	2	6	3		9	7			1					4			4
11	8	5	10	2	6	3		9	7		1						4			R
3	3	3	3	3	3	3		3	3		2	1					3			
		1	3					1												

Barrett	Brown	Callaghan	Clarke	Cohen	Conway	Dempsey	Drake	Earle	Haynes	Leggat	Macedo	McClelland	Nichols	Parmenter	Pentecost	Pearson	Robson	Seymour	Dyson	
10	4	5		2		3		9	7	11	1					8	6			2
11	8	5	10	2	6	3		9	7								4			3
9	7	6	10	2			3				1	5	11			6	4			4
3	3	3	2	3	1	3		2	2	1	1	2	1	1		2	3			
1		1	2		1			1		2			1							

1967-68

1	Aug	19	(h)	Wolves	L	1-2	Nichols		27,874
2		23	(a)	Sunderland	L	0-3			30,062
3		26	(a)	Chelsea	D	1-1	Brown		38,404
4		28	(h)	Sunderland	W	3-2	Barrett 2, Haynes		19,597
5	Sep	2	(a)	Leeds U	L	0-2			27,760
6		6	(a)	Sheffield W	L	2-4	Clarke 2		26,336
7		9	(h)	Everton	W	2-1	Moss, Barrett		25,366
8		16	(a)	Leicester C	W	2-1	Clarke, Haynes		16,441
9		23	(h)	West Ham U	L	0-3			29,234
10		30	(a)	Burnley	L	0-2			14,227
11	Oct	7	(h)	West Brom A	L	1-2	Clarke		17,316
12		14	(a)	Newcastle U	L	1-2	Clarke		27,664
13		21	(h)	Manchester C	L	2-4	Earle, Conway		22,108
14		28	(a)	Arsenal	L	3-5	Dempsey, Conway, Clarke		29,974
15	Nov	11	(a)	Coventry C	W	3-0	Clarke 2, Gilroy		31,311
16		18	(h)	Nottingham F	W	2-0	Clarke 2		22,413
17		25	(a)	Stoke C	W	1-0	Haynes		19,340
18	Dec	2	(h)	Liverpool	D	1-1	Clarke		29,330
19		16	(a)	Wolves	L	2-3	Gilroy, Moss		25,950
20		23	(h)	Chelsea	D	2-2	Gilroy, Moss		33,492
21		26	(a)	Tottenham H	D	2-2	Gilroy, Pearson		34,774
22		30	(h)	Tottenham H	L	1-2	Barrett		30,051
23	Jan	6	(h)	Leeds U	L	0-5			24,419
24		20	(h)	Leicester C	L	0-1			16,696
25	Feb	3	(a)	West Ham U	L	2-7	Clarke, Earle		32,230
26		10	(h)	Burnley	W	4-3	Clarke 2, Earle, Haynes		15,317
27		24	(a)	West Brom A	L	1-2	Barrett		18,500
28		28	(h)	Sheffield W	W	2-0	Clarke, Earle		15,391
29	Mar	8	(a)	Southampton	L	1-2	Haynes		29,051
30		13	(h)	Sheffield U	L	0-1			15,389
31		16	(a)	Manchester C	L	1-5	Clarke		30,773
32		23	(h)	Arsenal	L	1-3	Barrett		20,612
33	Apr	6	(h)	Coventry C	D	1-1	Earle		20,869
34		12	(a)	Manchester U	L	0-4			40,154
35		13	(a)	Nottingham F	D	2-2	Barrett, Clarke		20,638
36		15	(a)	Manchester U	L	0-3			60,465
37		20	(h)	Newcastle U	W	2-0	Clarke 2		14,670
38		23	(a)	Sheffield U	W	3-2	Barrett, Gilroy, Conway		20,641
39		27	(a)	Liverpool	L	1-4	Clarke		32,428
40	May	1	(h)	Stoke C	L	0-2			14,641
41		4	(h)	Southampton	D	2-2	Gilroy 2		13,451
42		21	(a)	Everton	L	1-5	Conway		38,337

P	W	D	L	F	A	W	D	L	F	A	Pts	Pos	Div		
42	6	4	11	27	41	4	3	14	29	57	27	22nd	1		Appearances
															Sub Appearances
															Goals

FA Cup

3	Jan	27	(h)	Macclesfield T	W	4-2	Clarke 2, Gilroy, Haynes	23,678
4	Feb	17	(h)	Portsmouth	D	0-0		39,381
R		21	(a)	Portsmouth	L	0-1		43,967

Appearances
Sub Appearances
Goals

League Cup

2	Sep	13	(h)	Tranmere R	W	1-0	Barrett	10,178
3	Oct	11	(a)	Workington	D	2-2	Haynes, Earle	11,357
R		16	(h)	Workington	W	6-2	Clarke 4, Callaghan, Barrett	8,614
4	Nov	1	(h)	Manchester C	W	3-2	Earle 2, Clarke	11,732
5		29	(h)	Huddersfield T	D	1-1	Gilroy	20,309
R	Dec	12	(a)	Huddersfield T	L	1-2	Gilroy	23,574

Appearances
Sub Appearances
Goals

Month End		Sep	Oct	Nov	Dec	Jan	Feb	Mar	Apr	Final
1967-68	**Pld**	10	14	17	22	24	28	32	39	**42**
	Pts	7	7	13	16	16	20	20	26	**27**
	Pos	20th	22nd	19th	21st	21st	22nd	22nd	22nd	**22nd**

340

Player appearance / scoring grid (shirt numbers by match). Column order left→right:

Macedo, Cohen, Dempsey, Brown, Nichols, Conway, Haynes, Callaghan, Barrett, Earle, Parmenter, Seymour, Pearson, Clarke, Ryan, Moss, O'Connor, McClelland, Mealand, Gilroy, Cunningham, Drake, Matthewson, Byrne, Salvage, Pentecost, Mullen, Murray, Kerrigan.

Mac	Coh	Dem	Bro	Nic	Con	Hay	Cal	Bar	Ear	Par	Sey	Pea	Cla	Rya	Mos	O'C	McC	Mea	Gil	Cun	Dra	Mat	Byr	Sal	Pen	Mul	Mur	Ker	#
1	2	3	4	5	6	7	8	9	10	11																			1
	2	3	4	5	6	10		8		11	1	7	9																2
	2	3	4	5	6	7		9		11	1	8	10																3
	2	3	4	5	6	7		9		11	1	8	10																4
	2	3	4	5	6		8		11		1	7	9	10															5
	2	3	7		6		5	11			1		10	4	8	9													6
	2	3	7		6		5	11	9		1		10	4	8														7
	2	3	7		6	10	5	11					9	4	8		1												8
	2*	3	7		6	10	5	11	12				9	4	8		1												9
		3	7		6	10	5	11			1		9	4	8			2											10
	2	3	7		6	10	5	11	8		1		9	4															11
	2	3	7		6	10	8	11			1		9	4				5											12
		3	7		6	10	5	11	8		1		9	4				2											13
	2	3	7		6	10	5	11			1		9	4					8										14
1	2	3	4		6	7	5	8*		11		12	9						10										15
1	2	3	4		6	7	5	11	8				9						10										16
1	2	3	4		6	7	5	11	8				9						10										17
1	2*	3	4		6	7	5	10	8	11		12	9						10										18
1		3	4		2	7	5	11	9			6			8				10										19
1		3	4		2	7*	5	11				6	9	12	8				10										20
1		3	4		2	7	5	11	8			6	9						10										21
1		3	4		2	7*	5	11	8			6	9		12				10										22
1		3*	4		2	7	5	11	8			6	9		12				10										23
1	2*	3	7		6		5	10	8	11				4					9	12									24
1		3	4		6	7				11		8	9	5					10		2								25
1		3	2		6	7	5	11	8				10	12					9*			4							26
1		3	2	5	6	7	8	11	10				9									4							27
		3	2	5	6	7	8	11	9		1		10									4							28
		3	2	5*	6	7	8	11	9		1			12	10							4							29
		3	2	5	6	7	8	11	9		1		10									4							30
		3	2	5	6	7	8	11	9		1		10									4							31
		3	2		6	7	5	11	8				10				1					4	9						32
1		3	6		2	7	5	10	8													4	9	11					33
1		3	7		2	6	5	10					8	4									9	11					34
1		3	7		2	6	5	10					8	4				12					9*	11					35
		3	6	12*		5*	10	9					8	4				2	11			11							36
		3	7		2	6	5	11	8				9	4			1		10*						12				37
			6	2	7		4	11	8				9	3			1	5	10										38
			6	2	7	8	4	11	9				10	3			1	5											39
			4	2*	7	8	6	11					9	3			1	5	10				12						40
1			4			7			8				10	3					9			5		11	2		6		41
		3	7			8							9	4				5*	9			4		11	2	12	6	10	42
18	17	38	42	13	42	34	35	40	26	8	16	9	36	20	8	1	8	8	18	0	1	10	4	5	2	0	2	1	
		1							1			2		4	1		1		1			1			2				
1	1	1	1	1	4	5		8	5			1	20		3				7										

Mac	Coh	Dem	Bro	Nic	Con	Hay	Cal	Bar	Ear	Par	Sey	Pea	Cla	Rya	Mos	O'C	McC	Mea	Gil	Cun	Dra	Mat	Byr	Sal	Pen	Mul	Mur	Ker	#
1		3	4		6	7	5*	11	8	12			9	2					10										3
1		3	10	2	7	6	5	11	8				9	4					10										4
1		3	2	12	6	7	5	11	8				10	4					9*										R
3		3	3	1	3	3	3	3	3				3	3					12										
			1							1																			
													2						1										

Mac	Coh	Dem	Bro	Nic	Con	Hay	Cal	Bar	Ear	Par	Sey	Pea	Cla	Rya	Mos	O'C	McC	Mea	Gil	Cun	Dra	Mat	Byr	Sal	Pen	Mul	Mur	Ker	#
	2	3	7		6	7	5	11	10				9	4	8		1												2
	2	3	7		6	10	5	11	8		1		9	4															3
	2	3	7		6	10	8	11			1		9	4				5											R
1	2	3	4		6	10	5	11	8			7	9						10										4
1	2	3	4		6	7	5	11	8				9						10										5
1		3	4		2	7	5	11	8			6	9						10										R
3	5	6	6		6	5	6	6	5		2	2	6	3	1		1	1	2										
					1	1	2	3					5						2										

341

1968-69

#	Month	Date		Opponent	Result	Scorers	Attendance
1	Aug	10	(h)	Bristol C	W 1-0	Gilroy	16,572
2		17	(a)	Aston Villa	D 1-1	Conway	21,450
3		21	(h)	Hull C	D 0-0		15,072
4		24	(h)	Bolton W	L 0-2		12,830
5		27	(a)	Sheffield U	L 0-1		17,932
6		31	(a)	Millwall	L 0-2		18,371
7	Sep	7	(a)	Oxford U	L 0-1		13,752
8		13	(h)	Crystal P	W 1-0	Macdonald	23,132
9		18	(a)	Derby C	L 0-1		26,771
10		21	(a)	Blackpool	D 2-2	Conway 2	15,765
11		28	(h)	Blackburn R	D 1-1	Macdonald	12,960
12	Oct	5	(a)	Birmingham C	L 4-5	Macdonald, Large 2, opp own goal	27,518
13		9	(h)	Sheffield U	D 2-2	Macdonald, Kerrigan	12,793
14		12	(h)	Norwich C	L 1-3	Macdonald	17,741
15		19	(a)	Middlesbrough	L 0-2		23,238
16		26	(h)	Bury	D 0-0		11,417
17	Nov	9	(h)	Portsmouth	D 2-2	Callaghan, Dempsey	14,601
18		16	(a)	Carlisle U	L 0-2		9,641
19		23	(h)	Huddersfield T	W 4-3	Halom, Jones, Byrne, Conway	11,394
20		25	(a)	Preston NE	D 0-0		11,724
21		30	(a)	Charlton A	L 3-5	Halom, Byrne, Ryan	17,271
22	Dec	7	(h)	Cardiff C	L 1-5	Barrett	13,191
23		14	(a)	Norwich C	L 0-2		13,022
24		21	(h)	Middlesbrough	L 0-3		13,333
25		26	(h)	Birmingham C	W 2-0	Callaghan, Halom	13,192
26		28	(a)	Bury	L 1-5	Jones	8,834
27	Jan	18	(a)	Portsmouth	L 1-3	Haynes	20,520
28	Feb	1	(h)	Carlisle U	L 0-2		12,863
29		15	(h)	Charlton A	L 0-1		14,921
30		19	(h)	Preston NE	W 2-1	Lloyd 2	11,726
31	Mar	1	(a)	Bristol C	L 0-6		15,349
32		8	(h)	Aston Villa	D 1-1	Dear	15,509
33		15	(a)	Bolton W	L 2-3	Dear, Lloyd	8,426
34		22	(h)	Millwall	W 2-0	Barrett, Conway	15,561
35		24	(a)	Cardiff C	W 2-0	Dear 2	20,747
36		29	(h)	Oxford C	L 0-1		14,854
37	Apr	2	(h)	Derby C	L 0-1		18,173
38		5	(a)	Blackburn R	D 2-2	Dear 2	7,863
39		7	(a)	Hull C	L 0-4		10,850
40		12	(h)	Blackpool	D 0-0		7,154
41		15	(a)	Huddersfield T	L 0-3		5,837
42		19	(a)	Crystal P	L 2-3	Dear, Large	36,521

P	W	D	L	F	A	W	D	L	F	A	Pts	Pos	Div
42	6	7	8	20	28	1	4	16	20	53	25	22nd	2

Appearances

Sub Appearances

Goals

FA Cup

3	Jan	4	(a)	Sunderland	W 4-1	Mullen 2, Brown, Haynes	27,091
4		25	(h)	West Brom A	L 1-2	Brown	31,204

Appearances

Sub Appearances

Goals

League Cup

2	Sep	3	(a)	Orient	L 0-1		12,901

Appearances

Sub Appearances

Goals

Month End		Sep	Oct	Nov	Dec	Jan	Feb	Mar	Apr	Final
1968-69	**Pld**	11	16	21	26	27	30	36	42	**42**
	Pts	8	10	14	16	16	18	23	25	**25**
	Pos	20th	22nd	19th	22nd	22nd	22nd	22nd	22nd	**22nd**

Seymour	Ryan	Dempsey	Matthewson	Callaghan	Brown	Haynes	Conway	Large	Gilroy	Barrett	Pentecost	Kerrigan	Salvage	Macdonald	McClelland	Byrne	Jones	Halom	Murray	Earle	Parmenter	Williamson	Cohen	Mullen	Lloyd	Horne	Tranter	Dear	Roberts	Moreline	#
1	2	3	4	5	6	7*	8	9	10	11	12																				1
1	2	3	4	5	6	7	8	9	10	11																					2
1	2	3	4	5	6	7	8	9	10	11																					3
1	2	3	4	5	6	7	8	9	10*	11		12																			4
1	5	3	4	7	6	8		9		10	2*		11	12																	5
1	2	3	4	5	6	7	8	9*		10		12	11																		6
1		3	4	5	6	7	8	9		11	2			10																	7
1		3	4	5	6	7	8	9	12	11	2			10*																	8
1		3	4	5	6	7	8	9		11	2			10																	9
	2	3	4	5	6*	7	8	9	10	11			12		1																10
		3	4	5	6	7	8	9		11	2			10	1																11
	5	3	4	7	6			9		11	2	8		10	1																12
1		3	4	5	6	7		9		11	2	8		10																	13
1		3	4	5	6	7				10	2	8*		9		12	11														14
1	5	3	4*	6	12		7	9		11	2			10		8															15
1	5	3		6	4	10	7	9*		11	2			12		8															16
	5	3		6	4		7	9		11	2		1		8	10															17
1	5	3		6	4	8	7				2					9	11	10													18
1	5	3		6	4	8	7				2					9	11*	10	12												19
1	5	3		6	4	8	7				2					9		10		11											20
1	5	3		6	4	8		12			2					9		10		7		11*									21
1	5	3		6	4	8	7			11	2					9		10													22
		3	4	5		8	7	12		11	2*				1	9				6		10									23
		3	4	5		8	7	12		11						9*				6		10	1	2							24
	2	5	6	3	4	10	7									11	8	9					1								25
	2	5	6	3	4	10*	7							12		11	8	9					1								26
		5	6	3	11	10	4	7								9							1	2	8						27
		6	3	4	10*	12	5							9			11			7			1	2	8*						28
	3	5	6	4	10	11	12									9				7			1	2	8*						29
	3	5		11	10		7																1	2	8	4	6	9			30
	3	5*		11	10		7												12				1	2	8	6	4	9			31
		3			10		2							6		7	11								8	4		9	5		32
		3			10		2	11								7				6*			1		8	4	12	9	5		33
		3			10		6									7				11			1		8	4	2	9	5		34
		3			10		6									7				11		12	1		8	4	2	9*	5		35
		3			10		6									7				11			1		8	4	2	9	5		36
		3			10		6									11				7			1		8	4	2	9	5		37
		3			10		6									11				7			1		8	4	2	9	5		38
		3					10									11				7			1	6	8	4	2	9	5		39
		3					10									7				11			1	6	8	4		9	5	2	40
		3					10									7				11			1	6	8	4		9	5	2	41
		3					11	9								7							1	6	8	4		10	5	2	42
18	21	27	24	40	35	28	34	19	5	29	16	3	2	10	14	12	18	10	2	13	1	10	6	2	15	13	9	13	11	2	
			1		1	4	1		1	2		3		2			1	2									1				
	1	1		2		1	5	3		1	2		1		5		2	2	3				3				7				

Seymour	Ryan	Dempsey	Matthewson	Callaghan	Brown	Haynes	Conway	Large	Gilroy	Barrett	Pentecost	Kerrigan	Salvage	Macdonald	McClelland	Byrne	Jones	Halom	Murray	Earle	Parmenter	Williamson	Cohen	Mullen	Lloyd	Horne	Tranter	Dear	Roberts	Moreline	#
	2		6	3	4	10		5		7						9	11	1					8								3
		4	3	11	10	8	5			7					6		9						1	2							4
1		2	2	2	2	1	2			2					1		2	1	2	1	1										
				2	1																			2							

Seymour	Ryan	Dempsey	Matthewson	Callaghan	Brown	Haynes	Conway	Large	Gilroy	Barrett	Pentecost	Kerrigan																			#
1	2	3	4	5	6	7	8	9		11		10																			2
1	1	1	1	1	1	1	1	1		1		1																			

1969-70

1	Aug	9	(h)	Bradford C	D 0-0			9,943
2		16	(a)	Bury	L 0-1			5,648
3		23	(h)	Gillingham	W 2-1	Haynes, Conway		8,648
4		27	(h)	Southport	W 3-2	Conway 2, Brown		9,143
5		30	(a)	Barrow	L 1-3	Richardson		5,665
6	Sep	6	(h)	Shrewsbury T	W 3-1	Conway 2, Barrett		8,990
7		13	(a)	Bristol R	L 2-3	Conway, Earle		10,633
8		16	(a)	Halifax T	W 8-0	Earle 5, Conway 2, Lloyd		5,809
9		20	(h)	Plymouth A	W 4-3	Conway 2, Lloyd, Haynes		12,843
10		27	(a)	Stockport C	W 4-1	Earle 3, Conway		4,231
11		29	(a)	Orient	L 1-3	Earle		18,861
12	Oct	4	(h)	Doncaster R	D 1-1	Brown		13,535
13		8	(h)	Bury	L 2-4	Conway, Lloyd		11,724
14		11	(a)	Bournemouth	D 2-2	Conway, Earle		8,429
15		18	(a)	Rotherham U	D 0-0			7,699
16		25	(h)	Barnsley	D 0-0			10,535
17	Nov	1	(a)	Brighton & HA	L 1-2	Haynes		17,760
18		8	(h)	Torquay U	D 1-1	Earle		10,000
19		22	(h)	Mansfield T	D 1-1	Conway		8,038
20		25	(a)	Luton T	L 0-1			16,485
21	Dec	19	(h)	Bristol R	W 3-1	Richardson 2, Earle		6,745
22		20	(a)	Shrewsbury T	D 1-1	Earle		3,847
23		26	(a)	Gillingham	L 0-2			8,265
24		27	(h)	Barrow	W 2-1	Richardson, Lloyd		9,559
25	Jan	2	(h)	Orient	D 1-1	Conway		12,308
26		10	(a)	Plymouth A	L 0-2			9,661
27		17	(h)	Stockport C	D 1-1	Richardson		7,435
28		27	(a)	Walsall	W 3-1	Lloyd, Halom, Earle		6,251
29		31	(a)	Doncaster R	W 1-0	Conway		8,180
30	Feb	6	(h)	Bournemouth	D 1-1	Earle		9,713
31		14	(a)	Bradford C	D 0-0			9,615
32		21	(a)	Barnsley	D 3-3	Conway, Earle, Gilchrist		9,676
33		28	(h)	Rotherham U	W 3-2	Halom, Lloyd, Barrett		8,142
34	Mar	14	(h)	Rochdale	W 2-0	Halom 2		6,708
35		18	(h)	Walsall	W 4-0	Earle 2, Halom, Brown		7,301
36		21	(a)	Reading	W 4-0	Halom 2, Barrett, Earle		16,431
37		27	(a)	Torquay U	D 1-1	Barrett		7,934
38		28	(h)	Tranmere R	D 1-1	Barrett		10,310
39		30	(h)	Brighton & HA	W 4-1	Barrett, Callaghan, Halom, Conway		17,933
40	Apr	3	(a)	Southport	W 2-0	Barrett, Conway		3,432
41		6	(a)	Mansfield T	W 3-2	Conway, Halom, Lloyd		10,322
42		8	(h)	Luton T	L 0-1			18,987
43		15	(h)	Halifax T	W 2-1	Conway, Halom		7,072
44		18	(a)	Rochdale	W 1-0	Halom		5,077
45		20	(h)	Reading	W 2-1	Earle 2		9,713
46		27	(a)	Tranmere R	L 0-1			5,665

P	W	D	L	F	A	W	D	L	F	A	Pts	Pos	Div	
46	12	9	2	43	26	8	6	9	38	29	55	4th	3	

Appearances

Sub Appearances

Goals

FA Cup

1	Nov	15	(a)	Exeter C	L 0-2		9,181

Appearances

Sub Appearances

Goals

League Cup

1	Aug	13	(a)	Orient	D 0-0		8,676
R		18	(h)	Orient	W 3-1	Conway 2, Earle	11,424
2	Sep	3	(h)	Leeds U	L 0-1		20,446

Appearances

Sub Appearances

Goals

Month End		Sep	Oct	Nov	Dec	Jan	Feb	Mar	Apr	Final
1969-70	Pld	11	16	20	24	29	33	39	46	**46**
	Pts	13	17	19	24	30	35	45	55	**55**
	Pos	9th	9th	14th	14th	14th	12th	8th	4th	**4th**

Seymour	Gilchrist	Callaghan	Horne	Roberts	Matthewson	Conway	Lloyd	Halom	Haynes	Jones	Brown	Large	Pentecost	Earle	Barrett	Williamson	Richardson	O'Leary	Tranter	Webster	Moreline	#
1	2	3	4	5	6	7	8*	9	10	11	12											1
1	2	3	4	5		7	12	9	10	11*	6	8										2
1	2		4	5	6	7			10		8		3	9	11							3
	2	6	4	5		7	12		10		8		3	9*	11	1						4
	2	6	4	5		7			10		9		3		11	1	8					5
1	2		4	5	6	7	10*	8	12				3	9	11							6
1	2		4	5		7	8	10*			3			9	11		6	12				7
1		3	4	12	5	7	8	10*			2			9	11		6					8
1		3	4		5	7	8	10			2			9	11		6					9
1		3	4	5		7	8	10*			2		12	9	11		6					10
1		3	4			7	8		10		6		2	9	11		5					11
1		3	4		5	7	8		10		2		12	9*	11		6					12
1		3		5		7	8	9	10		4		2		11		6					13
1	2		6		5	7	10	8			3			9	11		4					14
1	2		6		5	7	8		10		3			9	11		4					15
1	2		6		5	7	8	9	10		3				11		4					16
1	2		6		5	7	8		10		3			9	11		4					17
1	2	3	6		5	7			10		8			9	11		4					18
1	2	3	6		5	7			10		8			9	11		4					19
1			6	4	5	7			10		3			9	11		8		2			20
	2	6	4		5	7			10	12	3			9*	11		8			1		21
	2	3	4		5	7			10	12	6			9*	11		8			1		22
	2	6	4*		5	7			10		3			9	11		8		12	1		23
	2	6			5	7	12		10		3			9	11		8*		4	1		24
	2	6	4		5	7	8*	12	10		3			9	11					1		25
	2	3*	4			7	12	8	10		6			9	11		5			1		26
	2		4	5	6	7			10		3			9	11		8			1		27
			4		6	7	10	8			3		2	9	11		5			1		28
	12		4		6	7	10	8			3		2	9	11*		5			1		29
	12	6	4		5	7*	10	8			3		2	9	11					1		30
			4		5	7	10	8			3		2	9	11		6			1		31
	12		4		5	7	2	8*	10		3		2	9	11		6			1		32
			4		5	7	8	10			3		2	9	11		6			1		33
			4		5	7	10	8			3		2	9	11		6			1		34
			4		5*	7	10	8			3		2	9	11		6			1	12	35
					5	7	10	8			4		2	9	11		6			1	3	36
					5	7	10	8			4		2	9	11		6			1	4	37
	12				5	7	10	8			4		2	9	11		6*			1	3	38
	10				5	7		8			4		2	9	11				6	1	3	39
	6				5	7	10	8			4		2	9	11					1	3	40
	3				5	7	10	8			4		2	9	11					1	6	41
	3				5	7	10	8			4		2	9	11					1	6	42
					5	7	10	8			4		2	9	11				3	1	6	43
					5	7	10	8			4		2	9	11				3	1	6	44
					5	7	10	8			4		2	9	11				3	1	6	45
					5	7	10	8			4		2	9	11				6	1	3	46
18	20	28	29	9	39	46	30	23	27	5	44	1	25	41	44	2	31	0	7	26	11	
3	1		1				4	1			2	2		2					1	1	1	
1	1				21	7	11	3		3				22	7		5					

Seymour	Gilchrist	Callaghan	Horne	Roberts	Matthewson	Conway	Lloyd	Halom	Haynes	Jones	Brown	Large	Pentecost	Earle	Barrett	Williamson	Richardson	O'Leary	Tranter	Webster	Moreline	#
1	2*	3	6		5	7			10		8			9	11		4		12			1
1	1	1	1		1	1			1		1			1	1		1					
																	1					

Seymour	Gilchrist	Callaghan	Horne	Roberts	Matthewson	Conway	Lloyd	Halom	Haynes	Jones	Brown	Large	Pentecost	Earle	Barrett	Williamson	Richardson	O'Leary	Tranter	Webster	Moreline	#
1	2	3	4	5		7		9	10	11	6	8										1
1	2	6	4	5		7	12		10*		8		3	9	11							R
1	2		4	5	6	7	12		10		8*		3	9	11							2
3	3	2	3	3	1	3		1	3	1	3	1		2	2	2						
					2																	
					2								1									

1970-71

1	Aug	15	(a)	Barnsley	W	1-0	Barrett	8,805
2		22	(h)	Swansea C	W	4-1	Earle 2, Halom, Dunne	10,384
3		29	(a)	Walsall	L	2-3	Halom, Lloyd	6,176
4	Sep	2	(h)	Bradford C	W	5-0	Halom, Earle, Lloyd, Conway, Barrett	10,328
5		5	(h)	Chesterfield	W	2-0	Earle, Lloyd	13,175
6		12	(a)	Rochdale	W	2-1	Barrett, Conway	4,790
7		19	(h)	Doncaster R	D	1-1	Conway	13,642
8		23	(h)	Brighton & HA	W	1-0	Lloyd	13,856
9		26	(a)	Preston NE	D	1-1	Dunne	12,105
10		28	(h)	Tranmere R	W	2-0	Halom, Brown	10,968
11	Oct	3	(h)	Plymouth A	D	1-1	Earle	13,334
12		10	(a)	Shrewsbury T	W	1-0	Barrett	6,415
13		17	(h)	Barnsley	D	1-1	Lloyd	12,952
14		21	(a)	Reading	D	1-1	Halom	14,169
15		24	(h)	Halifax T	W	3-1	Lloyd, Morton, Earle	10,749
16		31	(a)	Torquay U	L	1-3	Johnston	7,598
17	Nov	7	(h)	Bury	W	2-1	Lloyd, Barrett	9,390
18		9	(a)	Port Vale	W	1-0	Lloyd	8,292
19		14	(a)	Rotherham U	D	1-1	Johnston	9,398
20		28	(h)	Aston Villa	L	0-2		16,021
21	Dec	5	(a)	Mansfield T	L	0-1		8,051
22		19	(a)	Swansea C	L	1-4	Johnston	10,625
23		28	(h)	Gillingham	W	1-0	Halom	7,071
24	Jan	2	(a)	Wrexham	D	2-2	Barrett, opp own goal	9,712
25		8	(a)	Tranmere R	W	3-0	Barrett 2, Halom	4,619
26		16	(h)	Reading	D	1-1	Earle	10,141
27		30	(a)	Aston Villa	L	0-1		33,340
28	Feb	6	(h)	Mansfield T	D	0-0		9,370
29		13	(a)	Bristol R	W	1-0	Conway	18,875
30		20	(h)	Port Vale	W	4-1	Barrett 2, Earle 2	10,389
31		26	(h)	Torquay U	W	4-0	Barrett 2, Conway, Matthewson	13,012
32	Mar	2	(h)	Bristol R	W	2-1	Johnston, Earle	15,871
33		6	(a)	Halifax T	L	1-2	Johnston	8,019
34		10	(a)	Brighton & HA	L	2-3	Conway, Johnston	14,413
35		13	(h)	Rotherham U	W	1-0	Earle	9,627
36		17	(h)	Wrexham	W	1-0	Barrett	8,856
37		20	(a)	Bury	L	0-2		4,121
38		26	(a)	Chesterfield	D	0-0		13,370
39	Apr	3	(h)	Walsall	W	1-0	Barrett	8,429
40		7	(h)	Rochdale	W	2-0	Earle, Conway	10,054
41		10	(a)	Gillingham	W	3-1	Barrett, Johnston, Conway	9,367
42		12	(a)	Plymouth A	D	1-1	Halom	11,712
43		17	(h)	Shrewsbury T	D	0-0		12,702
44		24	(a)	Doncaster R	W	1-0	Earle	4,399
45		28	(a)	Bradford C	W	3-2	Johnston 2, Lloyd	6,430
46	May	1	(h)	Preston NE	L	0-1		25,774

P	W	D	L	F	A	W	D	L	F	A	Pts	Pos	Div		
46	15	6	2	39	12	9	6	8	29	29	60	2nd	3		Appearances
															Sub Appearances
															Goals

FA Cup

1	Nov	21	(h)	Bristol R	L	1-2	Johnston	13,921

Appearances
Sub Appearances
Goals

League Cup

1	Aug	19	(h)	Orient	W	1-0	Conway	10,975
2	Sep	9	(a)	Darlington	W	4-0	Barrett 2, Halom, Conway	9,324
3	Oct	6	(h)	Queen's Park R	W	2-0	Barrett, Halom	31,727
4		27	(h)	Swindon T	W	1-0	Earle	22,576
5	Nov	17	(h)	Bristol C	D	0-0		16,281
R		24	(a)	Bristol C	L	0-1		23,249

Appearances
Sub Appearances
Goals

Month End		Sep	Oct	Nov	Dec	Jan	Feb	Mar	Apr	Final
1970-71	Pld	10	16	20	23	27	31	38	45	**46**
	Pts	16	23	28	30	34	41	48	60	**60**
	Pos	1st	1st	1st	3rd	4th	1st	2nd	1st	**2nd**

Football appearance/line-up grid (squad numbers by player and match).

Webster	Moreline	Callaghan	Brown	Matthewson	Dunne	Conway	Halom	Earle	Lloyd	Barrett	Richardson	Seymour	Pentecost	Davidson	Horne	Morton	Johnston	Roberts	Mansley	Tranter	No.
1	2	3	4	5	6	7	8	9	10	11											1
1	2	3	4	5	6	7	8	9	10	11											2
1	2	3	4	5	6	7	8	9	10	11											3
1	2	3	4	5	6	7	8	9	10	11											4
1	2	3	4	5	6	7	8	9	10	11											5
1	2	3	4	5	6	7	8	9	10	11											6
	2	3	4	5	6	7	8	9	10	11		1									7
	2	3	4	5	6	7	8	9	10	11		1									8
	2	3	7	5	6		8	9	10	11	4	1									9
	2	3	4	5	6	7	8	9	10	11		1									10
		3	2	5	6	7*	8	9	10	11	4	1	12								11
		3		5	6		8	9	10	11	4	1	2	7							12
		3	7*	5	6		8	9	10	11	4	1	2		12						13
		3	7	5	6		8	9	10	11	4	1	2								14
1		3	4	12	6		8	9	10	11	5		2				7*				15
1		3	4		6		8	9	10	7	5		2				11				16
1	12	3	4		6		8	9	10	11	5*		2				7				17
1		3	4	5	6		8	9	10	11			2				7				18
1	8	3	4*	5	6	12		9	10	11			2				7				19
1		3	4	5	6		8	9	10	11		1	2				7				20
	2	3	4	5	6		8*	9	10	11		1			7		12				21
	2	3*	12		6		9	8	10			1	4				7	5	11		22
1	2	8	4	5	6		9	7	10	11			3								23
1	2	8	4	5	6		9	7	10	11			3								24
1	2	8	4	5	6		9	7	10	11			3								25
1	2	6		5	4		8	9	10	11	12		3				7*				26
1	4	3		5	6	7*	8	9	10	11	12									2	27
1	4	3		5*	6	7	12	9	10	11							8			2	28
1	4	3	2	5	6	7		9	10	11							8				29
1	4	3	2	5	6	7		9	10	11							8				30
1	4	3	2	5	6	7		9	10	11							8				31
1	4	3	2	5	6	7		9	10	11							8				32
1	3	4	2	5	6	7		9	10	11							8				33
1	4	3	2	5	6	7		9	10	11							8				34
1	2	3	7*	5	4		12	9	10	11	6						8				35
1	2	3	4	5	6	7		9	10	11			12				8*				36
1	2	3	4	5	6	7		9	10	11			12				8*				37
1			4	5	6	7	8	9	10	11			3							2	38
1		3	4	5	6	7		9	10	11			2				8				39
1		3	4	5	6	7			10	11			2				8				40
1		3		5	6	7		9	10	11	12		2		4		8*				41
1		3		5	6	7	9*		10	11	12		2		4		8				42
1		3		5	6	7	9*		10	11	12		2		4		8				43
1		3		5	6	7	12	9	10	11			2		4		8*				44
1		3		5	6	7		9	10	11			2		4		8				45
1		3		5	6	7	12	9	10	11			2		4		8*				46
35	28	45	35	43	45	29	30	42	46	46	9	11	22	1	8	1	25	1	1	3	
	1		1	1							5		7	1		1					
		1	1	2	8	8	13	9	15							1	9				

Webster	Moreline	Callaghan	Brown	Matthewson	Dunne	Conway	Halom	Earle	Lloyd	Barrett	Richardson	Seymour	Pentecost	Davidson	Horne	Morton	Johnston	Roberts	Mansley	Tranter	No.
		3	4	5	6		8	9	10	11		1	2				7				1
		1	1	1	1		1	1	1	1		1	1				1				
																	1				

Webster	Moreline	Callaghan	Brown	Matthewson	Dunne	Conway	Halom	Earle	Lloyd	Barrett	Richardson	Seymour	Pentecost	Davidson	Horne	Morton	Johnston	Roberts	Mansley	Tranter	No.
1	2	3	4	5	6	7	8	9	10	11											1
1	2	3	4*	5	6	7	8	9	10	11					12						2
		3		5	6		8	9	10	11	4	1	2				7				3
1		3	4		6		8	9	10	11	5		2				7				4
	7*	3	4	5	6		8	9	10	11		1	2				12				5
		3	4	5	6		8	9	10	11		1	2	7							R
3	3	6	5	5	6	2	6	6	6	6	2	3	4	1		1	2				
					2	2	1		3												

347

1971-72

1	Aug	14	(h)	Watford	W	3-0	Earle 2, Johnston	13,568
2		21	(a)	Preston NE	L	0-2		16,425
3		28	(h)	Norwich C	D	0-0		10,668
4		31	(h)	Queen's Park R	L	0-3		21,187
5	Sep	4	(a)	Middlesbrough	L	0-2		20,682
6		11	(h)	Burnley	L	0-2		10,668
7		18	(a)	Swindon T	L	0-4		13,973
8		25	(h)	Orient	W	2-1	Barrett, Earle	9,153
9		28	(a)	Luton T	L	0-2		14,017
10	Oct	2	(a)	Sheffield W	L	0-4		14,983
11		9	(h)	Hull C	W	1-0	Earle	8,352
12		12	(h)	Oxford U	D	1-1	Callaghan	7,530
13		16	(a)	Watford	W	2-1	Conway, opp own goal	9,302
14		23	(a)	Portsmouth	L	3-6	Conway 2, Barrett	14,171
15		30	(h)	Blackpool	W	2-1	Conway, Lloyd	11,020
16	Nov	6	(a)	Bristol C	W	2-1	Cross, Barrett	17,265
17		13	(h)	Cardiff C	W	4-3	Conway 2, Earle, Cross	10,700
18		20	(h)	Charlton A	W	1-0	Barrett	13,359
19		27	(a)	Birmingham C	L	1-3	Conway	25,671
20	Dec	4	(h)	Carlisle U	L	0-1		8,101
21		11	(a)	Sunderland	L	1-2	Barrett	11,808
22		18	(h)	Middlesbrough	D	2-2	Cross, Barrett	7,571
23		27	(a)	Millwall	L	1-4	Lloyd	21,391
24	Jan	1	(h)	Swindon T	L	2-4	Earle 2	7,406
25		8	(a)	Norwich C	L	1-2	Earle	21,878
26		22	(h)	Luton T	W	3-1	Barrett, Johnston 2	11,328
27		29	(a)	Oxford U	L	0-1		8,113
28	Feb	12	(h)	Portsmouth	D	1-1	Cross	8,390
29		19	(a)	Blackpool	L	1-2	Conway	11,480
30		26	(h)	Bristol C	W	2-0	Callaghan, Earle	9,276
31	Mar	4	(a)	Cardiff C	L	0-1		13,122
32		11	(a)	Hull C	L	0-4		11,112
33		18	(h)	Preston NE	D	0-0		9,071
34		25	(a)	Burnley	D	1-1	Lloyd	10,082
35		28	(h)	Sheffield W	W	4-0	Cross 2, Earle, Mullery	7,947
36	Apr	1	(h)	Millwall	W	1-0	Barrett	20,154
37		3	(a)	Orient	L	0-1		16,024
38		8	(a)	Charlton A	D	2-2	Earle, Callaghan	9,055
39		18	(h)	Birmingham C	D	0-0		16,553
40		22	(a)	Carlisle U	L	1-3	Cross	6,067
41		25	(a)	Queen's Park R	D	0-0		20,605
42		29	(h)	Sunderland	D	0-0		12,360

P	W	D	L	F	A	W	D	L	F	A	Pts	Pos	Div		
42	10	7	4	29	20	2	3	16	16	48	34	20th	2	Appearances	
														Sub Appearances	
														Goals	

FA Cup

3	Jan	15	(a)	Queen's Park R	D	1-1	Conway	23,707
R		18	(h)	Queen's Park R	W	2-1	Cross 2	24,181
4	Feb	5	(a)	Huddersfield T	L	0-3		18,300

Appearances
Sub Appearances
Goals

League Cup

1	Aug	17	(h)	Cambridge U	W	4-0	Halom, Earle 3	8,360
2	Sep	7	(a)	Sheffield U	L	0-3		24,271

Appearances
Sub Appearances
Goals

Month End		Sep	Oct	Nov	Dec	Jan	Feb	Mar	Apr	Final
1971-72	Pld	9	15	19	23	27	30	35	42	42
	Pts	5	12	18	19	21	24	28	34	34
	Pos	22nd	17th	14th	18th	19th	20th	20th	20th	20th

Player appearance grid (shirt numbers worn per match). Columns left to right: Webster, Penetcost, Callaghan, Brown, Matthewson, Dunne, Johnston, Halom, Earle, Lloyd, Barrett, Horne, Moreline, Carlton, Conway John, Cross, Richardson, Conway Jim, Fraser, Stephenson, Mellor, Tranter, Mullery. Final column = match number.

Web	Pen	Cal	Bro	Mat	Dun	Joh	Hal	Ear	Llo	Bar	Hor	Mor	Car	CJo	Crs	Ric	CJi	Fra	Ste	Mel	Tra	Mul	#
1	2	3	4	5	6	7	8*	9	10	11	12												1
1	2	3	4	5	6	7	8	9	10	11													2
1	2	3	4	5	6	7	8*	9	10	11	12												3
1	2	3	4*	5	6	7		9	10	11			12	8									4
1	2	3		5	6	7		9	10	11			4	8									5
1	2*	3		5	6			9	10	11	12	4		7	8								6
1		3		5				9	10	11	4	2			8	6	7						7
1		3	2	5	6			9	10	11					8	4	7						8
1		3	2	5	6*			9	10	11			12		8	4	7						9
1		3	2	5	6	12		9	10	11					8*	4	7						10
1		3	2	5	6	12		9	10	11					8*	4	7						11
1	2	3		5	6			9	10	11					8	4	7						12
1	2	3		5	6			9	10	11					8	4	7						13
1	2	3		5	6	8		9	10	11						4	7						14
1		3	4	6				9	10	11					8		7	2	5				15
1		3	4	5				9	10	11					8	6	7	2					16
1		3	4	6				9	10	11					8*	12	7	2	5				17
1		3	4	6				9	10	11					8		7	2	5				18
1		3	2	6				9	10	11			4		8		7		5				19
1		3	2					9	10	11	6	4			8		7		5				20
1		3	4	12	6			9	10	11					8		7	2	5				21
1		3	4	12	6			9	10	11					8		7	2*	5				22
1		3	12	4	6			9	10	11*					8		7	2	5				23
1		3	4*	6				9	10	11			12		8		7	2	5				24
1		3	7	6	4			9	10	11					8			2	5				25
1		3		6	4	7		9	10	11		2			8	5							26
1		3		5	4	12		9	10	11*		2			8	6	7						27
1		3	4	6				9	10	11		2			8	5	7						28
1		3	4	5				9	10	11		2			8	6	7						29
		3	4	5				9	10	11		2			8	6	7			1			30
		3	2	5				9	10	11	7				8	6				1	4		31
		3	2	5				9	10	11	7				8*	6				1	12	4	32
		3	2	5	6			9	10	11	7				8					1		4	33
		3	2	5	6			9	10	11	7				8					1		4	34
		3	2	5	6			9	10	11	7				8					1		4	35
		3	2	5	6			9	10	11	7	12			8*					1		4	36
		3	2	5	6			9	10	11	7	12			8*					1		4	37
	2	3		5	6	7		9	10	11	4		8							1			38
	2	4		5	6	12		9*	10	11	7	3			8					1			39
	2	11	4	5	6	12		10*	9		7	3			8					1			40
	2	4		5	6			9	10	11	7	3			8					1			41
	2	6		5	4			9	10	11	7	3			8					1			42
29	14	42	28	39	30	8	3	41	42	42	13	13	5	1	35	16	22	9	10	13	1	6	
		1	1		5						3	2	3		1					1			
	3			3				11	3	8		7		8					1				

Web	Pen	Cal	Bro	Mat	Dun	Joh	Hal	Ear	Llo	Bar	Hor	Mor	Car	CJo	Crs	Ric	CJi	Fra	Ste	Mel	Tra	Mul	#
1		3		5	4	12		9	10	11		2			8*	6	7						3
1		3		5	4			9	10	11		2			8	6	7						R
1		3		5	4			9	10	11		2			8	6	7						4
3		3		3	3	1		3	3	3		3			3	3	3						
						1																	
															2	1							

Web	Pen	Cal	Bro	Mat	Dun	Joh	Hal	Ear	Llo	Bar	Hor	Mor	Car	CJo	Crs	Ric	CJi	Fra	Ste	Mel	Tra	Mul	#
1		3	4	5	6		8	9	10	11	12		7*						2				1
1	2	3		5	6	12		9	10	11		4	8	7									2
2	1	2	1	2	2	1	1	2	2	2	1	1	2	1					1				
						1								1									
												1	3										

349

1972-73

1	Aug	12	(a)	Sheffield W		L 0-3		23,109
2		19	(h)	Burnley		D 1-1 Went		10,285
3		26	(a)	Middlesbrough		W 2-1 Cross, Barrett		11,410
4	Sep	2	(h)	Preston NE		L 1-3 Richardson		7,640
5		9	(a)	Brighton & HA		L 1-2 Earle		15,615
6		16	(h)	Huddersfield T		D 1-1 Mullery		7,071
7		20	(h)	Hull C		W 2-0 Earle, Mullery		7,686
8		23	(a)	Millwall		W 3-1 Mitchell, Lloyd, Earle		12,242
9		26	(a)	Bristol C		D 1-1 Earle		14,210
10		30	(h)	Orient		D 1-1 Earle		10,991
11	Oct	7	(h)	Aston Villa		W 2-0 Mullery, Mitchell		17,576
12		14	(a)	Carlisle U		L 1-2 Mitchell		6,221
13		17	(h)	Queen's Park R		L 0-2		17,000
14		21	(h)	Blackpool		W 2-0 Strong, Earle		8,644
15		28	(a)	Sunderland		D 0-0		11,618
16	Nov	4	(h)	Bristol C		W 5-1 Earle, Mitchell 2, Strong, opp own goal		8,982
17		11	(a)	Hull C		D 2-2 Mitchell 2		9,405
18		18	(h)	Portsmouth		D 0-0		9,624
19		25	(a)	Cardiff C		L 1-3 Mullery		9,690
20	Dec	9	(a)	Oxford U		D 0-0		8,346
21		16	(h)	Nottingham F		W 3-1 Mitchell, Barrett, Mullery		8,255
22		23	(a)	Swindon T		D 2-2 Earle, opp own goal		9,489
23		26	(h)	Millwall		W 1-0 Conway (Jim)		16,093
24		30	(a)	Burnley		D 2-2 Went, Conway (Jim)		15,477
25	Jan	6	(h)	Middlesbrough		W 2-1 Mullery, Conway (Jim)		9,693
26		20	(a)	Preston NE		W 3-0 Earle 2, Barrett		5,759
27		27	(h)	Brighton & HA		W 5-1 Earle 2, Mitchell, Barrett, Conway (Jim)		12,008
28	Feb	10	(a)	Huddersfield T		L 0-1		6,469
29		17	(h)	Sheffield W		W 1-0 Earle		11,686
30		24	(a)	Nottingham F		L 1-2 Earle		8,810
31	Mar	3	(a)	Aston Villa		W 3-2 Barrett, Mitchell, Went		24,007
32		10	(h)	Carlisle U		W 1-0 Mitchell		9,835
33		17	(a)	Blackpool		L 0-2		8,019
34		24	(h)	Sunderland		L 1-2 Mullery		9,645
35		27	(h)	Luton T		L 0-1		7,442
36		31	(h)	Cardiff C		D 1-1 Conway (John)		6,262
37	Apr	7	(a)	Luton T		L 0-1		8,430
38		14	(h)	Oxford U		W 2-0 Earle, opp own goal		6,359
39		20	(h)	Swindon T		D 0-0		8,519
40		21	(a)	Portsmouth		W 2-1 Conway (John) 2		9,192
41		23	(a)	Orient		L 2-3 Barrett, Mullery		9,953
42		28	(a)	Queen's Park R		L 0-2		22,187

P	W	D	L	F	A	W	D	L	F	A	Pts	Pos	Div		
42	11	6	4	32	16	5	6	10	26	33	44	9th	2	Appearances	
														Sub Appearances	
														Goals	

FA Cup

3	Jan	13	(a)	Sheffield W	L 0-2		21,028

Appearances
Sub Appearances
Goals

League Cup

1	Aug	16	(a)	Reading	D 1-1 Richardson		8,884
R		23	(h)	Reading	D 1-1 Went		5,639
2R		28	(a)	Reading	W 1-0 Lloyd		8,174
2	Sep	5	(a)	Hull C	L 0-1		6,352

Appearances
Sub Appearances
Goals

Month End		Sep	Oct	Nov	Dec	Jan	Feb	Mar	Apr	Final
1972-73	Pld	10	15	19	24	27	30	36	42	42
	Pts	10	15	19	26	32	34	39	44	44
	Pos	16th	13th	10th	9th	4th	5th	6th	9th	9th

Mellor	Pentecost	Moreline	Mullery	Matthewson	Dunne	Conway Jim	Horne	Cross	Lloyd	Barrett	Callaghan	Went	Brown	Richardson	Earle	Cutbush	Conway John	Mitchell	Strong	Carlton	Lacy	Fraser	Pinkney	Shrubb	
1	2	3	4	5	6	7*	8	9	10	11	12														1
1		2	4		6			9	10	11	3	5	7	8											2
1		2			6			9	10	11	3	5	7	4	8										3
1		2			6			8*	10	11	3	5	7	4	9	12									4
1			8		6		4		10*	11	3	5		9	7	2	12								5
1			4		6				10	11	3	5			8	2	7	9							6
1			4		6				10	11	3	5		12	8	2	7*	9							7
1			4		6				10	11	3	5			8	2	7	9							8
1			4		6				10	11	3	5		12	8	2	7*	9							9
1			4		6				10	11	3	5			8	2		9	7						10
1			4		6		12		10	11	3	5			8	2		9	7*						11
1			4		6		12		10	11	3	5			8	2		9	7*						12
1			4		6			12	10	11	3	5			8	2		9	7*						13
1			4		6				10	11	3	5			8	2		9	7						14
1			4		6				10	11	3	5			8	2		9	7						15
1			4		6				10	11	3	5			8	2*		9	7	12					16
1			4		6				10	11	3	5			8	2		9	7						17
1	12		4		6				10		3	5			8	2	7	9	11*						18
1			4		6				10		3	5			8	2	7*	9	11		12				19
1			4		6	7			10	11	3	5			8	2		9							20
1			4		6	7			10	11	3	5			8	2		9							21
1	12		4		6	7			10	11	3*				8	2		9			5				22
1			4		6	7			10	11	3				8	2		9			5				23
1	12		4		6	7			10*	11	3	5			8	2		9							24
1			4		6	7	10			11	3	5			8			9				2			25
1			4		6	7				11	3	5			8			9				2	10		26
1			4		6	7				11	3	5			8			9				2	10		27
1	12		4		6	7*				11	3	5			8			9				2	10		28
1			4		6					11	3	5			8	2		9	7				10		29
1			4		6					11	3	5			8	2	12	9	7*				10		30
1			4		6					11	3	5			8	2		9	7				10		31
1			4		6*					11	3	5			8	2		9	7			12	10		32
1			4						10	11	3	5			8	2		9	12		6*		7		33
1			4						10	11	3	5		6	8	2		9	7*				12		34
1			4						12	11	3	5			8	2		9	7			10*		6	35
1			4				6			11	3	5			8	2	7	9*	12				10		36
1			6				4		10		3	5			8	2	12	9	11			7*			37
1			4			7	6		10	11	3	5			8	2	12		9*						38
1			4			7*	6		10	11	3	5			8	2	12	9							39
1	3		4				6		10	11		5			5	2	7	9							40
1	3		4		12		6		10	11		5			8	2	7	9*							41
1	3		4			7	6		10	11		5			8	2	12	9*							42
42	1	7	40	1	32	13	10	4	32	39	38	39	3	5	40	34	9	36	17		3	4	11	1	
	2	2				1	2	1	1		1		2		1	6		2			1	1	1		
		8			4			1	1	6		3			1	15		3	11	2					

Mellor	Pentecost	Moreline	Mullery	Matthewson	Dunne	Conway Jim	Horne	Cross	Lloyd	Barrett	Callaghan	Went	Brown	Richardson	Earle	Cutbush	Conway John	Mitchell	Strong	Carlton	Lacy	Fraser	Pinkney	Shrubb	
1	12		4		6	7	10			11	3	5			8			9				2			3
1			1		1	1	10			1	1	1			1			1				1			
		1																							

Mellor	Pentecost	Moreline	Mullery	Matthewson	Dunne	Conway Jim	Horne	Cross	Lloyd	Barrett	Callaghan	Went	Brown	Richardson	Earle	Cutbush	Conway John	Mitchell	Strong	Carlton	Lacy	Fraser	Pinkney	Shrubb	
1		2	4		6			8	10	11	3	5			9		7								1
1		2	4		6			9	10	11	3	5	7		8										R
1		2			6			9	10	11	3	5	7	4	8										2R
1					6		4		10	11	3	5		9	8	2	7								2
4		3	2		4		1	3	4	4	4	4	2	3	3	2	1								
								1			1		1												

1973-74

1	Aug	25	(h)	Millwall	W 2-0 Barrett, Conway (Jim)	12,072
2	Sep	1	(a)	Middlesbrough	W 2-0 Barrett, Earle	14,976
3		8	(h)	Orient	L 0-3	10,984
4		12	(h)	Blackpool	D 0-0	9,301
5		15	(a)	Cardiff C	D 0-0	11,251
6		19	(a)	Aston Villa	D 1-1 Slough	30,162
7		22	(h)	Bolton W	W 1-0 Busby	9,565
8		26	(a)	Oxford U	D 0-0	8,046
9	Oct	2	(h)	Aston Villa	W 1-0 Mitchell	11,776
10		6	(h)	Preston NE	D 0-0	10,520
11		13	(a)	Notts C	L 1-2 Earle	11,970
12		20	(h)	Sunderland	L 0-2	14,971
13		22	(a)	Blackpool	L 0-2	5,526
14		27	(a)	Carlisle U	L 0-3	7,147
15	Nov	3	(h)	Bristol C	W 2-1 Conway (John), Busby	9,613
16		10	(a)	Nottingham F	L 0-3	10,510
17		17	(h)	Portsmouth	W 2-0 Mitchell, Barrett	8,403
18		24	(a)	West Brom A	L 0-2	12,683
19	Dec	1	(h)	Hull C	D 0-0	5,636
20		8	(a)	Swindon T	D 1-1 Mullery	5,581
21		15	(a)	Sheffield W	W 3-0 Conway (John), Barrett, Busby	7,925
22		22	(h)	Oxford U	W 3-1 Cutbush, Busby 2	4,973
23		26	(a)	Luton T	D 1-1 Conway (John)	15,269
24		29	(a)	Orient	L 0-1	13,666
25	Jan	12	(h)	Cardiff C	L 0-1	7,413
26		20	(a)	Millwall	L 0-1	15,134
27	Feb	2	(h)	Sheffield W	W 4-1 Busby 3, Barrett	6,584
28		16	(h)	Notts C	W 2-0 Conway (Jim), Busby	7,515
29		23	(a)	Preston NE	W 1-0 Slough	9,545
30	Mar	5	(h)	Luton T	W 2-1 Lloyd 2	10,071
31		9	(h)	Carlisle U	L 0-2	6,731
32		16	(a)	Sunderland	L 0-1	30,439
33		19	(h)	Middlesbrough	L 0-4	18,114
34		23	(h)	Nottingham F	W 2-0 Busby, Conway (Jim)	9,884
35		30	(a)	Bristol C	W 1-0 Mullery	10,946
36	Apr	2	(a)	Bolton W	D 0-0	18,636
37		6	(h)	West Brom A	D 0-0	9,494
38		12	(h)	Crystal P	L 1-3 Moore	23,511
39		13	(a)	Portsmouth	L 0-3	12,054
40		16	(a)	Crystal P	W 2-0 Busby, Barrett	32,124
41		20	(h)	Swindon T	W 4-1 Cutbush, Howe, Barrett, Busby	7,080
42		27	(h)	Hull C	L 0-2	5,731

P	W	D	L	F	A	W	D	L	F	A	Pts	Pos	Div		
42	11	4	6	26	20	5	6	10	13	23	42	13th	2	Appearances	
														Sub Appearances	
														Goals	

FA Cup

3	Jan	5	(h)	Preston NE	W 1-0 Conway (John)	6,937
4		26	(h)	Leicester C	D 1-1 Mullery	26,231
R		30	(a)	Leicester C	L 1-2 Barrett	37,130

Appearances

Sub Appearances

Goals

League Cup

2	Oct	10	(a)	Oxford U	D 1-1 Barrett	7,101
R		16	(h)	Oxford U	W 3-0 Went, Lacy, Barrett	6,435
3		31	(h)	Ipswich T	D 2-2 Mullery, Barrett	8,964
R	Nov	14	(a)	Ipswich T	L 1-2 Earle	21,400

Appearances

Sub Appearances

Goals

Month End		Sep	Oct	Nov	Dec	Jan	Feb	Mar	Apr	Final
1973-74	**Pld**	8	14	18	24	26	29	35	42	**42**
	Pts	10	13	17	24	24	30	36	42	**42**
	Pos	4th	15th	14th	10th	16th	11th	11th	13th	**13th**

Appearances / team-sheet grid (shirt numbers by player and match).

Mellor	Cutbush	Slough	Mullery	Went	Dunne	Conway Jim	Earle	Busby	Lloyd	Barrett	Moreline	Mitchell	Lacy	Conway John	Webster	Fraser	Strong	Friend	Dowie	Moore	Callaghan	Howe	#
1	2	3	4	5	6	7	8	9	10	11													1
1	2	3	4	5	6	7	8	9	10	11													2
1	2	3	4	5	6	7	9	8*	10	11	12												3
1	2	3	4	5	6	7	8		10	11			9										4
1	2	3	4	5	7		8		10	11			9	6									5
1	2	3	4	5	7		8*	12	10	11			9	6									6
1	2	7	4	5		12		8	10	11	3		9*	6									7
1	2	3	4	5	7		8	9	10	11				6									8
1	2	3	4	5	7		8	9*	10	11			12	6									9
1	2	3	4	5			8*	12	10	11			9	6	7								10
1	2	3	4	5	8		9	12	10*	11			7	6									11
1	2	3	4	5	7		8	12	10*	11			9	6									12
1	2	3	4	5	7		8		10	11			9	6									13
1	2	3	4	5	7		12	8	10	11			9*	6									14
	2	3	4	5			8	9	10	11			6	7	1								15
	2	3	4	5	12		8	9*	10	11			6	7	1								16
	2	3	4	5	6		8		10	11			9	7	1								17
	2	3	4	5	6		8		10	11			9	7	1								18
1	2	10	4	5	8			9		11	3		6	7									19
1	2	10	4		6	8		9		11			5	7		3							20
1	2	10	4		6	8		9		11			5	7		3							21
1	2	10	4		6	8		9		11			5	7		3							22
1	2	10	4		6	8		9		11			5	7		3							23
1	2*	10	4		6	8		9	12	11			5	7		3							24
1		10	4		6	8		9		11		12	5	7*		2	3						25
1		8	4		6	7		9	10	11			5			2	3						26
1		8	4		6	7		9	10	11			5			2	3						27
1		8	4		6	7		9	10	11			5			2	3						28
1		8	4		6	7*		9	10	11			5			2	3	12					29
1		8	4		6			9	10	11			5			2	3	7					30
1		4			5	7		9	10	11			6	12		2	3	8*					31
1		4			6	7		9	10	11			5			2	3		8				32
1	2	3*	8		6	7		9	10	11			5				12			4			33
1	2		8		6	7		9	10	11			5				3			4			34
1	2		4		6	7		9	10	11			5				3			8			35
1	2		8		6	7		9*	10	11			5				3			4	12		36
1	2		4		6	7*		9	10	11			5	12			3			8			37
1	2		8		6	12		9	10	11			5*	7			3			4			38
1	8		4		3*	7		9	12	11						5	2			10	6		39
1	7		4			8		9	10	11						2	3			6	5		40
1	7		4			8		9	10	11						2	3			6	5		41
1	8*		4			7		9	10	11				12		2	3			6	5		42
38	34	33	40	19	35	25	15	34	34	42	2	11	32	13	4	17	17	2	1	10	4		
				1	2	1	4	2		1	2	1	2			1	1		1				
	2	2	2		3	2	12	2	7		2		3								1		

Mellor	Cutbush	Slough	Mullery	Went	Dunne	Conway Jim	Earle	Busby	Lloyd	Barrett	Moreline	Mitchell	Lacy	Conway John	Webster	Fraser	Strong	Friend	Dowie	Moore	Callaghan	Howe	#
1		10	4		6					11		9	5	7		2	3		8				3
1		8	4		6	7		9	10	11			5			2	3						4
1		8	4		6	7		9	10	11			5			2*	3		12				R
3		3	3		3	2		2	2	3		1	3	1		3	3		1				
													1						1				

Mellor	Cutbush	Slough	Mullery	Went	Dunne	Conway Jim	Earle	Busby	Lloyd	Barrett	Moreline	Mitchell	Lacy	Conway John	Webster	Fraser	Strong	Friend	Dowie	Moore	Callaghan	Howe	#
1	2	3	4	5	8			7	10	11			9	6									2
1	2	3	4	5	7		8		10	11			9	6									R
	2	3	4	5			8		10	11	12	9*	6	7	1								3
	2	3	4	5	6		8		10	11			9	7	1								R
2	4	4	4	4	3		2	2	4	4			4	3	2	2							
		1	1		1			3			1												

353

1974-75

1	Aug	17	(a)	West Brom A	W	1-0	Busby		11,408
2		20	(a)	Notts C	D	1-1	Mullery		9,368
3		24	(h)	Cardiff C	W	4-0	Conway (Jim) 2, Busby 2		8,119
4		28	(h)	Notts C	W	3-0	Slough, Conway (Jim), Busby		9,373
5		31	(a)	Millwall	L	0-2			9,936
6	Sep	7	(h)	York C	L	0-2			7,628
7		14	(a)	Orient	D	0-0			8,927
8		21	(h)	Norwich C	W	4-0	Busby, Fraser, Barrett, Lacy		9,414
9		25	(h)	Bristol R	D	0-0			8,706
10		28	(a)	Oldham A	L	0-1			12,750
11	Oct	5	(h)	Manchester U	L	1-2	Busby		26,513
12		12	(a)	Portsmouth	D	0-0			12,520
13		19	(h)	Bristol C	D	1-1	Mullery		8,960
14		26	(a)	Oxford U	L	1-2	Barrett		8,714
15	Nov	2	(h)	Aston Villa	W	3-1	Lacy, Busby, Lloyd		10,979
16		9	(a)	Hull C	L	1-2	Cutbush		7,571
17		16	(h)	Sunderland	L	1-3	Mullery		14,193
18		22	(a)	Sheffield W	L	0-1			12,373
19		30	(h)	Blackpool	W	1-0	Mullery		6,416
20	Dec	7	(a)	Nottingham F	D	1-1	Belfitt		10,057
21		11	(a)	Cardiff C	D	0-0			8,485
22		14	(h)	West Brom A	W	1-0	Mullery		6,730
23		21	(a)	Southampton	D	0-0			13,560
24		26	(h)	Orient	D	0-0			9,600
25		28	(a)	Bolton W	D	0-0			4,703
26	Jan	11	(h)	Nottingham F	L	0-1			9,159
27		18	(a)	Blackpool	L	0-1			6,710
28	Feb	1	(h)	Hull C	D	1-1	Dowie		5,739
29		8	(a)	Aston Villa	D	1-1	Busby		28,533
30		22	(a)	Sunderland	W	2-1	Busby 2		33,418
31		25	(h)	Sheffield W	W	2-1	Barrett, Mullery		8,550
32	Mar	4	(h)	Millwall	D	0-0			13,315
33		11	(a)	Bristol R	W	2-1	Mullery, Mitchell		11,765
34		15	(h)	Oldham A	D	0-0			13,186
35		22	(a)	York C	L	2-3	Slough, Busby		7,825
36		24	(h)	Southampton	W	3-2	Conway (Jim), Mullery, Barrett		11,939
37		28	(h)	Bolton W	W	2-1	Dowie, Mullery		9,453
38		31	(a)	Norwich C	W	2-1	Mitchell 2		29,909
39	Apr	12	(a)	Manchester U	L	0-1			52,971
40		19	(h)	Portsmouth	D	2-2	Mitchell 2		17,584
41		22	(h)	Oxford U	D	0-0			11,300
42		26	(a)	Bristol C	L	1-3	Barrett		11,538

P	W	D	L	F	A	W	D	L	F	A	Pts	Pos	Div		
42	9	8	4	29	17	4	8	9	15	22	42	9th	2		Appearances
															Sub Appearances
															Goals

FA Cup

3	Jan	4	(h)	Hull C	D	1-1	Conway (Jim)		8,897
R		7	(a)	Hull C	D	2-2	Busby 2		11,850
2R		13	(n)	Hull C*	W	1-0	Slough		4,929
4		28	(h)	Nottingham F	D	0-0			14,846
R	Feb	3	(a)	Nottingham F	D	1-1	Dowie		26,361
2R		5	(h)	Nottingham F	D	1-1	Slough		11,920
3R		10	(a)	Nottingham F	W	2-1	Busby 2		23,240
5		15	(a)	Everton	W	2-1	Busby 2		45,233
6	Mar	8	(a)	Carlisle U	W	1-0	Barrett		21,570
SF	Apr	5	(n)	Birmingham C†	D	1-1	Mitchell		55,000
R		9	(n)	Birmingham C‡	W	1-0	Mitchell		35,109
F	May	3	(n)	West Ham U	L	0-2			100,000

*Played at Filbert Street, Leicester. †Played at Hillsborough.

‡Played at Maine Road, Manchester. Final played at Wembley.

Appearances

Sub Appearances

Goals

League Cup

2	Sep	11	(a)	Wolves	W	3-1	Barrett 2, Busby		16,151
3	Oct	8	(h)	West Ham U	W	2-1	Mullery, Slough		29,611
4	Nov	13	(a)	Newcastle U	L	0-3			23,220

Appearances

Sub Appearances

Goals

League (Matches 1–42)

#	Mellor	Cutbush	Strong	Mullery	Lacy	Moore	Conway Jim	Slough	Busby	Lloyd	Barrett	Fraser	Mitchell	Howe	Belfitt	Conway John	Dowie	Scrivens	Bullivant
1	1	2	3	4	5	6	7	8	9	10	11								
2	1	2	3	4	5	6	7	8	9	10	11								
3	1	2	3	4	5	6	7	8	9	10	11								
4	1	2	3	4	5	6	7	8	9	10	11								
5	1	2	3	4	5	6	7	8	9	10	11								
6	1		3	4	5	6	7	8	9	10•	11	2	12						
7	1		3	4	5	6	7	8	9	10	11	2							
8	1		3	4	5	6	7	8	9	10	11	2							
9	1		3	4	5	6	7	8	9	10	11	2							
10	1		3	4	5	6	7	8•	9	10	11	2	12						
11	1		3	4	5	6	7	8	9	10	11	2							
12	1	2	3	4•	5	6	7	8	9	10	11		12						
13	1	2	3	4	5	6	7	8	9	10	11								
14	1	2	3	4	5	6	7	8	9•	10	11		12						
15	1	2	3	4	5	6	7	8	9	10	11								
16	1	2	3	4	5	6	7	8	9	10	11								
17	1	2	3	4		6	7	8	9	10	11				5				
18	1		3	4		6		8	9	10	11	2	7		5				
19	1		3	4	5	6		8	7	10	11	2				9			
20	1	2	3	4	5	6		8	7	10	11					9			
21	1	2	3	4	5	6		8	10		11					9	7		
22	1	2	3	4	5	6		8	10		11					9	7		
23	1	2	3	4	5			8	6	10	11					9	7		
24	1	2	3	4	5	6		8	10		11					9	7		
25	1	2	3	4	5	6		8	10	9	11						7		
26	1	2	3	4		6		8	10	9	11				5		7		
27	1	2	3	4	5	6			9	10		11		7	8				
28	1	2	3	4	5	6	7	10	9		11				8				
29	1	2	3	4	5	6		8	10	9	11						7		
30	1	2	3	4	5	6		8	10	9	12	11					7•		
31	1		3	4	5	6		8	10	9	7	11	2•	12			7		
32	1		3	4	5	6		8	10	9		11	2				7		
33	1		3	4	5	6			10	9		11	2	8			7		
34	1		3	4	5	6		8	10	9		11	2	12			7•		
35	1		3	4	5	6			10	9		11	2	8			7		
36	1		3	4	5	6		8	10	9		11	2•	12			7		
37	1		3	4	5	6		8	10	9•		11	2	12			7		
38	1		3	4	5	6			10	9		11	2	8			7		
39	1		3	4	5	6			10	9		11	2	8			7		
40	1	12	3•	4	5	6			10	9		11	2	8			7		
41	1	2		4	5	6		8•	9	10	11	3	7				12		
42	1	2		4	5	6		8	9	10	11	3				8•	7	12	
App	42	24	40	42	39	41	32	39	38	25	41	20	8	3	6	7	14	1	0
Sub		1											1		8		1	1	
Gls		1	9	2		4	2	11	1	5	1	5	1			2			

FA Cup

Mellor	Cutbush	Strong	Mullery	Lacy	Moore	Conway Jim	Slough	Busby	Lloyd	Barrett	Fraser	Mitchell	Howe	Belfitt	Conway John	Dowie	Rd
1	2	3	4	5	6	8	10	9		11		12			7•		3
1	2	3	4		6	8	10	9		11	5	7					R
1	2	3	4	5	6	8	10	9		11	7						2R
1	2	3•	4	5	6		8	9	10	11	7				12		4
1	2	3	4	5	6	8	10	9		11	7						R
1	2	3	4	5	6	8	10	9		11	7						2R
1	2	3	4	5	6	8	10	9	12	11	7						3R
1	2	3	4	5	6	8•	10	9	12	11	2					7	5
1		3	4	5	6	8•	10	9	12	11	2					7	6
1		3	4	5	6		10	9		11	2	7				12	SF
1		3	4	5	6	8	10	9		11	3	7				7	R
1	2		4	5	6	8	10	9		11	3	7					F
12	9	11	12	11	12	10	12	12	1	12	4	5	1		2	6	
											2				1	2	
						1	2	6		1					1		

League Cup

Mellor	Cutbush	Strong	Mullery	Lacy	Moore	Conway Jim	Slough	Busby	Lloyd	Barrett	Fraser	Mitchell	Howe	Rd
1		3	4	5	6	7	8	9	10	11	2			2
1	2	3	4	5	6	7	8	9	10	11				3
1	2	3	4		6	7	8	9	10•	11	12	5		4
3	2	3	3	2	3	3	3	3	3	3	1	1		
											1			
		1						1	1	2				

Month End	Sep	Oct	Nov	Dec	Jan	Feb	Mar	Apr	Final
1974-75 Pld	10	14	19	25	27	31	38	42	**42**
Pts	11	13	17	24	24	30	40	42	**42**
Pos	5th	13th	15th	11th	14th	14th	9th	9th	**9th**

1975-76

1	Aug	16	(h)	Blackpool	D	0-0			8,863
2		20	(h)	Carlisle U	W	3-0	Conway, Barrett, Slough		7,433
3		23	(a)	Bolton W	D	2-2	Busby, Mitchell		8,786
4		26	(a)	Sunderland	L	0-2			25,450
5		30	(h)	West Brom A	W	4-0	Mitchell, Howe 2, Busby		9,910
6	Sep	6	(a)	Oxford U	W	3-1	Conway, Busby, Mitchell		7,318
7		13	(h)	Bristol R	L	0-2			11,516
8		20	(a)	Hull C	W	2-1	Busby, Lloyd		8,471
9		27	(h)	Chelsea	W	2-0	Howe, Conway		22,921
10	Oct	4	(a)	Blackburn R	W	1-0	Howe		10,190
11		11	(h)	Nottingham F	D	0-0			10,149
12		18	(a)	Luton T	L	0-1			14,086
13		25	(h)	Orient	D	1-1	Howe		10,464
14	Nov	1	(a)	Portsmouth	W	1-0	Slough		11,441
15		8	(h)	Charlton A	D	1-1	Lloyd		15,466
16		15	(a)	York C	L	0-1			3,414
17		22	(h)	Luton T	W	2-0	Conway 2		9,626
18		29	(h)	Bristol C	L	1-2	Mullery		11,400
19	Dec	6	(a)	Oldham A	D	2-2	Howe, Conway		8,746
20		13	(h)	Bolton W	L	1-2	Slough		8,740
21		20	(a)	Blackpool	D	1-1	Mullery		6,379
22		26	(h)	Notts C	W	3-2	Mitchell 2, Slough		11,887
23		27	(a)	Plymouth A	L	0-4			24,054
24	Jan	10	(a)	Bristol R	L	0-1			7,863
25		17	(h)	Oxford U	D	1-1	Mitchell		6,783
26		31	(a)	Carlisle U	D	2-2	Mitchell 2		6,418
27	Feb	7	(h)	Sunderland	W	2-0	Busby 2		11,890
28		17	(a)	Charlton A	L	2-3	Mullery 2		11,536
29		21	(h)	York C	W	2-0	Lloyd, Slough		6,686
30		24	(a)	Southampton	L	1-2	Lacy		24,856
31		28	(a)	Orient	L	0-2			7,553
32	Mar	6	(h)	Portsmouth	L	0-1			6,928
33		9	(h)	Southampton	W	1-0	Mitchell		8,731
34		13	(a)	Nottingham F	L	0-1			11,445
35		20	(a)	Bristol C	D	0-0			19,935
36		27	(h)	Oldham A	W	1-0	Conway		5,856
37	Apr	6	(a)	Chelsea	D	0-0			23,605
38		10	(h)	Hull C	D	1-1	Mitchell		5,624
39		14	(a)	West Brom A	L	1-3	Scrivens		18,268
40		17	(a)	Notts C	L	0-4			8,819
41		19	(h)	Plymouth A	D	0-0			6,913
42		24	(h)	Blackburn R	D	1-1	Howe		5,914

P	W	D	L	F	A	W	D	L	F	A	Pts	Pos	Div		Appearances
42	9	8	4	27	14	4	6	11	18	33	40	12th	2		Sub Appearances
															Goals

FA Cup

3	Jan	3	(h)	Huddersfield T	L	2-3	Conway, Busby	10,299

Appearances
Sub Appearances
Goals

League Cup

2	Sep	9	(a)	West Brom A	D	1-1	Conway	10,877
R		24	(h)	West Brom A	W	1-0	Mullery	9,365
3	Oct	8	(h)	Peterborough U	L	0-1		9,805

Appearances
Sub Appearances
Goals

Month End		Sep	Oct	Nov	Dec	Jan	Feb	Mar	Apr	Final
1975-76	Pld	9	13	18	23	26	31	36	42	**42**
	Pts	12	16	21	25	27	31	36	40	**40**
	Pos	3rd	6th	7th	9th	10th	10th	10th	12th	**12th**

Mellor	Cutbush	Strong	Mullery	Howe	Moore	Conway	Mitchell	Busby	Lloyd	Barrett	Dowie	Slough	James	Kerslake	Lacy	Fraser	Camp	Bullivant	Scrivens	Margerrison	No.
1	2	3	4	5	6	7	8*	9	10	11	12										1
1	2	3	4	5	6	7		9		11	8	10									2
1	2	3	4	5	6	7	11	9			8	10									3
1	2	3	4	5	6	8	12	9	7	11		10*									4
1	2	3	4	5	6	8	7	9		11		10									5
1	2	3	4	5	6	7	11	9			8	10									6
1	2	3	4	5	6	7	8	9		11		10									7
1	2	3	4	5	6	7	11	9	8			10									8
1	2	3	4	5	6	8		9	7		11	10									9
1	2	3	4	5	6	8		9	7		11	10									10
1	2	3	4	5	6	8	7	9		11		10									11
1			4	5	6	8	7*	9	10	11	12	3	2								12
1			4	11	6	7		9	10		8		2	3	5						13
1		3	4		6	7		9		11	8	10	2		5						14
1			4		6	7		9	10	11	8	3	2		5						15
1		3	4	10	6	7		9		11	8		2		5						16
1		3	4	5	6	7		9		11	8	10				2					17
1		3	4	5	6	8		9		11	7	10				2					18
1		3	4	5	6	7		9		11	8*	10			12	2					19
1	3*	4	2		6	8		9		11	7	10			5	12					20
1	2	3	4		6	8				11	7	10*	12		5	9					21
1	2	3	4		6	8	7	9		11		10			5						22
1	2	3	4	12	6*	7	8	9		11		10			5						23
1	2	3	4		6	7	8	9		11		10			5						24
1	2	3	4	12	6	8	7	9		11*		10			5						25
1	2		4	5	6	7	8	9	10	11			3								26
1		3	4		6	8		9	7	11		10	2		5						27
1		3	4		6	8		9	7	11		10	2		5						28
1		3	4		6	8	9		7	11*		10	2		5		12				29
1		3	4		6	8	9		7	11		10	2		5						30
1		3	4		6	8*		9	7	11		10	2		5		12				31
1	2	3	4		6		7	9	10	11*	12	3			5						32
1	2	3	4		6	8	7	9	11			10			5						33
1	2	3	4	6		8	9*	7		11	12	10			5						34
1	2	3	4		6	7	8	9		11		10			5						35
1	2	3			6	8	10	9	7	11		4			5						36
1		3	4		6	8	7	9	10			11	2		5						37
1		3			6	7	8	9	10	11			2		5		4*	12			38
1	3*	12			6	8	7	9	4			10	2		5			11			39
1			6			8	7	9	4	11	10	3			5	2					40
1			6			8*	7		4	12	11	10	2		5	3	9				41
1		3			6		9*		4	10	8	2			5	7		11	12		42
42	22	36	36	28	33	39	26	37	25	32	14	40	14	1	26	5	3	1	2		
		1	2		1			1	4		1		1		1		1	2	1	1	
		4	7		7	10	6	3	1			5			1			1			

Mellor	Cutbush	Strong	Mullery	Howe	Moore	Conway	Mitchell	Busby	Lloyd	Barrett	Dowie	Slough	James	Kerslake	Lacy	Fraser	Camp	Bullivant	Scrivens	Margerrison	No.
1	2		4		6	8	7	9		11	10*	3	12		5						3
1	1		1		1	1	1	1		1	1	1	1		1						
												1									
					1		1														

Mellor	Cutbush	Strong	Mullery	Howe	Moore	Conway	Mitchell	Busby	Lloyd	Barrett	Dowie	Slough	James	Kerslake	Lacy	Fraser	Camp	Bullivant	Scrivens	Margerrison	No.
1		3	4	5	6	8	7	9		11	10		2								2
1	2	3	4	5	6	8	7	9	11		10										R
1	2	3	4	5	6	8	12	9	7*	11	10										3
3	2	3	3	3	3	3	3	3	2	1	1	3	1		1						
						1															
		1			1																

357

1976-77

1	Aug	21	(h)	Nottingham F	D	2-2	Lacy, Mitchell	9,437
2		24	(a)	Burnley	L	1-3	Barrett	11,484
3		28	(a)	Charlton A	D	1-1	Bullivant	10,699
4	Sep	4	(h)	Bristol R	W	1-0	Best	21,127
5		11	(h)	Wolves	D	0-0		25,794
6		18	(a)	Luton T	W	2-0	Barrett, Marsh	19,929
7		25	(h)	Hereford U	W	4-1	Slough, Evanson, Marsh 2	18,935
8	Oct	2	(a)	Southampton	L	1-4	Mitchell	28,489
9		16	(a)	Sheffield U	D	1-1	Mitchell	28,792
10		23	(h)	Hull C	D	0-0		18,671
11		30	(a)	Bolton W	L	1-2	Best	24,228
12	Nov	6	(h)	Cardiff C	L	1-2	Best	12,366
13		13	(a)	Plymouth A	D	2-2	Mitchell, Howe	25,335
14		16	(h)	Carlisle U	W	2-0	Marsh 2	9,215
15		20	(h)	Notts C	L	1-5	Slough	12,191
16		27	(a)	Blackpool	L	2-3	Mitchell 2	16,779
17	Dec	4	(h)	Oldham A	W	5-0	Mitchell 2, Maybank 2, Best	14,326
18		11	(a)	Orient	D	0-0		11,237
19		14	(h)	Blackburn R	W	2-0	Maybank, Best	8,543
20		27	(a)	Chelsea	L	0-2		55,003
21		28	(h)	Millwall	L	2-3	Mitchell, Howe	18,075
22	Jan	1	(a)	Cardiff C	L	0-3		20,268
23		3	(h)	Bolton W	L	0-2		12,594
24		15	(h)	Burnley	D	2-2	Slough, Barrett	8,815
25		22	(a)	Nottingham F	L	0-3		24,718
26	Feb	5	(h)	Charlton A	D	1-1	Mitchell	14,958
27		12	(a)	Bristol R	L	1-2	Mitchell	11,140
28		19	(a)	Wolves	L	1-5	Mitchell	25,865
29		26	(h)	Luton T	L	1-2	Warboys	11,071
30	Mar	5	(a)	Hereford U	L	0-1		6,590
31		11	(h)	Southampton	D	1-1	Lacy	13,408
32		19	(a)	Carlisle U	W	2-1	Slough, Mitchell	6,243
33		26	(h)	Sheffield U	W	3-2	Mitchell, Maybank 2	12,459
34	Apr	2	(a)	Hull C	L	0-1		6,158
35		8	(h)	Chelsea	W	3-1	Warboys, Best, Mitchell	29,690
36		9	(a)	Millwall	D	0-0		11,001
37		11	(h)	Plymouth A	W	2-0	Mitchell, Maybank	11,710
38		16	(a)	Notts C	D	0-0		14,847
39		23	(h)	Blackpool	D	0-0		10,956
40		30	(a)	Oldham A	L	0-1		9,466
41	May	7	(h)	Orient	W	6-1	Mitchell 4, Maybank 2	7,656
42		14	(a)	Blackburn R	L	0-1		9,406

P	W	D	L	F	A	W	D	L	F	A	Pts	Pos	Div		
42	9	7	5	39	25	2	6	13	15	36	35	17th	2		Appearances
															Sub Appearances
															Goals

FA Cup

3	Jan	8	(h)	Swindon T	D	3-3	Marsh, Howe, Barrett	16,460
R		11	(a)	Swindon T	L	0-5		23,880

Appearances
Sub Appearances
Goals

League Cup

2	Aug	31	(h)	Peterborough U	D	1-1	Barrett	10,222
R	Sep	7	(a)	Peterborough U	W	2-1	Best, Slough	16,476
3		22	(h)	Bolton W	D	2-2	Best, Mitchell	14,961
R	Oct	5	(a)	Bolton W	D	2-2	Mitchell, Howe	15,010
2R		20	(n)	Bolton W*	L	1-2	Opp own goal	9,345

*Played at St Andrew's,
Birmingham.

Appearances
Sub Appearances
Goals

Month End		Sep	Oct	Nov	Dec	Jan	Feb	Mar	Apr	Final
1976-77	Pld	7	11	16	21	25	29	33	40	**42**
	Pts	9	11	14	19	20	21	26	33	**35**
	Pos	4th	15th	15th	11th	17th	19th	17th	16th	**17th**

Teale	Cutbush	Strong	Slough	Lacy	Howe	Mitchell	Bullivant	Busby	Dowie	Barrett	Evanson	Mellor	Moore	Best	Marsh	James	Mahoney	Greenaway	Maybank	Peyton	Digweed	Camp	Jump	Margerrison	Warboys	Storey	Evans	#
1	2	3	4	5	6	7	8	9	10	11																		1
1	2	3	4	5	6	10	7	9	8*	11	12																	2
	2	3	4		5	10	7	9		11	8	1	6															3
	2	3	4	5				9		11	8	1	6	7	10													4
	2	3	4	5				9		11	8	1	6	7	10													5
	2	3	4	5	9					11	8	1	6	7	10													6
	2	3	4	5	9					11	8	1	6	7	10													7
		3	4	5	9	2				11	8	1	6	7	10*	12												8
	2	3	4	5	9	12				11*	8	1	6	7	10													9
	2	3	4	5	9	11					8	1	6	7	10													10
		3	4	2	5	9	11				8	1	6	7	10													11
		3	2	4	5	9				11	8	1	6	7			10											12
		3	4	5	9	11*					8	1	6	7	10	2		12										13
		3	4	5	9	11					8	1	6	7	10	2												14
		3	4	5	9	11					8	1*	6	7	10	2		12										15
1	2	3	4	5	9					11	8		6	7					10									16
	2	3	4	5	9					11	8		6	7					10	1								17
	2	3	4	5				9		11	8		6	7					10	1								18
	2	3	4	5				9		11	8		6	7					10	1								19
		3	4	5	2			9		11	10		6	7					8	1								20
1	2*	3	4	10	5			9		11	8		6	7			12	7										21
1	2	3	4	10	5			9		11	8		6					7										22
	2	3	4	5	9					11	8		6	7					10	1								23
	2	3	4	12	5	8				11			6	7	10					1		9*						24
12	2		4	5				9		11	8*		6	7	10					1			3					25
	2		4	5				9		11	8		6	7						1			3					26
	2		4	5				9		11	8		6	7						1			3	10				27
	2	3	5			8	4			11			6	7	10					1					9			28
	2	3	5			8*	4		7	11			6		10					1				12	9			29
		3	2	5		8	4			11	10		6							1					9	7		30
		3	8	5	10	11							6	7						1					9	4	2	31
		3	10	5	11								6	7					8	1					9	4	2	32
		3	8	5	10								6	7					11	1					9	4	2	33
		3	10	5	11								6	7					8	1					9	4	2	34
		3	11	5	10								6	7					8	1					9	4	2	35
		3	10	5	11								6	7					8	1					9	4	2	36
		3	11	5	10								6	7					8	1					9	4	2	37
		3	10	5	11	8							6	7						1					9	4	2	38
		3	10	5	11						12		6	7*					8	1					9	4	2	39
		3	11	5	10								6	7					8	1					9	4	2	40
		3	11	5	10								6	7					8	1					9	4	2	41
		3	4	5						11	8		6	7											9		2	42
5	17	42	42	26	23	38	18	5	3	20	29	13	40	32	16	3	1	4	15	23	1	1	3	3	15	12	12	
1			1		1	1					2					1	1	2						1				
		4	2	2	20	1				3	1			6	5			8						2				

Teale	Cutbush	Strong	Slough	Lacy	Howe	Mitchell	Bullivant	Busby	Dowie	Barrett	Evanson	Mellor	Moore	Best	Marsh	James	Mahoney	Greenaway	Maybank	Peyton	Digweed	Camp	Jump	Margerrison	Warboys	Storey	Evans	#
	2	3	4	5	9					11	8		6	7	10					1								3
	2	3	4	5	9	11				12	8*		6	7	10					1								R
	2	2	2	2	2	1				1	2		2	2	2					2								
											1																	
						1					1																	

Teale	Cutbush	Strong	Slough	Lacy	Howe	Mitchell	Bullivant	Busby	Dowie	Barrett	Evanson	Mellor	Moore	Best	Marsh	James	Mahoney	Greenaway	Maybank	Peyton	Digweed	Camp	Jump	Margerrison	Warboys	Storey	Evans	#
	2	3	4	5		7		9		11	8	1	6		10													2
	2	3	4	5				9		11	8	1	6	7	10													R
	2	3	4	5	9					11	8	1	6	7	10													3
		3	4	10	5	9	2		7	11	8	1	6															R
	2	3	4	5	9	11					8	1	6	7	10													2R
	4	5	5	1	5	3	3	2	1	4	5	5	5	3	4													
		1			1	2				1				2														

359

1977-78

1	Aug	20	(h)	Charlton A	D	1-1 Maybank	9,849
2		23	(a)	Oldham A	L	0-2	7,280
3		27	(a)	Bristol R	D	0-0	6,426
4	Sep	3	(h)	Blackburn R	D	0-0	10,095
5		10	(a)	Tottenham H	L	0-1	31,939
6		17	(h)	Notts C	W	5-1 Mitchell 3, Maybank, Evanson	6,601
7		24	(a)	Cardiff C	L	1-3 Maybank	8,810
8	Oct	1	(a)	Crystal P	W	3-2 Maybank 2, Gale	28,343
9		4	(h)	Burnley	W	4-1 Mitchell 2, Mahoney, Best	6,895
10		8	(h)	Blackpool	D	1-1 Mahoney	9,190
11		15	(a)	Luton T	L	0-1	12,800
12		22	(h)	Orient	L	1-2 Gale	9,128
13		29	(a)	Sheffield U	L	1-2 Gale	16,741
14	Nov	5	(h)	Sunderland	D	3-3 Mitchell, Best, Maybank	10,548
15		12	(a)	Stoke C	L	0-2	14,156
16		19	(h)	Hull C	W	2-0 Lacy, Gale	6,616
17		26	(a)	Southampton	L	0-2	21,085
18	Dec	3	(h)	Bolton W	W	2-0 Gale, Evans	8,216
19		10	(a)	Millwall	W	3-0 Gale, Evans, opp own goal	7,617
20		17	(h)	Stoke C	W	3-0 Evanson, Evans, Bullivant	8,014
21		26	(a)	Mansfield T	L	1-2 Mitchell	8,456
22		28	(h)	Brighton & HA	W	2-1 Money, Margerrison	21,695
23		30	(h)	Oldham A	L	0-2	10,099
24	Jan	2	(a)	Charlton A	W	1-0 Greenaway	14,590
25		14	(h)	Bristol R	D	1-1 Mitchell	8,424
26	Feb	4	(h)	Tottenham H	D	1-1 Greenaway	24,763
27		25	(h)	Crystal P	D	1-1 Evanson	14,090
28	Mar	7	(h)	Cardiff C	W	1-0 Gale	6,571
29		10	(h)	Luton T	W	1-0 Mahoney	7,996
30		15	(a)	Blackburn R	L	0-4	9,121
31		17	(a)	Orient	D	1-1 Margerrison	7,928
32		24	(h)	Sheffield U	W	2-0 Money, opp own goal	8,997
33		25	(a)	Brighton & HA	L	0-2	24,601
34		27	(h)	Mansfield T	L	0-2	7,088
35	Apr	1	(a)	Sunderland	D	2-2 Margerrison, Mitchell	11,951
36		4	(a)	Notts C	D	1-1 Gale	7,378
37		7	(h)	Southampton	D	1-1 Lacy	16,971
38		15	(a)	Hull C	W	1-0 Evans	3,961
39		18	(a)	Blackpool	W	2-1 Strong, Davies	4,695
40		22	(h)	Millwall	L	0-1	10,743
41		25	(a)	Burnley	L	0-2	9,462
42		29	(a)	Bolton W	D	0-0	34,110

P	W	D	L	F	A	W	D	L	F	A	Pts	Pos	Div		
42	9	8	4	32	19	5	5	11	17	30	41	10th	2	Appearances	
														Sub Appearances	
														Goals	

FA Cup

3	Jan	7	(a)	Burnley	L	0-1	11,124

Appearances
Sub Appearances
Goals

League Cup

1	Aug	13	(h)	Orient	L	0-2	4,691
		16	(h)	Orient	W	2-1 Maybank 2	4,388

(2 legged tie but both played at Fulham)

Appearances
Sub Appearances
Goals

Month End		Sep	Oct	Nov	Dec	Jan	Feb	Mar	Apr	Final
1977-78	**Pld**	7	13	17	23	25	27	34	42	**42**
	Pts	5	10	13	21	24	26	33	41	**41**
	Pos	16th	15th	16th	13th	12th	12th	12th	10th	**10th**

Appearances grid (player shirt numbers by match). `*` denotes substitute appearance.

Peyton	Evans	Strong	Storey	Lacy	Gale	Magerrison	Mitchell	Warboys	Maybank	Bullivant	Evanson	Greenaway	Best	Howe	Mahoney	Kerslake	James	McCurdy	Money	Hatter	Lovell	Davies	Mason	#
1	2	3	4	5	6	7	8*	9	10	11	12													1
1	2	3	4	5	6		11	9	10	7	8													2
1	2	3	4	5	6	7*		9	10	11	8	12												3
1	2	3	4	5	6		8	9	10	7			11											4
1	2	3	4	5	6		8	9	11	10	7													5
1	2	3		5	6		8	9	10	4	11	7												6
1	2	3		5	6	7		9	10	4	8		11											7
1	2	3		5	6		8	9	10		11		7	4										8
1	2	3		5*	6		8	9		12	11		7	4	10									9
1	2	3		5		4	8	9		11*	10		7	6	12						·			10
1	2	3		5	6		11	9			10		7	4	8									11
1	2	3		5	6		11	9		12	8		7	4*	10									12
1	2	3		5	6		8	9		4	11		7		10*	12								13
1	2	3		5			8	9	10	4	11		7				6							14
1	2	3		5			8	9	10	4	11		7	6										15
1	2	3		5*	6		8	9	10	4	12	7	11											16
1	2	3			6		11	9		4	8	7	5	12	10*									17
1	2	3			6	8	10	9		4	11	7	5											18
1	2	3			6	8	11	9		4	10	7	5											19
1	2	3			6	8	11	9		4	12	10	7*						5					20
1	2	3		5		8	11	9		4	7*	10			12			6						21
1	2	3		5		8	11	9		4*	10	7			12			6						22
1	2	3		5		8	11	9		4	10	7						6						23
1	2	3		5			11	9		4	8	10	7					6						24
1	2	3		5	6		11	9		4	8	10	7											25
1	2	3		5		8	11	9			4*	10	7		12			6						26
1	2	3		5		8	11	9			4	10	7					6						27
1	2	3		5		8	11				4	10	7		9			6						28
1	2	3		5		8	11	9				10	7		4			6						29
1	2	3		5		8	11	9			4	10			7			6						30
1	2	3		5		8	11	9			4	10			7			6						31
1	2	3		5		8	11	9			4	10			7			6						32
1	2	3		5			11	9			4	10*	7		8			6			12			33
1	2	3		5			11	9			4	10			7			6			8*	12		34
1	2	3		5			11	9			4	10	7		8			6						35
1	2	3		5	6		11	9			4	10	7		8									36
1	2	3		5	6		11	9			4	10	7					8						37
1	2	3		5	6		11	9			4	10	7					8						38
1	2	3		5	6		11	9			4	10	8									7		39
1		3		5	6		11	9			4	10	8						2			7		40
1		3		5	6		11	9			4	10							2		7	8		41
1				5	6		11	9*			4	10	7						2		12	10	3	42
42	39	41	5	38	38	40	39	4	12	32	39	23	10	10	13	1	1	23	5	2	4	1		
										3	2	1			4	2			2	1				
	4	1		2	8	3	9		6	1	3	2	2	3				2				1		

Peyton	Evans	Strong	Storey	Lacy	Gale	Magerrison	Mitchell	Warboys	Maybank	Bullivant	Evanson	Greenaway	Best	Howe	Mahoney	Kerslake	James	McCurdy	Money	Hatter	Lovell	Davies	Mason	#
1	2	3		5		8	11	9			4	10	7					6						3
1	1	1		1		1	1	1			1	1	1					1						

Peyton	Evans	Strong	Storey	Lacy	Gale	Magerrison	Mitchell	Warboys	Maybank	Bullivant	Evanson	Greenaway	Best	Howe	Mahoney	Kerslake	James	McCurdy	Money	Hatter	Lovell	Davies	Mason	#
1	3	2	5	6	7	8	9	10	4	11*		12												1
1	3	2	5	6	7	8	9	10	4	11*		12												2
2	2	2	2	2	2	2	2	2	2			2												
							2																	

361

1978-79

#	Month	Date		Opponent		Result	Scorers	Attendance
1	Aug	29	(a)	Bristol R	L	1-3	Margerrison	5,950
2		22	(h)	Wrexham	L	0-1		6,135
3		26	(h)	Burnley	D	0-0		5,407
4	Sep	2	(a)	West Ham U	W	1-0	Margerrison	25,778
5		9	(h)	Sheffield U	W	2-0	Mahoney, Margerrison	6,672
6		16	(a)	Sunderland	D	1-1	Margerrison	17,976
7		23	(h)	Millwall	W	1-0	Greenaway	8,917
8		30	(a)	Oldham A	W	2-0	Guthrie, Davies	6,972
9	Oct	7	(h)	Stoke C	W	2-0	Greenaway, Gale	12,531
10		14	(a)	Brighton & HA	L	0-3		24,576
11		21	(h)	Preston NE	W	5-3	Davies, Money, Lock, Guthrie, opp own goal	8,719
12		28	(a)	Crystal P	W	1-0	Greenaway	28,733
13	Nov	3	(h)	Blackburn R	L	1-2	Evans	12,583
14		10	(h)	Bristol R	W	3-0	Guthrie 2, Beck	10,296
15		18	(a)	Burnley	L	3-5	Evanson, Guthrie, Gale	10,566
16		21	(h)	West Ham U	D	0-0		26,597
17		25	(a)	Charlton A	D	0-0		11,440
18	Dec	2	(h)	Notts C	D	1-1	Guthrie	7,591
19		16	(h)	Newcastle U	L	1-3	Guthrie	8,575
20		23	(a)	Cardiff C	L	0-2		5,558
21		26	(h)	Cambridge U	W	5-1	Davies, Margerrison, Guthrie 3	7,814
22		30	(h)	Luton T	W	1-0	Opp own goal	8,591
23	Jan	20	(h)	Sunderland	D	2-2	Davies, Guthrie	11,260
24	Feb	6	(a)	Sheffield U	D	1-1	Margerrison	12,451
25		10	(h)	Oldham A	W	1-0	Davies	6,942
26		24	(h)	Brighton & HA	L	0-1		18,464
27	Mar	3	(a)	Preston NE	D	2-2	Kitchen, Guthrie	10,890
28		10	(h)	Crystal P	D	0-0		16,564
29		21	(a)	Leicester C	L	0-1		10,396
30		24	(a)	Wrexham	D	1-1	Kitchen	9,046
31		27	(a)	Orient	L	0-1		6,610
32		31	(h)	Charlton A	W	3-1	Kitchen, Davies, Evans	6,955
33	Apr	4	(a)	Stoke C	L	0-2		15,243
34		7	(a)	Notts C	D	1-1	Guthrie	9,465
35		11	(h)	Cardiff C	D	2-2	Kitchen, Lock	6,067
36		14	(a)	Cambridge U	L	0-1		6,523
37		16	(h)	Orient	D	2-2	Davies, Lock	8,052
38		21	(a)	Newcastle U	D	0-0		11,916
39		24	(a)	Millwall	D	0-0		7,397
40		28	(h)	Leicester C	W	3-0	Strong, Davies 2	7,002
41	May	5	(a)	Luton T	L	0-2		9,112
42		9	(a)	Blackburn R	L	1-2	Kitchen	4,684

P	W	D	L	F	A	W	D	L	F	A	Pts	Pos	Div		
42	10	7	4	35	19	3	8	10	15	28	41	10th	2	Appearances	
														Sub Appearances	
														Goals	

FA Cup

#	Month	Date		Opponent		Result	Scorers	Attendance
3	Jan	6	(h)	Queen's Park R	W	2-0	Margerrison, Davies	21,199
4		31	(h)	Manchester U	D	1-1	Margerrison	25,229
R	Feb	12	(a)	Manchester U	L	0-1		41,020

Appearances
Sub Appearances
Goals

League Cup

#	Month	Date		Opponent		Result	Scorers	Attendance
2	Aug	29	(h)	Darlington	D	2-2	Mahoney, Davies	3,894
R	Sep	5	(a)	Darlington	L	0-1		5,061

Appearances
Sub Appearances
Goals

Month End		Sep	Oct	Nov	Dec	Jan	Feb	Mar	Apr	Final
1978-79	Pld	8	12	17	22	23	26	32	40	42
	Pts	10	16	20	25	26	29	34	41	41
	Pos	4th	3rd	4th	5th	6th	6th	8th	7th	10th

362

Appearance grid (shirt numbers worn per match; * denotes substitute). Player columns read left-to-right: Peyton, Evans, Strong, Money, Banton, Lock, Bullivant, Gale, Margerrison, Evanson, Davies, Mahoney, Boyd, Guthrie, Greenaway, Beck, Lovell, Marinello, Kitchen, Mason, Hatter, Digweed. The match number is shown at the right of each row.

#	Peyton	Evans	Strong	Money	Banton	Lock	Bullivant	Gale	Margerrison	Evanson	Davies	Mahoney	Boyd	Guthrie	Greenaway	Beck	Lovell	Marinello	Kitchen	Mason	Hatter	Digweed
1	1	2	3	4	5	6	7	8	9	10	11											
2	1	2	3	10	5	4	7	6		11*	8	9	12									
3	1	2	3	10	5	4	7	6		11	8	9										
4	1		2	4	5	3	7	6	10	11	8	9										
5	1	2	3	4	5*	10	7	6	12	11	8	9										
6	1	2	3	5		4	7	6	10	11	8	9										
7	1	2	3	5		4	7	6	10	11*	8			9	12							
8	1	2	3	5		4	7	6	10		8			9	11							
9	1	2	3	5		4	7	6*	10	12	8			9	11							
10	1	2	3	5		4	7	6			8			9	11	10						
11	1	2	3	5		4	7*	6		12	8			9	11	10						
12	1	2	3	5		4	7	6		12	8			9	11	10						
13	1	2	3	5*		4	7	6		12	8			9	11	10						
14	1	2	3	5		4	7*	6		12	8			9	11	10						
15	1	2	3	5		4		6			8			9	11	10	7					
16	1	2	3	5		4		6	7		8			9	11	10						
17	1	2	3	5		4		6.		11	8			9	7	10						
18	1	2	3	5		4	8	6			7			9	11	10						
19	1	2	3	5		4	8			12	10*	7		9	11	6						
20	1	2	3	5		4	8	6			7			9	11	10						
21	1	2	3	5		4	8	6		12	7			9		10*			11			
22	1	2	3	5		4*	8	6	10		7			9	12				11			
23	1	2*	5	3		4		6	10	12	7			9		8			11			
24	1	2	5	6	3	4			10		7			9		8			11			
25	1	2	3	5		6	4		10		7			9		8			11			
26	1	2	3	5		4		6			7			9		8			11	10		
27	1	2	3	5		4	11	6						9		8			7	10		
28	1		2	5		3	4	6		11				9		8			7	10		
29	1	2	3	5		11	4	6	7	12			9*			8			10			
30	1	2	3	5		7	4	6	12	8			9*		11	10						
31	1	2	3	5		7	4	6						9	11	8			10			
32	1	2	3	5		4		6.		8	7			9		11			10			
33	1	2	3	5		4		6		11	7			9		8			10			
34	1	2	3	5		4		6		11*	7	12		9		8			10	3		
35	1	2				4		6		12	7		11*	9		8			10	3		
36	1	2	3	5		4		6	11	12	7			9		8			10*			
37	1	2	3	5		4		6		11	7			9		8			10			
38	1		2	5		4		6			7			9		8			10	3	11	
39	1		2	5				6			7			9		8	4		10	3	11	
40	1		2	5		4		6			7			9		8			10	3	11	
41		2	3	5		4		6			7			9		8			10		11	1
42		2	3	5		7		6			4			9		8		12	10*		11	1
Apps	40	35	41	42	7	39	28	36	20	16	32	7	1	34	14	32	2	8	17	4	5	2
Sub									6	7				2	2				1			
Gls	2	1	1	3		2	6	1	9	1	13	3	1			5						

#	Peyton	Evans	Strong	Money	Banton	Lock	Bullivant	Gale	Margerrison	Evanson	Davies	Mahoney	Boyd	Guthrie	Greenaway	Beck	Lovell	Marinello	Kitchen
3	1		2	5		3	4	6	10		7			9		8			11
4	1	2	3	5		6	4		10		7			9		8			11
R	1	2	3	5		6	4		10	12	7*			9		8			11
Tot	3	2	3	3		3	3	2	2		3			3		3			3
Sub									1										
									2	1									

#	Peyton	Evans	Strong	Money	Banton	Lock	Bullivant	Gale	Margerrison	Evanson	Davies	Mahoney	Boyd
2	1		2	4	5	3	7	6	10*	11	8	9	12
R	1		2	4	5	3	7	6	10	11	8	9	
Tot	2		2	2	2	2	2	2	2	2	2	2	
Sub													1
										1	1		

363

1979-80

						Result	Scorers	Attendance
1	Aug	18	(a)	Birmingham C		W 4-3	Davies 3, Guthrie	19,179
2		22	(h)	Orient		D 0-0		9,168
3		25	(a)	Sunderland		L 1-2	Gale	25,307
4	Sep	1	(h)	Preston NE		W 1-0	Marinello	7,940
5		8	(a)	Queen's Park R		L 0-3		17,105
6		15	(h)	Burnley		W 3-1	Davies 2, Lock	6,533
7		22	(a)	Leicester C		D 3-3	Davies 3	14,875
8		29	(h)	Luton T		L 1-3	Lock	9,944
9	Oct	6	(h)	Wrexham		L 0-2		7,091
10		9	(a)	Orient		L 0-1		5,090
11		13	(a)	Swansea T		L 1-4	Beck	12,960
12		20	(h)	Notts C		L 1-3	Davies	6,280
13		27	(a)	Chelsea		W 2-0	Beck, Davies	30,567
14	Nov	3	(h)	Birmingham C		L 2-4	Davies, Lock	8,243
15		10	(h)	West Ham U		L 1-2	Davies	16,478
16		17	(a)	Oldham A		W 1-0	Greenaway	5,473
17		24	(h)	Watford		D 0-0		10,126
18	Dec	1	(a)	Newcastle U		L 0-2		23,485
19		8	(h)	Shrewsbury T		W 2-1	Guthrie, Gale	5,337
20		15	(a)	Cambridge U		L 0-4		4,778
21		26	(a)	Cardiff C		L 0-1		8,105
22		29	(h)	Sunderland		L 0-1		9,591
23	Jan	12	(a)	Preston NE		L 2-3	Gale, Davies	7,912
24		19	(h)	Queen's Park R		L 0-2		11,539
25	Feb	2	(a)	Burnley		L 1-2	Gale	6,902
26		9	(h)	Leicester C		D 0-0		8,691
27		16	(a)	Luton T		L 0-4		9,169
28		23	(h)	Swansea T		L 1-2	Lock	6,145
29		26	(h)	Bristol R		D 1-1	Maybank	4,802
30	Mar	1	(a)	Notts C		D 1-1	Maybank	6,968
31		8	(h)	Chelsea		L 1-2	Lock	22,258
32		15	(a)	Wrexham		D 1-1	Davies	6,137
33		22	(a)	West Ham U		W 3-2	Maybank, Banton 2	30,030
34		28	(h)	Oldham A		L 0-1		5,855
35	Apr	4	(a)	Bristol R		L 0-1		7,289
36		8	(a)	Charlton A		W 1-0	Opp own goal	4,928
37		12	(h)	Newcastle U		W 1-0	Davies	7,250
38		15	(h)	Cardiff C		W 2-1	Lewington, opp own goal	5,161
39		19	(a)	Watford		L 0-4		15,898
40		22	(h)	Charlton A		W 1-0	O'Driscoll	3,766
41		26	(h)	Cambridge U		L 1-2	Mahoney	4,999
42	May	3	(a)	Shrewsbury T		L 2-5	Kitchen, Mahoney	6,328

P	W	D	L	F	A	W	D	L	F	A	Pts	Pos	Div	
42	6	4	11	19	28	5	3	13	23	46	29	20th	2	Appearances
														Sub Appearances
														Goals

FA Cup

3	Jan	8	(a)	Blackburn R		D 1-1	Money	9,826
R		15	(h)	Blackburn R		L 0-1		5,642

Appearances
Sub Appearances
Goals

League Cup

2	Aug	29	(a)	West Brom A		D 1-1	Davies	13,611
	Sep	5	(h)	West Brom A		L 0-1		11,542

Appearances
Sub Appearances
Goals

Month End		Sep	Oct	Nov	Dec	Jan	Feb	Mar	Apr	Final
1979-80	Pld	8	13	17	22	24	29	34	41	42
	Pts	8	10	13	15	15	17	21	29	29
	Pos	14th	18th	28th	22nd	22nd	22nd	21st	20th	20th

Football appearances and goals grid (shirt numbers by player and match):

Digweed	Strong	Mason	Bullivant.	Money	Gale	Marinello	Beck	Guthrie	Lock	Davies	Peyton	Peters	Banton	Mahoney	Kitchen	Greenaway	Hatter	Maybank	Wilson	Gale	O'Driscoll	Brown	Lewington	#
1	2	3	4	5	6	7	8	9	10	11														1
	3		4	5	6	7	8	9	10	11	1	2												2
	3		4	5	6	7	8	9	10	11	1	2												3
	3		4	5	6	7	8	9	10	11	1	2												4
	3		4	5*	6	7	8	9	10	11	1	2	12											5
	3		4	5	6	7	8		10	11	1	2		9										6
	3		4	5	6		8		10	11	1	2		9	7									7
	3*		4	5	6	7	8		10	11	1	2		9	12									8
	3		4	5	6	7	8	9		11	1	2		10										9
	3		4	5	6	7*	8		10	11	1	2		9	12									10
	3		4	5*	6		8		7	11	1	2		10		12	9							11
	3		4	5	6	7	8	9	10	11	1*	2			12									12
1	3		4	5	6	7	8	9	10	11		2												13
1	3		4	5	6	7	8	9	10	11		2*		12										14
1	3		4	5	6	7	8	9	10	11		2												15
1	3			5	6		8	9	10	11		2			7	4								16
1	3			4	6		8	9	10	11		2			7	5								17
1	3			4	6		8	9	10	11		2			7	5								18
1	3			4	6		8	9	10	11		2			7	5								19
	3			4	6		8	9	10	11	1	2			7	5								20
	3			4	6		8		10	11	1	2	5		7		9							21
	3			4	6	7	8	11*	9	1	2	5		12	10									22
	3			4	6		8	9	1	2	5			10	7	11								23
	3			4	6		8	9	1	2	5	11		10	7									24
	3			4	6		8	12	9*	1	2	5	11	10	7									25
	3			4	6		8	11	1	2	5		10	7										26
	3			4	6	12	8	11	1	2	5	9	9	7										27
	3	2*		6	11	8	4	9	1	12	5	10	7											28
	3	2		6	11	8	4	9	1	5	10	7												29
	3	2		6	11	9	1	5	10	4	7	8												30
	3	2	10	8	4	6	1	9	7	11	5													31
	3	2		6	8	4	9	1	5	10	7	11												32
	3	2		6	8	4	9	1	5	10	7	11												33
	3	2		6	8	4	9	1	5	10	7	11												34
	3	2		6	8	4	9	1	5	10*	7	12	11											35
	3	2		6	8	4	9	1	5	10	7	11												36
	3	2		6	4	7	1	5	10*	9	12	11												37
	3	2		6	8	4	9	1	5	10	7	11												38
	3		6	8	4	9	1	2*	5	12	10	7	11											39
1	3	2		6	8	4	9	5	10	7	11													40
1	3	2		6	8	4*	10	5	9	12	7	11												41
1	3		6	8	4	2*	5	10	9	12	7	11												42
11	41	1	15	41	42	17	40	15	38	39	31	28	21	10	4	8	6	19	2	14	8	1	10	
						1		1				1	1	1	3	5			2					
				4	1	2	2	5	15			2	2	1	1		3			1		1		

Digweed	Strong	Mason	Bullivant.	Money	Gale	Marinello	Beck	Guthrie	Lock	Davies	Peyton	Peters	Banton	Mahoney	Kitchen	Greenaway	Hatter	Maybank	Wilson	Gale	O'Driscoll	Brown	Lewington	#
	3		4	6		8	9	1	2	5		7	10	11										3
	3		4	6		8	9	1	2*	5	12	11	10	7										R
1	1		2	2		2	2	2	2	2	2	2	2											
				1																				

Digweed	Strong	Mason	Bullivant.	Money	Gale	Marinello	Beck	Guthrie	Lock	Davies	Peyton	Peters	Banton	Mahoney	Kitchen	Greenaway	Hatter	Maybank	Wilson	Gale	O'Driscoll	Brown	Lewington	#
	3		4	5	6	7	8	9	10	11	1	2												2
	3		4	5	6	7	8	9	10	11	1	2												2
	2		2	2	2	2	2	2	2	2	2	2												
								1																

365

1980-81

1	Aug	16	(a)	Rotherham U	D 2-2	Beck, Lock	4,436
2		20	(h)	Colchester U	W 1-0	Lock	4,155
3		23	(a)	Swindon T	W 4-3	Davies 2, Wilson, Mahoney	6,544
4		29	(h)	Hull C	D 0-0		4,592
5	Sep	5	(h)	Blackpool	L 1-2	Davies	4,940
6		13	(a)	Brentford	W 3-1	O'Driscoll, Brown, Davies	11,610
7		17	(a)	Exeter C	L 0-1		5,300
8		20	(h)	Walsall	W 2-1	Davies, Lock	4,573
9		27	(a)	Portsmouth	L 0-1		15,460
10	Oct	1	(h)	Exeter C	L 0-1		4,509
11		4	(h)	Burnley	L 0-2		4,673
12		7	(a)	Plymouth A	L 1-2	Beck	11,647
13		11	(a)	Gillingham	L 0-1		4,730
14		18	(h)	Oxford U	L 0-4		3,832
15		22	(h)	Millwall	D 1-1	Davies	4,095
16		25	(a)	Chester	W 1-0	Davies	5,126
17		28	(a)	Newport C	L 1-2	Beck	6,029
18	Nov	1	(h)	Chesterfield	D 1-1	Wilson	4,706
19		4	(h)	Plymouth A	D 0-0		3,507
20		8	(a)	Carlisle U	D 2-2	Beck, Hatter	3,665
21		11	(a)	Colchester U	L 2-3	Beck, Davies	2,543
22		15	(h)	Rotherham U	D 1-1	O'Driscoll	4,008
23		29	(a)	Barnsley	D 2-2	Peters, Goodlass	9,940
24	Dec	6	(h)	Huddersfield T	D 2-2	Davies 2	4,513
25		20	(a)	Reading	D 0-0		4,455
26		26	(h)	Sheffield U	W 2-1	Lock, Davies	6,323
27		27	(a)	Charlton A	D 1-1	Greenaway	11,067
28	Jan	10	(a)	Millwall	L 1-3	Davies	6,002
29		16	(h)	Barnsley	L 2-3	Mahoney, Wilson	5,263
30		31	(h)	Swindon T	W 2-0	Davies, Mahoney	4,785
31	Feb	7	(h)	Brentford	D 1-1	Beck	8,721
32		14	(a)	Blackpool	W 2-0	Mahoney, Goodlass	3,792
33		21	(h)	Portsmouth	W 3-0	Davies, Lock, opp own goal	9,921
34	Mar	1	(a)	Walsall	W 2-1	Beck, Peters	4,958
35		7	(a)	Burnley	L 0-3		5,472
36		14	(h)	Gillingham	W 3-2	Davies 2, Gale	5,445
37		17	(h)	Chester	L 0-1		3,387
38		21	(a)	Oxford U	L 0-2		3,646
39		28	(h)	Newport C	W 2-1	Davies, Wilson	4,570
40	Apr	4	(a)	Chesterfield	D 0-0		6,756
41		7	(a)	Hull C	W 1-0	Brown	3,263
42		11	(h)	Carlisle U	L 2-3	Banton, Coney	4,193
43		18	(h)	Charlton A	W 1-0	Coney	7,102
44		21	(a)	Sheffield U	W 2-1	Coney, Greenaway	10,898
45		25	(h)	Reading	L 1-2	Strong	4,601
46	May	2	(a)	Huddersfield T	L 2-4	Beck, Davies	6,965

P	W	D	L	F	A	W	D	L	F	A	Pts	Pos	Div	
46	8	7	8	28	29	7	6	10	29	35	43	13th	3	Appearances
														Sub Appearances
														Goals

FA Cup

1	Nov	22	(a)	Reading	W 2-1	Davies, Mahoney	7,485
2	Dec	13	(h)	Brentford	W 1-0	Greenaway	11,261
3	Jan	3	(a)	Bury	D 1-1	Mahoney	5,360
R		6	(h)	Bury	D 0-0		6,582
2R		12	(n)	Bury*	W 1-0	Davies	2,468
4		24	(h)	Charlton	L 1-2	Davies	17,050

*Played at The Hawthorns.

Appearances
Sub Appearances
Goals

League Cup

1	Aug	9	(a)	Peterborough U	L 2-3	Strong, Gale	3,662
		12	(h)	Peterborough U	D 1-1	Davies	3,477

Appearances
Sub Appearances
Goals

Month End		Sep	Oct	Nov	Dec	Jan	Feb	Mar	Apr	Final
1980-81	Pld	9	17	23	27	30	33	39	45	**46**
	Pts	10	13	18	23	25	30	36	43	**43**
	Pos	10th	18th	19th	15th	20th	18th	14th	13th	**13th**

Cricket batting-order grid (numbers indicate batting position; * = not out). Player columns left to right, match-row index at far right.

Peyton	Peters	Strong	Beck	Brown	Gale	Greenaway	Wilson	O'Driscoll	Davies	Lock	Mahoney	Hatter	Goodlass	Clement	Digweed	Corner	Banton	Lewington	Stannard	Day	Tempest	Coney	Parker	Hopkins	#
1	2	3	4	5	6	7	8	9	10	11															1
1	2	3	4	5	6	7	8	9	10	11															2
1	2	3	4	5	6		10	8	9	11	7														3
1	2	3	4	5	6		10	8	9	11	7														4
1	2	3	4	5	6	12	10	8	9	11*	7														5
1	2	3	4	5	6	10		8	9	11	7*	12													6
1	2	3	4	5*	6	12	10	8	9	11	7														7
1	2	3	4	5	6		10	8	9	11	7														8
1	2*	3	4	5	6	12	10	8	9	11	7														9
1	2*	3	4	5	6	12		8	9	10	7		11												10
1		3	4	5	6			8	9	10	7		11	2											11
1		3	4	5	7	12		8	9	10*	6		11	2											12
1		3	4	5	6		10	8	9		7		11	2											13
1		3	4	5	9	10	2	7	8	6			11												14
1		3	4	5	9	12	10*	7	8	6			11	2											15
1		3	4	5	6	9	10	7	8				11	2											16
	12	3	4	5	6	9*	10	7	8				11	2		1									17
1	12	2	4	5	6		10	7	8	3	9*		11												18
1	9	3	4	5	6	12	10	7	8				11	2*											19
1	2	3	4	5	9		10	8	7			6*	11		12										20
1	2	3	4*	5	9		10	7	8			6	11		12										21
1	2	3	4	5	9		8	10	7				11			6									22
1	9	2		4	5	10		12	8		3	7	6*	11											23
1	9	2		5	4	10		8	7	3			6	11											24
1	9	2			4	10		8	7*	3			6	11				5	12						25
1	12	2			4	10		8	7	3	5	6	11*					9							26
1		2			4	10		8	7	3	9	6						5	11						27
1		2						8	7	3	9	6	11	4				5	10						28
1	6		5	4		12	8	7	3*	9		11	2						10						29
	3		4	5	6	11	12	8*	7		9		2					10	1						30
	2	3	4	5	6	11*	12	8	7		9							10	1						31
	12	3	4	5	6		10	8	7	2*	9		11						1						32
	12	2		4	5	6	10	7	3		9			8*					1						33
8	3		4	5	6	10	9	7*		2								11	1	12					34
8	3		4	5	6	10	9*	7						11				1	2	12					35
8	3		4	5	6	10	9*	7				2						11	1	12					36
8	3		4	5	6	10	9	7		2								11*	1	12					37
4	3			5	6	10	8	7				9*						11	1	12					38
	3			5	6	4	10	8*	7	2								11	1	12		9			39
	3	8		5	6	4	10		7	2								11	1			9			40
	3	8	5	6*		4	10		7	2	12							11	1			9			41
	2	3	8			4	10		7		6						5	11	1			9			42
4	3	8	5				10	12	7	2*				6				11	1			9*			43
8	3		5			4	10	12	7					2			6	11	1			9	2		44
6	3	4		8			10*	7				12					5	11	1			9			45
6	3	4		8				12	7		9		10*				5	11	1					2	46
28	29	45	37	39	40	19	31	39	45	29	22	9	21	17	1	1	8	19	17	1		7	1	1	
5						7	4	3			1	1	1		2	1			1		5	1	3		
2	1	8	2	1	2	3	3	18	5	4	1	2		1								3			

Peyton	Peters	Strong	Beck	Brown	Gale	Greenaway	Wilson	O'Driscoll	Davies	Lock	Mahoney	Hatter	Goodlass	Clement	Digweed	Corner	Banton	Lewington	Stannard	Day	Tempest	Coney	Parker	Hopkins	#
1	2	3		5	9		8	7	4	10	6		11												1
1	9	2		4	10		8*	7	3		6		11					5		12					2
1		2				8	7	6	10	5	11	3	9					4							3
1		2				4	10*	8	7	3	9	6	11					5	12						R
1	6			5	4		8	7	3	9		11	2					10							2R
1				4	5	11	12	8	7	3*	9			2				6	10						4
6	2	5	1	3	5	4	6	6	6	5	4	5	2	4	2			4	2						
							1											1	1						
								1			3		2												

Peyton	Peters	Strong	Beck	Brown	Gale	Greenaway	Wilson	O'Driscoll	Davies	Lock	Mahoney	Hatter	Goodlass	Clement	Digweed	Corner	Banton	Lewington	Stannard	Day	Tempest	Coney	Parker	Hopkins	#
1	2	3	4	5	6	7	8*	10		9	12			11											1
1	2	3	4	5	6	7	12	10	11	9				8*											1
2	2	2	2	2	2	2		1	2	1	2			2											
							1						3												
		1			1			1																	

1981-82

1	Aug	29	(h)	Brentford	L	1-2	Davies	7,671
2	Sep	5	(a)	Lincoln C	D	1-1	Beck	3,034
3		12	(h)	Bristol C	W	2-1	Davies, Brown	4,169
4		19	(a)	Chesterfield	L	0-3		4,019
5		22	(a)	Wimbledon	W	3-1	Coney 2, Davies	5,554
6		26	(h)	Chester	W	2-0	O'Driscoll, Lewington	3,629
7		29	(h)	Southend U	W	2-1	Davies, Wilson	4,556
8	Oct	3	(a)	Oxford U	L	0-2		4,244
9		10	(a)	Huddersfield T	L	0-1		8,258
10		17	(h)	Newport C	W	3-1	Davies 2, Lewington	3,918
11		20	(h)	Exeter C	W	4-1	Davies 2, O'Driscoll, Brown	4,500
12		24	(a)	Burnley	D	2-2	Davies 2	4,224
13		31	(h)	Portsmouth	D	1-1	Wilson	7,542
14	Nov	3	(a)	Plymouth A	L	1-3	Davies	4,915
15		7	(a)	Carlisle U	W	2-1	Davies, Coney	4,385
16		14	(h)	Walsall	D	1-1	Brown	6,168
17		28	(h)	Millwall	D	0-0		8,343
18	Dec	5	(a)	Bristol R	W	2-1	Coney, Davies	4,489
19		30	(a)	Swindon T	W	4-1	Davies 2, Lock, O'Driscoll	5,641
20	Jan	20	(a)	Reading	W	3-0	Gale, Coney, Lewington	3,762
21		23	(a)	Brentford	W	1-0	O'Sullivan	10,830
22		30	(h)	Chesterfield	W	1-0	Davies	9,213
23	Feb	6	(a)	Bristol C	D	0-0		9,228
24		9	(h)	Wimbledon	W	4-1	Coney 2, Wilson, opp own goal	7,802
25		19	(a)	Southend U	D	0-0		7,715
26		23	(h)	Oxford U	D	0-0		5,959
27		27	(h)	Huddersfield T	D	2-2	Coney, Lock	5,963
28	Mar	7	(a)	Newport C	W	3-1	Brown, Wilson, Coney	5,178
29		10	(a)	Exeter C	L	0-1		3,367
30		13	(h)	Burnley	D	1-1	Davies	7,124
31		16	(h)	Plymouth A	L	1-3	Tempest	5,105
32		20	(a)	Portsmouth	D	1-1	Lock	10,712
33		27	(h)	Carlisle U	W	4-1	Brown 2, Davies, O'Driscoll	7,477
34	Apr	3	(a)	Walsall	D	1-1	O'Driscoll	3,120
35		6	(h)	Doncaster R	W	3-1	Coney, Davies, Brown	5,081
36		10	(h)	Gillingham	L	0-2		9,985
37		13	(h)	Swindon T	W	2-0	Brown 2	6,655
38		17	(h)	Bristol R	W	4-2	Davies, Lock, Brown, O'Driscoll	6,849
39		20	(a)	Preston N E	W	3-1	Davies 2, Lock	6,009
40		25	(a)	Millwall	L	3-4	Brown, O'Driscoll, opp own goal	6,484
41	May	1	(h)	Reading	D	2-2	Wilson, Lewington	6,773
42		5	(a)	Chester	W	2-0	Coney, Tempest	1,174
43		8	(a)	Doncaster R	L	1-2	Coney	4,729
44		11	(h)	Gillingham	D	0-0		7,174
45		15	(h)	Preston N E	W	3-0	Davies 2, Coney	7,585
46		18	(h)	Lincoln C	D	1-1	Brown	20,398

P	W	D	L	F	A	W	D	L	F	A	Pts	Pos	Div	
46	12	9	2	44	22	9	6	8	33	29	78	3rd	3	Appearances
														Sub Appearances
														Goals

FA Cup

1	Nov	21	(a)	Bristol R	W	2-1	Coney 2	6,497
2	Jan	2	(a)	Hereford U	L	0-1		4,619

Appearances
Sub Appearances
Goals

FL Cup

1	Sep	1	(a)	Bournemouth	W	1-0	Davies	3,935
1		15	(h)	Bournemouth	W	2-0	Beck, Wilson	3,583
2	Oct	7	(a)	Newcastle U	W	2-1	Wilson, Coney	20,242
2		27	(h)	Newcastle U	W	2-0	Lewington, Coney	7,210
3	Nov	10	(a)	Oldham A	D	1-1	Wilson	6,619
R		17	(h)	Oldham A	W	3-0	Coney 2, Hopkins	6,985
4	Dec	2	(a)	Tottenham H	L	0-1		30,124

Appearances
Sub Appearances
Goals

Month End		Sep	Oct	Nov	Dec	Jan	Feb	Mar	Apr	Final
1981-82	Pld	7	13	17	19	22	27	33	40	46
	Pts	13	21	26	32	41	48	56	69	78
	Pos	5th	7th	8th	4th	1st	2nd	3rd	2nd	3rd

Player appearance grid. Columns (left to right): Peyton, Hopkins, Strong, Beck, Brown, Banton, Davies, Day, Coney, O'Sullivan, Lewington, Wilson, Gale, Reeves, O'Driscoll, Scott, Tempest, Peters, Lock, Parker, Stannard. The right‑hand column gives the match number.

Pey	Hop	Str	Bec	Bro	Ban	Dav	Day	Con	O'Su	Lew	Wil	Gal	Ree	O'Dr	Sco	Tem	Pet	Loc	Par	Sta	No.
1	2	3	4	5	6	7	8*	9	10	11	12										1
1	2	3	4	5		7		9	10	11	8	6									2
1	2	3	4	5		7		9	10	11	8	6									3
1	2	3	4	5		7		9	10	11	8	6									4
1	2	3		5		7		9	10	11	8	6		4							5
1	2	3		5		7		9	10	11	8	6		4							6
1	2	3		5		7		9	10	11	8	6		4							7
1	2	3		5		7	12	9	10	11	8	6		4*							8
1	2	3		5		7	12	9	10		8	6		4*	11						9
1	2	3		5		7		9	10	11	8	6		4							10
1	2	3		5		7		9	10	11	8	6		4							11
1	2	3		5		7			10	11	8	6		4	9						12
1	2	3		5		7		9	10	11	8	6		4							13
1	2	3		5		7		9	10	11	8	6		4*		12					14
1	2	3		5		7		9	10	11	8	6		4							15
1	2	3		5*		7	12	9	10	11	8	6		4							16
1	2	3		5		7		9	10	11	8	6		4							17
1	2	3		5		7		9	10	11	8	6		4							18
1	2	3		5		7		9*	10	11	8	6		4		12					19
1		3		5		7*		9	10	11		6	8	4		12		2			20
1		3		5				9	10	11		6	8	4		7		2			21
1		3		5		7*		9	10	11	8	6		4		12		2			22
1		3		5				9	10	11	8	6		4		7		2			23
1		3		5		7		9	10	11	8	6		4				2			24
1	12	3		5		7		9	10	11*	8	6		4				2			25
1		3		5		7		9	10		8	6	11	4*		12		2			26
1		3		5		7		9	10		8	6	11	4				2			27
1		3		5		7		9	10		8	6	11	4				2			28
1		3		5		7		9	10		8	6	11	4				2			29
1	12	3		5		7		9	10		8	6	11*	4				2			30
1	2	3	12	5		7			10		8	6		4*		9		11			31
1	2	3		5		7			10		8	6		4		9*		11	12		32
1	2	3		5		7			10		8	6		4		9		11			33
1	2	3		5		7		9			8	6		4				11	10		34
1	2	3		5		7		9	10		8	6		4				11			35
1	2	3		5		7		9	10		8	6		4				11			36
1	2	3		5		7		9	10		8	6		4				11			37
1	2	3		5		7		9	10		8	6		4				11			38
	2	3		5		7		9	10		8	6		4				11			39
	2	3		5*		7		9	10		8	6		4		12		11	1		40
1	2			5		7*		9	10	11	8	6		4		12		3	1		41
1	2		12	5				9	10	11	8	6*		4		7		3			42
1	2			5				9	10	11	8	6		4		7		3			43
1	2		12	5				9	10	11	8	6		4		7		3*			44
1	2	3*		5		7		9	10	11	8	6		4		12					45
1	2	3*		5		7		9	10	11	8	6		4		12					46
44	**31**	**46**	**4**	**46**	**1**	**41**	**1**	**42**	**45**	**31**	**42**	**44**	**7**	**42**	**1**	**9**		**25**	**2**	**2**	
	4		1				3						1					5	1	1	3
		1	12		24			13	1	4	5	1			7			2		5	

Pey	Hop	Str	Bec	Bro	Ban	Dav	Day	Con	O'Su	Lew	Wil	Gal	Ree	O'Dr	Sco	Tem	Pet	Loc	Par	Sta	No.
1	2	3*		5		7		9	10	11	8	6		4		12					1
1	2	3		5		7		9	10	11	8	6		4							2
2	**2**	**2**		**2**		**2**		**2**	**2**	**2**	**2**	**2**		**2**							
																1					
							2														

Pey	Hop	Str	Bec	Bro	Ban	Dav	Day	Con	O'Su	Lew	Wil	Gal	Ree	O'Dr	Sco	Tem	Pet	Loc	Par	Sta	No.
1	2	3	4	5		7		9	10	11	8	6									1
1	2	3	4	5		7		9	10	11	8	6									1
1	2	3		5		7		9	10	11*	8	6		4		12					2
1	2	3		5		7		9	10	11	8	6		4							2
1	2	3		5		7		9	10	11	8	6		4							3
1	2	3				7		9	10	11	8	6		4		5					R
1	2	3		5		7		9	10	11	8	6		4							4
7	**7**	**7**	**2**	**6**		**7**		**7**	**7**	**7**	**7**	**7**		**5**				**1**			
																		1			
	1		1					1		4		1	3								

369

1982-83

							Scorers	Att.
1	Aug	28	(h)	Rotherham U	D	1-1	Davies	7,021
2	Sep	4	(a)	Shrewsbury T	W	1-0	Wilson	3,525
3		7	(h)	Queen's Park R	D	1-1	Lewington	15,004
4		11	(h)	Bolton W	W	4-0	Coney 2, Lewington, Houghton	5,688
5		18	(a)	Middlesbrough	W	4-1	Davies 2, Lewington, Houghton	6,445
6		25	(h)	Leeds U	W	3-2	Davies 2, Coney	12,798
7		28	(a)	Charlton A	L	0-3		6,790
8	Oct	2	(a)	Barnsley	L	3-4	Hopkins, Wilson, Davies	12,582
9		9	(h)	Blackburn R	W	3-1	Davies, Lewington, Wilson	5,698
10		16	(a)	Newcastle U	W	4-1	Davies 2, Coney, Houghton	29,490
11		23	(h)	Burnley	W	3-1	Lewington 2, Houghton	9,040
12		30	(a)	Crystal P	D	1-1	O'Driscoll	14,912
13	Nov	6	(h)	Oldham A	L	0-3		6,897
14		13	(a)	Grimsby T	W	4-0	Davies 2, Wilson, Gale	6,952
15		20	(a)	Wolves	W	4-2	Lewington, Davies 2, Wilson	14,448
16		27	(h)	Sheffield W	W	1-0	Davies	13,864
17	Dec	4	(a)	Leicester C	L	0-2		9,082
18		11	(h)	Derby C	W	2-1	Thomas, Carr	7,854
19		18	(a)	Carlisle U	L	2-3	Lewington, O'Driscoll	4,859
20		27	(h)	Cambridge U	D	1-1	Brown	9,105
21		28	(a)	Chelsea	D	0-0		29,797
22	Jan	1	(h)	Wolves	L	1-3	Lewington	17,196
23		3	(h)	Shrewsbury T	W	2-1	Davies, Thomas	7,786
24		15	(a)	Rotherham U	W	1-0	Brown	7,667
25		22	(h)	Middlesbrough	W	1-0	Wilson	8,431
26	Feb	5	(a)	Bolton W	W	1-0	O'Driscoll	6,748
27		19	(a)	Blackburn R	D	0-0		6,141
28		26	(h)	Newcastle U	D	2-2	Davies, Lock	14,277
29	Mar	5	(a)	Burnley	L	0-1		8,828
30		12	(h)	Crystal P	W	1-0	Brown	11,234
31		19	(a)	Oldham A	L	0-1		6,189
32		26	(h)	Grimsby T	W	4-0	Wilson 2, Lewington, Davies	8,096
33	Apr	2	(h)	Chelsea	D	1-1	Lock	15,249
34		5	(a)	Cambridge U	L	0-1		6,249
35		9	(h)	Charlton A	W	2-1	Davies, Brown	9,035
36		16	(a)	Leeds U	D	1-1	Houghton	24,328
37		19	(h)	Barnsley	W	1-0	Gale	9,003
38		23	(h)	Leicester C	L	0-1		24,251
39		30	(a)	Sheffield W	L	1-2	Wilson	12,531
40	Mar	2	(a)	Queen's Park R	L	1-3	Davies	24,431
41		7	(h)	Carlisle U	W	2-0	Wilson 2	10,045
42		14	(a)	Derby C	L	0-1		21,124

P	W	D	L	F	A	W	D	L	F	A	Pts	Pos	Div	
42	13	5	3	36	20	7	4	10	28	27	69	4th	2	Appearances
														Sub Appearances
														Goals

FA Cup

3	Jan	8	(a)	Oldham A	W	2-0	Coney, Houghton	8,087
4		29	(a)	Watford	D	1-1	Coney	24,574
R	Feb	1	(h)	Watford	L	1-2	Lewington	22,206

Appearances
Sub Appearances
Goals

League Cup

1	Sep	1	(a)	Southend U	L	0-1		2,671
		14	(h)	Southend U	W	4-2	Coney, Houghton, Davies, opp own goal	4,641
2	Oct	5	(h)	Coventry C	D	2-2	Gale, Brown	6,237
		26	(a)	Coventry C	D	0-0		8,217

Appearances
Sub Appearances
Goals

Month End		Sep	Oct	Nov	Dec	Jan	Feb	Mar	Apr	Final
1982-83	**Pld**	7	12	16	21	25	28	32	39	**42**
	Pts	14	24	33	38	47	52	58	66	**69**
	Pos	5th	3rd	2nd	3rd	3rd	3rd	3rd	3rd	**4th**

Peyton	Hopkins	Strong	O'Driscoll	Brown	Gale	Davies	Wilson	Coney	Houghton	Lewington	O'Sullivan	Parker	Lock	Tempest	Carr	Thomas	Rosenior	McDermott	Reeves	Scott	#
1	2	3	4	5	6	7	8	9	10	11											1
1	2	3	4	5	6	7	8	9	10	11*	12										2
1	2*	3	4	5	6	7	8	9	10	11		12									3
1	2		4	5	6	7	8*	9	10	11		12	3								4
1*	2		4	5	6	7	8	9	10	11		12	3								5
1	2		4	5	6	7	8	9	10	11											6
1	2		4	5*	6	7	8	9	10	11		12	3								7
1	2		4	5	6	7	8	9	10	11			3								8
1	2		4	5	6	7	8	9	10	11			3								9
1	2		4	5	6	7	8	9	10	11			3*	12							10
1	2		4	5	6	7*		9	10	11			3	8	12						11
1	2		4	5	6			9	10	11		8	3	7							12
1	2		4	5	6		8	9	10	11		12	3	7*							13
1	2		4	5	6	7	8	9	10	11			3								14
1	2		4	5	6	7	8	9	10	11			3								15
1	2		4	5	6	7	8	9*	10	11		12	3								16
1	2		4	5	6		8		10	11		12	3		7						17
1	2		4	5	6		8		10	11*		12	3	7	9						18
1	2		4	5	6	7	8		10	11			3		9						19
1	2		4	5	6	7	8	9	10	11			3								20
1	2		4	5	6	7	8	9	10	11			3								21
1	2		4	5	6	7	8	9	10	11			3								22
1	2		4	5	6	7	8	9	10	11			3*	12							23
1	2		4	5	6	7	8	9	10	11			3								24
1	2		4	5	6	7	8	9	10	11			3								25
1	2		4	5	6	7	8	9	10	11			3								26
1	2		4	5	6	7	8		10	11				9	3						27
1	2		4	5	6	7	8	9	10	11			3								28
1	2		4	5	6	7	8		10	11			3	9*	12						29
1	2		4	5	6	7	8	9*	10	11			3			12					30
1	2		4	5	6	7	8*	9	10	11			3			12					31
1	2		4	5	6	7	8	9	10	11			3								32
1	2		4	5	6	7	8	9	10	11			3								33
1	2		4	5	6	7*	8	9	10	11			3			12					34
1	2		4	5	6	7	8	9	10	11			3								35
1	2*		4	5	6	7	8	9	10	11		12	3								36
1	2		4	5	6	7	8	9	10	11			3								37
1	2		4	5	6	7	8	9*	10	11		12	3								38
1	2*		4	5	6	7	8	9	10	11		12	3								39
1			4	5	6	7	8	9	10	11		2	3*					12			40
1	2		4	5	6	7	8	9	10	11			3								41
1	2		4*	5	6	7	8	9	10	11			3					12			42
42	41	3	42	42	42	38	40	37	42	42		6	34	3	4	3	1				
											1	11		1	2	1		3	2		
	1		3	4	2	19	11	4	5	10			2		1	2					

Peyton	Hopkins	Strong	O'Driscoll	Brown	Gale	Davies	Wilson	Coney	Houghton	Lewington	O'Sullivan	Parker	Lock	Tempest	Carr	Thomas	Rosenior	McDermott	Reeves	Scott	#
1	2		4	5	6	7	8	9	10	11			3								3
1	2		4	5	6	7	8	9	10	11			3								4
1	2		4	5	6	7	8	9	10	11			3								R
3	3		3	3	3	3	3	3					3								
														2	1	1					

Peyton	Hopkins	Strong	O'Driscoll	Brown	Gale	Davies	Wilson	Coney	Houghton	Lewington	O'Sullivan	Parker	Lock	Tempest	Carr	Thomas	Rosenior	McDermott	Reeves	Scott	#
1	2		4	5	6	7	8	9	10	11			3								1
1	2		4	5	6	7		9	10	11		8	3								
1	2		4	5	6	7	8	9	10	11			3								2
1	2		4	5	6			9	10	11			3	8				7*	12		
4	4		4	4	4	3	2	4	4	4		2	3	1				1			
				1	1	1						1	1								

1983-84

1	Aug	27	(a)	Barnsley	L	0-3		9,851
2	Sep	3	(h)	Portsmouth	L	0-2		10,672
3		7	(a)	Manchester C	D	0-0		23,356
4		11	(a)	Crystal P	D	1-1	Tempest	11,327
5		17	(h)	Leeds U	W	2-1	Lock, Tempest	10,005
6		24	(a)	Grimsby T	L	1-2	Davies	5,769
7		27	(h)	Middlesbrough	W	2-1	Houghton, Tempest	6,452
8	Oct	1	(h)	Swansea C	W	5-0	Gale, Davies 2, Houghton, Tempest	7,253
9		8	(h)	Chelsea	L	3-5	Davies 3	24,787
10		15	(a)	Carlisle U	L	0-2		3,712
11		22	(a)	Shrewsbury T	D	0-0		4,767
12		31	(h)	Cardiff C	L	0-2		5,959
13	Nov	5	(a)	Newcastle U	L	2-3	Wilson 2	31,568
14		11	(h)	Sheffield W	D	1-1	Davies	9,687
15		19	(a)	Huddersfield T	L	0-2		8,914
16		26	(h)	Blackburn R	L	0-1		5,647
17	Dec	3	(a)	Cambridge U	D	1-1	Lock	3,031
18		10	(h)	Charlton A	L	0-1		6,140
19		17	(a)	Oldham A	L	0-3		4,516
20		26	(h)	Derby C	D	2-2	Rosenior 2	7,480
21		27	(a)	Brighton & HA	D	1-1	Sealy	15,076
22		31	(a)	Portsmouth	W	4-1	Carr, Davies 2, Rosenior	15,649
23	Jan	2	(h)	Grimsby T	D	1-1	Carr	7,351
24		14	(h)	Barnsley	W	1-0	Carr	5,085
25		21	(a)	Leeds U	L	0-1		11,421
26	Feb	5	(a)	Swansea C	W	3-0	Davies 2, Coney	7,350
27		11	(h)	Crystal P	D	1-1	Davies	9,119
28		19	(a)	Cardiff C	W	4-0	Coney 2, Rosenior 2	7,149
29		25	(h)	Shrewsbury T	W	3-0	Coney, Davies, Rosenior	5,149
30	Mar	3	(h)	Newcastle U	D	2-2	Scott, Davies	12,290
31		7	(a)	Sheffield W	D	1-1	Rosenior	20,440
32		17	(h)	Manchester C	W	5-1	Davies 4, Rosenior	9,684
33		24	(a)	Middlesbrough	W	2-0	Davies, Coney	5,435
34		31	(h)	Carlisle U	D	0-0		6,018
35	Apr	7	(a)	Chelsea	L	0-4		31,947
36		14	(h)	Huddersfield T	L	0-2		5,265
37		21	(a)	Derby C	L	0-1		12,178
38		23	(h)	Brighton & HA	W	3-1	Scott, Davies, Coney	7,742
39		29	(a)	Blackburn R	W	1-0	Davies	4,301
40	May	5	(h)	Cambridge U	W	1-0	Wilson	4,914
41		7	(a)	Charlton A	W	4-3	Scott, Houghton, Carr, Davies	6,151
42		12	(h)	Oldham A	W	3-0	Davies, Coney, Scott	5,089

P	W	D	L	F	A	W	D	L	F	A	Pts	Pos	Div		
42	9	6	6	35	24	6	6	9	25	29	57	11th	2	Appearances	
														Sub Appearances	
														Goals	

FA Cup

3	Jan	7	(h)	Tottenham H	D	0-0		23,398
R		11	(a)	Tottenham H	L	0-2		32,898

Appearances

Sub Appearances

Goals

Milk Cup

2	Oct	5	(a)	Doncaster R	W	3-1	Tempest, Davies, Scott	4,843
		26	(h)	Doncaster R	W	3-1	Davies 2, Lewington	3,891
3	Nov	8	(h)	Liverpool	D	1-1	Lock	20,142
R		22	(a)	Liverpool	D	1-1	Lock	15,783
2R		29	(h)	Liverpool	L	0-1		20,905

Appearances

Sub Appearances

Goals

Month End		Sep	Oct	Nov	Dec	Jan	Feb	Mar	Apr	Final
1983-84	Pld	7	12	16	22	25	29	34	39	42
	Pts	8	12	13	19	23	33	42	48	59
	Pos	13th	15th	20th	20th	19th	15th	14th	15th	11th

Stannard	Hopkins	Lock	O'Driscoll	Brown	Gale	Tempest	Wilson	Coney	Houghton	Parker	Carr	Marshall	Davies	Scott	Lewington	Peyton	Tapley	Rosenior	Sealy	Foley	Reeves	Cottington	#
1	2*	3	4	5	6	7	8	9	10	11	12												1
1		3		5	6	12	8	9*	10	2		4	7	11									2
1		3*		5	6	9	8		10	2	12	4	7	11									3
1			12	5	6	9*	8		10	2	3	4	7	11									4
1		3		5	6	9			10	2	8	4	7	11									5
1	12	3		5	6	9			10	2	8	4*	7	11									6
1		3*	4	5	6	9	8		10	2	12		7	11									7
1	12		4	5*	6	9	8		10	2	3		7	11									8
1			4	5	6	9	8*		10	2	3		7	11	12								9
1			4	5	6	9*	8	12	10	2	3		7	11									10
1	5		4		6		8*	9	10	2	3		7	12	11		·						11
1	5	6	4					9*	10	2	3	12	7	8	11								12
1	4	6		5			8	9*	10	2	3	12	7		11								13
1		3		5	6		8		10	2	4	9	7		11								14
1		3		5	6		8	7	10	2	4	9			11								15
	2	3			6		8		10			4	9*	7	11	1	5	12					16
	2	3	6					8	9	10		4	5	7	11	1							17
	5	3	4		6			9	10			8	2	7	11	1							18
	5	3			6				10			4	2		11	1		9	7	8			19
	5	3*			6				10			4	2	8	11	1		9	7	12			20
	5				6				10*		3	2	12	8	11	1		9	7	4			21
	5				6				10		3	2	4	8	11	1		9	7				22
	5				6		7		10*		3	2	4	8	11	1		9		12			23
	5		4		6						2	3	7	8	11	1		9		10			24
	5		12		6						2	3	4	8	11	1		9	7	10*			25
	5				6			11	9	2	3		4	7	10	1		8					26
	5				6		8		10	2	3		7	4	11	1		9					27
	5				6		8		11	2	3		7	4	10	1		9					28
	5				6		8		10	2	3		7	4	11	1		9					29
	5				6		8		10	2	3		7	4	11	1		9*					30
	5				6		8		10	2	3		7	4	11	1		9					31
	5				6	12	8		10	2	3		7	4	11*	1		9					32
	5				6		8		10	2	3		7	4	11	1		9					33
	5				6		8		10	2	3		7	4	11	1		9					34
	5		·		6	4	8		10	2	3		7		11	1		9					35
	5				6	4*	8		10	2	3		7		11	1		9		12			36
	5				6		8		10*	2	3	12	7	4	11	1		9					37
	5				6*		8		10	2	3	12	7	4	11	1		9					38
	5						8		10	2	3	6	7	4	11	1		9					39
	5				12		8		10	2	3	6	7	4	11	1		9*					40
	5			9			8		10	2	3	6	7	4	11	1							41
	5			9			8		10	2	3	6	7	4	11	1							42
15	31	15	10	13	35	13	14	26	40	34	38	21	35	31	32	27	1	22	5	2	2		
2		2			2		2	2	1			3	4	1	1		1			1	1		
		2			1	4	3	7	3			4		23	4			8	1				

Stannard	Hopkins	Lock	O'Driscoll	Brown	Gale	Tempest	Wilson	Coney	Houghton	Parker	Carr	Marshall	Davies	Scott	Lewington	Peyton	Tapley	Rosenior	Sealy	Foley	Reeves	Cottington	#
	5				6					2	3		7	4	8	11	1	9	10				3
	5		12		6					2	3		7	4	8	11	1	9	10*				R
	2		1		2					2	2		2	2	2	2	2	2	2				
			1																				

Stannard	Hopkins	Lock	O'Driscoll	Brown	Gale	Tempest	Wilson	Coney	Houghton	Parker	Carr	Marshall	Davies	Scott	Lewington	Peyton	Tapley	Rosenior	Sealy	Foley	Reeves	Cottington	#
1	5		4		6	9	8		10	2	3		7	11									2
1	5		4*		6		9	10		2	3		7	8	11				12				2
1	2	3			6		8		10	5	4	9	7		11								3
	2	3	12		6		8		10	5*	4	9	7		11	1							R
	2	3			6			9	10		4	5	7		11	1							2R
3	5	3	2		5	1	4	2	5	4	5	3	5	2	4	2							
			1																1				
		2			1							3	1	1									

1984-85

#	Month	Date		Opponent	Result	Scorers	Attendance
1	Aug	25	(h)	Shrewsbury T	L 1-2	Lock	4,898
2		27	(a)	Leeds U	L 0-2		14,207
3	Sep	1	(a)	Manchester C	W 3-2	Coney, Sealy, Wilson	21,071
4		4	(h)	Birmingham C	L 0-1		6,031
5		8	(h)	Blackburn R	W 3-2	Coney, Houghton, Wilson	4,439
6		15	(a)	Oxford U	L 2-3	Carr, Scott	8,082
7		22	(h)	Middlesbrough	W 2-1	Coney, Lewington	4,730
8		29	(a)	Brighton & HA	L 0-2		12,396
9	Oct	6	(h)	Huddersfield T	W 2-1	Davies, Houghton	4,377
10		13	(a)	Charlton A	W 2-1	Coney, Davies	6,619
11		20	(h)	Cardiff C	W 3-2	Davies, Lock, Wilson	5,358
12		27	(a)	Crystal P	D 2-2	Carr, Davies	8,035
13	Nov	10	(h)	Wimbledon	W 3-1	Carr, Coney, Davies	8,834
14		17	(a)	Grimsby T	W 4-2	Rosenior 3, Wilson	6,787
15		20	(a)	Carlisle U	L 0-3		2,994
16		24	(h)	Wolves	L 1-2	Houghton	7,049
17	Dec	1	(a)	Barnsley	L 0-1		6,742
18		7	(h)	Oldham A	W 3-1	Coney, Lewington, Wilson	4,472
19		16	(a)	Notts C	L 1-2	Marshall	4,917
20		22	(h)	Manchester C	W 3-2	Houghton, Lewington, Wilson	6,748
21		26	(h)	Sheffield U	W 1-0	Lewington	6,270
22		29	(a)	Birmingham C	D 2-2	Hopkins, Wilson	11,827
23	Jan	1	(a)	Portsmouth	D 4-4	Coney, Rosenior, Barnett, Lock	17,636
24		26	(a)	Shrewsbury T	L 1-3	Tapley	3,172
25	Feb	2	(h)	Brighton & HA	W 2-0	Houghton, Wilson	6,990
26		9	(a)	Blackburn R	L 1-2	Carr	11,023
27		19	(h)	Oxford U	W 1-0	Achampong	6,635
28		23	(h)	Carlisle U	W 3-2	Achampong 2, Rosenior	5,229
29	Mar	2	(h)	Crystal P	D 2-2	Hopkins, Lock	7,654
30		9	(a)	Cardiff C	W 2-0	Lock, Wilson	4,399
31		16	(h)	Charlton A	D 0-0		6,918
32		23	(a)	Huddersfield T	D 2-2	Houghton 2	4,843
33		30	(h)	Leeds U	L 0-2		7,901
34	Apr	6	(a)	Sheffield U	W 1-0	Rosenior	11,113
35		8	(h)	Portsmouth	L 1-3	Rosenior	12,542
36		13	(a)	Middlesbrough	L 0-2		4,443
37		16	(a)	Wimbledon	D 1-1	Wilson	5,811
38		20	(h)	Grimsby T	W 2-1	Sealy 2	3,632
39		27	(a)	Wolves	W 4-0	Houghton, Sealy 3	6,172
40	May	4	(h)	Barnsley	D 1-1	Wilson	3,721
41		6	(a)	Oldham A	L 1-2	Sealy	2,756
42		11	(h)	Notts C	W 1-0	Lewington	4,883

P	W	D	L	F	A	W	D	L	F	A	Pts	Pos	Div		
42	13	3	5	35	26	6	5	10	33	38	65	9th	2		Appearances
															Sub Appearances
															Goals

FA Cup

3	Jan	5	(h)	Sheffield W	L 2-3	Houghton 2	11,433

Appearances
Sub Appearances
Goals

Milk Cup

2	Sep	25	(h)	Carlisle U	W 2-0	Coney 2	3,340
2	Oct	9	(a)	Carlisle U	W 2-1	Davies, Houghton	2,818
3		30	(a)	Sheffield W	L 2-3	Carr, Hopkins	15,665

Appearances
Sub Appearances
Goals

Month End		Sep	Oct	Nov	Dec	Jan	Feb	Mar	Apr	Final
1984-85	**Pld**	8	12	16	22	24	28	33	39	**42**
	Pts	9	19	25	35	36	45	51	61	**65**
	Pos	16th	11th	9th	9th	11th	9th	10th	9th	**9th**

Peyton	Parker	Lock	Scott	Hopkins	Marshall	Davies	Wilson	Coney	Houghton	Rosenior	Sealy	Cottington	Carr	Lewington	Elkins	Kerrins	Stannard	Barnett	Hesford	Tapley	Achampong	Lee	Reeves	Match
1	2	3	4	5	6	7	8	9*	10	11	12													1
1	2	3	4	5	6	7	8	9	10	11														2
1	2	3	4	5	6	7	8	9	10	11														3
1	2	3*	4	5	6	7	8	9	10		11	12												4
1	2		4	5	6		8	9	10	7		12	3	11*										5
1	2		4	5	6*		8	9	10	7		12	3	11										6
1			4	5	6	12	8	9	10	7*			3	11	2									7
1	2		4	5	12	7	8*	9	10				3	11	6									8
1	2		4	5		7		9	10			8	3	11	6									9
1	2	6		5	4	7	8	9	10				3	11										10
1	2	6		5	4	7	8	9	10				3	11										11
1	2	6		5	4	7	8	9	10				3	11										12
1	2	6		5	4	7	8	9	10				3	11										13
1	2	6		5	4		8	9	10	7			3	11										14
1	2	6		5	4*		8	9	10	7			3	11	12									15
1	2	6*		5	4		8	9	10	7			3	11	12									16
	2	6		5	4		8	9	10	7			3	11			1							17
	2	6	4	5			8	9	10	7			3	11			1							18
	2	6	4	5		7	8	9	10				3	11			1							19
	2	6	4	5		12	8	9	10	7*			3	11			1							20
	2	6		5	4		8	9	10	7			3	11			1							21
	2	6*		5	4		8	9	10	7			3	11			1				12			22
	2	6		5	4		8*	9	10	7			3	11			1				12			23
	2	6	8	5	12			9*	10	7			3	11					1	4				24
		6	8	5	9			4	10	7			3	11	2				1					25
8		6		5	9			4	10	7			3	11	2				1					26
1	2	6		5		8			10	9			3	11	4						7			27
1	2	6		5		8			10	9			3	11	4						7			28
1	2	6		5		8			10	9			3	11	4						7			29
1	2	6		5		8			10	9			3	11	4						7			30
1	2	6	8	5					10	9*	12		3	11	4						7			31
1	2	6		5		8			10	9*	12		3	11	4						7			32
1		6	12	5	2	8			10				3	11	4						7	9*		33
1		6	7	5			8		10	9	2		3	11	4									34
1		6*	7	5			8		10	9	2		3	11	4							12		35
1	2			5		8			10		7	6*	3	11	4				8			12		36
1	2			5		8		9	10	7			3	11	4				6					37
1		12	2	5		8		9	10	4*			3	11	6				7					38
1	4			5	2	8		9	10	7			3	11	6									39
1	2		4	5		8		9	10	7			3	11	6									40
1	2		4	5		8		9	10	7			3	11	6									41
1	2		4	5		8		9	10	7			3	11	6									42
32	36	30	17	40	29	10	39	24	42	30	10	4	38	38	21	0	7	0	3	1	10	1	0	
			2			3	1						3	3		2	2				2			
		5	1	2	1	5	11	7	8	7	7		4	5		1			1	3				

Peyton	Parker	Lock	Scott	Hopkins	Marshall	Davies	Wilson	Coney	Houghton	Rosenior	Sealy	Cottington	Carr	Lewington	Elkins	Kerrins	Stannard	Barnett	Hesford	Tapley	Achampong	Lee	Reeves	
	2	6	8	5				9	10	7			3	11					1	4				3
	1	1	1	1				1	1	1			1	1					1	1				
									2															

Peyton	Parker	Lock	Scott	Hopkins	Marshall	Davies	Wilson	Coney	Houghton	Rosenior	Sealy	Cottington	Carr	Lewington	Elkins									
1	2		4	5		7	8	9	10				3	11	6									2
1	2	6		5	4	7	8	9	10				3	11										2
1	2	6*	12	5	4	7	8	9	10				3	11										3
3	3	2	1	3	2	3	3	3					3	3	1									
				1																				
			1		1		2	1					1											

1985-86

						Result	Scorers	Att
1	Aug	17	(h)	Leeds U		W 3-1	Scott 2, Coney	5,772
2		24	(a)	Middlesbrough		L 0-1		5,366
3		26	(h)	Grimsby T		W 2-1	Sealy 2	4,873
4		31	(a)	Barnsley		L 0-2		5,197
5	Sep	7	(h)	Portsmouth		L 0-1		9,331
6		14	(a)	Crystal P		D 0-0		6,381
7		17	(h)	Sheffield U		L 2-3	Coney, Sealy	4,259
8		21	(a)	Blackburn R		L 0-1		5,241
9		28	(h)	Brighton & HA		W 1-0	Carr	5,861
10	Oct	5	(h)	Shrewsbury T		W 2-1	Marshall, Pike	3,412
11		12	(a)	Wimbledon		L 0-1		5,953
12		19	(h)	Stoke C		W 1-0	Pike	4,007
13	Nov	2	(h)	Sunderland		L 1-2	Coney	5,795
14		9	(a)	Hull C		L 0-5		6,122
15		23	(a)	Huddersfield T		W 3-1	Barnett 2, Carr	4,650
16		30	(h)	Oldham A		D 2-2	Coney 2	3,544
17	Dec	7	(h)	Bradford C		W 4-1	Barnett, Marshall, Achampong, Carr	3,724
18		14	(a)	Leeds U		L 0-1		9,998
19		21	(h)	Middlesbrough		L 0-3		3,512
20		28	(a)	Sheffield U		L 1-2	Barnett	10,421
21	Jan	1	(h)	Norwich C		L 0-1		7,463
22		11	(a)	Portsmouth		D 1-1	Coney	13,666
23		18	(h)	Barnsley		W 2-0	Carr, Scott	3,580
24	Feb	1	(a)	Grimsby T		L 0-1		3,576
25		18	(a)	Stoke C		L 0-1		6,449
26	Mar	8	(a)	Shrewsbury T		L 1-2	Barnett	2,563
27		11	(h)	Blackburn R		D 3-3	Barnett, Marshall, Coney	2,535
28		15	(h)	Wimbledon		L 0-2		6,209
29		18	(a)	Millwall		D 1-1	Achampong	9,645
30		22	(h)	Crystal P		L 2-3	Coney 2	4,951
31		29	(a)	Norwich C		L 1-2	Coney	17,320
32		31	(h)	Millwall		L 1-2	Pike	4,581
33	Apr	2	(a)	Bradford C		L 1-3	Burvill	5,564
34		5	(a)	Sunderland		L 2-4	Coney, Burvill	11,338
35		8	(h)	Carlisle U		L 0-1		2,134
36		12	(h)	Hull C		D 1-1	Achampong	2,795
37		16	(a)	Brighton & HA		W 3-2	Brathwaite, Dreyer, Pike	6,255
38		19	(a)	Carlisle U		L 1-2	Dreyer	3,818
39		22	(h)	Charlton A		L 0-3		5,587
40		26	(h)	Huddersfield T		W 2-1	Scott 2	2,877
41		29	(a)	Charlton A		L 0-2		9,393
42	May	3	(a)	Oldham A		L 1-2	Coney	2,510

P	W	D	L	F	A	W	D	L	F	A	Pts	Pos	Div		
42	8	3	10	29	32	2	3	16	16	37	36	22nd	2	Appearances	
														Sub Appearances	
														Goals	

FA Cup

3	Jan	13	(a)	Sheffield U		L 0-2		7,004

Appearances
Sub Appearances
Goals

Milk Cup

2	Sep	24	(h)	Notts C		D 1-1	Barnett	2,324
	Oct	7	(a)	Notts C		W 4-2	Barnett, Marshall, Pike, Coney	3,054
3		29	(a)	Chelsea		D 1-1	Carr	19,669
R	Nov	6	(h)	Chelsea		L 0-1		20,190

Appearances
Sub Appearances
Goals

Month End		Sep	Oct	Nov	Dec	Jan	Feb	Mar	Apr	Final
1985-86	**Pld**	9	12	16	20	23	25	32	41	**42**
	Pts	10	16	20	23	27	27	29	36	**36**
	Pos	15th	16th	17th	21st	21st	21st	22nd	22nd	**22nd**

376

Cricket linear scorebook (fielding / bowling grid). Column headers are player names written vertically.

Peyton	Cottington	Carr	Scott	Hopkins	Parker	Marshall	Donnellan	Sealy	Coney	Houghton	Achampong	Hicks	Batty	Elkins	Grew	Barnett	Pike	Kerrins	Fishenden	Gore	Dreyer	Burvill	Brathwaite	Smith	#
1	2	3	4	5	6	7	8	9	10	11															1
1	2	3	4*		6	7	8	9	10	11	12	5													2
	2	3	4		6	7	8	9	10	11		5	1												3
	2	3	4	5	6	7		9	10	11	12		1	8*											4
	2*	3	4	5	6	7	12	9	10	11	8				1										5
	2	3	4	5		7		9	10		8			6	1	11									6
	2	3	4	5		7		9	10		8			6	1	11*	12								7
	2	3	4	5		7			10		8			6	1	11	12	9*							8
1	2	3		5		7		9			8	6		12		4	10	11*							9
1	2	3		5	4	7		9*			8	6				11	10	12							10
1	2	3	4	5	6	7		9			12	8*				11	10								11
1	2	3	4	5	6	7		9			8					11	10								12
1	2	3	4	5	6	7		9			8					11	10								13
1	2			5	6	7					8		4		3	11	10	9							14
1	2	10	4	5	6	7		9			8				3	11									15
1	2	10	4	5	6	7		9			8				3		11								16
1	2	10	4	5	6	7		9			8				3	11									17
1	2*	10	4	5	6	7		9			8				3	11	12								18
1	2	10	4	5	6	7		9			8				3	11									19
1	2	10	4	5	6	7					8	9			3	11									20
1	2	10	4	5	6	7	11				8				3*	12		9							21
1	2	10	4	5	6	7	3	9			8					11									22
1	2	10	4	5	6	7	3	9			8					11									23
1	2	3		5	6	7	10	9			8					11			4						24
1	2	3		5	6	7	10	9			8					11*	12		4						25
1	2	3	4		6	7	8	9				5*				11	10	12							26
1	2	3	4		6	7	10	9			12	5*				11	8								27
1	2	3	4		6	7	8	9			12					11	10		5*						28
1	2	3	4	6*	5		8	9				7				11	10	12							29
1	2	3	4	6	5		8*	9				7				11	10	12							30
1	2	3	4	6*	5	7		9				8				11	12			10					31
1	2	3	4*	5				9				8	6			11	12			10	7				32
1	2				5		8*	9								11	10	3	6	7		4	12		33
1	2				5		12	9				8				11	10		6*	4		7			34
1	2	3			5		4*	9				7				11	12		6	10		8			35
1	2	3			5		4					7				11	9	10		6		8			36
1	2	3*			5		4					7				11	9	10		6		8	12		37
1	2		3		5	7	4*			11						12	9	10		6		8			38
1	2					4	7	3		9						11	10	8		5		6			39
1	2					4	3	5		9		7					11	10		6		8			40
1	2					4	3	5		8*							9			6			12		41
1	2					4		5		9		8*					7	10		3		11	12		42
36	42	35	32	23	30	42	21	7	37	5	30	10	2	12	4	34	20	11	3	5	12	9	0	0	
									2			5			1	2	6	5				3	1		
		4	5				3				3	12			3	6	4					2	2	1	

Peyton	Cottington	Carr	Scott	Hopkins	Parker	Marshall	Donnellan	Sealy	Coney	Houghton	Achampong	Hicks	Batty	Elkins	Grew	Barnett	Pike	Kerrins	Fishenden	Gore	Dreyer	Burvill	Brathwaite	Smith	#
1	2	10	4	5	6	7	3*	9				8		12		11									3
1	1	1	1	1	1	1	1		1			1				1									
															1										

Peyton	Cottington	Carr	Scott	Hopkins	Parker	Marshall	Donnellan	Sealy	Coney	Houghton	Achampong	Hicks	Batty	Elkins	Grew	Barnett	Pike	Kerrins	Fishenden	Gore	Dreyer	Burvill	Brathwaite	Smith	#
1	2	3	4	5		7			10			8			6	11	12	9*							2
1	2	3	4	5	6	7		9				8				11	10								2
1	2	3	4	5	6	7		9				8				11	10								3
1	2	3	4	5	6	7		9				8				11	10								R
4	4	4	4	4	3	4		4				4			1	4	3	1							
	1				1			1								2	1								

1986-87

1	Aug	23	(a)	Rotherham U	D	0-0		3,279
2		30	(h)	Blackpool	L	0-1		3,903
3	Sep	6	(a)	Chester C	D	2-2	Parker, Scott	2,568
4		13	(h)	Brentford	L	1-3	Donnellan	4,791
5		16	(h)	Bolton W	W	4-2	Coney 2, Achampong, Scott	2,434
6		20	(a)	Notts C	W	3-2	Achampong 2, Coney	4,452
7		27	(h)	Middlesbrough	D	2-2	Scott 2	3,852
8		30	(a)	Walsall	D	1-1	Scott	4,110
9	Oct	4	(a)	Port Vale	W	1-0	Barnett	3,812
10		11	(h)	Swindon T	L	0-2		4,708
11		18	(a)	Wigan A	L	0-2		2,495
12		21	(h)	Bristol R	D	2-2	Oakes, Achampong	2,361
13		25	(h)	Bury	W	2-1	Marshall, Barnett	2,685
14	Nov	1	(a)	Doncaster R	L	1-2	Marshall	2,258
15		4	(a)	Chesterfield	L	1-3	Davies	2,249
16		8	(h)	Bristol C	L	0-3		4,453
17		22	(a)	Carlisle U	W	3-1	Coney 2, Davies	2,462
18		29	(h)	Darlington	W	3-1	Coney 2, Davies	3,367
19	Dec	13	(h)	Mansfield T	D	1-1	Davies	3,563
20		20	(a)	York C	D	1-1	Oakes	2,570
21		26	(h)	Gillingham	D	2-2	Marshall, Davies	5,887
22		27	(a)	Bournemouth	L	2-3	Kerrins, Barnett	6,670
23	Jan	1	(a)	Newport C	D	0-0		2,388
24		3	(h)	Carlisle U	W	3-0	Marshall, Coney, Barnett	3,700
25		24	(h)	Chester C	L	0-5		3,067
26	Feb	1	(a)	Brentford	D	3-3	Scott, Achampong, Carr	5,430
27		7	(a)	Bolton W	L	2-3	Hoddy, Achampong	4,128
28		14	(h)	Notts C	W	3-1	Barnett, Hicks, opp own goal	3,054
29		17	(h)	Rotherham U	D	1-1	Oakes	2,352
30		21	(a)	Middlesbrough	L	0-3		9,361
31		28	(a)	Walsall	D	2-2	Barnett, Donnellan	5,944
32	Mar	3	(h)	Doncaster R	D	0-0		4,154
33		7	(a)	Bury	L	1-2	Cottington	2,154
34		18	(a)	Bristol R	D	0-0		2,448
35		21	(a)	Swindon T	L	0-2		7,426
36		28	(h)	Port Vale	L	0-6		3,798
37	Apr	4	(a)	Bristol C	D	0-0		8,551
38		7	(h)	Blackpool	L	0-1		1,901
39		11	(h)	Chesterfield	W	3-1	Coney, Barnett, Parker	4,521
40		18	(h)	Newport C	W	2-0	Coney, opp own goal	4,234
41		20	(a)	Gillingham	L	1-4	Donnellan	6,123
42		25	(h)	York C	W	1-0	Barnett	4,107
43		28	(h)	Wigan A	D	2-2	Brathwaite, Barnett	3,609
44	May	2	(a)	Darlington	W	1-0	Donnellan	1,267
45		4	(h)	Bournemouth	L	1-3	Hopkins	9,239
46		9	(a)	Mansfield T	D	1-1	Davies	2,754

P	W	D	L	F	A	W	D	L	F	A	Pts	Pos	Div	
46	8	8	7	35	41	4	9	10	24	36	53	18th	3	Appearances
														Sub Appearances
														Goals

FA Cup

1	Nov	15	(a)	Hereford U	D	3-3	Barnett, Marshall, Coney	3,777
R		24	(h)	Hereford U	W	4-0	Marshall, Davies 2, Coney	3,592
2	Dec	6	(h)	Newport C	W	2-0	Oakes, Davies	4,052
3	Jan	10	(h)	Swindon T	L	0-1		7,077

Appearances
Sub Appearances
Goals

League Cup

1	Aug	26	(a)	Aldershot	W	3-1	Achampong, Scott, Coney	2,183
	Sep	3	(h)	Aldershot	W	2-0	Scott, Parker	2,093
2		23	(a)	Liverpool	L	0-10		13,498
	Oct	7	(h)	Liverpool	L	2-3	Scott, Coney	7,864

Appearances
Sub Appearances
Goals

Month End		Sep	Oct	Nov	Dec	Jan	Feb	Mar	Apr	Final
1986-87	**Pld**	8	13	18	22	25	31	36	43	**46**
	Pts	10	17	23	26	30	36	38	49	**53**
	Pos	13th	11th	12th	14th	14th	12th	20th	16th	**18th**

378

Vaughan	Marshall	Gore	Scott	Steggles	Parker	Barnett	Achampong	Coney	Kerrins	Lewington	Cottington	Oakes	Donnellan	Brathwaite	Hoddy	Hicks	Hopkins	Davies	Carr	Pike	Elkins	Skinner	Thomas	Batty	Langley	
1	2	3	4*	5	6	7	8	9	10	11																1
1	2	3*	4	5	6	7	8	9	10	11	12															2
1	2	3*	4	5	6	7	8	9	10	11	12															3
1	2		4		6		8	9	10	11	5	3	7*	12												4
1	2		4		6		8	9	10	11	5	3		7												5
1	2	5			6	7	8	9	10	11*	4	3			12											6
1	2		4		6	7*	8	9	10	11	3	5			12											7
1	2		4		6	7	8	9		11	5	3			10											8
1	2	10	4		6	7	8	9		11	5	3														9
1	2		4			7	8	9		11*	3	5	12		10	6										10
1	2		4				8	9	10	11	3	5			7	6										11
1	2		4		6	7	8	9	10	11	5		3													12
1	2		4		6	7	8	9	10	11*	3	5			12											13
1	2		4		6	7	8	9	10		5				3	11										14
1	2		4		6	7		9	10		5			8	3	11										15
1	2		4*		6	7	12	9	10		5			8	3	11										16
1	2				6	7		9	10		5	4		8	3	11										17
1	2				6	7		9	10		5	4	8	3	11											18
1	2				6	7		9	10		5	4*		8	3	11	12									19
1	2		4		6	7	9		10		5	8			3	11										20
1	2		4		6	7		9*	10		5	8			3	11	12									21
1	2		4		6	7		9	10		5	8			3	11										22
1	2		4		6	7		9	10		5	8			3	11*	12									23
1	2		4		6	7		9	10		5	8	12	3*		11										24
1	2	3	4			7*	8	9	10		6	5	12	11												25
1	2		4			7	8	9*	10		6	5		11	3	12										26
1	2		4			7	8	9			6	5	12	11*	3	10										27
1	2					7			10		6	5	4	3		8	9	11								28
1						7					6	5	4	3		9	10	8	11	2						29
1						7			2		6	5	4	3		9	10	8	11							30
1						7	5		2		6		4	3		9	10	8	11							31
1					5	7*			2		6		4	12	3		9	10	8	11						32
1					6				2		7*	5	4		3		9	10	8	11	12					33
1						2					7*	5	4		3		9	10	8	11*						34
1		4				7*		12	8	11	2	5	6			10	9			3						35
1	7				11*	12	9		4	2	5	8		6			3	10								36
1					2	7		9		4		5			6	8	3	10	11							37
1					2	7		9		4		5	12		6	8	3	10	11*							38
1					8	7		9		4		5	10	11	2	6	3									39
1		2			6	7		9		4		5	10	11		8	3									40
1		2			6	7		9		4		5	10	11*		8	3	12								41
1		2				7		9		4		5	10	11*	6	8	12	3								42
1		2				7		9		4		5	10	11*	2	6	12	3								43
1		8			11	7		9		4		5	10		2*	6	12	3								44
		2			6	7		9		4		5	12	11*	8	10	3						1	2		45
		8				7					5	11		6	10	3	9		4				1	2		46
44	29	7	30	3	31	42	19	36	29	25	21	41	25	7	11	20	20	18	21	12	9	2	1	2	1	
					2	1	1			2		5	2	4		3	4	1		1						
	4		6		2	9	6	10	1		1	3	4	1	1	1	1									

Vaughan	Marshall	Gore	Scott	Steggles	Parker	Barnett	Achampong	Coney	Kerrins	Lewington	Cottington	Oakes	Donnellan	Brathwaite	Hoddy	Hicks	Hopkins		
1	2				6	7		9	10		12	5	4		8*	3	11		1
1	2				6	7		9	10		12	5	4		8	3*	11		R
1	2				6	7		9	10			5	4		8	3	11		2
1	2	3	4		6	7	12	9	10			5			8*		11		3
4	4	1	1		4	4		4	4		4	4	4		4	3	3		
												1				2			
	2					1		2								3			

Vaughan	Marshall	Gore	Scott	Steggles	Parker	Barnett	Achampong	Coney	Kerrins	Lewington	Cottington	Oakes	Donnellan	Brathwaite	Hoddy	Hicks		
1	2	3	4		6	7	10	9	8	11	5							1
1	2	3	4		6	7	10	9	8	11	5							1
1	2		4		6	7	8	9		10	11	3			5			2
1	2		4		6	7	8	9			11	3		12	10*	5		2
4	4	2	4		4	4	4	4	3	4	4				2	1		
															1			
		3			1		1	2										

Fulham Against Other League Clubs

Fulham have played 96 clubs in the Football League since 1907-08. Below is Fulham's record against each club. Some clubs changed their names (eg Small Heath became Birmingham then Birmingham City) and some clubs modified their titles (eg Leicester Fosse became Leicester City). In all cases, the last name used by each club, for the most recent fixture against Fulham, cover all games under previous names. Since 1981-2 three points have been awarded for a win. A percentage success-rate is therefore shown instead of a points-won total, two points for a win being assumed throughout.

	P	HOME					AWAY					%
		W	D	L	F	A	W	D	L	F	A	
AFC Bournemouth	12	3	2	1	12	7	1	1	4	8	13	46%
Arsenal	28	5	4	5	28	24	0	1	13	13	38	27%
Aston Villa	34	10	5	2	34	20	4	5	8	22	30	56%
Barnsley	72	16	13	7	59	33	5	9	22	40	81	36%
Barrow	2	1	0	0	2	1	0	0	1	1	3	50%
Birmingham City	50	12	7	6	45	29	6	7	12	40	46	44%
Blackburn Rovers	52	11	10	5	53	32	5	5	16	22	47	45%
Blackpool	84	18	14	10	59	41	6	12	24	40	77	44%
Bolton Wanderers	40	10	3	7	33	24	4	5	11	21	31	45%
Bradford	34	10	4	3	36	21	7	5	5	25	22	63%
Bradford City	28	6	5	3	23	10	2	5	7	10	16	46%
Brentford	26	7	4	2	28	13	5	4	4	18	20	62%
Brighton & Hove A	26	11	0	2	32	9	2	2	9	12	30	54%
Bristol City	42	12	5	4	39	20	7	6	8	21	23	58%
Bristol Rovers	40	12	5	3	54	31	3	6	11	22	39	51%
Burnley	70	18	9	8	62	44	5	6	24	28	74	44%
Bury	54	14	7	6	58	30	6	7	14	31	44	50%
Cambridge United	8	2	1	1	8	4	0	1	3	1	7	25%
Cardiff City	38	10	3	6	37	27	6	3	10	19	24	50%
Carlisle United	26	7	1	5	20	12	3	2	8	16	27	44%
Charlton Athletic	40	8	6	6	26	26	5	7	8	24	33	49%
Chelsea	44	4	4	14	28	43	2	8	12	13	32	27%
Chester City	6	1	0	2	2	6	2	1	0	5	2	58%
Chesterfield	26	8	5	0	22	7	3	4	6	11	18	60%
Colchester United	2	1	0	0	1	0	0	0	1	2	3	50%
Coventry City	34	9	5	3	31	15	6	2	9	21	28	54%
Crystal Palace	32	7	6	3	25	17	4	6	6	21	26	53%
Darlington	6	3	0	0	9	2	2	0	1	3	6	83%
Derby County	42	10	7	4	38	24	2	6	13	26	52	44%
Doncaster Rovers	26	6	4	3	25	14	4	3	6	16	21	52%
Everton	26	6	4	3	19	16	0	4	9	10	30	38%
Exeter City	12	3	2	1	13	7	2	0	4	10	8	50%
Gainsborough Trin	10	4	0	1	18	2	2	2	1	6	6	70%
Gillingham	18	5	3	1	15	11	2	1	6	10	17	50%
Glossop North End	16	5	1	2	18	9	3	2	3	6	7	59%
Grimsby Town	40	12	3	5	42	26	7	3	10	32	28	55%
Halifax Town	4	2	0	0	5	2	1	0	1	9	2	75%
Hereford United	2	1	0	0	4	1	0	0	1	0	1	50%
Huddersfield Town	40	12	5	3	35	24	4	4	12	24	41	51%
Hull City	68	16	11	7	56	21	7	8	19	28	59	48%
Ipswich Town	12	3	2	1	19	7	4	1	1	14	10	71%
Leeds United	56	15	3	10	53	39	8	7	13	28	43	50%

380

	P	W	D	L	F	A	W	D	L	F	A	%
Leicester City	68	21	8	5	73	39	14	4	16	52	69	60%
Lincoln City	36	14	3	1	49	17	6	4	8	25	37	65%
Liverpool	28	4	6	4	17	15	0	3	11	13	39	30%
Luton Town	44	16	2	4	48	24	6	1	15	20	43	53%
Manchester City	30	7	3	5	35	30	3	2	10	21	39	42%
Manchester United	42	8	7	6	32	34	1	3	17	15	44	33%
Mansfield Town	10	1	3	1	4	5	2	1	2	7	7	50%
Merthyr Town	4	2	0	0	9	4	1	0	1	5	7	75%
Middlesbrough	40	9	3	8	31	30	7	2	11	24	39	46%
Millwall	32	9	4	3	20	11	4	5	7	18	23	55%
Nelson	2	0	1	0	0	0	0	1	0	1	1	50%
Newcastle United	38	10	5	4	41	30	5	5	9	26	37	53%
Newport County	14	5	0	2	15	8	2	3	2	13	12	61%
Northampton Town	10	3	0	2	9	10	2	1	2	11	12	55%
Norwich City	26	5	3	5	24	19	3	5	5	18	20	46%
Nottingham Forest	78	23	10	6	72	32	8	12	19	45	74	54%
Notts County	50	19	2	4	71	29	5	10	10	26	45	60%
Oldham Athletic	44	11	6	5	33	21	6	4	12	26	37	50%
Orient	68	15	12	7	56	32	9	8	17	32	46	50%
Oxford United	18	3	4	2	8	8	1	2	6	6	12	39%
Plymouth Argyle	44	11	6	5	49	33	2	6	14	25	52	43%
Portsmouth	34	2	7	8	17	24	3	5	9	17	34	32%
Port Vale	36	11	5	2	48	23	7	4	7	20	31	63%
Preston North End	36	9	3	6	26	20	5	4	9	20	26	49%
Queen's Park R	18	2	1	6	12	15	1	2	6	5	14	25%
Reading	14	2	3	2	11	11	2	2	3	11	9	46%
Rochdale	4	2	0	0	4	0	2	0	0	3	1	100%
Rotherham United	32	9	5	2	34	16	4	5	7	20	27	56%
Scunthorpe United	2	0	1	0	1	1	1	0	0	2	1	75%
Sheffield United	46	12	4	7	53	32	5	5	13	21	39	47%
Sheffield Wed	58	18	4	7	60	34	4	8	17	29	56	48%
Shrewsbury Town	14	5	1	1	13	6	2	2	3	7	11	61%
Southampton	46	12	9	2	35	22	1	4	18	20	55	42%
Southend United	10	2	2	1	8	8	3	1	1	8	7	65%
Southport	2	1	0	0	3	2	1	0	0	2	0	100%
South Shields	18	4	3	2	13	8	0	1	8	5	19	33%
Stockport County	32	14	1	1	43	8	7	2	7	23	21	70%
Stoke City	52	13	5	8	54	38	9	6	11	28	45	53%
Sunderland	34	6	4	7	27	25	3	6	8	17	28	41%
Swansea City	42	17	0	4	68	24	5	4	12	27	48	57%
Swindon Town	20	6	2	2	24	11	3	4	3	17	21	60%
Thames Association	4	2	0	0	12	2	0	2	0	0	0	75%
Torquay United	12	5	1	0	21	4	2	2	2	11	12	71%
Tottenham Hotspur	44	3	9	10	28	37	1	9	12	21	41	30%
Tranmere Rovers	6	2	1	0	4	1	2	0	1	4	1	75%
Walsall	16	6	2	0	23	9	2	4	2	13	13	69%
Watford	12	4	1	1	19	6	2	2	2	11	12	63%
West Bromwich A	48	9	4	11	30	25	5	3	16	29	64	36%
West Ham United	62	16	7	8	60	39	7	6	18	36	63	48%
Wigan Athletic	2	0	1	0	2	2	0	0	1	0	2	25%
Wimbledon	6	2	0	1	7	4	1	1	1	4	3	58%
Wolverhampton W	58	13	6	10	46	34	5	9	15	31	55	44%
Wrexham	6	1	0	2	1	3	0	3	0	4	4	42%
York City	6	2	0	1	3	2	0	1	2	3	5	42%
	2886	744	353	346	2732	1678	329	350	764	1627	2628	49%

Watney Cup

1970
Round 1
Aug 1 (h) v Derby County 3-5 a.e.t
Halom 2, Earle
Webster; Moreline(Pentecost), Callaghan, Brown(Tranter), Matthewson, Dunne, Conway (Jim), Halom, Earle, Lloyd, Barrett.
Att: 18,501

Anglo-Italian Cup

1973
Feb 21 v Como (a) 0-0
Mellor; Cutbush, Callaghan, Mullery, Went, Dunne, Strong, Earle, Mitchell, Pinkney, Barrett.
Att: 3,111
Mar 21 v A.S. Roma (h) 1-1
Strong
Mellor; Cutbush, Callaghan, Mullery, Went, Richardson, Strong, Earle, Mitchell, Lloyd, Barrett.
Att: 7,712
Apr 4 v Torino (a) 1-1
Strong
Mellor; Cutbush, Callaghan, Mullery, Went, Horne, Strong, Mitchell, Earle, Pinkney (Lloyd), Barrett.
Att: 10,000 approx

1974
May 2 v Bologna (h) 1-1
Conway
Webster; Cutbush, Moreline, Mullery, Went, Horne, Conway (Jim), Earle, Carlton, Lloyd, Barrett.
Att: 3,830

Les Strong

Jimmy Conway

382

John Mitchell

Alan Slough

Anglo-Scottish Cup

1975
Aug 2 v Norwich City (a) 2-1
Mitchell 2
Mellor; Cutbush, Strong, Mullery, Howe, Moore, Mitchell, Conway, Busby, Lloyd, Barrett.
Att: 6,728
Aug 5 v Bristol City (h) 2-2
Opp og, Mullery
Mellor; Cutbush, Strong, Mullery, Howe, Moore, Mitchell, Conway(Dowie), Busby, Lloyd, Barrett.
Att: 4,283
Aug 9 v Chelsea (h) 1-0
Mullery
Mellor; Cutbush, Strong, Mullery, Howe, Moore, Mitchell, Conway, Busby, Lloyd, Barrett.
Att: 13,080
Quarter-final
1st leg
Sep 16 v Heart of Midlothian (h) 3-2
Mitchell 2, Busby
Mellor; Cutbush, Strong, Mullery, Howe, Moore, Mitchell, Conway, Busby, Slough, Barrett(Dowie).
Att: 6,256
Quarter-final
2nd leg
Oct 1 v Heart of Midlothian (a) 2-2 (agg 5-4)
Slough, Mullery
Mellor; Cutbush, Strong, Mullery, Howe, Moore, Lloyd (Dowie), Conway, Busby, Slough, Scrivens.
Att: 14,517
Semi-final
1st leg
Oct 21 v Motherwell (h) 1-1
Conway
Mellor; James, Slough, Mullery, Howe, Moore, Mitchell(Dowie), Conway, Busby, Lloyd, Barrett.
Att: 9,672

Semi-final
2nd leg
Nov 4 v Motherwell (a) 3-2 (agg 4-3)
Opp og, Conway, Barrett
Mellor; James, Slough, Mullery, Lacy, Moore, Dowie, Lloyd, Busby, Conway, Barrett.
Att: 13,085
Final
1st leg
Nov 26 v Middlesbrough (a) 0-1
Mellor; Fraser, Strong, Mullery, Howe, Moore, Dowie, Conway, Busby, Slough, Barrett.
Att: 15,000
Final
2nd leg
Dec 9 v Middlesbrough (h) 0-0 (agg 0-1)
Mellor; Howe, Strong, Mullery, Lacy, Moore, Dowie, Conway, Busby, Slough, Barrett.
Att: 13,723

1976
Aug 7 v Chelsea (a) 0-0
Mellor(Teale); Cutbush, Strong, Slough, Howe, Lacy, Bullivant, Busby, Mitchell, Lloyd, Barrett.
Att: 12,001
Aug 11 v Orient (a) 1-2
Barrett
Teale; Cutbush, Strong, Slough, Lacy, Gale, Bullivant, Busby, Mitchell, Lloyd(Dowie), Barrett.
Att: 3,357
Aug 14 v Norwich City (h) 1-1
Dowie
Teale; Cutbush, Strong, Slough, Lacy, Gale, Bullivant, Mitchell, Busby, Dowie, Barrett.
Att: 4,425

1977
Aug 2 v Orient (h) 1-0
Warboys
Peyton; Storey, Strong, Bullivant, Lacy, Gale, Margerrison, Maybank, Warboys, Mitchell, Evanson.
Att: 3,700
Aug 6 v Chelsea (h) 1-0
Warboys
Peyton; Storey, Strong, Bullivant, Lacy, Gale, Margerrison, Maybank, Warboys, Mitchell, Evanson.
Att: 9,821

Les Barrett

John Dowie

Aug 10 v Norwich City (a) 1-0
Mitchell
Peyton; Storey, Strong, Bullivant, Lacy, Gale, Margerrison, Mitchell, Warboys, Maybank, Evanson.
Att: 3,755
Quarter-final
1st leg
Sep 13 v St Mirren (h) 1-1
Greenaway
Peyton; Evans, Strong, Storey, Lacy, Gale, Greenaway, Evanson, Mitchell, Maybank, Bullivant.
Att; 4,332
Quarter-final
2nd leg
Sep 26 v St Mirren (a) 3-5 (agg4-6)
Margerrison, Mitchell, Best
Peyton; Evans, Strong, Storey, Lacy, Gale, Bullivant, Maybank, Mitchell, Margerrison, Best.
Att: 9,800

1978
Aug 5 v Cardiff City (a) 0-1
Peyton; Strong, Lock, Money, Banton, Gale, Bullivant, Evanson, Margerrison, Davies, Boyd(Mahoney).
Att: 4,149
Aug 8 v Bristol Rovers (h) 2-1
Money, Margerrison
Pey'on; Strong, Lock, Money, Banton, Gale, Bullivant, Evanson, Margerrison, Davies, Boyd.
Att: 2,437
Aug 12 v Bristol City (h) 0-3
Peyton; Strong, Lock, Money, Banton, Gale, Bullivant, Davies, Margerrison, Evanson, Boyd.
Att: 4,324

1979
Aug 4 v Plymouth Argyle (h) 1-0
Marinello
Digweed; Mason, Strong, Money, Hatter, Beck(Greenaway), Bullivant, Lock, Marinello, Guthrie, Kitchen.
Att: 2,067
Aug 8 v Birmingham City (h) 0-5
Digweed; Mason, Strong, Money, Hatter, Beck, Bullivant, Lock, Marinello, Guthrie, Kitchen.
Att: 2,889
Aug 11 v Bristol City (a) 0-1
Digweed; Mason, Strong, Money, Banton, Beck, Bullivant, Lock, Marinello, Guthrie, Davies(Greenaway).
Att: 6,116

1980
Aug 2 v Bristol City (a) 0-2
Peyton; Peters, Strong, Beck, Brown, Gale, Greenaway, Lewington, Davies, Maybank, Lock(O'Driscoll).
Att: 1,929
Aug 4 v Notts County (h) 0-1
Peyton; Peters, Strong, Beck, Brown, Gale, Greenaway, O'Driscoll, Davies, Maybank (Mahoney).
Att: 1,516
Aug 5 v Orient (a) 2-1
Mahoney, Davies
Peyton; Peters, Strong, Beck, Brown, Gale, Greenaway, Lewington, Mahoney, Davies, O'Driscoll.
Att: 2,906

385

Full Members Cup

1985-6
Oct 15 v Shrewsbury Town (a) 0-0
Peyton; Cottington, Carr, Scott, Hopkins, Hicks, Marshall, Achampong, Kerrins(Thomas), Pike, Barnett.
Att: 1,340
Oct 22 v Oxford United (h) 0-2
Peyton; Cottington(Hicks), Carr, Scott, Hopkins, Parker, Marshall, Achampong, Coney, Pike, Barnett.
Att: 2,022

Kenny Achampong   Gary Barnett

Freight/Rover Trophy

1986-7
Preliminary Round
Dec 2 v Cambridge United (a) 4-0
Achampong 2, Coney, Gore
Vaughan; Marshall(Kerrins), Carr, Donnellan, Hicks, Parker, Barnett, Hoddy, Coney (Oakes), Gore, Achampong.
Att: 1,355
Preliminary Round
Jan 6 v Southend United (h) 1-2
Achampong
Batty; Hicks, Carr, Skinner, Gore, Thomas, Harlow, Achampong, Brathwaite, Cottington, Elkins(Hoddy).
Att: 1,456
1st Round
Jan 26 v Northampton Town (h) 3-2
Achampong, Barnett, Marshall
Vaughan; Marshall, Gore, Scott, Oakes, Cottington, Barnett, Achampong, Coney, Kerrins, Hoddy.
Att: 2,080
2nd Round
Feb 10 v Aldershot (a) 1-1 a.e.t.*
Pike
Vaughan; Marshall, Hicks, Donnellan, Oakes, Cottington, Barnett, Pike, Coney(Davies), Kerrins, Elkins.
Att: 2,571
*Aldershot won 11-10 on penalties.

Matches details not included in seasonal tables

FA Cup
1896-7
2nd Qualifying Round
Oct 31 v Swanscombe (a) 0-5
F.Kingsley; H.Shrimpton, E.Humphries, A.Frame,
H.Johnson, J.Shrimpton, W.A.Robertson, E.Withe-
ridge, J.Lindsey, A.Sermon, F.Hollands
Att: Not known

FA Amateur Cup
1897-8
1st Qualifying Round
Oct 16 v Eversleigh (h) 3-0
Robertson, Freeman 2
A.J.Maile; A.J.Mitchell, S.Aylott, J.Cox, J.Taylor,
A.Knight, W.Steers, E.H.Freeman, L.J.Moon, Withe-
ridge, W.A.Robertson
Att: Not known
2nd Qualifying Round
Oct 30 v Southall (a) 0-1
A.J.Maile; A.J.Mitchell, H.Shrimpton, J.Cox, A.Sermon,
A.Knight, W.Steers, E.H.Freeman, L.J.Moon, S.Aylott,
W.A.Robertson
Att: Not known

Football League
1939-40
Aug 26 v Bury (a) 1-3
Turner; Bacuzzi, Keeping, Evans, Hiles, Tompkins,
Higgins, Woodward, Rooke, O'Callaghan, Arnold.
Att: 9,000
Aug 28 v West Ham United (a) 1-2
Rooke
Turner; Bacuzzi, Keeping, Evans, Dennison, Tompkins,
Worsley, Woodward, Rooke, Finch, Arnold.
Att: 15,200
Sep 2 v Luton Town (h) 1-1
Rooke
Turner; Pitts, Bacuzzi, Evans, Hiles, Tompkins, Higgins,
Woodward, Rooke, O'Callaghan, Shepherd.
Att: 8,000

FA Cup
1945-6
Round 3 (1st leg)
Jan 2 v Charlton Athletic (a) 1-3
Rampling
Rickett; Bacuzzi, Lloyd, Freeman, Taylor, Wallbanks,
Rampling, Woodward, Rooke, Beasley, Shepherd.
Att: 30,000
Round 3 (2nd leg)
Jan 4 v Charlton Athletic (h) 2-1 (agg 3-4)
Rooke 2
Rickett; Bacuzzi, Lloyd, Freeman, Taylor, Wallbanks,
Rampling, Woodward, Rooke, Beasley, Shepherd.
Att: 20,000

*Joe Bacuzzi, whose career with Fulham spanned the
war.*

*England international goalkeeper, Hugh Turner, an
ever-present for Fulham in 1938-9, was one player
whose career at Craven Cottage was ended by the war.*

The War Years — 1915-1919

ALTHOUGH World War One began in August 1914, the football authorities decided to go ahead with the 1914-15 season on the normal Football League and FA Cup basis. They felt, as did most of the population, that the hostilities would be over by Christmas. It was a decision which, apparently, lost football a lot of public support. The season was, moveover, a very unreal one with attendances limited and clubs short of players. For the first time, gates for League matches at the Cottage were as low as 1,000, and it was almost with a sense of relief that this chapter in the club's history was brought to a close, with a 1-0 home defeat by Blackpool.

For four seasons the professional clubs then competed in regional Leagues, Fulham joining the London Combination. This comprised a varying number of sides, anything between ten (from 1917 to 1919) to 14 (in 1916-17). Only in the last two wartime seasons was there some structure to the organisation, with each club playing the others four times, making 36 games in the programme. Fulham easily held their own in this company, never finishing lower than sixth (out of 14 clubs in 1916-17), and once as high as third (out of ten clubs in 1917-18). This was really the least that could be expected, since only Spurs and Chelsea had spent the last peacetime season in a higher League.

For any sort of competitive football to exist at this time, the 'guest' system was absolutely essential. Few clubs could field a team made up of players whose registrations they held, and the use of 'guests' made it easier for clubs to fulfill fixtures. It was also a chance for the supporters to see stars they would never be able to watch in normal circumstances. Fulham drew on a nucleus of their pre-war regulars (Torrance, Russell, White and Reynolds), as well as having as guests former players like Fred Mavin and Mark Bell. Amongst the illustrious guests for Fulham in these years were such legendary names as Harry Hampton, George Elliott, Bill McCracken and Jackie Carr. So, also, were Gordon Hoare and Danny Shea, two players who were to sign for Fulham after the war.

The club's major achievement in these years came in 1919, in the London Victory Cup. After disposing of the Munitions League and Arsenal in the earlier rounds, Fulham defeated Spurs 2-0 in the semi-final, in front of a crowd of 45,000. In the Final, however, at Highbury, Chelsea were too strong, winning 3-0. The only 'real' Fulham players in the side that day were Charlton, Russell, Torrance and two wartime discoveries, Johnny McIntyre and Frank Penn.

Wartime regulars (from left) Arthur Reynolds, Wattie White and Frank Penn, a 'discovery' who served the Cottagers for 50 years.

Fulham Guest Players 1915-19

P.Allan (Clyde), E.J.Bassett (Notts County), Mark Bell (Clapton Orient), J.Bethune (Barnsley), Fred Blackman (Leeds City), S.Blackman (Bradford), P.Bratley (Liverpool), F.E.Bullock (Huddersfield), Jack Carr (Middlesbrough), J.F.Cumming (Manchester City), J.Darrell (Manchester United), Joe Dix (Clapton Orient), J.Dodds (Celtic), F.Drabble (Bradford), George Elliott (Middlesbrough), Eric Farnfield (Casuals), Percy Fender (Surrey), G.H.Fox (Queen's Park Rangers), James Galt (Everton), Jimmy Garden (Rangers), D.Greenaway (Arsenal), E.F.Grimsdell (Queen's Park Rangers), A.J.Grossart (Hibernian), Harry Hampton (Aston Villa), G.A.Handley (Bradford City), Neil Harris (Partick), H.Higginbottom (Luton Town), Gordon Hoare (Queen's Park Rangers), A.Hogg (Leeds City), George Holley (Sunderland), D.Howie (Bradford), George Hunter (Birmingham), W.Jennings (Bolton Wanderers), Wilf Low (Newcastle), Bill McCracken (Newcastle), J.McMasters (Celtic), Bobby McNeal (West Bromwich Albion), James Martin (Hearts), Fred Mavin (Bradford), James Molyneux (Chelsea), Jackie Mordue (Sunderland), Fred Morris (West Bromwich Albion), Tom Niblo (Newcastle), Ronnie Orr (South Shields), Danny Shea (Blackburn), R.Shields (Huddersfield), Jackie Sheldon (Liverpool), E.Simms (Luton Town), J.Smith (Bradford), Walter Smith (Manchester City), W.J.Stapley (Glossop), W.D.Tull (Tottenham Hotspur), Harry Tufnell (Barnsley), Tommy Urwin (Middlesbrough), George Walden (Clapton), Charlie Wallace (Aston Villa), W.Watson (Burnley), L.C.Weller (Everton), Fred Wheatcroft (Swindon), Jack Whitley (Chelsea), Robert Whittingham (Chelsea)

Danny Shea, a wartime guest who later rejoined Fulham in peacetime football.

World War One Summary
Leading Appearances

Jimmy Torrance	135
Fred Blackman*	125
Johnny McIntyre	83
Frank Penn	73
Harry Russell	65
Wattie White	47
Arthur Reynolds	42
William Taylor	42
E.F.Grimsdell*	40
Fred Mavin*	39
Danny Shea*	31
E.Bassett*	31
F.Drabble*	30
James Galt*	29
R.Gibson	29
Walter Smith*	29
A.J.Grossart*	28
J.McMasters*	28
Arthur Wood	26
Gordon Hoare*	25
Fred Morris*	24
Wilf Lowe*	22
R.Shields*	22
D.Howie*	20
George Martin	20

* Denotes guest player

Leading Goalscorers

William Taylor	29
Johnny McIntyre	28
Gordon Hoare	25
Wattie White	24
Fred Morris	24
R.Shields	18
Danny Shea	17
George Martin	16
Jimmy Torrance	15
Neil Harris	14
Harry Hampton	13
R.Gibson	10

1915-16

1	Sep	4	(a)	Watford	W 4-2 Taylor 2, Cannon 2	4,000
2		11	(h)	Millwall A	L 1-2 Taylor	8,000
3		18	(a)	Croydon C	L 2-3 Pearce, Taylor	2,617
4		25	(h)	Arsenal	W 4-3 White 2, Pearce, Sheldon	8,000
5	Oct	2	(a)	Brentford	D 2-2 Taylor, Cannon	2,900
6		9	(h)	West Ham U	W 1-0 Cannon	7,000
7		16	(a)	Tottenham H	L 1-3 Wheatcroft	4,200
8		23	(h)	Crystal P	W 5-0 Taylor 2, White 2, Cannon	5,000
9		30	(a)	Queen's Park R	L 1-2 Taylor	8,000
10	Nov	6	(h)	Chelsea	L 0-3	14,000
11		13	(h)	Watford	W 4-3 Shields 3, Taylor	3,500
12		20	(a)	Millwall A	D 0-0	5,000
13		27	(h)	Croydon C	W 2-0 Allan 2	1,500
14	Dec	4	(a)	Arsenal	L 1-2 Niblo	3,000
15		11	(h)	Brentford	W 4-3 Shields, Slade 2, Taylor	3,000
16		18	(a)	West Ham U	W 3-2 White, Taylor, Shields	3,000
17		25	(h)	Clapton O	W 4-0 White, Taylor 2, Slade	2,500
18		27	(a)	Clapton O	W 3-1 Taylor, Slade, Torrance	4,000
19	Jan	1	(h)	Tottenham H	L 0-2	5,500
20		8	(a)	Crystal P	D 2-2 Cannon, Taylor	8,000
21		15	(h)	Queen's Park R	L 0-1	5,000
22		22	(a)	Chelsea	D 1-1 Shields	25,000

P	W	D	L	F	A	W	D	L	F	A	Pts	Pos	Div	
22	7	0	4	25	17	3	4	4	20	20	24	5th	LC	Appearances
														Goals

23	Feb	5	(h)	Reading	W 6-0 White 2, Smith 2, Taylor 2	4,500
24		12	(a)	Clapton O	W 3-0 Taylor, Shields, Bresname	2,500
25		19	(h)	Tottenham H	W 3-1 Shields 2, Taylor	3,000
26		26	(a)	Millwall A	W 7-1 Taylor, White 3, Shields 2, Smith	3,500
27	Mar	4	(h)	Chelsea	L 0-1	11,500
28		11	(a)	Watford	L 0-2	1,000
29		18	(h)	Clapton O	W 4-0 Nicholl, White 2, Shields	4,500
30		25	(a)	Tottenham H	L 0-4	5,000
31	Apr	1	(h)	Millwall A	W 4-2 Shields, White 3	8,000
32		8	(a)	Chelsea	L 3-6 Shields 2, White	16,000
33		15	(h)	Watford	W 2-0 Taylor 2	4,500
34		21	(a)	Brentford	L 1-2 Walden	5,000
35		24	(h)	Brentford	W 1-0 Shields	4,000
36		29	(a)	Reading	W 4-0 Shields 2, White 2	1,000

P	W	D	L	F	A	W	D	L	F	A	Pts	Pos	Div	
14	6	0	1	20	4	3	0	4	18	15	18	4th	LC(Su)	Appearances
														Goals

Football appearances / line-up grid (shirt numbers by match). Best-effort reading.

#	Reynolds A	Bellamy J	Bullock FE	Tull W	Russell H	White W	Wood A	Cannon G	Pearce H	Taylor W	Torrance J	Sheldon J	Galt J	Grossart AJ	Blackman F	Martin G	Wheatcroft F	Bell M	Coquet E	Maughan W	Walker W	Marshall A	Shields J	Allan P	Niblo T	Nicholl J	Slade D	Bresname CJ	Stapley W	Smith J	Weller LC	Pike	Whitley J	Darrell J	Walden G	Martin J	Urwin T	Lee H
1	1	2	3	4	5	6	7	8	9	10	11																											
2	1	2	3	4	5	6	8	9		10	11	7																										
3	1	2		4	3	10	8		9	10			7	5	6																							
4	1	4	3		6	8			9	10	11	7	5		2																							
5	1		3		6	8		9		10	4	7	5		2	11																						
6	1			6	8	7	11		10	4		5	3	2		9																						
7	1			6	8	11		10	4		5	3	2	9	7																							
8	1			5	8	7	11	9	10	4		6	2			3																						
9	1			8	7		9	10	6	5	3	2								4	11																	
10	1		5	8	7	4	9	10	6		3									11	2																	
11	1		3	6	7		9	10	5											4	11	2	8															
12	1		3	7			10	6	5			11								4		2	9	8														
13	1		5	6	7		10	4		3				2							9	8	11															
14	1		9	10	8			4	5	3				7						2		11	6															
15	1		3	6		7	10	5			2									4	9	11	8															
16	1		6	8	10	4	5	3	2										7		9	11																
17	1		3	8	10	5			2											11	4			6	9	7												
18	1		2	6	8	10	5													11	3			4	9	7												
19	1	4	3	6	10	5		2												11				8	7													
20	1		3	6	11	10	5		2											4	9			8	7													
21	1		6	10	5		2													4	11	9		7	8	3												
22	1		3	8	10	4	5	6	2											11	9			7														
Apps	22	4	4	4	19	22	12	9	7	21	21	4	10	10	13	2	2	3	1	5	8	8	9	2	5	3	6	5	1									
Goals		6			6	2	14	1	1				1							6	2	1				4												

#	Reynolds A	Bellamy J	Bullock FE	Tull W	Russell H	White W	Wood A	Cannon G	Pearce H	Taylor W	Torrance J	Sheldon J	Galt J	Grossart AJ	Blackman F	Martin G	Wheatcroft F	Bell M	Coquet E	Maughan W	Walker W	Marshall A	Shields J	Allan P	Niblo T	Nicholl J	Slade D	Bresname CJ	Stapley W	Smith J	Weller LC	Pike	Whitley J	Darrell J	Walden G	Martin J	Urwin T	Lee H
1	1			3	8			10	11				5	6	2					4									7		9							
2	1			5	8			10	4				6	3												9			7	11	2							
3	1			6	8			10	4	5				2												9			7	11	3							
4	1				8			10	4		5	6	2													9			7	11	3							
5	1			3	8			10	4		5	6	2													9			7	11								
6	1			4				11	5	6	2															9		8	7			3	10					
7				6	8			4	5		2						11				9			10			7			3		1						
8	1				8			10	4	5	6	2								9	11					7			3									
9	1				8			10	4		2						11			9			6			7	5											
10	1			5	10			8	6		3						7			9		4										2	11					
11	1			5	8			10	4		2						11			9			7									3		6				
12	1				8	10			4		2				3					5		6											7		11	9		
13	1				10	8			4		2				3				5	9														6	11	7		
14	1			5	8			4			2									9						10	3						7	6	11			
Apps	13			10	13	2		9	14		7	6	14		2				1	4	13	1		4	1	10	1	6	7	1	1	2	3	3	3	2		
Goals				14				7					12							1	1					3												

391

1916-17

1	Sep	2	(h)	Reading	W 9-0	Hoare 5, G.Martin, Mordue, White 2	3,000
2		9	(a)	Millwall A	L 2-3	Hoare, G.Martin	6,000
3		16	(h)	Watford	W 7-0	Hoare 3, Gordon, White, Galt 2	4,000
4		23	(a)	Clapton O	W 3-0	Galt, White, G.Martin	4,000
5		30	(a)	Southampton	L 3-4	Taylor, Torrance 2	4,000
6	Oct	7	(h)	Queen's Park R	W 2-0	Taylor, Hoare	5,000
7		14	(a)	West Ham U	L 0-2		10,000
8		21	(h)	Tottenham H	W 2-1	Gibson, Hoare	4,000
9		28	(a)	Crystal P	L 0-1		1,200
10	Nov	4	(h)	Brentford	W 2-0	Taylor, Hoare	4,000
11		11	(a)	Chelsea	L 0-4		15,000
12		18	(h)	Arsenal	W 2-0	Hoare, G.Martin	1,500
13		25	(a)	Portsmouth	W 4-3	Bateman, Gibson 3	4,000
14	Dec	2	(h)	Millwall A	L 0-1		4,000
15		9	(a)	Watford	W 8-2	G.Martin 3, Gibson, Taylor 2, Mordue 2	2,000
16		23	(h)	Southampton	W 8-1	Hampton 3, Tufnell 3, Mordue 2	2,000
17		25	(a)	Luton T	L 0-1		4,000
18		26	(h)	Luton T	W 5-1	Hampton 3, Gordon 2	5,000
19		30	(a)	Queen's Park R	W 7-1	Hoare, Handley, Gordon, G.Martin 2, Watson, Gibson	3,000
20	Jan	6	(h)	West Ham U	L 0-2		8,000
21		13	(a)	Tottenham H*	L 0-1		4,000
22		20	(h)	Crystal P	W 4-3	Hoare 2, G.Martin, Tufnell	1,500
23		27	(a)	Brentford	D 1-1	Cannon	2,000
24	Feb	3	(h)	Chelsea	W 2-0	Hoare, Gordon	6,000
25		10	(a)	Arsenal	L 2-3	G.Martin, McIntyre	4,800
26		17	(h)	Luton T	W 4-2	Hoare 3, Tufnell	4,000
27		24	(a)	Brentford	W 4-1	McIntyre, Hoare 3	2,000
28	Mar	3	(h)	Queen's Park R	D 0-0		3,000
29		10	(a)	Chelsea	L 1-3	Torrance	5,000
30		17	(h)	Southampton	W 3-1	Tufnell, G.Martin 2	4,000
31		24	(h)	Watford	W 7-2	Gibson 2, J.Martin 3, Hutchins, A Smith	4,000
32		31	(a)	Luton T	W 3-2	G.Martin 2, Gibson	1,500
33	Apr	6	(h)	Millwall A	D 1-1	Smith	10,000
34		7	(h)	Brentford	L 0-2		5,000
35		9	(a)	Millwall A	L 0-2		6,000
36		10	(h)	Clapton O	W 2-1	Black, Holley	3,000
37		14	(a)	Queen's Park R	L 0-2		1,500
38		18	(a)	Watford	L 2-4	Platts, Penn	1,000
39		21	(h)	Chelsea	L 0-4		8,000
40		28	(a)	Southampton	W 2-1	Gibson, Brown	3,000

P	W	D	L	F	A	W	D	L	F	A	Pts	Pos	Div	
40	14	2	4	60	22	7	1	12	42	41	45	6th	LC	Appearances
														Goals

*Played at Homerton

Sams SM	Houghton J	Russell H	Gordon JE	Galt J	Martin J	Mordue J	White W	Hoare G	Martin G	Walker B	Torrance J	Blackman F	Bresname CJ	Reynolds A	McMaster J	Taylor W	Grossart AJ	Wood A	Gibson R	Taylor E	Handley A	Low W	Cannon G	Watson W	Holley G	Hampton H	Tufnell H	Fox GH	McIntyre J	Smith W	Catterson	Orr R	Jefferson RW	Dorrington J	Hutchins	Robinson	Wilson W	Smith A	
1	2	3	4	5	6	7	8	9	10	11																													1
1	3	2	6	5		11	10	9	8	7	4																												2
1	3		4	5	6		8	9	10		11	2	7																										3
	3		4	5	6		8	9	10		11	2	7	1																									4
	3		6	5		7	8			9	2		1	4	10																								5
1			4		5	7	6	9		11		2			10	3	8																						6
	3		4	5	6	7		9		11	10	4	2	7	1																							7
	3	4	5	6	7		9		11	10	2		1			8																						8
1	3		4	5	6	7	10	9		11	2			8																								9
1	3		5		7		9		11	4	2		6	10		8																						10
	3		5		7	8	9		11	6	2		4		10	1																						11
	3			7		9	10		5	2		6		8	1	11																						12
1	3			9		4	2		6		8		5																									13
	3	4		5		7	10		6	2		9		1		11																						14
1	3		11		10	6	2		7	8		9		5	4																							15
1	3		7		5	2		6		8				9	10	11																						16
1	3		7		5		11		8				6	10	9																							17
1	3	4	7		5		8		6	10	9	11																										18
1	3	4		5	9	8	2		7	11		6		10																								19
	3	4	8		5	2	10		9	1	11	6																										20
1	3	4	8		7	2	11		9	5		6		10																								21
1	3	4	8	10	5	2	11		7		6	9																										22
	3	4	8		5	2	6		7		9	11	10																									23
1	3	4	9		8	10	2		7	11	5	6																										24
	3		8	9	4	2	6		1	7		11	10																									25
		8	5	2	6	11		10	9	1	3	4	7																									26
		8	4	2	6	3	7	1	11	10	9	5																										27
		5	8	4	2	6	9	11	10	1	3	7																										28
	6	10	8	3	4	11	5	7	9	2	1																											29
	8	11	5	2	6	4	7	10	9	3	1																											30
	11	5	2	6	8	10	1	3	4	9																												31
	9	5	2	6	8	10	3	4	1	7																												32
	8	4	3	6	9	5	10	2	1	7																												33
	4	2	6	7	5	8	10	3	1	11																												34
	8	5	2	6	3	7	9	10	11																													35
	6	3	7	8	5	11																																36
	2	11	8	6	4	1	3	7																														37
	2	5	8	3	11																																	38
	2	6	8	11	10	1	9																														9	39
	2	3	9	5	6	1	8																														8	40
15	19	10	15	12	8	14	11	23	13	8	32	35	3	4	21	6	10	2	26	6	7	8	5	9	7	3	13	6	11	5	2	10	2	2	4	6	3		
			5	3	3	5	4	23	15		3				5				10		1			1	1	1	6	6		2					1			2	

Alf Marshall played number 5 in Match 11; James Nicholl played number 7 in Match 9; Green played number 4 in Match 12; Bateman played number 7 in Match 13 and scored once; Shaw played number 10 in Match 13; Joe Dix played number 11 in Match 13; Noble played number 8 in Match 14; Kennedy played number 4 in Matches 16 & 17; Ted Charlton played number 2 in Matches 17 & 18; Flavers played number 7 in Match 20; A.M.Ross played number 1 in Matches 23 & 28; G.Wilding played number 5 in Match 25; F.Johnson played number 7 in Match 31 and number 4 in Match 39; Quinn played number 11 in Match 32; Agarth played number 11 in Match 33; Humphries played number 4 in Match 36; Black played number 9 in Match 36 and scored once; Gibbs played number 5 in Match 37; W.Jackson played number 6 in Match 38; D.Greenaway played number 7 in Matches 38, 39 & 40; A.Brown played number 3 in Match 39 and number 11 in Match 40 and scored once; D.Howie played number 5 in Match 39; Jock Rutherford played number 4 in Match 40; F.W.Thompson played number 9 in Match 34, number 4 in Matches 35 & 38 and number 2 in Match 36; Pitt played number 1 in Matches 35 & 36; Frank Penn played number 10 in Matches 36, 37, 38 & 40 and scored once; H.Platts played number 9 in Matches 37 & 38 and scored once.

1917-18

1	Sep	1	(a)	West Ham U	L	1-6	Morris	8,000
2		8	(h)	Crystal P	W	7-1	Simms 3, Morris 3, Low	4,500
3		15	(h)	Queen's Park R	W	2-1	Edwards 2	4,000
4		22	(a)	Clapton O	W	5-1	Howie 2, Morris 3	2,000
5		29	(h)	Millwall A	W	3-1	Russell, Torrance, Greenaway	5,000
6	Oct	6	(a)	Tottenham H*	L	0-1		7,000
7		13	(h)	Chelsea	D	1-1	Morris	8,000
8		20	(a)	Brentford	W	3-1	Morris 2, Cumming	4,000
9		27	(h)	West Ham U	D	1-1	Howie	8,000
10	Nov	3	(a)	Crystal P	L	1-2	McIntyre	1,200
11		10	(a)	Queen's Park R	W	3-2	Morris 2, Cummings	3,000
12		17	(h)	Clapton O	W	3-0	Morris 3	3,000
13		24	(a)	Millwall A	L	1-2	Morris	4,500
14	Dec	1	(h)	Tottenham H	W	4-3	Morris 3, McIntyre	6,000
15		8	(a)	Chelsea	D	2-2	Morris, Hoare	10,000
16		15	(h)	Brentford	W	2-0	Morris, Howie	4,000
17		22	(a)	West Ham U	W	3-0	McIntyre 2, Cumming	8,000
18		25	(h)	Arsenal	D	1-1	Torrance	7,000
19		26	(a)	Arsenal	D	1-1	Morris	7,000
20		29	(h)	Crystal P	D	1-1	Torrance	3,000
21	Jan	5	(h)	Queen's Park R	W	1-0	Penn	5,000
22		12	(a)	Clapton O	D	1-1	Howie	1,500
23		19	(h)	Millwall A	W	4-2	Morris 2, Torrance 2	5,000
24		26	(a)	Tottenham H	W	1-0	Shea	14,000
25	Feb	2	(h)	Chelsea	L	0-2		6,000
26		9	(a)	Arsenal	W	3-0	McIntyre 2, Cannon	8,000
27		16	(h)	West Ham U	W	3-1	Shea 2, Mavin	8,000
28		23	(a)	Crystal P	L	2-5	McIntyre 2	3,000
29	Mar	2	(a)	Queen's Park R	W	1-0	Crockford	3,500
30		9	(h)	Clapton O	W	3-2	Taylor 2, Gordon	4,000
31		16	(a)	Millwall A	W	2-0	Elliott 2	5,000
32		23	(h)	Tottenham H	L	0-3		12,000
33		29	(a)	Brentford	W	3-2	Torrance 2, Shea	6,000
34		30	(a)	Chelsea	L	0-7		7,000
35	Apr	1	(h)	Brentford	L	4-6	Shea 3, Bassett	4,000
36		6	(h)	Arsenal	W	2-1	McIntyre, Shea	2,000

P	W	D	L	F	A	W	D	L	F	A	Pts	Pos	Div		
36	11	4	3	42	27	9	3	6	33	33	47	3rd	LC	Appearances	
														Goals	

*Played at Highbury

Football club season appearance grid (shirt numbers worn by each player per match). Match numbers appear at both the far left (implied) and far right of each row.

Match	Bailey W	Blackman F	Grimsdell EF	Hall W	Torrance J	Brown	Late JA	Edwards MW	Morris F	Taylor W	McIntyre J	Drabble F	Russell H	Low W	Simms E	Handley AM	Howie D	Greenaway D	Penn F	Mavin F	Cumming J	Wigmore	Elliott G	Harding	Green	Bradley	Carr J	Reynolds A	Smythe J	Burke J	Brandham J	Hoare G	Holley G	Smith W	Crockford H	Shea D	Martin G	Nicholl J	McMasters J	#
1	1	2	3	4	5	6	7	8	9	10	11																													1
2		2	3		7			8	10		6	1	4	5	9	11																								2
3		2	3	11				8	10		6	1	4		9		5		7																					3
4		2	3	4	5			8	9		6	1					10		7	11																				4
5		2	3		5			8	9		6	1	4				10		7	11																				5
6		2	3		5			8	9		6	1	4						11	10																				6
7		2	3		5				9		8	1	4				10		11	7	6																			7
8		2	3	4					10		8	1		6			5		11	7	9																			8
9		2	3	4	5				9		8	1					10		11	7	6																			9
10		2	3	4	5				9		8	1					10				6	11	7																	10
11		2	3	6	4				9		10	1					8				5	11		7																11
12			3						9		8						2		11		5	10			1	4	7	6												12
13		2	3	4					9		8	1					10		11	7	5												6							13
14		2	3	4					9		8	1					10		11	7	5												6							14
15		2	3	4					9		8	1							11	7	5												6	10						15
16		2	3	4					9		8	1					10		11	7	5												6							16
17		2	3	4					9		8	1					10		11	7	5												6							17
18		2	3	6					9		8	1		5			4		11										7						10					18
19		2	3	6					9		8	1		5			4		11										7						10					19
20		2	3	4	6				9		8			5					11										7						10	1				20
21		2	3	4					9		6	1					10		11	5	7														8					21
22		2	3	7	4				9		6	1					10		11	5															8					22
23			3	4	10				9		6								11	5														1	8					23
24		2	3	4	9						6	1							11	5															8		10	7		24
25		2	3		9						6	1					10		11	5															8			7	4	25
26		2	3		7						6	1							11	5															8		10		4	26
27			3		10						6	1							11	5															8	9		7	4	27
28		2	3		10				9		6	1							11	5															8			7	4	28
29		2	3	4					9			1							11	5															8		10	7	6	29
30			3		10						6	1							11	5															8			7	4	30
31		2	3	4							6	1							11	5										9					8		10			31
32		2		4	10							1							11	5										9					8				6	32
33			3		10				9		6								11	5														1	8					33
34			3						9								4			7	5													1	10					34
35		2	3						9		6	1									5														8					35
36		2							9		6	1							11		5														8					36
App	1	29	34	12	33	1	1	6	23	2	36	30	6	5	2	1	19	3	33	23	13	2	2	1	1	1	1	1	3	6	2	3	4	5	15	1	6	7		
Gls		7	2	24	2	9			1	1	3			4	1	1	1		3	2										2				1	8						

George Cannon played number 9 in Match 26 and scored once; D.Johnson played number 2 in Match 27; Jimmy Gordon played number 9 in Match 30 and scored once; E.J.Bassett played number 7 in Match 31, 32, 33, 35 and 36 and number 11 in Match 34 and scored once in Match 35; J.Dodds played number 3 in Match 32, number 2 in Match 33 and 34; Mark Bell played number 4 in Match 33; Arthur Wood played number 8 in Match 34 and number 10 in Match 35 and 36; J.Bethune played number 3 in Match 36; T.Smith played number 7 in Match 6; E.Symes played number 6 in Match 34 and number 4 in Match 35 and 36.

1918-19

1	Sep	7	(h)	Tottenham H	D	2-2	Bassett, Torrance	9,000
2		14	(a)	Chelsea	L	2-4	Mavin, Hampton	8,000
3		21	(h)	Arsenal	L	1-2	Shea	8,000
4		28	(a)	Crystal P	L	0-1		6,000
5	Oct	5	(h)	Queen's Park R	D	3-3	Shea, Bassett, Torrance	4,000
6		12	(a)	Millwall A	W	1-0	White	4,000
7		19	(a)	Clapton O	W	4-1	McIntyre 3, Shea	2,000
8		26	(h)	West Ham U	D	2-2	Shea, Penn	4,000
9	Nov	2	(a)	Tottenham H	L	0-1		6,000
10		9	(h)	Chelsea	L	1-2	McIntyre	10,000
11		16	(a)	Arsenal	W	3-1	Hampton 2, Shea	5,000
12		23	(h)	Crystal P	W	5-1	Higginbottom, McIntyre, Shea, Hampton 2	7,000
13		30	(a)	Queen's Park R	W	3-0	McIntyre 2, Hampton	6,000
14	Dec	7	(h)	Millwall A	L	0-1		7,000
15		14	(h)	Clapton O	W	5-1	Shea 3, Harris 2	3,000
16		21	(a)	West Ham U	L	1-2	Harris	10,000
17		25	(a)	Brentford	L	1-2	Wood	10,000
18		26	(h)	Brentford	L	1-4	McIntyre	20,000
19		28	(h)	Tottenham H	W	3-1	McIntyre, Elliott, Penn	7,000
20	Jan	4	(a)	Chelsea	L	0-3		25,000
21		11	(h)	Arsenal	W	3-1	Hampton, McIntyre, Martin	10,000
22		18	(a)	Crystal P	W	4-1	Bassett, McIntyre 2, Pearce	6,000
23		25	(h)	Queen's Park R	W	1-0	McIntyre	12,000
24	Feb	1	(a)	Millwall A	D	1-1	Harris	10,000
25		8	(a)	Clapton O	W	4-0	Harris, Bassett, Tee 2	5,000
26		15	(h)	Brentford	W	3-2	Harris 2, Bassett	25,000
27		22	(a)	Tottenham H	W	2-0	McIntyre, Harris	6,000
28	Mar	1	(h)	Chelsea	W	6-2	Torrance, McIntyre, Harris 3, opp own goal	26,000
29		8	(a)	Arsenal	L	0-5		22,000
30		15	(h)	Crystal P	D	1-1	Torrance	15,000
31		22	(a)	Queen's Park R	W	1-0	Harris	11,000
32		29	(h)	Millwall A	W	2-0	McIntyre, Taylor	15,000
33	Apr	5	(h)	Clapton O	W	2-0	Farnfield, Harris	12,000
34		12	(a)	Brentford	L	0-5		15,000
35		18	(h)	West Ham U	D	1-1	Walker	20,000
36		21	(a)	West Ham U	L	1-2	Harris	15,000

P	W	D	L	F	A	W	D	L	F	A	Pts	Pos	Div		Appearances
36	9	5	4	42	26	8	1	9	28	29	40	4th	LC		Goals

Victory Cup

37	Mar	24	(h)	Munitions Lgue	W	3-0	Penn, Torrance 2	3,000
38		31	(a)	Arsenal	W	4-1	McIntyre, Elliott 2, Whittingham	22,000
39	Apr	19	(a)	Tottenham H	W	2-0	Whittingham 2	45,000
40		26	(n)	Chelsea	L	0-3		36,000

Match 40 (Final, Victory Cup) played at Highbury

Appearances
Goals

Fulham team which met Brentford on 12 April 1919. From left: Unknown, Penn, Morris, Harris, Gibson, Wallace, McIntyre, Mavin, Russell, Charlton, Grimsdell, Nixon, Phil Kelso (manager), unknown.

Player appearance and position grid (shirt number played by each player per match). Columns are players; rows are match numbers (shown at both left and right).

Match	Smith W	Blackman F	Blackman S	Bratley P	Low W	McIntyre J	Bassett EJ	Shea D	Cannon G	Torrance J	Penn F	Molyneux J	Mavin F	Hampton H	Wood A	Coquet E	Russell H	Marshall A	Hall W	Crockford H	Higginbottom H	Fender P	White W	Hatfield	Symes E	Kelso P	Wilson S	Simms	Reynolds A	Hogg A	Orr R	Harris N	McNeal R	Elliott G	McCracken B	Brown A	Martin G	Langtry A	Pearce B	Match
1	1	2	3	4	5	6	7	8	9	10	11																													1
2		2	3	6		4		10	8	7	1	5	9	11																										2
3	1		3			6	7	8		10	11	5	9			2	4																							3
4		2				6	7	8		10	11	1	5					3	4	9																				4
5	1	2	3	4	5	6	7	8		10	11										9																			5
6		2				6	7	8			11	5	9												1	10														6
7		2	3	4				10	7	8	6	11	5	9								1																		7
8		2	3					10	7	8	6	11	5	9								1	4																	8
9		2	3					10	7		6	11	5									1			4	8	9													9
10		2	3	4	5			10		8	6	11		9									7				1													10
11		2						10		8	6	11		5	9	7		4							3				1											11
12		2	3	4	5			10		8	6	11		9									7				1													12
13		2	3		5			10		8	6	11		9									4				1													13
14	1	2		4				10	7	8	6	11	5													9			3											14
15		2						10	7	8	6	11	1	5											4				3	9										15
16		2	3		5			10	7	8	6	11																	1	9	4									16
17			2		5			10	7		4	11			8												9		1	3		6								17
18		2			5			10	7		6	11			8										4		9		1	3										18
19		2		3	8	7				6	11	5								10					4				1			9								19
20	1	2				7				4	11	5																				6	8	3	9	10				20
21	1	2				8	7				11	5	9				4												3			6				10				21
22	1					8	7				5	11					4			10									3			6					2	9		22
23	1	2				8	7				5						3															9	6				10			23
24	1	2					7				5	11					3															9	6				10		8	24
25	1	2				10	7				5	11					3															8	6							25
26	1	2				8	7				5	11					3			10												9	6							26
27	1	2				8	7				5	11					3															9	6							27
28	1	2				8	7				5	11					3															9	6							28
29	1	2				8	7				5	11					3								4							9	6							29
30	1	2				10	7				5	11					3															9	6						8	30
31		2				8	7	10	5	11							4														1	9	6							31
32	1	2				8				10	11	5		7		4																	6							32
33						8				5	11					2																	9							33
34						6				11	5					4																	9							34
35	1	2														10		5															9							35
36	1					10										7	6	5															9							36
Totals	18	31	11	9	9	33	25	16	2	32	32	3	15	10	7	1	16	4	1	4	4	2	1	2	6	1	2	4	3	6	6	15	15	2	1	1	4	1	3	
Goals						16	5	9		4	2		1	7	1						1		1									14		1			1		1	

Match	Smith W	Blackman F	Blackman S	Bratley P	Low W	McIntyre J	Bassett EJ	Shea D	Cannon G	Torrance J	Penn F	Molyneux J	Mavin F	Hampton H	Wood A	Coquet E	Russell H	Marshall A	Hall W	Crockford H	Higginbottom H	Fender P	White W	Hatfield	Symes E	Kelso P	Wilson S	Simms	Reynolds A	Hogg A	Orr R	Harris N	McNeal R	Elliott G	McCracken B	Brown A	Martin G	Langtry A	Pearce B	Match
37						8					11	5				2																9						9		37
38	1	2				10					5	11				3																				6	9			38
39	1	2				10						11		9		5																7	6							39
40	1	2				10					5	11				4																7	6	9						40
Totals	3	3				3					3	4	1	1	4																	3	3	2						
	1					2	1																									2								

W.Jennings played number 4 in Matches 23, 24, 25, 26, 27, 28 & 30; Willie Walker played number 11 in Matches 23, 35 & 36; Jack Tee played number 9 in Match 25 and scored twice; William Taylor played number 10 in Matches 27, 28 & 29 and number 9 in Match 32 and scored once; E.F.Grimsdell played number 2 in Matches 34 & 36 and number 3 in Matches 32, 33 & 37; Wilf Nixon played number 1 in Matches 33 & 34; Harry Bagge played number 4 in Matches 33, 35, 36 & 39 and number 6 in Match 37; A.J.Grossart played number 3 in Match 31 and number 6 in Matches 33 & 35; R.Gibson played number 7 in Matches 33, 34 & 37; Eric Farnfield played number 10 in Match 33; Ted Charlton played number 3 in Matches 34, 35, 36, 39 & 40; Charlie Wallace played number 8 in Matches 34, 35 & 36; Fred Morris played number 10 in Match 34; Jones played number 7 in Match 35; George Hunter played number 4 in Match 38; Jack Carr played number 7 in Match 38 and number 8 in Match 40; Robert Whittingham played number 8 in Matches 38 & 39 and scored three goals; Wood played number 1 in Match 37; Pitts played number 4 in Match 37; Lynes played number 10 in Match 37.

Walker, the Portsmouth goalkeeper, fists the ball over the bar as Fulham's Ronnie Rooke storms in during the first League South 'B' match in October 1939. Right: The programme for that match.

The War Years — 1939-1946

WHEN the 1939-40 season kicked off, few people expected it to be completed. It was an unreal atmosphere, polluted by the ever-darkening war clouds. On Saturday, 2 September 1939, Fulham entertained Luton in a Second Division match, and the kick-off was delayed until 6pm at the request of the authorities. When Ronnie Rooke scored Fulham's equaliser, it proved to be the last goal scored in the League before war was declared the following day. On the Cottagers' left-wing for that match was Ernie Shepherd, who was making his League debut. With the abandonment of the League programme, he had to wait seven years to play in his first 'official' League game.

There was a total blackout of civilian football when war broke out, in marked contrast to the response to World War One. This lasted only a few days and contingency plans for regional competitions were implemented, with limitations placed on the size of crowds. By 21 October 1939, the League's regional competitions were ready to start playing: Fulham began in League South 'B' in 1939-40, finishing fifth out of ten clubs. This was one of ten regional Leagues which, by the following season, were converted into just two, a Northern and Southern section. With League placings based on goal-average (because clubs were not able to fulfill the same number of fixtures), Fulham's average of 0.849 (62 for, 73 against from 30 games) earned 23rd place out of 34.

In 1941-2, Fulham participated in the breakaway London League and managed 24 points from 30 games, good enough for 11th position amongst 16 clubs. For the remainder of the war, Fulham competed in the Southern section of the League, along with 17 other clubs, finishing 14th, 9th and 11th respectively. In 1945-6, a 42-game season was restored, and in the Football League South, Fulham managed their best performance, eighth place.

The Cup competitions were marginally more rewarding. In 1939-40, the Cottagers got to the semi-final of the League Cup, only to lose 4-3 to West Ham, the eventual winners. In the London Cup of 1941-2, Fulham failed to qualify for the semi-finals from their group only on goal-average. These were the best achievements the club could manage during the whole of the 1939-46 period.

Like virtually every other club, Fulham were dependent on the guest system: in some matches, the entire team comprised players officially registered with other clubs. There were, however, some Fulham players whose best years were in this period and whose only international recognition came in wartime fixtures. Ronnie Rooke, who dominated the scoring with an amazing 212 goals in 199 appearances, played for England against Wales in October 1942. The stylish Joe Bacuzzi was Fulham's most capped wartime player, whilst Eddie Perry and Vivian Woodward each played once for Wales.

Many Fulham players saw active service, and four lost their lives. Ernie Tuckett and George Fairbairn were killed in action: both were on the books in 1939, although neither was in the first-team squad. Dennis Higgins was the established right winger when war broke out, and was killed in North Africa in 1942, as was one of his predecessors, Jimmy Temple, who left Fulham in 1931. Perhaps the most tragic story concerns Jimmy Tompkins, Fulham's outstanding left-half of the late 1930s. When war started, he was a private in the Territorial Army, but by 1944, had been promoted to major. He was killed in Normandy in June 1944, in the D-Day landing. Weeks later his wife was killed by a flying bomb in London. In the late 1950s, their son Neil, who was briefly on Fulham's books, died during his National Service in Germany.

World War Two Summary
Leading Appearances
(Excludes League Cup 1940-41 and FA Cup 1945-6)

Ronnie Rooke	199
Len Jones*	121
Harry Freeman	111
Joe Bacuzzi	104
Harry Duke*	101
Ernest Hiles	101
James Evans	90
Viv Woodward	90
Jim Taylor	88
Joe Conley*	85
Jack Finch	79
Jack Watson*	55
Jim McCormick	51
John Arnold	46
Mike Keeping	46
David Thomas*	44
Jim Tompkins	43
Tom Holley*	41
Ernie Shepherd	38
Pat Gallacher*	34
Taffy O'Callaghan	33
Sam Malpass	32
G.C.Dean*	31
Charles Leyfield*	31
Ernie Muttit*	30
Horace Rickett*	25
Dennis Rampling	24
Pat Beasley*	23
Frank Boulton*	23
George Matthewson*	22
R.M.Cowan*	22
Anthony Lowes*	21

* Denotes guest player

Leading Goalscorers

Ronnie Rooke	212
Joe Conley	43
Viv Woodward	41
David Thomas	21
John Arnold	16
Tom Kiernan*	16
C.G.Dean	15
Pat Gallacher	14
Jack Stamps*	14
Jim McCormick	12
Jock Dodds*	11
Jack Finch	11
Harry Potts*	11
Peter Buchanan*	9
Charles Leyfield	9
Len Jones	9
Pat Beasley	6
Harry Freeman	6
Anthony Lowes	6
Wally Sloan*	6
Jim Taylor	6
Taffy O'Callaghan	5
Chaplie Revell	5
Dennis Rampling	5
Eddie Perry	5

* Denotes guest players

Derby County forward Jack Stamps (right), guested for several clubs including Fulham, Southampton and Aldershot. Stamps, who netted 14 wartime goals for the Cottagers, was to win fame as the man who scored twice in the first post-war FA Cup Final in 1946, when Derby beat Charlton 4-1 after extra-time.

Fulham Guest Players 1939-46

Sam Abel (Queen's Park Rangers), Jimmy Allen (Aston Villa), Cliff Bastin (Arsenal), Pat Beasley (Huddersfield), R.J.E.Birkett, J.Blair (Morton), Albert Borass (Chesterfield), J.E.Burrows (Mansfield), Leslie Boulter (Brentford), Frank Boulton (Derby County), G.H.Bremner (Arsenal), F.Briggs (Wrexham), James Brisco (Hearts), J.Broadhurst, Alan Brown (Huddersfield), J.Brown (Hibernian), William Buchan (Blackpool), Peter Buchanan (Chelsea), K.Buckham, Vic Buckingham (Tottenham Hotspur), Ambrose Buckley (Doncaster), Harry Burgess (Chelsea), Tom Bush (Liverpool), Louis Cardwell (Blackpool), Tommy Cheetham (Brentford), Arthur Chesters (Crystal Palace), Jack Chisholm (Tottenham Hotspur), Wilf Chitty (Reading), William Cobley (Aston Villa), Ernest Collett (Arsenal), Leslie Compton (Arsenal), Joe Conley (Torquay), Wilfred Copping (Leeds United), Harold Cothliff (Torquay), R.M.Conan (Rangers), Albert Cox (Sheffield United), Freddie Cox (Tottenham Hotspur), Stan Cullis (Wolves), Arthur Cunliffe (Hull), Horace Cumner (Arsenal), Albert Dawes (Crystal Palace), Fred Dawes (Crystal Palace), C.G.Dean (Southampton), John Devlin (Hibernian), Ephraim 'Jock' Dodds (Blackpool), Ted Drake (Arsenal), Allenby Driver (Sheffield Wednesday), Edward Duggan (Luton Town), George Duke (Luton Town), Harry Duke (Norwich), Alex Farmer (Queen's Park Rangers), Harry Ferrier (Barnsley), Len Flack (Norwich), Fred Ford (Millwall), Joseph Foxall (West Ham United), C.Fuller, Pat Gallacher (Bournemouth), W.G.Gibson (East Fife), Albert Gibbon (Tottenham Hotspur), George Green (Charlton), J.Griffiths, W.M.Griffiths, J.A.Grundy, Reg Halton (Bury), Dave Hamilton (Newcastle), William Hamilton (Preston North End), Les Henley (Arsenal), A.H.Hickman (Aston Villa), Frank Hindle (Blackburn Rovers), Harold Hobbis (Charlton), S.G.Hobbus, Tom Holley (Leeds United), John Holliday (Brentford), Harry Hollis (Charlton), Idris Hopkins (Brentford), James Horton (Aldershot), Leslie Howe (Tottenham Hotspur), Arthur Hudgell (Crystal Palace), William Hughes (Birmingham), D.R.Humphries, John Humphries (Everton), Douglas Hunt (Brentford), Doug Jarvis (Leytonstone), Joseph James (Brentford), William Jessop (Preston North End), Joe Jopling (Charlton), Charles Jones (Southend), Eric Jones (West Bromwich Albion), F.Jones (Ipswich), George Jones (Sheffield United), Len Jones (Plymouth Argyle), Stan Jones (Blackpool), J.Jordan (Queen's Park Rangers), Phil Joslin (Torquay), W.Kay, Lawrence Kelly (Aldershot), Tom Kiernan (Albion Rovers), Norman Kirkman (Burnley), David Kinnear (Rangers), Peter Kippax (Burnley), Fred Kurz (Grimsby), Fred Laing (Luton Town), F.C.Lester (Sheffield Wednesday), Charles Leyfield (Doncaster), Archie Livingstone (Bury), Adam Little (Rangers), Cliff Lloyd (Wrexham), Lodge, Anthony Lowes (Sheffield Wednesday), George Ludford (Tottenham Hotspur), Walter Lumby (Stockport), George Lunn (Aston Villa), A.H.Machin, Mackie, H.McClusky (Celtic), Jimmy McCormick (Tottenham Hotspur), O.McCullough, J.McDermott, James McInnes (Liverpool), Joe Mallett (Queen's Park Rangers), Tommy Manley (Brentford), D.K.Martin (Notts County), Bill Mason (Queen's Park Rangers), George Matthewson (Bury), Fred Marsdale (Bournemouth), D.Mangnall, John Meadows (Burnley), Joe Millbank (Crystal Palace), G.Mills (Chelsea), Milsom, Ken Moody (Grimsby Town), Norman Moore (Grimsby Town), Morgan, James Morris (Stockport), M.R.Muir (Rochdale), A.Muir (Albion Rovers), Ernie Muttitt (Brentford), Bill Nicholson (Tottenham Hotspur), Frank O'Donnell (Aston Villa), Oswald Parry (Crystal Palace), J.Osborne (Romford), Sid Ottewell (Chesterfield), R.W.Palmer, George Poland (Liverpool), Harry Phipps (Charlton), Harry Potts (Burnley), J.Poulter, Robert Pryde (Blackburn Rovers), Edwin Reay (Queen's Park Rangers), Robert Redfern (Bournemouth), Charles Revell (Charlton), Horace Rickett (Chelmsford), James Richardson (Millwall), George Robinson, Albert Robson (Crystal Palace), R.Rodger, Robert Royston (Plymouth), Len Salmon (Burnley), James Ganders (Charlton), Fred Sargent (Tottenham Hotspur), Reg Savage (Nottingham Forest), G.Scaife, D.R.Sears, George Skinner (Tottenham Hotspur), Sharp (Partick Thistle), Albert Sibley (Southend), Joshua Sloan (Tranmere), C.Smith, Edward Smith (Millwall), J.Smith (Burnley), Leslie Smith (Brentford), Trevor Smith (Crystal Palace), Richard Spence (Chelsea), W.Sperrin, Alan Squires (Preston North End), Jack Stamps (Derby County), Fred Steele (Stoke City), Frank Swift (Manchester City), Bill Sneddon (Brentford), F.Taylor, Albert Tennent (Chelsea), J.R.Thomson (Everton), David Thomas (Plymouth), Bob Thomas (Brentford), Ernie Toser (Millwall), G.Trewick, G.Tunnicliffe (Derby Amateurs), James Wallbanks (Millwall), Ralph Ward (Tottenham Hotspur), George Wardle (Exeter), J.Watson (Brentford), Jack Watson (Bury), Sam Weaver (Chelsea), J.W.Whatley, W.Whitfield, W.Whittacker (Brentford), George Wilkins (Brentford), Jimmy Wilson (Chelsea), Ray White (Tottenham Hotspur), G.T.Wilshaw (Port Vale), Billy Wright (Wolves), Albert Young (Arsenal).

401

1939-40

1	Oct	21	(h)	Portsmouth	W	2-1	Rooke 2	6,468
2		28	(a)	Queen's Park R	D	2-2	Rooke 2	5,000
3	Nov	4	(h)	Aldershot	W	3-1	Fisher 2, Finch	5,000
4		11	(a)	Bournemouth	L	1-2	Arnold	3,000
5		18	(h)	Chelsea	L	1-3	Perry	8,000
6		25	(a)	Southampton	L	2-5	Arnold, Woodward	4,000
7	Dec	2	(h)	Brighton & HA	W	7-4	Perry 4, Burgess, Tompkins, Woodward	5,000
8		9	(a)	Reading	L	1-6	Muttitt	3,000
9		16	(h)	Brentford	L	2-4	Woodward, Burgess	5,000
10		23	(a)	Portsmouth	L	1-3	Mills	1,964
11		25	(h)	Queen's Park R	L	3-8	Mills, Woodward, D.S.Thomas	6,006
12		26	(a)	Aldershot	D	3-3	Arnold 2, D.S.Thomas	3,000
13		30	(h)	Bournemouth	W	5-2	Taylor, D.W.J.Thomas, Woodward 2, Wilkins	3,000
14	Jan	6	(a)	Chelsea	D	1-1	Rooke	6,240
15		13	(h)	Southampton	W	4-1	Arnold, Rooke 2, Woodward	1,734
16		20	(a)	Brighton & HA	D	1-1	Rooke	1,500
17	Feb	14	(a)	Brentford	W	5-2	Woodward, Rooke 3, Arnold	
18	May	13	(h)	Reading	W	6-2	Rooke 3, Woodward, Ottewell, opp own goal	1,500

P	W	D	L	F	A	W	D	L	F	A	Pts	Pos	Div
18	6	0	3	33	26	1	4	4	17	25	18	6th	Sth 'B'

19	Feb	10	(h)	Portsmouth	W	3-2	Finch, Rooke, Arnold	3,842
20		17	(a)	Millwall	L	0-2		3,862
21		24	(a)	Southampton	W	4-0	Taylor, Arnold, Woodward, Rooke	3,000
22	Mar	2	(h)	Arsenal	D	1-1	Woodward	8,000
23		9	(a)	West Ham U	L	0-5		8,000
24		16	(h)	Charlton A	W	2-0	Woodward, Arnold	6,663
25		22	(a)	Chelsea	W	4-1	Rooke 2, Woodward, opp own goal	15,000
26		23	(h)	Tottenham H	L	2-3	Arnold, opp own goal	8,000
27		25	(h)	Chelsea	W	4-3	Rooke, opp own goal, Cranfield 2	10,000
28		30	(a)	Brentford	L	0-5		6,956
29	Apr	6	(a)	Portsmouth	W	3-0	McCormick, Woodward 2	5,007
30		10	(a)	Tottenham H	L	1-3	Rooke	2,000
31		13	(h)	Millwall	W	2-0	Rooke, McCormick	8,000
32		18	(a)	Charlton A	L	5-7	Rooke 2, Woodward 3	776
33	May	22	(a)	Arsenal	L	1-2	Ottewell	
34		27	(h)	West Ham U	W	2-1	Rooke, McCormick	4,000
35	Jun	3	(h)	Brentford	L	3-5	Ottewell 2, Rooke	
36		6	(h)	Southampton	L	1-2	Ottewell	

P	W	D	L	F	A	W	D	L	F	A	Pts	Pos	Div
18	5	1	3	20	17	3	0	6	18	25	17	7th	Sth 'C'

League War Cup

1	Apr	20	(h)	Brentford	W	4-1	D.W.J.Thomas, Arnold 2, Rooke	12,000
		27	(a)	Brentford	W	2-1	Woodward, Jones	7,865
2	May	4	(a)	Norwich C	D	1-1	Rooke	6,000
		11	(h)	Norwich C	W	1-0	McCormick	8,220
3		18	(h)	Nottingham F	W	2-0	Rooke, opp own goal	8,708
4		25	(h)	Everton	W	5-2	Woodward 2, Rooke, McCormick, Arnold	14,705
SF	Jun	1	(n)	West Ham U*	L	3-4	Woodward, Rooke 2	32,799

*Semi-final played at Stamford Bridge

APPEARANCES

Arnold J 36, Bacuzzi J 18, Boulton FP 11, Brown 3, Burgess H 7, Cann H 19, Chesters A 1, Cothliff HT 1, Cox FJA 4, Cranfield HR 3, Dennison RS 1, Evans JL 42, Flack DW 7, Finch J 34, Fisher LP 2, Freeman HG 7, Green GH 2, Griffiths J 7, Higgins D 2, Hiles EC 40, Jones LJ 4, Keeping AEM 44, Mason WS 1, McCormick J 8, McCormick R 4, Mills GR 4, Muttitt E 1, O'Callaghan E 3, Ottewell S 5, Perry E 5, Pitts H 1, Reay EP 3, Rooke RL 35, Rozier AT 1, Scott HS 1, Shepherd E 1, Smith J 1, Stuart R 2, Taylor JG 42, Thomas DS 6, Thomas DWJ 3, Tompkins JJ 25, Turner H 3, Weaver S 2, Whatley WJ 1, Wilkins GE 2, Woodward V 43, Worsley 6.

GOALS

League: (91) 27 Rooke; 19 Woodward; 10 Arnold; 5 Ottewell, Perry; 3 McCormick J; 2 Burgess, Cranfield, Finch, Fisher, Mills, Taylor, Thomas DS; 1 Muttitt, Thomas DWJ; Tompkins, Wilkins; 4 OG.
League Cup: (18) 6 Rooke; 4 Woodward; 3 Arnold; 2 McCormick J; 1 Jones, Thomas, OG.

1940-41

1	Aug	31	(h)	Queen's Park R	W 3-1	Woodward, Rooke 2	3,000
2	Sep	7	(a)	Arsenal	L 0-5		3,000
3		14	(h)	Arsenal	L 0-1		1,000
4		21	(a)	Millwall	L 1-4	Woodward	600
5		28	(h)	Luton T	D 3-3	Woodward, Rooke, Richfield	800
6	Oct	5	(a)	Charlton A	L 0-3		500
7		12	(h)	Clapton O	W 3-1	Birkett, Thomas 2	400
8		19	(a)	Brentford	L 3-8	Miller 2, Thomas	1,000
9		26	(h)	Reading	D 1-1	Finch	300
10	Nov	2	(a)	Reading	L 1-2	Rooke	2,000
11		9	(h)	Charlton A	L 1-2	Finch	150
12		16	(a)	Queen's Park R	W 5-2	Thomas 2, Rooke 2, Taylor	1,000
13		23	(h)	Brentford	W 3-0	Thomas 2, Rooke	600
14	Dec	7	(h)	Millwall	L 3-5	Woodward, Thomas, Rooke	600
15		14	(a)	Luton T	W 4-3	Thomas, Fisher 2, Hiles	400
16		21	(h)	West Ham U	L 1-2	Woodward	1,000
17		25	(a)	Chelsea	L 2-5	Woodward, Osborne	3,441
18		28	(a)	West Ham U	L 1-2	Rooke	2,500
19	Jan	4	(h)	Queen's Park R*	W 4-1	Revell, Rooke, Keeping, opp own goal	1,000
20		11	(a)	Queen's Park R*	W 7-5	Rooke 4, Woodward, Evans, Robson	2,256
21		25	(a)	Crystal P*	L 2-5	Revell, Beasley	2,000
22	Feb	1	(h)	Brentford*	W 4-1	Revell, Rooke, Beasley, O'Callaghan	2,400
23		8	(a)	Brentford*	L 4-7	O'Callaghan 2, Keeping, Smith	2,000
24	Mar	1	(a)	Crystal P*	L 1-4	Robinson	2,500
25		8	(a)	Norwich C	L 0-2		1,380
26		15	(a)	Aldershot*	L 1-3	Freeman	3,000
27		22	(a)	Aldershot*	L 2-4	Rooke, Cullen	3,500
28		29	(a)	Crystal P	D 1-1	Rooke	3,000
29	Apr	5	(a)	Portsmouth	D 3-3	Rooke 3	3,099
30		11	(h)	Chelsea*	W 4-0	Woodward 2, Rooke, O'Callaghan	5,000
31		13	(a)	Millwall	D 0-0		
32		19	(a)	Chelsea*	L 3-4	Rooke 2, Woodward	2,712
33		26	(a)	West Ham U	W 1-0	Rooke	3,000
34	May	3	(a)	Aldershot	D 3-3	Rooke 2, Revell	2,000
35		10	(a)	Brentford	W 3-2	O'Callaghan, Revell, Woodward	2,670
36		17	(h)	Millwall	W 4-1	Revell, Rooke 2, Woodward	2,140
37		24	(h)	Southend U	W 8-2	McCormick, Revell, Rooke 4, Halton 2	1,000
38		31	(a)	Millwall	L 0-6		1,800
39	Jun	2	(h)	Queen's Park R	W 3-2	Miller, Rooke 2	2,500
40		9	(a)	Tottenham H	L 1-2	Revell	4,000

P	W	D	L	F	A	W	D	L	F	A	Pts	Pos	Div
30	6	2	4	33	21	4	4	10	29	53	†	23rd	Sth RL

League War Cup

1	Feb	15	(a)	Watford	L 1-4	Robson	5,000
		22	(h)	Watford	W 2-1	O'Callaghan, Rooke	2,500

†Positions fixed on average points as clubs played differing number of games.
Matches marked thus * were in the London Cup and did not count towards the South Regional League. Fulham finished 5th out of 6 clubs in the London Cup Qualifying Group 'A' and so did not qualify for the semi-finals.

APPEARANCES
Arnold J 2, Bacuzzi J 10, Bastin CS 1, Birkett RJE 3, Bonass AE 1, Boulton FP 12, Briggs F 5, Buckham K 1, Cardwell L 3, Collett E 1, Cranfield HR 2, Cullis S 9, Duke GE 1, Evans JL 7, Finch J 17, Fisher LP 11, Flack DW 7, Freeman HG 7, Griffiths WM 1, Grundy JA 5, Halton RL 3, Hammond RAC 1, Hiles EC 31, Hobbus SG 4, Hughes WM 2, Jobling J 1, Joslin PJ 8, Kay W 1, Keeping AEM 2, Lunn G 1, Malpass ST 7, Matthewson G 5, McCormick J 1, McCormick R 3, Miller JW 6, Morris R 5, Muttitt E 10, O'Callaghan E 9, O'Leary V 15, Osborne J 2, Pavitt WE 1, Penn F 1, Poulter J 1, Revell C 14, Richfield M 2, Robinson GH 2, Rodger R 2, Rooke RL 27, Rozier AT 1, Scaife G 14, Smith JT 2, Spence R 3, Taylor JG 7, Thomas DWJ 14, Thomson JR 1, Trewick G 1, Weaver S 3, Whittaker W 3, Wilson J 1, Woodward V 29. (League Cup appearances unknown, 2).

GOALS
League: (62) 24 Rooke; 9 Thomas; 8 Woodward; 5 Revell; 3 Miller; 2 Finch, Fisher, Halton; 1 Birkett, Hiles, McCormick J, O'Callaghan, Osborne, Richfield, Taylor.
League Cup: (3) 1 O'Callaghan, Robson, Rooke.
London Cup: (32) 10 Rooke; 4 Woodward; 4 O'Callaghan; 3 Revell; 2 Beasley, Keeping; 1 Cullen, Evans, Freeman, Robinson, Robson, Smith, OG.

1941-42

1	Aug	30	(h)	Aldershot	L 2-6	Rooke 2	3,500
2	Sep	6	(a)	Millwall	W 4-2	Muttitt, Cranfield, Rooke 2	5,000
3		13	(h)	Arsenal	L 2-5	Cranfield, Rooke	10,473
4		20	(a)	Queen's Park R	W 5-2	Sibley, Rooke 4	5,500
5		27	(h)	Reading	D 2-2	Rooke 2	6,019
6	Oct	4	(h)	Brighton	L 2-3	McCormick, Morgan	2,500
7		11	(h)	Brentford	W 4-3	Gallacher 2, Hiles 2	6,000
8		18	(a)	Crystal P	L 1-3	Hiles	5,000
9		25	(a)	Clapton O	L 1-2	E.Jones	2,000
10	Nov	1	(h)	Tottenham H	D 2-2	Rooke 2	6,000
11		8	(a)	Portsmouth	L 3-5	Gallacher, Richardson, Rooke	6,324
12		15	(h)	Chelsea	L 1-4	Freeman	4,994
13		22	(a)	Charlton A	D 3-3	Rooke 2, Gallacher	3,069
14		29	(h)	West Ham U	L 1-3	L.Jones	4,468
15	Dec	6	(a)	Watford	W 5-3	Thomas, Gallacher 2, Conley 2	1,000
16		13	(a)	Aldershot	L 3-4	Rampling, Rooke 2	3,000
17		20	(h)	Millwall	W 4-3	Rooke 4	1,000
18		25	(a)	Arsenal	L 0-2		10,578
19		27	(h)	Queen's Park R	L 0-3		3,771
20	Jan	3	(a)	Reading	L 1-4	Gallacher	4,000
21		10	(a)	Brighton	W 7-3	Dean, Finch 2, Gallacher 2, Rooke 2	2,500
22		17	(a)	Brentford	W 3-2	Dean 3	3,000
23		31	(h)	Clapton O	W 5-1	Dean, Conley 3, Finch	1,921
24	Feb	14	(h)	Portsmouth	L 2-7	Conley 2	4,404
25		21	(a)	Chelsea	W 5-1	Rooke 2, Finch, Gallacher, Woodward	3,255
26		28	(h)	Charlton A	L 4-7	Dean 2, Rooke, Gallacher	3,091
27	Mar	7	(a)	West Ham U	D 1-1	Kiernan	2,500
28		14	(h)	Watford	L 1-3	Finch	2,462
29		21	(a)	Portsmouth*	L 1-9	Kiernan	6,215
30		28	(h)	Chelsea*	W 1-0	Conley	5,886
31	Apr	4	(h)	Portsmouth*	W 2-1	Conley 2	5,167
32		6	(a)	Chelsea*	D 2-2	Conley 2	10,986
33		11	(h)	Crystal P*	W 4-1	Woodward 2, Conley, Gallagher	6,000
34		18	(a)	Crystal P*	W 4-3	Rooke 3, Foxall	3,378
35	May	2	(a)	Tottenham H	L 1-7	Conley	3,754
36		23	(h)	Crystal P	W 4-3	Conley 4	3,000

P	W	D	L	F	A	W	D	L	F	A	Pts	Pos	Div
30	4	2	9	36	55	6	2	7	43	44	24	11th	LL

Matches marked thus * were in the London War Cup and did not count towards the London League. Fulham finished second on goal-average, behind Portsmouth, in the London War Cup Qualifying Group 4 and thus did not qualify for the semi-finals.

APPEARANCES
Abel S 1, Bacuzzi J 10, Beasley A 1, Bonass AE 2, Briggs CE 1, Buckingham VF 1, Compton LH 1, Conley JJ 20, Cranfield HR 6, Cullis S 9, Cumner RH 2, Dean CG 14, Duffy 6, Duke HP 25, Evans JE 3, Finch J 10, Ford FG 1, Foxall JS 5, Freeman HG 13, Gallacher P 29, Gibbons AH 1, Griffiths WM 2, Hamilton W 1, Hiles EC 24, Holley T 1, Holliday J 2, Howe LF 1, Jones EN 7, Jones L 24, Joslin PJ 4, Keen ERL 2, Kelly L 1, Kiernan T 5, Lester FC 2, Lodge 1, Ludford G 1, McCormick J 6, Mackie 1, Malpass ST 7, Marsden F 1, Matthewson G 18, Milsom J 1, Milton GW 1, Morgan 1, Muttitt E 7, Neary HF 1, Nichols E 1, Parry O 1, Poland G 1, Pryde RI 2, Rampling DW 4, Richardson JR 6, Rooke RL 25, Scaife G 2, Sharp 3, Sibley A 12, Skinner G 1, Smith E 2, Smith C 1, Sneddon WC 1, Stevens AH 1, Swift FV 5, Taylor F 4, Thomas DWJ 4, Tickridge S 1, Tompkins JJ 10, Tuckett EW 1, Wallbanks H 1, Walsh 1, Ward RA 1, Whatley WJ 11, Whitfield 6, Wilson J 1, Woodward V 2, Young AA 1.

GOALS
League: (79) 27 Rooke; 12 Conley; 11 Gallacher; 7 Dean; 5 Finch; 3 Hiles; 2 Cranfield; 1 Freeman, Jones E, Jones L, Kiernan, Morgan, Muttitt, McCormick, Rampling, Richardson, Sibley, Thomas, Woodward.
League Cup: (0) Nil.
London Cup: (14) 6 Conley; 3 Rooke; 2 Woodward; 1 Foxall, Gallacher, Kiernan.

1942-43

1	Aug	29	(a)	Luton Town	L	1-3	Freeman	2,000
2	Sep	5	(h)	Brentford	W	3-1	Conley, Thomas, Gallacher	4,600
3		12	(a)	Reading	L	1-4	Martin	4,000
4		19	(h)	Millwall	W	4-1	Rooke, Dean 2, Conley	4,500
5		26	(a)	Chelsea	L	2-4	Jones, Rooke	10,635
6	Oct	3	(h)	Arsenal	L	3-4	Rooke, Dean, Conley	11,000
7		10	(a)	Crystal P	W	4-2	Finch, Conley, Rooke, Dean	5,500
8		17	(h)	Charlton A	L	2-4	Holliday, Muttitt	5,500
9		24	(a)	Southampton	L	2-4	Arnold, Conley	7,000
10		31	(h)	West Ham U	L	2-3	Conley, Rooke	5,500
11	Nov	7	(a)	Portsmouth	D	1-1	Tompkins	5,844
12		14	(h)	Watford	W	2-0	Rooke 2	3,000
13		21	(a)	Clapton O	L	2-4	Neary, Freeman	2,500
14		28	(h)	Luton T	W	6-2	Thomas, Leyfield 3, Rooke, Driver	1,500
15	Dec	5	(a)	Brentford	L	2-4	Conley, Finch	2,500
16		12	(h)	Reading	W	5-2	Driver 2, Rooke 2, Leyfield	3,000
17		19	(a)	Millwall	W	6-2	Dean, Broadhurst 3, Ottewell, Conley	3,000
18		25	(a)	Queen's Park R	L	1-2	Conley	4,000
19		26	(h)	Queen's Park R	W	4-2	Thomas 2, Rooke, Conley	7,919
20	Jan	2	(h)	Chelsea	W	3-1	Rooke 2, Conley	9,800
21		9	(a)	Arsenal	L	2-7	Rooke, Conley	8,332
22		16	(h)	Crystal P	L	1-2	Ottewell	3,824
23		23	(a)	Charlton A	L	0-2		3,500
24		30	(h)	Southampton	L	2-8	Conley 2	2,513
25	Feb	6	(a)	West Ham U	L	1-2	Conley	5,200
26		13	(h)	Portsmouth	L	2-6	Rooke 2	4,837
27		20	(a)	Watford	W	4-1	Rooke, Dean 2, Ottewell	2,500
28		27	(h)	Clapton O	D	1-1	Holley	4,000
29	Mar	6	(h)	Charlton A*	W	3-1	L Jones 2, Rooke	5,030
30		13	(a)	Aldershot*	L	1-4	Rooke	5,000
31		20	(h)	Portsmouth*	D	2-2	Rooke 2	5,810
32		27	(a)	Charlton A*	L	1-6	Rooke	4,500
33	Apr	3	(h)	Aldershot*	D	2-2	Rooke, Hobbis	7,727
34		10	(a)	Portsmouth*	W	3-1	Thomas 2, Conley	7,265

P	W	D	L	F	A	W	D	L	F	A	Pts	Pos	Div
28	7	1	6	40	37	3	1	10	29	42	22	14th	L Sth

Matches marked thus * were in the League War Cup South Qualifying Group 4 and did not count towards the League South table. Fulham finished fourth out of six clubs and did not qualify for the semi-finals.

APPEARANCES
Arnold J 1, Bacuzzi J 13, Broadhurst R 1, Buckley A 6, Bush TW 12, Conley JJ 32, Conway J 1, Copping W 2, Costello W 1, Davie J 1, Dean CG 14, Drake EJ 2, Driver A 5, Duke HP 34, Evans JL 19, Farmer A 1, Ferrier H 1, Finch J 18, Freeman HG 20, Gallacher P 3, Hiles EC 3, Hobbis HHF 1, Holly T 20, Holliday JW 2, Jones L 29, Kirkman N 1, Kurz FJ 1, Lester FC 5, Leyfield C 7, Lloyd C 5, Ludford G 1, Malpass ST 7, Martin DK 1, McCulloch O 1, McInnes JS 4, Merrett GE 1, Milton GW 5, Muir A 3, Muttitt E 6, Neary HF 2, Nicholson WE 1, O'Donnell F 3, Ottewell S 9, Palmer RW 1, Pilkington SH 1, Pitts H 1, Rampling DW 1, Rooke RL 26, Rozier AT 2, Salmon L 1, Savage RE 1, Smith C 1, Smith JT 2, Sneddon WC 2, Sperrin W 1, Stevens AH 2, Thomas DWJ 10, Thomson JR 3, Tompkins JJ 4, Tuckett EW 4, Watson JF 1, Whitfield W 2, Wilson J 2, Woodward V 1.

GOALS
League: (67) 17 Rooke; 15 Conley; 7 Dean; 4 Leyfield, Thomas, 3 Ottewell, Broadhurst, Driver, 2 Finch, Freeman, 1 Arnold, Gallacher, Holliday, Jones, Martin, Muttitt, Neary, Tompkins, Halley.
League Cup: (12) 6 Rooke, 2 Jones, Thomas 1, Conley, Hobbis.

1943-44

1	Aug	28	(a)	Luton T	D	2-2	D.W.J.Thomas, Leyfield	4,000
2	Sep	4	(h)	Brentford	W	4-3	Stamps 2, D.W.J.Thomas, Rooke	7,737
3		11	(a)	Aldershot	D	2-2	Rooke, Dean	6,000
4		18	(h)	Millwall	W	4-1	Rooke 2, Stamps, Leyfield	
5		25	(a)	Chelsea	L	0-3		11,717
6	Oct	2	(h)	Arsenal	L	3-4	Rooke 2, D.W.J.Thomas	17,994
7		9	(h)	Crystal P	L	4-5	Rooke 3, Leyfield	8,000
8		16	(a)	Charlton A	D	1-1	Conley	8,000
9		23	(a)	Southampton	W	3-2	Stamps, Rooke 2	7,000
10		30	(h)	West Ham U	L	2-6	Stamps, Rooke	10,000
11	Nov	6	(h)	Brighton	W	6-2	D.W.J.Thomas, Rooke 2, Conley, Malpass, L.Jones	5,000
12		13	(h)	Watford	D	0-0		3,901
13		20	(a)	Clapton O	W	3-1	Rooke, Duggan 2	2,000
14		27	(h)	Luton T	W	4-1	Stamps 2, D.W.J.Thomas, Stevens	1,000
15	Dec	4	(a)	Brentford	D	1-1	Stamps	7,510
16		11	(h)	Aldershot	D	2-2	Stamps 2	3,000
17		18	(h)	Queen's Park R	D	2-2	Rooke, Stamps	6,000
18		25	(a)	Tottenham H	L	0-2		16,629
19		27	(h)	Tottenham H	L	0-2		
20	Jan	1	(a)	Millwall†	L	1-5	Rooke	3,973
21		8	(a)	Brighton	W	6-3	Taylor, Quested 2, Rooke 3	3,000
22		22	(a)	Arsenal	D	1-1	O'Callaghan	8,116
23		29	(a)	Crystal P	L	2-6	Rooke, Muttitt	7,000
24	Feb	5	(h)	Charlton A	W	5-1	Rooke 3, Conley, L.Jones	5,000
25		12	(h)	Southampton	W	6-2	Conley 2, Holley 2, Kiernan 2	5,000
26		19	(a)	Reading*	L	0-3		4,000
27		26	(h)	Luton T*	W	2-0	Rooke, Kiernan	3,000
28	Mar	4	(a)	Clapton O*	W	4-0	Stevens, Rooke, Flack, Devlin	2,000
29		11	(h)	Reading*	L	3-4	Rooke, Devlin 2	7,000
30		18	(a)	Luton T*	L	2-3	Rooke 2	3,000
31		25	(h)	Clapton O*	L	4-5	Kiernan 2, Rooke 2	5,000
32	Apr	1	(a)	West Ham U	L	2-3	Kiernan, Rooke	5,000
33		10	(h)	Chelsea	L	2-3	Kiernan 2	
34		22	(a)	Queen's Park R	D	3-3	Stamps, Kiernan 2	4,000
35		29	(a)	Watford	W	6-3	Stamps 2, Kiernan 3, Rampling	2,198
36	May	6	(h)	Clapton O	W	3-1	Conley 2, Kiernan	2,000

P	W	D	L	F	A	W	D	L	F	A	Pts	Pos	Div
30	7	3	5	47	35	4	6	5	33	38	31	9th	FLS

†Match 20 played at Selhurst Park.
Matches marked thus * were in the League War Cup South Qualifying Competition Group 'D' and did not count towards the Football League South.
Fulham finished third out of six clubs and thus did not qualify for the semi-finals.

APPEARANCES
Allen JP 2, Bowpitt T 3, Brophy HF 1, Brown J 8, Buchan WRM 7, Chick W 1, Cobley WA 1, Copping W 2, Conley JJ 30, Cowan RM 7, Cox AEH 18, Dean CG 3, Devlin J 4, Duggan EJ 1, Duke HP 23, Evans JL 11, Flack WLW 6, Freeman HG 4, Fuller C 1, Halton RL 1, Henley L 1, Hickman AH 3, Hiles EG 1, Holley T 20, Horton JC 1, Humphreys J 1, Humphreys PR 2, James J 1, Jones L 31, Jones VC 2, Joslin PJ 5, Kiernan T 11, Kinnear D 1, Laing FJ 1, Lester FC 8, Leyfield C 15, Lloyd C 16, Lumby WCM 1, Malpass ST 7, Mangnall D 1, Manley T 6, Millbanks JH 2, Milton GW 2, Muttitt E 3, O'Callaghan E 10, Phipps H 1, Quested WL 1, Rampling DW 4, Rooke RL 32, Royston R 1, Sears DR 1, Shepherd E 3, Stamps JD 15, Stevens AH 8, Summers J 4, Taylor JG 1, Taylor TE 8, Thomas DWJ 11, Thomas RA 2, Tompkins JJ 4, Wallbanks H 11, Wallbanks J 1, Ward TA 1, Watson J 1, Watson JF 3, Weaver S 1, Whittaker W 2, Wilson J 3, Woodward V 1,

GOALS
League: (80) 25 Rooke; 14 Stamps; 11 Kiernan; 7 Conley; 5 Thomas D; 3 Leyfield; 2 Duggan, Jones L, Holley, Quested; 1 Dean, Malpass, Muttitt, O'Callaghan, Rampling, Stevens, Taylor.
League Cup: 7 Rooke; 3 Devlin, Kiernan; 1 Flack, Stevens.

1944-45

1	Aug	26	(h)	Chelsea	W	7-4	Rooke 4, Potts 2, O'Callaghan	10,000
2	Sep	2	(a)	Reading	L	4-5	Conley 2, Rooke 2	4,000
3		9	(h)	Queen's Park R	D	2-2	R.Thomas, Rooke	8,000
4		16	(a)	Brighton	W	7-1	Rooke 4, Leyfield, Potts 2	4,500
5		23	(h)	Crystal P	W	6-2	Rooke 4, Flack, O'Callaghan	8,000
6		30	(a)	Watford	W	2-1	Potts 2	4,840
7	Oct	7	(h)	Southampton	W	4-3	Rooke 3, Leyfield	8,000
8		14	(h)	Arsenal	D	4-4	Arnold, R.Thomas 2, opp own goal	16,000
9		21	(a)	Charlton A	W	3-1	Potts, Rooke 2	7,000
10		28	(h)	Clapton O	W	5-2	Cheetham 3, Potts 2	6,000
11	Nov	4	(h)	Brentford	L	0-2		25,000
12		11	(h)	West Ham U	L	4-7	Potts 2, Arnold, Lowes	10,359
13		18	(h)	Portsmouth	L	0-2		8,986
14		25	(a)	Tottenham H	L	1-2	L.Jones	14,300
15	Dec	2	(a)	Chelsea	L	0-2		18,000
16		9	(h)	Reading	L	2-3	Lowes, J.Wilson	8,000
17		16	(a)	Queen's Park R	D	4-4	Dodds 2, Watson, Lowes	10,000
18		23	(h)	Luton T	W	3-2	Dodds 3	5,000
19		26	(a)	Luton T	L	1-3	Opp own goal	5,000
20		30	(h)	Brighton	L	2-3	O'Callaghan, Dodds	4,000
21	Jan	6	(a)	Crystal P	W	2-0	Gallacher, Jessop	6,000
22		13	(h)	Watford	L	0-2		4,000
23		20	(a)	Southampton	L	0-3		6,000
24		27	(a)	Arsenal†	L	3-8	Dodds 2, Lowes	5,246
25	Feb	3	(h)	Millwall*	L	1-3	Sloan	8,000
26		10	(a)	Brighton*	W	3-1	Sloan 2, Rooke	7,000
27		17	(h)	Brentford*	W	1-0	Rooke	15,000
28		24	(a)	Millwall*	L	0-1		9,000
29	Mar	3	(h)	Brighton*	W	5-2	Dodds 3, Livingstone 2	9,000
30		10	(h)	Brentford*	W	5-2	Lowes, L.Jones, Kippax 3	10,380
31		24	(a)	Clapton O	D	0-0		2,500
32		31	(a)	Brentford	W	3-2	Sloan 3	8,780
33	Apr	14	(a)	West Ham U	L	2-3	Rooke, Lowes	8,000
34		21	(a)	Portsmouth	L	1-3	Opp own goal	7,983
35		28	(h)	Tottenham H	L	2-4	Rooke 2	8,000
36	May	5	(h)	Charlton A	W	5-3	Rooke 2, Steele 2, Weston	1,500

P	W	D	L	F	A	W	D	L	F	A	Pts	Pos	Div
30	6	2	7	46	45	5	2	8	33	38	26	11th	FLS

†Match 24 played at White Hart Lane.
Matches marked thus * were in the League War Cup South Qualifying Group 2 and did not count towards the Football League South. Fulham finished second, behind Millwall, and thus did not qualify for the semi-finals.

APPEARANCES
Abel S 1, Adams BK 1, Arnold J 7, Bacuzzi J 18, Bewley DG 2, Blair J 1, Borrows JE 1, Boulter LM 6, Bowpitt T 1, Briggs F 2, Briscoe JER 1, Buchanan PS 1, Buckingham VF 7, Buckton T 1, Cheetham TM 6, Chitty W 1, Conley JJ 3, Cowan RM 15, Cox FJA 1, Cunliffe A 2, Dawes AG 1, Dawes FW 3, Dodds E 9, Duke HP 18, Flack WLW 10, Freeman HG 20, Gage A 2, Gallacher P 2, Gibson WG 3, Hamilton DS 1, Hiles EC 1, Hollis H 2, Hopkins 12, Hudgell AJ 1, Hunt DA 1, Jarvis DH 2, Jessop W 8, Jones C 1, Jones EN 2, Jones F 2, Jones GH 1, Jones L 33, Jones S 3, Jones VC 1, Jordan J 1, Kiernan T 1, Kippax FP 5, Laws WC 1, Leyfield C 9, Livingstone A 4, Lloyd C 12, , Lowes AR 20, Mallett J 1, McCormick J 3, McClusky H 1, Meadows JR 1, Millbank JH 2, Miller JW 3, Moody KG 1, Moore NW 1, Morris J 1, Muir MR 1, Muttitt E 3, Neary HF 2, O'Callaghan E 10, Potts H 10, Preskett J 2, Rampling DW 2, Redfern R 1, Rickett HF 10, Robson AP 1, Rooke RL 15, Shepherd E 1, Sloan JW 11, Smith J 3, Smith LGF 1, Squires A 1, Steele FC 1, Taylor JG 3, Tennant AE 1, Thomas DWJ 2, Thomas RA 4, Toser E 1, Tunnicliffe G 2, Wallbanks H 1, Watson JF 26, Weston AL 1, White R 1, Whittaker W 1, Wilson J 3, Wright H 1.

GOALS
League: (79) 25 Rooke; 11 Potts; 8 Dodds; 5 Lowes; 3 Cheetham, O'Callaghan, Sloan, Thomas R; 2 Arnold, Conley, Leyfield, Steele; 1 Flack, Gallacher, Jessop, Jones L, Watson, Weston, Wilson; 3 OG.
League Cup: (15) 3 Dodds, Kippax, Sloan; 2 Livingstone, Rooke; 1 Jones J, Lowes.

1945-46

1	Aug	25	(a)	Derby C	L	2-5	Rooke 2		15,000
2		30	(a)	Newport C	W	5-1	Rooke 3, Collins, Frost		5,000
3	Sep	1	(h)	Derby C	W	2-1	Sargent, McCormick		20,000
4		8	(h)	Leicester C	W	1-0	Taylor		18,000
5		12	(a)	Nottingham F	D	1-1	Wardle		14,000
6		15	(a)	Leicester C	W	1-0	Taylor		14,000
7		22	(a)	Coventry C	L	1-3	Rooke		14,113
8		29	(h)	Coventry C	W	2-0	Rooke, McCormick		22,000
9	Oct	6	(h)	Luton T	W	4-1	Buchanan 2, Wardle, Rooke		15,000
10		13	(a)	Luton T	D	2-2	Rooke 2		10,000
11		20	(a)	Aston Villa	L	0-3			15,000
12		27	(h)	Aston Villa	L	1-4	Rooke		32,500
13	Nov	3	(h)	Arsenal	W	5-2	Rooke 3, Jessop, Shepherd		30,000
14		10	(a)	Arsenal	L	0-2			19,000
15		17	(a)	Charlton A	L	2-4	Rampling, Rooke		20,000
16		24	(h)	Charlton A	L	2-4	Shepherd 2		35,000
17	Dec	1	(h)	Swansea T	W	5-2	Shepherd 3, McCormick, Miller		18,000
18		8	(a)	Swansea T	D	2-2	Shepherd, Rooke		15,000
19		15	(h)	Plymouth A	W	4-0	Rampling 2, Shepherd, Rooke		15,000
20		22	(a)	Plymouth A	W	2-0	Rooke, Rampling		2,000
21		25	(a)	Portsmouth	D	2-2	Freeman, Rooke		11,841
22		26	(h)	Portsmouth	W	5-2	Rooke 4, Shepherd		22,324
23		29	(h)	Nottingham F	D	3-3	McCormick, Freeman 2		20,000
24	Jan	12	(h)	Wolves	W	3-1	Woodward 2, Shepherd		34,099
25		19	(a)	Wolves	L	0-2			18,000
26	Feb	2	(h)	West Ham U	L	0-1			30,000
27		9	(h)	West Brom A	L	1-4	Opp own goal		15,000
28		16	(a)	West Brom A	L	1-3	Beasley		20,000
29		23	(a)	Birmingham C	L	0-2			25,000
30	Mar	9	(h)	Tottenham H	D	1-1	Rooke		30,000
31		16	(a)	Tottenham H	W	3-1	Beasley, Buchanan 2		23,211
32		23	(a)	Brentford	W	2-1	Buchanan, Rooke		23,400
33		30	(h)	Brentford	D	2-2	Rooke, Beasley		30,000
34	Apr	6	(h)	Chelsea	W	3-2	Shepherd, Beasley, McCormick		35,000
35		13	(a)	Chelsea	D	0-0			35,000
36		15	(h)	Birmingham C	W	3-2	Taylor, Buchanan, Woodward		14,000
37		19	(a)	Millwall	W	1-0	Shepherd		25,000
38		20	(h)	Southampton	W	3-1	Woodward 2, Beasley		15,000
39		22	(h)	Millwall	W	7-0	Rooke 2, Woodward 2, Buchanan 2, Shepherd		18,783
40		27	(a)	Southampton	D	1-1	Shepherd		10,000
41		29	(a)	West Ham U	W	5-3	Rooke 3, Shepherd 2		8,000
42	May	4	(h)	Newport C	W	3-1	Buchanan, Woodward, Beasley		15,000

P	W	D	L	F	A	W	D	L	F	A	Pts	Pos	Div
42	13	4	4	60	35	7	6	8	33	38	50	8th	FLS

FA Cup

3	Jan	5	(a)	Charlton A	L	1-3	Rampling		30,000
		7	(h)	Charlton A	W	2-1	Rooke 2		20,000

The FA Cup was played on a two-legged, home and away basis. Fulham's line-ups for the third round tie against Charlton can be found on page 387.

APPEARANCES
Bacuzzi J 37, Beasley A 24, Bewley DG 12, Bremner GH 1, Brown AW 1, Buchanan PS 25, Chisholm J 2, Collins W 1, Evans JL 8, Evans O 13, Ferrier H 4, Freeman HG 42, Frost GC 2, Gage A 4, Hiles EC 1, Hindle FJ 1, Holben G 2, Hunt DA 1, Jarvis D 7, Jessop W 1, Jones EN 9, Little A 1, Lloyd C 15, Lowes AR 1, Machin AH 1, Malpass ST 4, McCormick J 31, McDermott J 3, Miller JW 4, Morris J 1, O'Callaghan E 1, Rampling DW 15, Rickett HF 17, Rooke RL 41, Sanders JA 1, Sargent F 1, Shepherd E 35, Stevens E 1, Taylor JG 37, Thomas DS 1, Wallbanks H 28, Wardle C 4, Watson JF 25, Wilkins GE 1, Woodward V 16, Worsley H 1.

GOALS
League: (93) 31 Rooke; 16 Shepherd; 9 Buchanan; 8 Woodward; 6 Beasley; 5 McCormick; 4 Rampling; 3 Freeman, Taylor; 2 Wardle; 1 Collins, Frost, Jessop, Miller, Sargent, OG.
FA Cup: (3) 2 Rooke, 1 Rampling.

Fulham in 1945-6, when the League was getting back to some sort of normality with a 42-match programme. Back row (left to right): Frank Penn (trainer), Jim Taylor, Harry Freeman, Horace Rickett, Joe Bacuzzi, Sam Malpass, Dave Bewley. Front: Peter Buchanan, Jimmy McCormick, Ronnie Rooke, Pat Beasley, John Miller, Jack Watson. Penn, of course, had begun his career as a wartime guest during 1915-19.

England captain Johnny Haynes is chaired off the Wembley pitch by Peter Swan (left) and Jimmy Armfield after the resounding 9-3 win over Scotland in April 1961, a victory which clinched the Home International Championship. Mick McNeill is the other England player, whilst team manager Walter Winterbottom follows the group.

Fulham Internationals

Superior number in front of score (e.g. ¹2-1) represents goals scored by player in match.

England

John Arnold (1)

Scotland	Apr	1933 Glasgow	1-2

Albert Barrett (1)

Northern Ireland	Oct	1929 Belfast	3-0

George Cohen (37)

Uruguay	May	1964 Wembley	2-1
Portugal	May	1964 Lisbon	4-3
Republic of Ireland	May	1964 Dublin	3-1
USA	May	1964 New York	10-0
Brazil	May	1964 Rio de Janeiro	1-5
Northern Ireland	Oct	1964 Belfast	4-3
Belgium	Oct	1964 Wembley	2-2
Wales	Nov	1964 Wembley	2-1
Netherlands	Dec	1964 Amsterdam	1-1
Scotland	Apr	1965 Wembley	2-2
Hungary	May	1965 Wembley	1-0
Yugoslavia	May	1965 Belgrade	1-1
West Germany	May	1965 Nürnberg	1-0
Sweden	May	1965 Göteborg	2-1
Wales	Oct	1965 Cardiff	0-0
Austria	Oct	1965 Wembley	2-3
Northern Ireland	Nov	1965 Wembley	2-1
Spain	Dec	1965 Madrid	2-0
Poland	Jan	1966 Liverpool	1-1
West Germany	Feb	1966 Wembley	1-0
Scotland	Apr	1966 Glasgow	4-3
Norway	Jun	1966 Oslo	6-1
Denmark	Jul	1966 Copenhagen	2-0
Poland	Jul	1966 Chorzow	1-0
Uruguay	Jul	1966 Wembley	0-0
Mexico	Jul	1966 Wembley	2-0
France	Jul	1966 Wembley	2-0
Argentina	Jul	1966 Wembley	1-0
Portugal	Jul	1966 Wembley	2-1
West Germany	Jul	1966 Wembley	4-2
Northern Ireland	Oct	1966 Belfast	2-0
Czechoslovakia	Nov	1966 Wembley	0-0
Wales	Nov	1966 Wembley	5-1
Scotland	Apr	1967 Wembley	2-3
Spain	May	1967 Wembley	2-0
Wales	Oct	1967 Cardiff	3-0
Northern Ireland	Nov	1967 Wembley	2-0

Johnny Haynes (56)

Northern Ireland	Oct	1954 Belfast	¹2-0
Northern Ireland	Nov	1955 Wembley	3-0
Spain	Nov	1955 Wembley	4-1
Scotland	Apr	1956 Glasgow	¹1-1
Brazil	May	1956 Wembley	4-2

Sweden	May	1956 Stockholm	0-0
Finland	May	1956 Helsinki	¹5-1
West Germany	May	1956 Berlin	¹3-1
Wales	Nov	1956 Wembley	¹3-1
Yugoslavia	Nov	1956 Wembley	3-0
Republic of Ireland	May	1957 Wembley	5-1
Denmark	May	1957 Copenhagen	¹4-1
Republic of Ireland	May	1957 Dublin	1-1
Wales	Oct	1957 Cardiff	²4-0
Northern Ireland	Nov	1957 Wembley	2-3
France	Nov	1957 Wembley	4-0
Scotland	Apr	1958 Glasgow	4-0
Portugal	May	1958 Wembley	2-1
Yugoslavia	May	1958 Belgrade	0-5
USSR	May	1958 Moscow	1-1
USSR	Jun	1958 Göteborg	2-2
Brazil	Jun	1958 Göteborg	0-0
Austria	Jun	1958 Göteborg	¹2-2
USSR	Jun	1958 Göteborg	0-1
Northern Ireland	Oct	1958 Belfast	3-3
USSR	Oct	1958 Wembley	³5-0
Scotland	Apr	1959 Wembley	1-0
Italy	May	1959 Wembley	2-2
Brazil	May	1959 Rio de Janeiro	0-2
Peru	May	1959 Lima	1-4
Mexico	May	1959 Mexico City	1-2
USA	May	1959 Los Angeles	¹8-1
Northern Ireland	Nov	1959 Wembley	2-1
Yugoslavia	May	1960 Wembley	3-3
Spain	May	1960 Madrid	0-3
Hungary	May	1960 Budapest	0-2
Northern Ireland	Oct	1960 Belfast	5-2
Luxembourg	Oct	1960 Luxembourg	¹9-0
Spain	Oct	1960 Wembley	4-2
Wales	Nov	1960 Wembley	¹5-1
Scotland	Apr	1961 Wembley	²9-3
Mexico	May	1961 Wembley	8-0
Portugal	May	1961 Lisbon	1-1
Italy	May	1961 Rome	3-2
Austria	May	1961 Vienna	1-3
Wales	Oct	1961 Cardiff	1-1
Portugal	Oct	1961 Wembley	2-0
Northern Ireland	Nov	1961 Wembley	1-1
Austria	Apr	1962 Wembley	3-1
Scotland	Apr	1962 Glasgow	0-2
Switzerland	May	1962 Wembley	3-1
Peru	May	1962 Lima	4-0
Hungary	May	1962 Rancagua	1-2
Argentina	Jun	1962 Rancagua	3-1
Bulgaria	Jun	1962 Rancagua	0-0
Brazil	Jun	1962 Vina del Mar	1-3

George Best (left), football's wayward genius, won five full caps for Northern Ireland as a Fulham player, whilst current Fulham captain, Jeff Hopkins (above), had made 13/1 appearances for Wales up to the end of 1986-7.

Bedford Jezzard (2)		
Hungary	May 1954 Budapest	1-7
Northern Ireland	Nov 1955 Wembley	3-0

Jim Langley (3)		
Scotland	Apr 1958 Glasgow	4-0
Portugal	May 1958 Wembley	2-1
Yugoslavia	May 1958 Belgrade	0-5

Len Oliver (1)		
Belgium	May 1929 Brussels	5-1

Frank Osborne (2)		
Northern Ireland	Oct 1922 The Hawthorns	2-0
France	May 1923 Paris	4-1

Jim Taylor (2)		
Argentina	May 1951 Wembley	2-1
Portugal	May 1951 Goodison Park	5-2

Northern Ireland

George Best (5)		
Holland	Oct 1976 Rotterdam	2-2
Belgium	Oct 1976 Liège	0-2
West Germany	Apr 1977 Cologne	0-5
Iceland	Sep 1977 Belfast	2-0
Holland	Sep 1977 Belfast	0-1

Bobby Brennan (1)		
England	Oct 1950 Belfast	1-4

Johnny Campbell (2)		
England	Oct 1950 Belfast	1-4
Scotland	Nov 1950 Glasgow	1-6

Joe Connor (1)		
England	Mar 1904 Belfast	1-3

Ted Hinton (5)		
Scotland	Nov 1946 Glasgow	0-0
Wales	Apr 1947 Belfast	2-1
Scotland	Oct 1947 Belfast	2-0
England	Nov 1947 Goodison Park	2-2
Wales	Mar 1948 Wrexham	0-2

Hugh Kelly (2)		
England	Nov 1949 Maine Road	2-9
Wales	Mar 1950 Wrexham	0-0

Jack McClelland (1)		
Mexico	Jun 1966 Belfast	4-1

Alex Steele (2)		
Wales	Feb 1929 Wrexham	2-2
Scotland	Feb 1929 Belfast	3-7

Scotland

Graham Leggat (11)

Wales	Oct	1958 Cardiff	[1]3-0
Northern Ireland	Nov	1958 Glasgow	2-2
England	Apr	1959 Wembley	0-1
West Germany	May	1959 Glasgow	[1]3-2
Holland	May	1959 Amsterdam	[1]2-1
Northern Ireland	Oct	1959 Belfast	[1]4-0
Wales	Nov	1959 Glasgow	[1]1-1
England	Apr	1960 Glasgow	[1]1-1
Poland	May	1960 Glasgow	2-3
Austria	May	1960 Vienna	1-4
Hungary	Jun	1960 Budapest	3-3

Jimmy Sharp (1)

Wales	Mar	1909 Wrexham	2-3

Wales

Gordon Davies (11/4)

Turkey	Nov	1979 Izmir	0-1
Iceland	Jun	1980 Reykjavik	4-0
Spain (sub)	Mar	1982 Valencia	1-1
France (sub)	Jun	1982 Toulouse	1-0
England	Feb	1983 Wembley	1-2
Bulgaria	Apr	1983 Wrexham	1-0
Scotland	May	1983 Cardiff	0-2
Northern Ireland	May	1983 Belfast	[1]1-0
Brazil	Jun	1983 Cardiff	1-1
Rumania (sub)	Oct	1983 Wrexham	5-0
Scotland (sub)	Feb	1984 Glasgow	1-2
England	May	1984 Wrexham	1-0
Northern Ireland	May	1984 Swansea	1-1
Iceland	Sep	1984 Reykjavik	0-1
Iceland	Nov	1984 Cardiff	2-1

Jeff Hopkins (13/1)

Northern Ireland	May	1983 Belfast	1-0
Brazil	Jun	1983 Cardiff	1-1
Norway	Sep	1983 Oslo	0-0
Rumania	Oct	1983 Wrexham	5-0
Bulgaria	Nov	1983 Sofia	0-1
Yugoslavia	Dec	1983 Cardiff	1-1
Scotland	Feb	1984 Glasgow	1-2
England	May	1984 Wrexham	1-0
Northern Ireland	May	1984 Swansea	1-1
Norway	Jun	1984 Trondheim	0-1
Israel	Jun	1984 Tel Aviv	0-0
Iceland	Sep	1984 Reykjavik	0-1
Iceland (sub)	Nov	1984 Cardiff	2-1
Norway	Jun	1985 Bergen	2-4

Cliff Jones (2)

Italy	Oct	1968 Cardiff	0-1
Rest of the UK	Jul	1969 Cardiff	0-1

Billy Richards (1)

Northern Ireland	Dec	1932 Wrexham	4-1

Sid Thomas (4)

England	Oct	1947 Cardiff	0-3
Scotland	Nov	1947 Glasgow	2-1
Northern Ireland	Mar	1948 Wrexham	2-0
Scotland	Oct	1948 Cardiff	1-3

Republic of Ireland

Jimmy Conway (17/1)

Spain	Oct	1966 Dublin	0-0
Turkey	Nov	1966 Dublin	2-1
Spain	Dec	1966 Valencia	0-2
Czechoslovakia	Nov	1967 Prague	2-1
Austria (sub)	Nov	1968 Dublin	2-2
Hungary	Jun	1969 Dublin	1-2
Scotland	Sep	1969 Dublin	1-1
Czechoslovakia	Oct	1969 Prague	0-3
Denmark	Oct	1969 Dublin	1-1
Hungary	Nov	1969 Budapest	0-4
Poland	May	1930 Dublin	1-2
West Germany	May	1970 Berlin	1-2
Italy	May	1971 Dublin	1-2
Austria	May	1971 Dublin	1-4
Uruguay	May	1974 Montevideo	0-2
Chile	May	1974 Santiago	2-1
Norway	Mar	1976 Dublin	3-0
Poland	May	1976 Poznan	2-0

John Dempsey (7)

Spain	Dec	1966 Valencia	0-2
Czechoslovakia	May	1967 Dublin	0-2
Czechoslovakia	Nov	1967 Prague	2-1
Poland	May	1968 Dublin	2-2
Poland	Oct	1968 Katowice	0-1
Austria	Nov	1968 Dublin	2-2
Denmark *	Dec	1968 Dublin	1-1

*Abandoned after 51 minutes

Jimmy Dunne (1)

Austria	May	1971 Dublin	1-4

Robin Lawler (8)

Austria	Mar	1953 Dublin	4-0
Luxembourg	Oct	1953 Dublin	4-0
France	Nov	1953 Paris	0-1
Norway	Nov	1954 Dublin	2-1
Holland	May	1955 Dublin	1-0
Norway	May	1955 Oslo	3-1
West Germany	May	1955 Hamburg	1-2
Yugoslavia	Oct	1955 Dublin	1-4

Turlough O'Connor (1)

Czechoslovakia	Nov	1967 Prague	[1]2-1

Sean O'Driscoll (2/1)

Chile	May	1982 Santiago	0-1
Brazil	May	1982 Uberlandia	0-7
Trinidad (sub)	May	1982 Port of Spain	1-2

Gerry Peyton (20/1)

Spain (sub)	Feb 1977 Dublin	0-1	
Bulgaria	Oct 1977 Dublin	0-0	
Turkey	Apr 1978 Dublin	4-2	
Poland	Apr 1978 Lodz	0-3	
Denmark	May 1979 Dublin	2-0	
Bulgaria	May 1959 Sofia	0-1	
West Germany	May 1979 Dublin	1-3	
Argentina	May 1979 Dublin	0-0	
Wales	Sep 1979 Swansea	1-2	
Bulgaria	Oct 1979 Dublin	3-0	
England	Feb 1980 Wembley	0-2	
Cyprus	Mar 1980 Nicosia	3-2	
Switzerland	Apr 1980 Dublin	2-0	
Argentina	May 1980 Dublin	0-1	
Cyprus	Nov 1980 Dublin	6-0	
Belgium	Mar 1981 Brussels	0-1	
Czechoslovakia	Apr 1981 Dublin	3-1	
Holland	Sep 1981 Rotterdam	2-2	
France	Oct 1981 Dublin	3-2	
Trinidad	May 1982 Port of Spain	1-2	
Wales	Mar 1986 Dublin	0-1	

Wartime Internationals
England

Joe Bacuzzi (13)

Wales	Nov 1939 Cardiff	1-1	
Wales	Apr 1940 Wembley	0-1	
Scotland	Feb 1941 Newcastle	2-3	
Wales	Apr 1941 Nottingham	4-1	
Scotland	May 1941 Glasgow	3-1	
Wales	Jun 1941 Cardiff	3-2	
Scotland	Oct 1941 Wembley	2-0	
Wales	Oct 1941 Birmingham	2-1	
Scotland	Jan 1942 Wembley	3-0	
Scotland	Apr 1942 Glasgow	4-5	
Scotland	Oct 1942 Wembley	0-0	
Wales	Feb 1943 Wembley	5-3	
France*	May 1946 Paris	1-2	

*Victory International

Ronnie Rooke (1)

Wales	Oct 1942 Molineux	1-2	

Wales

Eddie Perry (1)

England	Apr 1941 Nottingham	4-1	

Viv Woodward (1)

England	Jun 1941 Cardiff	¹2-3	

Under-23 Internationals
England

Les Barrett (1) v Greece, 1967.
Allan Clarke (5) v Wales, Austria, Greece, Bulgaria, Turkey, 1967.
George Cohen (8) v Hungary, France, Scotland, Holland, 1960; Scotland, West Germany, 1961; Yugoslavia, Rumania, 1963.
Johnny Haynes (8) v Italy, Scotland, 1955; Denmark, Scotland, 1956; Scotland, Romania, Czechoslovakia, 1957; Bulgaria, 1958.
Tony Macedo (10) v Italy, West Germany, 1959; Hungary, France, Holland, East Germany, Poland, Israel, 1960; Italy, West Germany, 1961.
Alan Mullery (3) v Italy, 1961; Holland, 1962; Belgium, 1963.
Bobby Robson (1) v Denmark, 1956.

Northern Ireland

Brendan Mullen (1) v Italy, 1969.

Under-21 Internationals
England

Cliff Carr (0/1) v Republic of Ireland (sub), 1985.
Dean Coney (2/2) v Turkey (sub), 1985; Rumania (sub), Turkey, Denmark, 1986.
Tony Gale (1) v Poland, 1982.
Paul Parker (7/1) v Finland, Turkey, Israel (sub), Republic of Ireland, Rumania, Finland, 1985; Turkey, Denmark, 1986.

Wales

Jeff Hopkins (4/1) v France (sub), Holland, 1982; Norway, Yugoslavia, Bulgaria, 1953.

Viv Woodward won a wartime cap for Wales.

Football League

Joe Bacuzzi (1)
Scottish League	Oct 1941	Blackpool	3-2

Allan Clarke (2)
Scottish League	Mar 1967	Glasgow	[2]3-0
Belgium League	Sep 1967	Brussels	[1]2-2

George Cohen (4)
Scottish League	Mar 1964	Sunderland	2-2
Italian League	May 1964	Milan	0-1
League of Ireland	Oct 1965	Hull	5-0
Irish League	Sep 1966	Plymouth	[1]2-0

Andy Ducat (1)
The Army	Nov 1921	Leyton	4-1

Johnny Haynes (13)
Scottish League	Apr 1954	Chelsea	[1]4-0
League of Ireland	Sep 1954	Dublin	[1]6-0
Scottish League	Oct 1955	Sheffield	4-2
League of Ireland	Dec 1955	Liverpool	5-1
Irish League	Apr 1956	Belfast	2-5
Irish League	Oct 1956	Newcastle	[1]3-2
Irish League	Oct 1957	Belfast	[1]4-2
Irish League	Nov 1958	Liverpool	[1]5-2
League of Ireland	Mar 1959	Dublin	0-0
Italian League	Nov 1960	Milan	2-4
League of Ireland	Oct 1961	Bristol	[1]5-2
Italian League	Nov 1961	Manchester	0-2
Scottish League	Mar 1962	Villa Park	[1]3-4

Bedford Jezzard (3)
League of Ireland	Mar 1953	Dublin	2-0
Danish Combination	May 1953	Copenhagen	[1]4-0
Scottish League	Apr 1954	Chelsea	[2]4-0

Len Oliver (1)
The Army	Oct 1926	Millwall	4-1

Frank Penn (1)
The Army	Oct 1926	Millwall	4-1

Arthur Reynolds (1)
Southern League	Oct 1914	Highbury	2-1

Jim Taylor (3)
Scottish League	Mar 1948	Newcastle	1-1
Scottish League	Nov 1950	Glasgow	0-1
League of Ireland	Apr 1951	Dublin	1-0

On four occasions, Fulham have had two players in an England team (Haynes and Jezzard against Ireland in 1955 and Haynes and Langley (against Scotland, Portugal and Yugoslavia in 1958). This has happened once for Northern Ireland (Campbell and Brennan against England in 1950) and seven times for Wales (Davies and Hopkins against Northern Ireland, Brazil, Rumania, Scotland, England and Iceland in 1983 and 1984). The record, however, was set for the Republic of Ireland in November 1967 when Conway, Dempsey and O'Connor all played against Czechoslovakia.

Full-back George Cohen, at home with just some of the momentoes of 37 England appearances.

Summary of Fulham's Cup Record

FA Cup	Stage of Fulham's Exit	Lge Cup
1	Final	-
4	Semi-finals	-
5	6 Round 5	2
1	5 Round 4	5
26	4 Round 3	7
33	3 Round 2	9
2	2 Round 1	4
2	1 Round -	-

NB. Cup rounds prior to 1925-6 converted to modern equivalents.

FA Cup		Status of Opponents	Lge Cup	
W	L		W	L
15	29	Higher division	6	12
22	26	Same division	6	6
34	15	Lower division	12	9

NB. Fulham's FA Cup record in their Southern League days is excluded because it is not possible to compare fairly the status of various Leagues outside the Football League.

When the Football League Cup was introduced in 1960-61, Fulham were one of the First Division clubs that entered. In their first round tie, played on the opening night of the competition, Fulham lost 2-1 at Bristol Rovers, but their goal, scored early in the match by Maurice Cook, was the first-ever scored in the League Cup.

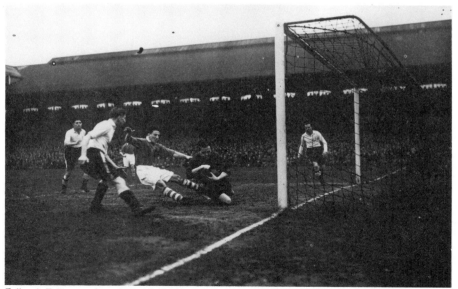

Fulham's Kelly saves from O'Linn during the FA Cup third round match against Charlton Athletic at Craven Cottage in January 1950.

Fulham's Record Scores

Competition	BIGGEST VICTORY		BIGGEST DEFEAT	
	HOME	**AWAY**	HOME	AWAY
Division One	10-1 v Ipswich Town, Dec 1963	5-2 v Aston Villa, Mar 1966, v Blackpool, Oct 1960	6-1 v Sheffield Wednesday, Jan 1961	9-0 v Wolves, Sept 1959
Division Two	8-1 v Swansea Town, Jan 1938	6-1 v Doncaster Rovs, Mar 1958	6-1 v Bradford, Feb 1914	7-0 v Liverpool, Nov 1955, v Nottm Forest, Aug 1927
Division Three	10-2 v Torquay United, Sept 1931	8-0 v Halifax Town, Sept 1969	6-0 v Port Vale, Mar 1987	6-1 v Notts Cnty, Sept 1930
FA Cup	6-0 v Bury, Jan 1939	8-3 v Luton Town, Jan 1908	4-0 v Burnley, Jan 1927	6-0 v Newcastle Utd, Mar 1908
League/Milk/ Littlewoods	5-0 v Northampton, Oct 1965, v Wolves, Oct 1966	4-0 v Darlington, Sept 1970	3-1 v Reading, Oct 1964	10-0 v Liverpool, Sept 1986

The first season under the new offside law brought a flood of goals and on 26 September 1925, a total of 194 goals were scored in 44 Football League games. Fulham lost 4-0 to Second Division leaders, Chelsea. This picture shows Fulham goalkeeper Tom McKenna punching clear at Stamford Bridge.

Fulham's Scoring Rates

The following table shows how Fulham's scorers compare in terms of goals per game.

		Gls	App	Gls/app
1	Frank Newton	81	88	0.92
2	Roy Dwight	57	80	0.71
3	Ronnie Rooke	77	110	0.70
4	Allan Clarke	57	100	0.57
5	Bedford Jezzard	154	306	0.50
6	Graham Leggat	134	280	0.48
7	Jim Hammond	150	342	0.44
8	Gordon Davies	136	313	0.43
9	Maurice Cook	97	248	0.39
10	Jimmy Temple	61	168	0.36
11	Steve Earle	108	327	0.33
12	Bob Thomas	57	177	0.32
13	Trevor Chamberlain	64	204	0.31
13	John Mitchell	61	194	0.31
15	Arthur Stevens	124	412	0.30
15	John Arnold	63	213	0.30
17	Dean Coney	72	246	0.29
18	Johnny Haynes	157	657	0.24
19	Bobby Robson	80	370	0.22
20	Jim Conway	76	360	0.21
21	Les Barrett	89	491	0.18

Bob Thomas

Frank 'Bonzo' Newton established the record for scoring in consecutive games in 1932-3, with 12 goals in nine matches. The closest challengers are Bedford Jezzard and Roy Dwight, who scored in the first seven games of 1954-5 and 1956-7 respectively.

In 1921-2 and 1922-3 goalkeeper Arthur Reynolds kept clean sheets in six straight League matches, although he conceded two goals in a Cup-tie in 1921-2 during the League sequence. In nine consecutive home League games between March and October 1920, Fulham did not concede a goal, and Reynolds was again the custodian.

Fulham appears to have had a special attraction for many of its players. A surprisingly high number of players have returned to the Cottage after leaving it for other clubs. Amongst the most famous are Jimmy Sharp (1904-05 and 1909-13), Frank Newton (1931-33 and 1934-35), Bobby Robson (1951-56 and 1962-67), Alan Mullery (1959-64 and 1972-76), Rodney Marsh (1963-66 and 1976-77), Bill Dodgin jnr (1951-52 and 1961-63) and Gordon Davies (1978-84 and 1986-). Others who had two playing spells at The Cottage include Harry Lee, Robert Ferguson, Arthur Telford, Jimmy Bowie and Wally Hinshelwood. In 1987, two more returned, Jim Stannard from Southend and Leroy Rosenior from Queen's Park Rangers.

Fulham's Hat-trick Specialists

In League and Cup games since 1907, Fulham have recorded 122 hat-tricks, scored by 48 different players. The 15 who have scored 3 or more trebles are as follows:

	3gls	4gls	5gls	6gls	Hat-tricks
Jim Hammond	8	2	0	0	10
Ronnie Rooke	6	2	0	1	10
Graham Leggat	6	2	0	0	8
Bedford Jezzard	3	2	1	0	6
Johnny Haynes	5	1	0	0	6
Roy Dwight	5	1	0	0	6
Frank Newton	4	0	0	0	4
Maurice Cook	4	0	0	0	4
Steve Earle	3	0	1	0	4
Bill Haley	3	1	0	0	4
Gordon Davies	3	1	0	0	4
Arthur Stevens	3	0	0	0	3
Trevor Chamberlain	3	0	0	0	3
Bert Pearce	3	0	0	0	3
Eddie Perry	2	1	0	0	3

Jim Hammond

Ronnie Rooke

Graham Leggat

Fulham's Leading Appearances

	League		FA Cup		League Cup		Total	
1	Haynes	594	Haynes	43	L.Barrett	36	Haynes	657
2	Lowe	473	Lowe	33	S.Brown	29	Lowe	511
3	Penn	428	Cohen	33	Peyton	28	L.Barrett	487/4
4	L.Barrett	420/3	Penn	32	Callaghan	27	Penn	460
5	Cohen	408	L.Barrett	31/1	Strong	26	Cohen	459
6	Oliver	406	Macedo	31	Gale	24	Oliver	434
7	Reynolds	399	Mullery	31	Davies	22	Strong	424/3
8	A.Barrett	388	A.Barrett	30	Earle	21/2	Reynolds	420
9	Stevens	385	Strong	28	Lloyd	20	A.Barrett	418
10	Strong	370/3	Oliver	28	Haynes	19	Stevens	412
11	Mullery	363/1	Stevens	27	Conway	18	Mullery	411/1
12	S.Brown	346/5	Fryer†	26	Cohen	17	Peyton	395
13	Macedo	346	Hammond	26	Mellor	17	S.Brown	392/5
14	Peyton	345	Conway	25	Mullery	16	Macedo*	391
15	Robson	344	Langley	23	Wilson	15	Robson	370
16	Torrance	336	Goldie	22	Dunne	15	Conway	356/4
17	Langley	323	Peyton	22	Slough	14/1	Langley	356
18	Hammond	316	Hill	21	Lock	14	Torrance	355
19	Conway	312/4	Reynolds	21	Cutbush	14	Hammond	342
20	Gibbons	299	Davies	21	Dempsey	14	Callaghan	332/4

*Macedo's total includes 14 League Cup appearances. †Fryer's FA Cup appearances include some made when Fulham were in the Southern League.

Les Barrett holds the Fulham record for consecutive League appearances, with 148 between August 1969 and November 1972. This run stretched to 167 games when Cup appearances are included. The previous record was held by goalkeeper Ernie Beecham with 122 League appearances between 1926 and 1928. In addition to these two, eight other players have notched centuries of consecutive appearances for Fulham: Reynolds, Jezzard, Lloyd, Dempsey, Gibbons, Langley, Mellor and Peyton.

Eddie Lowe, second only to Johnny Haynes in the list of appearances for Fulham.

Johnny Haynes

Bedford Jezzard

Fulham's Leading Scorers

	League		FA Cup		League Cup		Total	
1	Jezzard	154	Stevens	14	L.Barrett	12	Haynes	157
2	Haynes	146	Hill	11	Earle	10	Jezzard	154
3	Hammond	141	Hammond	9	Coney	10	Hammond	150
4	Leggat	127	Haynes	9	Davies	9	Davies	136
5	Davies	120	Rooke	8	Clarke	7	Leggat	134
6	Stevens	110	Busby	7	Conway	6	Stevens	124
7	Earle	98	Harrison	7	Key	5	Earle	108
8	Cook	89	Penn	7	Dempsey	3	Cook	97
9	Newton	77	Davies	7	Halom	3	L.Barrett	89
10	Robson	77	Cook	6	Mullery	3	Newton	81
11	L.Barrett	74	Coney	6	Wilson	3	Robson	80
12	Rooke	69	Chamberlain	5	Dyson	3	Rooke	77
13	Conway	67	Clarke	5	Metchick	3	Conway	76
14	Chamberlain	59	Leggat	5			Coney	72
15	Arnold	58	A.Barrett	5			Chamberlain	64
16	Temple	58	Arnold	5			Arnold	63
17	Mitchell	57					Temple	61
18	Coney	56					Mitchell	61
19	Thomas	55					Clarke, Dwight	
20	Dwight	54					& Thomas	57

NB. Some players scored a number of goals in the FA Cup for Fulham (T.Meade 15, J.Connor 7, H.Fletcher 5, D.Lloyd 5 and B.Tannahill 5) but all or most of them were in the qualifying rounds when Fulham were in the Southern League.

Fulham Attendances 1907-1987

HOME ATTENDANCES					AWAY ATTENDANCES		
Average	Highest	Lowest	Season	Division	Average	Highest	Lowest
18,000	40,000	8,000	1907-08	Two	8,000	16,000	500
18,500	40,000	6,000	1908-09	Two	10,500	20,000	4,000
14,500	25,000	10,000	1909-10	Two	8,000	20,000	3,000
14,500	35,000	4,000	1910-11	Two	10,500	50,000	2,000
13,000	42,000	3,000	1911-12	Two	9,000	35,000	2,000
12,500	25,000	5,000	1912-13	Two	7,500	15,000	2,000
14,500	35,000	5,000	1913-14	Two	11,500	35,000	5,000
6,500	14,000	1,000	1914-15	Two	6,000	10,000	1,000
15,000	30,000	4,000	1919-20	Two	12,000	40,000	2,000
18,500	40,000	4,000	1920-21	Two	15,500	25,000	8,000
20,500	34,000	10,000	1921-22	Two	14,500	25,000	8,000
20,000	35,000	14,000	1922-23	Two	12,500	24,000	5,000
15,500	22,000	7,000	1923-24	Two	12,500	25,000	6,000
15,500	30,000	5,000	1924-25	Two	15,500	45,000	5,000
16,500	43,000	5,000	1925-26	Two	12,500	50,000	4,000
17,000	40,500	3,500	1926-27	Two	13,500	38,000	5,000
17,500	40,000	8,000	1927-28	Two	15,500	60,000	5,000
18,000	30,000	10,000	1928-29	Three	10,500	20,000	4,000
15,000	30,000	3,000	1929-30	Three	10,000	22,000	2,000
12,500	22,000	6,000	1930-31	Three	8,500	27,000	3,000
17,000	25,000	8,000	1931-32	Three	10,500	27,000	5,000
22,000	43,500	10,000	1932-33	Two	16,500	47,000	4,000
17,000	36,000	6,000	1933-34	Two	15,000	35,000	5,000
17,500	30,000	10,000	1934-35	Two	14,000	35,000	3,000
17,500	40,000	6,000	1935-36	Two	16,000	55,000	4,000
18,000	30,000	8,000	1936-37	Two	16,500	56,000	4,000
18,500	39,500	10,000	1937-38	Two	18,000	40,000	6,000
19,500	49,335	3,000	1938-39	Two	21,000	64,000	5,000
24,954	40,339	10,260	1946-47	Two	21,569	47,658	8,036
22,682	41,500	9,878	1947-48	Two	24,590	54,071	9,031
28,844	40,000	19,000	1948-49	Two	25,330	50,133	13,179
35,000	44,000	25,000	1949-50	One	34,000	54,726	15,000
32,500	42,000	24,000	1950-51	One	34,122	58,000	18,997
33,000	46,000	16,000	1951-52	One	30,096	55,531	8,260
24,500	40,000	10,000	1952-53	Two	20,449	30,160	3,155
23,000	30,000	12,000	1953-54	Two	18,991	36,092	9,391
23,500	33,500	11,500	1954-55	Two	20,271	44,372	7,000
19,807	31,500	9,000	1955-56	Two	20,332	35,496	10,000
21,052	33,700	8,000	1956-57	Two	19,958	36,735	8,410
20,680	42,289	7,700	1957-58	Two	20,712	51,701	8,028
26,931	40,000	18,300	1958-59	Two	23,267	43,926	7,638
30,386	44,695	17,398	1959-60	One	30,503	52,150	15,007
22,964	38,000	13,006	1960-61	One	24,386	56,210	8,692
24,401	43,355	12,630	1961-62	One	24,523	37,988	10,641
21,938	39,961	8,954	1962-63	One	23,454	60,578	10,000

422

HOME ATTENDANCES					AWAY ATTENDANCES		
Average	Highest	Lowest	Season	Division	Average	Highest	Lowest
21,163	41,769	11,165	1963-64	One	23,426	49,520	9,503
17,692	36,291	10,162	1964-65	One	24,749	45,402	11,972
21,160	38,960	9,735	1965-66	One	23,783	46,382	10,497
24,426	47,290	14,570	1966-67	One	26,739	51,673	13,518
22,702	40,154	13,451	1967-68	One	28,824	60,465	14,227
14,238	23,132	7,154	1968-69	Two	16,733	36,521	5,837
10,258	18,987	6,708	1969-70	Three	8,938	18,861	3,432
12,004	25,774	7,071	1970-71	Three	10,209	33,340	4,121
11,146	21,187	7,406	1971-72	Two	14,580	25,671	6,067
10,267	17,576	6,262	1972-73	Two	11,933	24,007	5,759
10,129	23,511	4,973	1973-74	Two	13,448	32,124	5,526
10,808	26,513	5,739	1974-75	Two	15,361	52,971	4,703
9,740	22,921	5,856	1975-76	Two	12,754	25,450	3,414
14,589	29,690	7,656	1976-77	Two	18,077	55,003	6,158
10,550	24,763	6,161	1977-78	Two	13,939	34,110	3,961
10,063	26,597	5,407	1978-79	Two	11,966	28,733	4,684
8,438	22,258	3,766	1979-80	Two	12,781	30,567	5,090
5,061	9,921	3,387	1980-81	Three	6,709	15,460	3,263
6,945	20,398	3,629	1981-82	Three	5,698	10,830	1,174
10,838	24,251	5,688	1982-83	Two	12,529	29,797	3,525
8,180	24,787	4,914	1983-84	Two	11,615	31,947	3,031
6,158	12,542	3,721	1984-85	Two	8,335	21,071	2,756
·4,610	9,331	2,134	1985-86	Two	7,211	17,320	2,510
4,078	9,239	2,352	1986-87	Three	3,950	9,361	1,267

HOME ATTENDANCES		Division	AWAY ATTENDANCES	
Highest	Lowest		Highest	Lowest
47,290 v Man Utd March 1967	8,954 v Blackpool March 1963	ONE	60,578 v Everton May 1963	8,260 v Huddersfield Dec 1951
49,335 v Millwall October 1938	1,000 v Barnsley Nov 1914	TWO	63,962 Newcastle Nov 1938	500 v Glossop Apr 1908
30,000 v Swindon Mar Charlton Apr Brentford Oct 1930	2,352 v Rotherham Feb 1987	THREE	33,340 v Aston Villa Jan 1971	1,174 v Chester May 1982

423

Best and Worst League Seasons

VICTORIES

Most home wins   18   1958-59
Most away wins   10   1907-08
Most wins   27   1958-59

Fewest home wins   5   1951-52
Fewest away wins   1   1923-24; 1927-28;
                                 1964-65; 1968-69
Fewest wins   7   1968-69

DEFEATS

Most home defeats   11   1967-68; 1979-80
Most away defeats   20   1927-28
Most defeats   26   1985-86

Fewest home defeats   1   1912-13; 1948-49
Fewest away defeats   6   1907-08; 1931-32
Fewest defeats   9   1931-32; 1948-49;
                                 1958-59

DRAWS

Most home draws   9   1947-48; 1969-70;
                                 1981-82
Most away draws   9   1934-35; 1952-53;
                                 1986-87
Most draws   17   1986-87

Fewest home draws   0   1914-15
Fewest away draws   0   1912-13; 1927-28;
                                 1960-61
Fewest draws   4   1956-57

POINTS

Most home points   45   1981-82*
                          37   1958-59
Most away points   33   1981-82*
                          24   1931-32
Most points   78   1981-82*
                          60   1958-59; 1970-71

Fewest home points   16   1967-68
Fewest away points   2   1927-28
Fewest points   25   1968-69

GOALS SCORED

Most home goals scored   72   1931-32
Most away goals scored   44   1957-58
Most goals scored   111   1931-32

Fewest home goals scored   19   1979-80
Fewest away goals scored   10   1920-21
Fewest goals scored   39   1973-74

GOALS CONCEDED

Most home goals conceded   41   1967-68; 1986-87
Most away goals conceded   67   1927-28
Most goals conceded   98   1967-68

Fewest home goals conceded   8   1921-22
Fewest away goals conceded   20   1922-23
Fewest goals conceded   32   1922-23

Three points for a win. Equivalent when two points for a win: 57 total, 33 at home and 24 away.

⊞ Picture Parade
Fulham action down the years

Alex Fraser on the ball in the FA Cup first round tie against Reading on 4 February 1905.

Jack Papworth gets the ball under control against Oldham Athletic in January 1924.

Heads high as Fulham shock West Ham by drawing this Second Division match in October 1937. Fulham had yet to win a game that season and they would have broken their duck but for a missed penalty.

Roy Bentley scores against Rotherham United in September 1956. It was Bentley's debut after joining Fulham from Chelsea.

George Cohen clears the danger against Nottingham Forest at Craven Cottage in March 1962.

427

Sean O'Driscoll nets a spectacular goal against Carlisle in March 1982 as Fulham march towards promotion.

Peter Scott, from the penalty spot, scores one of his two goals against Middlesbrough in September 1986.

SUBSCRIBERS

4	Dennis Turner	53	Peter King	102	Sue Ballard
5	Alex White	54	Alan Cartwright	103	Andrew S Victory
6	Johnny Haynes	55	Nicholas Jenkins	104	Brian Blackman
7	R A Rundle	56	John Barrett	105	Graham Blackman
8	D J Bell	57	William Moss	106	Peter Reason
9	John Henry Hilton	58	B S Massey	107	Edward Bennett
10	Derek Hyde	59	Carlo Roberto	108	Andrew R Wilson
11	John A Harris	60	M Taylor	109	Derek Hicks
12	Kåre M Torgrimsen	61	J J Hall	110	David Smithers
13	William Needs	62	W P J Clark	111	Joseph W Palmer
14	Patricia Arthur	63	John Shirley	112	Jeffrey Palmer
15	W O'Connell	64	Steven Leven	113	Robert Wauters
16	Roger Hudson	65	Jack Mills	114	Geoffrey Green
17	Derek T Bryant	66	Richard Shore	115	Barry Sklan
18	Dave Parine	67	I F Woolley	116	Graham Weight
19	Peter Heffernan	68	Peter I Plummer	117	Steve Wears
20	John MacDermott	69	Robert Bruce	118	John Crome
21	K Beaven	70	Roy M Costan	119	Nick Navratil
22	Anthony William Camilleri	71	Scott P Trotman	120	Miss Jane Blight
23	Vincent Heywood	72	Graham Collins	121	D Fribbins
24	C D Wannell	73	Graham Goldsmid	122	Graham Skipp
25	John Rickard	74	Robin Peter Fribbins	123	Steve Barry
26	David Amos	75	John David Clarke	124	Brian Matthews
27	Paul A Rogers	76	G E Clark	125	M (Spike) Ross
28	Robert Hingley	77	David L Maryon	126	Jon Barnes
29	Robert J Murphy	78	Stephen Hills	127	Alan Andrew Smith
30	R D Waters	79	Reginald A Ambrose	128	Ian A Clarke
31	William T F Nash	80	Alan Morris	129	Peter McDonagh
32	Melvin Tenner	81	D J Ridgwell	130	Vaughan Webb
33	John A Saunders	82	P T Petherick	131	D Booth
34	Kay Williams	83	R Maitland Earl	132	R Booth
35	Anthony David Gilroy	84	John William Doust	133	Clifford Moore
36	M A Krzyzak	85	Nigel Batchelor	134	Craig Foley
37	Colin Stevens	86	J L Jones	135	George Mallison
38	Alan Stevens	87	R G Cain	136	Thomas Dixon
39	Rosemarie Conroy	88	Yvonne & Ken Simpson	137	Stephen Holloway
40	Paul Watkins	89	Peter Busby	138	John Edward Warner
41	E Borkowski	90	R L Brooks	139	Philip Howard Bennett
42	Peter & Stephen O'Brien	91	Steve Knight	140	C Schluter
43	B Longhurst	92	Tom & Heather Young	141	J E Gribble
44	Ray Crawford	93	D R Gutteridge	142	Richard Bampton
45	Robert Alfred Fennell	94	D G Gutteridge	143	Robin Stieber
46	Richard Kilford	95	Michael C Best	144	Graeme Ogston
47	Philip Hankers	96	R J Shelley	145	Peter Donnison
48	G Andrews	97	Jim Nott	146	Michael Yuill
49	Peter Hyams	98	David Nott	147	Jim Sims
50	Miss M Pitcher	99	Joe Cotter	148	Alex Sims
51	Martin Bradshaw	100	S Newell	149	Andy Sims
52	Dennis Colchester Butler	101	Ms L A Burgess	150	Ali Sims

151	Gary Collier	207	Ian Campbell	264	Michael Robert Rust
152	Miss S Maidwell	208	J J Stobbs	265	Mrs Alice Lee
153	Peter Ward	209	Simon Blackie	266	Rodney Hunt
154	Michael J Neale	210	Mrs M M King	267	Barry Leach
155	D W Garner	211	D King	268	Joseph Aloysius Evinson
156	Graham Preston	212	P A McNeela	269	B O Showan
157	Percy F Preston	213	Peter Robinson	270	D K Showan
158	Raymond Charles Brooks	214	David Pearce	271	Bruce Nigel Dunn
159	Michael John Brooks	215	David Stannard	272	Chris Finn
160	P W Barker	216	Eric McKenzie	273	G R White
161	Peter Thomas Yates	217	Carol Grover	274	Keith Alan Couling
162	Ernest J Brotherston	218	Mike Dymond	275	David A Barrows
163	Robert S Reed	219	Stephen J Murray	276	John Motson
164	C W Cox	220	Gerard Curran	277	Neil Farrell
165	S N Woodward	221	Daniel William Young	278	David Jessop
166	F Vass	222	Robert D Wemyss	279	Michael Duthie
167	Helge Eriksen	223	K M Wilkins	280	B R Hough
168	Martin Andrew Lee	224	N P Weeden	281	James W O Aplin
169	L V J Timms	225	M J Weeden	282	Marc Taylor
170	Derek Bradley	226	R W Weller	283	John Taylor
171	Steve Jex	227	John Gillett	284	Alastair R A Finn
172	Dean Antony Gadd	228	Ian Matheson	285	Simon Carthew
173	T J Turner	229	Barry & Paul Taylor	286	Ralph Mortimer
174	Stephen Peterman	230	Michael Heatley	287	John Weir
175	I W Clay	231	The Hawkins Family	288	Duncan Watt
176	Dave Wilson	232	The Hawkins Family	289	Anthony Harris
177	Steve Johnson	233	The Hawkins Family	290	Philip T Jackson
178	Miss L P Haycock	234	Spike Denton	291	Steve Whiston
179	C B Haycock	235	Derek M Cordle MBE	292	Paul Elford
180	Neil Parmenter	236	Simon Cox	293	Frederick John Hermon
181	Nicholas Spokes	237	R E Booth	294	Jeremy Pruce
182	John Delaney	238	Malcolm Tarrey	295	A F Child
183	Ian Jordan	239	Edward Wauters	296	Edward J Larking
184	Ian Mills	240	Ken Hawkes	297	Miss J E Peters
185	T Bermingham & Miss W Mitchell	241	Jonathan Kelly	298	Bert Crane
		242	L H T Roberts	299	A E Walmsley
186	James T McCrann	243	James P Crennin	300	Brian C Jennings
187	T J Burden	244	Bob Bovington	301	Philip Baker
188	Tim Burden	245	Martin Del-Bo	302	George Baker
189	Neal Christie	246	Paul Buttler	303	Phil Soar
190	B P Robbins	247	C J Green	304	Gordon Small
191	R T Britnell	248	Stephen Smith	305	Frederick J Lee
192	S Nejand	249	P J Nickless	306	John Treleven
193	M A Gower	250	Norman William Reynolds	307	J Gardiner
194	Ian Gary Crouthers	251	Mark Gilronan	308	Gary James
195	Paul Stone	252	P J Lowings	309	K J Dowie
196	K M Edwards	253	Ian Gregory	310	Michael Lownsbrough
197	Barrie M Gale	254	Dennis Bone	311	RF, SA & AF Jones
198	R Wicks	255	Terry Kilroy	312	Gary Fordrey
199	R Wicks	256	John Michael Burnett	313	Alan Wicks
200	R Wicks	257	R A Lewis	314	Robin Rebbeck
201	R Wicks	258	Brian Pickering	315	Dean Stimpson
202	R Wicks	259	Roger Martin Puckey	316	Domenico Polimeno
203	S Dearsley	260	E G Wyatt	317	T Gillingham
204	P J Dearsley	261	Pete Everett	318	Gillingham Shoes
205	Colin R Cooper	262	Michael V Huband	319	E T Tidy
206	David Crankshaw	263	J Wattam	320	Paul Martinez

321	Brian E Hollingsworth	377	Paul Hooper	434	Ron Bryant
322	Derek Brewer	378	Robert M Page	435	Reg Evans
323	Roger Wettone	379	John & Monica Page	436	W T Alexander
324	Paul Ratcliffe	380	David J Page	437	Roger John Southgate
325	Paul Ratcliffe	381	John Corner	438	David Daly
326	Barry J Warren	382	Ian Gray	439	Malcolm Hartley
327	Douglas Lamming	383	David Keats	440	Keith Lowe
328	Andrew Charman	384	P G Beadle	441	John O'Connor
329	D J Elliott	385	J D Sullivan	442	John A Pearson
330	Michael Riches	386	J D Watkins	443	O Frost
331	Stanley Brian Harry	387	Chris Copus	444	Mick Cox
332	B H Standish	388	Tony Sheridan	445	Vic Reed
333	P L M Lunn	389	Ron Bourley	446	M & N Simonds
334	Julian Morris	390	Ray Bourley	447	D Tilley
335	Brian C Sibley	391	Raymond A Kelly	448	H W Scott
336	D J Martin	392	Peter Pickup	449	Robert Brian Dark
337	S P Tomlin	393	Gareth Protheroe	450	Douglas Tilbury
338	Stewart Fell	394	Harald Lohr	451	Joe Nienaltowski
339	J F Burrell	395	Ian Griffiths	452	Derek Moth
340	Graham Turpin	396	M Swart	453	John Harrison
341	F Enticknap	397	A C Seal	454	Terry Frost LCIOB
342	John Edward Spreadbury	398	Ian Trevor Prior	455	D Wheatley
343	Keith Dunkin	399	Christopher O'Leary	456	R J Gamble
344	David Downs	400	B Couldrick	457	G J Carter
345	Bob Lipscombe	401	P F Flood	458	Leonard Overfield
346	Peter E Newman	402	Ashley Laurence Prust	459	Alan Garner
347	A Martinez	403	Desmond J Howlin	460	Alan Warner
348	Ray Green	404	Gavin James Botten	461	A Wheatley
349	Leslie Carter	405	Paul G Sheldrake	462	William Guard
350	Dennis Rouse	406	Doug Champ	463	Ian Pettit
351	Theo, Darren & Neil Morris	407	G Allcock	464	David Tross
352	Frank Core	408	John Woodland	465	P Martin
353	James R Symonds	409	Stewart J Parker	466	A McClelland
354	R J B Nosworthy	410	Stephen John Murrell	467	Richard Michael Granville
355	Barbara Bowden	411	R C Mitchell	468	E J Haywood
356	David J F Salisbury	412	Stephen Flinn	469	Dave Hillam
357	Anthony Ramos	413	Colin Flinn	470	Søren Skafte Jensen
358	R H White	414	John Lennon	471	Mrs B M Humphris
359	Christer Svensson	415	Jack Lennon	472	Kieran Doherty
360	J Musgrove	416	A M Krupnik	473	Brian Williams
361	Richard Stocken	417	Michael Kay	474	Robert James French
362	Paul Dillon	418	Col GHT Shrimpton CBE TD	475	D J Harrison
363	Denis J Flavin	419	D Staniforth	476	J R Huntingford
364	Juri Pawlovich Lukosiak	420	Nigel James Minto	477	Peter Bird
365	Geir Juva	421	Paul Hatcher	478	R G Woolman
366	Keith Coburn	422	David Johnson	479	Mark Stoddart
367	Peter J & Matthew	423	Lars-Olof Wendler	480	Alfred Frank Laurence
	S Strangeman	424	Miss Abigail Close	481	Leonard R P Stock
368	Alan & David Squire	425	Mrs Sarah Haynes	482	C D Jeffries
369	Richard D N Wells	426	Roy Close	483	M J Turner
370	Dennis Andrews	427	Olivia Woodward	484	Christopher H K Paris
371	Stephen George Surridge	428	Andrew Stanley	485	D J Gardner
372	Philip R Pinhey	429	Mark John Lewis	486	G Williams
373	Tony Doubledee	430	Antony Lembo	487	J Ringrose
374	A B Gilbert	431	David Lloyd	488	A F Bailey
375	J W Kettle	432	Moira & Frederick Furness	489	Alan Rustad
376	Stephen W Stenson	433	Peter Baxter	490	R T A Naylor